Emigrants on the Overland Trail

Emigrants on the Overland Trail

The Wagon Trains of 1848

Michael E. LaSalle

Truman State University Press

Kirksville, Missouri

Copyright © 2011 Truman State University Press, Kirksville, Missouri, 63501
All rights reserved
tsup.truman.edu

Cover art: William Henry Jackson (1843-1942), *Crossing the South Platte River*, undated, water-color. Image courtesy Scotts Bluff National Monument.

Cover design: Teresa Wheeler

Library of Congress Cataloging-in-Publication Data

LaSalle, Michael E., 1945–
Emigrants on the Overland Trail : the wagon trains of 1848 / Michael E. LaSalle.
    p. cm.
Includes bibliographical references and index.
ISBN 978-1-935503-95-8 (pbk. : alk. paper) — ISBN 978-1-61248-021-3 (ebook)
1. Overland Trails—Description and travel. 2. Pioneers—West (U.S.)—Diaries. 3. Pioneers—West
(U.S.)—Biography. 4. West (U.S.)—Description and travel. 5. Overland journeys to the Pacific.
6. Overland Trails—History—Sources. 7. Frontier and pioneer life—West (U.S.)—History—
Sources. I. Title.
F593.L288 2011
978'.02—dc23

                                                                        2011037737

For Yvonne, my wife and colleague

Contents

Illustrations, Tables, and Maps

Acknowledgments

A special debt of gratitude is owed to my late mother, who years ago gave me a transcribed copy of Thomas Corcoran's letters (her great-great-uncle). Little did she know that it would someday lead to this book. I am indebted to Travis Boley and Jim Riehl of the Oregon-California Trails Association for the use of the association's database to identify the known diarists/narrators of the 1848 overland emigration. Without their writings, there would not have been nearly as much of a story to tell. We are also fortunate that the following trail scholars (most of whom are now deceased) gathered and preserved a great deal about the emigrant trails before it disappeared: LeRoy R. Hafen, Paul C. Henderson, William J. Ghent, Dale L. Morgan, Charles L. Camp, George R. Stewart, Charles Kelly, Irene D. Paden, Aubrey L. Haines, Merrill J. Mattes, John D. Unruh Jr., Louise Berry, and Gregory M. Franzwa. Appreciation must also be expressed to the Oregon-California Trails Association and to Trails West for their ongoing efforts to promote and preserve the trails.

Materials for this book came from a variety of historical societies, libraries, archives, and collections. I am indebted to all of them, particularly for the help from Maria Ortiz, Ruth Lang, and Sharon Hiigel of the Fresno City and County Historical Society; Judy Green and Scott Daniels of the Oregon Historical Society; Cheryl Gunselman of the Washington State University Library; Robert Manasek at the Scotts Bluff National Monument; Breon Mitchell of the Lilly Library, Indiana University–Bloomington; Patty Mosher with the Galesburg (IL) Public Library; Sarah Elder of the St. Joseph Museum; Tod Ruhstaller of the Haggin Museum; Kimberly Harper of the State Historical Society of Missouri; Lisa Marine from the Wisconsin Historical Society; Erica Cook with the Idaho State Archives; Debra Kaufman of the California Historical Society; Catherine Hansen Tracy of the California State Library; Allison Akbay from Stanford University; Heidi Orchard at the Utah State Archives; and Ann Buttars with the Utah State Library. Special thanks is owed to a couple of Oregon residents and trail scholars: Jim Riehl, a dedicated member of OCTA, and Stephenie Flora, who maintains a valuable website called Oregon Pioneers. Both read the manuscript and offered many insightful suggestions and corrections. To Wendell Huffman and Kristin Johnson I owe thanks for valuable information about Peter Lassen and the Donner party. For their interest and encouragement, I wish to thank my friends Ray Carlson and Lorraine Alcorn. I thank Truman State University Press and Nancy Rediger, its director, for agreeing to publish the book. Barbara Smith-Mandell, the Press's acquisitions editor, first opened the door and then as my copy editor, labored through my manuscript, rendered valuable recommendations, endured my argumentative nature, and indulged me more than I deserved. I was fortunate to have the talented Judith Sharp as my book designer and Teresa Wheeler as my cover designer, and Tom Willcockson of Mapcraft as my excellent cartographer.

I thank my children for their encouragement when rough spots in the trail seemed to bog me down, and my wife, Yvonne, to whom this book is dedicated, for being my indefatigable traveling companion, navigator, and overall sounding board and sympathizer.

Michael E. LaSalle
Hanford, California
September 10, 2011

Introduction

This book tells the story of the men, women, and children who loaded up their covered wagons and went west in 1848. There have been many books dealing with the Oregon and California Trails and the California gold rush, but until now, no book has been exclusively devoted to the wagon trains of 1848. Prominent trail historians regarded that year as "lost" because few diaries, journals, or other narratives had surfaced, and no book devoted more than a chapter to the year. Recently, a number of additional diaries, journals, and other narratives have come to light, including a long letter written by my great-great-great-uncle Thomas Corcoran that recounted some of his experiences during his 1848 overland trip to California. A copy of his letter has been in my family's possession for years and is what inspired me to learn more about the year Thomas made his great journey.

There were eighteen distinct wagon companies in 1848, traveling like knots in a long rope that stretched over three hundred miles from front to back. This book relies predominantly on seven diarists, each of whom traveled with a different wagon company. Their diaries and journals are an invaluable gift to the American people. The diarists ranged from a college-educated teacher to a barely literate ox driver. One was a young mother and another, the most entertaining of all, was a French priest on his way to Oregon to become an Indian missionary. These diaries and journals are far from masterpieces of writing. The travelers wrote with simple voices and in the language of ordinary folks, recording events with a quiet absence of boastfulness and exaggeration. They rarely expressed emotion, although a discerning reader can sense what was going on in their minds and hearts. I have included many of their daily entries, unedited and in full, to let the reader hear each writer's voice and experience their wide-ranging differences in tone and style, including their erratic spellings, odd punctuation (or the complete lack thereof), and often nonexistent sentence structure.

It is easy to underestimate the difficulty of the trail, to undervalue the emigrants' struggles, and to underappreciate their courage. The West could not be settled by the weak, the squeamish, or the fainthearted; the sensible and cautious tended to stay home. Of those who did set out for the West, few fully grasped what lay ahead, having little conception of the distance, the difficulties, and the dangers.

These ordinary people demonstrated that the human spirit, under the influence of good leadership, could surmount unprecedented hardships and obstacles. They may have been slowed from time to time, but they never faltered. They showed that hardship and privation were not barriers; they were just annoying challenges.

These men, women, and children were pioneers in the true sense of the word, venturing where most were unwilling to go. But somebody had to go first. Somebody had to put down roots and establish the rudiments of American civilization so others could follow. In 1845, an eastern newspaper editor concocted the term "manifest destiny" to describe the popular notion that America was destined to spread into adjacent territories and bring its superior institutions to these far-flung lands.[1] Many historians have asserted that this phrase explained westward emigration, that it was what uncorked all that bottled-up energy and rallied Americans to leave their homes, but I say "buffalo chips." Consider that for each person who headed west in 1848, another seven thousand Americans stayed home. The decision to go west had little to do with devotion to manifest destiny or with responding to a patriotic call to duty and everything to do with people deciding to do something for themselves.

The reasons for this westering urge were numerous, but most could be assigned to a few broad categories: Some were inherently restless, perpetually dissatisfied by nature, those who thought they would always find something better somewhere else. These people tended to remain discontented no matter where they alighted; if they had been content, they would have stayed home. Others were adventurers, thrilled at the prospect of going somewhere—anywhere—to escape the drudgery of their present state. Still others went west because of their health. Large numbers had lived in the Ohio, Mississippi, and Missouri River valleys, where mosquito-borne illnesses such as malaria spread their misery. They heard that Oregon and California were free of the "fever and ague" (malaria) that plagued the Midwest. Some had contracted "lung fever," for which California's dry climate was reputed to be one's best chance for a cure.

It is a misconception that the overland emigrants were a poor, landless people seeking free land. Most already had land. They were farmers from Ohio, Indiana, Illinois, Iowa, and Missouri who sold their farms and reinvested most of the proceeds in outfitting themselves for the trip. It took a considerable sum in those days—about $1,000—to buy a wagon, yokes of oxen, and provisions to support a family on the five-month journey.

As of 1848, emigrants had been traveling by covered wagon to Oregon and California for about eight years. People had expected 1848 to be a boom year for emigration, but instead numbers were down. The war with Mexico and the fate of the Donner party in 1846 may have had a chilling effect. There were also men who had gone to Oregon in earlier years and returned east in '46 and '47. Often disillusioned, they spread the word that the trip was a killer and Oregon a land of incessant rains. The Whitman massacre and the ensuing Cayuse war in the Oregon Territory occurred at the end of 1847, but word of those events did not arrive in St. Joseph until the emigrants of 1848 were well along the trail.

Table 1: Number of emigrants per year, 1840–1850[2]

Year	To Oregon	To California	Total
1840	13	0	13
1841	24	34	58
1842	125	0	125
1843	875	38	913
1844	1,475	53	1,528
1845	2,500	260	2,760
1846	1,200	1,500	2,700
1847	4,000	450	4,450
1848	**1,300**	**400**	**1,700**
1849	450	25,000	25,450
1850	6,000	44,000	50,000

The California-bound emigrants of 1848 did not leave their homes to become gold miners. Even though James Marshall had discovered gold at Sutter's Mill in January 1848, word of that discovery did not reach the California-bound wagons until they were almost there. What set 1848 apart was that it was the last year the trail was uncrowded. In 1849, the gold rush changed everything.

I have traveled where our diarists traveled, and have seen what they saw. We should travel the trail—all or part of it—and see where the covered wagons once rumbled through dense clouds of dust. Much of the route is still vast, open, and unspoiled. Anyone with a sense of history will be moved by it. They will be inspired by those who trod it. It will promote a sense of pride in those leather-tough people who traversed it 160 years ago.

I urge the reader to acquire Gregory M. Franzwa's *Maps of the Oregon Trail* (1990) and *Maps of the California Trail* (1999). I also recommend *Emigrant Trails West: A Guide to the California Trail to the Humboldt River* (2007) and *A Guide to the California Trail along the Humboldt River* (2007), both published by Trails West, Inc. These books contain superb maps that show the precise location of the trails, mile by mile, and are a valuable supplement in following our diarists' progress. We are indebted to an earlier generation of trail scholars, people like Dale Morgan, Charles Camp, Irene Paden, Aubrey L. Haines, Merrill Mattes, Gregory M. Franzwa, the people connected with Trails West, and countless other volunteers who have pored over trail journals, interviewed local ranchers and "old timers," and walked the landscape looking for swales, ruts, and other evidence of the roads. Organizations like the Oregon-California Trails Association and Trails West have promoted the trails and fought to preserve them. To these people and organizations the nation owes a great debt, but only continued vigilance will preserve what remains.

The Oregon and California Trails are some of America's greatest treasures, and the overland emigration of 1848 is one of the great stories of America, a story as great and as big as the West itself. The covered wagon will always be a symbol of America and the era when the nation began settling the Far West. These emigrants came to represent the American spirit and character, and this book is a heartfelt tribute to what they accomplished.

Table 2: The wagon companies of 1848

Company	Narrators*	Departed
Allsopp	J. P. C. Allsopp (R)	April 10, from Independence
Greenwood		early April, from Bellevue (Council Bluffs)
Cornwall	P. B. Cornwall (B)	
	Thomas Corcoran (L)	April 12 (est.), from Bellevue (Council Bluffs)
Adams	W. L. Adams (L)	
	Inez Parker (R)	April 26 (est.), from Bellevue (Council Bluffs)
Smith	Edward Smith (D)	April 28, from Independence
Wambaugh	Riley Root (D)	
	John McPherson (D)	
	Rufus Burrows (R)	
	John Trullinger (R)	April 28, from St. Joseph
Gates		April 29 (est.), from St. Joseph
Kelly	R. Kelly (R)	April 29 (est.), from Independence
Miller	William Anderson (D)	April 30, from St. Joseph
Walker		May 5 (est.), from St. Joseph
Bristow		May 5 (est.), from St. Joseph
Purvine	William Porter (D)	
	Richard Cheadle (L)	May 6, from St. Joseph
Watt	Keturah Belknap (D)	May 7, from St. Joseph
Hanna		?
Delaney		?
Chiles	Richard May (D)	May 10, from Independence
Stone	Father Lempfrit (D)	
	James D. Miller (R)	May 13, from St. Joseph
Hensley		May 20 (est.), from Independence
Lassen		May 13 or 20, from Independence

*(D) = diary/journal; (L) = letter; (R) = reminiscence; (B) = biography

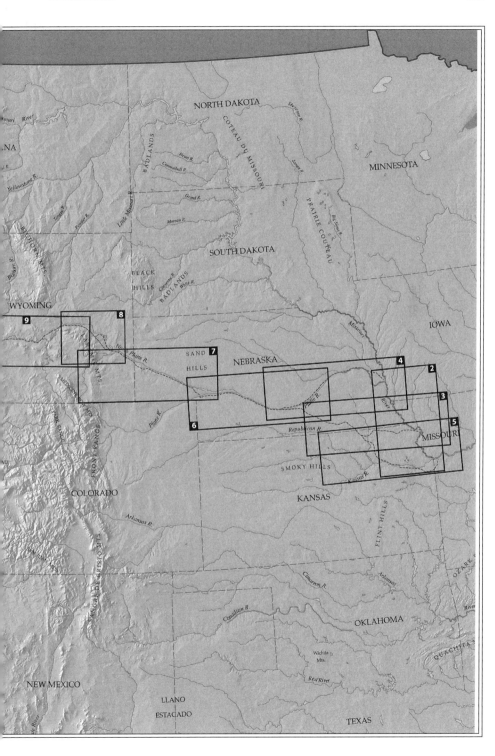

CHAPTER 1

Just Five Months to Get There

APRIL 1848

SECOND WEEK OF APRIL 1848
Thomas Corcoran and P. B. Cornwall, at Sarpy's Ferry,
Council Bluffs area, along the Missouri River

Just as the sun was about to slide behind the bluffs, two young men stood on the east bank of the Missouri River. They were at Sarpy's Ferry, nine miles north of the mouth of the Platte River. Their wagon party had already ferried across the roiling, quarter-mile-wide Missouri, and they were waiting for the flat-bottomed boat to return for them.

Thomas Corcoran fidgeted nervously with the reins of his jet-black mare and began a deep, breath-sucking, uncontrollable cough that doubled him up. His companion, P. B. (Pierre Barlow) Cornwall, looked at him with concern and asked if he was going to be all right. Thomas nodded uncertainly, trying to recover his breath, and wiped the bloody spittle from his mouth. The promise of a life-saving climate in California had drawn him away from his family and put him on the trail west. He suffered from an especially severe case of what he called "lung fever." Judging from his symptoms, it was probably what is now called histoplasmosis, caused by spores from a fungus (*Histoplasma capsulatum*) released when farmers turned the virgin prairie soils. Inhaled into the lungs, the spores could become a yeast and produce a moderate to severe lung affliction, which in its most serious form, could resemble the late stages of tuberculosis.[1] A doctor had warned Thomas that he would soon fill a grave beside his father unless he left immediately for a drier climate. Much of what we know about Thomas' journey comes from an evocative letter he sent to his sister, Elizabeth Lonergan.[2] Thomas was illiterate and had to dictate his letters.

As the ferry was nearing the east bank, two sober-faced men approached. According to Thomas, a man by the name of Doc Hann handed him a paper. Hann was suing Thomas, claiming his trespassing cattle had damaged Hann's land. The summons

1

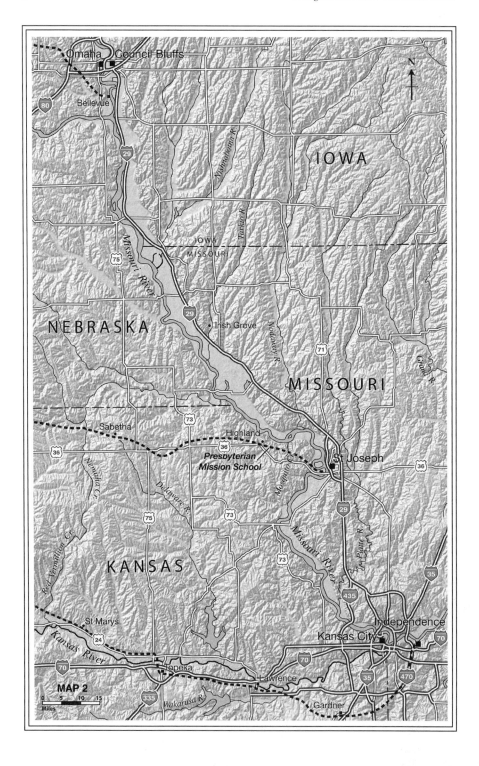

ordered Thomas to appear in court in sixty days or forfeit sixty-five dollars. The other man, Hann's son-in-law, grabbed Thomas' mare, intending to take her as restitution.

P. B. Cornwall pulled out his six-shooter and knife, and told Thomas to climb on his mare and get on the ferry. Doc Hann stepped back, nervously clearing his throat. Just who did he think he was, Hann asked Cornwall. "A better man than ever made you," P. B. answered coldly, fixing him with a withering stare. He joined Thomas on the ferry, and the two young men were safely deposited on the far bank.[3]

A few days earlier, P. B. Cornwall had attended a going-away party hosted by Thomas' sister. When Thomas left his family's sod cabin in northwest Missouri to join Cornwall and his small party, he was so sick that Elizabeth had to saddle his mare, Slipper, and help him mount. His mother "could hardly shake hands with" him, certain her twenty-three-year-old son would die along the trail with no friend to bury him. The separation was heart-wrenching, but if Thomas was to survive, he had to go.

The youngest of ten children, Thomas Corcoran was born in Kilcoltrim, County Carlow, Ireland in 1825. His family immigrated to Quebec in 1828. Then in 1841, Thomas, his parents, an older brother, and his sister, Elizabeth, heard of better opportunities in Missouri.[4] After arriving at a small trading post that would become St. Joseph, the Corcorans traveled sixty miles north to an area that would soon be organized as Atchison County. They came to rest at Irish Grove, where other Irish immigrant families had also come to settle. It was a picturesque place on bluffs overlooking the Missouri River. But as pretty as it was, Irish Grove had problems. The place was gaining a reputation for unhealthfulness—a country where swarms of mosquitoes infested the stagnant pools along the river. The settlers were plagued with malaria—what they called "fever and ague"—which they thought was caused by

Portrait of Thomas Corcoran (1825–1904), ca. 1876. Photograph taken by the Society of California Pioneers, when Thomas was about fifty years old. Courtesy of the Haggin Museum, Stockton, California.

"bad air" and was an inescapable part of life.[5] But the Corcorans' neighbor, Martin Murphy Sr., did not feel the disease was inescapable. After losing a wife and granddaughter to malaria, he concluded that Irish Grove was an unhealthy place to live.[6] Father Christian Hoecken, a Jesuit missionary with the nearby Pottawattamie tribe, had heard that California was a Catholic country and a healthful place to raise a family. On his urging, the Murphys and some neighbors left for California in 1844.[7]

Lung fever could also be a problem, and the Corcoran family had come down with it. At one time, they were so sick that Father Hoecken had to come and nurse the family back to health. In 1844, Thomas' father, Francis, died at age sixty. While the cause of his death is unknown, the prevalence of malaria and lung fever in the area suggests some possible causes.[8]

Money was scarce in Missouri in those years. The economy was largely one of subsistence and barter, and most settlers lacked the cash to purchase the government land on which they settled. In 1846, word reached Irish Grove that war had been declared against Mexico and President Polk had ordered the raising of a volunteer Missouri regiment to be trained at Fort Leavenworth. Thomas crossed the Missouri River and traveled to the fort, where he worked as a teamster, driving freight wagons for Colonel Stephen W. Kearny's Army of the West as it marched to Santa Fe. At the end of his tour of duty, he returned to the humid air of Irish Grove and his lung fever returned with a vengeance.[9]

P. B. Cornwall was born in Delaware County, New York, in 1821. When he was fifteen, he left home to work as a cook on a Lake Ontario steamer. At eighteen, he traveled to the Wisconsin Territories to try his luck at fur trapping. The following year, in 1840, his father died and left him a mercantile store in Manchester, Ohio. After operating the store for seven years, P. B. sold it, but the proceeds were insufficient to pay his creditors. At the beginning of 1848, P. B. was twenty-six and mired in debt.[10]

P. B. had read John C. Fremont's *Report of the Exploring Expedition to the Rocky Mountains.* It told of his experiences in 1842 as a captain in the U.S. Corps of Topographical Engineers, when he and his team of engineers and *voyageurs* were sent to explore the Rocky Mountains, Oregon, and California. Fremont's sobriquet, the Great Pathfinder, was misleading; he mostly followed trails already used by Indians, trappers, and mountain men. The Great Publicist would have been more accurate. His superbly written book, published in 1845, was produced with the

Daguerreotype portrait of Pierre Barlow (P. B.) Cornwall (1821–1904), ca. 1851. From *Life Sketch of Pierre Barlow Cornwall* (San Francisco: A. M. Robinson, 1906).

assistance of Jessie, his learned wife and the daughter of Senator Thomas Hart Benton. A curious, hungry public read this gallant, epic adventure and many a reader was moved by its romanticized description of the West, including Henry Wadsworth Longfellow, who wrote: "[H]ighly entertaining and exciting. . . . What a wild life and what a fresh existence! But, ah, the discomfort!"[11]

Like many others, P. B. credited Fremont's *Report* with inspiring him and his sixteen-year-old brother, Arthur, to leave Ohio early in the spring of 1848. They had decided to go to Oregon to make their new start.

Much of the information about P. B.'s 1848 journey west comes from a biography written by his son in 1906, after P. B.'s death.[12] According to that account, it was early April when the Cornwall brothers arrived in St. Joseph, then a settlement of about 1,800 year-round residents.

For many years, Independence, Missouri, had been the most prominent jumping-off point for travelers to the Far West. Beginning in the early 1820s, traders and merchants set out from Independence with their huge, lumbering, wide-wheeled freight wagons, and rumbled down the Santa Fe Trail for Taos and Santa Fe. The first parties to head for the Oregon Territories departed from Independence in 1838, and the first wagon party bound for California left from there in 1841.[13]

But nothing stays the same for long. The fledgling settlement of St. Joseph also sat along the Missouri River, where it could be supplied by steamboats coming up from St. Louis. It was also sixty miles farther north than Independence, making it a shorter overland route to Oregon and California. All it needed was merchants to outfit wagon companies.

The shops and stores came, and the first westward-bound wagons departed from St. Joseph in 1844. By the following year, its reputation as a jumping-off place had been established. Its just-founded newspaper, the *St. Joseph Gazette*, reported on May 2, 1845, that a company of Oregon emigrants, consisting "of one thousand persons, one hundred wagons and about two thousand cattle," were camped just outside of town.

The eager merchants of St. Joseph published an "article" in the *Gazette*'s issue of March 6, 1846. The lengthy promotion, directed to "all those who are desirous of emigrating to Oregon or California," invited people to select "St. Joseph as the place to which they should direct their course, possessing as it does, all the facilities for furnishing such necessities as may be required for the journey." The article boasted that St. Joseph possessed "13 large mercantile establishments, which are capable of furnishing every article in the Grocery and Dry Goods line that may be required for the outfit, at prices as cheap as the emigrant can bring them from St. Louis." It had a "large Flour Mill, . . . large Beef and Pork packing establishments," and "a sufficient number of Blacksmiths, Wagon Makers, Saddlers and other mechanics, who are always prepared . . . to make or repair any article in their line . . . and at prices that will give satisfaction." As if that wasn't enough, readers were assured that St. Joseph was "the *nearest* and *best* route," being "upwards of ONE HUNDRED MILES nearer than *any other point* on the western frontier."

By 1847, St. Joseph had fully developed its outfitting capabilities. That, together with its unabashed self-promotion, resulted in 867 wagons departing from there that year.[14] Even bigger things were predicted for 1848. The January 21, 1848, issue of the *Gazette* mentioned that "[a]ppearances indicate that a large emigration will be made to Oregon during the present year.... We anticipate that many hundreds will congregate at this place before the first of May, and cross the river here."

When P. B. and Arthur Cornwall stepped off the steamboat at St. Joseph in early spring of 1848, they would have seen what Riley Root, an Oregon-bound emigrant of that year, reported: a little river town with over twenty stores, three taverns, three boardinghouses, two flour mills, two sawmills, eight blacksmith shops, a couple of wagon shops, and plenty of prairie grass nearby upon which to graze oxen, mules, and horses.[15] In short, St. Joseph had everything an emigrant needed for a journey across the plains—and everything needed to eclipse Independence as the gateway to the Far West.

According to the Cornwall biography, P. B. and his brother arrived at St. Joseph with little more than Fremont's *Report*, "a Bible, a dictionary and copies of Moore, Byron, and Burns." They outfitted themselves, buying "horses, provisions, clothing, muskets, rifles . . . and miscellaneous articles of general use and Indian trading."

Although P. B. had Fremont's *Report* and its maps, he decided to hire a guide. St. Joseph had those for sale too. Each spring, men with impressive credentials would hang around Independence and St. Joseph and offer themselves as pilots to Oregon or California.

In its December 3, 1847, issue, the *Gazette* mentioned "that Mr. Moses Harris (a gentleman of a good deal of Oregon, California and Rocky Mountain distinction) is now in St. Joseph, and will remain here during the winter.... We believe that Mr. H. intends returning to Oregon next spring, and if so, his services as a pilot shall by all means be engaged by the emigrants."

One couldn't do much better than to be piloted by "Black" Harris. With dark skin and coal-black eyes, hair, and whiskers, the frontiersman came by his nickname fairly. As a young man, he had learned his skills as a fur trapper in the upper Missouri region in the 1820s. He was part of the Ashley-Henry brigade of trappers from 1823 through 1827, working in the Rockies with some of the most famous mountain men ever: Jedediah Smith, Thomas Fitzpatrick, Jim Bridger, William Sublette, and James Clyman. Harris continued as a trapper until beaver became scarce, then offered his knowledge of the western trails to travelers taking wagons to Oregon. He guided a large wagon party leaving Independence for Oregon in the spring of 1844, then remained in Oregon in 1845 and 1846. He and seven companions returned to the States in the spring of 1847, and at South Pass he joined Commodore Robert F. Stockton and his party returning east after Stockton had "conquered" California.[16]

The Stockton party arrived in St. Joseph on October 23, 1847, and Harris hung around the small town, as the *Gazette* article had noted.

Two months later, the January 21st *Gazette* reported that "Mr. Harris is still in the neighborhood of St. Joseph, and will pilot a company to Oregon or California. St. Joseph is still his headquarters, and he will start from this place as the most eligible." But the Cornwalls did not sign on with the legendary "Black" Harris. They hired William O. Fallon instead.

Cornwall's biography reported that "Tom Fallon, woodsman, hunter, scout and freelance, who had already traversed the west, was engaged as guide" (it got Fallon's first name wrong).[17] Fallon was described in Thomas Corcoran's letter as a former Rocky Mountain trapper and Indian "interpreter."

Fallon's résumé was not to be taken lightly either. He was a big man, sometimes referred to as Big Fallon or Le Gros. Yet he was considered "cat-like in his quickness and grace."[18] The master historian of the West, Bernard DeVoto, called him "as fantastic a mountain man as the [fur] trade ever produced, a giant who had preceded even the Ashley men into the mountains and had roamed the entire West ever since."[19] Like "Black" Harris, Fallon had been an experienced mountain man and trapper, having been employed by Ashley-Henry, the American Fur Company, and Hudson's Bay Company.[20] He was later reported as traveling with a trading company in 1835, and with wagon trains going to Oregon in 1842 and 1844.[21] He was in California in 1846 and 1847, and led the fourth relief party into the snowbound Sierras to save whoever was left of the stricken Donner party. In 1847, he had acted as a guide for General Stephen W. Kearny's party, which left California in June and arrived at Fort Leavenworth in August, completing the journey in only sixty-four days.[22]

It is not without significance that William Fallon was married to an Oglala Sioux and was fluent in French and a number of Indian dialects.[23] This was an important asset. Travelers wanted a guide who, in addition to knowing the trail, knew the Indian character—one who could keep his composure when Indians approached, and could tell the difference between a hostile war party on the prowl and a harmless hunting group. In short, the Cornwalls had hired an exceptionally qualified guide.

Weather played a pivotal role in determining when wagon companies began their journeys west. They would ordinarily not leave until spring weather had produced enough new grass to support their livestock. When the Cornwalls arrived in St. Joseph, they were early, but they were not the only emigrants waiting to leave. On January 21, the *Gazette* reported that "about forty families are in St. Joseph and the neighborhood, awaiting the spring time, when they will set out for that country or California." It would be some time before any wagon parties would depart. A cool, dry spring meant the new grass was behind schedule. Even if the Cornwalls were rash enough to leave before the new grass appeared, Fallon was experienced enough to know that it would have been terribly reckless for three people to strike out alone across Indian Territory. They needed the protection of a wagon company.

Fallon and the Cornwalls could have patiently waited in St. Joseph for a wagon train to form, but for some reason, they decided to leave St. Joe and head 120 miles north to Council Bluffs. "[I]n April, 1848," Cornwall's biography explained, they "left 'St. Joe,' going by way of Council Bluffs where were encamped some five hundred Oregon immigrants."[24] Considering how ideal St. Joseph was for embarking on a journey west, their decision to go north to Council Bluffs seems odd, but the Cornwall biography fails to explain. P. B. does not appear to be a patient person; his behavior suggests he was a restless fellow, unwilling to wait around. He must have believed the Oregon-bound emigrants at Council Bluffs would depart sooner than those congregating in St. Joseph.

Fallon may have played a role in the decision. In leading the fourth relief party to the Donner camp in April 1847, he would have witnessed gruesome sights. When Fallon and General Kearny's eastbound party came across the Donner camps two months later, they had to collect and rebury scattered bones uncovered by melted snow.[25] Fallon had seen the unspeakable and must have related these images to the Cornwalls.

It is undeniable that the Donner party made some foolish decisions that caused them to arrive in the Sierras late. But the snows came unusually early in '46, and were of unprecedented severity and duration. With limited experience crossing the Sierras, it is understandable why many may have assumed such early and severe snows were the norm. News of the Donner tragedy may have generated a heightened sense of urgency among some guides in 1848 to get their parties started as early as possible and not to dawdle on the trail. Perhaps Fallon was one of these. "Just five months to get there" would have sounded like sage advice.

In the meantime, a party of wagons was leaving Independence. J. P. C. Allsopp had recently been discharged from the U.S. Navy after serving in the Mexican War. He was traveling with a stag company, a group "of young men of Southern birth" who had arrived at Independence in the spring and had joined a party of twenty-five wagons. Allsopp wrote a short reminiscence in the 1880s—the only one known to have left a record of the group's journey. He was not the party's leader, but since there is no other name by which to identify it, it will hereafter be referred to as the Allsopp company. They left Independence on April 10, and because of its early departure, it would have been a good group for the Cornwalls to join. But the Cornwalls had likely not heard about it.

In any event, Fallon and the two Cornwall brothers departed St. Joseph and traveled north to Council Bluffs through a sparsely populated landscape that until 1836 had been exclusively reserved for Indians. Traveling on horseback, they probably took the stage and mail road that passed through Irish Grove in Atchison County. Since Thomas and his family lived less than a mile west of where the road passed through the Irish community, it is likely that the Cornwalls came in contact with Thomas when they passed through there, perhaps while stopping for food and rest.[26] One can picture Thomas talking with them, and telling them of his poor health and his need to go to a dry climate. He might have mentioned that his former neighbors Martin Murphy, Patrick Martin, and John Sullivan had left Irish Grove with their families in 1844 to go to California. He surely would have explained that the group had traveled to Council Bluffs, where they formed the Stephens-Townsend-Murphy party.[27] Thomas may have also confided with an embarrassed grin that he was looking forward to seeing his former neighbor Ellen Murphy, a darling girl two years older than he was.[28]

When the Cornwalls left Irish Grove, Thomas was with them. They may have seen him as an asset—another person, another horse, another rifle. Perhaps he had told the Cornwalls of his experience as a veteran of Colonel Kearny's Army of the West. There had to be some value in that, even if he had only been a teamster driving a freight wagon. Maybe it was just because P. B. liked him. But considering Thomas' shaky constitution and the severity of his sickness, one wonders how P. B. could have seen him as anything but a burden and a liability.

When Cornwall and his entourage finally arrived at Council Bluffs, they would have come to the rim of the bluffs and gazed upon the Missouri River floodplain below. Bluff to bluff, it was about five miles across. It would have been a much different landscape than exists today. Imagine the scene in 1848. Blink away the skyscrapers of the Omaha skyline, the office buildings, the congested freeways, the glittering casinos, and the tall exhaust stacks of the power plants. Reimagine the vegetation. The rolling land, stretching back from the bluffs on both sides of the river, was largely prairie grassland. Trees, mostly oak, black walnut, ash, and elm, would only be found along the creek bottoms. The floodplain was a flat, grassy meadow, interspersed with areas of mosquito-infested marshes. Along the riverbanks grew narrow bands of tall cottonwoods. The river, a churning ribbon of brown, muddy water, was generally much wider, shallower, and slower moving than it is today. Its course has changed a great deal since 1848, owing to its current, constantly eating away at the far edge of a bend, and depositing sand and silt on the near bank. Over time, each bend pushed farther forward, becoming more extreme and acute, until the raging waters of the next inevitable flood shot across and scoured out a shortcut. When the floodwaters receded, the former bend was left abandoned like an orphan, and in subsequent floods would gradually fill in with silt.

Both Corcoran's letter and Cornwall's biography expressly used the name Council Bluffs for the place from which their party departed, even though there was no town or settlement by that name in those days. The name referred to the general area, so-called because Lewis and Clark, pausing about forty miles north of the mouth of the Platte in August 1804, held a council with chiefs of the Otoe tribe at the foot of some high bluffs just west of the river and a few miles north of present-day Omaha.

Returning from the Upper Missouri, Lewis and Clark brought glowing reports of abundant beaver in the Upper Missouri tributaries. As a result, beaver trapping brigades moved west to the Rocky Mountains. Fur companies established new outposts in the Council Bluffs area and came to rely on a growing legion of *engagés*, and free or independent trappers operating in the Rocky Mountains. In 1822, the Missouri Fur Company established a trading post at a place called La Belle Vue (Beautiful View) on a high bluff on the west side of the Missouri River. The place soon came to be called Bellevue.[29] Following a trail that Indians had used for centuries to reach their buffalo hunting grounds, the fur companies began supplying their trappers in the Rockies from their Bellevue and Council Bluffs outposts. In time, a clearly marked, easily traveled wagon trail was established connecting Bellevue to the fur country beyond the Continental Divide.

The Cornwalls, Fallon, and Corcoran descended the bluffs and moved across the river bottom, dodging the swamps and quagmires, then forded Mosquito Creek. They encountered a group of emigrants camping on a dry, grassy spot. This was the "five hundred Oregon-bound immigrants" Cornwall's biography mentioned, although evidence shows there were substantially fewer.[30]

Two-and-a-half-year-old Inez Eugenia Adams was too young to remember much, but many years later, she wrote a recollection based on stories her parents had told her of the trip, including her own memory of sleeping in a tent on the prairie grass at Council Bluffs.[31] Her father, W. L. Adams, had left Galesburg, in Knox County, Illinois, in March 1848, with a large party of about fifty wagons that included friends and acquaintances from towns and communities near Galesburg. A college-educated schoolteacher, Adams had declined an offer to become a college administrator. Determined to emigrate to Oregon, he outfitted himself with a covered wagon, four yoke of oxen, and two milk cows (one a fourteen-year-old cow named Rose) and painted the words "Hic Transit" on his wagon cover.[32]

Cornwall discovered that the Oregon emigrants "were not going to break camp for some two weeks to come. This was longer than he was willing to wait."[33] So P. B. and his companions left the Oregon camp, followed the road through a band of tall cottonwoods that bordered the river, and came to Trader's Point, a filthy little trading post belonging to Peter A. Sarpy.[34]

Just beyond the post, on the eastern bank of the river, was the landing for Sarpy's Ferry, the southernmost ferry in the Council Bluffs area. It had been in existence since at least 1840, and was the one the Murphys probably used in 1844 when they set out for California.[35] In 1848, the Missouri channel was farther west than it is today, and the location of Sarpy's Trader's Point, long since washed away, is at today's Gifford's Point, near Camp Gifford Road and west of the present river channel.[36]

Twenty miles north of Sarpy's Ferry was a large encampment of Mormons who had escaped Nauvoo by the thousands in February 1846. Many had used Sarpy's Ferry to cross the Missouri River, but Sarpy's small ferry was inadequate to transport all of the estimated two thousand Mormon wagons, so the Mormons constructed their own ferry upriver from Sarpy's. By 1848, the Mormons were operating three ferries—the upper, middle, and lower.[37]

While neither Cornwall's biography nor Corcoran's letter specified which ferry they used, it is almost certain they used Sarpy's "Gentile ferry," which was the southernmost and therefore the most convenient.[38] Besides, non-Mormons tended to not do business with Mormons unless it was necessary. And the feeling was mutual; the Mormons were bitter over the years of persecution by Gentiles, particularly Missourians, whom they commonly reviled as "Missouri Pukes." The Mormons were also convinced that God would soon inflict retribution on the Gentiles, so they tended to stay away from them, not wanting to be too close when God's lightning bolts began to strike.

After disembarking from the ferry, P. B. and Thomas would have ascended a draw through the towering western bluffs. From the top of the draw, they could have looked out through the fading light and seen the orange glow of the campfires of the Oregon-bound emigrants on the east side of the river. Twenty miles to the north were the Mormons' "Winter Quarters," and six miles to the northeast, across the river, in a notch where Mosquito Creek descended through the eastern bluffs, were a few other Mormon camps. The two young men should have been able to make out columns of smoke curling into the sky from the Mormon campfires and chimneys. In the next several weeks, 2,400 Mormons would leave the area to join fellow Saints at Salt Lake. But since they had not nearly as far to travel and wished to avoid contact with the Gentiles, it would be a while before the Mormons would begin to stir in earnest.

Anxious to join their companions, the two men continued along the top of the bluff until they arrived at the tiny settlement of Bellevue. Although it was the eastern terminus of the long Council Bluffs trail to the Far West, there wasn't much there besides a Presbyterian Indian mission and the Council Bluffs Indian Agency. The federal government had established the Indian Agency in 1823 to serve the Omaha, Otoe, Missouri, and Pawnee tribes. The agency's compound at Council Bluffs consisted of a number of deteriorating buildings and some small fields. One of its functions was to distribute government annuities to the tribes;[39] another was to mediate the never-ending disputes between tribes and negotiate peace treaties that never lasted. The agency maintained a blacksmith shop and a number of cabins that housed a blacksmith, a translator, a teacher, and some farmers, all employed by the agency. For twenty-five years, the agency had been trying, with disappointing success, to teach trades and modern farming practices to the local natives.

When Reverend Moses Merrill and his wife arrived in Bellevue in 1833 as Baptist missionaries, the fur traders' whiskey had already affected most of the local Indians.

After seven disheartening years, during which Merrill complained of his inability to stem the Indians' intemperance, he died a broken man and his wife returned east. Reverend Ambler Edson and his wife came in 1841 to fill Merrill's shoes, but they gave up a year later and abandoned the place for much the same reason.[40] Bellevue was then without missionaries until 1846, when the Presbyterian Board of Missions sent Reverend Edward Kinney. His efforts were evident when the Cornwall party arrived; his mission house was rising handsomely and would be completed by the end of the year.[41]

Cornwall and Corcoran must have been exhausted from the day's travels. Riding into the camp established by their fellow travelers, Thomas might have looked toward the West, where the emigrant trail disappeared into a vast grass-covered sea and the pink and crimson sky met the far-off horizon. He might have felt his breath quicken just a little, worried that in his sickened state this journey might be too much.

P. B. Cornwall was determined to not languish here any more than he had been prepared to languish in St. Joseph. According to his biography, he was "desirous of getting well on [his] way before the tide of emigration began." By staying ahead of it, he believed he would be assured of "the choice of grass for their animals and camping spots for themselves." What he needed, however, was protection from the Indians, so he was looking for some emigrants with wagons with whom he could travel. And he succeeded. He had been "joined by Orrin Kellogg, his son Joseph and two young men named Hathaway."[42]

The large Kellogg family was also anxious to get away early. The party of fourteen had as many as four wagons. Orrin Kellogg and his son Joseph had gone to Oregon in 1845 and returned to Wood County, Ohio, in 1846; they were now escorting the rest of the family back to the Willamette Valley. The party included Orrin's wife, Margaret, his younger sons, Edward, Elijah, George, Jason, and daughter Phoebe. There was also Orrin's oldest son, Joseph, and his wife, Estella, and their two young children, Orrin and Charles, and Orrin's son-in-law, Sylvester Hathaway, married to Orrin's daughter Charlotte, and Sylvester's brother, Daniel.[43] Biographical sketches of the Kelloggs written years later reported that the family left Ohio in November 1847 and traveled by steamer to St. Joseph, where they spent the winter. The Kelloggs left St. Joseph the next spring, and although they mentioned traveling with Cornwall, they did not mention going through Council Bluffs.[44] Yet Corcoran and Cornwall were both clear that they had departed from Council Bluffs, where the Kelloggs had joined them.[45]

Corcoran wrote to his sister that their party also included a young man named Young "that lived in Hayes Grove," but there is no other information about Young or anyone else who may have been part of this small group. With perhaps no more than thirteen men, they might have worried whether the group was large enough to make it safely through Indian Territory.

Around the campfire that evening, the two groups might have gazed at each other, studying each unfamiliar face in the flickering amber-orange light. They were probably sizing each other up, wondering whether it was such a good idea throwing in with people they didn't know. But despite the uncertainty, it must have seemed better to travel with a few strangers than to face Indians alone.

While Thomas was bringing a rifle and a good-looking mare, it was important that everyone be able to pull his weight and it was impossible for him to hide his poor health. Some of the party must have eyed him apprehensively, wondering whether it was such a good idea having him along.

CHAPTER 2

St. Joseph, a Rising Star
APRIL 15

APRIL 15, 1848

James Clyman, Wayne City landing on the Missouri River,
two miles north of Independence, Missouri

Imagine James Clyman standing on the hurricane deck of the stern-wheeler *Tamerlane*. He leans against the railing, having made his way up to get away from the main deck crammed with wagons, crates, a few head of livestock, and shoulder-to-shoulder people. The brass bell and shrill whistle echo across the water as the big steamboat pulls away from the Wayne City landing on the south bank of the Missouri River. Enjoying the cool breeze, Clyman squints past the brick and wood buildings along the landing and traces the steep road that winds its way up the bluffs. Independence, just out of sight beyond the bluffs, is two and a half miles away on the edge of the frontier.

In his younger years, Clyman had been a trapper, hunter, and frontiersman of the first rank—complete with fringed buckskin tunic, leggings, and moccasins—a companion of such legendary names as Jedediah Smith, Jim Bridger, William Sublette, and Thomas Fitzpatrick. Clyman "possessed the keenest sight of any man I ever knew," one friend claimed. Another regarded him as "a splendid rifle shot." He was tall, over six feet, rawboned, very powerful, walked with a long, quick stride, and possessed an uncommon endurance that had saved his life on a number of occasions.[1] As a young trapper returning from the Rocky Mountains in 1827, Clyman guided his fellow trappers down the Sweetwater and Platte Rivers, then passed Independence just as it was being established. In the spring of 1844, he came to Independence and joined a wagon train bound for Oregon.[2] After spending a stint in Oregon, he traveled to California, then guided an eastbound party in the spring of 1846, arriving in Independence on July 23. As soon as he reached the town, he hastened to Noland's Tavern to wash the trail dust down his throat.[3] He was getting up in years now and may have lost some of his strength and endurance, but probably not much. His travels through the West during 1844 through 1846 confirmed that, even in his midfifties, his hunting abilities had not diminished much and he was still quite capable of living off the land in rugged circumstances.

In 1848, the fifty-six-year-old Clyman decided to leave his home in Milwaukee, Wisconsin, and return to California. This time he was bypassing Independence, and going on to the recently established St. Joseph, which he had heard was the up-and-coming place to "jump off."

As the *Tamerlane* struggled against the stubborn current of the half-mile-wide river, there was a thud and the boat lurched as it glanced off a submerged tree trunk that the pilot had somehow missed. But the steamer kept going, having suffered no ill effects. Like all the steamboats that plied the Missouri, the *Tamerlane* was specially designed to navigate the shallow, muddy river. It was a flat-bottomed vessel with a shallow draft, and the pilot stood high in the wheelhouse so he would have a good view of the ever-changing channel

Portrait of James Clyman (1792–1881), ca. 1870s. Frontispiece from *James Clyman: An American Frontiersman* (San Francisco: California Historical Society, 1928). Courtesy of California Historical Society, FN-00794/CHS2010.217.

that meandered back and forth. It was a dangerous river, due to the shifting sandbars and ever-eroding current that uprooted trees from its banks. Submerged sand dunes on the bottom of the channel never stayed put; they were always moving, but skilled pilots could see where they were.

When a bank of the river caved in, as happened regularly, whole trees fell into the water and were carried along by the current. Some lodged in the river bottom. These snags were especially dangerous—one could tear through a boat's hull. Because of this, steamboats usually traveled only during daylight hours, moving slowly upstream at ten miles per hour. The pilot kept a sharp eye out, searching for any floating debris, a telltale "boil," or any other disturbance in the water's surface that signaled a hidden snag or sandbar.

During his travels in 1844 through 1846, Clyman had been a dedicated diarist, filling the pages of nine journals with his keen observations. His thoughts and actions in 1848, however, would largely remain obscure because, for some reason, he would not keep a journal this year. Perhaps he felt that he had seen it all before and could add little to his previous writings. But he was taking his nine journals to California, safely protected in his *parfleche*, a waterproofed carrying bag of well-oiled buffalo hide.

Since Clyman kept no written record of his travels in 1848, it is not certain that he was a passenger of the *Tamerlane*, but the odds are great that he was. It is known that he left Milwaukee in the spring of 1848 for St. Joseph.[4] It made no sense for him to make a long overland trip on horseback from Milwaukee when all he had to do was book passage on the nearest steamboat to the Mississippi, then voyage downriver to St. Louis, then up the Missouri to St. Joseph. Records indicate that there were about twenty steamboats traveling the Missouri River that year. Because the volume of commerce dropped off as one went further upriver, most of those steamboats did not go beyond Weston (at present-day Kansas City) or Fort Leavenworth. Those going as far as St. Joseph or Council Bluffs were fewer and ran more infrequently.[5] A steamer took between eight and thirteen days to travel the 449 miles of winding river from St. Louis to St. Joseph, much of the time being taken up with loading and unloading passengers and cargo, and with stopping periodically to "wood the boat" to keep the boiler fires going. Clyman is believed to have traveled with a wagon company that left St. Joseph shortly after the *Tamerlane* arrived in St. Joseph.

A young man by the name of Rudolph Friederich Kurz wrote in his journal that he left St. Louis aboard the *Tamerlane* on April 5 and arrived at St. Joseph on April 18.[6]

Kurz was fascinated with frontiersmen. If Clyman had been a passenger on the *Tamerlane*, Kurz would have been attracted to the man a friend described as an exemplar of an earlier age, usually dressed in a frontiersman's signature costume and with his knife, tomahawk, and a treasured muzzle-loading Hawken rifle never far from his reach.[7] In his heavy accent, Kurz might have introduced himself to Clyman, informing him that he was a young artist from Switzerland who had come to study and paint Indians on the American frontier. Clyman was known to be a man of few words, but he might have told the young foreigner that he knew a great deal about Indians.

With plenty of time on this slow-moving boat, Clyman might have told Kurz some of his harrowing Indian exploits. Folding his arms, with his dark blue eyes staring into space, the old frontiersman might have begun by relating his experience with the Ashley-Henry expedition of 1823. He could relate how he was a part of that ill-fated brigade of seventy trappers and boatmen who traveled up the Missouri in keelboats that spring. He could describe how they encountered a large Arikara village along the river, how thirteen of his companions had been killed in the ensuing battle, and how he had escaped death by outrunning and outlasting a party of Arikara warriors who chased him on foot across endless miles of prairie. And that story could have been the first of many.

———————————

On April 18, the *Tamerlane* steamed up to the St. Joseph landing, the boat's crew pulling in the lines to the rhythm of one of their jubilee songs.[8] The boat tied up on the east side of the river, a hundred or so yards south of where Blacksnake Creek entered the river at the foot of the Blacksnake Hills.

No matter which steamboat Clyman arrived on that April, he would have traveled with passengers of all stripes: tradesmen and traders, mountain men and mechanics, and emigrants bound for Oregon or California. Amid the soft hissing of steam from the now-quiescent boilers, a long line of passengers would have hurried down the tottering gangplank, followed by rumbling wagons. Then came the barrels, kegs, crates, boxes, bales, and sacks of goods, off-loaded by a host of stevedores.

The young Swiss recorded what he saw: "Though the town [St. Joseph] was founded only six years ago, there are evidences already of a rapidly expanding and flourishing city. . . . Upon my arrival the principal streets are much enlivened by fur traders and emigrants on their way to regions, as yet little known, in Oregon and California." The long-bearded fur traders were the most colorful characters in town, according to Kurz, wearing funny-looking furry caps and fringed, embroidered buckskins.[9]

Home to about a thousand residents in 1848, St. Joseph was still a young town, founded as recently as 1842 by Joseph Robidoux. The son of a St. Louis-based fur trader, Robidoux began accompanying traders up the Missouri River in 1799, when he was but sixteen years old.[10] He set up his own trading post in the Council Bluffs area in 1809, and became such a successful trader that the American Fur Company thought his trading post stood in the way of its long-term aspirations, so it bought him out. Drawn to St. Michael's Meadow at the foot of the Blacksnake Hills, Robidoux built a cabin there about 1829 and began trading goods for furs with the local Indians.[11] He kept twenty French *engagés* busy, sending them onto the plains of Kansas and Nebraska to trade beads, mirrors, pots, pans, knives, and brightly colored cloth to the Indians for furs and buffalo hides.

Portrait of Joseph Robidoux (1783–1868). Courtesy of St. Joseph Museums, Inc., St. Joseph, Missouri.

Under the Indian Intercourse Act of 1834, that area had been designated Indian Territory and no white man was allowed to live there except federally licensed traders such as Robidoux. Nevertheless, scores of white squatters, perhaps up to two hundred families, had settled in the area anyway. Then came the Platte Purchase of 1836, where the American government purchased two million acres from the Sac, Fox, and Iowa tribes, and thousands of white settlers rushed into the area, joining the hundreds of illegal squatters.[12]

Robidoux's trading post, located where the river made a broad curve to the east and facing a large, flat meadow, was an ideal spot for a town. The river cut its deepest channel against the eastern bank, making it an excellent landing for steamers. He had a town plat drawn up designating streets, blocks, and lots covering 160 acres, and named the town St. Joseph in honor of his patron saint.[13]

After recording his plat map in St. Louis in July 1843, Robidoux immediately began selling lots. Stores and shops quickly sprang up to serve the growing population of farmers in the area. The town opened a new era in 1844, when a wagon train assembled in St. Joseph and departed for Oregon. By May 1845, the town had its first newspaper, the *St. Joseph Gazette,* which reported that the town had a population of 682.[14]

Wagon trains ordinarily left during an extremely narrow window of time. Although it would have varied slightly from year to year, depending on the weather, rarely would any wagon company leave St. Joseph before April 25, owing to the lack of new grass. And rarely would one leave after May 25 because of fears of early snows in the Cascades or Sierras. Consequently, there would be about one month of frantic activity, then things would abruptly return to normal.

When Clyman and Kurz stepped off the *Tamerlane* on April 18, the town was no longer quiet, not like when the Cornwall brothers had been there a few weeks earlier. The crowded town was beginning to bustle, enlivened with the energy of large numbers of recently arrived emigrants.

Clyman must have strode through the muddy streets with his characteristic long, quick stride, inhaling the sweet aroma of fresh horse and ox manure hanging in the humid air. He would have eyed the freight wagons that lumbered down the streets and the saddle horses tied to the storefront hitching rails, stamping their feet and swishing their tails to keep flies from alighting. He probably nodded to other mountain men in their fringed buckskins, but walked grim-faced past Sac and Fox Indians who leaned languidly against the saloon walls.

Clyman had never been here before and perhaps he was struck by the newness of the buildings. But new or not, at least one 1849 visitor was not favorably impressed, describing the town as "dirty" and "uninviting."[15] A multitude of shops lined the littered streets, offering almost anything an emigrant might need, and the town resounded with the ringing of iron against iron in the blacksmith shops. Some of the emigrants would be inquiring about whom they might join up with, as it was deemed imperative to join a company large enough to get them safely through Indian Territory.

Excited emigrants rushed from store to store, trying to complete the details of outfitting themselves for the journey. Stories of the Donner party and its terrible fate in the Sierra snows had been making the rounds, some true and some grotesquely embellished. In any event, there was a prevailing sense of urgency to get going.

One emigrant, loud and uncouth, haggled with an oxen trader, another pleaded with a blacksmith, and another made inquiries with a dry goods clerk. After all, this was a once-in-a-lifetime undertaking. It had to be the most exciting, trying, unnerving, and daunting thing these emigrants had ever done—or would do—in their lives. If they survived the journey, they could feel a smug pride at their accomplishment, something that ought to be seen as heroic in the eyes of their "meek-hearted" friends and relatives who stayed behind. It is no wonder that emotions ran high.

If Clyman had bothered to wander beyond the town limits, he would have observed clusters of parked, canvas-covered wagons, white cotton tents pegged into the ground, and large numbers of cattle, horses, and mules grazing on the outlying prairie.

Emigrants leaving homes west of the Mississippi, such as Iowa and Missouri, usually came overland in their own ox-drawn wagons loaded with many of the provisions they would need. Emigrants from east of the Mississippi River, such as Illinois, Indiana, or Ohio, usually sold their farms—and just about everything else—and traveled to the closest river port to board steamers that would carry them to St. Louis. Changing to smaller steamers, they ascended the Missouri until they arrived at St. Joseph, a town eager to outfit them with whatever they needed. Indeed, they had heard that it was often cheaper to buy wagons, yokes of oxen, and all the needed provisions in St. Joseph than to bring them on a steamer. Some of the St. Joseph prices were listed in a February 9, 1849, *Gazette* article that came out a few months before the full impact of gold rush prices hit:

> Wagons—$65.00–95.00
> Oxen per yoke—$30.00–40.00
> Mules—$30.00–60.00
> Flour, per cwt.—$1.50–1.75
> Coffee, per lb.—$.06–.08
> Sugar, per lb.—$.05–.06[16]

In planning for the journey, the emigrants had a long laundry list of questions. What kind of wagon? What should pull it—horses, mules, or oxen? What tools? How much flour, bacon, etc., etc.? What medicines? What firearms and how much powder and lead? In recent years, through trial and error and the lessons of hard knocks, the answers had pretty much been settled upon. In anticipation of these questions, the *Gazette* on March 19, 1847, published an article summarizing its recommendations for any emigrant who was still scratching his head in uncertainty. It is hard to know how many of the 1848 emigrants read it, but it is certain that it and similar versions abounded everywhere. If an emigrant had never seen or heard of such a list, a St. Joseph shopkeeper would have been only too glad to enlighten him.

The *Gazette* article read:

Subjoined you will find a list of the principle [sic] articles necessary for an outfit to Oregon and California, which may be useful to some of your readers. It has been carefully prepared from correct information derived from intelligent persons who have made the trip.

The wagons should be new, made of thoroughly seasoned timber, and well ironed and not too heavy with good light beds, strong bows, and large double sheets. There should be at least four yoke of oxen to each wagon—one yoke to be considered as extra, and to be used in cases of emergency. Every family should have at least two good milch cows, as milk is a great luxury on the road.

The amount of provisions should be as follows; to each person except infants:

200 lbs of bread stuff (flour and crackers)
100 lbs of Bacon
12 lbs of Coffee
12 lbs of Sugar

Each family should also take the following articles in proportion to the number, as follows:

From 1 to 5 lbs Tea
From 10 to 50 lbs Rice
From ½ to 2 bushels Beans
From ½ to 2 bushels dried fruit
From 1 to 5 lbs Salaratus
From 5 to 50 lbs Soap

Cheese, Dried Pumpkins, Onions and a small portion of Corn meal may be taken by those who desire them. The latter article, however, does not keep well.

No furniture should be taken, and as few cooking utensils as are indispensably necessary. Every family ought to have a sufficient supply of clothing for at least one year after their arrival, as everything of that kind is high in those countries. Some few cattle should be driven for beef, but much loose stock will be a great annoyance. Some Medicines should also be found in every family, the kind and quantity may be determined by consulting the family physician.

I would suggest to each family the propriety of taking a small sheet-iron cooking stove with fixtures, as the wind and rain often times renders it almost impossible to cook without them; they are light and cost but little. All the articles may be purchased on good terms in this place.

As an unattached bachelor, James Clyman would not be buying a wagon or oxen. Instead, he was probably looking to buy a good horse, or maybe two, as one was never sure what kind of misfortune might befall one on the trail. Someone might have mentioned Joseph Robidoux. The old Frenchman was not only the father of the town, he was also the father of many children—seven by his French wife and allegedly sixty by Indian consorts.[17] To support all this and his addiction to playing cards, Robidoux remained active in the trading business. He often placed ads in the *Gazette*, such as this one that appeared on June 2, 1848:

Horses wanted! I will purchase 20 or 30 head of horses on reasonable terms. Ponies suitable for the mountain trade preferable. —Jos. Robidoux

Clyman might have gone to the old Frenchman's stable, and if Robidoux was there, he would have encountered a man about his age, very French in appearance, with a dark, weathered face, scruffy graying whiskers, a large nose that didn't quite fit, and a broad-brimmed black hat that slouched over his dark eyes. Clyman had a keen eye and fond appreciation for good horseflesh, so he wouldn't have settled for anything mediocre.

It is possible that the two men had met years before. Robidoux's trading post in the 1820s was on the Missouri River, seven miles below Fort Atkinson, and he visited the fort often, looking for business. Perhaps they met when Clyman passed through the fort in 1823 as part of Ashley's ill-fated trapping brigade. Or perhaps in 1824, when Clyman stumbled, starving and half dead, into the fort after leaving the Sweetwater River valley in today's Wyoming and trekking alone on foot for eighty days over seven hundred miles.[18] But even if the two had not met, they should have been aware of each other's reputation; both were renowned along the Missouri. If the two met at Robidoux's stable, it would have been an interesting discourse between two men who had played significant roles in the opening of the West.

CHAPTER 3

Load the Wagons
APRIL 9–MAY 6

APRIL 9–25, 1848
Keturah Belknap, Van Buren County, Iowa

It was dawn and the rear end of a covered wagon was backed up against the steps of a log farmhouse in southeastern Iowa. Twenty-eight-year-old Keturah Belknap was helping her husband, George, load the wagon. As she carried items to the wagon, she mulled the bittersweet memories of the home she was leaving. Many she recorded in a journal, a detailed and touching account that gives us a unique glimpse into the life of one of the many remarkable women who left for Oregon in 1848.[1]

Keturah was nineteen in 1839 when she married George in Allen County, Ohio. That same year, she and George, along with his parents, Jesse and Jane Belknap, left Ohio to establish new farms on the prairie of southeastern Iowa. For eight years they worked arduously to clear the land and improve their farms. Keturah and George had four children during that time: Hannah born in 1841, John in 1843, Jesse in 1845, and Martha in 1846.

In November 1843, Keturah wrote, "I have experienced the first real trial of my life. After a few days of suffering our little Hannah died [at 2 ½ years old] of lung fever so we are left with one baby." Then in June 1845, she wrote, "I have had to pass thru another season of sorrow. Death has again entered our home; this time it has claimed our dear little John for its victim [at two years of age]." And then in October 1847, she recorded, "My dear little girl, Martha, was sick all summer and the 30th of October she died, one year and one month old. We now have one little boy left [Jesse]."

In the spring of 1847, she wrote: "Spring '47. The past winter there has been a strange fever raging here (it is the Oregon fever) it seems to be contagious and it is raging terribly, nothing seems to stop it but to tear up and take a six months trip across the plains with ox teams to the Pacific Ocean."

Some of the Belknaps' neighbors and relatives left for Oregon in May 1847, but George and Keturah traveled to Ohio by steamer so she could pay a last visit to her parents. "I knew it would be my last visit," she lamented, "but I kept all those thots buried in my own breast and never told them that the folks at home were fixing to cross the plains. . . . It was hard for me to not break down."

Upon their return to Iowa, Keturah wrote: "We found the folks all excitement about Oregon. . . . Our home was sold waiting our return to make out the papers. . . . There was nothing done or talked of but what had Oregon in it."

A decade earlier, most people knew little about the Far West, but by 1848 some of the first emigrants to Oregon had returned east, many reporting a depressing view of the place. After all, the returnees tended to be the most dissatisfied element of a generally dissatisfied class. The fact that they had gone to Oregon in the first place suggested that they were restless spirits, readily drawn to new exploits like moths drawn to the light. They were often malcontents, people who wanted something— anything—new. They had trouble finding peace and satisfaction; wherever they alighted, they quickly reentered the state of dissatisfaction. In short, they were people with "itchy feet."

James Clyman commented on this when he arrived in the Willamette Valley in the fall of 1844: "I never saw a more discontented community, owing principally to natural disposition," he wrote. "Nearly all, like myself, having been of a roving discontented character before leaving their eastern homes." Indeed, when Clyman left Oregon for California in 1845, he wrote that the majority of those who accompanied him were "thoroughly disgusted with Oregon." And when Clyman left California in 1846, a number of westbound emigrants encountering Clyman's eastbound group noted in their diaries that the returnees were disparaging California.[2]

Yet, Keturah's diary contains no evidence that negative reports had reached her family or infected them with doubts or misgivings. Rather, the Belknaps seemed to be the kind whose blood was readily stirred by the mysterious unknown. With George and Keturah losing three of their four young children, the decision to move may have been prompted by health considerations, much as it had for Thomas Corcoran and the Murphys.

Keturah started preparing for their journey during the fall, making a year's worth of clothing for her family: "November 15, 1847. Have cut four muslin shirts for George and two suits for the little boy. With what he has that will last him (if he lives) until we will want a different pattern." George worked at getting ready, too: "The men are busy making ox yokes and bows for the wagon covers and trading for oxen."

Keturah also made a strong cover for the wagon out of heavy white linen and a muslin cover as well: "we will have to double cover so we can keep warm and dry." While Keturah worked on the wagon covers, George was out "practicing with the oxen," getting them "used to running together."

They loaded the wagon on April 9, 1848. "I am the first one up," she recorded, "breakfast is over; our wagon is backed up to the steps. . . . The wagon looks so nice, the nice white cover drawn tight to the side boards with a good ridge to keep from sagging."

They loaded their wagon with boxes containing dishes and provisions, a medicine chest, and a chest filled with clothes. They loaded four homemade linen sacks, each filled with 125 pounds of flour (500 pounds total) and one sack filled with 125 pounds of cornmeal. Smaller sacks were loaded, containing dried apples and peaches, beans, rice, sugar, and coffee. Their feather tick bed was thrown on top of everything, and a place was left vacant on the wagon floor for Keturah's chair, where she would sit as the wagon bumped its way across the plains.

"Tuesday, April 10, 1848. Daylight dawned with none awake but me. . . . Our wagon is ready to start." She was visited by Dr. Walker who gave her advice and encouragement. "Don't fret," she recorded him as saying, "whatever happens don't fret and cry; courage will do more for you then anything else."

The party set out with Jesse and Jane Belknap in the lead, followed by George and Keturah with their wagon. Then came George W. Bethers with one wagon, John W. Starr with one wagon, Mr. Prather with two wagons, Chatman Hawley with two wagons, and Abraham Newton with two wagons.[3] They could have gone directly west to Council Bluffs, a closer jumping-off place, but they did not. Instead, they chose to go south to St. Joseph, but did not explain why. Was it because it would have taken them through an area where a host of Mormons were camped?

Keturah commented on their wonderful oxen: "We have two yoke of well-trained oxen; all there is to do is to hold up the yoke and tell Old Buck and Bright to come under and they walk up and take their place as meek as kittens." Their second yoke was a pair of matched, black four-year-old steers named Dick and Drab, and they brought along three milk cows, one of which was named Brock.

She wrote on the following day that "[w]e are in Missouri now; see once in a while a log hut and some half dressed children running away to hide." She added that "[t]he road is good and I am standing the ride fine." She may have been alluding to the fact that she was now pregnant.

Nearing the Missouri River twelve days later, Keturah wrote on Sunday, April 23, that "the men come in from the stock and say there has been a band of sheep herded on the range for two days and they have spoiled the grass so the stock wont feed on it." She had just referred to a flock of three hundred sheep belonging to the Watt family. Joe Watt, his parents, two brothers, four sisters, and a few others, were also going to Oregon. They were bringing two large freight wagons, each drawn by five yoke of oxen, a herd of loose cattle, a band of sheep, and a number of extra hands as drivers and herders.[4]

One of ten children, Joe Watt was born in 1817 in Knox County, Illinois. The family moved to Missouri in 1838, when Joe was only twenty. Senator Lewis Linn from Missouri had introduced a bill into Congress to encourage people to emigrate to Oregon by offering 320 acres to anyone settling there (640 acres per married couple). By 1843, Joe's father was thinking about it, but he could not raise enough money to outfit his large family for such a long trip. Joe decided that he would try it alone.

With a new pair of boots, $2.50 in his pocket, and a few pins and fishhooks to trade with the Indians, Joe and two friends joined a wagon train to Oregon in 1844. Joe hired on as an ox driver. By the time the train reached eastern Oregon, Joe owned a rifle and one cow as a result of some astute trades. But the emigrants' provisions were failing, and the family for which he drove felt they could no longer feed him. Joe and one of his friends decided that they had to strike out on foot alone. He left his cow with the train and asked his other friend to look after her. Joe and his companion struggled on alone through the Blue Mountains of Oregon with but a loaf of bread between them. They barely managed, shooting some prairie chickens and trading gunpowder to some Indians for potatoes. When they at last straggled into The Dalles along the Columbia River, Joe tried to get passage on a raft going down the river. Having no money, he offered to work for his passage. The boatman took one look at him and remarked that he looked like a worn out ox that was too weak to work. Taking pity on him, the boatman asked him if he could sing, to which Joe replied yes. The boatman took him aboard and had him sing songs to the other passengers as they rafted down the river.

Joe staggered into Oregon City in the Willamette Valley in November 1844 with nothing but his rifle, a pair of buckskin pants that were worn away below the knees, a red blanket for a coat, and the scant remains of a hat. While wandering the streets, he met Dr. John McLoughlin, the chief factor of the Hudson's Bay Company. Calling Joe a vagabond, McLoughlin ordered his clerk to give the boy a suit of clothes, then hired him to lay bricks. With his earnings, Joe repaid the kind Dr. McLoughlin, then took a carpentry job at a nearby Catholic mission. With these earnings, he purchased a crate of Seth Thomas clocks that had come in by ship. He peddled these clocks to the settlers along the river and used the proceeds to purchase sixty bushels of wheat. Because the year's wheat harvest had produced a surplus, he was able to purchase the wheat at a reduced price. Exceedingly wet conditions ruined the next year's crop, and wheat became dear. Joe sold his at a considerable profit. Dazzled with the opportunities he saw in the Willamette Valley, he returned home to Missouri to fetch his family. With over $2,000 in his pocket, he had more than enough to bring them out. He had noticed that Oregon had few sheep, but an abundance of lush pastures and a strong demand for woolen goods. He decided that when he returned, he would bring a large flock of sheep with him. Now in the spring of 1848, Joe was leading this party and a large flock of sheep to Oregon.

Seventeen-year-old Richard Cheadle was also traveling in the Watt party. Leaving Ottumwa, Iowa, on April 4, Cheadle came with one wagon and his twenty-year-old single sister, Sarah. His older sister, Adaline, and Adaline's husband, Aaron Chamberlin, came too, bringing one wagon. Years later, Cheadle wrote in a reminiscence that as they traveled through Missouri, they were soon joined on the road by Mr. Greenwood of Burlington, Iowa, with two wagons and by L. L. Blain of Albany, Missouri, with two wagons.[5] Twenty-five miles north of St. Joseph, the Cheadle group joined the Watt party. After this, they were joined by the Jackson brothers, George, Benjamin, and Andrew. Then Daniel Simonds and Mr. Roberts from Indiana were added, bringing the Watt group to about thirteen wagons.

The Belknap family and friends and their nine wagons also decided to join, increasing the size of the Watt company to about twenty-two wagons. Because April 23 was the Sabbath, Keturah wrote that many in the company wanted to stay in camp, but there was some disagreement. "[On the 23rd] Mr. [George] Jackson's voice is heard," she wrote. "He says if we stay it will break the Sabbath worse than if we go on so we all started but had only gone about 5 miles when a little boy was run over by the wagon and killed. We then stopped and buried the child." Loud recriminations likely erupted from those who were certain the calamity was caused by dishonoring the Lord's Day.

On Tuesday, April 25, the Watt company was nearing St. Joseph. "Will get to the river tomorrow," Keturah reported. "They say there are some Mormons here that give us some trouble with our stock. They might want a good horse so we think it best to put a good guard out."

April 25, 1848
Riley Root, Wambaugh company, St. Joseph, Missouri

On April 25, Riley Root was getting ready to cross the Missouri River at St. Joseph. At fifty-three-years-old, Root was a widower and a college-educated man who had been a surveyor, farmer, and teacher.[6] He was going to Oregon alone just to have a look around. His journal began the account of his travels:

> I left home in Knox county, Illinois, the 3d day of April, 1848, for Woodstock in Fulton county, a distance of about 20 miles, where I staid one day with my eldest daughter. I then started for the Mississippi river . . . by the way of La Harp, a distance of fifty miles, over which route most of the way to La Harp is as handsome prairie as I have seen in the State. . . . From this place I passed down the river to Quincy, where I stopd with a design to visit my youngest daughter of sixteen years of

Portrait of Riley Root (1795–1870). Courtesy of Galesburg Public Library, Galesburg, Illinois.

age, who is attending school at the Mission Institute, about two miles east of Quincy.... From Quincy I went to St. Louis for the purpose of obtaining a boat to go to St. Josephs on the Missouri river, where most of the emigrants meet before leaving the United States for Oregon.

Root accompanied what appeared to be the first party of wagons to cross the river that spring: "On the 25th of April," he wrote, "I crossed the Missouri river at St. Josephs into the Indian territory, with several wagons of emigrants, who intended to travel out a short distance and organize for the route. This day we have traveld as far as the bluffs of the river, a distance of 5 miles, and encamped for the night."

Emigrants crossed their wagons and livestock at St. Joseph by way of a ferry. The ferry landing on the east bank of the Missouri was where today's Francis Street ends at Riverfront Park. An 1849 gold rusher described the ferry's location as "the finest place I have seen on the river for crossing an eddy on both sides."[7]

After crossing the river on April 25, Root wrote that his group traveled five miles across a heavily timbered river bottom and through soft and miry ground in places. They likely stopped at Peter's Creek, where it descended through a notch in the bluffs, at a place where companies usually encamped on their first night after crossing the river.

April 26, 1848
Keturah Belknap, Watt company, St. Joseph, Missouri

Keturah and her family crossed the river next day:

[April 26] Wednesday. All are on the stir to get to the wharf before the other company gets here, and now begins the scene of danger. The river is high and looks terrific; one wagon and two yoke of oxen are over first so as to have a team to take the wagons out of the way; it is just a rope ferry. All back safe. Now they take the wagons and loose horses. They say it will take about all day to get us over. Next the loose cattle that go as they are in a dry lot without anything to eat. When they get the cattle on the boat they found one of our cows [Brock] was sick; she had got poisoned by eating the Jimpson weeds. She staggered when she walked on the ferry and in the crowd she was knocked overboard and went under but when she came up the boat man had his rope ready and throwed it out and lassoed her and they hauled her to land but she was too far gone to travel so the boatman said he would take our wagon and stock over for the chance of her so they hauled her up to the house and the last we saw of her a woman had wrapped her in a warm blanket and had a fire and was bathing her and pouring milk and lard down her. She could stand alone the next morning so we bade farewell to the Missouri River and old Brock. The Watts company will stay here till the Jacksons [George, Benjamin and Andrew] get over the river and we will move on to fresh grass and water.

The ferry Keturah mentions was probably a scow-shaped, flat-bottomed boat, like the ones described by emigrants in 1849, with barely enough room for one wagon or a few head of livestock. Keturah described their transportation as a "rope ferry," probably meaning that it was guided across the river by means of ropes sliding along the length of a long, heavy hemp hawser stretched across the breadth of the river. The St. Joe end of the hawser was fastened to a stout tree on the bank some distance upstream from the point of crossing. The current pushed the ferry both downstream and westward across the river.[8] Each time a steamer needed to pass, though infrequent, the hawser had to be taken down, then reattached—not an inconsiderable task.

No 1848 diarist mentioned how much the ferry charged, but we know the St. Joseph town council had set ferry rates in 1846 at one dollar per wagon with four oxen or horses, 12 cents per person, 25 cents per mule or horse, and 6 cents per cow or ox.[9] Each ferry trip over and back took a long time, which is why Keturah wrote that the livestock and wagons in her party "will take about all day to get over." She explained that "[t]he Watts company will stay here till the Jacksons get over the river and we will move on to fresh grass." While pausing on the west side of the river, Richard Cheadle reported that a Mr. Holdridge and Mr. Armpriest joined the Watt company, increasing its size to around twenty-four wagons.[10]

In the early morning hours of April 27, a dreary mist would have hung over the slow-moving river as people were beginning to move their cattle and wagons toward the ferry landing. Soon the mad rush was now on as every description of wagon, all loaded to the gills and some with extra baggage hanging on their sides, rolled forward to take its place in line. This was when a wagon owner might experience misgivings, and perhaps even panic. Was his wagon loaded too heavy or did it carry too little? What had he forgotten? Most travelers were bringing what they thought they needed to set up new homes in the West, and they would learn later that they had brought too much—far too much.

There are no good descriptions of the crossing here in 1848, but the river should have been wider than it was at Council Bluffs. By the time it flowed past St. Joseph, it would be as much as a third of a mile across, having gained the waters of the Platte, Nishnabotna, Big Nemaha, Little Nemaha, Tarkio, and Nodaway Rivers, in addition to a number of lesser streams.

In a way, this river crossing was a symbolic passage—the crossing of a barrier separating the past from the future and the familiar from the unknown. They were crossing to the place where their hopes and dreams would begin, but by crossing the river they were effectively cutting themselves off from family and friends with no way to stay in touch, and most had little conception of the distance, difficulties, and dangers that lay ahead.

April 27, 1848
William Wright Anderson, Miller company, St. Joseph, Missouri

William Wright Anderson was in one of the many parties crowding up to the ferry landing on April 27. In his wonderfully detailed diary of the journey, Anderson notes that they crossed the Missouri at St. Joseph on the twenty-seventh, after which he and his company traveled five miles through the wooded bottomland to the bluffs, where they likely encamped on Peter's Creek. Anderson's journal does not explain why he caught the pioneering itch, but we know that he was a young bachelor hired to drive a team of oxen for Isaac Miller from Miami County, Indiana.[11] With three wagons and five yoke of oxen for each wagon, Isaac and his brother, Christian, would have needed to hire help.

William Bristow, Bristow company, and Bolivar Walker,
Walker Company, St. Joseph, Missouri

Two other wagon companies, one captained by William Bristow and the other by W. Bolivar Walker, crossed the river at St. Joseph, probably after the Watt company. There are no known diaries or other narratives by anyone in these two companies, so it is not known how many wagons were in each. It is known, however, that Bolivar Walker and his brother, Claiborne, had gone to Oregon in 1845. Bolivar returned to Pike County, Missouri, to bring the rest of the family out in 1848, including another brother, Walter.[12] It was also reported that Bristow's party "left St. Joseph on May 3rd."[13] If that is true, they must have camped at Peter's Creek on the evening of May 3, and then made it to Mosquito Creek on the fourth, departing that campground on the morning of the fifth. The Walker and Bristow companies must have been traveling close to each other; later the two parties combined into one company consisting of twenty-four wagons.[14]

May 2–6, 1848
William Porter, Purvine company, St. Joseph, Missouri

William Porter was a college-educated thirty-six-year-old who brought along a tiny notebook, only four inches by six inches, in which he recorded details of his journey. According to a letter he later wrote to his parents, William, his wife, Sarah, and their four children left Pike County, Illinois, on April 7, 1848. They were accompanied by his brother Stephen, his wife's sister and her husband, Dr. Joseph and Cassandra Coffey Blackerby, Porter's and Blackerby's father-in-law N. Coffey and his family, and H. N. V. Holmes. The group had traveled overland by wagon pulled by oxen, then crossed the Mississippi River at Louisiana, Missouri, and arrived at St. Joseph on April 23. They did not seem terribly rushed, as they lingered outside town for six days. Porter recorded that they went into town on the twenty-eighth and "laid in meal [grain], etc.," and fed oats and corn to their ox teams to rebuild their strength after the long pull across Missouri.

Porter wrote that someone named Samuel Tucker crossed the river on April 30, and that "Holmes and Blackerby crossed on the 1st of May." Porter then explained that he and his brother Stephen crossed on May 2, while John Purvine (with five wagons) of Scott County, Illinois, and Mr. Hooker of Morgan County, Illinois, crossed on May 3 and 4. When all were across on the fourth, Porter reported that "[w]e all went out to Peter's Creek six miles from St. Joseph." On the fifth, they left Peter's Creek, traveling "12 to 14 miles to a small creek [Mosquito Creek] and camped." The party organized, electing John Purvine as their captain and William Porter as lieutenant. Isaac Ball, Jacob Conser, Norris Humphreys, Wesley Shannon, Harvey Rudolph, and Charles Benson also joined the "Purvine company." Consisting of up to twenty-four wagons, the Purvine company departed Mosquito Creek on the morning of May 6.[15]

Many parties had been arriving at the ferry landing simultaneously, causing a great deal of congestion. In the days leading up to this, men had been visiting small clumps of families camping just outside town, looking for people with whom they could form a company of at least twenty wagons for protection. On the other hand, some crossed the river first, then tried to find a company to join. Because of the mass of wagons trying to ferry across at the same time, some already-formed companies were unable to cross on the same day and got separated. In such cases, the first across would have to linger on the river's west side for a number of days until the last of their party made it over.

The bottleneck at the ferry was at its worst between April 27 and May 4. Despite the congestion, there was no incentive for the ferry operators to build additional ferryboats. It would not have added to the number of emigrants or wagons needing to cross, and would have earned no extra revenue for the ferrymen. Besides, the ferrymen understood that impatient emigrants were less likely to complain about the rates being charged.

Despite the problems, the emigrants of 1848 had an easy time compared to those of 1849. Because of the gold rush, St. Joseph went from "bustling" in the spring of 1848 to "bedlam" in the spring of 1849. Where two hundred wagons crossed at St. Joseph in 1848, over two thousand would cross there in 1849.[16] J. Goldsborough Bruff was in St. Joseph on May 7, 1849, when he wrote: "As far as we could see . . . the country was speckled with white tents and wagon covers of the emigrants. There were but two very indifferent scows at the ferry, and these were being plied from earliest day till midnight, every day; had been so for weeks, and from the mass here, would continue for several weeks more."[17] And the numbers would grow even more in succeeding years.

CHAPTER 4

The Talk Before the Walk
APRIL 27–MAY 7

APRIL 27, 1848

Riley Root, Wambaugh company, Mosquito Creek, Indian Territory, Kansas

After spending the night at Peter's Creek on April 25, Riley Root and his party ascended the winding ravine of Peter's Creek and came out upon the rolling, treeless prairie. They rumbled over new grass until they reached a hollow along Mosquito Creek (also called Spider Creek), where they encountered a band of tall trees growing along this steep-banked stream. Because of its distance from Peter's Creek and its ample supply of wood and water, this was the customary place on Mosquito Creek for companies to camp the second night after crossing the Missouri. In his journal, Root reported his party's stay at Mosquito Creek:

> The next day [26th] we pursued our journey as far as Musketoe creek, a distance of 8 miles, where we encamped. Next day, Friday, 27th, we organized into a company of 15 or 20 wagons, with such regulations as we deemed necessary for our safety through the Indian country, and tarried there for the night.

Near the campground was the coffin of a dead Indian resting high up in the branches of an oak, an inviting target for young boys to throw rocks at. The corpse had been there awhile; C. W. Cook had made a note of it in his diary on April 30 of the previous year: "[H]ere an old dead Indian warrior wrapped in his rug, and sitting high up in an oak tree was a striking example of their peculiar mode of interment."[1]

Root must not have found the Indian in the tree particularly interesting, as he didn't mention it. While his party had been languishing in camp on April 27, Root may have been growing impatient. Oregon was far away, and standing around batting at the bothersome flies wasn't getting them any closer. The emigrants had been waiting on a committee composed of M. N. Wambaugh, John McPherson, and Robert Houston, who had been named to draw up the rules by which this company of wagons would be governed. Why was it taking so long? Had there been murmuring that this had been a terrible waste of time, that they really needed to get going if they were going to beat the early Cascade and Sierra snows?

At last, the rules were presented, debated, and adopted. The *St. Joseph Gazette* printed the entire "Mosquito Creek Resolution" in its May 12 issue, reporting that the compact had been unanimously adopted by the company on April 27. It was reported that M. N. Wambaugh was elected camp master and John McPherson, John Trullinger, Thomas Patton, and E. E. Brock were elected sergeants.[2]

The resolution contained nine points.

1. A Camp Master shall be elected and it shall be his duty to select places of encampment and shall determine the order of traveling.
2. All men over 14 years shall be placed on a guard list and details of guards shall be made up from this list by rotation.
3. Four Sergeants shall be selected, whose duty it is to see that the guards are at their posts.
4. A list of families shall be made in alphabetical order. The family at the top shall take the lead on the first day, followed by the others in alphabetical order. Each day thereafter, the lead shall change with the leader of the previous day falling to the rear. No wagon shall start until the Camp Master gives the order. The company shall keep as close together as possible.
5. Everyone shall exercise caution with their firearms.
6. If a majority of the Company is dissatisfied with the Camp Master, a meeting shall be called to consider his replacement.
7. Any question submitted at a meeting shall be decided by a majority vote.
8. The Camp Master shall be relieved from performing guard duty, and for causes deemed sufficient, he may excuse anyone else from standing guard.
9. The Company may accept any emigrant who may arrive after this date.

At the last minute, they also saw fit to adopt one other rule: "[A]ll dogs be tied up securely every night to prevent alarms &c."

The company had just formed a democratic government in its simplest form, whose purpose was to impose a set of rules that would apply to a group of self-reliant and independent-minded strangers as they came together to cross territory where no other law existed. While there may have been some grumblings, most probably accepted the need for a "constitution" as a bulwark against chaos and lawlessness on the trail, not so much against the criminal, but to resolve fair disputes between otherwise law-abiding travelers.

Election of company officers could be hotly contested. Authority-craving aspirants could wage intense campaigns, with impassioned speeches, debates, and murmurings before votes were cast. In some cases, votes were counted by a simple raising of hands; a more dramatic procedure was having candidates stand apart from the crowd. At a signal, the emigrants would rush to stand behind their favorite, and the one attracting the largest following was the choice.[3] The disgruntled losers often proved a troublesome lot, quick to spread whispers of criticism or otherwise sow seeds of discord when things went poorly.

The Mosquito Creek resolution was signed by forty-one men: Wambaugh, Riley Root, Levi Hardman, Stephen Broadhurst, Reuben Dickens, Jordan Dickens, John Dickens, Jeremiah Dickens, Jesse Dickens, Thomas Patton, Daniel Trullinger, N. H. Trullinger, John Trullinger, Gabriel Trullinger, J. McPherson, Thomas Adams, J. C. Austin, Thomas Bateman, D. C. Baker, E. E. Brock, Robert Brock, Tarlton Brock, Peter Cline, John J. Crook, W. W. Harper, Robert Houston, James Houston, Milton Houston, Newton Houston, L. D. C. Lanterette, Levi Lewfleur, John Miller, G. W. Mullen, David Parks, Absalom Parks, John Parks, Ira Patterson, Samuel Patterson, Henry Shields, Hamilton Sharp, and N. C. Wilcox.[4]

One of the larger groups was the Dickens family. Reuben Dickens was a forty-nine-year-old Baptist preacher from Franklin, Missouri, who brought his wife, Nancy, and eight children: Jeremiah (25), Jehu (24), John (22), Joshua (20), Annie (18), Jesse (16), Jordan (14), and Ella (11). Elder Dickens had hired Thomas Patton to drive one of his ox teams, and Tom would soon take a fancy to Dickens' oldest daughter, Annie.[5]

The Trullinger family was another large group. Daniel Trullinger brought his wife, Elizabeth (whose uncle, Andrew Johnson, would later become president of the United States) and their ten children: Gabriel (24), Nathan H. (22, married to Frances), John (20), Amanda (18), Mary Jane (15), Elizabeth (12), twins Eliza and Evangeline (10), Daniel (8), and Sarah (5). The Trullingers had left Iowa with several cows, chickens, pigs, and horses, and three wagons, one of which was so large it had to be drawn by four yoke of oxen.[6]

Another large family, one that would later play an important role in Thomas Corcoran's fate, was the Parks family. David Parks, recently of Cass County, Indiana, was heading to Oregon with his wife, Catherine, and their seven young sons: John (18), Absalom (17), David Jr. (16), Charles (13), Isaac (6), William (4), and Daniel (1).

Fourteen-year-old Rufus Burrows came with his mother and stepfather, Rufus Hitchcock, and an uncle, Street Rice. Even though neither Hitchcock nor Rice appeared as signers of the Mosquito Creek Resolution, Burrows' reminiscence written years later described them as traveling with Captain Wambaugh's company.[7]

Daniel Hunsaker, his wife and three children, together with four wagons, sixteen yokes of oxen, and 125 head of loose cattle, were also part of the Wambaugh company, even though Hunsaker is not shown as a signer of the resolution.[8]

John McPherson, elected one of the sergeants of the company, was a young Scotsman, teacher, and bachelor. He would keep a detailed journal of the journey. Upon his arrival in California, he loaned it to the *Californian*, a San Francisco newspaper, which published a few excerpts that show him as an observant man and a superb writer. He later became a freelance journalist, poet, and historian in the Bay area.[9] It is unfortunate that the rest of his journal has disappeared—it would have been a valuable contribution to the story of the Wambaugh company's travels.

And then there were the McCombses. Lambert McCombs had sold his farm in St. Joseph County, Indiana, in 1847, and traveled with his family to Independence to spend the winter. His family consisted of his wife, Hannah, a married daughter, Martha, and her husband, Levi Hardman, and four younger, unmarried children: Rebecca, Hannah, Israel, and Frank. While in Independence, Lambert read a letter published in a local newspaper that would change his fortunes, a letter written by James Clyman in 1846 upon his return from the Far West. The letter described the Napa Valley of California in such romantic terms that Lambert decided that was where he wanted to settle.[10] Lambert moved his family to St. Joseph in the early spring, and at some point, his son-in-law, Levi Hardman, hired a young bachelor named Stephen Broadhurst to drive one of his ox-drawn wagons. In another case of frontier romance, Stephen managed to attract McCombs' daughter Rebecca, and before they left St. Joseph, the couple found a preacher and were secretly married. Both Hardman and Broadhurst were signers of the Mosquito Creek Resolution, while curiously McCombs was not.

Much of the information about members of the company comes from recollections written years later by Eva McCombs, a McCombs family descendant, and by George Broadhurst, son of Stephen and Rebecca. Both Eva and George claimed that it was James Clyman who piloted the McCombses, Hardmans, and Broadhursts to California. Other than those references, it is difficult to find evidence of Clyman's presence; however, he wrote a letter dated December 25, 1848, from California to a friend in Milwaukee. Most of his letter understandably dwelled on what was occupying everyone's mind at the time—the gold in California and the "immense richness of the mining regions." He penned only a few words about his trip, almost an afterthought: "[W]e left the west of Missouri on the 1st day of May and arrived here on the 5th of September without accident or interruption of any kind worthy of notice."[11]

Clyman's statement that they left on May 1 is curious. Was it an incorrect date, a weakness that often manifested itself in his earlier journals? Did he leave Mosquito Creek with the Wambaugh company on April 28, in which case he simply misrecollected the date? If he was correct about the May 1 date, then he couldn't have left with the Wambaugh company. Yet, it is known that at some point he was connected with McCombs, Hardman, and Broadhurst. Since Hardman and Broadhurst signed the Mosquito Creek Resolution, they are known to have started with the Wambaugh company.

Could Clyman have started with another party that caught up to the Wambaugh company later? Not likely. If Clyman had been with a party that left St. Joseph on May 1, his group would have had to overtake and pass two significant companies that had left before May 1 in order to catch up to Wambaugh. William Anderson was a diarist in the Miller company, which left St. Joseph on April 30, one of the two companies ahead, yet he never mentioned being passed by any group. With no evidence that shows otherwise, we will assume that Clyman was traveling with the Wambaugh company from the beginning.

If Clyman was present while the Wambaugh company was organizing, one can imagine the old frontiersman sitting on a rotting cottonwood limb at Mosquito Creek, cleaning his Hawken rifle and ignoring the organizational proceedings. His Hawken was his prized possession, a superb percussion cap instrument, made by the Hawken brothers of St. Louis. Heavy at 13½ pounds, with a 38" long barrel and a 17/32" rifled bore, it fired a bullet that ran 32 to the pound. Together with its double-set hair trigger, and a range of up to five hundred yards, it provided the keen-eyed Clyman with the ideal hunting tool.[12]

Since Clyman was an experienced overlander who had been on a number of western expeditions, he didn't need a refresher course on how a wagon train should be run. His skills at surviving in the West were exceptional, having learned from some of the best. Yet, he had also spent a number of years in Illinois and Wisconsin, where he acquired a certain patrician polish not normally found in other mountaineers.

If Clyman had been present during this organizational meeting, one wonders why, with all of his qualifications, he wasn't elected camp master instead of Wambaugh. "Captain Wambo," as some called him, was far from a greenhorn. He had traveled to Oregon in 1844, in the same company as Clyman, which meant that they were familiar with each other. But whether they were close friends or jealous rivals is unknown. From Oregon, Wambaugh had traveled to California in 1846, arriving at Sutter's Fort on June 26. Then he enlisted in John C. Fremont's California Battalion and was made lieutenant, second in command of F Company under Captain Lansford Hastings. Once the California war wound down, Wambaugh was discharged. He bought land in the Santa Clara Valley, then returned to Missouri in the spring of 1847, traveling east with Commodore Robert Stockton's party.[13]

Emigrants were usually midwestern farm families who needed someone to show them more than the way to get to their destination. As camp master, it would be Wambaugh's role to show them how to make camp, guard livestock, ford rivers, hunt for meat, deal with Indians, and generally how to survive in the deserts and mountains of the West. Emigrants were prone to get lost, would wander alone too far from their wagons, would eat bad food, drink poisonous water, and drown while fording rivers. The job of camp master would not be easy. Many of the emigrants were independent personalities, used to being self-governed, with little taste for authority.

Anyone not willing to stay on his farm in Illinois probably wouldn't be easy to keep in line in the wagon train either.

While Clyman's role in this company is uncertain, it is doubtful he would have wanted to be camp master. He may have considered it beneath the station of someone of his stature and skills. He was much more admirably qualified to be a guide, pilot, or hunter—things he may have felt took more ability and knowledge than being a hand-holding nanny to a bunch of nagging tenderfoots. Yet, even as the company's guide, he would not have been immune from being badgered. Imagine being pestered for five months with, "Hey, Clyman, how much farther to the next crick?"

What might Clyman have thought about these people milling around their Mosquito Creek camp? He jotted down some thoughts about some westbound emigrants he encountered while returning from California in 1846, revealing his opinion of emigrants in general: "It is remarkable how anxious these people are to hear [about] the Pacific country, and strange that so many of all kinds and classes of People should sell out comfortable homes in Missouri and Elsewhere pack up and start across such an emmence Barren waste to settle in some Place of which they have at most so uncertain information, but this is the character of my countrymen."[14]

While the emigrants waited in camp for the rules committee to complete their work, they would have had time to wonder about what their journey would be like. The road west was almost mythical, steeped in rumors, legends, and folklore. Because of Clyman's experience, he was in a position to rectify many of their illusions, but whether he was approached for enlightenment is unknown.

Root's diary specified that the Wambaugh company consisted of only fifteen to twenty wagons. George Broadhurst, on the other hand, the son of Stephen and Rebecca Broadhurst, wrote years later that there were sixty wagons in the Wambaugh company. Rufus Burrows also wrote years later that the company consisted of fifty-one wagons, two hundred people, 250 head of oxen to pull wagons, two to three hundred head of loose cattle, and fifty saddle horses.[15] But a lot happens on the trail. Some companies break up and some consolidate with others. Broadhurst's and Burrows' recollections likely referred to the size of their company at a later time. Since Root's entries can be verified as accurate on most things, his number of fifteen to twenty wagons at this point in the journey is likely to be correct.

April 28–29, 1848
William Anderson, Miller company, Mosquito Creek,
Indian Territory, Kansas

William Anderson, the young, single man employed by Isaac Miller to drive one of his wagons, began his diary by explaining that they crossed the Missouri at St. Joseph on April 27 and they camped that evening at the bluffs, probably on Peter's Creek. The next morning: "April 28th we started early this morning, and traveled on to

Musqueto creek a distance of 14 miles here we camped soon after starting this morning we passed a large company [Gates company] that seemed to be busily engaged in organizing."

When the Miller party arrived at Mosquito Creek on the afternoon of April 28, the Wambaugh company was gone, having left earlier that day. Anderson noticed the dead Indian in the tree: "I beheld an Indian coffin in the forks of a standing tree, having a curiosity to look at it I clime upt it and raised the lid and looked in and saw skeleton and some beads this coffin was dug out of a log and covered with a broad slab or punckin. I took one bead for a relick but one of the girls in our company got it away from me and I never saw it again."

The next morning, April 29, they waited at Mosquito Creek for the rest of their party to join them. During that time, Anderson said they "spent the day watching the cattle and shooting gofers and other game that came in our way." He noted that the large company he mentioned passing the previous day, the one he called the "Gates company," passed them that evening. Then, according to Anderson, "the balance of our company came up and we proceeded to organize." Anderson did not identify who were elected as officers of his company, but a reminiscence written in 1927 reported the company was captained by Charles Miller.[16] It was likely a misrecollection caused by the passage of time. More likely, Isaac Miller, Anderson's employer, was the one elected captain of their company. Charles Miller was Isaac's son and was only eighteen at the time.[17]

The large Isaac Winkle family traveled with the company, including Isaac's daughter and son-in-law Elizabeth and William Grayson Porter (and their one-year-old son, Isaac), and William Porter's seventeen-year-old brother, McCauley Porter.[18]

David Presley, Adam Stephens, William Stephens, Sanford Stephens, Thomas Wyatt, Isaac Wyatt, William Ransom, Isaac Owens, Benjamin Cleaver, Isaac Winkle, John Ramsey, and Mr. Sutherland also traveled in the Miller company.[19] Altogether, the Miller company started with about twenty-three wagons.

Anderson reported that their company departed Mosquito Creek on the morning of April 30, traveling just behind the Gates company, which had departed Mosquito Creek the day before. There were no known diaries from the Gates party, but a September 1848 article in the *Oregon Spectator* suggests that Thomas Gates was its captain.[20]

May 5–6, 1848

William Porter, Purvine company, Mosquito Creek, Indian Territory, Kansas

This William Porter traveling in the Purvine company is not the same William Porter who was traveling in the Miller company. According to this William Porter's diary, the Purvine company spent the night of May 4 at Peter's Creek, then resumed their journey the next morning: "May 5th. Left Peter's Creek six miles from St. Joseph, and traveled 12 to 14 miles to a small creek [Mosquito Creek] and camped. Here is an Indian buried in a tree, good camping ground."

While this is the last reference in the 1848 diaries to the Indian of Mosquito Creek, the remains would be noted again in 1849, in the diary of Vincent Geiger: "At 4 o'clock we came to Spider Creek [Mosquito Creek], a very small stream but and excessively bad crossing. In the forks of a tree on the bank of this stream, about thirty feet high, there is a coffin containing the bones, beads &c. of an old Indian Chief who died about four years ago."[21]

According to Porter, the Purvine company departed Mosquito Creek on the morning of May 6. There are no known diaries from the William Bristow or Bolivar Walker companies, but Bristow later reported that he left St. Joseph on May 3. Walker and Bristow merged their companies shortly after leaving St. Joseph. Assuming both of these companies made the same daily progress as most other companies, they should have made it to Peter's Creek on May 4, and to Mosquito Creek on the fifth. Thus, they probably left Mosquito Creek on May 6, the same day as the Purvine company.

May 6–7, 1848
Keturah Belknap, Watt company, probably at Mosquito Creek, Indian Territory, Kansas

Keturah Belknap had written that once they crossed the Missouri, they had to wait for the Jackson brothers to cross. Richard Cheadle, also traveling in the Watt company, explained in his reminiscence that they "crossed the Missouri River on May 4," perhaps suggesting that the Jacksons had crossed by then as well. It would appear that the Watt party was finally ready to move away from the river by May 5, and may have camped at Peter's Creek that evening. In that case, they likely made it to Mosquito Creek by the evening of the sixth. Thus, Keturah's undated entry could have been describing the morning of May 7:

> We will now form a company and make some laws so all will have their part. Some of the oxen are getting tender-footed; they have been trying to shoe them but gave it up. I have washed and ironed and cooked a nice skillet of corn bread (enough for two dinners for George, Jessie, and I). This morning the roll is called and everyone is expected to answer his name. They have quite a time with the election of officers. Every man wants an office. George Jackson and Joe Watts are pilots; they have both been over the road before and have camping places noted down so now we take the trail again. The order is for the first one hitched up [to] "roll out." So we are ahead on the lead today. Then Beathers are next but tomorrow we will be behind.

If the Watt company organized at the Mosquito Creek campground and departed from there on May 7, it means the Walker, Bristow, and Purvine companies were traveling a day or two ahead of them.

On May 5, the *St. Joseph Gazette* reported: "For the last two weeks [April 20–May 4] our town has been literally crowded with Oregon and California emigrants, laying in their supplies before crossing the mountains. At the time of our writing, two hundred and ten wagons have crossed at this place."

Most of these wagons can be accounted for from information found in the known diaries and journals. It is estimated that the Wambaugh company had about twenty wagons. Although it is not known how many wagons were in the Gates company, Anderson referred to it as "large," perhaps meaning as many as forty. The Miller company had twenty-three wagons, Watt had twenty-four, the combined Walker and Bristow companies had twenty-four, and the Purvine company had twenty-four. This accounts for a total of 155 wagons, but is still fewer than the *Gazette* reported.

Table 3: Wagon companies leaving St. Joseph area by May 7, 1848

Company (Diarist)	Number of Wagons	Departed from Mosquito Creek
Wambaugh (Root)	20	April 28
Gates	40 (est.)	April 29
Miller (Anderson)	23	April 30
Walker	} 24	May 5 (est.)
Bristow		May 5
Purvine (Porter)	24	May 6
Watt (Belknap)	24	May 7 (est.)
Total	155	

CHAPTER 5

A Vast Green Sea
APRIL 28–MAY 13

APRIL 28–MAY 12, 1848

Riley Root, Wambaugh company, Mosquito Creek, Indian Territory, Kansas

On the morning of April 28, men's voices rang out and whips cracked as the Wambaugh company departed from the Mosquito Creek campground. Wagons creaked and rumbled as this band of adventurers began what would be a long and arduous journey. Falling onto the westward trail, the wagons climbed toward the top of the hill, the oxen straining up the incline. A few miles farther, they descended into the Wolf River Valley where the trail crossed the stream, then ascended out of the valley and swung northwest. A company like Wambaugh's, consisting of twenty or so wagons, could easily stretch a half mile from front to back, a train of still-bright wagon covers rising and falling with the contours of the land. A company like Wambaugh's, consisting of twenty or so wagons, could easily stretch a half mile from front to back, a train of still-bright wagon covers rising and falling with the contours of the land. Such a sight, with its dramatic sweep and movement, would inspire many American artists in the years to come.

The party soon came upon the Presbyterian Mission School for the Iowa, Sac, and Fox tribes, twelve miles from Mosquito Creek and two miles east of the present-day town of Highland, Kansas. The three-story limestone and red brick building, which is still there today, had been constructed two years earlier, but probably still seemed out of place on the raw prairie. About a mile southwest was the Great Nemaha Indian Subagency, where the subagent of the federal Office of Indian Affairs and various government employees resided. Both the mission and subagency had been established in 1837, just after the Platte Purchase of 1836, when the Iowa, Sac, and Fox tribes gave up their lands east of the Missouri River in exchange for this land and other considerations.[1]

According to Root's journal, the party "tarried at the mission" on April 29 and 30, but he did not record why. Two years later, Root would return to Illinois from

Oregon and publish a book containing his diary and some detailed observations about various aspects of his journey. He described what he called "Iowa and Sack Mission Boarding School" as a building "106 feet in length by 40 in width, with a basement for cooking and dining-rooms." The upper stories were classrooms, library, printing press room, and dormitories. While the mission's schoolmaster, S. M. Ervin, showed Root his young Indian students, Root wrote that someone else living at the mission lamented that "it is with great difficulty youth are persuaded to tarry long enough at the school to acquire any valuable education."[2]

On May 1, the Wambaugh company left the mission and traveled fifteen miles. Although they may have been the first company to travel it that spring, the trail had been used for years and the hundreds of wagons in earlier years had etched unmistakable marks across the windswept grasslands, meandering over the graceful curves of the ground, across braided hills, rises, knolls, ravines, creeks, and creeklets.

It is fortunate that the precise route of the trail was mapped many years ago by devoted trail historians who poured through thousands of emigrant diaries, interviewed hundreds of old-timers, and studied the marks still remaining on the land.[3] The route had an inherent logic to it, hewing to the high ground—the dividing ridges that lay between the system of creeks that drained away on the left hand and those that drained away on the right. By following the country's backbone, travelers avoided many of the creeks, gullies, and ravines that were a problem for wagons to traverse. Though small, these obstacles were often no small chore. Crossing the water was not so much of a problem, but heavily laden wagons were not easy to control on the steep banks and other severe inclines. They would have to be braked and held back as they descended the near bank, even let down by ropes. Once across, wagons would have to be hitched to extra teams of oxen and pulled up the far bank.

The prairie looked quite different than it does today. In the mid-nineteenth century, the prairie was a seemingly endless expanse of new grass, a banner of green rippling gently as far as the eye could reach. It was treeless, except where narrow bands of trees grew along the folded creases where the creeks and streams ran. It was on this section of the trail that one emigrant remarked that the long lines of wagons, their white covers well-trimmed, looked not unlike vessels gliding over the swells of a vast green sea.[4]

In the fall, when the grasses were mature and dry, recurring prairie fires were ignited by lightning strikes or by Indians who had learned that new grass did better if it emerged from fire-scorched earth. New tree seedlings would perish in the hot blazes and only the larger, established trees along the waterways survived.

The resulting tallgrass prairie was unfamiliar to most of the emigrants, a vast ecosystem often markedly different from the lands that they had left behind. In this world, the big bluestem grass grew, along with switchgrass, Indian grass, and flowers like leadplant, stiff goldenrod, primrose, spiderwort and many more. Each species occupied a different place, a different height, and a different role, but together

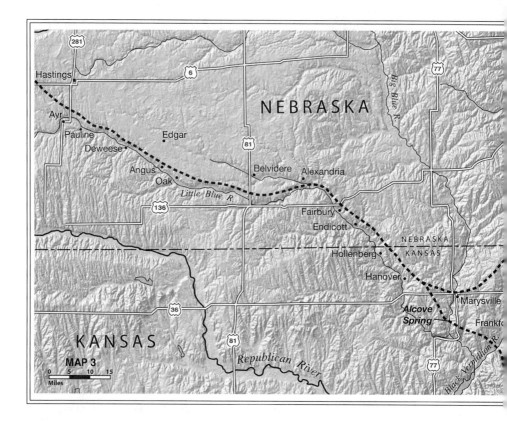

produced a dense mat of vegetative material, filled with the buzzing, humming, and flittering of bugs, butterflies, and birds.[5] An artist may have been moved by the beauty and a botanist may have thrilled at the opportunity to examine new species, but the emigrants probably looked at the prairie differently. Even as they marveled at its bigness and appreciated its beauty, the emigrants probably saw the prairie primarily as an immense solitude that would take forever to cross.

The Wambaugh company followed a trail that meandered generally north of and parallel to today's Highway 36. Riley Root tended to chronicle just the essentials— date, miles traveled, place camped. His truncated journal entries recorded their progress:

Tuesday, May 2— 20 miles.

Wednesday, May 3— 15 miles, to Nemahaw creek.

Thursday, May 4— we staid at the same place.

Friday, May 5— 13 miles over a very crooked road.

Saturday, May 6— 20 miles.

Sunday, May 7— 14 miles to camp, 4 miles to Blue creek [Big Blue River], and 10 more to camp.

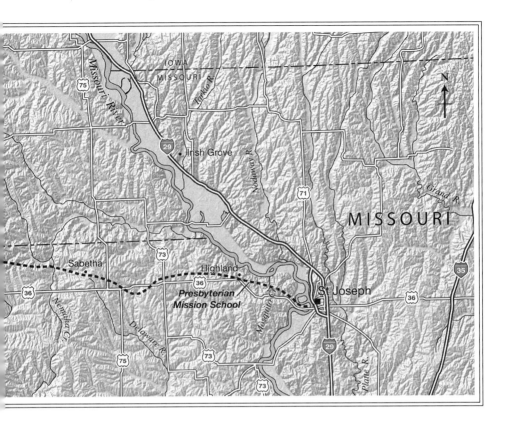

It is remarkable that, at the end of an exhausting day, the diarists could rally them-selves sufficiently to drag a notebook out of its waterproof covering and pick up a pen and bottle of ink. It is no wonder that many of their jottings were short and devoid of elaboration.

After fording the Big Blue River on the west side of today's Marysville, Kan-sas, on May 7, the Wambaugh company steadily ascended onto a high open pla-teau. About eight miles beyond the river, where two ridges came together, the St. Joseph road joined the trail coming up from Independence, but Root's journal did not mention the location. The Allsopp party coming from Independence should have crossed the place a few days earlier and the Wambaugh company should have fallen onto some freshly made wagon marks. James Clyman now found himself on familiar ground, having passed that way two years earlier when he returned from California on his way to Independence.

During the gold rush of 1849, thousands of wagons would merge at this junc-tion of the roads. Some gold rushers mentioned the spectacle in their diaries. James Pritchard wrote,

By noone today [May 11, 1849] we came to where the St. Joseph road & Indipen-
dance road came together. It was allarming to see the long strings of wagons
that were on the road. I counted just passing before us as we came into the St.
Jo. road 90 Ox teams in one string. And as far as the Eye could reach forward and
back the road was just lined with them. It would appear from the sight befor us
that the Nation was disgorgeing it self and sending off its whole inhabitance.[6]

Root's entry for May 7 reported that the Wambaugh company encamped ten
miles west of their crossing of the Big Blue River. It was likely on Cottonwood Creek,
two miles past the junction of the roads, and on today's Highway 243, two miles east
of present-day Hanover, Kansas.

From here, the conjoined roads continued along high ground, tracing a line that
traveled north and above the valley of the Little Blue River, a roughly thirty-foot-
wide tributary of the Big Blue. Edwin Bryant, a former newspaper editor who traveled to California in 1846, praised the valley when it came into view:

Late in the afternoon we reached the summit of a ridge, overlooking a valley,
through which winds a small rivulet, the banks of which are fringed with timber. The view from the ridge of the beautiful valley below appeared almost like
a creation of enchantment. Involuntary exclamations of pleasure and admiration escaped from the lips of the whole advance party as soon as the scene
became visible.[7]

The trail generally followed the high side of an inclined plane that tilted gradually toward the Little Blue, staying high enough to avoid the innumerable ravines and
gullies that ran into the valley. Wagon companies ordinarily descended to the river in
the afternoon to camp closer to water and firewood.

According to Root's journal, his company made twenty miles on May 8, camping that night at a stream he called the "Wyatt." John C. Fremont's *Report* had given
the creek that name, but it would later be called Rock Creek, as it is known today.
The place of their encampment was three miles northeast of present-day Endicott,
Nebraska.

The Wambaugh company made fourteen miles on May 9, camping on Little
Sandy Creek, five miles northwest of present Fairbury, Nebraska. According to Root,
they traveled eighteen miles on May 10 to the "Little Fork of L. [Big] Sandy," just
south of today's Belvidere, Nebraska. They traveled eleven miles on May 11, camping
along "Blue Creek" (Little Blue River), about where the present small community of
Oak, Nebraska, is situated. On May 12, they traveled another twelve miles, continuing to stay near the Little Blue, and camped about five miles south of present-day
Edgar, Nebraska.

APRIL 30–MAY 12, 1848
William Anderson, Miller company, Mosquito Creek, Indian Territory

While camping back at Mosquito Creek on April 29, William Wright Anderson's Miller company had "organized" and the Gates company had just passed them by. Anderson had a more active pen than Root, and he described the following day: "April 30th having our officers elected and rules and regulations layed down— agan started on our journey   we traveled 6 miles to day and camped on a branch [likely the Wolf River]   we saw a good many indians on this branch   they came sneaking around our camp after night and the guard took one prisoner."

The Miller company was traveling two days behind Root and his Wambaugh company, and one day behind Gates. They had not yet reached the Presbyterian Mission School, but were passing through an area where many Sac Indians were to be found. Emigrants in other years mentioned seeing Sacs along this section of the trail, often wrapped in red blankets, with heads shaved except for a crown lock tied up with feathers and other ornaments. They sometimes approached the emigrants to solicit "tolls" or tribute, arguing that the travelers were using their wood and their livestock were eating their grass. Some emigrants expressed annoyance with the Indian sub-agents for putting such crazy ideas into the Indians' heads.[8]

In the morning of May 1, the Miller company experienced their first mishap. "We found one of Isaac Miller's oxen dead," Anderson wrote about his employer, "so we yoked up a cow and turned our Indian captive loose and started agan." He added that as soon as they departed their camp, a host of Indians waiting on the hill came down and devoured the carcass.

The Miller company stayed along the high ground during the day, but rolled over a woodless, waterless land. Oxen could do without water during the day, provided they had access to it at night. A guide who knew the trail would try to adjust the distances traveled each day so that as evening approached he could lead his company to a creek or stream that lay below the main trail, and thus provide the camp with water and wood. Yet, there were a few stretches along this part of the trail where a "dry" camp was unavoidable, especially if there had been no recent rains. Such a stretch existed between the Wolf River and Walnut Creek, a distance of almost thirty miles. The Miller camp on the evening of May 1 would have been about four miles east of the present town of Hiawatha and in the middle of that waterless stretch.

It was only their second night out, so while the emigrants' spirits should have been high, the oxen still fresh and strong, and their wagons still new, there may have been some aching muscles and sore bottoms in camp that night. Even people (and oxen) accustomed to hard work needed time to get acclimated to walking all day or bumping over the prairie on a hard wooden seat.

They were clearly in Indian territory now, and it was common practice for companies to protect themselves and their livestock from the natives by forming their wagons, tongue-to-tail, into an enclosure, or "corral," when they came to a halt for the night. In some companies, the practice was for the lead wagon to circle to the left, while the next one went to the right, and so on until they had formed an oblong circle. The travelers pitched their tents outside the circled wagons and sent the children out to collect firewood. Campfires were usually established outside the perimeter of the tents and the women would then begin to cook. This was a routine that would be followed with few exceptions over the next five months. Once the wagons were circled, the oxen would be led to the stream and allowed to drink, and as soon as their thirst was quenched, they were led or driven into the corral to spend the night unyoked. That night, however, the Anderson party did not camp by a stream and they corralled their cattle, thirsty and restless, within the circled wagons.

A well-regimented, well-disciplined company would post guards every night to keep an eye on the livestock and to prevent a surprise Indian attack. Most emigrants reported detesting night guard duty, but it was an important job. As the guards listened into the night for any sound that did not belong, they would also listen for any change in their animals' behavior, a horse snorting nervously or a dog barking at a faint but suspicious noise.

Anderson described the night of May 1:

> [W]e traveled about 16 miles and camped in the open Pereri [prairie] without wood and but very little watter   no watter for our stock at all   we concluded to caral [corral] our cattle to keep them from straying off in search of watter so we formed a caral with the waggons leaving three gaps in it   at dark the cattle were drove in and a gard placed at each gap . . . about 11 o'clock when everything was still and the cattle all laying down and as dark as a stack of black cats all at once one of the girls sleeping in one of the waggons kicked a basket of tin dishes out the fore part of the waggon   it fell on the tung [tongue] from there on the ground making a tremendous racket   in an instant every ox was up and runing out and gone   here we cattlemen boys and dogs sooke sooke hoah hoah hoah over the pereri for about a mile   when we succeeded in getting round them and drove them back into the caral where we kept them a few minutes when one knocked a yoke down that was sitting up against the waggon and here they all went agan   we got them up and they broke out a third time so we gave it up and never carraled our cattle any more to guard inside our waggon carall.

It was an inauspicious start for the Miller camp. Cattle were a combustible lot, their temperaments varying from docile to skittish. The slightest unexpected noise could startle even the most placid. And when the first bolted, they all bolted. The whole experience that night must have been quite disheartening.

Some companies eschewed the practice of confining their livestock to a corral and instead allowed them to remain loose during the night. If they were in an area where the threat of Indian pilferage was not serious, if they were camping near a stream or river, and if the grass was adequate, such a procedure worked reasonably well. At the end of an exhausting day and after drinking their fill and snatching a few mouthfuls of grass, the tired animals would tend to lie down and stay down for much of the rest of the night. When they did get up, they would graze nearby, having no reason to wander. In these circumstances, it was a matter of chasing the oxen into the wagon enclosure in the morning to be yoked. Over time, the emigrants learned which cattle could be trusted to remain nearby. Those that were inveterate wanderers might be the only ones kept corralled through the night.

The morning usually started with the camp master shouting "Catch up!" A lively commotion ensued as the men drove their animals into the corral to be cornered and truckled to the yoke. The catch did not always go smoothly as some oxen simply did not like being "caught up." Before hitching the oxen to their wagons they might be led to water one more time. It was not uncommon to discover in the morning that some of the loose cattle and horses had strayed off (or were chased off by Indians), in which event, a party was sent off to look far and wide for them.

One group of animals the emigrants had to keep a particularly keen eye on were horses that had been purchased in St. Joseph. Still close to home, their instincts were to make a run for it at night. If not corralled or otherwise tightly hobbled and watched, they would be gone by daybreak, on their way to some comfortable, hay-filled stable in St. Joseph.

While these things were going on, the women were preparing a breakfast of coffee, fried bacon, and bread, which was used to sop up every last trace of bacon grease. Not knowing where the next creekless, woodless camp would be, the emigrants learned to send their children out to collect extra firewood and throw it into their wagons. With breakfast finished, fires burning out, and oxen shuffling patiently, the teamsters would crack their whips. Shouts of "Gee-up, gee-haw" would resound up and down the train, and the line of wagons would lurch forward and resume rumbling down the trail.

It is interesting that Riley Root's entry of May 1 reported that they camped fifteen miles beyond the mission, just a few miles ahead of Anderson's camp that night. Therefore, Root's camp should have been dry too, but he had recorded no disagreeable conditions or incidents.

After their troubles the night of May 1, Anderson wrote that they traveled ten miles the following day and came to "a small branch" (Walnut Creek?), where they camped: "[O]ur cattle having no watter for the last 24 hours and not knowing how soon we should again come to watter, we remained here until May the 3rd."

While some of the smaller creeks on the trail may not have had names, many did and their names were usually announced by guides who had been over the trail before. Anderson's failure to identify these creeks by name and his statement that they did not know "how soon we should again come to watter" are signs that they were not being guided by anyone who had traveled this road before.

A few days later an article appeared in the May 5 issue of the *St. Joseph Gazette*:

Major [Moses "Black"] Harris came in from the front camp of the Oregon emigrants, having been recalled by Maj. Gillespie of the U. S. Marine Corps, for the
purpose of making arrangements to go with Col. Fremont, who is expected here
by the 15th next month. Maj. H. reports the different trains for Oregon and California getting on well, except the last one, some 35 miles from this place, which
he found in utter confusion, having no leader, at a place distant from water and
nearly all their cattle lost, either driven off by the Indians, or strayed off during
the night in search of water.

It appears that some front-running company had lost the services of Black Harris, a superbly qualified pilot. It appears he had been leading a company traveling
ahead of Anderson's, but there is no evidence of any party leaving St. Joseph that
was known to be traveling ahead of Wambaugh. Since men like Wambaugh and
Clyman were too experienced to have needed Harris as their pilot, it is possible,
however, that Harris had been the pilot for the Gates party, the next in line.

As to the company that Harris "found in utter confusion," one cannot help but
suspect that he was referring to Anderson's Miller company, which would have been
about thirty-five miles from St. Joseph on May 1 when Harris would have encountered them on his return to St. Joe. Harris wasn't hesitant in saying that this company
lacked a leader, and the cattle problems that Harris mentioned sounded strikingly
similar to Anderson's accounts.

John C. Fremont had recently been convicted of insubordination in his court
martial in Washington, DC. He resigned his military commission in protest and
undertook a civilian assignment to find a practical railroad route through the southern Rockies on behalf of a group of investors. It sounded as if Fremont might have
asked his friend Major Gillespie to track down the renowned Black Harris to help
navigate him across the southern Rockies. Curiously, Harris and Gillespie did not
end up traveling with the Fremont expedition after all. It was lucky for them, since
the expedition would end in disaster later that year in the deep winter snows of the
Rocky Mountains.[9] Black Harris is next mentioned the following year, in an April
20, 1849, *Gazette* article, which mentioned him arriving from Fort Laramie after a
very successful buffalo hunting and trading expedition. A few weeks later, he was
in Independence, Missouri. He was getting ready to lead a party to California when
he died on May 6, 1849, in a cholera epidemic that was spreading among the crowds
gathering to begin their trip to the California goldfields.[10]

As for the progress of the Miller company, William Anderson described the next
day as another miserable one:

May the 3rd when we again started and traveled 14 miles when we were overtaken by a storm which gave us a complete drenching and we were forced to
camp on the plains out of sight of timber without any fire all wet and cold and
shivering   thus we passed the night the rain pouring down in torrents the most

part of the fore part of the night   I was on gard until midnight then crawled under a waggon and lay until morning and not a dry thread on me.

Anderson recorded that, after traveling only six miles on May 4, they encamped likely on a small stream just south of present-day Sabetha, Kansas. They traveled eighteen miles on May 5, traveling through hilly country where, in places, drifts of exposed limestone, like dull-colored teeth, peeked out from under lips of grass. They camped on "a small beautiful stream the banks of which were lined with timber." Based on Anderson's estimated distances, this stream should have been Nemaha Creek. It was bordered by low, scrubby oak, and despite its steep, muddy banks, it was a fairly easy stream to cross. The trail crossed the creek about one-half mile south of the present-day bridge on Highway 71.[11] As of May 5, Anderson's party was about fifty miles out of St. Joseph, while the Wambaugh company was about sixty miles out. The Gates company should have been somewhere in between.

On May 6, the mishap-prone Miller company experienced another problem: "May the 6th we traveled 15 miles and camped here," Anderson reported. "[O]ne of our company Mr. Cleaver had the misfortune to loose a yoke of cattle   they were young cattle and some troublesome to yoke   on the next morning they were found dead with the yoke turned in   turning the yoke they fell with their heads under them." This was an example of why turning cattle loose at night, despite its risks and headaches, was the best routine. Cattle simply had an uncanny knack of getting themselves into bad scrapes if they were tied up or otherwise restrained at night.

The next day, May 7, Anderson reported that they traveled sixteen miles "over a beautiful roling perari road and encamped by a small grove of timber by which ran a beautiful little branch [likely Lilly Creek, a few miles east of Marysville]."

During the day on May 8, perhaps just west of where the trail crossed the Big Blue River at today's Marysville, seven bedraggled, eastbound men hove into sight of the Miller company. Riding their jaded mules and looking like they hadn't seen a razor, soap, or water in quite some time, the group was led by Joe Meek, a six-foot-two-inch, broad-shouldered, shaggy bear of a man. Meek brought jarring news from Oregon that would spread through the camp like a prairie wildfire. Anderson recorded the encounter:

May the 8th we traveled 15 miles to day we met a Mr. Meeks and 6 other men on their way from Oregon to Washington City [Washington, DC]   they said that the Cyuse Indians were at war with the Oregon settlers and that they were going to try to get some assistance from the united states   they had bin 62 days on the road from Oregon City and were then 100 miles from the Missouri River   they said that they had to live on mule flesh for some time before they came into bufalo country   we camped this day on the west side of a branch of big blue river [west of present-day Marysville, Kansas]   here was a grave of a child that the emigrants of last year burried.

Meek and his fellow travelers would have been besieged with every imaginable question. The Indian war in Oregon was sobering news. Of more immediate concern, however, Meek probably warned the Miller party to be on the lookout for Pawnees ahead, who had confronted them while they were traveling down the Platte River. George Ebbert, one of Meek's traveling companions, reported that the Pawnees had "tried to rob us by trying to intimidate us into giving up our guns."[12]

Joe Meek had been born in Virginia in 1810, and went west when he was only eighteen. He was hired on as a trapper by William Sublette of the Rocky Mountain Fur Company in 1828. One of the West's truly larger-than-life figures, Meek was noted as a raconteur of the first order. Indeed, some of his yarns were so extraordinary that they smelled of shameful fabrication. As a loyal employee of the Rocky Mountain Fur Company, later assimilated by the American Fur Company, Meek toiled for twelve years in the mountain streams and creeks, including his notorious month-long drunks at the annual rendezvous. His far-flung beaver hunting had taken him as far as California with Joseph Walker in 1834.

By 1840, Meek was only thirty years old, but the fur trade was dying and he emigrated to Oregon to settle down. In the Willamette Valley, Meek tried his hand at farming, a difficult transition for a man who had only known the rough, free life of hunting, trapping, and Indian fighting. Needing to supplement his income, Meek got himself elected sheriff and then tax collector for the valley's communities. In 1846, he was elected to the legislature of Oregon's new provisional government.[13]

On December 8, 1847, shocking news arrived in the Willamette Valley. The Cayuse Indians had massacred the Whitmans at the Whitman mission. The fledgling provisional government acted immediately, forming a volunteer militia to send to Walla Walla. They designated Joe Meek to hasten east to Washington, DC to ask for military help. The legendary mountainman and his companions paused at the Whitman mission as they headed east and viewed the gruesome scene. Meek must have suffered a particularly heart-wrenching grief. He had left his young, half-Indian daughter, Helen, with Mrs. Whitman to be educated, and he found her among those who had died. Joe and his party left the mission on March 4 and continued their march eastward.[14] They encountered a party of hostile Bannock warriors, but talked their way past them. During much of their early journey, they slogged through deep snow and suffered intense cold. They traveled through country that was devoid of buffalo and other game. Faced with starvation, they were forced to eat skunks, and when one of their horses gave out, they ate him too. They were provided with food when they arrived at Peg Leg Smith's trading post along the Bear River in today's Idaho. They continued on to Fort Bridger and were provided with fresh mules. They then proceeded on to Fort Laramie. They had a tense encounter with a Sioux camp at Ash Hollow. Then it was a party of Pawnees along the Platte River. Continuing down the Platte, they were soon starving again. They resorted to eating their greasy *parfleches*, and were on the verge of consuming one of their mules when, according to party member George Ebbert, they met the first emigrant wagon train and were able to eat ham and eggs instead. Ebbert wrote that they met three other companies before they reached St. Joseph, the last one of which he said was led by Joe Watt. They knew Joe from when he lived in Oregon.[15] The Meek party arrived at St. Joseph on May 10.[16] By then they had to have passed a minimum of seven companies: Wambaugh, Gates, Miller, Walker, Bristow, Purvine, and Watt, although a few of them may have been traveling so close to one another that Ebbert considered them to be the same company.

Curiously, Riley Root made no mention of his company meeting Meek, not surprising since Root was such a miser with his words. But in a reminiscence written in 1890, John Trullinger, a Wambaugh company member, asserted that their party had met Meek and his men on the trail.[17]

James Clyman had left the fur trade and the Rocky Mountains in the fall of 1827, a year before Meek began his trapping career. Although Meek would have missed Clyman by a year, both belonged to the same exclusive fraternity of former trappers and both would have had a number of friends in common: Jedediah Smith, William Sublette, Jim Bridger, Thomas Fitzpatrick, and Black Harris. Meek might also have met Clyman when he was in Oregon in 1844 to 1845. If the two met on the trail in 1848, they would have had plenty to talk about, but with Meek's reputation for loquaciousness, compared to Clyman's taciturn soft-spokenness, it might have made for a very one-sided conversation.

In reading Meek's and Ebbert's accounts of their wintry trek through what is now Eastern Oregon, Idaho, and Wyoming, one common thread was quite apparent; they regarded all the Indians they encountered—Bannocks, Snakes, Crows, Sioux, and Pawnees—as potential threats. They would have been unsure whether a general uprising against whites was spreading like a wildfire across the entire west. With that in mind, it is likely that Meek and his friends would have admonished Clyman, Wambaugh, and all the emigrant companies they met to be cautious and vigilant as they headed west.[18]

Returning to William Anderson, he wrote that his Miller company traveled eleven miles on May 9, twelve miles on May 10, and eighteen miles on May 11. On the eleventh, he wrote that they encountered Little Sandy Creek, about five miles northwest of present Fairbury, Nebraska. After traveling three miles on the twelfth, he recorded that the road had become "dusty," that they crossed the "big sandy," and then camped eleven miles beyond it. They should have spent the night about four miles southwest of present Alexandria, Nebraska.

May 6–12, 1848

William Porter, Purvine company, Mosquito Creek, Indian Territory, Kansas

When William Porter and his Purvine company rolled away from Mosquito Creek on the morning of May 6, they were probably a day behind the Walker and Bristow companies, six days behind the Miller company, and eight days behind Wambaugh. Porter described the next two days' travel:

> 6th. Started with the intention of going only 8 miles—we crossed a small stream about as large as Bay Creek on which are some Indians making some attempt to farm. Three miles further is what is called the agency [Nemaha Indian Sub-agency] at which place we arrived about noon, and not knowing the distance across the prairie we continued on till 11 o'clock in the night and then stopped without wood or water. You should leave this agency early in the morning. There is a farm at this agency which appears to be conducted poorly.
>
> 7th. Retraced 4 or 5 miles of our road for the purpose of getting to wood and water off the road to the left. Water plenty, but wood scarce. Two of our company went back to the agency to get their wagons repaired, and we were lying by today.

The Nemaha Indian Subagency, established near the Presbyterian Mission School, was like most Indian agencies at the time. It maintained a staff consisting of an interpreter, a gunsmith, a blacksmith to make or repair guns, farm implements, and wagons, and farmers to teach the Indians agricultural skills. Porter suggested that some in his company had need of the blacksmith.

Porter's company, like Anderson's, was probably not led by someone familiar with what lay ahead, causing them to be unprepared for the "dry" camp they faced on the night of May 6. Porter's entry for the seventh went on to prescribe advice for any future emigrant:

> Start early in the morning from the mission and if you see no prospects for timber turn from the road to camp. Keep the plainest road which is very good at this time. We traveled 12 or 15 miles into the prairie today. Here are several branches to the road any one of which will be right. Keep the best which lies on the dividing ridge.

Porter had noted that much of the terrain along this stretch was wide and open, so the trail was rarely one narrow ribbon. This is why wagon trains frequently fanned out, moving off the main trail to travel across fresh, virgin grass as a means of avoiding dust or mud. Porter continued:

> 7th and 8th. Lay by waiting for the return of part of our company from the agency.
> 9th. Traveled 15 or 16 miles and camped off the road about two miles to the right [perhaps at Walnut Creek].

10th. Traveled 20 miles and camped on Wolf River [more likely the Nemaha].

11th. Traveled 20 or 25 miles, passing good camping places and camped on the road.

12th. Traveled 12 or 14 miles and camped off the road. Poor grass and water.

Although Porter failed to mention meeting Joe Meek and his men, his letter to his parents reported that "Andrew Rodgers was killed with the Whitman's family." The fact that Porter mentioned Rogers as among those killed in the Whitman massacre suggested that the Porter family knew him. Does it also not seem likely that Porter learned of his death from Meek?

It is certain that the Bristow company met Meeks. When William Bristow arrived in Oregon City in September, he reported to the *Oregon Spectator* newspaper that he and his men met Meek about sixty miles west of St. Joseph on May 7, although the date was probably wrong. More likely, the Bristow company encountered Meek on about May 8 or 9.[19]

MAY 9, 1848
Keturah Belknap, Watt company, Nemaha River, Indian Territory, Kansas

After crossing the Missouri River on April 26, Keturah Belknap's diary went silent for almost two weeks. As she grew heavier with child, she may have found the trip more difficult. Her next entry was undated, but it was probably around May 9 when her Watt company met Meek and his eastbound party at or near the Nemaha River, about fifty miles west of St. Joseph. She described the encounter:

> Just as we were ready to sit down to supper, Joe Meek and his posse of men rode into camp. They were going to Washington D. C. to get the government to send soldiers to protect the settlers in Oregon and they told us all about the Indian Massacre at Walla Walla called the "Whitman Massacre." They had traveled all winter and some of their men had died [one of Meek's fabrications] and they had got out of food and had to eat mule meat so we gave them all their supper and breakfast. The captain divided them up so all could help feed them. Father B. [Belknap] was captain so he and George took three so they made way with most all my stuff I had cooked up.

Joe Watt also mentioned the Meek encounter in a recollection written many years later. According to Watt, Meek announced upon his arrival that "[t]he Cayuse Indians have broken out and are murdering far and near, sparing neither man, woman, nor children."[20]

For many emigrant men, it was difficult enough to get their wives to leave family and friends and a solid, cozy house to become pioneers. And now this? Is this what they had to look forward to after crossing a cursed wilderness—a bunch of Indians slaughtering settlers by the scores in Oregon? According to Keturah, Meek's chilling report was the last straw for some:

> [S]ome want to turn back and others are telling what they would do in case of an attack. I sit in the wagon and write a letter as these men say if we want to send any word back they will take it and drop it in the first Post Office they come to so I am writing a scratch to a lady friend. While I'm writing I have an exciting experience. George is out on guard and in the next wagon behind ours a man and woman are quarreling. She wants to turn back and he wont go so she says she will go and leave him with the children and he will have a good time with that crying baby, then he used some very bad words and said he would put it out of the way. Jus then I heard a muffled cry and a heavy thud as something was thrown against the wagon box and she said "Oh you've killed it" and he swore some more and told her to keep her mouth shut or he would give her some of the same. Jus then word came, change guards. George came in and Mr. Kitridge went out so he and his wife parted for the night. The baby was not killed. I write this to show how easy we can be deceived. We have a rest and breakfast is over. Meek and his men are gathering their horses and packing, . . . The woman was out by the roadside with a little buget [buggy?] and her baby asleep in the wagon under a strong opiate.

May 3–11, 1848
Father Lempfrit, Stone company, St. Joseph, Missouri

A different sort of fellow showed up in St. Joseph on May 3. He was Honoré-Timothée Lempfrit, a French Catholic priest who had recently arrived in America. Belonging to the order of the Oblates of Mary Immaculate, the forty-five-year-old priest was being sent by his order to serve as a missionary among the Indians in Oregon. He kept a wonderfully descriptive diary that was only recently discovered and translated from French to English.[21] He came from an ancient country, with cathedrals, chateaus, stone villages, and rock walls, where almost every hectare was filled with country roads and carefully manicured fields and gardens. The priest was now about to enter the American West, a strange new world, vast, empty, and wild, and, other than the almost imperceptible fingerprint of the primitives, it was virtually untouched by the hand of man. His recorded reactions and impressions are delightfully fresh and captivating—almost childlike and naïve.

Father Lempfrit's diary reported that he took the *Tamerlane* up the Missouri River from St. Louis, but it would have been the steamboat's next trip after delivering Rudolph Kurz to St. Joseph. Lempfrit and a fellow priest, Father Lionnet, had left St. Louis, then a city of about 65,000, on April 26, 1848. They arrived at St. Joseph on May 3, and spent the next few days with Father Scanlon, the town's priest. Lempfrit wrote that he said Mass and heard a few confessions. He described the settlement as four years old and with about one thousand inhabitants. By the time he arrived, most of the emigrant parties had already crossed the Missouri River and were gone. Things in town were beginning to quiet down and return to normal.

Lempfrit heard that there was an Irish Catholic emigrant in town by the name of David O'Neil who was with a small group that was getting ready to leave for Oregon. Lempfrit found O'Neil and they struck a deal. For fifty dollars, O'Neil agreed to carry both priests' baggage in his two already overstuffed wagons and would provide them with meals. Father Lempfrit then went and bought himself a tent and a "pretty little black pony" on which to ride across the plains.

The day before they left St. Joseph, Father Lempfrit entered in his diary that:

> On the 10th, towards midday, we saw a cavalcade arriving which we at first took to be Indians, but little by little we discerned them to be white men. These presumed Indians were a delegation from the Oregon states on their way to Washington to ask for help from the United States against the Oregon Indians. We learned that the Indians of Walla Walla were in rebellion and had massacred Doctor Whitman with his wife and children, in all eleven persons.

This was all Lempfrit wrote about the arrival of Joe Meek's party at St. Joseph. But one has to wonder how he reacted to the news. After all, he was going to Walla Walla. How did he feel about going to a place where he might experience martyrdom much sooner than he had planned?

The *St. Joseph Gazette* reported Meek's arrival in its May 12 issue:

> Yesterday morning [May 10] our town was startled with news that the Indians in the Oregon Territory are waging a most fearful warfare upon the whites in that country. Mr. Meek has come in with an escort of six men, as the bearer of despatches from the Governor of Oregon, to the President, having left there on the 5th day of March. He reports that four tribes of Indians numbering about three thousand warriors were united against the whites and that four battles had been fought, the army of the Oregonians numbering five hundred, under the command of Col. Neal Gilliam. . . . Mr. Meek received his papers in December, but was unable to leave the country before March, because the Indians were between him and the Mountains.

Meek had left Anderson's Miller company at the Big Blue River on May 8. To arrive at St. Joseph on the tenth, he and his companions had traveled about one hundred miles in two days, a remarkable feat worthy of his larger-than-life reputation. He and two of his friends, Ebbert and Leabo, continued traveling east on steamboats and trains, first to St. Louis, then on to Washington, DC, still attired in their smelly buckskins and wolfskin caps and spreading the alarming news as they headed east. Upon arriving in Washington, Meek immediately saw the president. It wasn't hard, since they were distantly related. After they got him cleaned up, Meek appeared before Congress to plead for help. When he returned to Oregon months later, he had been made a U.S. marshal by the president.[22]

The O'Neil family and the two priests were part of a small company of eleven wagons captained by David Stone that crossed the Missouri River on May 11. Much of the information regarding the composition of the Stone company came from a reminiscence written years later by James D. Miller, who was eighteen at the time. Miller explained that when his father, Joseph, got the Oregon "fever," he sold his farm near Fort Wayne, Indiana, and brought the family and their wagons by steamer down the Ohio River to St. Louis, then up the Missouri to Weston. Buying horses and teams of oxen in Weston, they traveled overland to St. Joseph. There, they bought their provisions: two hundred pounds of flour and one hundred pounds of bacon for each person, cornmeal, dried apples and peaches, beans, salt, pepper, rice, tea, coffee, sugar, a medicine chest and "plenty of caps, powder and lead."[23]

Like Father Lempfrit, Miller recalled encountering Joe Meek's party at the St. Joseph ferry, erroneously reporting it as May 4. "Meek's story of the wholesale massacre," Miller recorded, "made us blue and discouraged, thinking we would go hundreds of miles possibly to meet the fate of Dr. Whitman and others."[24]

According to Miller, Captain Stone's company consisted of Stone, his wife, two children, and two wagons. David O'Neill, probably a widower, traveled with his two young sons and two wagons. There was George A. Barns, his wife, and one wagon; George Smith with two wagons; and William Smith. Then there was the largest family: the Millers, consisting of three wagons, Joseph A. Miller, his wife, and four children: Charles, Jefferson, James D. (eighteen at the time), and young Annie.

The company was accompanied by a number of single men: George Hedger, George Wallace, L. D. Purdeau, James Costello, Charles Costello, Lawrence Burns ("the Irishman"), and the two priests. Miller reported Jacob Conser as in their company, although Jacob has also been mentioned as being in the Walker company.[25] Conser could have started with Walker and later dropped back to join the Stone company, or he could have started with Stone and hustled forward later to join Walker. All told, Miller claimed that there were thirty-one men "able to bear arms."[26]

Father Lempfrit described the day they crossed the Missouri River:

> It was May 11th that we crossed the river to go and camp that same day from where the caravan was stationed. Our conductor, O'Neil had allowed several animals to stray when we were crossing the river, consequently we were obliged to remain in the same place for several days until they had been recovered. I passed an excellent night under our tent. In the afternoon I went hunting and was quite lucky.

The Stone party was the last company to leave St. Joseph in 1848. According to the *Gazette*, 210 wagons had crossed the river at St. Joseph as of May 5. Adding eleven wagons from the Stone company increases the total to 221. But the total for the year was still down substantially from the 867 wagons that had crossed there in 1847.[27] There were two more companies that probably left from St. Joseph. Assuming twenty-five wagons each would bring the total to 216 wagons, very close to the number reported by the *Gazette*.

Table 4: Companies known to have departed from St. Joseph in 1848

Company (Diarist)	Number of Wagons	Departed From Mosquito Creek
Wambaugh (Root)	20	April 28
Gates	40 est.	April 29
Miller (Anderson)	23	April 30
Walker } Bristow	24	May 5 (est.)
Purvine (Porter)	24	May 6
Watt (Belknap)	24	May 7
Stone (Lempfrit)	11	May 13 (est.)
Total	166	

CHAPTER 6

Indian Troubles
APRIL 12–MAY 10

APRIL 12–MAY 10, 1848
Thomas Corcoran and P. B. Cornwall, Cornwall company,
Bellevue, Indian Territory, Nebraska

P. B. Cornwall and Thomas Corcoran were last seen sleeping on the heights of Bellevue near the Council Bluffs Indian agency. They left Bellevue on about April 12, starting west ahead of all but perhaps one or two early emigrant companies. Would Cornwall's sense of urgency and the pace he set ensure that his party would cross the western mountains before October 31, the dreadful date that trapped the Donners?

Neither Cornwall's biography nor Corcoran's letter detailed their trip out of Bellevue, but the trail west was easy to follow. It is almost certain that Cornwall and his companions followed the trail west where it gradually descended off the Bellevue plateau and snaked through open prairie. Heading more north than west until it struck Big Papillion Creek, the trail then followed the east bank of the creek as it wound northwest for about twenty miles. After crossing the creek at an easy ford, the trail turned more west than north. They continued about ten miles to the Elkhorn River, about two miles south of where today's Highway 36 crosses the river. Heavily timbered along its banks, the Elkhorn was over one hundred feet wide with a swift, deep current. Two years earlier, the Mormons had sent work details from their camps in the Council Bluffs area to begin improving the trail for the great Mormon migration that was to follow. Ramps were dug into the banks of the smaller creeks and bridges were built over the others. When the Cornwall party arrived at the Elkhorn, they should have come to the crude ferry and wooden landing abutments the Mormons had built the year before.[1] The ferry had been used heavily in 1847, helping get the first wave of Mormon emigrants on their way to the Salt Lake valley. It seems doubtful that the Mormons would have kept men camping around the ferry this early in the spring, as they would not begin their 1848 emigration until May 26. With no ferrymen present, it would not be surprising if enterprising young men like Cornwall and his companions helped themselves to the use of the flat-bottomed raft.

Once across the Elkhorn, the trail aimed toward a tall post rising into the air about three-quarters of a mile west, a signal the Mormons had planted to show the location of a small bridge they had built over tiny Rawhide Creek.

About ten miles beyond the Rawhide, the trail struck the north side of the Platte River, just southwest of where the town of Fremont stands today. The year before, the Mormons had marked this place with the "Liberty Pole," a forty-foot-tall cottonwood pole flying a white flag. Capable of being seen from afar, it was used to direct Mormon companies to this assembly point from which they continued west in 1847. The trail continued close to the Platte for another twenty or so miles, coming at last to Shell Creek, a couple of miles east of present-day Schuyler, Nebraska. Once again, the Cornwall party would have benefited from another Mormon improvement—a small bridge across the twelve-foot-wide, three-foot-deep, tree-fringed creek.[2]

For the next twelve miles, the Platte River drifted away from the road. There would be no water for the travelers until the road rejoined the Platte at the mouth of the Loup River. The previous year, William Clayton, one of the Mormon diarists of 1847, mentioned encountering a large Pawnee village situated at the mouth of the Loup.

Neither Cornwall nor Corcoran mentioned the Pawnee village, but it is because the Pawnees had moved it during the past year. In fact, the travelers did not mention any encounters with Indians during this section of the trail, suggesting nothing unusual occurred. But the small Cornwall party was taking chances, as one of the Mormon wagon drivers had been shot and killed the year before by Omaha Indians somewhere between Winter Quarters and the Liberty Pole.[3]

The old trapper/trader trail crossed the Loup's mouth. But because of the width, depth, and the speed of the river's current, it was a dangerous obstacle for wagons. That was why the Mormons chose not to cross it here in 1847 or 1848. Instead, they headed along the Loup's northern side for about twenty-eight miles before fording at an easier place.[4] It is impossible to know whether Cornwall's party crossed the Loup at its mouth or took the Mormon route. Neither Cornwall's biography nor Corcoran's letter explained. It is more likely that the party, being under Fallon's guidance, kept to the old trail and forded where the Loup entered the Platte.

West of the Loup, the old trail continued up the Platte's broad floodplain. Ranging between ten and fifteen miles wide, the plain was as smooth and free of obstacles as one could hope for. Indeed, it was so flat and smooth that, other than keeping the Platte close by on the left, one did not need to travel along any particular course. There was adequate water, wood, and grass for hundreds of miles.

When they left Bellevue, Thomas Corcoran had entered into an agreement with Orrin Kellogg's son, Joseph. Thomas would pay him to carry his clothing and blankets in his wagon and to provide him meals. Thomas remained quite ill during this early part of the trip, explaining in his letter to his sister that his cough was so bad

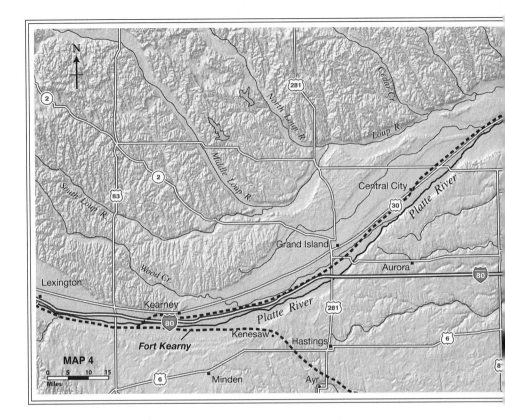

MAP 4

0   5   10   15
Miles

that he continued to cough up blood: "Every night, we would stand guard in two hour shifts. After I stood guard for about a week, the boys went to the wagon train captain and told them I coughed so much at night that they would stand guard, so I didn't have to stand guard anymore."

Gradually, the Platte curved to the southwest. It remained very wide and shallow, a complex river of braided channels and sandbars. In most places it was treeless, except for a thin fringe of cottonwoods along its banks. The islands, protected from the recurrent prairie fires, were often thickly wooded, and the travelers must have seen great flocks of ducks and geese in the river's wetlands, a significant stopping point along their migratory route. At length, Cornwall's party came into view of Grand Island, noticing it first from a distance as a dark green blister on the horizon. About forty miles long and ranging up to five miles wide, the island was formed by the Platte dividing into two principal channels. Near the head of Grand Island, the Oregon Trail, the chief highway of travel from Independence and St. Joseph, came up and struck the south side of the Platte.

About twenty miles west of the head of Grand Island, the Cornwall party came to a place that was frequently used as a ford across the Platte. Although the river was

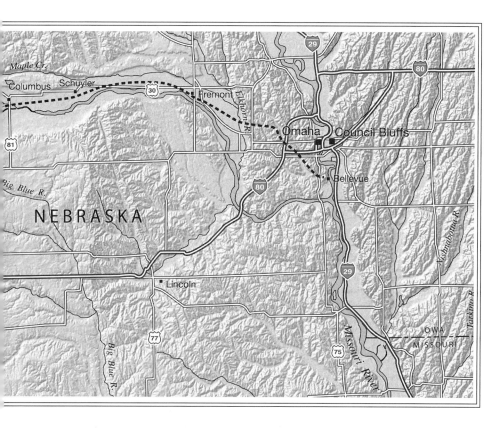

described as about a mile wide at that spot, it consisted of a large number of shallow channels separated by narrow sandbars; the water was rarely more than knee-deep and the channels had hard bottoms. This crossing of the Platte was about 220 miles from Bellevue and about fourteen miles west of where the army would soon establish Fort Childs, later called Fort Kearny.[5] During the gold rush, Fort Kearny was an important army outpost, a welcome pause for the thousands of gold rushers that would travel the trail in the years to come.

Cornwall's biography suggested that they used this ford to cross the Platte because of the Pawnee Indians, declaring that "it was their custom to separate into small bands and wander about seeking opportunities to rob and murder. No tribe on the continent ever obtained more justly the fear, hatred and contempt of the white man."[6] Fallon may have been concerned that the diminutive Cornwall party was too small to adequately defend itself, and may have hoped they could soon merge with a larger wagon train making its way up the Oregon Trail.

After crossing to the southern bank of the Platte, the Cornwall party commenced traveling along the great Oregon road. They were now in antelope and buffalo country, and the party sent men out to hunt during the day. Despite his health problems,

Thomas Corcoran explained in his letter that he and others spent all day hunting out on the prairie while the wagons plodded slowly along the dusty trail. By evening, according to Thomas, he and the others would return to the wagons, "bringing plenty of fresh meat for the whole party for supper, breakfast and dinner."[7]

There is a Corcoran family story that the illiterate Thomas memorized poetry as he heard it read around the campfire at night. One can imagine P. B. reading from his books by "Moore, Byron, and Burns" while Thomas listened intently and committed the verses to memory. During the following day's hunt, he would have plenty of time to recite the memorized verses to himself as he rocked along in the saddle.

"About three hundred miles to the westward of their starting point [Bellevue]," Cornwall's biography recounted, "the party met the famous scout, Joe Meek, on his way from Oregon to the Capitol at Washington [DC], in search of federal aid for the settlers in the first Indian war of the northwest. The story he told of the ferocity of the Indians was not calculated to encourage the emigrants."[8] In a couple of biographical sketches, the Kelloggs also corroborated meeting Meek along the Platte.[9]

Since Corcoran, Cornwall, and the Kelloggs eschewed dates, we must estimate when they encountered Meek and his party. If the Cornwall biography is correct in its estimate of meeting Meek three hundred miles from Bellevue, the location would have been slightly east of where the Platte River branches into south and north forks (a few miles southeast of present-day North Platte, Nebraska). Meek had left the Whitman mission on March 4 and arrived at St. Joseph on May 10. These dates translate into an average rate of travel of thirty miles per day. This rate of travel suggests that Meek would have encountered Cornwall just below the forks of the Platte on about April 29. If an estimated rate of travel for Cornwall's wagons was seventeen miles per day, it would indicate that the Cornwall party left Bellevue around April 12.

Of all the companies leaving from Independence and St. Joseph, the leading group should have been Allsopp's, who reported that his party arrived at Fort Laramie on May 31. Therefore, on April 29, when Cornwall's company likely met Meek, Allsopp's group should have been traveling along the Little Blue River and Wambaugh's would have just left St. Joseph. It is quite evident, therefore, that the impatient Cornwall had left Bellevue so early that he and his companions were way ahead of the St. Joseph and Independence wagon trains. This will turn out to have been a bad idea.

During Cornwall's meeting with Meek around April 29, Meek is certain to have warned Fallon and Cornwall about a band of Pawnees his party had encountered not far to the west who had tried to rob them. Meek also likely reported a village of Sioux camped at Ash Hollow, a few days' travel west of the troublesome Pawnees.

Leaving Meek, Cornwall's group must have continued on with trepidation. Thomas Corcoran wrote that they were traveling along the Platte, having not yet reached its south fork, when they ran into the Pawnees:

The Pawnee Indians were trying to steal from us. They kept shooting around us all day. We traveled all night to get to the Sioux Indians who were friendly with the whites. I slept in a wagon part of the night with my rifle and pistol by my side, ready for an attack. Other men rode on each side of the wagons. We came to a half-about at daybreak near a little bend in the Platte River. The sleeping men were awakened and rode guard while the others slept. Shortly after sunrise, I walked about a mile ahead of the wagon train and saw about six Indian warriors coming down on us. I hurried back to camp and told them what I had seen. They corralled the wagons and made a line of defense with them. We had an interpreter with us by the name of Fallon. He went out to meet them. They told him that they had been fighting with the Sioux Indians that morning and about sixty of their tribe had been killed. They told us that we must give them provisions and clothing. We told them we had nothing to give them. They had their bows strung and were all ready to fire on us. They were all around us and each of us had a pistol in one hand and a rifle in the other, waiting to see who would fire first. They got around in front of the wagon in which I slept and one of them took hold of my blankets. He was going to carry them off. I got up on the tongue of the wagon and pushed him away. They then made a break and stole all of Young's blankets. This was the Young that lived in Hayes Grove. Then we leveled our rifles at them and they took to their heels and ran. We then hitched our teams to the wagons and drove to the Sioux village and arrived that evening. The Sioux were glad to receive white travelers and they hoisted the American flag on a pole. They told us that we could go thru their Nation in peace but not to kill any more buffalo than we need to eat. They said that they were their cattle.

In contrast, Cornwall's version, written by his son fifty-eight years later, described a much more dramatic scenario:

All were in high spirits when, without warning, they [Cornwall's party] suddenly rode over a rise on the prairie almost in the midst of a camp of two thousand Pawnees. Within a trice they were surrounded, made prisoner and deprived of their arms. . . . Fallon, who could speak the Pawnee dialect, wisely concealed this fact for obvious reasons. For a day and a night and a part of the next day the immigrants were kept under close guard while the Indian chiefs, sitting about in a council, smoked and debated as to what disposition should be made of them. Fallon, hearing their speeches, ascertained that the younger braves insisted upon having the lives of the prisoners as a fitting reprisal for those of two Indians of their tribe who had recently been killed at Fort Smith on the Arkansas [River]. The old chiefs spoke against this sanguinary procedure and the council was long and heated in its discussions.[10]

Cornwall's biography went on to explain that P. B. asked to be taken to the council, where he addressed the chiefs and warned them that Colonel Loring's regiment, an army as numerous as "leaves on the trees," was just behind them and that if any harm should come to him and his friends the army "would bring a stiff reckoning upon the Pawnees."

The chiefs decided to release the party, and Cornwall and his companions resumed their journey. They drove all day and through the night, not daring to slow down. When the early light of dawn arrived, they discovered that fifty Pawnee braves had followed them on ponies all through the night. Then "began a running fight which lasted all day," in which Cornwall claimed he was shot through his right leg by an arrow. The party kept their wagons rolling all that day and through another night. The next morning, the men and their animals, at the point of "sheer exhaustion," spotted sixty mounted Indians crossing the Platte and riding toward them. Recognizing them as Sioux, Fallon exclaimed, "Boys, I think we are saved." Indeed, one of them was Fallon's father-in-law.[11]

The mention of Colonel Loring's name is interesting. Loring led a company of mounted riflemen from Fort Kearny to Oregon in 1849.[12] How Cornwall knew of Colonel Loring is only speculation, but it may be that while Cornwall was traveling to Council Bluffs, he heard the army was getting ready to send troops west to establish a new fort on the south bank of the Platte that would later be named Fort Kearny. Loring's name may have come up in connection with that project.

The Cornwall biography continued describing the party's meeting with the Sioux, reporting that when they learned that the hated Pawnees were just beyond, the Sioux galloped off in pursuit. Later that night, the Sioux rejoined the Cornwall party and camped the night with them. According to Cornwall, the Sioux were "loaded down with the spoils of the enemy who they had met and defeated after a fierce battle. They were naked except for their clouts; their heads were shaved clean save for a band of bristling hair in the center that stood high and extended from their foreheads backward. In all the splendor of their war paint they sat about in buffalo robes, boasting of their deeds of prowess and valor." Afterwards, the Cornwall party was escorted by their Sioux "allies" the rest of the way to Fort Laramie.[13]

Recording events after so many years, it is perfectly understandable that Cornwall and Corcoran would recall differently the details of the same incident, but the differences between the two versions are too extreme to be reconcilable; they do not seem to be describing the same event. We need to look at other sources to see what further light can be shed on the incident.

During the first week of June, a man by the name of John S. Shaw rolled into St. Joseph with a party of wagons. A few days later, on June 9, 1848, the St. Joseph Gazette published the news:

Mr. Shaw arrived here on Monday [June 5] from Fort John [Laramie] on [the] Platte River. On his way in he met about 300 wagons of Oregon and California emigrants and 200 wagons of Mormons. All were getting on well. The first company was 500 miles from the settlements, and the last one about 150. A company of California-bound emigrants numbering about sixty, had a little difficulty with the Pawnees, but no person was injured.

There is a copy of an old newspaper clipping in a file in the St. Joseph Public Library that curiously does not identify the date or the newspaper in which it appeared, but it is essentially the same report as above, except it contains the following additional information:

[A] party of fifty Pawnees robbed one of their number, a Mr. Greenwood, of a cow, clothing and some smaller articles and whipped another man. Our informant [Mr. Shaw] states that there would have been no danger, but the emigrants were afraid of the Indians and suffered themselves to be treated in that manner.

Shaw was a trader of buffalo robes. In 1846, he was bringing a party of wagons east along the Platte River when he was robbed by the Pawnees of his cargo of 140 packs of buffalo robes. Undaunted, he traveled up the Platte the next year with his men and wagons, and was returning from Fort Laramie in the spring of 1848, his wagons again filled with robes and tongues, when he encountered the emigrant companies heading west.[14] Encounters with Shaw would be reported by William Porter on May 21, by Edward Smith on May 22, and by Father Lempfrit on May 28. The "last party" Shaw reported meeting 150 miles from St. Joseph would have been the Chiles company, which had started from Independence. According to diarist Richard M. May, a member of the Chiles party, they encountered Shaw on May 29, about twenty miles beyond Rock Creek. In contrast, neither Riley Root in the Wambaugh company nor William Anderson in the Miller company had mentioned meeting Shaw's party.

Based on the dates of these encounters, Shaw's wagons were traveling east at an average rate of about seventeen miles per day. When Shaw reported to the *Gazette* that he met the first emigrant party five hundred miles from the settlements, it should have been near Chimney Rock, which is about five hundred miles west of St. Joseph. Shaw's average rate of travel would have put him at Chimney Rock on about May 6.

We have already estimated that Cornwall met Meek just east of the Platte forks on April 29. Perhaps a day or so later, the Cornwall party encountered the Pawnees. Assuming Cornwall continued west at a rate of travel of seventeen miles per day, and figuring one day of delay caused by their encounter with the Pawnees and Sioux, Cornwall's group would have passed Chimney Rock about May 7, about the same day as Shaw did. It is reassuring to see these dates closely match.

There is one more narrative that adds something to this incident. Rufus Burrows, the fourteen-year-old traveling with the Wambaugh company, wrote a reminiscence many years later. Some of it is consistent with John Shaw and some is not. Because so many years had passed, we must be wary of some of Burrows' details:

Our emigrant train [the Wambaugh company] had various experiences on the way to California. On account of one sick man, Mr. Huntsucker, the train was delayed for a while. In order to get better feed for their stock, Mr. Greenwood, his family and a young man by the name of P. B. Cornwall, went on ahead of the train for one day. The next day after leaving the main train, this little party met five or six hundred Pawnee Indian warriors who had been out on a big buffalo hunt, and also intruding on the Sioux Indian grounds. Not knowing of the large train behind, the warriors took all Greenwood had in his wagon and let him go on. As he started, Cornwall walking behind the wagon, four or five young warriors, wanting to give him a scare, shot five arrows at him; Cornwall then stopped and picked them up, taking them along. Greenwood, having been across the plains many times before and knowing the country well and that there was a Sioux Indian village just a short distance ahead, and also knowing that they were at peace with the whites, went on to the Sioux village. After reaching there, Cornwall took his five arrows and went to the Sioux Chief and presented them to him, the Chief exclaiming, 'Pawnee, Pawnee, Pawnee.' Then taking the arrows he said, 'When the sun goes down, we will give them their arrows back with some of our own with them,' meaning an Indian battle. The old Chief then gave a loud yell. All of his warriors came running to him. After a little time and a few gestures, they commenced to scatter. Just a short while before the sun went down, those Indians, warriors, braves in their war paint and many feathers, came riding up on their horses and circled about their Chief. They all started back on the road to find the Pawnees. After traveling quite a distance they discovered the camp, but did not make an attack then, but waited until near the break of day, when they surrounded the Pawnee camp. A fierce battle ensued, the Sioux killing about fifty of the Pawnee and forcing the rest, about four or five hundred in number, to flee, leaving a large number of Indian ponies and a quantity of dried buffalo meat, which the Sioux took as the spoils of war.[15]

With hair-pulling frustration, we compare Burrows' "five or six hundred" Pawnees with Cornwall's "two thousand," Shaw's "fifty," and Corcoran's "six." The most obvious problem with Burrows' version, however, is his suggestion that his Wambaugh party was traveling only a day behind Cornwall. That is impossible. On April 29, the estimated date of Cornwall's encounter with the Pawnees, the Wambaugh company was only two days out of St. Joseph—more than three hundred miles and at least three weeks away. Could we be wrong in supposing that Cornwall was so far ahead? Did he and his party leave Bellevue so much later that they met Wambaugh's company somewhere along the Platte, as Burrows seemed to suggest? This is not possible if Shaw passed Greenwood or Cornwall near Chimney Rock on about May 6 and if one accepts Cornwall's and Kellogg's claims that they encountered Meek along the Platte. Wambaugh's party would not arrive at the forks of the Platte, near where Cornwall met Meek and the Pawnees, until May 22. Cornwall couldn't have encountered Meek on the Platte as late as May 22 because Meek arrived in St. Joseph on May 10.

Sifting through each particle of evidence, forgiving the narrators for faulty recollections, and being mindful of each possible motive to tinker with the truth, it is possible that Burrows had heard the Greenwood and Cornwall stories while sitting around a campfire many weeks later. Perhaps he thought it would impress his friends and grandchildren if his story placed him in greater proximity to the danger.

Is it possible that Cornwall and Corcoran were traveling separately at the time, and that they were describing two separate, discrete encounters with Pawnees? The answer is no because both Cornwall and Corcoran mentioned being with Fallon when he communicated with both the Pawnee and Sioux. Despite their major disparities, they must have been describing the same incident.

Caleb Greenwood, whom both Shaw and Burrows mention, was affectionately known as "Old Greenwood," perhaps the most colorful figure on the trail in 1848. He was about eighty-five years old at the time, and, like Joe Meek, was regarded as the consummate confabulator, a disciple of picturesque language. Journalist Edwin Bryant encountered him in California in 1846, describing him as about "six feet in height, raw-boned and spare in flesh, but muscular, and notwithstanding his old age, walks with all the erectness and elasticity of youth." Bryant went on to describe this impossibly ancient mountain man as having a flowing white beard and being dressed in tanned buckskins "nearly equal to the age of its wearer."[16] A female emigrant in 1845 recounted that Greenwood and his sons dressed the same as Indians, and that she was as much afraid of them as she was of the Indians.[17]

Old Greenwood's early history is so obscure it is almost mythological. He may have been born in Virginia in about 1763; no one is quite sure. The first place his name crops up is in an account book for a trapping brigade along the Middle Missouri River in 1811. When most of the beaver trapping activity shifted to the Rockies in the 1820s, Greenwood, like James Clyman, was hired to trap in one of William Ashley's brigades. While Clyman was scrambling up Rocky Mountain canyons, wandering from stream to stream, and looking into every nook and cranny for beaver during 1824 through 1827, Greenwood was doing the same thing, only farther north. In about 1826, Caleb married Batchicka, a Crow woman, and is believed to have lived among the Crows in the Yellowstone River country in Montana as a free trapper until about 1834.

In the summer of 1834, Greenwood is mentioned in the journal of Reverend Moses Merrill, the Baptist missionary at Bellevue. Merrill wrote that the old trapper came to his mission, complaining that the Crows were having troubles with the Sioux, and that the Sioux had taken his horses. He needed a job and had come to offer his services as an Indian interpreter.[18]

It appears that Greenwood and his family then settled somewhere near Bellevue, maybe even in northwestern Missouri, between 1834 and 1844. He may have tried his hand at farming. But in 1844, shortly after Batchicka died, the Stephens-Townsend-Murphy party hired him to pilot them from Bellevue to as far through the Rockies as he could.[19] Old Greenwood and Batchicka had had seven children and it appears that he took his four oldest sons with him in 1844: John (about 18), Britton (about 17), Governor Boggs (named after Missouri governor Lilburn Boggs, about 9), and William Sublette (about 6). He left his three youngest children—James Case (about 3), Angeline (about 2), and Sarah (about 1)—to be cared for by either friends or relatives. Greenwood and his sons continued to travel with the Stephens-Townsend-Murphy party when they entered California in the fall of 1844. The next spring, the Greenwoods left California and headed east to meet westbound emigrants at Fort Hall. Caleb offered his services as a guide to California and succeeded in recruiting fifty wagons of emigrants, charging $2.50 per wagon.[20] After getting this wagon party safely over the Sierras in the fall of 1845, he and his sons spent the winter in California, then joined Lansford Hasting's eastbound party the next spring. Somewhere near Fort Laramie, the Greenwoods picked up another party of emigrants and led them back to California, crossing over Donner Pass about five weeks ahead of the early storms that trapped the Donner party. Old Greenwood and his sons led the second relief party sent to rescue the stranded Donner emigrants.[21] Old Greenwood and his sons left California in the spring of 1847 to fetch the rest of his children. For the trip back east, Old Greenwood served as one of Commodore Stockton's guides when the Stockton party left California on July 19 and arrived at St. Joseph on October 27, 1847.[22]

After gathering up his youngest children in the spring of 1848, Greenwood and his family started for California. It seems most likely that Caleb departed from Bellevue since all of his known connections were there. His fifth son, James Case Greenwood, was born about 1841, almost certainly named for James Case, a farmer employed by the Bellevue Indian Agency in 1836. Case lived among the Otoes about ten miles south of Bellevue, then spent a few years at the agency's Pawnee post along the Loup River until he was fired in 1846 because they discovered he was a Mormon.[23] In 1844, Elisha Stephens, a Bellevue Indian Agency blacksmith, had hired Greenwood to pilot his Stephens-Townsend-Murphy party out of Bellevue.[24]

If Greenwood and his family left from Bellevue, one wonders whether they were part of Cornwall's party from the outset, but it does not seem likely. Neither the Cornwall nor the Kellogg biography mentions Greenwood, and besides, Cornwall already had Fallon as his guide. Although Fallon and Greenwood would have been acquainted, perhaps even friends, Fallon might not have appreciated having a rival guide traveling with him. And because Old Greenwood had been making his living as a trail guide during the previous four years, it seems that he would have lined up his own party of emigrants to guide. Indeed, the newspaper account of John Shaw's arrival at St. Joseph reported that Greenwood was with "a company of

California-bound emigrants numbering about sixty," which could represent a party of ten to fifteen wagons.

If judged by the total number of miles traveled over the trail between Missouri and California, Old Greenwood and his sons could have fairly claimed that they were the most knowledgeable and experienced guides on the trail that year. While Greenwood was certainly capable of traveling through Indian country alone—he had done it many times—he may have wanted to travel under the protection of a wagon train because he had his young children with him, and was probably unwilling to expose them to risks he might have been willing to take by himself.

Assuming that John Shaw was correct that it was Greenwood whom the Pawnees had robbed of his cow and clothing, Greenwood and his party had, like Cornwall, also left early. This would not be surprising as Greenwood and his sons had slogged through snow in the Sierras many times, twice heading east and thrice going west. Like Fallon, they had witnessed the appalling Donner spectacle, and had probably had enough of deep Sierra snows. Caleb had every incentive to cross the mountains into California early this year.

Because Burrows wrote that Cornwall and Greenwood were together at the time of the Pawnee incident, one might wonder whether Greenwood's and Cornwall's parties had merged sometime before they ran into the Pawnees. But Corcoran only mentioned Young's blankets' being stolen. If Greenwood, whose cow and clothing were stolen, had been traveling with Cornwall and Corcoran, surely Corcoran would have mentioned that theft, one of much greater magnitude.

So it would seem that the Greenwood and Cornwall parties were traveling separately, perhaps only a day apart, and that Greenwood's party was in the lead. His group was likely the first one accosted by the Pawnees. If so, Greenwood probably hastened on, and when he met the Sioux, informed them of the Pawnees, much as Burrows described. Corcoran said the Pawnees complained about having fought the Sioux earlier that morning and that sixty of them had been killed. It was probably the survivors of that Sioux attack who molested the Cornwall party.

As for the Cornwall biography, its version is just too epic and dramatic when compared to the others. Perhaps P. B.'s son, the biography's author, felt the finer points of accuracy should take a backseat to breathtaking drama.

In view of Greenwood's long history of living among and around Indians for about forty years, one might be surprised that he let the Pawnees take his cow and clothing. His advanced age suggests that he had learned how to survive among Indians, and one of the more essential qualities of a successful mountain man was the ability to avoid an unnecessary fight. Perhaps he understood that the Pawnees, if dealt with correctly, were more of a pest than a danger. And with his children present, perhaps his primary concern was to have this episode end safely. For all of 1848, there is no other event described by a number of narrators in such a perplexing and contradictory manner. Until an authoritative, first-person, contemporary account comes to light that resolves all these disparities, it will have to remain a fascinating mystery.

Regardless of what really happened with the Pawnees, there is one thing that is indisputable: the tribe was in a very sad and pitiable state in 1848. Looking back on the tribe's long history, one might think they had been the architects of their own misfortune. The Pawnees had once been a large and menacing tribe, the scourge of the plains, numbering as many as 20,000 in the 1700s.[25] The historical record is filled with accounts of Pawnees sending raiding parties far and wide, stealing horses and taking scalps from virtually every tribe that bordered their territory: Arapaho, Comanche, Cheyenne, Apache, Kiowa, Kansa, Shawnee, Osage, Arikara, Ponca, Otoe, and Omaha. These raids were followed by ceaseless reprisals and counter-reprisals. Regarded as arrogant troublemakers, the Pawnees had earned the enmity of all their Indian neighbors. They had no friends or allies, nor did they seem to feel they needed any.

After they had been the dominant tribe for years, things began to change in 1832 when the Pawnees were ravaged by a catastrophic smallpox epidemic that killed thousands. Even though the epidemic decimated their ranks, they failed to perceive their vulnerability and managed to enflame the powerful Sioux.

Not originally a plains tribe, the Sioux were newcomers to the area. Prior to 1700, they barely eked out an existence in the woods of northern Minnesota, hunting deer on foot with bows and arrows. Provided with firearms by French traders, their Cree, Assiniboine, and Chippewa enemies drove the Sioux south and west out of their ancestral home.[26] In due time, the Sioux discovered that the Arikara tribe to their west possessed firearms, rode horses, and hunted buffalo on the western prairies. Seeing it as a better way of life, the Sioux continued to gradually push west over a period of a hundred years, eventually defeating the Arikara and muscling their way past them into what is now eastern South Dakota. The Sioux stole horses, figured out how to ride them, and began hunting buffalo with these new tools. With better diets and living conditions, their birthrates climbed and infant deaths plummeted. In a generation, Sioux numbers had grown markedly. By the early 1800s, even though the Sioux were still not regarded as a particularly large tribe, they were formidable fighters who had become a force with which to be reckoned. As early as 1804, Lewis and Clark were aware of the Sioux's reputation as the greatest and fiercest of the tribes that they would meet. In a slow and bloody process, the Oglala branch of the larger Sioux tribe pushed the Crow and Kiowa out of the Black Hills of western South Dakota and made it their new home.[27]

William Sublette and Robert Campbell, like James Clyman, had once been fur trappers working for William Ashley's Rocky Mountain Fur Company. Forming their own partnership, Sublette and Campbell became suppliers and carriers for the fur trade, and purchased a large quantity of trade goods in St. Louis in the spring of 1834. They set out with a pack train for the summer rendezvous in the Rocky

Mountains. Upon reaching the Laramie Fork, Sublette and Campbell left thirteen men there to build a crude stockade near where the Laramie Fork emptied into the North Platte River, and named it Fort William. Campbell sent two men to visit the Oglala Sioux in the Black Hills to invite them to send some of their people south to trade at their new outpost. Led by their chief, Bull Bear, about one hundred lodges of Sioux came south and set up camp near the fort, the first entrance of Sioux into the region. The next year, most of the remaining Oglala lodges moved south to camp near the stockade as well. By 1835, about two hundred Oglala Sioux lodges, representing one to two thousand Sioux, were encamped on the plain around Fort William.[28]

Previous to 1834, the American Fur Company had enjoyed a virtual monopoly of trade with the Sioux. Seeing the new Fort William as a threat to their long-term relationship with the tribe, the company purchased the stockade from Sublette and Campbell in 1835 and renamed it Fort John. But because of its location along the Laramie River, most people began calling it Fort Laramie.[29]

For generations, the Pawnees had lived along the Platte, Loup, and Republican Rivers. They planted corn, squash, and beans in their villages each spring before traveling to their favorite buffalo hunting grounds south of the forks of the Platte River. In the late summer, they would return to their villages to harvest their crops, then return to the forks region for their fall and winter hunts.[30]

When the Oglala Sioux moved into the area of the Laramie Fork, they began sending their own hunting parties to the forks of the Platte in 1835. Finding it rich in buffalo, they decided to claim it as exclusively theirs. The Pawnees sent a war party to attack the Sioux in 1837, and the Sioux retaliated by sending war parties against Pawnee hunting parties whenever they found them, igniting a bloody, full-blown war between the two tribes. Although the Sioux had been raiding Pawnee villages periodically since the 1820s, mostly to steal horses, 1837 marked the beginning of a large number of particularly malignant attacks against Pawnee villages and hunting parties.[31] By 1840, according to a government estimate, Pawnee numbers had declined to about six thousand.[32]

Despite government assurances of protection from the Sioux, five hundred Sioux warriors descended on Pawnee villages in the summer of 1841 while most of the Pawnees were away hunting and massacred scores of Pawnees, mostly women, children, and old people. Over the next several years, the Sioux continued to attack Pawnee villages.[33] It was as if the Sioux were determined to eradicate the tribe. It was no longer a fair fight.

By 1848, the thirteenth year of the war, the bedeviled Pawnees were virtually homeless, a broken and mangled tribe with no friends. The 1848 report of Bellevue Indian agent, John Miller, put the fast-dwindling tribe at only 2,500.[34] Small bands of uprooted and disheartened Pawnees were now wandering the plains, killing buffalo wherever they could and badgering emigrant wagon trains for food and blankets. Although emigrants had been molested by Pawnees for years, 1848 would be a particularly sad year as the Pawnees hounded wagon trains, begging for food and clothing, and pilfering anything that was not closely watched or guarded. It was difficult not to be moved by their plight, but the Pawnees' persistent begging and sticky fingers quickly destroyed any goodwill the emigrants might have felt. And the Pawnees could also be dangerous. Pawnee hunters had caught Oregon-bound emigrant Edward Trimble alone in 1846 when he had foolishly gone off alone to look for lost stock near the forks of the Platte, and they killed him. The story of his fate was widely published in Missouri newspapers and was likely well known among this year's travelers.[35] Although Pawnee warriors were still fierce and capable of mounting an attack on a wagon party, their old chiefs usually held them back. They had been warned against provoking the anger of the whites, but as long as there were hot-blooded young warriors looking for an opportunity to distinguish themselves, emigrants had every reason to remain vigilant as they passed through Pawnee territory.

A number of whites had tried to help the Pawnees. Baptist missionaries tried to "civilize" them in the 1830s and early 1840s, encouraging them to give up buffalo hunting and engage in full-time, European-style farming at permanent villages; and they set up demonstration farms to show them how. Ever since about 1834, the Bellevue Indian Agency had been delivering annual annuities to the Pawnees. In 1840, the agency sent a group of white farmers, blacksmiths, and teachers to the Pawnees, and tried to persuade them to remain in permanent villages on the Loup, far away from the Oregon Trail. But to the Pawnees, becoming full-time farmers and giving up their traditional ways, notwithstanding the disastrous consequences of keeping them up, was simply unthinkable.

Sadly, things only got worse for the Pawnees. With the beginning of the gold rush in 1849, the Pawnees would come in contact with cholera carried by the gold rushers. Carried back to their villages, the disease killed a quarter of their already severely diminished population.[36]

After making it through Pawnee territory in April 1848, the Cornwall party, and probably the Greenwood party as well, encountered Mr. Shaw and his freight wagons near Chimney Rock on or about May 6. From there, it was only seventy miles to Fort Laramie. It appears that Greenwood and Cornwall reached the fort around May 10, about three weeks ahead of the Allsopp company. Cornwall's small group, as well as Greenwood's, probably had had enough close calls with Indians and it appears they decided to sit tight at the fort and wait for a larger wagon train they could join.

CHAPTER 7

Independence,
a Star in Decline
APRIL 29–MAY 20

APRIL 29–MAY 11, 1848
Edward Smith, at Lone Tree, 28 miles southwest of Independence, Missouri

It is easy to imagine Edward Smith sitting on a wagon tongue at the end of the day on April 29. Tired and covered in dust, he nestled a brand new journal in his lap. Bound in a hard, marble-patterned cover, it was thirteen inches high and eight inches wide. He opened it, turned to the first page, and took up his pen. Dipping it into his ink bottle, he paused a moment to gather his thoughts. He then began to write at the top in large, bold letters: "A Journal of Scenes and incidents on a Journey from Missouri to California in 1848."[1]

Having given it a title, Smith continued: "April 29 left the frontiers and arrived at the Elm grove at 6 oclock PM it is a lone tree with the top cut off." Smith raised his head and cocked his ear, listening for a moment, then added, "greatly annoyed by wolves around our camp."

The "frontiers" Smith mentioned probably refers to a camp at the Blue River crossing, about twelve miles south of Independence. On the morning of April 29, his small party resumed their trip and, after traveling sixteen miles across the open prairie, they reached the "lone tree" he mentioned, located where the Santa Fe–Oregon Trail crossed Cedar Creek, about twenty-eight miles from Independence. Once a proud and beautiful tree in a wide and lonely grassland, the "Lone Elm" or "Lone Tree" was a single tree that had been hacked away by travelers over the years until it had been reduced to a plucked prairie hen—little more than a limbless, barkless trunk. Emigrants would continue to hew away at it until 1852, when a diarist sadly noted that there was "no Lone Tree to be found."[2]

Edward Smith did not record in his journal who he was or where he came from. Strangely, he would not even mention his family in his journal until near the end of

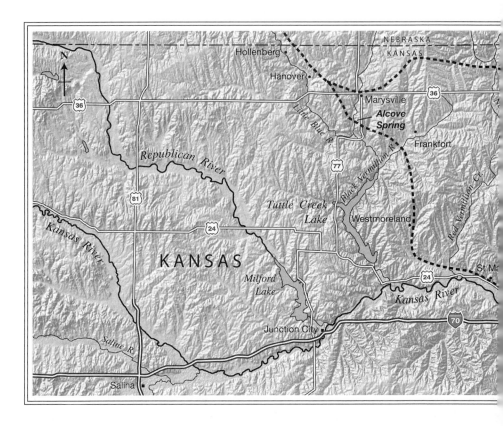

his trip. An 1850 census shows that he would have been forty-one years old in 1848, and was accompanied by his wife, Jane, and four children: Mary A. (13), Mary S. (11), Alicia (7), and John (2). Bound for California, Smith took two wagons, and was traveling with one other family with one wagon. Obviously, neither he nor his traveling companions were familiar with the trail. That such a tiny party would dare venture into Indian Territory alone was a sign either of uncommon courage or of uncommon foolishness.

When Smith arrived in Independence, he would have found a handsome, flourishing town, about two and a half miles south of the Wayne City landing on the Missouri River. He did not describe the settlement or its stately brick courthouse set on a large, grassy square protected by a rail fence. Around the courthouse were crowded establishments that served the trader, trapper, and emigrant. There were wagon shops and blacksmith shops. There were stables selling oxen, horses, and mules. There were butcher shops, dry goods stores, inns, and taverns.

In contrast to St. Joseph, the settlement of Independence had been established for some time. In the 1810s, American trappers knew that the streams of the southwestern Rockies teemed with beaver. Operating in the mountains around Taos, New Mexico, the trappers were treated as intruders by the Spaniards and were arrested

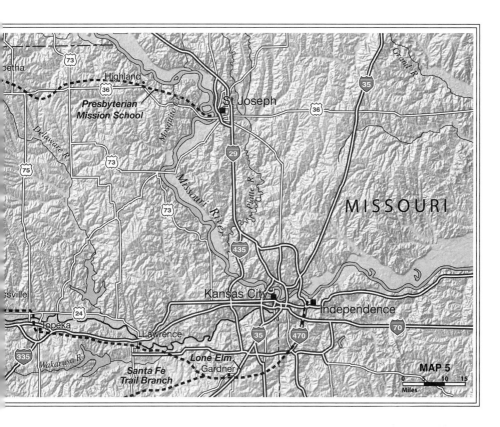

if caught. Notwithstanding, word spread that the commercial possibilities of trade with Santa Fe and Taos were limitless. Bold, enterprising people like Hugh Glenn, Jacob Fowler, Thomas James, and William Becknell set out in 1821 from Franklin, Missouri, on a nine-hundred-mile trip to Santa Fe with pack trains loaded with manufactured goods. Upon arriving, they found that the Mexican revolution had occurred and the Mexicans, unlike the Spaniards, welcomed them. When Becknell returned to Franklin, he brought back 10,000 Mexican silver dollars and the rush to Santa Fe was on.[3]

By 1825, traders were routinely traveling to and from Santa Fe along the new trail. The initial pack trains later gave way to long caravans of large, wide-tired freight wagons. Needing a closer place on the Missouri River to support this thriving trade, the settlement of Independence was born in 1827. The next year the new boomtown had grown to over five hundred people. This eastern terminus of the Santa Fe Trail grew from 2,800 residents in 1830 to 4,500 by 1836.[4]

In 1827, an epic winter journey would open the way for a new role for Independence. In January of that year, William Sublette and Black Harris departed the Great Salt Lake Valley, and began a 1,500-mile overland return to St. Louis. Snowshoe-clad through the early part of their trek, they traveled along the south bank of the Platte

River. Near Grand Island they left the Platte and crossed to the headwaters of the Little Blue River. From there, they followed the river southeast to the Big Blue River, crossed it, then continued south until they struck the Kansas River. After fording the Kansas, they encountered the Santa Fe Trail and followed it east into Missouri. The new route became known as Sublette's Trace, and opened a new trail from Missouri to the Platte River and beyond.[5]

A few weeks after Sublette and Harris arrived in Independence, Sublette headed west again, this time guiding a party of sixty men with pack mules outfitted by the American Fur Company. He retraced his steps to the Platte, and followed it west, eventually reaching Bear Lake in the Rockies, where the fur trappers' rendezvous was held that year. Upon the conclusion of the monthlong drunk, trapper James Clyman was assigned the task of guiding a group of traders and trappers and seven thousand pounds of beaver furs back to Missouri. No doubt following Sublette's careful instructions, Clyman led them east over Sublette's Trace, and the party arrived in Lexington, Missouri, about October 1, 1827. As their journey was nearing an end, the first log structures were being built in Independence.[6] From that time, Sublette's Trace became an established route to and from the trappers' annual rendezvous in the Rocky Mountains during the 1830s.

By 1840, however, the age of the fur trapper was ending. The year 1840 held the last great rendezvous. On May 12, 1841, a new era dawned, that of the emigrant wagon train. A group of sixty people with thirteen wagons and carts left Sapling Grove, twenty miles southwest of Independence. It was the first expedition to attempt to reach California with wagons. Under the direction of Thomas Fitzpatrick, the party included John Bartleson, John Bidwell, Joseph Chiles, Charles M. Weber, and a small group of Jesuit priests led by Father Pierre-Jean De Smet. When the Bartleson wagon party reached Soda Springs in present-day Idaho, the company divided. Fitzpatrick took the missionaries and about a third of the emigrants on to Oregon, while the rest followed Captain Bartleson to California.[7]

In the spring of 1842, Dr. Elijah White led a larger wagon party to Oregon with a group that included such men as Lansford Hastings and William O. Fallon. Sublette's Trace would soon become known as the Oregon Trail. The next year, 1843, was called the year of "the Great Emigration" because two large parties totaling 150 wagons and 1,100 people left Independence for Oregon. Also driving three thousand head of loose cattle with them, their expedition would thereafter be called the "cow column."[8] In 1844, Black Harris led a large party of 350 emigrants out of Independence to Oregon, a party that included James Clyman and M. N. Wambaugh.[9] By now, Independence had become the dominant outfitter for wagon parties heading for the Far West, and remained so in 1845 and 1846.

But 1847 would see a change. Independence, the shining star of jumping-off points and the Queen City of emigrants, would lose its crown to St. Joseph. The *St. Joseph Gazette* bragged in its June 25, 1847, issue that "[t]he wagons that crossed at this point number 867, and at Independence 433, making in all 1,300 wagons now on the prairie." Independence was a star in decline. Again in 1848, fewer emigrants would leave from it than from St. Joseph. While Independence would see a resurgence of emigrant activity in the next few years because of the gold rush, it would never regain its preeminence.

Edward Smith's party was not the first one to leave Independence in 1848. That honor belonged to the J. P. C. Allsopp party, which had left on April 10. This group of young Southern bachelors was traveling with a party of emigrants and their twenty-five wagons.[10] By April 29, the Allsopp company should have been almost two hundred miles ahead of Edward Smith. In fact, the Allsopp train may have already crossed the Big Blue River to the northwest.

After leaving the doomed Lone Tree to its fate on the morning of April 30, Smith added to his journal: "[April] 30 Started half Past seven arrived at the Misharawi [?]   at 5 oclock PM saw several Indians on the Praries   met some men from fort Man [Fort Mann] who informed us we were on the Santa Fee Road."

How embarrassing. Eight miles west of the Lone Tree (two miles west of present-day Gardner, Kansas, near Highway 56) the trail split. The Santa Fe Road veered to the southwest, while the Oregon Trail continued straight.[11] How could Smith's party have made such a blunder? For over twenty years, heavy freight wagons bound for Santa Fe had been making such deep, clear tracks that the place where the less-traveled Oregon road departed the main road apparently went unnoticed by Smith.

Smith described his humiliating return to the fork so that he could take the one that would lead them to California:

> May the 1st turned back and traveled about 8 miles and struck the great oregon Road. Traveled on the Road about ten miles encamped on a Small stream [likely Captain Creek]   Rain at night   the Praries are the most beautiful Eyes ever beheld.

After Smith's tiny party backtracked on the morning of May 1, another party was leaving Indian Creek, a campsite about thirty miles southwest of Independence. This group of about twenty-three Oregon-bound wagons was led by Reverend Clinton Kelly, and was still about eight miles from reaching the trail's fork when Smith returned to it. Reverend Kelly was a forty-year-old Methodist minister from Kentucky, and was taking his wife and perhaps as many as twelve children and three wagons. No diary is known to exist from anyone in the Kelly company, although Kelly's youngest son wrote an article many years later about his family's journey. The article explained that there were thirty men in the party, including men by the name of Richardson, Cox, Catlin, Wells, Huntley, Brown, and Welch.[12] Edward Smith would soon be referring to Kelly's company as the "oregon company" behind him.

A Journal of Scenes and incidents on a journey
from Missouri to California in 1848

april 29 left the frontiers and arrived at the Elm grove
at 6 oʼclock P M it is a lone tree with the top
Cut off and a few gooseberry Bushes good water

30 Started half Past Seven arrived at the Mishaway
at 3 oclock P M saw several Indians on the Baries
Met some men from fort Man who informed us we were on the

May 1st Santa fe Road May the 1st turned back and traveled about
8 miles and Struck the great oregon Road traveled on the
Road about ten miles encamped on a small Stream Rain
at night the Baries are the most Beautiful Eyes ever

2 beheld May 2 very foggy in the morning clear about nine
crossed the Wahkarushi and encamped at 12 oClock
at night 3 Pottowattemies encamped near us

3 W Remained in Camp about 29 Caw Indians came
in Camp gave them something to eat and they
went off after a short stay of about one hour
at nine we were visited by a severe Rain Storm accompanied by
high winds and severe thunder and lightning

thurs 4 started early and travelled 21 miles without wood or
water and encamped at the Mary Springs in the Barie

frid 5 Remained in Camp and in the evening we were joined
by 23 waggons all bound for oregon except one

Sat 6 moved about 15 miles encamped on a stream calld
By the Indians Chungaluney encamped at about 4 oclock

Sun 7 P m about four miles took us to the River 3 waggons
ferried over the oregon, Company forded the River
this day Mr Smith and family and two Brothers
left the oregon Company and joined ours we now
number 3 families and 4 waggons 8 men besides
women & Children after Crossing the River the
Co encamped on the Barie at a small creek we
travelled 3 miles and encamped near the lodge

Mon 8 of Some Pottowattemies Indians & Remained
in Camp untill 2 oclock P m to nold 12 miles and encamped
on cross creek the most delightfull River Bottom I ever beheld

tues 9 we travelled along the River Bottom over the same delightful
Country in the afternoon came on a cold rain Storm and
after traveling 13 miles we encamped near some

First page of "Edward Smith Diary, A Journal of Scenes and incidents on a Journey from Missouri to California in 1848." Mss. 18, Courtesy of Fresno City and County Historical Society, Fresno, California.

On May 2, the day after getting themselves onto the proper road, Smith's tiny party crossed the Wakarusa River. He recorded that Pottawattamie Indians were camping near them that night. The Pottawattamies were new to the area, having arrived there just five months earlier. Originally from Illinois and Indiana, the tribe had been forced by the federal government, under the terms of the Treaty of Chicago of 1833, to leave their ancestral homes and emigrate to southwestern Iowa. Thirteen years later, in June 1846, because of growing pressure from white settlers, the Office of Indian Affairs entered into a new agreement with the chiefs of the tribe. In exchange for giving up six million acres in Iowa and part of Missouri, the tribe of about two thousand were to receive $850,000 in annuities, payable over thirty years, and were to be given almost 500,000 acres along the Kansas River in eastern Kansas. Edward Smith had likely noticed a group of Catholic Pottawattamies who had been led to this place along the Wakarusa in November 1847 by the Jesuit missionary Father Christian Hoecken, the same priest who had encouraged Martin Murphy to leave Irish Grove and take his family to California in 1844, and who had nursed Thomas Corcoran and his family when they suffered their bouts of lung fever.[13]

There were two places where Oregon-bound emigrants usually crossed the Wakarusa River. One was five miles southeast of present-day Lawrence, Kansas, and the other was about three miles south of Lawrence.[14] It is impossible to know which one Smith's party had used. He did not complain about the crossing's difficulty, but both crossings were renowned not for the width or depth of the water, but rather for the deep, almost perpendicular, banks. Considering it too much work to dig ramps down the banks, emigrants instead lowered their heavily laden wagons down the twenty-foot banks with ropes and then double-teamed their oxen to pull wagons up the other side.

Smith wrote on May 3 that they remained in camp. A group of Kansa Indians appeared and begged for food. This tribe, estimated at about 1,700 in 1845 by the American Indian Mission Association (Baptist), had resided along the Kansas River for centuries.[15] That night, Smith's party was "visited by a severe Rain Storm accompanied by high winds and severe thunder and lightning." It was likely the same storm system William Wright Anderson had complained about on May 3.

On May 4, Smith's party traveled twenty-one miles without wood or water and encamped at "Marry Springs in the Prarie." For reasons not specified, the Smiths did not move on the fifth, but "laid by" instead. This allowed the Kelly company to overtake them that evening. Smith noted it in his journal: "[W]e were joined by 23 waggons all bound for Oregon except one."

Smith's party advanced about fifteen miles on the sixth and encamped on Shunganunga Creek. Though small and narrow, the Shunganunga was much like the Wakarusa—it flowed through a deep trench that was difficult for wagons to cross. It is currently channeled through the city of Topeka, Kansas.[16]

Smith recorded the following day:

sun 7— about four miles took us to the River   3 waggons ferried over   the
oregon [Kelly] company forded the River this day. Mr. Smith and family and two
Brothers left the oregon company and joined ours   we now number 3 families
and 4 waggons 9 men besides women & children   after crossing the River the
co. encamped on the Prarie at a small creek   we traveled 3 miles and encamped
near lodge of some Pottawattomie Indians.

Smith was referring to crossing the Kansas River, a major river that was ordinarily
two hundred yards wide. In 1842, Captain John C. Fremont described it as having an
"angry current, yellow and turbid."[17] The approach to the river was through a dense
forest about three-quarters of a mile wide, and composed mostly of oak, linden, and
hickory. In earlier years, the Kansas had been a difficult river to ford except during
times of exceptionally low water. Emigrants were grateful when the Frenchman
Papin and his two half-Indian sons established a ferry there in 1844. In 1846, they
were reported to be charging one dollar per wagon. Big enough to carry one fully
loaded wagon at a time, the ferry consisted of a platform of long poles lying across
two large dugout canoes. Though the ferry was a big help, the emigrants had to lower
their wagons down the steep banks to the ferry landing by means of ropes, and then
double-up teams of oxen to pull them up the opposite bank and across the adjacent
sandy marsh. The livestock had to swim. The Papin ferry is believed to have been
located where the Topeka Avenue Bridge in Topeka now crosses the river.[18] After
crossing, Smith's party moved along the northern side of the Kansas River, across
what Fremont had described in 1842 as "handsome open prairie."[19]

The Smith party had been fortunate as far as weather was concerned. James
Clyman's party in 1844 had not been so lucky. It had rained during fifteen of the
first thirty-one days after leaving Independence, forcing them to face raging creeks
and rivers, record-breaking floods, and roads that were hopeless quagmires. Where
it took the Smith party eight days to travel from Independence to the Kansas River
crossing, it had taken Clyman's party thirty-one. In his 1844 journal, Clyman had
lamented that "the prairie has become so soft that it will [not] bear the weight of a
man in many places. . . . it is almost enough to discourage the stoutest and bravest
amongst us." His party made it across the Kansas River just in time, as the incessant
rains rendered it impossible to cross thereafter. It was now "8 or 10 miles wide," he
recorded.[20]

Smith reported remaining in camp until two in the afternoon on May 8. Then
they traveled twelve miles and "encamped on cross creek the most delightful River
Bottom I ever beheld." This would have been near today's Rossville, on Highway 24.
On the ninth, they traveled thirteen miles through a cold rainstorm along the Kansas River bottom. After a long day of slogging through ankle-deep mud, with heads
bowed in the face of the daylong downpour, they finally stopped and "encamped near
some Pittowatttemy Indians on a small stream [likely Lost Creek]." This was about
one mile north of today's Belvue, on Highway 24.

During the day on May 9, Smith passed a spot where Father Hoecken would later move his Catholic Pottawattamies from the Wakarusa River. He would establish a mission there that would later be called St. Mary's.[21]

On May 10, Smith reported that they

remained in camp waiting for the [Kelly] company until 11 oclock am   traveled 5 miles to the Little Vermillion [Red Vermillion River] and encamped late in the evening   the oregon co. [Kelly] came in   Much dissatisfaction Prevails among them   already dissolution is threatened.

Dissatisfaction, as Smith called it, could easily arise within a wagon company. In the communities the emigrants had left, they had been able to pick their friends. Here on the trail they were often thrown together with people they had not previously known and whom they rapidly grew to dislike. With the travelers suffering from stress and fatigue, unintended insults or incidents of carelessness and thoughtlessness could easily create discord. Even the most trivial provocations could cause weary emigrants to erupt in anger. If a person had an inclination toward pettiness, selfishness, recklessness, or some other annoying trait, the hardships of the trail would surely magnify it.

In this case, it may have been that the Kelly company was moving too slowly for some. Like a convoy of ships, the fleetest could only move at the pace of the slowest. In any given company, there were always those who were maddeningly slow to get up in the morning, were slow to catch up, or were disorganized, inefficient, or inept. Fear of being caught in the mountain snows kept a keen sense of urgency foremost in many minds. Any kind of dawdling, whether caused by human foolishness, misbehavior, or incompetence, could prove fatal. It made many of the emigrants edgy and unforgiving.

Smith did not record his experience crossing the Red Vermillion River, but Louis Vieux had built a toll bridge there sometime in 1847 or 1848. Although he charged one dollar per wagon, most were pleased to pay it. It made the crossing of this very deep-gorged stream much easier and less treacherous.[22]

It was through here in 1846 that journalist Edwin Bryant praised the beguiling beauty and richness of the land. He admired the thick grass of the upland prairies and the black soils of the bottomlands. He wrote that "It is impossible to travel through this country without a sensation of regret that an agricultural resource of such immense capacity . . . is so utterly neglected and waste[d]." After passing through a large village of about four or five hundred Kansa Indians, Bryant also wrote that "they all appeared to be the most unblushing and practised beggars. There was scarcely an object which they saw, from a cow and calf to the smallest trinket or button upon our clothing, that they did not request us to present to them." He was puzzled why these starving people "give no attention to agriculture," and "have not the smallest appreciation of the great natural wealth of the country over which they roam." He could not understand why they were so determined to continue their ancestral ways of hunting game, which was now getting scarce, when they could rid themselves of their privation by simply taking up the raising of cattle and the growing of crops.[23]

Smith's journal continued on May 11, in which he described a stream into which flowed the water from a number of "fine springs of cold water." These were probably Scott Springs, about twelve miles beyond the crossing of the Red Vermillion, and located near present-day Highway 99 and about a mile south of Westmoreland.

Along this beautiful stretch of trail, diarists often acclaimed the profusion of prairie wildflowers, a vibrant, sparkling array of millions of larkspur, pink verbena, wild indigo, honeysuckle, and wild rose. Strolling beside their wagons, women and children often wandered a ways into the prairie to enjoy the peaceful tranquility of the grass bending in the warm, gentle breezes, to sniff at the wondrous wildflowers, to festoon their hair with garlands of blooms, and to pick bouquets to carry with them.

Near midday, the wagon companies would "noon," a standard routine that diarists mentioned from time to time. This was a time for oxen to rest and emigrants to eat. The women would pull out food they had prepared that morning or earlier. After eating, people would collapse in the grass in the warm sun (although it was wise to first look carefully for snakes), resisting the temptation to drift off amidst a chorus of birds and the humming of countless insects.

The Smith party traveled sixteen miles on May 11. When they encamped, Smith noted that the Kelly company was camping about five miles behind them. Early in the morning of the twelfth, Smith and his companions resumed their travels and soon came to the Big Vermillion River. They found a broad, deep river bottom about a mile in width, about a third of which was overgrown with timber. They forded the river about noon, then stopped on the north side to camp for the night at a place about six miles southwest of today's Frankfort, Kansas.

May 10–12, 1848
Richard M. May, Chiles company, Independence, Missouri

Not quite two weeks after the Smith party had departed, another wagon train left Independence. This caravan of twenty-eight wagons destined for California was headed by thirty-eight-year-old, six-foot-four-inch Joseph Ballinger Chiles, who was among a handful of men well-qualified to lead a wagon party to California. Intimidatingly tall with red hair and steely gray eyes, Chiles possessed a self-assurance that induced unquestioned submission to his authority.

Chiles was born in Kentucky in 1810; he married in 1830, and a year later moved himself and his wife to Jackson County, Missouri, where he began farming not far from Independence. In 1836, his wife, Polly Ann, died, leaving him with four young children.[24] Brooding and lonely, Chiles felt he needed a change of scenery. When a number of his friends began talking of emigrating to California in 1841, he decided to go. Leaving his farm and children with relatives, he joined the Bartleson-Bidwell party, leaving Sapling Grove in the spring of 1841.[25] After blazing new routes and experiencing daunting hardships, including abandoning their wagons, the starving and exhausted group made it across the Sierras and into the great valley of California.

Chiles stayed in California long enough to get acquainted with such people as General Vallejo and John Sutter, then returned to Independence in 1842. In 1843, he returned to California, this time leading his own wagon party. He spent the next three years in California, becoming enamored with a quaint little valley northeast of Napa. Set upon acquiring it, he became a

Portrait of Joseph Ballinger Chiles (1810–85). Reproduced from Helen S. Giffen, *Trail-blazing Pioneer* (San Francisco: J. Howell, 1969). Source of original photograph unknown.

Mexican citizen, applied for a Mexican land grant, and began making improvements. By 1847, he was ready to return to Missouri to fetch his children. He traveled to Sutter's Fort in the summer of 1847 and joined Commodore Robert F. Stockton's party. Along with the Greenwoods, he was one of the men hired to help guide Stockton's party of forty-six men back to Missouri, and they arrived in late October.

In May 1848, Chiles had his children with him, seven years older than when he first left them: James (17), Elizabeth (15), and Fannie and Mary (both over 8). Chiles' brother, Christopher ("Kit"), came along as well. They were traveling with at least one wagon and two carriages.

Mike McClellan and his family were part of Chiles' company. Mike was a longtime resident of the Independence area, a neighbor of Chiles, and a nephew of the celebrated trapper, mountaineer, and guide Joseph R. Walker.[26] A descendant of John Preston suggests that Preston, the Campbell family, and Jerome Davis (who had been to California before) were also traveling with the Chiles party.[27] And then there was Thomas S. Bayley, a Mississippi schoolteacher who was going to Oregon to improve his health. He was taking his four sons and had agreed to carry three hundred letters addressed to Oregon residents that had been accumulating in the Independence post office. As Bayley's reward, the post office told him he could keep whatever he could collect from the intended recipients.[28]

Richard M. May kept a wonderful diary that began by explaining how he traveled on the steamer *Haydee* and arrived at the Wayne City landing on May 10. Disembarking, he traveled two and a half miles into Independence, and discovered that Chiles and his company of twenty-eight wagons had already departed. May explained that he would have to hurry:

> I went on horseback and employed a Mr. Stowe to purchase a yoke of oxen and 2 wagons and other articles of outfit for which I paid him $100. All things being collected together, we left Independence the 12th of May, but previously dispatched a message to Joseph Childs [Chiles] who was at the head of a train for that distant land and informed him that I was on the way who promptly sent word that he would wait or travel slowly until I reached him.[29]

When May left Independence on the twelfth, hurrying to catch up to Chiles, Edward Smith and the Kelly company were already about 140 miles along the trail. The Chiles company were somewhere in between.

Mid-May 1848

Major Samuel J. Hensley, Hensley company, Independence, Missouri

About a week after Richard May departed, thirty-two-year-old Major Samuel J. Hensley left Independence. He was leading a company of eighteen wagons and a train of pack mules. Like Chiles, Hensley was an experienced frontiersman, also from Jackson County, Missouri. He had traveled with the Chiles party to California in 1843 and, like Chiles, had stayed there for three and a half years. In California, he had been employed by John Sutter, then played a prominent role in the Bear Flag Revolt. He was made captain in Fremont's California Battalion that secured the state in 1846, then returned to Missouri in 1847, traveling east with Joseph Chiles, Peter Lassen, and the Greenwoods in Commodore Stockton's entourage. Like Stockton, Hensley continued on to Washington, DC, to testify in Fremont's court-martial.[30] It is remarkable how many of these trail guides had at one time or another been connected with each other. Intending to return to California, Hensley was now leading his own company. It was the last party to leave from Independence for the Far West this year.

Peter Lassen, a former resident of Chariton County, Missouri, had gone to California in 1839. Shortly after his arrival, this former Danish immigrant became an early employee of Captain John Sutter. He watched with envy as Sutter profited each fall with the arrival of emigrants at his fort. So he hatched his own plans and obtained a Mexican land grant for a rancho about one hundred miles north of Sutter's Fort. In the summer of 1847, he joined Commodore Stockton's eastbound party. Believing he could entice a party of emigrants to follow him back to his rancho, Lassen returned to his former Missouri home.[31] His arrival was celebrated in the November 4, 1847, issue of the *Brunswicker,* Brunswick, Missouri's local newspaper:

> The *Meteor* [a steamer] last Sunday, brought down our old county man Peter Lawson [Lassen], who has been absent to California since the spring of 1839. He came in a train of Commodore Stocton [*sic*] who was also on board, and is on his way overland to Washington [DC]. Mr. Lawson left California on the 19th July . . . [h]e brings in a young Indian chief with him to show him sights and will take him back next spring.

Lassen was ready to return to California the next spring. On May 4, 1848, the *Brunswicker* reported that "[Peter] Lawson, [William] Meyers and their company left here last Friday for California. Some seven teams in all will go from Chariton and Carroll counties. The rendezvous is St. Joseph." Evidence suggests that Lassen and his "seven teams" did not go to St. Joseph, but rather traveled to Independence and attached themselves to either Captain Chiles' or Major Hensley's company.

Table 5: Companies leaving from Independence in 1848

Company	Number of Wagons	Departed From Independence
Allsopp	25	April 10
Smith	3	April 28
Kelly	20 (est.)	April 29
Chiles	30 (est.)	May 10 (est.)
Hensley	18	May 20 (est.)
Total	96	

CHAPTER 8

Through
the Tallgrass Prairie
MAY 13–30

MAY 13–27, 1848
Riley Root, Wambaugh company, along the Little Blue River,
Indian Territory, Nebraska

"Saturday, 13th— 9 miles, still on Blue creek," Root recorded. After camping beside the Little Blue River on the night of May 12, Riley Root's Wambaugh company continued along the Little Blue, camping on the thirteenth near the Little Blue, about four miles east of present-day Deweese, Nebraska. The blue prairie across which Root's party lumbered on the thirteenth quivered under a scorching sun. The wagon covers, no longer white, were clad in a drab veneer of chalky dust. The oxen struggled to pull the heavy wagons, their tongues hanging out and their sides heaving. The Wambaugh company, on the road for just over two weeks, were still in the prairie's stubborn grasp. The oxen were fatigued and most of the emigrants were sinking under the tedium of marching across an endless sweep of grass, without a tree in sight. As they walked beside their wagons, they might be entirely focused on putting one foot in front of the other, slipping into a languid sleepwalking trance and noticing little beyond the next few feet of dusty trail.

On May 13, the Wambaugh company would have crossed the 98th meridian, an invisible line that signaled a subtle transformation in the countryside. In his 1844 journal, James Clyman noted that, after crossing Rock Creek, the soils changed from heavy and sticky to light and sandy.[1] The land reflected a changing climate as well. The drier winds cracked their lips and sucked the moisture out of the wood in their wagons, making wagon tongues brittle and more likely to break. The more farsighted had lashed a spare pole under the belly of their wagon and brought plenty of axle grease, but most had not. Rattling wagon boxes and creaking wagon wheels sounded as if they might come apart; greaseless wheels squeaked and grated. Iron tires were becoming so loose on the shrunken wheels that something had to be done. Some tried taking wheels off and submerging them in creeks overnight, but this was a lot of work after a long day on the trail. Simply wetting them was ineffective, as they dried out rapidly, so they resorted to other tricks. Some drove wooden shims between the wheels and tire irons, but they never seemed to last. William Porter, in his letter to his parents, described another way: "The most common way is to nail a thin hoop on the felloe on part of its circumference and heat the tire and put it on."

The plant and animal life were changing too. The travelers began seeing jackrabbits and prairie dogs, pronghorn antelope and buffalo instead of deer and elk, and more wolves, lizards, and rattlesnakes. Short, curly buffalo grass and cactus were also appearing for the first time.[2] Marching beneath the withering sun, the emigrants' hands and faces had undergone a change. In such clear, dry air, the sun was brighter and the travelers developed a burnished tan despite broad-brimmed hats and calico bonnets. Some joked that exposure to the sun and wind had put a little "bark" on their faces, while others teased about looking like Indians. But the word "Indian" tended to bring an uneasiness to their sunburned countenances. They knew they were about to pass through Pawnee country and tensions were building. Stories of Indian attacks, often apocryphal or at least exaggerated, must have circulated through the wagon train and would have struck fear in even the stoutest of hearts.

Riley Root recorded that they traveled ten miles on May 14 and killed their first buffalo. Clyman might have tried to locate the spot on the Little Blue River where he had caught a couple of dozen catfish in 1844, or where he had spotted some beaver working in the stream. Based on Root's estimated distances, their camp on the evening of the fourteenth was about five miles northwest of today's Deweese, Nebraska.

On May 15, Root wrote that they had traveled twelve miles, but complained that "[f]eed has not been sufficient to give our cattle a full supply." William Porter's letter to his parents reported that the "[g]rass is not as good as it commonly is." At the end of the day on the fifteenth, the Wambaugh company camped about three miles north of present-day Ayr, Nebraska. Root noted that "[a]t this place a few wagons, which had been traveling behind us, came up and joind our party, making in all about thirty wagons." Those wagons probably came from the Gates company. Since Root had estimated their party as having "15 or 20" wagons when they left Mosquito Creek, this entry suggests that ten to fifteen wagons had just joined them, and had reduced the Gates company by the same number.

Root's entry revealed how companies sometimes reconfigured. Larger trains might break into smaller segments. Smaller groups, feeling insecure, might try to join others. Some emigrants were fast-moving and impatient, others were slow and plodding. There were breakdowns and needs for repairs. Sometimes the travelers or their stock just needed a rest. Some felt impeded by the slow pace of others and muttered about those who held them back, and those who were pushed faster and harder than they wished muttered about those who drove them at such a rate. The slow movers

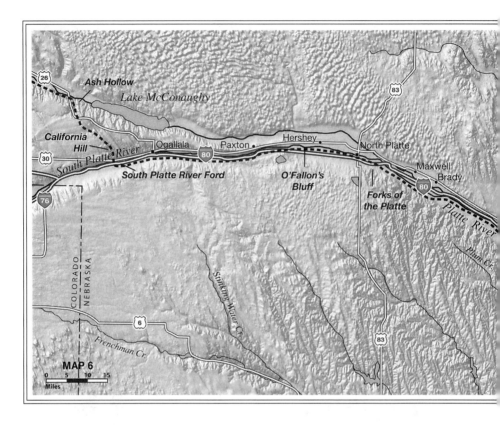

often pulled over and waited for more suitable traveling companions, while the faster wagons might hasten forward to join those ahead. Nothing stayed the same.

As evening closed in on the fifteenth, the men would have returned to camp after tending the livestock and found a seat near the campfire. While the women prepared the evening meal and children cavorted with the dogs, the men would have lit their pipes and sipped freshly brewed coffee. Tobacco and coffee may have been luxuries, but they were things these people were not going to do without, so they usually brought plenty of both.

As the sun sank slowly behind the distant horizon, the most melancholy feelings could rise like a chilly mist from a swamp. Gazing toward the west, the emigrants might contemplate how far they still had to go and wonder how they, their oxen, and wagons could possibly make it. Perhaps a group of men gathered to talk guardedly about the hardships and dangers they knew awaited them, while a homesick woman paused in her work to look up at the night sky and find some solace in familiar stars twinkling back at her, just as they had at home. If they were lucky, someone might get out a fiddle and play a lively tune to distract them from their worries and lift their spirits.

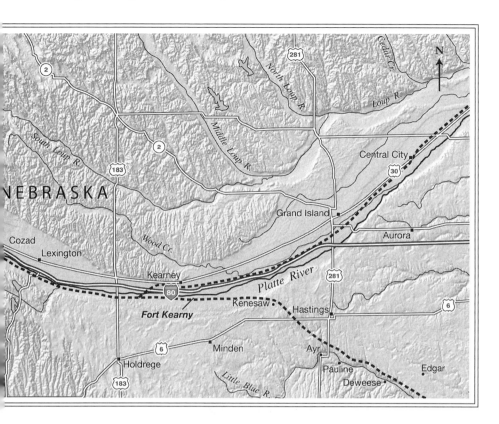

After the women finished their chores and put the children to bed, some might gather to talk, while elsewhere the orange light of a flickering candle leaked through a torn wagon cover where a woman was putting things in order. Others may have sat down by a dying fire to compose a letter, hoping to meet someone traveling east who could carry their letters to a post office in St. Joseph or Independence.

While a symphony of frogs croaked by the river, someone might have noticed the normally stoic James Clyman molding bullets by the fire and observed that his face looked unusually taut. Clyman had crossed this spot four years earlier and recorded in his journal that they had "passed the great Pawnee Lodge trail leading south," a great, wide mark rubbed across the prairie. For centuries, thousands of Pawnees, with their horses and dogs, had been traveling south each year to where they would hunt and raid, and then return.[3] Crossing the trail meant the emigrants were now solidly in Pawnee country, where Clyman had once come close to losing his life. As a young trapper in 1824, he was returning alone from the Rockies and trying to reach Fort Atkinson. He made his way along the south bank of the Platte River, trying to sneak through Pawnee territory undetected. He was unsuccessful. A group of young Pawnee warriors took him prisoner and were preparing to kill him when a seasoned older warrior, admiring Clyman's stone-faced bravery, interceded and escorted him back to the trail. This was just one of Clyman's several close calls with Indians and he felt he understood their character very well. Returning from California in July 1846 with his small party, Clyman recorded his apprehension: "Here we are 8 men and 2 women and one boy this day entering into an enemies country who if possible will Butcher every individual or at least strip us of every means of comfort or convenience."[4]

After leaving the Little Blue River on May 16, the company traveled over a high, waterless dividing ridge. They would have first seen the Platte River as a long, wavy line on the horizon, a range of broken hills formed over thousands of years from sand blown out of the riverbed by strong winds. From the hills, they would have had a sweeping view of the long-anticipated Platte River Valley. According to Root, the Wambaugh company traveled twenty-eight miles; the twentieth mile "brought us to Platt river," about five miles east of where Fort Kearny would soon be built. Only two weeks later Lt. Colonel Powell would arrive with three companies from the Oregon battalion and commence making adobe blocks to build the fort.[5]

In his book, Root noted that on May 16 they passed buffalo robes and other articles strewn along fifteen miles of trail. The emigrants learned that the Pawnees had been hunting buffalo and drying meat for the winter when a Sioux raiding party rode down on them and they scattered in a panic. Root seemed sympathetic, describing the Pawnees as a feeble race that was "liable to be driven about by the Sioux at all times," and noting that "[t]heir pressing necessity for food and clothing makes them more inclined to trouble the emigrant trains than they otherwise would, and whenever they meet with a train that is feeble in numbers, they fall on them and plunder their food and clothing."[6]

Young Rufus Burrows, traveling with the Wambaugh company, recorded a more detailed account of this encounter with the Pawnees:

> The fleeing Pawnees on the road back to the[ir] village met the main train, and on seeing it most of them stayed back a short distance. But a few came up to the train, begging and bothering us so that we could not go ahead. The Pawnees did not know we had given them a lot of stuff as we passed their village, so Captain Wambo said to them, "We gave you all we could when we passed through your village; and now get out of the road and let us go on, as we have a long way to go." ... Wambo ... said to the [Indian] boy, "What do they want?" He [the Indian boy] replied, "We want blood." Wambo said, "What for?" The young Indian replied, "That Mormon wagon ahead sent the Sioux back and they killed fifty of our warriors, also took our ponies and a lot of buffalo meat." At this Wambo gave orders to corral the wagons at once, then saying to the young Indian, "We are ready, come on." This was on the open prairie.[7]

Burrows continued describing the tense confrontation:

Warriors backed up about three hundred yards, parleying. The Indians only having bows and arrows, the older and wiser of them did not want to fight, but the
young warriors parlayed all day, trying to get them to fight, but at last gave it up
and left just as the sun went down. Our train then hurried up and started for the
Sioux village, knowing that they were at peace with the whites and would afford
better protection.[8]

Although Burrows clearly mentioned passing a Pawnee village, Root's journal entries
did not mention it.

After striking the Platte, Root reported that the company traveled "8 more
[miles] to camp on the banks of the Platt river" at the end of the day on May 16.
The Greenwood and Cornwall parties had traveled through here about three weeks
earlier, while Allsopp's group was about four days ahead. Root also reported that the
company had covered 248 miles between St. Joseph and where they struck the Platte.

The Platte River Valley was a change, a welcome interlude from the rolling undu-
lations of the high prairie. The smooth, flat river plain ranged from three to five miles
wide and was bordered on each side by sandy bluffs. The river itself varied from one to
two miles wide and the river bottom, having been washed and blown away, grain by
grain, over the ages, lay hundreds of feet below the high prairie plateau on either side.
Willows and short, scrubby cottonwoods grew on the tiny islets within the channel,
while most of the outside riverbank was devoid of wood. The river was unlike any
the emigrants had seen: unbelievably wide and shallow, with islands and sandbars,
and always muddy. Some called it "the river that flows upside down," or described it
as "too thick to drink, too thin to plow." Women, examining the prospects of doing
some long overdue laundry, would have taken one glance at the muddy brown water
and joked that clothing would come out dirtier than it went in.

The modern traveler will see a different landscape in the Platte River valley. The
once grassy plain is now irrigated fields of corn, soybeans, and alfalfa, with widely
spaced farmhouses sheltered by windbreaks of trees. Because of dams and the great
volumes of water pumped out to support towns and agriculture, the Platte River has
dwindled to a mere shadow of its former self; in most places, it is less than a hundred
yards wide. The once-treeless riverbanks now support dense stands of trees, mostly
cottonwood and willow. Even the bluffs overlooking the river bottom now support
many trees, the result of eliminating prairie fires. The region has not lost its charm; it
is still exceedingly beautiful, but in an entirely different way.

Root reported traveling twenty-two miles on May 17 and fifteen miles on the
eighteenth. Travel up this long, flat plain, grand only in its length and solitude,
would have been unchanging as far as the eye could see. The only variation would
be occasional patches of alkali, areas encrusted with white, powdery, shimmering
salts. In the absence of recent rains, wagon trains stirred up huge clouds of dust that
were hard on the lungs and irritating to the eyes. It could be so bad that wagon trains

often spread out and traveled abreast rather than single file to avoid choking on each other's dust.

The Wambaugh company camped the night of May 18 on Plum Creek, although they should have found its water brackish and disagreeable.[9] On the nineteenth, they laid by, although Root did not explain why. On the twentieth, they traveled eighteen more miles, and Root complained about the scarcity of wood and grass.

As the emigrants continued their march up the Platte River Valley, they would have rolled through a veritable boneyard of bleached buffalo bones. In 1841, John Bidwell wrote:

> The scenery of the country of the Platte is rather dull and monotonous, but there are some objects which must ever attract the attention of the observant traveler; I mean the immense quantity of buffalo bones, which are everywhere strewed with great profusion, so that the valley, throughout its whole length and breadth, is nothing but one complete slaughter yard.[10]

Five years later, in 1846, Edwin Bryant made a similar observation while traveling up the valley: "The bones of buffalo, whitened by the action of the atmosphere, are seen every few yards."[11]

These skeletal remains should have still been abundantly evident in 1848, but curiously none of the year's diarists mentioned them. Some inventive pioneers found they could communicate with wagons behind them by scribbling messages across the broad foreheads of those bleached-white skulls and setting them on stakes driven into the ground beside the trail.

Indians had hunted buffalo within this valley for ages, but it had been only in the past few decades that America's demand for buffalo hides had exploded, giving rise to a robust new business that employed many who had formerly trapped beaver in the Rockies, and the large-scale slaughter of buffalo had been going on for a number of years. Hunters, interested only in harvesting hides and tongues, left the rest of the carcasses for wolves and vultures to feast upon, but the scavengers could only eat so much and countless tons of meat were left to rot in the sun. The Lewis and Clark expedition of 1804 killed their first buffalo where the Platte flowed into the Missouri.[12] But in 1848, forty-four years later, the vast herds in the lower Platte River Valley were gone, their bones the only sign of their prior abundance. These emigrants would have to travel west to where the Platte River forked (three hundred miles west of the Missouri), before they would see the first of the large buffalo herds remaining along the trail.

Traveling across the gentle landscape, the Wambaugh party made one of their better days on the twenty-first, traveling twenty-five miles and camping about one mile south of where today's I-80 and Brady Road intersect. On May 22, they made another twenty-five miles, passing where the Platte divided into its north and south forks. They camped that night just above the forks, about one mile south of present-day North Platte, Nebraska. Root noted that it rained all day and night. They were experiencing a mighty rainstorm that was slowly moving up from the south, and it would be mentioned by each of the other diarists, some of them describing its fierceness in great detail.

The plains were known for their storms and their spectacular displays of lightning and thunder. Root wrote that the storm scared their cattle, and his company was forced to spend most of May 23 looking for their scattered livestock. They did not get them all rounded up "till three o'clock," according to Root, and they only traveled two miles that day.

On May 24, the Wambaugh company traveled twelve miles and came to where Root would describe them crossing the south fork of the Platte:

> This fork at this place is about half a mile wide, and the quick-sands gave way so rapidly under our cattle's feet, that we found it necessary to travel quickly over it, for fear of sinking deeply into it. By my reckoning here, the distance from St. Josephs to the crossing is 375 miles. After we crossd the river, we traveld five miles up the north side of the river and encampd for the night without any wood for cooking our food, except a few small willows.

John McPherson recorded in his journal that the Wambaugh company numbered thirty-nine wagons when they crossed the South Fork, and it took them two hours and twenty minutes to cross.[13] Back on May 15, Root had reported wagons coming up from behind that had increased the size of their company to thirty. So where did the extra nine wagons come from? Since there is no evidence of any other company wedged between Wambaugh and Gates, it would appear that they came from the Gates party.

The ford where Wambaugh crossed his wagon train, called the "lower crossing," was about eighteen miles above the forks and about one mile south of present-day Hershey, Nebraska. Although Captain Wambaugh chose to lead his company across here, the popularity of the crossing was declining as it gave way to an "upper crossing" about thirty-five miles farther up the South Fork.

On May 25, the Wambaugh company traveled eighteen miles along the north bank of the south fork and stopped to camp about five miles west of present-day Paxton, Nebraska. They traveled twenty-two miles on the twenty-sixth, and camped about where Brule, Nebraska, is today. Root mentioned the site as having good grass but no wood. A knowledgeable pilot would know there would be no wood here and would have instructed everyone to toss extra firewood into the backs of their wagons before leaving their previous camp.

On May 27, Root and his company left the South Platte and angled northwest eighteen miles over a high, dry prairie to reach Ash Hollow on the North Platte. They traveled another four miles up the North Platte and camped. In contrast to the shallow, lazy South Fork, they found that the North Fork was narrower, colder, and ran with more urgency.

MAY 13–27, 1848
William Anderson, Miller company, Little Blue River, Indian Territory, Nebraska

On May 13, the Miller company was still traveling along the Little Blue River. They had crossed Little Sandy Creek the day before and were running about thirty miles and two days behind Wambaugh. They traveled ten miles on the thirteenth and camped beside the Little Blue, about three miles northwest of present Hebron, Nebraska. Here, William Anderson noted, "there had been a person buried some years before   the wild beasts had scratched him up and his bones lay scattered around   ther was a board laying near on which was carved the name Robason."

The following day, the Miller company experienced another minor mishap, as Anderson described:

> May the 14th we traveled 17 miles . . .   just before we camped [about five miles south of present Edgar, Nebraska] Isaac Owens came verry near upsetting his waggon   there was sort [short] turn to make round a deep washed gorge   in making the turn the fore wheel ran off the bank   fortunately he stopped the team just as the axel tree struck the ground and saved it from being mashed to pieces then took the team loose and puled the waggon back and pried up the front wheel and got it out without any injury about this time   it commenced raining and it pored down in torents and continued all night.

The much-needed rain Anderson reported on May 14 is mentioned by all the other diarists, save Riley Root, who might have thought it too trivial to record. Anderson wrote that the rain continued on the fifteenth; it must have been enough to slow them down, as they only traveled six miles that day. Their likely campsite was about three miles east of present-day Deweese, Nebraska.

The following day, Anderson described the Miller company's encounter with the Pawnees:

> May the 16th we traveled 14 miles   soon after starting we met a party of them much dreaded Pawnee Indians   we stoped and held a talk and gave them some presents and started on agan   they followed on and attempted to steal several articles and then left us (they snatched Moses Millers knife out of his Belt and he drawed his pistel and made him give it back agan and they attempted to pull some clothing out of the wagons so we used our ox whips on them and they left sooner than otherwise would have done)   In the evening some of our men that were on ahead of the train came riding back and hallowed to us to corel [corral] the stock on the inside and every man with his rifle stood ready for the charge beheld when they came up it was the same little band that we had met in the morning numbering about 25 men   they came galloping up within one hundred yards and turned and rode round   two of our men went to them they

gave us to understand by sines that they had a battle with the sue [Sioux] Indians
a few days before   they warned us to guard our horses close or the sues wood
steal them   we gave them some bread and meat and made them go over the
river an camp and this was the point where the road left the river   we remained
here all night and kept a strong guard out to guard the stock and Indians   they
remained quiet at their camp all night.

It is possible the Miller company had encountered the same group of Pawnees
the Wambaugh company had met two days earlier. Even though Anderson understood from the Pawnees' sign language that they had battled the Sioux "a few days
before," one wonders if the badly mauled warriors were referring to the attack that
took place on about May 1, two weeks earlier and about one hundred miles farther
west. Or had there been a later attack by the Sioux? It seems as if the Pawnees had
been working their way along the trail, determined to try their luck with other wagon
companies. There seemed to be a pattern. After asking for presents, they would beg
for food, then see what they could snatch without being caught. They might leave if
the emigrants, with rifles leveled, demanded it, but they might continue to follow,
looking for any opportunity.

Ordinarily, emigrants were generous, but under the circumstances, they might
lean toward being tightfisted. So early in the trip, they might be unwilling to give up
even a cup of flour, not knowing whether it might be the difference between living or
dying as they crossed the mountains at the end of the journey. There was too much
uncertainty and too much at stake to be very charitable.

On May 17, the Miller company "traveled over a high roling peraire to the Platte
river a distance of 25 miles." Reaching the river at long last, Anderson continued,
"this river is over a mile wide the ground here is almost white in places with a salty
substance [alkali] and the grass was so salty that the stock would not eat much of it."
Rumbling across the alkali flats kicked up particularly irritating dust, making the
oxen sneeze and irritating the travelers' eyes. At night, they would have hacked and
coughed, trying to rid their lungs of the caustic stuff.

The Miller camp on May 17 should have been along the river about seven miles
northwest of present Kenesaw, Nebraska. On the eighteenth, they traveled twenty-
one miles up the Platte and, according to Anderson, saw "a great many antelope."

On May 19, they traveled only five miles. Anderson wrote:

I had a curiosity to know something about the width of this river so I puled off
my pants and waded to the opposite shore   in the deepest places I found it was
only about 3 feet deep   as I came back I steped it and found it to be over 2000
steps across [about a mile] the most singular river I ever saw.

The place where Anderson waded is roughly where P. B. Cornwall's party probably
forded three weeks earlier.

On May 20, Anderson's company traveled fourteen miles across a land that was bounteous in little except rattlesnakes. During the day, their hunters killed an antelope and two wild geese. Killing an antelope on the open plain was no small feat. The fleetest of all four-legged animals on the plains were incredibly wary, with sensitive ears and notes; they would be gone the moment they detected movement or picked up a scent, making it extremely difficult to get within rifle-range.

The Miller company's camp on the evening of May 20 would have been about five miles southeast of present-day Overton, Nebraska. During the night, it began to rain and the next morning the sky remained the color of lead. The emigrants pulled overcoats and cloaks out and fastened them to their chins, then leaning into the cold, wet wind with lowered heads, they resumed their travels. Their heavy-breathing oxen, straining at the overloaded wagons, were in no hurry, and the teamsters had given up goading the animals to go faster, and let the tired beasts set their own pace.

Despite the bad weather, the Miller company managed sixteen miles on May 21 and camped about three miles south of today's Lexington, Nebraska. Anderson wrote that the storm "drove our cattle to the bluffs and caused us some trouble to get them agan." They rounded up their scattered cattle and still managed to make eighteen miles on the twenty-second, ending the day about five miles west of present Cozad, Nebraska. On May 23, they continued their journey through a country that offered little of interest. They spent the day rumbling beside the Platte, making fifteen miles and camping about four miles southeast of present-day Brady, Nebraska. They were about twenty miles and one day behind Wambaugh.

On the morning of May 24, the Miller company was about twenty miles downstream of the forks. This meant that they were nearing the great buffalo herds that congregated along the south fork. Because a woman in the company had gone into labor, the wagon train stayed in camp all day. Taking advantage of the pause, and perhaps not wanting to listen to the sounds of a woman in the throes of labor, Anderson and five others decided to go hunting. Giving chase to a buffalo, they shot him behind the shoulder, and he "ran a piece and fell." They "shot several rifle balls aganst his forehead (but they didnt enter the skull)," Anderson wrote. "[They] went up and shaved the hare and dirt off his forehead then shot another ball and it went through the skull." The hunters took some meat but "left the rest for the wolves to devour."

Over the years, packs of wolves had learned to follow wagon trains, skulking just out of rifle-range and waiting for the remains of any buffalo, antelope, or ox to fall their way. The emigrants often complained that at night, the howls sounded as if there were hundreds of wolves out there, and it made their flesh crawl. While out hunting on May 24, Anderson and his companions came across eleven head of stray cattle that "the company before us" had lost, so they "took charge of them," thinking they could return the cattle when they overtook the company ahead.

The woman safely delivered her child, and since she and her newborn were "all right," the Anderson company resumed their march on May 25, and met the owners of the lost cattle. "[S]o weakened by the loss of the 11 head of cattle that [they] would not be able to get through," Anderson wrote, the owners were determined to find their errant beasts and were searching back along the trail. Anderson helped them drive their cattle forward and soon "overtook ther train which was 12 waggons." He wrote that his company then passed them; he described them as "a company of California emigrants."

Were these California emigrants a detachment from the Wambaugh company? Not likely. First, Root had written that they had recovered all their cattle scattered by the storm. Second, it would have been poor form for Wambaugh to continue on while leaving twelve of his wagons behind to fend for themselves. Third, Anderson indicated that they returned the strays to their owners while still east of where the Wambaugh company crossed the river. But instead of the California men crossing where Wambaugh had, Anderson wrote that they continued up the south bank of the south fork and were heading toward the "upper crossing." Thus the evidence is that these twelve wagons came from the Gates party, the remnants of which should still be ahead of Miller. It was originally estimated that the Gates company had started with about forty wagons. Then it was learned from Root and McPherson that perhaps as many as twenty wagons had joined them from Gates. If these twelve "California" wagons had also come from Gates, it suggests that all that may have remained of the original Gates party might have been as few as ten wagons. There is a larger story here, but no one to tell it.

On May 25, Anderson reported that they traveled eighteen miles, another day in sight of the familiar bluffs that bounded the river. That night, they encamped near the forks. Since Wambaugh's company had reached this same point on the twenty-second, Anderson's company was now traveling three days behind them.

Also on May 25, Anderson noted seeing "numerous bufalo paths leading from the bluffs to the river these paths are about 14 inches wide and 1 to 3 inches deep and smooth as though they had bin cut with a spade." On May 26, Anderson reported passing the "lower crossing" of the South Platte six miles after leaving camp that morning, but the company did not follow Wambaugh by crossing here. Anderson mentioned that just beyond the lower crossing the "bluffs rise between the north and south forks of the platte," confirming that the "lower crossing" was just before reaching O'Fallon's Bluff, a low, sandstone ridge that pushes out to the South Platte River and forces the trail to ascend a gentle draw. The bluff may have been named for Benjamin O'Fallon, an early Indian agent, or it may have been named in the 1820s for William O. Fallon, who was piloting the Cornwall party in 1848.[14] Wagon ruts can be seen today running up the draw and over O'Fallon's Bluff at the eastbound rest area on I-80 between Hershey and Sutherland, Nebraska.

The Miller party continued sixteen miles over O'Fallon's Bluff and along the south bank of the South Platte on May 26. During the day, the California company of twelve wagons overtook and passed them. Anderson did not mention traveling across Alkali

Lake (seven miles west of present-day Paxton, Nebraska), a large area of white alkali, but he did note passing "through a great many [prairie] dog towns." During the day, he and his friends "dug a den of young wolves out and found a large rattlesnake in with them." He seemed amazed at discovering that rattlesnakes shared burrows and dens not only with wolves but also with prairie dogs and gray ground owls.

They were now in the heart of buffalo country, and Anderson wrote that on the twenty-sixth they "saw a great many buffalo to day and our hunters killed one of them today." He reported that they traveled only four miles on May 27, but did not explain why.

MAY 13–27, 1848

William Porter, Purvine company, Big Blue River, Indian Territory, Kansas

On May 13, William Porter and his Purvine company were one day behind the Walker and Bristow companies and had reached the Big Blue River just west of present-day Marysville, Kansas. Perhaps the company's young boys tried their hand at fishing in the river, home to some very large catfish. They had to be careful approaching the riverbanks, where water moccasins often lay quietly in the thick grass. Just before crossing the Big Blue, Porter wrote that "Denton drove Charlie's [Charlie Benson] wagon against a stump, and broke the tongue, and in crossing the river, the wagon upset, and detained us some time." By the end of the day, they had made sixteen miles.

On May 14, Porter and his company passed the junction of the Independence and St. Joseph roads, but Porter did not mention it. He did, however, note seeing their first antelope. After traveling fifteen miles, they camped near Cottonwood Creek, two miles east of present-day Hanover, Kansas. Slowed by rain on the fifteenth, they traveled only nine miles, probably camping about four miles northeast of present-day Hollenberg, Kansas. They traveled fifteen miles on May 16 and stopped near Rock Creek (at today's Rock Creek Station State Historical Park). Porter inserted a warning in his diary for future emigrants: "If you come to a rocky branch [Rock Creek] in the after part of the day, better not pass till the next day," pointing out that until they reached Little Sandy Creek, there would be no water for twenty miles beyond Rock Creek. Porter noted that on the seventeenth they "[t]raveled 20 miles and camped on a sandy creek." Because the spring of 1848 was so dry, they "had to dig for water" in the bottom of Little Sandy Creek. Their camp would have been approximately five miles northwest of today's Fairbury, Nebraska. Over the next three days, Porter recorded no exceptional incidents, but noted making eighteen miles on May 18, eighteen miles on the nineteenth, and fifteen miles on the twentieth.

On May 21, Porter and his Purvine company finally departed the Little Blue and headed across the prairie on a beeline to the Platte River. That day, they "met a company [John Shaw] from the mountains today loaded with [buffalo] robes. Stormed." After traveling fifteen miles, they stopped about seventeen miles short of the Platte River and spent the night on the divide between the Little Blue and the Platte.

According to Porter, the Purvine company finally reached the Platte River on May 22, having just passed through the country where the Wambaugh and Miller companies had been troubled by Pawnees a week before. Porter made no mention of them, so the Indians may have left the area along the trail, or perhaps had not ventured out in the miserable rain.

The Purvine company traveled another five miles up the Platte River on the twenty-second before stopping to camp. Porter wrote that they had to cross the river to get wood, and that it continued to rain "all night with very heavy wind. Wagons covers leaked middling badly."

May 23 was a day of clear skies and bright sun, and Porter wrote that they only traveled seven miles up the Platte that day, then paused to dry out their clothing, bedding, and just about everything else. They removed wagon covers, articles stored in wagon boxes, and anything else that was wet. Their cornmeal was damp and had to be thrown away. On May 24, they traveled fifteen miles, and on the twenty-fifth they traveled eighteen. Porter wrote that they camped at "a place where Mr. Watt's company had buried a child the day before," an event Keturah Belknap did not mention in her diary. This is our first evidence that the Watt company had moved ahead of the Purvine company, likely doing so on May 7 or 8, when the Purvine company had remained in camp. On May 26 and 27, Porter's company continued up the Platte River bottom without incident, going eighteen and sixteen miles, respectively.

May 13–27, 1848

Edward Smith, Big Vermillion River crossing, Indian Territory, Kansas

Edward Smith and his small party of four wagons lazed in their camp on the north side of the Big Vermillion River on May 13, while the Kelly company "came up with us   they Broke an axletree   In the evening we formally joined the [Kelly] Co." On May 14, Smith's party traveled with the Kelly company and made fourteen miles. Smith reported that they camped that night

> on the right [west] bank of the Big blue River near a fine spring of very cold water [Alcove Springs]   here we Passed the grave of an old lady who had died here and was Buried on the left [east] Bank of the river under a hickory tree about one foot in diameter on the right hand side about 4 rods from the road   the name inscribed on the tree is Sarah Keys aged 70 years Died in May 1846.

Edwin Bryant was traveling in 1846 with what would later be known as the Donner party, and he described the death of Sarah Keys. She and her son-in-law, James R. Reed, were members of that party, and Reed would become a principal character in the tragedy that would befall the party later that year. Mrs. Keys was very sick when the party left Independence, but she was determined to see her son who had emigrated to Oregon a couple of years earlier. She didn't make it, dying here, at a place

Bryant's party named Alcove Springs. Bryant described the area beside the Big Blue River as extremely beautiful, with large oak, cottonwood, walnut, and sycamore trees growing in a half-mile-wide band along the river. After mentioning that a boy caught a three-foot catfish in the river, Bryant wrote that he and some companions wandered up a rivulet about three-quarters of a mile to a place where the spring waters spilled over a rock ledge and fell ten feet into a basin. Waiting for Sarah Keys to expire, they chiseled "Alcove Springs" on top of the rock ledge,[15] and James Reed carved his name and the date into a nearby rock. The waterfall and both rock engravings can still be seen about six miles south of Marysville, Kansas, on the east side of the Big Blue River, on East River Road.

Smith's entry for May 14 revealed that they crossed the Big Blue River at Alcove Springs and camped on its west bank that evening. On the fifteenth, his company traveled fourteen miles through a "light rain" and "encamped on a small stream [Cottonwood Creek, east of Hanover, Kansas] now nearly dry." During their travels that day, Smith reported that they "struck the Emigrant Route from St. Josephs fresh tracks as if 200 waggons had passed a few days before." Smith's estimate of the number of wagons that preceded them through the "junction" was astonishingly accurate.

On May 15, the Allsopp party should have been 260 miles and twenty days ahead of Smith and Kelly, while the Wambaugh company was about ninety miles and seven days ahead. The Gates company, followed by the Miller company, were about seventy miles and six days ahead. The Watt, Walker, and Bristow companies should have been about twenty miles and two days ahead, while Porter's Purvine company was about ten miles and one day ahead of Smith and Kelly. Behind Smith were Father Lempfrit and the Stone company. They were still on the St. Joseph Road, but it is hard to say exactly where, as Father Lempfrit rarely recorded miles traveled. The Stone party would cross the Big Blue River on May 21, about six days later. As for the Chiles and Hensley companies, they were still rumbling up the Independence road and would cross the Big Blue River on the twenty-second, a day after the Stone company.

Edward Smith noted that on the morning of May 16 they discovered that "some of the cattle were gone." They found them five miles away, which delayed them from leaving camp until two in the afternoon. As a result, they only made eight miles on the 16th, and set up camp about four miles east of present-day Hollenberg, Kansas.

On May 17, Smith's company left camp at eight in the morning and rolled until five in the afternoon. Smith complained that they "traveled at a snail's gallop," and only made nine miles that day. They camped "on the open Prarie," near today's Rock Creek Station State Historical Park. He reported finding "two cows strayed from a co one day ahead   in the evening two men came and got the cows." The cows and men were probably from the Purvine company, only one day ahead.

Smith and his party started early in the morning of May 18 and traveled all day, making eighteen miles. Once they passed Rock Creek, Smith recorded, as Clyman had in 1844, that the soil was becoming "more sandy." They ended their day on Little Sandy Creek, about five miles northwest of today's Fairbury, Nebraska.

Smith wrote that his party made twelve miles on May 19, and saw "several Elk and antelope." Water was scarce and Smith noted that "the grass was very short." The occasional tree might mark the location of a tiny green pool of slimy, stagnant water, which they usually found unfit for drinking, with tadpoles, mosquito larvae, and other disagreeable creatures swimming in it. When they came to "a dry creek bed" (Big Sandy Creek), they were forced to dig deep pits in the bottom to find water for their stock, just as the Purvine company had done. They camped approximately one mile east of present Belvidere, Nebraska.

The Smith company made seventeen miles on May 20 and

> encamped in a beautiful bend of the [Little Blue] river where a small company
> of the oregon Emigrants were encamped   they did not move today on account
> of the Indians intending to drive their cattle off but they drove off the Indians.

It appears that the Pawnees were still in the neighborhood. The "oregon Emigrants" Smith mentioned were likely from the Kelly company. They could not have been Porter's company, as it had camped about twenty-six miles ahead of Smith's party on the night of May 20.

On May 21, Smith's party made twelve miles, and Smith expressed displeasure that their party was making slow progress, perhaps because of having to search for strayed cattle so often. "Sun 21— we started at 8 A M," he wrote. "[T]raveled until 12 at a very slow rate finding that we were not averaging more than 12 miles a day I and Mr. Lindsey & families left the Co and overtook another Co who were in the habit of guarding there cattle so we joined that Co." That night, they camped about two miles north of today's Angus, Nebraska.

The company Smith and Lindsey joined was clearly not the Purvine company, as it was about thirty miles ahead of Smith. The only other party known to be traveling close by was Kelly, which could have split up due to dissention, with the faster travelers moving ahead.

On the evening of the twenty-first, Smith reported a lone rider straggling into camp. Dr. Atkinson had been traveling alone on horseback since leaving St. Joseph—a reckless and dangerous plan. Perhaps Dr. Atkinson realized he was entering Pawnee territory, and it was time to seek the safety of others.

Something else arrived in Smith's camp that evening, something the diarists universally complained about. At about ten o'clock, Smith reported,

> we were visited by one of the severest thunder and Lightening storms I have ever
> seen   the Rain descended in torrents and all the tents were prostrated at once
> the wagons being scarcely able to Resist the Storm.

Smith's party resumed traveling along the Little Blue on May 22, and the rain returned. After traveling sixteen miles, they camped about three miles east of present-day Pauline, Nebraska. From that spot, they left the Little Blue and headed on a northwesterly bearing for the Platte. That evening they were joined in camp by "a party of mountain traders." Judging by the dates on which other diarists recorded meeting John Shaw, Smith was probably referring to Shaw's wagons. During the night, Smith complained, "we were again visited by a terrific Rain storm."

Oddly, Smith has still not mentioned his wife and children. He did not comment on how his family was faring in the punishing storms, or whether his wife and little ones were having a hard time. Women and children ordinarily did not ride in the wagons, but walked beside them. Slogging along the trail on rainy days, they must have been miserable, soaked to the skin, shivering in the wind, slipping and sliding in shoes wet and heavy with clinging mud. When it rained at night, it would have been impossible to maintain campfires or keep dry, and sleeping was out of the question if one was wet to the skin and cold.

The morning of May 23 brought some relief—a clear day with a warm, bright sun. Smith reported that they "remained in camp" that day, taking advantage of the warm day for "drying the wet beding and clothing." No doubt the travelers and their stock also needed a day of rest. The distant horizon foretold how far they still had to go and must have discouraged even the most robust personality.

The next morning, on May 24, the Smith party returned to the trail, but it began raining again. Eight miles out of camp, along Thirty-Two-Mile Creek, Smith related that they "met a party of Pawnees   gave them some tobacco and bread." Continuing another twelve miles, they "camped in the open Prarie wild sage for fire wood." Their camp would have been about four miles southeast of present Kenesaw, Nebraska.

It took only ten miles of travel on May 25 for the Smith party to pass over the sandy hills and descend to the banks of the Platte. Smith mentioned that the "waters were very much swollen By the Recent Rains and ran swiftly by   verry turbid and muddy." They traveled up the river plain another six miles. Seeing riders approaching and supposing them to be Indians, Smith reported that they hastily formed their wagons into a "coral." But their alarm was misplaced as the riders turned out to be "some Mountain traders."

They traveled sixteen miles up the Platte on May 26. Smith did not record their miles on the twenty-seventh, but mentioned that they saw two buffalo, and that the Kelly company they had left on the twenty-first caught up to them. According to Smith, the group then divided into two separate parties, one that camped three miles ahead and one that camped two miles behind. With so many detachments, "go-aheads," and "drop-backs," these companies were beginning to lose their identity. Sadly, Smith failed to mention how many wagons were now in his party, in the one ahead, or in the one behind, or to identify any of their leaders.

Smith reported camping on the evening of May 27 "near a small creek [likely Plum Creek] with some timber on the head."

MAY 12–30, 1848

Father Lempfrit, Stone company, somewhere just west of St. Joseph, Missouri

On May 11, Father Lempfrit and his companions in the Stone company had just left St. Joseph. Before reaching the Presbyterian Mission School on the twelfth, the French priest got a close-up look at some Indians and noted their predilection for gaudy dress and adornment:

> 12th May. Around 10 o'clock we were surrounded by Indians called Pawnee. If I would not have been in America I would have believed myself present at carnival time, a real masquerade! They were daubed with red, white and yellow; some had their skin painted in long lines rather like the zebra, some had one eye red, the other white, and others had their faces painted in four or five colours. Their chief wore on his chest three big tin medals, these bore the effigy of George III, King of England. The chief's hair was dressed in the form of a horse's mane, the hair at the back was drawn up towards the front, and instead of a large hairpin he stuck a sheaf of green reeds through his hair. This handsome head of hair was adorned with . . . a long dragoon's sword sheath from which he hung a sheaf of reeds. At St. Joseph I had procured a pretty little black pony for myself. I had a beautiful saddle with a fur [horse] blanket that was very attractive to the Indian chief; he eyed it with envy.

It is almost certain Lempfrit was mistaken about the tribe. Considering the location and their description, he was more likely describing Sacs than Pawnees.

Lempfrit's group resumed their journey the next morning:

> 13th May. I took the lead with my little pony. We came into vast and beautiful prairieland [where there were] some very pretty little hills. Unfortunately, my horse was too nimble, and I found myself too far ahead. The caravan had halted at 6 o'clock that evening. I was alone in that immense prairie—it was as if I were alone in the world. Not the smallest sound came to tear me away from my reveries. I waited in vain until 9 o'clock in the evening. In Europe, the Christian soul rejoices when hearing the sound of the bells; here there is absolute silence, it is as if nature is in suspended animation. I started to feel afraid and decided to return on my tracks. It was not until very late at night that I caught sight of our campfires [likely a few miles west of the Indian Mission School].

This man in black cloth was once again riding ahead on his spirited black pony. Having grown up in France, where virtually every corner was filled with the works of men and no place was too remote to hear the clanging of church bells, Lempfrit was

drawn to the open plains. It is no surprise that the profound silence and solitude of
the western prairie entranced him, even as he might have found it unsettling. But did
this guileless soul not appreciate the dangers of wandering off alone?

Captain Stone and his small party had left St. Joseph late, the last to leave from
there that year. Whether Stone was concerned about arriving late at the western
mountains is hard to say, but he did seem concerned about traveling through Indian
Territory with such a small company. He asked Father Lempfrit and an "Irishman"
(likely Lawrence Burns) to ride forward and ask the company ahead to wait for them:

> 14th May. There were only 11 waggons in our caravan; another of 21 waggons
> was three days ahead of us. The captain [Stone] proposed to me that I take the
> lead with an Irishman and go and request the captain of that caravan to wait for
> us. I was told that the caravan was only 45 miles away, that is why we took only
> a small quantity of food with us. I had three biscuits and a roasted starling—we
> left at 8 o'clock in the morning. We covered twenty-five miles without meeting
> up with the caravan. We arrived at a little village called Nemaha. There I found a
> good Canadian who gave us dinner.

Lempfrit's reference to a company three days ahead of them could have been to
the Purvine company. According to William Porter's diary, the Purvine company
camped on a creek (probably the Nemaha) on May 10, which means they were more
like four days ahead of Lempfrit's party.

After eating with the Canadian on Nemaha Creek, Lempfrit and his companion
resumed their chase, but when night fell, they stopped to spend the night sleeping on
"the edge of a meadow." Years later, James D. Miller, a member of the Stone company,
noted that one or two houses occupied by "traders and half-breeds" stood on Nemaha
Creek, something that no other diarists mentioned that year.[16]

Lempfrit and the Irishman resumed their pursuit early the next morning:

> [May 15] We were going down a hill. . . . [B]efore long a piercing scream came to
> our ears; my companion [the Irishman] is terrified, he thinks the Indians are after
> us. "Indian, Indian," he cries, taking off at a gallop. I followed him. Fear had led
> astray this poor man's senses, he was out of his mind. He did not stop until he
> reached the edge of a forest more than ten miles away. As it was dark we were
> able to go no further. I wanted at least that we take cover in the thickness of the
> forest. Impossible! My friend was so fearful of the Indians that he wanted to bed
> down in open country. We set our horses free to graze, attaching them with a
> rope long enough for them to find sufficient grass. Then we ate the remainder of
> our provisions. The weather was stormy, we were without shelter and I had only
> my coat to protect me from the rain. We both wrapped ourselves up in it. I would
> have slept quite well but for my Irishman who could not sleep a wink, believing
> at every moment that he heard Indians coming upon us unexpectedly. I told
> him to arm himself with the sign of the cross he set about doing this endlessly,

he kept waking me up to show me that he knew how to make it well, asking me if it was properly done like this. . . . About 4 o'clock in the morning I woke up absolutely soaked by the rain that had been falling throughout a good part of the night. We at once saddled our horses in order to resume our search. We went thirty miles without eating anything.

By afternoon on the sixteenth, Father Lempfrit and his companion paused to study the wagon tracks and concluded that they were still at least a day behind their quarry:

[May 16] Without provisions we lost heart; we thus resolved to return. The Irishman still had a piece of bacon that we roasted on the fire, and we ate it with great relish. We went to bed down a few miles from there, then the next day we traveled the whole day without eating anything. . . . Great was our joy when half an hour later, we found our people. Nearly all of them were asleep. They made haste to prepare something for us to eat, as we were in dire need of food. What made me suffer the most during those three or four days was being deprived of tobacco. I had forgotten to refill my tobacco pouch, with the result that I spent two complete days without having any. Those who have the unfortunate habit of taking snuff will be able to understand what I had to endure.

It seems that Lempfrit and his companion had been sent on a fool's errand, as the company they had been sent to overtake was too far ahead. And while the captain's idea might have had merit, he may have picked the wrong people for this assignment.

The Stone company resumed their travels on the seventeenth. Lempfrit complained of being tired from his three-day jaunt, then reported that their wagon's axle broke, forcing them to pause. They cut a limb from a tree and fashioned a replacement. Lempfrit had little to say about their travels on May 18 and 19, and since he rarely estimated mileage, it is futile to estimate where the company camped during those nights.

On May 20, the irrepressible priest could not seem to abide the plodding pace of the oxen-drawn wagons, yearning instead for some tranquil sightseeing. Apparently undaunted by his previous frights, he once again mounted his little black pony and galloped forward into the open spaces, making sure this time that the fainthearted Irishman did not accompany him.

20th May. Today, a strange adventure befell me. I had taken the lead with my pony. I came into a huge plain. By midday I had not yet found the smallest stream and I was dying of thirst. The caravan was late and I urged my horse hoping to come to come across some little spring. Around four o'clock I stopped to say my office [prayers]. My horse was grazing about ten paces away from me. All of a sudden I see him rear up on his hind legs, absolutely terrified, immediately I notice two moving shadows that seemed to me like the top of two barouches. At first I thought that it was the caravan's vehicles arriving, but while I reflected that we had no waggons covered in blue, I could discern two objects, one white, the other blue. So I went up to my horse to get my spyglass. What was my surprise when, with the aid of my glass, I unmistakably distinguished two Indians creeping along, with blankets over their heads. The wind was blowing up the blankets in a way that made them appear like carriages to me. I was frightened. I mounted my horse, departed at a gallop, and made for a forest in which to hide whilst waiting for the caravan to arrive. Towards 7 o'clock in the evening I thought I could see three men coming. Indeed these were our people. I told them about my adventure and they laughed uproariously!

One cannot help but wonder how Lempfrit's companions regarded the priest's reckless sense of adventure. Did they respect him despite his recklessness, or dismiss him as an odd and feckless duck?

Lempfrit had barely reached camp that evening when a fierce storm arrived:

The night of the 20th to the 21st was both frightening and catastrophic. A terrible storm broke around 8 o'clock that evening. The rain came down in buckets and the wind blew with extreme violence. Our tent was just about carried away by the hurricane a score of times. Since they had failed to put out the fire, large burning embers were being picked up by the wind and tossed as far as our waggons. We narrowly escaped being burnt alive. An hour later, water was streaming into our tent, and as I was crouched down in order to hold down the tent's sides I could soon feel my knees soaking in the water that was pouring over our bedding. So I let go my hold to go find shelter in the waggon, and I spent the rest of the night there, chilled to the marrow.

Even though the rain continued on May 21, Lempfrit and his company continued onward, arriving at the Big Blue River just west of present-day Marysville, Kansas:

Later in the day we came upon a beautiful river in the forest, and we crossed this without any accidents. Not too far away from there we found a spring that had excellent water, the first we have happened upon since we joined the caravan. On a little knoll I saw a cairn, the grave marker of a child who had been drowned while crossing the river.

James D. Miller of the Stone company also mentioned in his reminiscence that a couple of traders' "adobe houses" were located at the Big Blue River crossing, something no other diarist mentioned.[17]

After crossing to the west side of the Big Blue on the afternoon of May 21, the Stone company was a full eight days behind William Porter's Purvine company. Instead of catching up to them, the Stone company had fallen even farther behind.

Lempfrit wrote that rain and thunder continued on May 22. He found a turtle from which he "made excellent stew," and complained that "the rains of these last few days have brought on several cases of fever. I am treating my patients." Lempfrit had once worked in the monastic infirmaries of France, which is perhaps why the company looked to him as their doctor. The next two days, he wrote:

> 23rd May. We have had a very bad night. The storm ceased only at daybreak. Because of the violence of the wind we had not been able to light a fire.
>
> [May 24] [b]ad weather all day, still raining. . . . [Wolves] prowl around our camp all night long and their howling gives us the shivers.

Ordinarily, heavy rains on the prairie would soften the ground and create thick mud that made travel possible only through the extreme exertion of man and beast. But by May 20 to 24, when these ferocious storms hit, most of the wagon trains were traveling across sandy soils that rapidly absorbed the water.

Lempfrit wrote that "nothing of interest" happened on May 25 and 26. On May 27, he reported that they met "two wagons loaded with furs on their way to St. Louis," likely John Shaw. He also noted that the night of the twenty-seventh was windy. "My patients are becoming more numerous," he wrote, and "Mr. Lionnet [his companion priest] is unwell." A raw, cold wind blowing against wet clothing was sapping these tired people of their body heat, and lengthy exposure to wet and cold was bringing on illness. Small-bodied women and children were especially susceptible to colds, bronchitis, whooping cough, and pneumonia.

Despite Father Lempfrit's chafing at the trail's miseries and tribulations, he praised the area along the Little Blue River, citing the

> very pretty little roses and some jasmine. . . . The further we go, the more picturesque the country becomes. One might say that Nature has taken great pleasure in beautifying these wild regions, I said to myself while gazing upon places so lovely, that she must smile to herself that man has so late discovered some of her most beautiful creations.

MAY 12–29, 1848

Richard May, Chiles company, on the trail just west of Independence, Missouri

On May 12, Richard May and his friends had just left Independence, hastening to catch up to the already departed Joseph Chiles' train. They made only ten miles their first day out. After his entry on the twelfth, May made no entry in his diary until May 21, when he happily reported that "[o]n that day we had the joy and pleasure of arriving at Capt. Childs' [Chiles] who very kindly had us take supper with him."

It apparently had taken May and his friends ten days to close the distance, and he and the Chiles company crossed the Big Blue River at Alcove Springs on May 22. May noted passing the "junction" of the Independence and St. Joseph roads ten miles beyond where they crossed the Big Blue. May also noted the great storm:

On the 22nd we traveled about 14 miles and near 2 o'clock passed the junction of the St. Joseph road. It rained all day and in the evening it fell in torrents. I just thought as I was driving the team along this is the sweet portion of traveling to California. This day one of my steers became weary and sullen and we turned him out.

With all the rain, the trail had turned into a path of thick mud by now, and the Chiles company must have proceeded with great difficulty. They continued four miles past the junction and stopped to camp two miles east of present-day Hanover, Kansas. They were traveling about one day behind Father Lempfrit and the Stone company.

The next morning, May 23, May went back and found his ailing ox. He recorded that it was "still raining and the wind blowing very hard but having on my rain cloak and cap," but admitted he was not suffering seriously. Because of the rain, they stayed in camp all day on the twenty-third. From May 24 through May 26, Richard May recorded nothing of consequence, except that on the twenty-fifth his oxen strayed and he and his friends found them seven miles away. His company only traveled seven miles on May 25 and twelve miles on the twenty-sixth. Their campsite on May 26 could have been Rock Creek. May did not make an entry on May 27. On May 28, he reported that they traveled ten miles, but they "lay by all day" on May 29. Then he reported that they traveled twelve miles on May 30. On that day, he also reported that they had encountered Shaw's wagons on May 28 and 29:

> [May 30] We met yesterday [May 29] and the day before [May 28] 22 wagons from the mountains laden with buffalo robes and tongues principally. One train of 7 wagons belongs to Mr. Shaw who commanded the steamer, *Tobacco Plant*, who I have seen a few times on the river. Mr. Millington was in company with the train, who gave me a pair of mockisons and through Capt. Childs I received of them a piece of dried buffalo. I did not forget to requite them for their favor by giving them some coffee and sugar, a sufficiency to last them to the States.

Major Samuel J. Hensley and his company were traveling a few days behind the Chiles caravan. But we know nothing of their progress due to the absence of narrators in his party.

———————————

At the end of May, the Greenwood and Cornwall parties were relaxing near the protective walls of Fort Laramie, waiting for the first large wagon party to come along. As of May 27, the next wagon train on the trail would have been Allsopp's, and it was probably nearing Chimney Rock, about seventy miles from Fort Laramie. The hindmost parties, Chiles and Hensley, had about one hundred miles to go before they reached the Platte River. From front to back, Greenwood's and Cornwall's parties excepted, the wagon trains on the Oregon Trail were spread over four hundred miles.

Table 6: Location of each known company as of May 27, 1848

Company (Diarist)	Location
Greenwood	at Fort Laramie
Cornwall	at Fort Laramie
Allsopp	about 70 miles from Fort Laramie
Wambaugh (Root)	at Ash Hollow
Gates	somewhere between Wambaugh and Miller
12 California wagons	approaching upper crossing of South Fork of Platte
Miller (Anderson)	approaching upper crossing of South Fork of Platte
Walker	nearing the forks of the Platte
Bristow	nearing the forks of the Platte
Watt (Keturah Belknap)	nearing the forks of the Platte
Purvine (Porter)	nearing the forks of the Platte
Smith (Smith)	probably at the mouth of Plum Creek, along Platte
Kelly (Smith)	nearing the forks of the Platte
Stone (Lempfrit)	about 40 miles from reaching the Platte
Chiles (May)	about 100 miles from reaching the Platte
Hensley	slightly behind Chiles
Lassen	traveling either with Chiles or Hensley

CHAPTER 9

Black Beasts, Black Faces
MAY 28–JUNE 3

MAY 28–JUNE 3, 1848
Riley Root, Wambaugh company, west of Ash Hollow, Nebraska

On the morning of May 28, the Wambaugh company was along the North Platte, four miles west of Ash Hollow and on the eastern fringe of a great meadow, getting ready to return to the trail. The strong fragrance of sage and cedar hung in the early morning air. Through the mist, they could make out columns of smoke rising from lodges in the Sioux village two miles to the west. Riley Root described the encounter in his book: "Near Ash Hollow on the Platt, we passd two bands of them not many miles distant from each other, consisting of 40 or 50 lodges each." The Sioux had established their camps so that their lodges straddled the trail, making it impossible for the wagons to avoid them. According to Root, Captain Wambaugh ordered his wagon train to stay close and admonished the men to "keep their guns where they could lay their hands on them at a moment's warning." He warned that no one but he was to speak to the Indians.[1] Although Cornwall's biography had described the Sioux as "allies," Root's account suggested that Wambaugh wasn't so sure. Years later, Joe Meek would inform his biographer that when he and his party traveled east in April 1848, they were told at Fort Laramie about the Sioux camp near Ash Hollow. "The Sioux are a bad people," a French trapper warned them.[2] Assuming Meek was not spinning another yarn, it is likely he would have passed this warning on to Wambaugh and Clyman when he met them on the trail on about May 7.

Even without Meek's warning, Wambaugh and Clyman would have been well aware that the Sioux had a dark side. Like many tribes, they had a history of sending warriors to steal horses and take scalps from neighboring tribes, and had demonstrated a willingness, especially against the Pawnees, to massacre women and children, and mutilate bodies.[3]

As recently as 1842, Dr. Elijah White's Oregon-bound wagon party had been stopped west of Independence Rock by a band of 350 Sioux warriors. According to

John C. Fremont, the warriors had set out with the express intention of attacking Dr. White's party. But Thomas Fitzpatrick was Dr. White's guide, and the Sioux held "Broken Hand," as they called Fitzpatrick, in high esteem. In deference to Fitzpatrick, the Sioux allowed the wagon train to proceed unharmed, but not without warning them that "[this] path was no longer open, and that any party of whites which should hereafter be found upon it would meet with certain destruction."[4]

Because of this and other incidents with passing emigrants, Colonel Stephen Kearny and several companies of mounted dragoons arrived at Fort Laramie in 1845, where 1,200 Sioux and their chiefs waited to meet with him. This was the first time most Sioux had seen the white man's warriors, with their long knives and intimidating cannon. The chiefs told Kearny that their hostility arose from wagon trains driving buffalo from their hunting grounds along the North Platte, and Kearny warned that the army would severely punish the Sioux if any harm came to any white travelers in the future, and drove his point home by firing off his cannons.[5] Despite Kearny's show of strength, a Sioux raiding party attacked a group of white missionaries on the Loup River the very next year.[6]

James Clyman's experiences over the years had taught him to be cautious toward all Indians in general. One of his friends from Milwaukee reported that Clyman

> seldom laughed or showed any emotion, except when an Indian was in sight, when an expression would appear on his face not difficult to interpret, and one that most certainly boded no good to the Indian.[7]

This is not to suggest that Clyman hated Indians, but rather he distrusted them, feeling that it was prudent to always be on guard. Seeing Wambaugh's alarm, the members of his company must have felt anxious as they advanced toward the Sioux camp.

John Richard, a short French trader, had been traveling with the Wambaugh party, according to Root, "much of the way from St. Joseph," and was returning to Fort Laramie with his wagons filled with trade goods. Richard was based near Fort Laramie and known for running whiskey and trading robes. Riley Root related that Richard had "gone ahead, arrivd at the [Sioux] band several days before us, informing them that we were coming and advising them to peace, with the expectation of receiving a gift from us as indicative of friendship." As Wambaugh's wagons neared the village, Root noted that its two chiefs were seated on the ground awaiting the emigrants, or *meneaska,* as the Sioux called them. A number of blankets were spread on the ground, ready to receive the gifts.[8]

Richard appeared to be playing the role of a peace envoy, but his motives were likely not purely altruistic. He was, after all, a trader by profession, and it was in his interest to ensure that the two cultures maintained a harmonious relationship, and that any misunderstandings or indiscretions were avoided.

While some of the emigrants may have seen these gifts as expressions of friendship, others did not and chafed at what they saw as a demand for tribute. When George

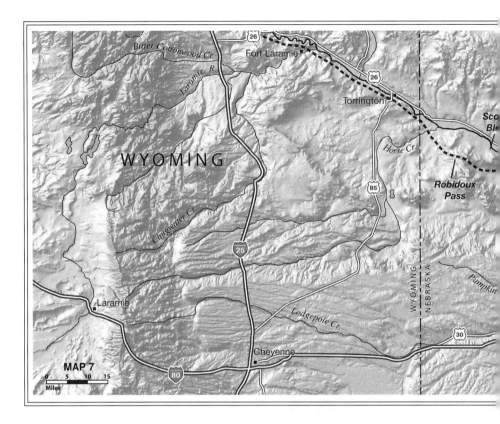

MAP 7

Curry, on his way to Oregon in 1846, paid "tribute" to a Sioux village near Fort Laramie, he expressed indignation at their hypocrisy: "Their country, forsooth! Did they not steal it from the Cheyennes, and do they not hold possession of it because they are the more powerful?"[9]

Root reported that his Wambaugh company "bestowd their gifts of flour, corn meal, beans, bacon, and every such thing, as they pleasd to give." Afterwards, the chiefs proceeded to distribute the bounty among the village's families.[10] Root noted the two chiefs' names as "Whirlwind and Badwoon." The latter was most likely Bad Wound, reported by Francis Parkman in 1846 as a member of Whirlwind's village.[11] In 1856, Bad Wound would be listed as the head chief of the Oglala Sioux by General W. S. Harney of the U.S. Army, and mentioned by other reporters as a principal Oglala chief as late as 1865.[12] Whirlwind was an older man, but must have been an imposing figure; in 1846, Parkman described him as "a tall, strong man with heavy features."[13] Whirlwind was still around in 1850, when gold seeker Walter Pigman encountered him in a camp of three hundred Sioux at Ash Hollow. Pigman claimed that Whirlwind, at 250 pounds, was the largest man he had ever seen.[14]

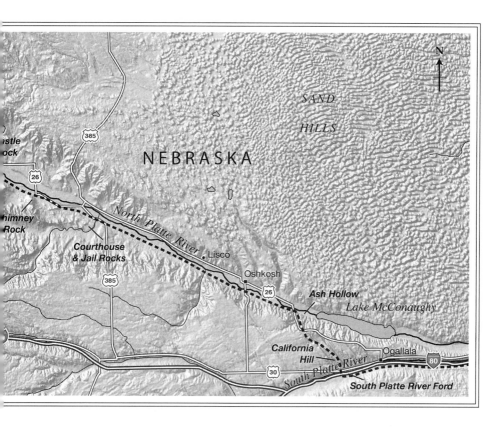

Francis Parkman first encountered the Sioux in June 1846, at a village led by Chief Smoke that was located where the Oregon Trail crossed Horse Creek, about 120 miles west of Whirlwind's 1848 camp near Ash Hollow. After receiving a law degree from Harvard, Parkman had gone west to "observe the Indian character" for a book he wanted to write.[15] He was a bright, talented writer, and his descriptions of the Oglala Sioux are unrivaled masterpieces. Of Smoke's village at Horse Creek, he wrote:

> Warriors, women, children swarmed like bees; hundreds of dogs, of all sizes and colors ran restlessly about; and close at hand the wide, yellow stream was alive with boys, girls and young squaws, splashing, screaming and laughing in the water.[16]

Parkman described the old squaws as "withered, witchlike hags," who, their beauty long gone, worked like slaves pitching lodges, catching horses, and cooking food. Young warriors strutted about naked except for clouts and moccasins and their heads shaved but for a narrow band of bristling hair along the center. Black face paint showed that they had recently taken a Pawnee scalp. They sported bullskin shields, feathered lances, strong bows, and dog-skin quivers filled with arrows. Their ponies were saddled, but in place of bridles, they tied braided ropes around the ponies' lower jaws. The best

John Mix Stanley (1814–72), *Prairie Indian Encampment*. Oil on canvas, ca. 1870. Courtesy of Detroit Institute of the Arts, Detroit, Michigan.

warriors were rewarded with the most attractive young girls, who were richly adorned with metallic trinkets and baubles that sparkled in the sun.[17] The scene that greeted Riley Root was probably much the same as what Parkman had observed two years earlier. But Parkman also foresaw the Sioux's bleak future. As an emigrant wagon train crossed Horse Creek, he wrote that it moved "in slow procession by the encampment of the people who they and their descendants, in the space of a century, are to sweep from the face of the earth."[18] Even then Parkman understood that the Sioux and their way of life were doomed.

In 1804, the Oglala branch of the Sioux was reported to number only 360. By 1825, they numbered 1,500, and in 1835 had grown to about 2,000 people.[19] The Oglala were generally split into two major bands—one led by Chief Bull Bear and the other by Chief Smoke—and each band was composed of several villages that were constantly on the move. Chief Bull Bear had led his band of about one hundred lodges from the Black Hills to the Fort Laramie plains in 1834, and was followed there the next year by the other principal Oglala band of about one hundred lodges, presumably led by Chief Smoke. Each village had its own chief, whose influence could extend beyond his village, depending on the degree to which he commanded respect. Mahto-Tatonka, or Bull Bear, was clearly the Oglalas' dominant chief at the time, but he was not well liked. He was a bully and a cold-blooded despot; whenever he fancied someone's horse or young squaw, he would simply take them and not hesitate to kill anyone who showed the slightest objection. He had more than thirty sons, some of whom were already showing their father's ruthless nature, and his power came from fear of him and his menacing brood.[20]

The year 1840 represented a turning point in the Sioux's fortunes, when the unscrupulous John Richard started the flow of alcohol among the Oglalas of the North Platte and gifts of whiskey became white traders' way of cementing trading relationships with the various bands. Trading, selling, or even giving whiskey to Indians was against the law, but the nearest authorities were five hundred miles away. Who was going to enforce the law? Alcohol was especially destructive to the Sioux, leading to bouts of intoxication and drunken brawls among warriors, resulting in killings and long-lasting feuds between families, villages, and bands.[21]

In the fall of 1841, Bull Bear visited Smoke's village, and after a round of heavy drinking, Bull Bear challenged old Smoke to fight. Knowing he would lose, Smoke refused and Bull Bear killed three of Smoke's horses. Months later, when Bull Bear and his entourage were drunk, Red Cloud, a nephew of Smoke, shot Bull Bear. The killing split the Oglala into two quareling factions and the acrimony persisted for decades. Indeed, forty years later, the two groups remained divided even as they shared a reservation.[22]

Tunica, also known as Whirlwind, succeeded Bull Bear as chief. In 1845, a war party set out to raid the Snakes (Shoshones), but the entire party, including Whirlwind's son, Male Crow, was wiped out. Enraged at the death of his son, but with his band severely weakened, Whirlwind sent a war pipe to all of the far-flung the Teton Sioux tribes, summoning them to join him in an all-out war against the Snakes.[23] Witnessing these events, Parkman wrote "War is the breath of their nostrils." In summer 1846, large war parties of Brule Sioux from South Dakota and Miniconjous Sioux from north of the Black Hills came to join the Oglala, assembling on the wide plains around Fort Laramie. Parkman was led to believe that a total of five to six thousand Sioux would eventually assemble.[24] About this time, emigrant George L. Curry noted that

> [t]he plains surrounding the fort [Laramie] were covered with the lodges of the Sioux, who were preparing to send out a large war-party against the Crows [Snakes]. There were about two thousand in number.[25]

Edwin Bryant had his own estimate when he passed through Fort Laramie that year, recording that there were about six hundred lodges and three thousand Sioux camping around the fort.[26]

Both Bryant and Parker were impressed with the appearance of the Sioux. Many observers claimed that the Sioux, taller and better dressed, were a cut above what they had seen in the Pawnees. Bryant wrote: "The men are powerfully made and possess a masculine beauty which I have never seen excelled." Parkman concurred, describing them as "naked and splendidly formed," often "over six feet tall." Bryant was especially taken by their young women, smitten by their "regularity of feature and symmetry of figure." He went on to note that the Sioux were conscious of their superior physical attributes, which made them "arrogant and exacting toward their more feeble neighbors; and have thus, probably acquired a reputation for cruelty and duplicity."

Parkman was anxious to witness their ceremonies of war and the spectacle of a great Indian battle. He chased around from village to village, sitting in Whirlwind's lodge and in the lodges of other village chiefs. For countless hours he listened as the chiefs debated, passed the war-pipe, called on the Great Spirit, drank, and quarreled about their plans, and awaited Whirlwind's instructions. This went on for weeks, for which the impatient Parkman lambasted the Sioux as being "like children that did not know their own minds. They were no better than a body without a head."[27]

The white traders, in the meantime, were vehemently opposed to an Indian war. They heavily depended on the Sioux, Snakes, and Crows to hunt buffalo in wintertime, when the dark beasts' coats were thick and shaggy, and trade the buffalo robes for blankets, tobacco, flour, sugar, coffee, and other luxuries.[28] Fearing the effects of such a war, the traders lobbied Whirlwind long and hard, and he eventually lost his zeal for war.[29] And then there was the whiskey problem. Somehow, the Sioux had come into a generous supply. "It was like a spark dipped into a powder magazine," Parkman wrote. A drunken spree erupted, and Parkman reported that the Sioux began "quarreling, breaking up and dispersing."[30] Whether it was because of the drunken brawls or because they had reached the limits of their patience, the Sioux began to return home. As the massive war party disintegrated, Parkman harshly excoriated the ditherings of old Whirlwind. The vacillating chief had "two hearts," as the Sioux would say.[31] His leadership had been discredited and his influence crumbled. Disgusted, Parkman wrote that only half a dozen lodges remained loyal and the rest removed themselves to other villages.[32] In fairness, it may have been difficult for any chief to hold such a large and disparate body of Sioux to one purpose; perhaps not even the ironfisted, despotic Bull Bear could have pulled it off.

Not only was Whirlwind's status in the tribe diminished, he was now destitute. He had purchased the support of the other chiefs by giving away all of his horses and other property. Discredited and impoverished, Whirlwind moved what was left of his followers to Horse Creek.[33] Now, in the late spring of 1848, the Wambaugh company had encountered Whirlwind and the up-and-coming Bad Wound west of Ash Hollow with perhaps as many as three hundred villagers.

On May 28, after paying their tribute, the Wambaugh company left the Sioux village and resumed their journey. They traveled another nine miles that day, and stopped to camp at a place that would be about two miles southwest of present-day Oshkosh, Nebraska. The next day, they traveled seventeen miles over a "Sandy road" and

Notice Chimney Rock in the left distance, while wagons circle into their nightly corral beside the North Platte River in the right distance. William Henry Jackson (1843–1942), *Approaching Chimney Rock*. Watercolor painting, 1931. Courtesy of Scotts Bluff National Monument, SCBL-25.

camped about a mile south of today's Lisco, Nebraska. In 1848, this section of trail was devoid of trees. Because of the total absence of wood, Root reported that they "[b]urnt buffalo excrement for cooking."[34] When traveling through areas where there was no wood, but plenty of buffalo, children were assigned the job of gathering up the dry buffalo chips in sacks or baskets or tossing them into blankets slung beneath a rolling wagon. At first, people wrinkled up their noses at the strange, foul-smelling smoke, but once they got over the thought of where the chips came from—they were just undigested plant fiber—they found them a suitable fuel. Edwin Bryant claimed they were "an excellent substitute for wood," burning with a "lively blaze," and producing "a strong heat."[35]

The Wambaugh company rolled thirteen miles on May 30, camping along the North Platte, perhaps three miles west of Lisco. On May 31, they traveled twenty-one miles and observed that the terrain was changing again. After hundreds of miles of uninspiring grassland, the land was giving way to drier, sparser vegetation. The great air masses moving eastward were forced to rise as they passed over the Rockies, cooling, condensing, and precipitating. Squeezed of much of its moisture, the drier air continued east, blowing as strong, unchecked winds. With less rain, plants like sagebrush and cacti began making their appearance. Clumps of grasses such as little bluestem, western wheatgrass, needle-and-thread, and blue gramma were replacing the big bluestem and buffalo grass of the prairie. Indeed, green grass was getting harder to find, appearing only around springs and in creek bottoms. The emigrants were moving from a landscape of greens to one of tans, and from a world of flatness to one with vertical dimensions.

The Wambaugh company was now about to encounter some astounding geological formations. Buttes of rock, sand, and clay, resembling fortresses and redoubts, were beginning to appear on either side of the trail. Aeons of wind, ice, and rain had been washing away a landscape that had been uplifting for millions of years, leaving three-hundred-foot-high formations that rose above the plain like great sentinels. Root and his party rolled by Courthouse Rock, Jail Rock, and Chimney Rock on the thirty-first, probably camping at Pumpkin Creek at the end of the day. He entirely failed to mention the first two ziggurats, but that is not unexpected. With an intervening high ridge, only their tops could be seen from the trail. One would have to leave the trail and ascend the ridge to see them in their full grandeur.

Root did comment on Chimney Rock, however, one of the great landmarks along the Oregon Trail. Indeed, there was no other feature along the trail that was more often mentioned by emigrants in their diaries than this funnel-shaped spire that jutted over three hundred feet into the sky. While many emigrants were moved to stare in awe and wonder at this needle-like formation, Root would only comment that it was "fast crumbling down."

The young Scotsman John McPherson was in Root's party, and he did not give Chimney Rock such short shrift. One of the excerpts from his journal that was later published in a San Francisco newspaper was about his visit to this landmark:

> About 10 o'clock [AM] we were opposite Chimney Rock. Curiosity being enlisted, I walked to examine it. Its formation is of sand and clay and although Geologists would no doubt take considerable interest in its examination, I confess I paid little attention to it. Standing, however, at the base of the shaft on the conical pedestal, the scene around possessed some interest. Away about three miles distant, the caravan moved slowly over the plain in one unbroken line, characteristic of military order. The Platte glittering in the sun-beams appeared to flow calmly, like an innocent boy's career, ere he has entered into the turmoil of life to mingle with the great sea of humanity. The antelope would ever and anon, bound in their gaiety over the prairie, and far away, a small herd of buffalo was seen at great speed, hotly pursued by one of the company mounted on his charger.[36]

On June 1, the Wambaugh company put in an exceptionally long day of travel. They entered a large valley, at the western end of which stood Scott's Bluff, a massive, uplifted spine of sandstone and white chalky marl. The face of its northern escarpment was high and steep, pushing hard against the North Platte River and forcing the trail to make a wide, sweeping swing along the southern fringe of the bluffs. They came to a picturesque basin that afforded a gentle passage over the bluffs, a place later called Robidoux Pass. Root wrote that they nooned there at a refreshing spring.

Again we are treated to McPherson's prose:

> About seven miles from camp, we left the river and struck into a beautiful basin, encircled by bluffs [Scotts Bluff] of the most romantic aspect. Stately towers would present their fronts on the summit of the ridge, and occasionally the remains of a dilapidated fortress, looking vulnerable in their decay. From the fissures of the hills, beautiful cedars raised their heads, green as the grass-platted earth. On an elevated point, there stood a turret from which a sentry gazed intently on the plain. . . . [A]s we were about to ascend toward the pass, the sun was descending from his meridian, appearing loath to leave the pinnacle of his glory, encircled by a luminous halo, cast his beams upon the earth, and the bluffs now envisioned by a girt of gold, looked proudly up, as they caught the reflection of the liquid fire.[37]

Clyman had been through this pass many times before. In late July 1844, while on his way to Oregon, he recorded in his journal that his party camped by the spring. He took his rifle and guarded a "Beautifull covey of young Ladies & misses while they gathered wild currants & choke cherries which grow in great perfusion in this region and of the finest kind."[38]

Although Clyman was fifty-six years old in 1848, he was still a bachelor. He may have struck up an awkward conversation with the twenty-six-year-old Hannah McCombs, one of Lambert McCombs' daughters. Sometime during this trip, a romance sprang up between this improbable couple. Hannah was regarded for her busy, helpful, capable character, and Clyman especially admired capable people. Perhaps Clyman suggested that if Hannah would like to gather a basket of choke cherries and wild currants, he knew of such a place and would be pleased to escort her there.

The James Clyman–Hannah McCombs attraction was not the only blossoming romance in the company. Tom Patton, the young teamster hired by Reverend Reuben Dickens, had developed a liking for eighteen-year-old Annie, one of the minister's daughters. And she returned his interest; they were known to have arranged surreptitious meetings at the campfire once her hawkeyed father retired for the night.[39]

Leaving the spring at what would be later named Robidoux Pass, the company of wagons continued through the basin and over the pass. The pass was named after either a son or nephew of Joseph Robidoux the founder of St. Joseph. This Robidoux would establish a blacksmith and trading post here a few months later in 1848.[40] Coincidentally, Francis Parkman had mentioned in 1846 that a blacksmith by the name of Robidoux carried on his trade at Fort Laramie.[41]

It must have been a clear day as the company surmounted the pass, as Root noted on the summit that he was able to discern the dark-shadowed form of Laramie Peak far to the west. Descending the other side, the company traveled down a "good road" that eventually led them back to the North Platte. At the end of this very long day of travel-ing thirty-four miles, they camped in a wide, lush meadow through which the clear water of Horse Creek ran swiftly. Even though Root did not mention it, travelers often cursed the thick clouds of mosquitoes that resided here.

Three years later, the meadow at Horse Creek would host a massive convention of Plains Indians. In 1851, the U.S. Office of Indian Affairs felt the need to tamp down a growing unrest and hostility that the tribes living along the trail were exhib-iting toward each other. The government offered presents to all tribes who sent del-egations to this grand council. A great throng, estimated at ten thousand—Sioux, Crows, Snakes, Cheyenne, and Arapahos—arrived and set up their lodges. Not sur-prisingly, the Pawnees declined to come. After two weeks of feasting, passing the pipe, and pledging peace, the chiefs "touched the pen" to a peace treaty between the government and tribes, then took their presents and returned home. The peace between the tribes held for all of two weeks.[42]

One observer at the council there wrote that

> a large band of Sioux Chiefs, braves and men, nearly a thousand in number, came down the Platte. . . . In the center rode their principal chiefs, who carried an old American flag, which they say was given to them by General Clark [William Clark of Lewis and Clark fame] in the early days of his superintendency.[43]

Thomas Corcoran had mentioned that when they arrived at the Sioux camp after being pursued by the Pawnees, "the Sioux were glad to receive white travelers and they hoisted the American flag on a pole." The same flag?

The following day, June 2, the Wambaugh company left their camp on Horse Creek and followed the trail along the Platte, much of it through clouds of chalky dust that enveloped the train, covering all in a thin layer of white. The river coursed between tall, stately cottonwoods, tempting the travelers to pause and sit in their cool shade. The road led through sandy hills, where, according to Root, "little grass grows except wild wormwood and prickly pear." After fifteen miles of travel, they stopped at a spot beside the river that had "plenty of wood for fuel." As they lit their camp-fires beneath the trees, and the women began boiling water for coffee and making the evening meal, the soft rustle of the leaves overhead and the sweet smell of the river's water must have been a delight to be savored. Their camp would have been about two miles southeast of today's Torrington, Wyoming.

On June 3, the Wambaugh company arrived at Fort Laramie. On that day, the footsore oxen drew their wagons up some barren hills. As they reached the summit, the view opened below to a swiftly running stream called the Laramie Fork. A wide meadow spread beyond it and on the right side of the grassy expanse, the travelers would have seen a low, clay-walled fort. But this was not Fort Laramie. The dilapi-dated, abandoned structure, originally built by trader Lancaster P. Lupton as early as

1839 or 1840, was Fort Platte, an early attempt at establishing a worthy competitor to Fort Laramie. It failed and was abandoned in 1845.[44]

Then the Wambaugh party spotted a large, adobe-walled structure built on a curve of the Laramie Fork, about a mile west of the Fort Platte ruins. This was Fort Laramie. The wagon company had traveled 570 miles during thirty-seven days of dreary solitude, and the fort must have looked like a welcome oasis, a sanctuary, an outpost of civilization. A mighty cheer must have risen from the dry, dusty throats of the Wambaugh party as the teamsters goaded their weary oxen to hurry on.

The meadow near the fort was dotted with a number of dust-covered wagons. The Wambaugh company was far from the first to arrive. The Greenwood and Cornwall parties had been here since about May 9 or 10, more than three weeks earlier. J. P. C. Allsopp reported that his group arrived at the Fort on May 31, three days earlier. There is also evidence that another party was there, but the discussion of that one will come later.

May 28–June 3, 1848
William Anderson, Miller company, west of the forks of the Platte

On May 28, William Anderson and his Miller company were still trundling along the south bank of the South Fork of the Platte, traveling fifteen miles that day. The twelve California wagons had gone on ahead, but they felt nervous. Fearing that they were too small, Anderson wrote that "travel[ing] among the Indians and having some difficulty with them they asked permission to join our company to travel as far as fort hall with us." They were accepted and Anderson reported that the Miller company thereby grew to "35 waggons 275 head of cattle 300 head of sheep and 35 head of horses."

While they traveled on the twenty-ninth, Anderson reported observing "numerous herds of buffalo." Seeing a large herd crossing the river, Anderson and seven other men

> ran down and concealed ourselves behind a little nole to wait for them to come within gunshot   they however got wind of us somehow and turned and ran back across the river agan   we ran up to the bank of the river and fired at them   they were too far off though we could see the balls splash in the watter at there heels   the buffalo made a great splashing in the watter the nois of which resembled that of some great watter fall.

More than anything else, the buffalo symbolized the Great Plains. John Bidwell described the South Forks area in 1841 as "completely clouded by these huge animals."[45] A year later, the Fremont expedition encountered the first large herds about forty miles east of the forks, which Fremont described as "[s]warming in immense numbers over the plains."[46] When James Clyman reached the forks in 1844, he "found the Buffalo in great Quantities."[47] In 1846, Francis Parkman wrote that the hills through this region were "dotted with thousands of buffalo," while another 1846 traveler claimed to have seen "millions of buffalo."[48] That man may have been exaggerating about the number of buffalo, but it was no exaggeration that the area abounded in mosquitoes and buffalo gnats. The many pools of stagnant water along the edges of the South Platte spawned immense swarms that pestered the emigrants, seeking moisture around their eyes and mouths. Edwin Bryant described their bites as terribly "afflictive."[49]

By 1848, the emigrants were still encountering great herds of buffalo roaming the plains south of the South Fork. They needed to "make meat," but they also looked forward to the hunt as an irresistibly exciting sport. Being somewhat dull-minded creatures, buffalo were not especially difficult to approach. Hunters would ride toward a herd concealed by a gentle rise, then as soon as the herd came into view, whip their fresh horses into action and dash forward, but their horses got winded rapidly. Unlike the Indians, the emigrants had not learned to gallop their ponies back and forth before coming within sight of the herd to warm them up and get them to their second wind.

Bulls, young and old, often grazed apart from the main herd and would be the first to raise their shaggy heads at the sound of the oncoming hunters. They would stare for just a moment before turning to flee ungallantly. Just beyond were the cows and calves whose tender meat the hunters favored. Closing in on the fringes of the panicking herd, the hunters would plunge into a churning current of stampeding beasts and clouds of dust to single out their targets and take their shots. Some cows would fall at once, but others kept running until their punctured lungs filled with blood and they slumped to the ground, bloody froth pouring from their mouths and nostrils. Troops of wolves always shadowed the herds, and were quick to scavenge whatever was left after the hunters had taken the choicest parts. That night the emigrants would feast on tongues and roasted hump ribs.

Buffalo hunting was dangerous, and for more than just the buffalo. Chasing hell-bent across the prairie was flirting with disaster. The plains were riddled with prairie dog and rodent holes, and creased with sudden gulches. A wounded buffalo might wheel suddenly, and charge horse and rider. Indian ponies were trained to avoid the sharp horns, but emigrants' horses were not, and many an emigrant and his horse were hurt. But some of the buffalo hunting stories were merely funny. Keturah Belknap wrote that Dr. Baker, a member of their party, was hunting when

> he jumped off and threw down the bridle to give his game another shot and away went the horse with the buffalo, but in about two weeks the company that was behind sent word to Dr. Baker that the horse had come to them with the saddle still on but turned under his belly.

William Henry Jackson (1843–1942), *Crossing the South Platte*. Watercolor painting, 1930s. Courtesy of Scotts Bluff National Monument, SCBL-23.

In his letter to his sister, Thomas Corcoran had described his own experience hunting buffalo, shortly after his party's encounter with the Pawnee. His lungs must have been improving in the drier air of the Platte River Valley.

> When we came to the south fork of the Platte River, I came across a band of buffalo and ran a calf down and caught it with my rope. Slipper [his mare] threw me and when I recovered, the buffalos were bellowing all around me. I got my horse and got safely away with the calf. I tried to bring the calf back to camp alive but it gave out on the way and I had to kill it. I tied the loins and hindquarters to the back of my saddle and struck out for camp. When I got to the South Fork, the oxen teams were already across the river. The river was a half mile wide and looked like a running sea of water. I was a little frightened for I could not swim. I ventured in and found that it did not average more than three or four feet deep, so I got to the other side safely.

William Anderson and the Miller company came to the "upper crossing" of the South Fork of the Platte River on May 29.

> May the 29th we traveled 1 mile which brought us to the [upper] crossing of the south fork of platte river which was neer half a mile wide   the bottom of this

river is verry sandy mostly quick sand which makes it verry bad fording   however we commenced crossing by putting two teams to one waggon and by the
middle of this after noon we were all a cross and but one wagon tung broke   not
knowing how far it was to watter we camped for the night (one man hated to
wade so bad that he got on his lead ox and the ox scared and threw him flat in
the middle of the river wetting him all over and filled him full of cus words but he
soon got shut of them).

Both Corcoran and Anderson described the South Platte as a half-mile wide
where they crossed. Fording a river with wagons was dangerous and had to be done
with caution. With a given volume of water, wider meant shallower and narrower
meant deeper, so wagon train fords were usually at a wide spot in the river, one with a
decent "bottom." But even at the better spots, there was still quicksand. After plunging down the riverbank, the ox drivers had to keep their frightened oxen moving forward feverishly to keep the sucking sands from swallowing up their oxen and wagons.

In 1848, the South Platte River was a half-mile wide, with no trees to speak of.
Now it is an unmemorable channel, with much of its upstream water diverted for
municipal and agricultural uses, and the narrow stream almost completely obscured
from view by a tangle of brushy willows and cottonwoods along the banks. The river
in 1848 may have been shallow, but it was often deep enough for its muddy water to
boil and swirl around the wheels. Near the middle, where the water was deepest, wagons and oxen could come dangerously close to floating, with water often rushing into
the wagon box and getting things wet. The top-heavy wagons, sensitive to gusts of
wind and changes in current, were prone to rocking precariously. Frightened women
would clutch at their children and anything else they could get their hands on, praying the unsteady wagons would not pitch them into the muddy water.

To get the wagons across quickly, the drivers had to double- and triple-team their
wagons. Then they would surround their loose livestock and force them into the water.
When it got deep enough, the animals' instincts took over, and they would begin to
swim. By the time they reached the other side, the oxen were exhausted. Anderson
reported that they pitched camp almost immediately to give the animals that afternoon and night to recruit. The matter-of-fact writings of Corcoran and Anderson did
not do justice to the danger of crossing the South Platte, and they probably understated the difficulty because it would have seemed unmanly to do otherwise.

The "upper crossing" where the Miller company forded was located about four
miles west of present Brule, Nebraska. Once the gold rush began, it later became
known as the Lower California crossing because another crossing further upstream,
near present-day Julesburg, Colorado, came into use. The new crossing near Julesburg would become known as the Upper California crossing.[50]

On the morning of May 30, the Miller company, together with the twelve
California-bound wagons that had joined them, resumed their journey. The trail now
headed north. As it left the South Platte, it ascended a steep, almost two-mile hill,

later called California Hill. Evidence of wagon ruts up this hill can be seen today north of Highway 30, and about four miles west of present Brule, Nebraska.

After the tiring pull out of the South Platte Valley, the Miller company continued another fifteen miles across the tablelands that lay between the two forks of the Platte. In that waterless, gently rolling landscape, the grass was short and thin, and rattlesnakes by the hundreds lay silently coiled along the trail, striking at the feet of the approaching oxen. The eye could look in all directions across this dreary scene and find absolutely nothing of interest except the blooming blue lupine. At last, the company arrived at the head of the large canyon called Ash Hollow. Anderson described the place as

> a deep ravine that has steep rocky cliffs on each side that rises to the height of 200 feet in the bottom of this hollow   there are a good many ash trees and bushes from which it derives its name   the river here [North Platte] is near ¾ of a mile wide.

To descend into the ravine, the wagons had to come down an abnormally steep incline, what would later be called Windlass Hill. The men had to lock all four of their wagon's wheels, while dozens of hands grabbed the taut ropes and eased the heavy wagon down. Beginning in 1849, and for the next twenty years, tens of thousands of wagons would descend Windlass Hill. The pulverizing effect of the wagon wheels and years of heavy rains eventually washed away the crumbled sand and left deep, jagged scars that remain today.

The trail continued along the bottom of the hollow for about two miles, following a marshy route along Ash Creek, a tiny stream fed by a number of cold springs. After so many miles of dry and monotonous prairie, the emigrants must have exulted in the picturesque hollow. The hollow and the many small ravines feeding into it were filled with vegetation of all sorts: grapevines, wild cherries, plums, wild currants, and gooseberries. Ash trees grew along the stream and an abundance of wild roses and other wildflowers in full bloom filled the air with their heady perfume. Scattered in the rocks above were cedars, their sweet-smelling wood available to fuel their campfires. Buffalo chips would not be needed here.

In the years to come, emigrants and gold rushers were informed that there would be no wood for the next sixty miles, so they would lay in wood at Ash Hollow. In 1854, a traveler sadly noted that the once-famed "forest of ash trees, like every other place near the road, had been stript of its wood."[51] Today, Ash Hollow has returned to its former glory; leaving it alone for the last 140 years has done wonders.

Anderson's party traveled a total of twenty miles on May 30, passing through Ash Hollow and ending the day about one mile west of it. The next morning, the thirty-first, they traversed the meadow west of the hollow and passed the spot where the Wambaugh company had encountered Chief Whirlwind's camp three days earlier, but the Sioux were no longer there.

The Miller company traveled fifteen miles along the Platte, struggling across an expanse Anderson described as "verry sandy." The horses sank fetlock deep in the sand, while the oxen strained at their wagons, their narrow wheels sinking eight to ten inches in the road. Near the end of the day, Anderson reported that his company passed an Indian village and that they camped one mile beyond it. He and some friends went to call on the village, hoping to do some trading, and learned that Whirlwind was the name of their chief. He had moved his encampment nine miles west from where the Wambaugh company had encountered it.

Anderson described his experience with the Sioux:

[May 31st] pased a sue Indian village of about 30 lodges and camped one mile above them   they swarmed around us with buffalo robes mockasons and dressed elk skin pants to trade for flower [flour] fruit and meal   for half a dozen dried apples they would give a good pare of mockasons so we carried on a brisk trade with them for about three hours   when night came on and the old chief at our request took them all back to there village they invited us to come down with them to ther village so 4 of us went with them to ther village   we went into the chief whirlwinds lodge and sat down in a circle and one of them cut up a lot of willow bark and tobacco and put it in a large pipe and smoked a puff or two and pased it round   ther lodges are made of poles and dressed buffalo hides   they have some 15 or 20 poles 15 feet long stood up on end with the tops tied together and the skins sewed to gether so that when they are pulled down over the poles they will be stretched tight and then fastened down to the ground with small stakes and a trap door at the bottom and a small hole at the top for the smoke to escape.

David Presley, his wife, and their twelve children were traveling with the Miller company. The story is told how the Sioux squaws were especially drawn to their son Ransome, an adorable little boy with light, curly locks and deep blue eyes. The squaws brought ponies to the family, offering to swap them for the child.[52]

It was hard to find an emigrant family that didn't have at least one dog with them. The dogs were frequently troublesome and could just as easily provoke a stream of curses as they could praises. Francis Parkman remarked how the Sioux villages were filled with "hundreds" of them,"[53] so one can easily imagine the Indian dogs encountering the emigrants' pack of canines. How could it not have produced a melee? And who would have dared intervene? Oddly, not a single 1848 diarist mentioned such matters in their jottings.

When the sun rose on the morning of June 1, Anderson and his company pulled out, leaving Whirlwind's village behind. The old chief would die, presumably of old age, about three years later.[54] According to Anderson, "several white traders" and their "two wagons . . . loaded with buffalo robes" left the Sioux camp and joined his company as they continued west. This was probably John Richard and his confederates. They must have remained with the Sioux after the Wambaugh company had moved on.

Both Edwin Bryant and Francis Parkman mentioned Richard in their 1846 chronicles. Richard operated a small trading post called Fort Bernard that was located about eight miles southeast of Fort Laramie, sheltered beneath a canopy of cotton-woods growing along the south bank of the North Platte River. Calling it a fort seems ludicrous; both Bryant and Parkman described it as a dismal compound of rough logs; Bryant called it "inferior to an ordinary stable."[55] It burned down in the winter of 1846/47, and no diarist will mention the structure in 1848 when passing the location.[56] As for Richard himself, Parkman described him in 1846 as "a little, swarthy, black-eyed Frenchman . . . athletic . . . vigorous," wearing a deerskin frock, leggings, and moccasins, with black, curling hair falling below his shoulders.[57] Emigrants usually recorded his French name phonetically as "Rashaw," "Reshaw" or "Risaw."

After leaving Whirlwind's camp on June 1, Anderson wrote that his company traveled fifteen miles, then camped beside the North Platte at a spot that was likely four miles west of present-day Oshkosh, Nebraska. Anderson wrote that they passed a spring-fed creek after traveling six miles on June 2. After another nine miles, they came to another creek, probably Pumpkin Creek. They had now entered this country of strange and mysterious formations. They stopped

> opposite a solitary wall or as it is sometimes caled the cort house rock   its about 5 miles from the river   it has the appearance at a distance of some great build-ing with a great many windows and doors in it   on the east side of this there is a nother smaler one which has the appearance of an outer building.

After variously calling it McFarlan's Castle, Parker's Castle, and Castle Rock, emigrants finally seemed to settle on calling it Courthouse Rock.[58] Anderson's description suggested he had ridden over the intervening ridge to see it in its entirety. It was common to misjudge its distance in the clean, dry air, so emigrants frequently left their wagons and took a lazy stroll over the ridge to examine the massive bastion more closely. After failing to come appreciably closer after an hour of hard trudging, many returned to their wagons in discouragement.

Anderson reported passing another Indian village on June 2:

> [W]e gave them some presents such as flower and meat, and pased on   we also saw a company of these Indians moving ther lodges   they fastened there long poles to each side of ther horse leaving one end to drag on the ground then these they tied there baggage and young ones   there dogs were loaded in the same manner.

Not only did the Sioux use their dogs as beasts of burden, they also used them as an emergency food supply. Dogs were valuable in converting excess or unwanted buffalo meat. When the Sioux ran short of buffalo meat, they could always eat their dogs. In fact, boiled puppy was considered a special delicacy.[59]

The Anderson party traveled sixteen miles on June 3, and stopped to camp opposite Chimney Rock. This fragile finger pointing heavenward had inspired thousands of passersby to write about it, from early fur trappers in the 1830s to emigrants traveling by as late as the 1860s. Projecting about 350 feet above the surrounding plain, it was, technically, not even a rock. It was primarily made of hardened sand and clay. Some diarists in earlier years had expressed concern that the thin upper section looked precarious and unstable, and they were right. Sometime in 1849 it was struck by a bolt of lightning, and the topmost thirty feet came crashing down. Another six feet of the pinnacle came tumbling down years later when it was blasted by another bolt of lightning.[60]

With some daylight left, Anderson wrote that "4 of us two boys and two girls concluded we would take a walk out to the chimney rock and look at it." They found the distance deceiving and it was dark by the time they got there. They carved their names in the soft material at its base, then returned to camp, not arriving until ten o'clock. It was a long walk, according to Anderson, but "pretty good exercise after driving an ox team through the dust all day." Anderson's adventure with another man and two girls may have been prompted by geological curiosity, but it would be naïve to assume that single emigrants were uninterested in the opposite sex. Even at the end of a long day of travel, they might find the energy for courting.

Late May 1848
Keturah Belknap, Watt company, along the Platte River

Ever since Keturah's Watt company had encountered Joe Meek and his men about May 9, her diary had fallen silent. Perhaps it was the rigors of the trip or the burdens of her pregnancy or both. When they neared the Platte River, they were entering Pawnee country, and Keturah finally managed an undated entry:

> This is the 4th week we have been on the road and now we are among the Pawnee Indians so we must get into larger company so we can guard ourselves and stock from the prowling tribes and renegade whites that are here to keep away from the law. They seem to have their eyes on a good horse and follow for days then if they are caught they will say they got them from the Indians and by paying them something they would give the horse up, then try to make us believe that they were sent out to protect the emigrants.

Keturah did not mention any encounter with the Pawnees, but she brought to light a little-reported fact: some of the frontier's most disagreeable and dissolute characters were white men who lurked just beyond the settlements, out of reach of the law, yet close enough to bedevil and prey upon the emigrants.

Richard Cheadle wrote that somewhere along the Platte River his Watt company was traveling in close proximity to the Walker, Bristow, and Purvine companies.[61] William Porter recounted a story years later that Watt's sheep were spoiling the grazing for the cattle, so the companies insisted that Watt keep his sheep behind them. Porter wrote that someone taunted Watt by leaving him a message penciled on a buffalo skull posted beside the trail for him to read when he passed by: "Watts and his sheep, going to pasture / Says Watts to his sheep, can't you go faster?"[62]

Keturah's next entry was not dated, but it dealt with their passage along the South Fork of the Platte. She described the danger that large buffalo herds posed to wagon trains.

> [W]e have to keep out an advance guard to keep the [buffalo] herd from running into our teams. The road runs between the bluff and the river and it is just the time now when the buffalo are moving to the river bottom for grass and water. A herd passed us a few days ago; the guard turned them so they crossed the road behind us.

After grazing all day on the waterless plains above the bluffs, the thirsty buffalo returned to the river in the late afternoon, often at stampede speed. If a wagon train happened to be between them and the water, the thundering herd could easily crash through a line of wagons, leaving destruction in its wake. It wasn't just the damage that the emigrants feared; their own loose livestock were inclined to run off with the stampeding buffalo, as if they preferred the company of their free-ranging brown cousins.

May 28–June 3, 1848
William Porter, Purvine company

On May 28, William Porter and his Purvine company were about six days and 105 miles behind the Wambaugh company, and were about three days and fifty-five miles behind Anderson's Miller company. They were also about a day and twenty miles behind the Walker-Bristow company. At this point, Purvine might have moved ahead of the Watt company. On that day, William Porter reported seeing his first buffalo along the Platte River. On the twenty-ninth, he mentioned passing "through a large [prairie] dog town and saw forty or fifty buffalo." After making eighteen miles that day, they camped near the forks.

The Purvine company traveled another sixteen miles along the south fork on May 30 and camped. "Water but no wood, except the buffalo chips which are very plentiful," Porter wrote. He mentioned seeing "plenty of buffalo today." On May 31, they traveled fifteen miles, and Porter recorded that "I saw hundreds of buffalo and I killed one which is the first that has been killed in the company. It was a young cow and eats excellent."

William Porter was not the first to praise the fine, naturally salty taste of buffalo meat from a fat cow or heifer. Edwin Bryant agreed, writing that their meat was
"superior to our best beef." Years earlier, fur trappers had learned that females were
fat as a result of grazing on the lush spring grass. The bulls, on the other hand, were
sexually active at this time. In trying to breed females in heat and fending off the
challenges of other bulls, they spent so little time eating that their meat was lean,
dry, and tough.[63] Porter also observed that when they encountered buffalo meat left
behind by other hunters, the hot sun had seared the surface, leaving the meat inside
"sweet and good."[64]

––––––––––––

Fremont's 1845 *Report* addressed the dramatic reduction in the buffalo herds. He
remarked that between the years of 1824 and 1836 one "would be always among large
bands of buffalo" between the Missouri River and the Rocky Mountains.[65] By 1842,
he noted that "the buffalo occupy but a very limited space, principally along the eastern base of the Rocky Mountains." A partner in the American Fur Company advised
Fremont that during the previous eight years (1834 to 1842), the American Fur Company, Hudson's Bay Company, and a few smaller enterprises shipped a combined total
of 90,000 buffalo robes annually, and 800,000 buffalo hides were shipped during
those eight years. Fremont was quick to add that the hides came from thick-coated
cows killed during the cold months of November through February, and he estimated that hunters removed hides from only one-third of all females killed. Indeed,
the total number of buffalo killed during the decade, he concluded, was "immense."[66]
John Bidwell had seen a grim future for the buffalo as early as 1841, warning that they
"are fast diminishing. If they continue to decrease in the same ratio that they have
for the past 15 or 20 years, they will ere long become totally extinct."[67] Edwin Bryant
expressed the same concern in 1846, describing the buffalo as "a retreating and fast
perishing race."[68]

Bidwell had mentioned that the Indians "behold with indignation the shameful
and outrageous prodigality of the whites who slaughter thousands merely for their
robes and leave the meat." But the Indians were not completely innocent bystanders.
Lured by white traders offering trade goods and trinkets for buffalo hides, the Indians often killed more buffalo than they needed for meat, and took the extra hides to
the traders. Between the white and red hunters, tons and tons of meat were being left
to spoil in the sun.[69]

When the 1848 emigrants encountered John Shaw's party and their twenty-two
wagons, they were witnessing firsthand the immense quantities of buffalo robes and
tongues still leaving the prairie. Riley Root could see that "the country is drying up
and buffalo becoming less abundant." When Root arrived at Fort Laramie, the fort's
bourgeois, or manager, told him that the American Fur Company alone had shipped
over 80,000 buffalo robes out of the West in 1847. From all sources, 110,000 robes

were shipped to St. Louis that year, a staggering confirmation that the slaughter continued unabated.[70] The 1848 overland emigrants would not have played a significant role in reducing the buffalo herds. The trail touched the main buffalo range for scarcely one hundred miles, and the wagon trains passed through within the space of a month; thus, the numbers they killed were truly insignificant.[71] As for the future, however, swarms of gold rushers and professional buffalo hunters would cause the great buffalo herds along the forks of the Platte to eventually vanish.

Returning to William Porter, he recorded that June 1 was a "very cold and windy day." During the day's travels, his company leaned into a bitter wind. By the end of the day, they had made only fourteen hard-won miles and must have pulled close to the warmth of their campfires that night. According to Porter, their camp was "near the crossing," and he estimated that they had traveled 430 miles since leaving St. Joseph.

Porter wrote little about the next two days, except that after traveling three miles on June 2, they "crossed South Fork without any serious accident." Once the emigrants crossed the South Platte, they left the big buffalo herds behind. On June 3, they rolled the twenty-mile distance across the high prairie and made it to Ash Hollow, where they set up camp beside the North Platte River.

MAY 28–JUNE 3, 1848

Edward Smith, Smith party, near the forks of the Platte River

Back on May 28, Edward Smith and his small party were drawing near the forks of the Platte:

> sun 28— this morning is quiet   cool wind from the northwest started at 5 and traveled until ½ half past 6 and encamped on the Bank of the River supposed to be the lower end of Brady Island   we saw 5 Buffalo on the Prarie   Dr. Atkinson went out to kill one and was drove in by the Pawnee Indians.

If they camped at the lower end of Brady Island, as Smith recounted, their camp would have been about three miles south of the present community of Brady, Nebraska.

The Smith party returned to the trail early on May 29. Three hours later there was a cry of "Indians!" Apprehensively, they reached for their guns and circled the wagons. Much to their chagrin, they discovered that the approaching images were nothing more than five oxen and two cows that had strayed from a company ahead.

On May 30, Smith reported quarreling in his party, but he did not give a reason. It could have been anything. The crushing effect of exhausting days, piled one-on-one, must have made it difficult for people to remain civil with each other.

Smith wrote that at noon on the thirtieth "we see 3 horsemen coming towards us   they proved to be Capt. Bristow and two men the owners of the cattle." This revealed that the Walker-Bristow company was not far ahead. Smith went on to explain that a herd of buffalo had stampeded the Walker-Bristow livestock and caused twenty-five of their wagons to run. The Smith party ended the day "about 2 miles below the junction of the north and south forks of the Platte River." William Porter had reported that his Purvine company camped about sixteen miles up the south fork on the thirtieth. Richard Cheadle had written that his Watt company had "formed a connection" with the Walker and Bristow companies between the Blue and South Platte. All of this suggests that the Walker-Bristow, Purvine, and Watt companies, representing over seventy wagons, were probably all traveling together, and were one day ahead of Smith at this point.

The following day, May 31, Smith and his companions traveled sixteen miles, and camped near the lower crossing of the south fork, a mile or two south of present-day Hershey, Nebraska. He complained of "innumerable swarms of Buffalo" near their camp, and of suffering through "a severe gale accompanied with thunder and lightening" that night.

On June 1, Smith and his companions continued up the South Fork:

> the Buffalo continued in sight all day, about noon I went back to bring up my dog which had staid   I saw many Indians   I found a steer   he and four Buffalo were coming to water   the Buffalo stoped on the hill   the steer came down and I drove him about 8 miles to the wagons.

The next day, June 2, Smith continued to travel with a segment of the original Kelly company. They traveled about ten miles and then camped beside the river, where Smith complained about "mirriads of Musketoes." He reported that they "overtook the Bristow co." here, and he was probably referring to the combined cavalcade of Walker-Bristow, Purvine, and Watt.

Smith and his party traveled four miles on June 3, then crossed the south fork of the Platte at the "upper crossing." At one o'clock, they left the ford and proceeded the fifteen-mile distance to Ash Hollow and the North Platte. We have already learned from Porter's diary that his company crossed the South Fork the day before. By the end of the third, there must have been a rather large collection of wagons—probably over a hundred from the Walker-Bristow, Purvine, Watt, Smith, and Kelly parties—all camping in the vicinity of Ash Hollow.

MAY 28–JUNE 3, 1848
Father Lempfrit, Stone company, somewhere north
of the Little Blue River, Nebraska

Lempfrit's diary entries rarely provided mileages, so it is difficult to know precisely where he and his company were on May 28, except that they had not yet reached the Platte River. He wrote that he said Mass in his tent on Sunday the twenty-eighth, then traveled "through enchanting country." Nearing the Platte on the twenty-ninth, he recorded making twenty-five miles that day, "without finding a single drop of water." When they stopped to camp, he saw "some lovely mountains in the distance." He was referring to the low range of sand hills that rose up just before the trail dropped into the Platte River Valley.

Lempfrit's company spent a "dry" camp on the night of May 29 on the divide between the Platte and the Little Blue. The next morning, the thirtieth, he complained that their "animals are dying of thirst." The incorrigibly impatient priest was determined to hazard another jaunt by himself, and he again rode ahead on his pony. Ascending to the summit of the sand hills, he wrote that he then gazed upon "one of the most beautiful panoramas I have seen in my life. With the help of my spyglass I discerned the lovely banks of the River Platte." The wagons from the Stone party soon caught up to him and they descended to the river, where their thirsty livestock could finally drink. Since there was no wood along the river, the company spent the night without a campfire.

When Lempfrit's party commenced their journey up the Platte the following day, May 31, the priest wrote that near noon,

> someone came galloping up to fetch me to come to the aid of the Captain's son who had fallen from the waggon. He said the boy had broken his legs. I take off at a gallop and reach a spot near where the people were gathered together. I examined the injury. Luckily no bones were broken, it was the tendons that were hurt. I think my patient is now all right.

On June 1, Lempfrit complained of a difficult night:

> It has been stormy the whole night. A violent wind prevented us from sleeping. Several of our people are sick from having drunk bad water. Going ahead, I saw a little wolf [coyote] that alarmed my small pony. Shortly afterwards, I see two Indians coming towards us, carrying guns. They were hunters. I gave them my hand and one of them pressed it against his heart. I gave them some tobacco. . . . The same day we see a large buffalo. One of our men goes ahead to kill it. He misses his shot, and then we noticed that there were more of them lying down behind the one who was keeping watch.

Cold, wet weather was taking its toll on the travelers. Filthy water teeming with nasty microbes, spoiled food, and dirty cooking utensils frequently led to diarrhea, or "watery bowels," as some emigrants were inclined to describe it.

Lempfrit's company traveled along the Platte on June 2 without incident. Another storm arrived that night, causing him to be "awakened at the moment when our tent was about to be carried off by the violence of the wind." He made no entry on June 3.

MAY 29–JUNE 3, 1848

Richard May, Chiles company, at Little Sandy Creek, Nebraska

On May 29, the Chiles company was lagging far back. They were about eighty miles behind the Stone company. "[L]ay by all day," Richard May wrote on the twenty-ninth, "in consequence of an express coming on [from Major Hensley] to Capt. Childs desiring to stop a day or two until they could overtake him."

On the thirtieth, the Chiles company continued twelve miles up the trail and camped again on the Little Blue. "We saw several antelope yesterday and today," May wrote, "but our sharp shooters could not take them with their rifles." He recorded that his three yokes of oxen had strayed "forward on the road 7 miles again." Blaming his lead ox, May decided to stake him at night, hoping that would cure the problem.

The Chiles company traveled about ten miles on May 31, after which May recorded his impressions of the country through which they had passed the previous days:

> The landscape on the [Little] Blue River is delightful, the lowlands being as level as a bowling green and as rich as could be wished. The high prairie is undulating and every way calculated for agricultural purposes. . . . In traveling up [the Little] Blue River in all the branches we crossed emptying into it we found coarse sand and gravel and seldom any water in them. The prairie all the way to this point is handsomely decorated with wild flowers which would give a botanist employment and diversion. The dull monotony of a prairie journey is quite tiresome, it being so very uniform that the variety we seek is nowhere to be found. The crack of the whip the clanking of the chains and the still more disagreeable shriek of wagons is all that the sense of hearing conveys to the mind. Now and then the lark and quail will give you one of their best and sweetest notes to cheer you while journeying in these endless prairies.

May noted that his company finally left the Little Blue on June 1, and began crossing the divide between it and the Platte. It would be a day of disagreeable weather:

> It has been a blustering day, the wind blowing a strong gale and rained in the evening. I find by experience that it requires some knowledge of cattle to get along in a train. An experienced driver has less difficulty than those unacquainted with the business of driving. Our traveling community are all cheerful and in a good humor this evening although several tents were blown to the ground. We number, men women and children, 112 and of that number these are 37 men and we are in hourly expectation of being overtaken by a train of 18 wagons and 12 men with pack mules [Major Hensley's company].

After traveling twelve miles on the first, the Chiles company camped on the plain about four miles after they had left the Little Blue. On June 2, they completed their excursion across the divide and ascended to the rim of the sand bluffs above the Platte River. At the summit of the bluffs, May remarked how they could see "the river very distinctly for many miles to the right and the left." After completing a day of traveling fourteen miles on June 2, they finally came to rest beside the Platte at a place where May estimated that Grand Island was two-thirds below their camp and one-third above it.

May reported a memorable event the next day:

> 3rd of June. We traveled about 12 miles … we passed 4 companies of the Oregon Battalion. They were laying off a fort, the point being selected heretofore. The tended field in the open prairie had quite an imposing appearance. The train of government wagons, 23 in number, 12 of which were employed in transporting artillery and the fixtures belonging to the camp. … I have lived to see one Pawnee Indian. He came into camp this morning begging something to eat. We fed him and no doubt he would steal all my property tonight if he could. The fort spoken of is to be called Childs.

The Chiles party was passing through late enough to witness Lt. Col. Ludwell Powell arriving with 175 troops from the First Missouri Volunteers, also called the Oregon Battalion, to begin building Fort Childs. Within months, the fort, built on land purchased from the Pawnees for $2,000 in trade goods, would be renamed Fort Kearny after the recently deceased General Stephen W. Kearny.[72] The new fort would try to keep Pawnees from harassing the flood of gold rushers who would travel up the Platte River in the years to come.

Table 7: Location of companies on the evening of June 3, 1848

Company (Diarist)	Location
Greenwood	at Fort Laramie
Cornwall	at Fort Laramie
Allsopp	at Fort Laramie
Wambaugh (Root)	at Fort Laramie
Gates	near Scotts Bluff
Miller (Anderson)	at Chimney Rock
Walker	at Ash Hollow
Purvine (Porter)	at Ash Hollow
Watt (Belknap)	at Ash Hollow
Smith (Smith)	at Ash Hollow
Kelly	at Ash Hollow
Stone (Lempfrit)	along the Platte, somewhere below the forks
Chiles (May)	just west of Fort Childs (Fort Kearny)
Hensley	just behind Chiles
Lassen	traveling with Chiles or Hensley

CHAPTER 10

Come, Come Ye Saints
MAY 26

MAY 26, 1848
Mormons' Winter Quarters, north of present-day Omaha, Nebraska

The Mormon wagon train departing the Council Bluffs area on the morning of May 26, 1848, was a marvel of organization, meticulously divided into companies of hundreds, and led by captains of hundreds, fifties, and tens. Angling their wagons up the bluffs, they headed west toward the Platte River, finally on their way to the Promised Land—Zion, as they called it. Above the clanking of chains and the huffing of straining oxen could be heard a chorus of voices singing "Come, come ye Saints, no toil nor labor fear." They were in a jubilant mood, as well they should. At last, they were pulling away from Winter Quarters, a pit of privation and wretchedness that had sorely tested their mettle, and shaking themselves free of two dreadful years along the Missouri River.

No story about the overland emigration of 1848 would be complete if the Mormons were ignored. They—at least some of them—played a significant role in the overland emigration of 1848, especially for those bound for California. We therefore need to take a backward glance at what brought the Camp of Israel to the Council Bluffs area in the first place.

In 1831, the Mormon Prophet Joseph Smith Jr. established their New Jerusalem near Independence, Missouri, declaring it to be the site of the original garden of Eden. Hostile mobs soon drove them out, and they resettled in Daviess and Caldwell Counties, Missouri, where, according to Smith, Adam and Eve had lived after being expelled by God from Eden.[1] But in 1839 the Camp of Israel was again driven out by mobs and forced to move. Settling in western Illinois by the Mississippi River, they began building their holy city, Nauvoo.

For the next five years, the Mormons were pretty much left alone. Unhindered, they organized like an industrious hive of bees, working with one mind to build fine houses, establish productive farms, and construct a splendid temple made of white limestone blocks.[2] But they seemed to eventually irritate their non-Mormon neighbors and wear out their welcome. There was something about them that made Gentiles uncomfortable. Perhaps it was what was seen as a heretical religion or strange practices, or a holier-than-thou smugness. But more than anything else, it seemed to be their practice of polygamy.[3] Nothing could stir up shocked whisperings more than this titilating practice of having multiple bed partners.

Not only did people come to disapprove of the Mormons, they came to fear them. As a large, centrally directed body, the Mormons could wield great political and economic influence, and they often did. When their leadership told them whom to vote for, they did so obediently. They conducted commerce in much the same manner, often buying and selling in large quantities. They could influence trade, crush competitors, and affect markets. In short, they were inclined to make enemies, and soon became targets for those who reveled in the ugly sport of bullying and terrorizing. Militias and night-riding mobs attacked them, ran off their stock, and set fire to their houses, barns, and haystacks. But the Mormons would not take it lying down. They formed their own militias and struck back, beginning a period of endless recriminations and counter-recriminations, reprisals and counter-reprisals.[4]

Shortly before their leader Joseph Smith was murdered in a Carthage, Illinois, jail in 1844, he was already thinking that his Saints would have to move again. Even though he had once declared that Israel's Promised Land was in Missouri, and later declared that it was really in Illinois, he admitted that God's ways were mysterious, and by 1844 he was again declaring that it was really somewhere else. By February 1844, the Prophet's mind had already flown to the Far West. Smith told the Quorum of the Twelve Apostles that they should send parties to California and Oregon to have a look around. They even considered Texas. They must find a place, he said, "where the devil cannot dig us out," or, as Brigham Young later expressed it, a place where they would "not be likely to be infringed upon."[5]

In order for this embattled religious sect to survive, they would need far more than plans on where to move the church—they would need strong, smart leadership. Even though forty-five-year-old Brigham Young was the senior member of the Quorum of Twelve, Joseph Smith's murder opened a door to a number of rivals, each claiming visions or revelations that proved that God had anointed him as Smith's successor. A destructive struggle for leadership began to infect the congregation and fracture the fragile church. James J. Strang emerged as a strong candidate, with a substantial following.[6]

Just when it seemed that chaos would prevail, Brigham Young suddenly underwent a transfiguration in the eyes of a majority of the church's leaders. He now looked bigger and stronger, and sounded wiser, and so they confirmed him as the new president of the Camp of Israel. Once it became clear to Strang that he had been rebuffed, he left the church in a huff and took a couple of thousand church members with him to Wisconsin.[7]

What at first seemed misfortune was really a blessing, for in losing Joseph Smith this precarious church gained Brigham Young. To get these beleaguered people through the next couple of years required a genius of organization with lion-like strength and temperament, traits that Young possessed. By the summer of 1845, there were an estimated 17,000 Mormons living in and around Nauvoo. Knowing they would have to leave soon, the church leadership decided to send a party of three thousand men and their families (approximately 12,000 persons) to upper California the following spring.[8]

During the fall of 1845, the Mormons began to prepare in earnest for their western exodus the following year, but fate did not give them that much time. In the face of growing pressure from their enemies, the Quorum of the Twelve Apostles proclaimed that the Saints would abandon Nauvoo as soon as the grass began to grow, hoping that this would stay their enemies until they were able to depart the next spring.

First, they had to sell their fixed property—farms, houses, and shops—often getting only ten cents on the dollar. They also began building and acquiring the implements of emigration: wagons, oxen, mules, horses, and supplies. They cut and dried oak for wagons, soaked hickory in brine for their axles and wagon bows, and harvested hemp along the river to make miles and miles of rope. They hammered at their forges and anvils, producing chains and iron wagon wheel tires by the thousands. The women busied themselves sewing wagon covers, tents, clothing, and flour sacks. An inventory of their progress taken on November 23, 1845, disclosed that about 1,500 wagons were completed and almost 2,000 more were in various stages of completion.[9]

In the meantime, the church leadership continued to debate where they would go. In an October 1845 letter to the brethren, the Twelve suggested they were considering Vancouver Island along the Pacific. By December, they had decided to send an advance party to prepare the way "in some good valley in the neighborhood of the Rocky Mountains." Then rumors began spreading that the Mormons' enemies were planning imminent arrests or assassinations of the Twelve. In a panic, the Twelve Apostles met on February 2, 1846, and agreed that they could not wait until spring. The exodus had to begin at once even though they were not fully ready to leave and had not decided where in the West they would go.[10]

On February 4, the first families began lining up to cross the Mississippi River. Wagons loaded to the brim with furniture, books, tools, and food crowded at the landings. Such haste to leave meant that many were ill-prepared and under-provisioned. Flatboats, scows, and skiffs began ferrying people, wagons, and livestock across the mile-wide river. As they made it to the other side, they moved to a camp about seven miles west of Nauvoo, in a grove of timber on Sugar Creek.[11] Waiting for further instructions, they huddled around blazing fires and brooded beneath their blankets. For many, this had been the fourth time in fifteen years that they had been uprooted from their homes.

It took weeks to get all the people, wagons, and livestock across. At first, the weather was uncommonly mild, but then the temperature plummeted. It got down to twelve below one night, and the river froze with ice two-and-a-half feet thick. For a while, a mass of Saints and their wagons and belongings could cross on the ice.[12] By February 17, about two thousand Saints had collected at the Sugar Creek camp. On that day, the Lion of the Lord mounted his wagon in the middle of the camp, and addressed his people:

> All the Camp of Israel . . . we have called you together this morning for the purpose of giving you some instructions with regard to the order and organization of the camp. . . . It takes a long time to move so large a body of people as this. It will not do to start off helter-skelter without order and decorum—if we should but few would reach the place of destination . . . we will number Israel and organize them into companies of tens, of fifties, of hundreds and place captains over them. . . . We do not intend to make a great many laws or bye laws to violate but we will have order and will not suffer men to run from one wagon to the other.[13]

Despite Young's moving speech, he let his people continue to shiver at the Sugar Creek campground while he waited for more to cross the river. It was not until March 1 that he finally gave the signal for the first wagons to begin the slow and difficult crawl across four hundred miles of frozen Iowa landscape. Wagon companies moved out in stages, and the raw, bitter cold gave way to incessant rain that fell nearly every day for eight weeks.[14] Wagons stalled in the thick mud, forcing them to double- and triple-team their yokes of oxen. Creeks and rivers raged. Five miles might be a good day's travel; sometimes they only made one. Rain soaked through wagon covers, and tents blew down as the pegs would not hold in the soft ground. Shoes and clothes didn't dry out for days on end. Often camping far from wood, they were forced to eat cold food and sleep in wet clothing on soaked bedding.

A string of permanent camps, with such names as Garden Grove and Mt. Pisgah, were established along the trail as way stations to help those behind. A large number of Saints stopped at them simply because they could go no further across what Young described as a "great mud hole." The endless rains, the constant exposure, the always-wet clothing, and months of slogging through the thick, foot-sucking muck, took their toll. Scores came down with colds, diarrhea, whooping cough, and pneumonia; some were so utterly exhausted and sick that they lay in their wagons and died. Despair curdled into bitter complaints and tempers erupted into violence. The spirit of sharing or giving aid to their brothers and sisters began to dry up.[15] The Iowa trail would forever be remembered as the Mormons' *via dolorosa*, their road of sorrow. And more and more Mormons continued to pour across the Mississippi.

On June 2, the leading companies, consisting of about five hundred wagons, picked up an Indian trail and followed it to the Missouri River, arriving at the Missouri on June 13. It had taken four months to travel four hundred miles—a snail's pace of less than three miles per day, and a reflection of the difficulty of the trail and the exhaustion of man and beast. Although they could rejoice at having arrived at the Missouri, they had been terribly worn down from their long journey.[16]

Coming to the edge of the bluffs overlooking the Missouri, the advance party gazed down upon a quarter-mile-wide river, and a wide, grassy floodplain of the Council Bluffs area. They sought out Peter Sarpy at Trader's Point below Bellevue and inquired about the use of his ferry, the only one in the area. They talked with him about Indians and the overland trail west to the Rocky Mountains. With more than two thousand wagons to ferry across, one at a time, the river crossing was going to take a very long time.[17]

It had been Brigham Young's original goal to have his people reach the Missouri River by April, and proceed to the sanctuary of the Far West by year's end. But it was obvious now that to go all the way into the West this year was unthinkable. The church leadership conferred and decided that they had to stop, regroup, and lick their wounds. They would have to spend the rest of the summer settling people in camps along both sides of the river, and build winter-tight shelters, plant fall crops, and cut prairie grass to feed between 10,000 and 30,000 head of livestock during the coming winter.[18]

As more and more wagons showed up at the Missouri, camps sprung up at every suitable location, near wooded creeks and springs, often within sight of Pottawat-tamie Indian villages. The federal Indian Intercourse Act of 1834 expressly prohib-ited whites from entering and occupying Indian lands unless properly licensed by the Office of Indian Affairs.[19] The Mormons, thousands of them, with huge numbers of wagons and tens of thousands of head of livestock, were on Indian land illegally, a problem Young would have to deal with.

Young forbade his people to come in contact with the Indians. And he admon-ished them, at all costs, to avoid intentional or inadvertent insults or offenses, but to "hold their tongues" in their dealings with any non-Mormons.[20] Since Mormons car-ried a deep bitterness toward Gentiles, a moment of weakness could too easily erupt into incendiary words. Young's policy was one of silence; he and his designees would do the talking.

Young met with the local Indian agent and assured him that the Mormons' pres-ence here was strictly temporary. To demonstrate his intention of moving on, Young continued to ferry Mormons across the river, using Sarpy's ferry at Trader's Point to convey wagons and families, while they swam their livestock across. In the mean-time, Young ordered the building of a larger ferry a few miles farther upstream. It wasn't just that Sarpy's ferry was too small; with what he charged, he would have drained them of their scant funds.[21] By June 29, the Mormons completed a large ferry capable of carrying two wagons at a time. But still, the movement of so many people and wagons across the river would take time.

Back in Washington, DC, President Polk had his hands full. Congress had authorized war against Mexico, but rumors were flying within the War Department that upwards of 10,000 Mormons were headed for California or perhaps Oregon, or both. The department was alarmed at the prospect of this religious sect helping the Mexicans defend California or helping Great Britain hold the Oregon country, or both.

With a shrewdness few men could match, Brigham Young had taken steps, even before they left Nauvoo, to capitalize on Washington's uneasiness. He had to engender sufficient fear in Washington to elicit an offer of government help in exchange for the Mormons' loyalty, but he dared not overplay his hand. If he generated too much fear, he could risk being attacked by the U.S. Army. In late January 1846, Young dispatched Jesse C. Little as his envoy to Washington, authorizing him to tell President Polk that Mormons were available to build forts and bridges, establish ferries, haul freight, or even serve in the U.S. Army against Mexico or Britain. But the offer contained a carefully worded threat:

> [We] are true-hearted Americans . . . and have a desire to go under the outstretched wings of the American Eagle. We would disdain to receive assistance from a foreign power . . . unless our government shall turn us to be foreigners. . . . [I]f I cannot get it in the land of my fathers, I will cross the trackless ocean where I trust I shall find some friends to help.[22]

Colonel Thomas Kane, a non-Mormon who was sympathetic to the Mormons' plight, volunteered to act as an agent for Mormon causes. As a son of a close friend of the president, Kane was granted a meeting with Polk and he "told him all." He let it be known that he had seen a letter in which the Hudson's Bay Company, a British trading firm in the Oregon country, was offering assistance to the Mormons, and hinted that the Mormons had been invited to settle on Vancouver Island.[23] Polk must have shuddered. Whether he liked the Mormons or not, he had to prevent that from happening. He asked Kane to return to Council Bluffs at once and see what could be done to keep the Mormons loyal. At the same time, he got his cabinet to authorize Colonel Stephen Kearny, commander of Fort Leavenworth, "to receive into service as volunteers a few hundred of the Mormons who are now on their way to California."[24] Kane arrived at Fort Leavenworth in mid-June carrying Secretary of War W. L. Marcy's dispatch to Col. Kearny:

> It is known that a large body of Mormon emigrants are enroute to California for the purpose of settling in that country. You are desired to use all proper means to have a good understanding with them, to the end that the U.S. may have their cooperation in taking possession of, and holding that country. . . . You are hereby authorized to muster into service such as can be induced to volunteer; not, however, to a number exceeding one-third of your entire force.[25]

In turn, Kearny dispatched Captain James Allen to travel to the Mormon camps on the Missouri to "endeavor to raise from among them four or five companies to join me in my expedition to that country." His plan was to take the Mormon units with him to Santa Fe, then on to California. On July 1, 1846, Captain Allen arrived at the Mormon camp and met with Young and other church leaders. Young could have jumped at Captain Allen's request, but he displayed reluctance at first. He needed government permission for his Saints to winter on Indian land on both sides of the river and he intended to bargain for it. Although it was beyond the scope of his authority, Allen gave Young the permission he requested.[26]

Young knew he was going to have a difficult time getting the support of his people. He would have to deal with men like Lucious M. Scovil, who still seethed from the federal government's inaction when mobs and militias were tormenting the Saints in Missouri and at Nauvoo. In April 1846, Scovil had written that "I disdain this government as I do the gates of hell . . . I desire to see this government go to the shades of oblivion." Most Mormons were incensed at the notion of helping the United States government, while others were simply leery that this was a government subterfuge. Hosea Stout wrote in his diary that he suspected Captain Allen's visit was nothing more than a pretense to spy on the Mormons' size and strength.[27]

Nevertheless, Young persuaded the Twelve Apostles that the government's offer was a godsend and should be accepted. And why wouldn't he feel that way? It had been his idea after all to send Jesse Little to plant this seed in President Polk's head. The arrangement would address a number of problems. First, it gave Young leverage to get government permission for the Mormons to overwinter on Indian lands. Second, he was still thinking about settling in California, where there would be a great benefit in already having a large group of Mormon men there to prepare for them. Third, the church and its people were impoverished, and this was a way to get five hundred men fed, clothed, and transported to California, all at government expense. Fourth, each recruit would be paid for his service, and Young planned to collect their pay and bring it back to Council Bluffs to purchase food. According to Young's calculations, it would be a goodly sum, about $50,000. Last, it gave Young an excuse as to why the Saints would not reach the Rocky Mountains by the end of 1846, as he had promised.[28]

Recruiting five hundred men was not going to be easy. When Young first asked for volunteers, he got only a handful. So he resorted to threats: he would send old men and women if he must. Three weeks later, he had finally secured five hundred able-bodied "volunteers."[29] On July 21, 1846, this newly formed Mormon Battalion, accompanied by a few women as laundresses, marched out of camp and headed toward Fort Leavenworth. They had been assured by Young that their families would be well cared for. Parley Pratt followed closely, sent by Young to collect the men's first pay as soon as they received it.[30] A few members of this Mormon Battalion would later play a dramatic role in the discovery of gold in California and pioneer a new way over the Sierras, an improved route that some of our 1848 California emigrants will follow.

As the Army of the Lord marched out of sight, Young breathed a deep, unwinding sigh of relief. He could now turn to other pressing matters, the first of which was to get the Saints situated in suitable quarters for the winter. Sarpy's ferry and the Mormon-constructed ferry were both running night and day, continuing to move people and wagons to the west side of the river.[31]

By the end of July 1846, thousands of Mormons had managed to ferry to the west side of the Missouri and were now encamped there. Although Captain Allen had told Young that the government was agreeable to the Mormons' remaining on the west side of the Missouri temporarily, the land belonged to the Omaha tribe. Young understood that he needed to strike an agreement with the tribe as well. A council was held on August 28, 1846, between the Mormon leaders and Big Elk, the principal chief of the Omahas. The Mormons sought permission to stay for up to two years. Big Elk saw benefits in the arrangement. His tribe consisted of only a few hundred families, having been decimated by a succession of smallpox epidemics and the ravages of alcohol. To make matters worse, they were frequently attacked by the Pawnee and Sioux, their longtime enemies. Big Elk thought the presence of the Mormons would help keep these raiding parties at a distance, and he received assurances from Young that the Mormons would not kill much of their game. He and the "Big Red-headed" chief, Brigham Young, concluded their agreement, shook hands, and passed the peace pipe.[32]

Although a number of temporary camps had been set up, the church leaders wanted to consolidate their winter quarters into one large camp that would be close to the river. On September 11 the Twelve decided on a spot eighteen miles upriver from Bellevue. In Mormon fashion, they laid out the new site on paper: a grid of broad, straight streets that created five-acre blocks, each divided into twenty lots. After selecting their lots, families began building their shelters. They ranged from elaborate, two-story log cabins with plank floors to small, dirt-floored shanties. The more unfortunate created shelters by digging caves into the bluffs' steep embankments. But they ran into problems. Due to the scarcity of bricks and stones, few built fireplaces or chimneys, and many cabins would fill with smoke, forcing them to cook outdoors. When the heavy rains came, torrents of water gushed down the slopes, often flooding the dirt-floored cabins.[33]

Where once there had been a grassy meadow, by the end of December there were shelters of different sizes and shapes, and in varying degrees of completion. Winter Quarters now consisted of 538 log cabins, 83 sod shanties, and 3,483 inhabitants. While much had been accomplished to prepare for winter on the west side of the Missouri, Young still had to worry about those east of the river. Conditions were growing more desperate for the 1,000 to 1,500 Mormons who had not yet left Nauvoo. They tended to be the old, sick, and feeble, those who had no one to look after them, and those who were so poor they had no means to leave. And there were also the stubborn who refused to sell their farms or houses to the Gentiles for a pittance. While those remaining in Nauvoo had become a source of vexation for Young, they were not the only ones he had to worry about. There were the multitudes stranded in smaller camps and settlements strung along the Iowa trail. Some had stayed at these way stations to help refugees yet to come, but now they themselves needed help. Many others, too worn out or discouraged to go any farther, had stopped at other places to overwinter. Almost any grove or glen where there was water and a supply of wood had become a place to hunker down. So desperate were their needs that these people became an albatross around Young's neck. He could neglect them no longer, so he sent parties eastward to rescue the "poor camps."[34]

With four thousand at Winter Quarters on the west side of the river, about 2,500 in various camps and settlements on the east side at Trader's Point and its immediate vicinity, and four hundred camping on the Niobrara River, it is estimated that about seven thousand Mormons spent the winter in and around the Council Bluffs area. Coupled with those hunkered down along the Iowa Trail and those still at Nauvoo, there were about twelve thousand Mormons at about eighty different locations strewn across the landscape, trying to survive the winter and awaiting Young's next orders.[35]

It was not long before starving Omaha children came into Winter Quarters begging for food, and the hearts of many Mormon women were moved to pity. But Young was firm; the people must leave the Indians alone, and above all, they must not give them "ardent spirits." He was afraid that intermingling could eventually lead to an incident that could jeopardize their temporary sanctuary.[36]

For good reason, the Omahas lived in constant fear of the Sioux and Pawnee. The Sioux had recently attacked a village of Omahas sixty miles north of Winter Quarters and had killed seventy-three. In another incident, a Sioux war party attacked some Omahas within gunshot of Winter Quarters. Young warned his people to stay out of their conflicts and not take sides. But compassion made noninvolvement difficult, as the Mormons sympathized with their Indian hosts. One Mormon was moved to write, "the sufferings of these poor miserable beings was immence and excited the sumpathey of our people."[37]

Although the Omaha were a quasi-agricultural people who raised corn, beans, melons, and squash, they ordinarily sent hunting parties each summer three hundred miles west to hunt buffalo along the Platte River, even though they were vulnerable to attack from the Pawnee and Sioux. But with the Mormons living nearby this year, the Omaha braves discovered the Mormons' docile, four-legged creatures grazing in the vicinity and soon the Indians were "killing two or three oxen per day." In answer to the Mormons' complaints, Big Elk responded: "[T]hey [my braves] are just like the wolves of the prairie for when they are hungry they don't know better than to take what is handiest." Eventually, a meeting was called regarding the depredations and the mounting friction between the two groups. The Mormon High Council's minutes recorded Big Elk's complaint:

You cut hay but people must buy it if one wants to warm . . . you can take our wood . . . eat up our grass kill our game scare it away come to live where we used to hunt . . . [we] must not kill your cattle but our game all scared away.[38] You cut hay but people must buy it if one wants to warm . . . you can take our wood . . . eat up our grass kill our game scare it away come to live where we used to hunt . . . [we] must not kill your cattle but our game all scared away.

As tensions with the Indians increased, the church leadership suspected John B. Miller, the Indian subagent for the Pottawattamies, and R. B. Mitchell, the Bellevue subagent for the Omahas and Otoes, were behind it. They were certain that the agents were anti-Mormon bigots who were inciting ill feelings among the natives.[39]

And there were other ill feelings—those held by virtually all non-Mormons. Most believed that the Mormons were trespassers and interlopers, with no legal right whatsoever to inhabit Indian lands. A group of Missourians wrote a letter to President Polk in July 1846, complaining of

a set of men denominating themselves Mormons hovering on our frontier, well armed, justly considered as depredating on our property, and in our opinion, British emissaries, intending by insiduous means to accomplish diabolical purposes. . . . [W]e consider it the duty of our common American father . . . to take the necessary measures to disarm and expel them from our border.[40]

Although the Mormons had assured the Indian agents that their occupation was temporary, their lack of definitive dates and plans for departure led the agents and their superiors to be distrustful of their real intentions. In the Office of Indian Affairs in Washington, DC, Commissioner William Medill worried that the Mormons' stay might not be so temporary and instructed his St. Louis–based superintendent, Thomas Harvey, to pay them a visit.[41] While Harvey had been led to believe that the camps were being built on the east side of the river only, he was astonished to find a camp being established on the west side, on Omaha land, and was amazed at its size and appearance of permanency.

During his visit, Harvey complained to Young that this settlement was being built illegally, without the permission of the Office of Indian Affairs and in clear violation of the Act of 1834. Brigham answered that Captain Allen, a representative of the president, had given them permission, and that the Indian chiefs had consented to their stay as well. Harvey had not been aware of Captain Allen's permission, but he pointed out that the army did not have the authority to grant such permission. An angry Young insisted that the Mormons had a right to be there and he "would not be neither drove or pushed."[42]

Harvey was furious too. His report to Commissioner Medill, describing the Mormons' settlement and Young's intransigence, caused a great rumble to reverberate among various branches of government.[43] This would not be the last Young would hear about this, and he knew that forces were growing against their presence. He sensed an urgency to get on with their westward migration as soon as spring weather would allow, but for now, he had no choice but to get his congregation ready for winter.

The members of the Mormon Battalion received their first pay in August at Fort Leavenworth. Each was paid $42 in clothing money or, as Young had calculated, about $21,000 total. Parley Pratt, whom Young had sent to collect it, managed to come back with only $5,835. The men giving it stipulated that it was to go to their families. Young was outraged at their paltry contributions. He was determined to spend it for the benefit of all and leaned heavily on the families to whom the contributions were sent. He managed to pry $4,400 loose, arguing that the Saints were in this together and the money had to be consecrated for the use of the camps as a whole.[44]

The battalion money, together with contributions from others, was used to buy goods and groceries in large quantities and at wholesale prices in St. Louis. "[W]e will make every dollar sent us count as good as two or three at ordinary traffic," Young explained. On the arrival of over sixty tons of supplies from St. Louis, a store was opened and the goods were sold to the people at a markup that was explained as necessary to create profits that would pay for the cost of a flour mill they were building nearby. Many grumbled, however, especially the families of the Battalion members, believing church leaders were lining their pockets.[45]

Young's agents continued to follow the Mormon Battalion to Santa Fe to collect from their next payday. Largely because many of the men's wives had written letters complaining about what had happened to the first collection, Young's agents only managed to collect $1,277 this time. With winter now upon them, the Camp of Israel faced daunting trials. They had insufficient food and supplies, and those who had enough were asked to share with those who did not.[46] While this brought out the best in some, others murmured that they were having to share with wastrels who had foolishly squandered their food.

Because the amount of money collected from the battalion at Fort Leavenworth and Santa Fe was such a huge disappointment, the Mormons resorted to other resources. They had large numbers of cattle, which allowed them to trade beef to the Indians for buffalo robes and deerskins from which they could make clothing. The women formed work groups to make baskets out of willows and some of the men made tables, which they traded for grain and other needs. Necessity trumped principle and men were sent downriver to find work among those cursed Gentiles, building fences, painting buildings, clearing stumps, and threshing wheat on the farms of many "Missouri Pukes."[47]

Disease became a heavy tax on this uprooted church. Before the onset of winter, the mosquitoes were so thick along the Missouri Bottoms—or "Misery Bottoms," as they often called it—that they would totally encrust a horse's neck. The mosquitoes were good at spreading malaria and other diseases among the people. As the winter progressed, they ran out of vegetables and had to survive on coarsely ground flour and beef. The freezing weather killed the mosquitoes, accounting for a sharp drop in viral and bacterial diseases, but the people began to experience scurvy and other afflictions brought on by bad nutrition.[48]

There were many deaths in the Mormon camps, a disproportionately high number of them being children and infants. With sickness and death all around, the dark-spirited John D. Lee wrote in his diary in early March 1847, that this was a "time of deep affliction and sore lamentation with this people, for daily more or less of them are consigned to the tomb." By the time the Mormons finally abandoned Winter Quarters in June 1848, it was estimated that one thousand had died, a death rate of about one in twelve.[49]

Brigham Young tried to keep news of their sufferings from leaking to the outside world, not wanting to give that apostate James Strang anything to gloat about. Further, Young feared that news of their misery would filter back to the East Coast and England and would discourage prospective converts and emigrants.[50] Sensing the gloom into which his people had sunk, Brigham Young had to periodically refresh his flock's spirits with dramatic exhortations, perhaps needing to exhort himself as well. On April 16, 1847, he wrote,

> We are willing to take our full share of trouble, trials, losses, and crosses, hardships and fatigues, warning and watching, for the kingdom of heaven's sake; and we feel to say; Come, calm or strife, turmoil or peace, life or death, in the name of Israel's God we mean to conquer or die trying.[51]

But not all of the Saints were calmed, reassured, or inspired by Young's words. The complaints and grumblings kept coming, especially the particularly persistent complaint about how Young had grabbed away much of the Mormon Battalion's pay. One disgruntled Saint wrote that the money was "clinched by these vultures to enable them to live in affluence and splendor."[52]

With a view to mollifying the most disenchanted members of the congregation, Young called a meeting in November 1846. He sensed the need to respond to an epidemic of denunciations, restore their confidence in his leadership, and reassure them that their leaders had good plans for their future. He told them of his dream about the Rocky Mountains, that they would soon "go in safety over" them.[53]

During the course of their winter miseries, the church leadership continued to meet and debate where they would take their people. They had to get them out of there before the angel of death got them all or U.S. soldiers came to drive them out, but they still did not know where their new Zion would be. So they studied their maps, reread Fremont's book, and conferred with trappers and traders who knew the West. The one they talked to the most was veteran fur trader Peter Sarpy, interrogating him about his many trips into the Rockies and the Great Basin.[54]

The Twelve Apostles also conferred at length with Father Pierre-Jean De Smet, the Belgian missionary who had spent many years among the Indians of the West.

"They asked me a thousand questions," the priest related, indicating that they seemed most pleased with his account of the Great Basin.[55] By now, the Mormons had crossed Oregon and California off their list, realizing that those regions would eventually fill up with the hated Gentiles, but they dared not let word of their destination escape their small circle. They had five hundred Mormon soldiers on their way to California, and did not want such news to reach and dishearten those poor souls. They also didn't want the soldiers' families grousing that Young had sent their loved ones off on a wild goose chase. And then there was the U.S. government. Young was certain that, so long as he expected that thousands of Mormons would soon arrive in California, the president would have reason to stay on good terms with the Mormons on the Missouri.

By January 1847, Young and the Twelve Apostles had developed a plan for an advance party of companies to leave in the coming summer. Comprised of the most able-bodied men and their families, augmented by some widows, orphans, and battalion families, it would be led by captains of hundreds, fifties, and tens. This meant that the sickest, poorest, and least well-connected families would have to stay behind to spend another winter, underprovisioned and among what they felt was a tribe of begging, pilfering Indians. And it was this group that expressed their displeasure.[56]

But Brigham Young was tired of nagging Saints. According to John D. Lee's journal, Young erupted:

> You poor stinking curses, for you are cursed and the hand of the Lord shall be upon you and you shall go down to hell for the murmuring and bickering. This people means to tie my hands continually as they did last year so that we can't go to the place of our destination. They are already coming to me saying can't you take me along? Don't leave me here, if you do I am afraid I shall die, this is such a sickly place. Well, I say to them, die, who cares?[57]

Despite Young's outburst, he and the Twelve altered their original plan. The advance party would be cut down to only able-bodied men: carpenters, millwrights, and farmers. Brigham Young and most of the Twelve would lead 144 men and boys, three women and two children, seventy-two wagons, sixty-six oxen, ninety-three horses, fifty-two mules, nineteen cows, some chickens, and seventeen dogs. The first of this pioneer party left on April 5, 1847. When they arrived at their destination, wherever that might be, they were to lay out a city, plant crops, and begin construction of dwellings and flour and saw mills, all to prepare for the families that were to soon follow.[58]

After a somewhat easy, uneventful trip up the Platte River and Sweetwater River valleys, the party reached the Continental Divide at South Pass on June 27, 1847. Here, they encountered the inimitable Black Harris, who was returning to the States. The crusty former trapper knew the Rockies as well as anyone, so they asked where they should go that would be best for farming and settling. Imagine Harris stroking his bushy, coal-black beard and gravely pondering the question. According to Mormon William Clayton, Harris opined that the Cache Valley would be best.[59]

Leaving Harris, the pioneers continued on. At Little Sandy Creek, about twenty miles beyond South Pass, the party encountered another legend of the Rockies, Jim Bridger. "Old Gabe" had been a trapper ever since the 1820s and was a former companion of such mountain legends as William Sublette, James Clyman, Jedediah Smith, Thomas Fitzpatrick, and Joseph Walker. His trading post, Fort Bridger, lay about 130 miles farther on, and he may have been even more informed about all the nooks and crannies of the Rocky Mountains than Harris was.

The company examined Bridger intensively, while the company clerks took exhaustive notes. Bridger spoke most favorably of the Sevier Valley in central Utah and the Bear River Valley in today's Idaho. He was not particularly encouraging when asked about the Salt Lake Valley, saying it was too cold to grow corn. William Clayton expressed frustration at Bridger's "imperfect and irregular descriptions," perhaps because they had plied him with too much liquor.[60]

On the Green River, about three miles above the Big Sandy River, the party next encountered fellow Saint Sam Brannan. At Young's instruction, Brannan had taken a group of Mormons by ship from New York City to California. When they arrived in San Francisco Bay on July 19, 1846, they found the adobe hamlet of Yerba Buena under American control. After settling his people, Brannan hurried east to find his brethren so he could proclaim what a wonderful paradise they had found.[61] But Brannan's exuberance for California proved its final kiss of death. That was exactly what Young wished to avoid, explaining that he did not want to lead his people to a place that would soon fill with Gentiles.

In the end, Young decided on the Great Salt Lake Valley. They arrived there on July 30, 1847, and work crews began laying out and building Zion. Young returned east to meet the first westbound wagon companies that had already left Winter Quarters. The party of 1,700 people would join the pioneer party in the Salt Lake Valley in a few months and help establish a community that would be ready to receive more Saints, including the group that would come in the spring of 1848.

This brings us back to the large wagon train leaving Winter Quarters on May 26, 1848. It was led by Brigham Young himself and consisted of 397 wagons and 1,229 persons. Two other Mormon wagon parties would leave later that year, one on May 29 with 226 wagons and 662 persons, and another on June 30 with 169 wagons and 526 persons. A total of 2,417 Mormon emigrants would go west in 1848 to join the 1,800 Saints who had preceded them to the Salt Lake Valley in 1847.[62]

Even after the Mormon wagon companies of 1848 left Winter Quarters, many thousands still remained behind in the Council Bluffs area.[63] Generally, they were the ill, the impoverished, and those with less influence. They had been told to remain there another year, or more, until the Salt Lake settlement was sufficiently well-established to support them. Despite their grumblings, this group obediently stayed, prepared to languish even longer at that dismal place. In the years to come, the Council Bluffs area would continue to be the place where most Mormons, from far and wide, would set out on their journey to the Great Salt Lake Valley.

CHAPTER 11

The Babylon of the West
JUNE 3–17

JUNE 3, 1848
Thomas Corcoran and Caleb Greenwood,
on the plain beside Fort Laramie, Wyoming

On the afternoon of June 3, the Greenwood and Cornwall companies had been at Fort Laramie for about three weeks. It is interesting that P. B. Cornwall, who had been so eager to begin his journey early, languished at Fort Laramie for so long. His zeal for haste may have been dampened by his experience with the Pawnees and by Joe Meek's chilling reports of Indian uprisings farther west. Or perhaps the Kelloggs, concerned about the safety of their families, had insisted on waiting until a large Oregon-bound company came along.

With time on their hands, it would not be surprising if Thomas Corcoran had listened to Caleb Greenwood spin a few yarns. The old mountaineer was famous for his stories and it was easy to get him started. At eighty-five years of age, it was remarkable that Greenwood was still living. Many trappers and mountain men had not survived, often because of bad luck, but more often than not, the survivors were stronger, tougher, smarter, and more careful that those who hadn't made it. Greenwood's survival through decades of blizzards, starvation, grizzly bears, and Indians had earned him legendary status.

The old mountain man's face was largely hidden behind a flowing white beard, while his long white hair, greasy and tangled, hung from beneath a mangy wool cap. His tanned buckskins shined with a black luster that came from the hot drippings of years of elk, bear, and buffalo fat.[1] He would have likely recounted his early years as a trapper and his later years as a pilot for wagon parties going to California. If he had mentioned traveling with a party to California in 1844, Thomas' eyes surely would have lit up. His interest in the Murphys was more than casual. The two families had emigrated from Ireland in the 1820s and had settled in Frampton, Quebec, where Thomas Corcoran and Daniel Murphy had received their first communion together.

It was because of the Murphys that the Corcorans moved to Irish Grove in Missouri, and it was likely because of them that Thomas chose California as the place for his lungs to heal.

"Did you encounter the Murphy family?" Thomas may have asked. "Yup," Caleb would have confirmed; he had indeed traveled with them to California. "And Ellen Murphy?" Caleb's twinkling eyes and toothless smile would have said it all. "Yup," he might have croaked. "Pretty as paint, she was. . . . Pretty as paint."

The conversation might have broken off when the men, squinting into the distance, noticed a cloud of boiling dust on the low bluffs to the southeast. Then riders on horseback appeared, followed by the dull gray of a dusty wagon cover, then another and another, as a long line of wagons descended the hills. It was the Wambaugh company arriving at Fort Laramie.

June 3–15, 1848
Riley Root, Wambaugh company, Fort Laramie, Wyoming

Riley Root's journal entry reported that his Wambaugh company traveled seventeen miles on June 3 over "a good road," and had rolled past Fort Laramie and established their camp on the plains about one mile west. There are a number of trails over the bluffs leading to the fort. It is difficult to know which trails existed in 1848, and which the Wambaugh company used, but the train would have come across a series of low hills, then made a rapid descent to the Laramie River below. John McPherson's description of the Wambaugh company's arrival was one of the excerpts published in the *Californian*:

> About 3 o'clock . . . on descending a hill, we arrived in view of Fort Laramie. With the bleak hills by which it is encircled, and the impetuous Laramie Fork of the Platte, rolling at their base, and sweeping by the fort, it possessed considerable interest. This stream is very rapid, but we were fortunate to have crossed without accident. Fort Laramie is situated on the left bank of the above named stream, which runs in a serpentine course for a considerable distance through as bleak and sterile a region as can well be imagined. . . . Scarcely a stinted shrub can be seen upon the hills. On the banks of the stream tho' the eye alights on groves of Cotton-wood, whose green leaves tremble in the breeze, throwing an air of animation over the otherwise desolate and lifeless scene.[2]

Although McPherson mentioned cottonwoods, he called the area "bleak and sterile," and "desolate and lifeless." In the fourteen years since the first stockade was erected, countless trappers, traders, emigrants, and Indians had been cutting down trees for construction and firewood. Today, cottonwoods and willows again grow in a thick band along the fringe of the great meadow and populate the borders of the Platte and Laramie Rivers (both much narrower now).

James F. Wilkins (gold rusher), drawing of Fort Laramie, 1849. Courtesy of Wisconsin Historical Society, WHi-3935.

The temperamental Laramie Fork was unpredictable. If the river was running low, it was a cinch to wade. But if heavy rains had recently visited the mountains above, the river could be a raging monster—as much as two hundred yards wide, deep, ice cold, and swift and turbulent. When the river was in that condition, many people drowned and many animals and wagons were swept away when they foolishly tried to cross. It was best to wait a day or two for the torrent to subside. From McPherson's account, it sounds like the Wambaugh company found the river in one of its middling stages—dangerous, but survivable.

Fort Laramie was built on a tongue of river bottom, a grassy plain between the junction of the North Platte River and the Laramie Fork. It was a historic crossroads and strategic location toward which travelers naturally gravitated. It had everything a traveler could want: grass, wood, and clear water. And it was along the trail back to Missouri. It was a popular place for Indians, trappers, and traders to periodically congregate, communicate, recreate, and intoxicate.

The first to make a written description of the location was Robert Stuart in 1812.[3] William Sublette and Robert Campbell recognized it as an ideal place to establish a trading post, and in 1834 their men chopped down hundreds of cottonwoods, sank the logs upright into the ground, and formed a rectangular stockade they christened Fort William. The American Fur Company purchased the fort in 1836 and renamed it Fort John, but almost everyone insisted on calling it Fort Laramie.[4] In the years that followed, the post became a major center where Indians and trappers came in large numbers to trade buffalo robes and furs for blankets, guns, powder, lead, tobacco, and other dry goods.[5] But the soft wood of the palisades began rotting almost as soon as they were planted in the damp ground. By 1841 the company was forced to rebuild the fort. They brought Mexicans up from Santa Fe who built in the style they knew best—with adobe blocks. The new fort, 125 feet wide and 150 feet long, was constructed on higher ground, two miles above the Laramie Fork's junction with the Platte, and one mile west of the original stockade.[6] Standing high and majestic, the new fort stuck out as quite extraordinary in the barren landscape. The new adobe fort had barely been completed and occupied when Captain Fremont visited in 1842:

> [The fort] is a quadrangular structure, built of clay, after the fashion of the Mexicans, who are generally employed in building them. The walls are about 15 feet high, surmounted by a wooden palisade. . . . There are two entrances, opposite each other . . . one of which is a large and public entrance; the other smaller and more private—a sort of postern gate. Over the great entrance is a square tower with a loophole, and, like the rest of the work, built of earth. At two of the angles, and diagonally opposite each other, are large square bastions, so arranged as to sweep the four faces of the walls.[7]

Fremont praised the fort's "white-washed" walls and commended its very "clean appearance." But, of course, it was only a year old then.[8] James Clyman passed this place many times from 1825 through 1827, before any fort existed. When he arrived at the fort on his way to Oregon in 1844, he did not remark in his journal how dramatically the location had changed in the seventeen years since he had last passed through. He seemed impressed, however, with the fort's "white Battlments." Departing two days later, he recounted how he "soon lost sight of the white washed mud walls" of this great adobe fortress.[9]

Although beaver trapping had declined dramatically by 1848, there were many white trappers in the Rockies who traveled to the fort in June and July to trade, resupply, and have fun. Each time a group of trappers arrived, they would celebrate with a "blow out," as Francis Parkman called their nights of revelry and carousing. The riotous, drunken sprees were stoked by kegs of Taos Lightening brought by traders from New Mexico and sold for four dollars a pint, and the night echoed with the sounds of swearing, shouting, and fighting. The next morning, clumps of stuporous men with "swollen eyes, bloody noses, and empty pockets" lay sprawled within the walls of this Babylon of the West.[10]

As soon as the last adobe brick had been laid in 1841, the effects of rain and snow had begun deteriorating the mud blocks. By 1846, both Edwin Bryant and Francis Parkman were describing the walls only as sun-dried bricks of clay.[11] Neither they nor any of the 1848 diarists mentioned the walls as "white-washed." Gold rusher J. Goldsborough Bruff wrote in his journal on July 12, 1849, that the fort, now eight years old, "has suffered much from time and neglect."[12] Eastbound Mormon William Kelly paused at the fort on May 28, 1849, and described the fort as a

> wretched reality—a miserable cracked, dilapidated, adobe, quadrangular enclosure, with a wall about twelve feet high, three sides of which were shedded down as stores and workshops . . . propped all around on the outside with beams of timber, which an enemy had only to kick away and down would come the whole structure.[13]

Francis Parkman's description of an emigrant wagon train arriving at the fort in 1846 was probably typical. Parkman wrote that, as the wagon train appeared in the distance, the fort's deputy *bourgeois* (manager), James Bordeaux, grabbed his spyglass and watched the wagons "steadily advancing from the hill":

> They gained the river, and, without turning or pausing, plunged in, passed through, and slowly ascending the opposing bank, kept directly on their way by the fort. . . . [G]aining a spot a quarter of a mile distant, they wheeled into a circle. For some time our tranquility was undisturbed. The emigrants were preparing their encampment; but no sooner was this accomplished, than Fort Laramie was taken by storm. A crowd of broad-brimmed hats, thin visages, and staring eyes, appeared suddenly at the gate. Tall, awkward men in brown homespun; women with cadaverous faces and long lank figures, came thronging in together, and, as if inspired by the very demon of curiosity, ransacked every nook and corner of the fort. . . . The emigrants prosecuted their investigations with untiring vigor. They penetrated the rooms, or rather dens, inhabited by the astonished squaws. Resolved to search every mystery to the bottom, they explored the apartments of the men. . . . Having at length satisfied their curiosity, they next proceeded to business. The men occupied themselves in procuring supplies for their onward journey; either buying them, or giving in exchange superfluous articles of their own.[14]

Some of the roofless cells that lined the interior of the fort's walls were living and sleeping quarters, others were storerooms. And then there was the all-important blacksmith shop. The interior courtyard was divided roughly in half, one side of which was used to keep the American Fur Company's small herd of horses, mules, and cattle at night after they had spent the day grazing on the adjacent plain.

Riley Root penned his own description of the fort, its inhabitants, and surroundings:

There is nothing interesting about the fort. It is built of sun-dried bricks, with timber sufficient to support the bricks and form the doors and windows, and done in the coarsest manner. Within this wall, which is about 12 or 14 feet high, are the dwellings and other necessary rooms for the accommodation of the fort. Within this area, also stands a large rude press, for pressing robes and peltry for market. In another apartment is a yard for horses and cattle. What is most attractive is, within these dwellings can be seen the white man and the rusty-looking Indian woman, living lovingly together, whilst the little papooses are playing together happily. Without these walls are seen no appendages. The eye can rest on nothing all around but a dreary waste.

Root was describing the company employees—clerks and others—usually of French blood, who had taken Sioux wives. The immense open plain around the fort was often covered with throngs of Sioux, and their lodges, horses, and dogs, much like when Colonel Kearny and his troops were there in 1845, or when Bryant and Parkman came in 1846. There must have been very few Sioux on that day in 1848, as Root would surely have mentioned such a spectacle. Curiously, Root entirely failed to note the Greenwood, Cornwall, or Allsopp parties, which were likely camping somewhere near when his party arrived. His observation that the area surrounding the fort was a "dreary waste" corresponded with McPherson's description of its being "bleak and sterile." Root and McPherson also viewed the company's long-haired employees similarly. McPherson wrote,

> Fort Laramie is occupied by the servants of the [American Fur] company, principally Canadian French who, of all others, are the best adapted for trading with the rough tribes with whom they have intercourse.... [They are] happy with their squaws and yellow offspring. They appeared to take great pleasure in guiding us through the fort, which appeared simply to consist of small square rooms, capable of affording scanty accommodations for themselves and [their] squaws.[15]

The Wambaugh company lingered at the fort for three more days. During that time Root described them as busy.

> [June] 4th, 5th, and 6th—Staid at the same place [Fort Laramie], and shod several oxen, which had become lame by traveling. However, as the road some of the way after that, provd worse than any we had passd, and our oxen not becoming lame by traveling over it, we concluded that their lameness must be attributed in part to the alkali over which they so frequently passd. The fort has a blacksmith shop and some few tools. For the use of which our company paid 7 ½ dollars for one day and a half.

After traveling more than five hundred miles since leaving St. Joseph, most recently over sand, gravel, and alkali, many of the Wambaugh company's oxen had limped up to the fort. Besides shoeing the sore-footed animals, the emigrants would need to replace oxen that had died or strayed, or were too lame for simple shoeing. The company kept a supply of extra oxen, often acquiring the seriously lame ones for next to nothing. After a year to heal while grazing on the adjacent plains, the oxen could be sold or traded to any desperate emigrant who was prepared to pay dearly.

The blacksmith shop was important for more than shoeing horses, mules, and oxen. Wagons old or new, ruggedly or shoddily built, were showing the effects of thousands upon thousands of jarring bumps along the trail. The blacksmith shop would have rung with the sound of pounding and clanging as emigrants crowded around the forges, taking off loose iron tires, cutting and heating, and then snuggly resetting them on shrunken wheels.

When the Wambaugh company arrived at the fort on June 3, there must have been a flurry of visits with the Greenwood, Cornwall, and Allsopp parties who were camped somewhere near. After a few handshakes, the newcomers were likely invited to sit down and have a cup of coffee. They shared gossip, exchanged news, swapped stories, and discussed their concerns and plans for moving on. The upcoming route through dangerous Crow and Snake country must have been discussed, especially among the guides. Certainly, James Clyman and Caleb Greenwood must have met and talked. Clyman knew the old man, in fact, knew him well. They may have first become acquainted when both were trappers in the 1820s. Then in 1844, Clyman traveled west with the Nathaniel Ford company at the same time Greenwood was traveling to California with the Stephens-Townsend-Murphy party. There is evidence that the two companies traveled together for a period of time.[16]

In the spring of 1846, Clyman and Greenwood both traveled with Lansford Hastings' eastbound party. The soon-to-be-infamous Hastings, acting as "pilot," had already published his *Emigrant's Guide to Oregon and California* in 1845. It was an encyclopedia of ignorance and falsehoods, the most dangerous of which was recommending a shortcut across the Great Salt Desert, a route he had not even tried.

According to Clyman's journal, there had been a great deal of argument within the 1846 Hastings party over whether to try this frightening route across the Salt Desert. Because the Greenwoods were heading east "to catch emigrants," it did not fit into their plans. He and his sons left the Hastings party and turned north on the trail to Fort Hall.[17] Somewhere east of Fort Hall, the Greenwoods met a party of emigrants and were hired to take them to California. The rest of Hastings' party, including Clyman, left the Humboldt about nine miles west of today's Elko, Nevada, and began a torrid, scorching trip just south of the Great Salt Lake, an area Clyman described as "the [most] desolate country perhaps on the whole globe."[18] Needless to say, he didn't much care for what became known as Hastings' Cutoff. Having barely made it with just horses and mules, Clyman knew it would be madness to try that route with ox-drawn wagons.

Clyman had served with James Reed and young Abraham Lincoln in the Black
Hawk War in 1832. When Clyman stopped at Fort Laramie on his way east in 1846,
he encountered Reed and his ill-fated Donner party. Reed had a copy of Hastings'
recently published *Guide* and asked Clyman what he thought of Hastings' "nigher
route to California." According to Clyman, he told Reed to "take the regular wagon
track [through Fort Hall] and never leave it." Clyman warned him against taking
"the great desert," but Reed rebutted, "It is of no use to take so much of a roundabout
course."[19] Reed placed greater stock in Hastings' recommendation. After all, he had
published a book, while Clyman had not. Reed's decision would cost the Donner
party dearly.

Greenwood should have also known Captain Wambaugh. Like Clyman, Wambaugh traveled with the Ford company to Oregon in 1844, and Wambaugh and
Greenwood both returned to the States from California with Commodore Stockton's eastbound party in the spring of 1847.[20]

Somehow, Thomas Corcoran's arrangement with the Kellogg family had fallen
apart. His letter explained that Joseph Kellogg wanted out of their earlier arrangement to provide him with board: "Orrin's son [Joseph Kellogg], the man I agreed to
board with went back on his bargain. He said it was too much for his family to cook
for so many." Looking for a new arrangement, Thomas met David Parks, who was
traveling with the Wambaugh party:

> [At Fort Laramie] we were joined by a company from Ohio. I made arrangements
> to board with one of the Ohio men, whose name was Parks, for one and a half
> dollars a week all of the way across. They would also carry my clothes and blan-
> kets. They were a very good family. I sold my provisions at Fort Laramie and
> made $150 in the transaction.

After three days of resting and refitting at Fort Laramie, Riley Root wrote that
he and his Wambaugh company left the fort on June 7. Thomas Corcoran's letter
seems to confirm that he traveled with the David Parks family from here on. Indeed,
this and other evidence suggests that the entire Cornwall party elected to join the
Wambaugh company. Cornwall's biography mentions that they were also joined
at the fort by Jeemes Walker and Frank McClellan, nephews of trapper, mountain
man, explorer, and guide Joseph R. Walker.[21] In September 1847, Joseph Walker had
left Independence, accompanied by his brother, Sam, their nephew Frank McClellan, and Sam's twenty-one-year-old son, James (or Jeemes).[22] They were headed for
California. Joseph Walker had been to California a number of times, and Frank had
accompanied Joseph Chiles there in 1843, but young Jeemes had never been west
before. It seemed an odd plan for a mountaineer of Joe Walker's experience to begin
this trip in the fall, when they were bound to meet deep snows and possibly blizzards
in the Rockies and Sierras; nevertheless, the party set out. In November, they got
bogged down in deep snow west of Fort Bridger. They had no choice but to hunker

down on Henry's Fork, a tributary of the Green River. They erected lean-to shelters and spent the winter there. It was miserable and Sam died. Jeemes later wrote that they "passed a forlorn and miserable Winter." When the snows melted in the spring, Joseph inexplicably stayed in the mountains, while Jeemes and Frank headed east to Fort Laramie, where they joined the combined Wambaugh and Cornwall parties.[23]

It appears that Caleb Greenwood also attached his party to the Wambaugh company at Fort Laramie. With Wambaugh, Clyman, Fallon, and McClellan all having been to California before, they wouldn't have needed Greenwood as a guide. Or would they? Greenwood would have been a valuable pilot for any wagon company going to California. He and his sons had traveled the 170-mile section of trail from the Raft River to the Humboldt River at least four times, so the Greenwoods had something to offer. Besides, the emigrants were about to cross a country known to be frequented by Crow hunting and raiding parties. Caleb Greenwood had lived among this tribe for almost a decade. He had married a Crow woman, spoke their language, and had seven half-Crow children, making him the ideal interlocutor for this segment of the journey.[24]

As for J. P. C. Allsopp, he reported in his reminiscence that his company arrived at the fort on May 31, and that

> [h]ere we rested a few days, and having heard that the Indians might trouble us, we held a council of war, and appointed scouts, who were to ride ahead of the party to warn the main body of approaching danger.

An eastbound Oregonian later encountered these westbound wagon companies, and his journal entry suggests that Allsopp's party had left the fort around June 4, a few days before Wambaugh's.[25]

When the combined Wambaugh, Cornwall, and Greenwood parties finally got underway on June 7, it would have been a rather large procession. Earlier, on May 15, John McPherson had reported thirty-nine wagons in their company. The Cornwall group may have added as many as four (the Kellogg family's). Shaw's report to the St. Joseph *Gazette* on June 9 noted that Greenwood had been traveling with a party of sixty persons, which could mean about ten wagons. This would mean a combined total of between fifty and sixty wagons. Interestingly, George Broadhurst, Stephen's son, wrote years later that the Wambaugh company consisted of sixty wagons, while Rufus Burrows recalled having fifty-one. Such recollections were likely referring to the company's size after it left Fort Laramie. Over the next forty-five days, this large party would travel together between Fort Laramie and Fort Hall, a distance of 570 miles.

The Wambaugh party was now a remarkable group with no fewer than eight seasoned men and boys who had been to California before: Captain Wambaugh, James Clyman, William O. Fallon, Frank McClellan, Caleb Greenwood, and Greenwood's three oldest sons. With so many strong personalities, it would have been fascinating to understand its hierarchy of leadership and authority. Fallon may have been

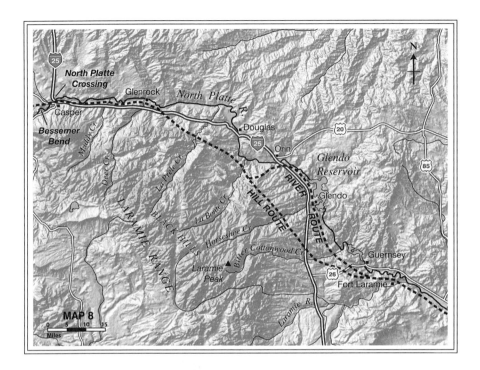

married to a Sioux woman and fluent in their language, but logic suggests that his value would quickly diminish once they left Sioux country.

The elaborate detail of McPherson's journal would have added much to the story of these parties leaving the fort, but because his journal is apparently lost to history, other than what the San Francisco newspaper published, we have only Riley Root's writings, and he sadly lets us down.

Leaving the fort's safety and comfort must have been disquieting to many of the emigrants, especially the women. Most understood that the easy part of the journey was over and the country ahead would be harsher, the grass and water scarcer, and the trail rougher. Root described the day they left the fort:

> [June] 7th— Left Larimie fork about noon, and passd over the bluffs 2 miles to Platt river. From thence we passd on about 4 miles farther and encamped, with plenty of wood, of yellow pine and cedar. During the night, it was so cold as to produce ice in our cooking vessels. About 4 miles farther on, is Black Hills Gap, where the river passes through high, precipitous rocks. At this place, also, the Black Hills commence.

The road leaving the fort led over a ridge between the Laramie River and the North Platte. At the top of the ridge, the trail divided into two forks: the "river route," and the "hill" or "plateau" route. The left fork—the hill or plateau route—continued west along the top of the ridge and eventually moved away from the Platte River and traversed higher ground closer to the foot of the Laramie Range, a chain of mountains looming about twenty miles to the west. This was no ordinary set of hills. The mountain range, commanded by Laramie Peak at over 10,000 feet, was imposing compared to anything they had encountered so far. This range of peaks and its outlying foothills were called the Black Hills (not to be confused with the Black Hills of South Dakota) because the dark forests on their upper slopes had appeared black from a distance to the early mountaineers.

Root provided few details of the day's march, which is unfortunate because they passed a number of interesting topographical features. Because the key landmarks he named and his estimate of the miles between these locations match this road perfectly, it is clear that his Wambaugh company took the right fork—the river route—and descended the bluffs to the North Platte River bottom. From Root's descriptions, it appeared that his company descended off the dividing ridge, perhaps at Mexican Hill, and traveled along the river bottom beside the North Platte. After about five miles, they would have come to Register Cliff, an almost mile-long cliff of sandstone facing the river.[26] Emigrants would frequently camp here and inscribe their names on the cliff face. Today one can reach the cliff by taking Road 109S south of present-day Guernsey, Wyoming, then traveling about two miles southeast.

About a mile and a half west of the cliff, the trail ascended a hill composed of outcroppings of the same sandstone.[27] In the years that followed 1848, the grinding action of thousands upon thousands of wagons during the gold rush and thereafter eventually incised seven-foot-wide, five-foot-deep ruts over portions of the hill. Widely regarded as one of the most spectacular vestiges of the Oregon Trail, these ruts are preserved today about a half mile south of Guernsey. Yet no 1848 diarist would record anything about either Register Cliff or the rutted hill, likely because neither place yet showed sufficient signs of human activity to merit mentioning.

Beyond the ruts, the trail descended and crossed Warm Springs Creek, an ordinarily dry stream bed about twelve miles from Fort Laramie. From here, a wagon train could either continue northerly up the river route, or it could turn southwesterly and travel up the limestone-walled Warm Springs canyon about two miles, where it would rejoin the hill route. About a mile and a half up this canyon, one would encounter Warm Springs. Although the waters from these springs were a tepid seventy degrees, they were considered "warm" in comparison to the frigid waters of the Platte. Since the springs were fourteen miles from the fort, it was a popular place for emigrants to stop and camp for the night. It was also a good spot to do laundry, and came to be called the "Emigrants' Laundry Tub."[28]

According to Root, the place of their first encampment after leaving the fort was four miles below Black Hills Gap, indicating that they spent the night very near Register Cliff. They were off again on June 8 and Root reported a long day in which they traveled twenty-two miles. Those taking the river road, such as the Wambaugh company, struggled over the sandstone ridge where the deep ruts remain today, crossed the sand and gravel bed of Warm Springs Creek, then followed the trail north, crossing present-day Highway 26 about two miles west of Guernsey. With a number of experienced guides, the Wambaugh party would have had no problem picking up the faint trail north of the creek. Inexperienced travelers, however, apparently had more difficulty in the early years. Edwin Bryant, traveling with a small group in 1846, complained that "[c]ontrary to our expectations, we found no trail near the river."[29]

North of Warm Springs Creek, the uplifting of the Black Hills had caused the North Platte River to carve a deep canyon. Upon reaching the hills' eastern border, the river poured through what Root called Black Hills Gap, a narrow canyon with red rock walls rising about three hundred feet above the level of the river. Because of this, the trail quit the river and climbed the rising topography. Although the road was never more than four miles from the canyon for the next twenty miles, the river was inaccessible during much of this stretch.

After leaving Warm Springs Creek on the morning of June 8, the wagon train rambled over a series of gently rolling hills. While the country east of Fort Laramie had been a great expanse of grassland prairie, west of it was a rougher, drier land with sandy soils that supported much less grass; here sagebrush, the prevalent vegetation, suffused the air with a pungent, herbal scent.

Ten miles of marching across this rolling country brought the company to Bitter Cottonwood Creek as it rushed down from the Laramie Mountains. The crossing was about a mile above where it tumbled into the deep canyon of the Platte. Abundant driftwood debris lined the creek's banks, flushed down from the mountains by periodic torrents. When James Clyman's party camped at the Bitter Cottonwood in 1844, he described the creek's water as "mean tasted." Early explorers had discovered that their horses would not eat the leaves of the tall, straight, narrow-leafed cottonwoods that lined the creek; hence, the "bitter" appellation.[30] Today, the creek is simply named Cottonwood Creek. To follow the trail, turn north off Highway 26 two miles west of Guernsey onto Wendover Road, and follow the dirt road northwest about six miles to where the road crosses the creek.

In all directions, the travelers would have seen buttes, ravines, gulches, and flats. Along the creeks were thickets of brush and groves of cottonwoods, and along the ridges were sagebrush, stunted pine, and cedar, all perfect sanctuaries for elk and black-tailed deer. High among the canyons and rocky crags of the Laramie Mountains west of the trail lived mountain lion, grizzly bear, and bighorn sheep, but the need to keep moving discouraged hunting expeditions into those areas. Besides, hostile Crow and Snake raiding parties had been known to lurk there.

One can hardly imagine Clyman, the consummate hunter, passing up an opportunity in 1848 to hunt this area with his treasured Hawken rifle, to test whether his keen eye and steady aim remained as sure as they used to be. We only have the

Riley Root's account to rely on and he never once mentioned who hunted for his company or how they fared. One story is told, however, relating to hunters in the Wambaugh company. George Broadhurst, the son of Stephen Broadhurst (teamster for Levi Hardman), said that Captain Wambaugh had appointed Levi as one of the company's scouts and hunters. He was to ride a mile off the trail and keep an eye open for trouble. He was also expected to bring fresh meat into camp at the end of the day. After a number of unproductive hunting days, Levi finally brought a tough old owl into camp. Wambo made Levi boil it and drink the juice. "No man questioned the captain," Broadhurst declared. "[H]e was boss."[31]

Bitter Cottonwood Creek would have been an ideal place to stay, but the Wambaugh party pushed on, ascended the twisting trail another eight miles over parched ridges and hills where limestone, sandstone, and marly white clay peered out from beneath the soils. With almost sixty wagons, the Wambaugh train would have stretched a mile or so along the trail, raising dense clouds of white limestone dust. Limestone becomes mildly caustic when it comes in contact with moisture, and as fine dust it irritates eyes and lungs. The dust would have aggravated Thomas Corcoran's condition, so he may have ridden at the front of the lumbering column rather than beside the Parks family wagon.

After a long day of twenty-two miles on June 8, Root recorded that they "encampd at a spring of the best water west of St. Joseph." This should have been Red Springs, located five miles south of the present-day community of Glendo, Wyoming, and one half mile east of Highway 319.

The emigrants set out in the morning of the ninth on another long day, and made twenty miles "over a tolerably good road." About three miles after leaving Red Springs, they crossed Horseshoe Creek, a swift, clear stream with abundant grass and wood. It was here that a Mormon emigrant in 1847 had noted the smell of wild mint spicing the air.[32] Although Root did not mention it, other travelers remarked about the bitter cottonwoods and abundant grass growing on both sides of the stream. The trail crossed the creek about where present-day I-25 crosses it. Three miles east of the trail crossing, the Platte River continued to meander through its narrow canyon.

The Wambaugh company pushed on past Horseshoe Creek and soon came to a fork in the trail. Companies could either leave the river route and travel west up Whiskey Gulch until it merged with the hill route, or continue northerly up the river route (as the Wambaugh company did), passing through where the modern community of Glendo stands. From Glendo, the trail pretty much followed the route of today's I-25 for another twelve miles. Along here, the trail descended to where "[o]ccasionally we saw the river," Root wrote. At the end of the day on the ninth, Root reported that they "encamped on it [Platte River] at night, with but little grass for our cattle." This would have been about three miles southeast of today's Orin, Wyoming, just east of today's I-25.

William Henry Jackson (1843–1942), *La Bonte Creek*. Watercolor painting, 1937. Courtesy of
Scotts Bluff National Monument, SCBL-30.

On the morning of June 10, the Wambaugh company followed the river road as it
turned away from the river and headed southwesterly up a ridge that divided Indian
Creek from Spring Creek. Root mentioned Laramie Peak looming in the distance
straight ahead. He described the road as "quite smooth" and wrote that the country
was "almost destitute of vegetation, except the wild sage." In this country, sage was
everywhere, and would be for most of the rest of the journey. Tough as barbwire, sage
was the plant best able to survive in the arid west; it could tenaciously cling to life in
a mean environment—dry summers, frozen winters, and gravelly soils.

Ten miles after leaving the North Plate, the river road rejoined the hill road at
a spot that today is very remote and far from public roads. The conjoined trails then
headed northwesterly about six more miles before descending to what some of our
diarists called Big Timber Creek, but it was also called Beaver Creek or La Bonte
Creek (its modern name). After traveling a total of seventeen miles on the tenth, they
camped at La Bonte Creek, where there was good grass, clear water, and wood. Their
camp would have been about a mile and a half east of Highway 94, and nine miles
south of present-day Douglas, Wyoming.

The emigrants of 1848 were probably unaware that they were enjoying the benefits of Mormon "road gangs" that Brigham Young had put to work the previous year,
or at least the diarists never mentioned it. Working the rough hill route through the
Black Hill country, the Mormon work crews had rolled rocks out of the way and

leveled the steepest approaches to streambeds to help the Mormon wagon trains that would follow.[33] Since the Mormons had taken the hill route, the Wambaugh company would not have benefited from the Mormons' labor until they joined the hill road six miles south of La Bonte Creek.

Leaving La Bonte Creek on the morning of June 11, the Wambaugh party followed the trail across a prominent ridge to what would become known as the "red earth country." On both sides of the trail were hills and buttes with alternating strata of hardened clay and sandstone, some white and some as red as bricks. Emigrants often wrote that dust from pulverized red rock ran like "streams of blood" during rainstorms and some called the area "Uncle Sam's brickyard."[34] The company passed to the east of Knob Hill, a pyramidal hill of gray limestone that seemed out of place among so much red-tinted rock and soil.

The Wambaugh company marched on during the eleventh, across broken, arid country where yellow and pink-blossomed prickly pear and aromatic sagebrush grew. Fremont had noted in 1842 how the sage suffused the air with its distinctive scent, which he described as resembling camphor and turpentine.[35] During that day's travels, the Wambaugh party leaped across Wagon Hound Creek, a steep-banked stream that meandered through a narrow valley between hills of bright red rock and sand. Continuing on, the trail weaved, navigating the many inclines, draws, and rocky outcroppings. In the distance, the emigrants would have seen conical hills and small buttes of piled rock and hardened clay that protruded from the landscape at odd angles and in many colors, some as red as bricks, others as chalky limestone, and others as ashen gray. The Black Hills, now much diminished in size and steepness, continued to shadow them a few miles west of their line of march. Forming a detached spur, these hills are now called Sheep Mountain. On the right lay a series of chalk buttes, and beyond them, about six miles away, lay the Platte River. It was along this stretch of trail that Root noted they finally lost sight of Laramie Peak, which had been a steadfast landmark for ten days.

After traveling eighteen miles, Root's party made camp along La Prele Creek, which Root called Mike's Head Creek. The twenty-foot-wide La Prele provided abundant grass after a day of crawling across a country with little edible vegetation. Today the location of their camp can be reached by taking exit 151 off of I-25, ten miles west of Douglas, then traveling south on Natural Bridge Road. The trail crossed the road about three miles south of I-25, while the trail's crossing of La Prele Creek was about one mile east of that point.

Leaving La Prele on the morning of June 12, the Wambaugh company continued to travel across undulating, dry country on a route that would soon rejoin the North Platte. The last remnants of the Black Hills, with its exposed strata of white granite and red sandstone, were slowly receding on their left. About six miles beyond La Prele Creek, they crossed, with difficulty, the steep-sided, eight-foot-wide Box Elder Creek (very close to where I-25 crosses it today). Four years earlier, Clyman had described Box Elder Creek as "thickly set with . . . Timber, well Stored with current and choke cherries & a number of Large grissly Bears."[36] Three miles farther, they crossed Fourche Boise Creek, about thirty feet wide and two feet deep. Nine miles farther, they reached the Platte River. From La Bonte Creek to this point on the Platte, a distance of almost twenty-five miles, the course of the trail very closely matches that of major power lines that cross through there today.

After traveling four miles beside the Platte, the Wambaugh company came to Deer Creek. Root seemed pleased, praising the location for having "plenty of wood, good water and grass for our stock." Indeed, Deer Creek had been a well-regarded campsite for a number of years, especially because its wide bottomland grew an abundance of grass, which would keep the livestock satisfied and not inclined to wander. The year before, Mormon William Clayton praised the creek's grass and timber, and expressed delight when he pulled a mess of silvery fish from the creek. They were probably Rocky Mountain herring, also known as Rocky Mountain whitefish, Williamson's whitefish, and grayling.[37]

The Wambaugh company left Deer Creek on the next morning of June 13, following the trail where it crossed the stream just north of present-day Glenrock and its railroad tracks. Riley Root reported that they traveled sixteen miles along the Platte on the thirteenth, crossing a number of deep ravines with difficulty. Root wrote very little besides complaining about the lack of grass. The company laid by on the fourteenth, as high winds forced them to stay in camp all day. On June 15, they resumed their march along the river for another five miles and camped in a low area beside the river. Their camp would have been just north of today's I-25, about one mile east of exit 182. It had been one week and 130 miles since they had left Fort Laramie, and this was where they would cross the North Platte River, a dangerously wide, deep, and swift obstacle.

June 3–15, 1848
William Anderson, Miller company, at Chimney Rock, Nebraska

On June 3, William Anderson and his Miller company had not yet reached Fort Laramie. On the day the Wambaugh company arrived at the fort, the Miller company was still seventy miles away and still traveling with the twelve California-bound wagons that had joined them on the south fork of the Platte on June 2. Those twelve wagons would remain with the Miller company for the next two hundred miles, increasing the Miller party to thirty-five wagons. Anderson did not mention the Gates company, but they, with a diminished number of wagons, probably remained just ahead of Miller.

The Miller company camped near Chimney Rock on the evening of the third and returned to the trail on the morning of the fourth. During the day, they plodded past an avenue of towering, fortresslike buttes that had been given names like

Smokestack Rock, Castle Rock, Table Rock, and Coyote Rock. The modern traveler speeds by them in minutes, but the slow-moving emigrant of the mid-nineteenth century had all day to gaze at them. Yet, for the most part, the diarists' writings about them were muted or colorless, perhaps owing to their fatigued states. Anderson must not have been inspired because he altogether failed to note them.

After only traveling eight miles along the Platte on June 4, the Miller company stopped to camp even though the sun was still high in the afternoon. The trail left the Platte at this point and headed across a long, waterless stretch toward Robidoux Pass. Anderson explained their decision: "[O]ur Indian trader Rashaw [John Richard] told us we should not find any more watter under 15 miles, so we camped."

At dawn on June 5, the Miller company rolled out of camp early and began moving away from the Platte on a smooth trail that led toward Robidoux Pass. Fourteen miles ahead was Scotts Bluff, a white, turreted city looming eight hundred feet over the valley floor and bathed in the golden light of the early morning sun. Sometime past noon, the company arrived at the wide draw through which they would ascend to pass over the bluff's southern end. After nooning beside a spring that gushed into a ravine, the company resumed their march. From the summit of the pass, they could catch their last glimpse of Castle Rock, still visible twenty miles to the east. To the west, they had their first sighting of Laramie Peak, commanding the western horizon a hundred miles away.

Anderson wrote in his journal how Scotts Bluff got its name, but he did not indicate from whom he heard the story:

> [T]hose bluffs drive ther name from a melancholy incident that took place amongst a company of trappers and traders on there way to the states   one of ther party by the name of Scott was taken verry sick and was unable to go any farther so he begged his companions to go on and leave him as it was imposable for him to get well and as they were scares of provision much delay here might prove fatal to them by starvation   so they gave him some provision and bid him good by for the last time and left him   his bones was afterwards found on the top of these bluffs where it was supposed he cralled to before he died   they have ever since bin caled scotts bluffs.

Several versions of this story had been handed down by word of mouth over the years by various trappers and emigrants, with no two versions exactly alike: Hiram Scott was a fur trapper in the 1820s, a clerk of the American Fur Company, or maybe not. He was a young man, or he was an old man. He died of an illness, or from starvation, or from wounds inflicted by Indians. He first suffered his affliction while in the Black Hills, or on the Platte, or at the bluffs. He was left to die by his companions, or was not, or did not have any companions. He got to the place of his death by walking or by crawling. He moved twenty miles before dying, or maybe it was fifty or one hundred miles. He died at the foot of the bluffs, or at the summit.[38] You get the idea.

Making it over Robidoux Pass, the Miller company pressed on, traveling another ten miles across a mildly undulating plain. At the end of a long, exhausting day, the company finally reached Horse Creek, with its abundant water, grass, and mosquitoes, having traveled twenty-five miles. The company had been inhaling dust for hundreds of miles, some of it lung-burning alkali, and had labored through withering heat for many days. The concerned teamsters watched as their oxen, heads down and tongues hanging out, struggled to pull the heavy wagons. The grass had been diminishing as they moved westward and the oxen had been losing weight, burning up more energy each day than they replaced during their night's scant grazings. Even the emigrants seemed thinner, their tanned faces growing more gaunt and hollow.

Tired inattentiveness may have contributed to two tense incidents that occurred when the Miller company arrived late that evening at Horse Creek. In descending a steep bank into the creek, Anderson reported a gun sliding out of one of the wagons and disappearing into the murky waters. Somehow, they found it. As they circled their wagons for the night, there was another incident: "[W]hile coreling [corralling] there was a gun went off in one of the wagons   the ball pased through the cover and over our heads with a whis to it." Always alert to the sudden appearance of Indians, emigrants kept their arms loaded and within easy reach, but such precautions created other risks.

After a much-needed rest, the company got a late start on the morning of the sixth. They traveled five miles and reached the North Platte River, then traveled over "a roling sandy plain" to where they camped near the river. On the morning of June 7, the Miller company traveled fifteen miles up the Platte during a heavy rain, as Anderson described. He saw "several indian coffins up in some scrubby trees that stood along the bank of the river." Some called them "nests of the dead"—hoisted high in the limbs of cottonwoods to get them out of reach of wolves. To most, these were merely a curiosity, but emigrant journals note that young boys saw them as targets for rock-throwing.

Also on June 7, the Miller company passed the site of Fort Bernard beside the North Platte. Even though its former occupant, John Richard, was traveling with them, Anderson did not mention the spot, likely because there was nothing left to see. Judging by Francis Parkman's disdainful description of the place in 1846, it would have been no great loss. They camped that evening beside the river, stopping about three miles from where the Laramie fork joined the North Platte, meaning that, oddly, they camped just short of reaching Fort Laramie. The next day, however, Anderson described his Miller company and the twelve California-bound wagons making their way to Fort Laramie:

> June the 8th we traveled about 3 miles which brought us to fort laramy situated on the west bank of laramy river about 1 ½ miles from its junction with the north platte   one half mile below fort laramy is the ruins of old fort John   here Rashaw and his men stoped   they had been down trading with the sue Indians   we camped near fort laramy in order to have our wagons repared and to

trade some but the smith of the fort was not about so I went in the shop and
done what work the company wanted done   Mr. [Isaac] Miller and my self had
started with a set of smith tools and finding that the team would not be able
to get through with them and meeting with a chance we sold them to rashaw
down at his fort and took a yoke of cattle in part payment for the tools   so we
spent the day in trading off things as we could do without to lighten our load and
at night had a great dance.

From Anderson's entry, it sounds like John Richard ("Rashaw") accompanied
them across the Laramie Fork, but instead of going to Fort Laramie, he set up his trading operation at the ruins of an earlier fort, which Anderson calls Fort John. While
Anderson described these ruins as "one half mile below fort laramy," some historians
believe the site of the old Fort John stockade is at least one mile east of Fort Laramie.
The ruins of Fort Platte, on the other hand, were one mile northeast of Fort Laramie.[39]
With the old stockade's cottonwood logs rotting away, and with thousands of Sioux,
trappers, and emigrants needing firewood, probably little of the old log stockade would
have remained in 1848. Indeed, just a year later, a gold rusher described passing "on our
right . . . the bare mud walls of an old deserted fort [Fort Platte] and on our left & one
mile up Laramie's fork was the fort of that name [Fort Laramie]."[40] He made no mention
whatsoever of the old stockade. Anderson must have been mistaken; Richard probably
stopped at the ruins of Fort Platte rather than at old Fort John.

Anderson failed to report the presence of any other wagon companies near the
fort when his company arrived on June 8. The Wambaugh company, together with
the Cornwall and Greenwood groups, had left the day before. The Allsopp party was
most certainly long gone as well. As for the Gates company, it cannot be ascertained
whether it was there or had already left.

The Miller company camped near Fort Laramie to be near its blacksmith shop,
where their wagons could get much-needed attention. Apparently Isaac Miller and
William Anderson were blacksmiths who were hauling the heavy tools of their
trade—anvils, hammers, tongs, etc.—to set up business in Oregon. While it was
astonishing how much most emigrants had managed to cram into their twelve-foot
by four-foot wagons, that accomplishment had proved to be imprudent. With their
oxen weakening and the terrain becoming more daunting, it was just too much; hard
choices had to be made.

Miller and Anderson had made the wrenching decision to lighten their load by
disposing of everything they "could do without," which unfortunately included their
blacksmithing tools. They acquired another yoke of oxen, doing business with the
traders Francis Parkman had excoriated as "a set of mean swindlers."[41] What had gone
wrong? Had they lost some oxen? Were some ill or lame? Or were they just afraid that
their oxen had grown too weak to haul such a heavy load? Anderson does not explain.

Other emigrants with weakened oxen were also concluding that they could
not continue with all that they had started with. The fort was well known as a place

where emigrants tried to sell or trade away what they could do without. And if no one wanted it, they simply threw it away. Tools, chests of drawers, oaken chairs, and sets of china, all sentimentally precious, were now burdensome curses. Here, much of it would be unceremoniously dumped, discarded, and abandoned on the plain around the fort.

While the Wambaugh party had stayed at the fort three days, the Miller company lingered very little, resuming their journey the day after they arrived.

> June the 9th being refitted and our loads some what lighter, we again started on our long and tedious journey   we traveled 19 miles to day 8 miles up the north platte then 2 miles over the bluffs to the big spring   9 miles further we came to a small stream called bitter cotton wood from the timber of that name that grows on its banks   on this branch we camped.

Calling their journey "long and tedious," Anderson hints at weariness. It probably seemed as if they had been traveling forever, but dishearteningly, they had only gone a third of the way.

The Miller company pushed hard on June 9, their first day out, traveling nineteen miles. They traveled along the river route, following Wambaugh's tracks, and got as far as Bitter Cottonwood Creek, meaning that they ended the day about twenty-eight miles behind the Wambaugh company. It is believed that the Miller company had no experienced guide or pilot, but with a large number of wagons not far ahead, they didn't need one. The thousands of hooves and hundreds of wagon wheels ahead left unmistakable marks to follow.

Anderson and his Miller company departed the Bitter Cottonwood on the morning of June 10 and traveled fourteen miles. He reported that "our hunters killed an elk to day." They ended the day at a "good camp" on Horseshoe Creek, unwilling to pass by its broad, handsome meadow. It was where the large Wambaugh party had camped the night before.

On June 11, Anderson reported traveling twelve miles. Eight miles after leaving Horseshoe Creek, they "approached" the Platte, near where Elkhorn Creek crosses today's I-25 and about six miles north of Glendo. He wrote that they

> were obliged to take to the bluffs agan on account of there near approach to the river   here was what was caled the dalls of the platte river   it is 150 yards wide   the banks of each side rise to the height of 200 feet perpendicular through this narrow passage   the mighty waters of the north platte rush through with a tremendous roar.

One mile east of here is the Glendo Reservoir, which is impounded in the Platte River canyon.

Traveling another four miles, the Anderson party descended to the river's edge, where they camped on the night of June 11, about five miles southeast of present-day

Orin, and just east of I-25. Anderson's entry for the eleventh clearly confirms that the Miller company was following Wambaugh's path along the river route. Judging by the location of their camp on the night of the eleventh, they were not keeping pace with Wambaugh, having now fallen thirty-five miles behind.

Leaving their camp on the Platte on the morning of June 12, the Miller company traveled beside it for a few miles, then nooned at a spring about a quarter mile west of the road. They then picked up the trail where it turned left and headed southwesterly up the ridge between Indian and Spring Creeks, over what Anderson described as a "pretty good" road. The tracks of the large Wambaugh party ahead were fresh and clear. They passed through wide expanses of gray-green sage, its aromatic scent filling their nostrils. After traveling sixteen miles, the Miller company arrived at "big timber [La Bonte] creek," where they camped in the same spot the Wambaugh company had camped two nights earlier.

Anderson recorded on June 13 that they "traveled 18 miles   4 miles brought us to marble creek [Wagon Hound Creek]   the road was verry hilly and rough   to day we are now traveling through the black hills   we camped on a stream caled mikes head [La Prele Creek]." Anderson did not bother to mention that they passed through "red earth country" that day, or that La Prele Creek had good water and ample wood and grass.

"June the 14th we traveled 12 miles," Anderson entered in his journal, "and camped on a small clear stream [Little Box Elder Creek] flowing from the black hills here." The camp would have been along the creek, just south of I-25's exit 156. During their travel on June 14, Anderson reported that their "hunters killed a buffalo and in packing some of the meet in on horse back one of the packs turned and the horse took fright and ran off and fell over a precipice on his side which injured one of his hind legs verry much but he soon got over it." This is the first mention of buffalo in more than 150 miles, and the fresh meat was surely welcomed in camp. During their stay here, Anderson reported that one of their young boys discovered a pistol lying by the stream. From its appearance, Anderson conjectured, it "had bin lost by the emigrants of the year before   he cocked it and puled the trigger and it fired as clear as though it had just been loaded."

That wasn't their only discovery. Anderson described a grim scene:

> at this camp there had bin a grave   the corps [corpse] had bin dug up by the Indians for the purpose of getting what cloths there was round it   the bones lay scattered around on the ground with some bunches of long light coloured hare which led us to believe it had bin a woman at this camp.

Before the Miller company left their camp on the morning of the fifteenth, there was more excitement:

> Before leaving camp this morning we discovered a buffalo passing from the branch up over the bluffs   three of us ran round behind a hill and got within

150 yards of him and two of us fired   both shots took effect   he ran a piece and
another shot was fired in behind the shoulders   the blood streamed from his
nose   he ran some 40 or 50 yards and fell   two more balls ended his life making 5 balls shot through his lungs.

After departing their camp on Little Box Elder Creek on the morning of June
15, Anderson wrote that they had traveled three miles when they came to the edge of
the North Platte River. They traveled close to the river for seven miles, then crossed
Deer Creek, but instead of camping at this haven of good water, wood, and grass, they
continued another ten miles. It had been a tiring day of twenty miles, and Anderson
complained that they camped where "grass and wood was scarce." Sometime during
the day's travel, they had come across another stomach-churning discovery:

we pased another grave to day the body of which was dug up and the bones
scattered around on the banks of the platte   the hare was yet on its skull which
gave it the appearance of a boy probably some 10 or 12 years old.

These remains must have been particularly haunting. Not just that the remains
were scattered or that they were of a child, but because these graves were more than
seven hundred miles from any civilized place and would be lost to the ages. Seeing
these violated graves taught the emigrants to use exceptional measures to protect
their dead from the predations of wolves and Indians, even from the desecrations of
white grave-robbers. The emigrants learned to dig deep graves within the trail. Then
they would drive their wagons over the refilled graves, letting their innumerable oxen
hooves and wagon wheels obliterate all evidence.[42] The number of emigrants who
died along the trail as of 1848 was small in comparison to the numbers that would
die in the coming years, largely because of cholera. Some trail historians estimate
that between 20,000 and 30,000 died on the road during its history, representing an
average of one grave for every five hundred to seven hundred feet of trail.[43]

EARLY JUNE 1848
Keturah Belknap, Watt company, probably west of Ash Hollow, Nebraska

Keturah Belknap, tired and heavy with child, had been neglecting her diary again,
but she did take time to make a short, undated entry when her Watt company encountered Indians:

Now we are on to the Pawnee Indians. They say they are a bad set. We must
pass right thru their villages; they came out by the thousands and want pay for
crossing their country. They spread down some of their skins and wanted every
wagon to give them a little something and they went to dividing it amongst
themselves and got into a fight.

Although she identified the Indians as Pawnee, the scene she painted sounded similar to what the other wagon parties experienced at Whirlwind's and Bad Wound's camps west of Ash Hollow. Recalling that Keturah's party had met Joe Meek, who warned that the Sioux at Ash Hollow were "bad people," one wonders if it was just coincidence that Keturah described the Indians as a "bad set."

June 3–15, 1848
William Porter, Purvine company, west of Ash Hollow, Nebraska

Late in the afternoon of June 3, William Porter's Purvine company arrived at Ash Hollow. With a few hours of daylight remaining, they continued a couple of miles before pitching camp on the long meadow beside the Platte. Even though Wambaugh's company had visited Chief Whirlwind's camp in this same meadow six days earlier, the Sioux were no longer there. Whirlwind had them on the move; his Sioux camp was heading toward Fort Laramie.

According to Porter, their oxen ran off the next morning before they broke camp and it was noon before they tracked them down and caught them. Resuming their travel late that day, they had gone only eight miles when disaster struck: "4th ... nineteen teams ran away with their wagons," Porter reported. "Broke Mr. Ball's leg and crippled a number of oxen. Frightful sight." Isaac Ball had broken his leg when he leaped from his wagon to "head off the crazed cattle."[44]

In a letter to his parents three weeks later, Porter explained the incident and gave them advice in case they decided to come to Oregon the following year. He intimated how the run-away occurred on June 4:

> A small dog or two will be useful till you cross the Missouri river, after which they are more than useless. They have caused our company to divide. They have caused Walker and Bristow's companie's team to run away twice and ours once. It is a remarkable thing that teams, especially on the Platte, are apt to become frightened very easily and run off. Walker and Bristow's company had 24 teams to run at once, killing some oxen and crippling others, besides other damage. Our company had 19 teams (all except Purvine's 5 wagons) to run. Isaac Ball of St. Charles Co., Mo. had his thigh broken. He is doing well. It is a frightening sight to see so many teams running. When you stop for dinner or any cause, loose the cattle from the wagons. If there is about to be a general run away, turn your oxen from the road and give them a fair start and stick to the wagon; otherwise you are liable to be run over and wrecked. The cattle will run about 200 yards and stop.

This terrifying scene makes one wonder if the emigrants shouldn't have traded their dogs to the Sioux for a buffalo robe or two. With all the ill-treatment, oxen should have been mean-tempered beasts, but most were placid and docile, with strong herding instincts. These traits usually served the emigrants well, but when something startled or frightened them, their instinct as a prey species kicked in, and they would panic. There was nothing to do but let them run themselves out.

After the stampede, the company traveled no farther, camping instead beside the North Platte about three miles southwest of present-day Oshkosh, Nebraska. The next day went much better, as Porter recorded them traveling "16 miles over bad roads, passing through an Indian village of about 250 Indians, all came out for presents and to trade." In all probability, this was Whirlwind's camp. As for poor Isaac Ball, how he must have suffered as his freshly fractured thigh bumped along in the back of his wagon over rough roads.

In another part of his letter, Porter mentioned that the Walker and Bristow companies had been traveling with his Purvine company for "some time" as protection against the Indians, although he failed to specify exactly where they had consolidated. Later entries will suggest that, although they were traveling together, they kept their separate identities, perhaps traveling as separate divisions.

On June 6, the companies made sixteen miles, and Porter reported passing through a hailstorm and a second Indian camp. They ended the day camping about three miles east of Pumpkin Creek, and northeast of Courthouse Rock, which Porter only described as a "Solitary tower." Complaining about rain, wind, and cold on the seventh, Porter reported that they traveled eighteen miles that day and camped near Chimney Rock.

On June 8, they made fifteen miles. Because of the long stretch of dry country ahead, they, like the companies before them, stopped and camped about six miles east of present-day Gering, Nebraska, where the trail swung away from the Platte. Even though Porter did not mention this, it will be seen later that Edward Smith's small party was closing in on the Walker, Bristow, and Purvine companies. Smith would also camp on the night of the eighth where the trail left the Platte.

On the morning of June 9, the Walker-Bristow and Purvine companies headed over a smooth road across the valley east of Scotts Bluff, and passed the spring at Robidoux Pass. Calling it a day after traveling fourteen miles, the Purvine company camped just west of the pass. Porter did not report it, but Smith's journal shows that he and his party left very early on the morning of the ninth, apparently passing the Watt, Walker-Bristow, and Purvine companies while they all lay in camp. Smith's small group pressed on, and after an exhausting day of twenty-six miles, ended up spending the night of the ninth at Horse Creek. Smith was now twelve miles ahead of the four companies he had passed earlier in the day.

On June 10, Porter reported that his party made its way across the undulating plain west of Robidoux Pass for twelve miles, stopping to spend the night in the lush meadow along Horse Creek. Although thankful for the "good grass," Porter complained about having to go two miles up the creek to find driftwood to use as firewood. Other travelers had mentioned that no trees grew along Horse Creek, but floods periodically washed driftwood down from the hills above and deposited them along the creek's banks. Today, one will find an entirely different scene, with a heavy growth of trees and brush along the banks of this narrow creek.

According to Porter, their companies traveled sixteen miles beside the North Platte River on June 11, then selected a campsite beside the river where there was plenty of firewood but scarce grass. They only had to travel twelve miles on June 12 to reach Fort Laramie. Porter noted in his diary that he had tallied 580 miles from St. Joseph to the fort. Riley Root had estimated the same distance at 570 miles, remarkably similar.

Porter wrote almost nothing about the fort, except that they left it the next day. Despite their run-aways, battered wagons, and injured oxen, they didn't stay at the fort long enough to do much in the way of repairing, trading, or recuperating. Porter and his Purvine company left Fort Laramie on June 13, but Edward Smith also recorded that he saw the companies of Watt, Walker-Bristow, and Kelly leaving the fort on that morning as well. As for the Wambaugh company, it was now leaving Deer Creek, eighty-five miles ahead, while the Miller company was leaving LaBonte Creek, fifty-five miles ahead.

Porter's group made twelve miles on their first day out of Fort Laramie, stopping to camp at Warm Springs, which Porter called "Big Springs." From there, they traveled ten miles on June 14 and set up camp at "bitter cottonwood [creek]." Contrary to what others had written, Porter complained about the creek's "[p]oor grass," although he did report seeing "considerable elk sign today."

On June 15, the large caravan of Walker-Bristow, Watt, and Purvine traveled fourteen miles and camped at Horseshoe Creek. Porter called it a "good camp," adding that they "[s]et two wagon tires. Jackson Purvine commenced driving Ball's team today." Porter explained in his letter to his parents how they dealt with their loose tire irons: "[T]ake off the tire, raise or open the felloe, take pieces of good firm sole leather, cut round holes in them, slip into the hole and slip it on to the spoke, and two or three pieces, according to the circumstances, between the felloes and put on the tire," concluding that this seemed "to do well."

Next to Riley Root, William Porter was the stingiest with his words. One wonders what was he was thinking. People like Porter had probably never seen land and hills so dry and parched, and had never seen geological formations like the buttes, cliffs, and vertiginous mountain ranges that they had been passing recently, yet Porter made no comments about them.

June 4–17, 1848
Edward Smith, Smith party, west of Ash Hollow, Nebraska

Edward Smith's small party, probably still traveling with the Kelly company, began to stir early on the morning of June 4 along the river and just west of Ash Hollow. The Watt, Walker, Bristow, and Purvine companies were camped just a few miles ahead, in the same long meadow where Wambaugh's company had met Whirlwind's camp seven days earlier. Smith's entry for June 4 was:

> Sun 4— we started early and traveled about 4 miles found grass and halted for Breakfast and grazing   the scenery on the north fork is Romantic in the extreme The Capt [Kelly?] gave orders to move forward   at one oclock six got Ready   the Balance Refused and we traveled about 5 miles and encamped   the Pike and Scott County [Purvine] company wagons Ran away   Bruised some oxen feet and Broke the thigh of a man by the name of Ball.

Smith is suggesting continued disharmony in what is believed to be the Kelly company. He implies that six wagons, including his, rolled out of the meadow that morning, while a majority of the company stubbornly refused to budge, perhaps determined to rest and recruit their tired livestock at this wonderful oasis. With so many independent-minded spirits in these companies, it is understandable that some would insist on doing what they thought was best despite the recommendations of their leader.

After traveling only nine miles on June 4, Smith's tiny group of six wagons stopped to camp. With the Purvine party camping about twelve miles west of Ash Hollow, it appeared that Smith came to a halt only three miles behind them. There must have been some communication between the two camps as Smith had obviously learned of their run-away accident.

On the fifth, Smith's party again only traveled nine miles, while the Walker, Bristow, and Purvine companies made sixteen. Near the end of the day, Smith reported encountering a Sioux camp, presumably Whirlwind's. Smith's party exhibited a reckless spirit in separating from the main company the day before, and by marching through Sioux country by themselves. Wambaugh, Clyman, and Meek were wary of the Sioux, and even Francis Parkman in 1846 had warned against revealing a "timorous mood," which might embolden the Sioux to try their mischief. If the emigrants assumed a bold, confident bearing, Parkman argued, the Indians would be "tolerably safe neighbors."[45] Considering what the Sioux warriors had recently done to the Pawnees, their capacity for violence should not be ignored.

Smith's small party moved on heedlessly and in due course encountered the Sioux camp:

> the Indians Received us in a sitting Posture on the ground in a semi Circle   we gave them a few presents with which they seemed highly Pleased ... Many Indians visited the camp during the afternoon and evening   the road during the day was very sandy hard Rolling all day.

Even though his party was small enough to be virtually helpless, Smith expressed no apprehension and no hint that they found the Sioux's attitude menacing.

The Smith party camped about six miles west of present-day Oshkosh on the evening of June 5. On the sixth, Smith reported traveling fifteen miles and camping near a second Indian village, where they "were visited by a severe hailstorm it fell about one inch in thickness." When the storm passed, Smith observed that they could see Courthouse Rock and Chimney Rock in the distance; the latter he estimated to be thirty miles distant.

Smith mentioned that they rolled out of camp at seven o'clock on the morning of June 7 and "halted for noon opposite the Court House this is an isolated Bluff about 7 miles south of the River." In the afternoon, they traveled nine more miles and camped at five o'clock beside the river, where they were drenched by another rainstorm. The next day, they were off shortly after sunrise:

> Thurs [June] 8— we started at ½ Past six   in about 8 miles we passed the Celebrated chimney Rock which appears to be fast crumbling to Ruins and in a few more years this natural chimney will be seen no more   nothing but the base will be seen to Point the traveler to the spot where it once stood in the afternoon   we traveled about 10 miles and encamped where the Road leaves the River and runs through a gap in the hills called Scotts Bluffs.

In reporting that they camped on June 8 where the trail leaves the North Platte, Smith confirmed that his party had again closed in on the Watt, Walker, Bristow, and Purvine companies. Although Smith did not mention their presence or proximity, they would have been camping at or near the same spot.

Smith reported leaving camp very early on June 9:

> June frid 9— we started at ½ past six and halted for noon at the spring immerging from the Bluff [at Robidoux Pass]   the Lofty Peak of Larimie range in Plain view   at night we halted about dusk at Horse creek   we found good grass and no wood   during the day we passed the grave of an emigrant named Jesse Right aged 36 years   died 11th of July 1847 . . . he belonged to oscaloosa co.

Smith's party pushed very hard on the ninth, traveling about twenty-six miles. He and his oxen must have been very tired when they finally stopped at Horse Creek. Since Porter reported that they camped about twelve miles short of Horse Creek that same evening, the Smith party must have passed them during the day, although neither Smith nor Porter mentioned the event. Smith probably moved ahead of the Watt, Walker-Bristow, and Purvine companies by leaving very early that morning and traveling late in the evening. With almost seventy wagons in the other four companies and the availability of grass becoming a problem, Smith might have decided it was important to move ahead of such a huge number of hungry, grass-cropping animals.

On June 10, Smith reported that they traveled "late," adding that there was plenty of wood but "very Poor grass." The eleventh should have been a day of particular excitement as the Smith party arrived at the Laramie River, just across from the fort:

> Sat 11— started at 6 the country is very sandy and grass very short arrived at the Junction of Laramie fork at 12 and encamped 4 companies gone ahead of us at night Capt Wattes [Watt] Co with sheep came in.

It seems odd that, with the fort in view, Smith abruptly stopped and camped before crossing the Laramie River. Perhaps the river was running high at the time.

Smith's entry for June 11 creates an uncertainty. He reports that "4 companies gone ahead of us." Does he mean that four wagon parties had already departed from Fort Laramie as of the eleventh. And if so, which companies? Was it the Allsopp, Wambaugh (with Greenwood and Cornwall groups), Gates, and Miller companies, all of which had left on and before June 9? Or was he referring to a different group of unnamed companies that had arrived and left the fort after the Miller company left on June 9, but before Smith arrived on June 11? The latter seems unlikely because no other companies appear anywhere in the historical record.

Smith reported crossing the river the next day:

> Mon 12 I crossed the Larime fork and struck camp called fort Platte as Lupton fort now occupied by John Reshaw [Richard] & Pike & Scott Co. [Purvine company] and Walkers [with Bristow] and Kellys Co arrived during the day some repairing wagons & we Remained in camp."

Smith made it very clear that the Watt, Purvine, Walker-Bristow, and Kelly companies arrived after he did and probably in that order. This confirms that Smith had indeed passed them earlier. With Joe Watt's company coming in ahead of them all, it looks like Watt was no longer willing to keep his grass-fouling sheep at the rear.

For reasons that Smith did not explain, he remained either at Fort Platte or Fort Laramie for five days:

> tues 13— nothing occurred worthy of note, we Remained at the fort all
>   the companies [Watt, Walker-Bristow, Purvine, and Kelly] Left to day.
> Wed 14— the same as yesterday.
> thurs 15— in the morning the horses started for the Rising of the Sun
>   and after a chase of about 7 miles we came up with them about
>   noon Delaneys Company arrived and encamped 1 ½ miles above
>   Fort John or Laramie.
> frid 16— Capt Hannahs company arrived at fort Platte about noon and
>   encamped at fort John we remained in camp.
> Sat 17— the horses started again for the east got about 3 miles from
>   camp Capt Hannahs co Left about 10 oclock.

In reporting that the Watt, Walker-Bristow, Purvine, and Kelly companies all departed the fort on June 13, Smith corroborated Porter's entry that his Purvine company left Fort Laramie on that date. When Smith wrote that "we Remained," it is unclear if he meant that only he and his family remained, or if his entire party of six wagons remained at the fort.

Smith's entries for June 15 and 16 contain the first record of "Delaneys Company," and of "Capt Hannah's company." He will again mention Hannah's company being at Deer Creek on June 24. Interestingly, Bancroft's 1886 *History of Oregon* contains a list of emigrants who arrived in Oregon in 1848, including "S. Hanna."[46]

Until this point, Edward Smith had been pushing himself and his family at a hard pace, and seemed unforgiving toward those who plodded and delayed. Yet he now inexplicably lingered at the fort, remaining there until June 27, a total of seventeen days. In remaining at the fort during this period, he provided unmatched information about the identity and order of seven separate wagon companies, including dates of arrival and departure for all but one.

June 4–17, 1848

Father Lempfrit, Stone company, somewhere along the Platte River, Nebraska

Father Lempfrit reported that he said Mass on Sunday morning, June 4. He virtually never reported the miles traveled each day, so we must estimate where he and his Stone company were that morning. His party had struck the Platte River late in the day on May 30. They did not cross the South fork of the Platte until June 10, so it took them eleven days to travel about 170 miles, or an average rate of sixteen miles per day. At that rate, their camp on the morning of the fourth should have been a few miles south of present-day Cozad, Nebraska, along the south bank of the Platte.

After celebrating Mass, Lempfrit reported that they had to locate three horses that had strayed during the night before resuming their march. They soon met someone coming down the trail:

> About 1 o'clock we meet a nice Frenchman, Mr. Montaland, a native of Angers who is clerk at Fort Laramie. This worthy gentleman seemed quite desirous of turning back so that he could go a little way with us and have a conversation. . . .
> As he was on his way to France, I confided some letters to my superiors and my friends in France to his care.

In 1846, Francis Parkman had described "Monthalon" as Fort Laramie's "clerk, a sleek, smiling Frenchman."[47] One can sense Lempfrit's joy in meeting a countryman, with whom he could converse comfortably in his native language.

At the end of the day on June 4, the Stone company should have camped somewhere southeast of today's Brady, Nebraska. On the morning of June 5, after treating Monthalon to a breakfast of buffalo steaks, Father Lempfrit reported that the man took "his leave of us." After resuming their trek, Lempfrit noticed that "Buffalos begin to become more numerous, we meet up with them on all sides." In camp that night, probably somewhere south of present-day Maxwell, Nebraska, Lempfrit noted that the night was very cold and complained about the lack of firewood and being unable to build campfires. They had to use "the dried dung of buffalo" for their cooking, and he lamented that the "smoke has an offensive smell that is most disagreeable."

On the morning of June 6, the Stone company continued up the broad river plain, picking up small pieces of wood along the way and tossing them into the wagons. They saw buffalo "in the hundreds," which Lempfrit observed would leave the river during the day to graze on the plains above the bluffs. The priest seemed fascinated with these strange animals and reported that his fellow traveler, Mr. O'Neil, took an interest in one in particular:

> To look at, one would assume that these quadrupeds cannot run, swift and powerful horses however have to be used to overtake them. The cow especially runs with great agility, and very few horses are suitable for hunting the cows. This afternoon, as we are traveling through a ravine, we came upon a cow in labor. Master O'Neil took possession of the baby calf without difficulty—for he had a cow newly in milk, and he brings it to her to suckle. The cow examines it for a moment, rather fearful, then she decided to let it feed. From this time onwards the little buffalo follows the cow as if it were his mother. Everyone plays with the young buffalo, he looks just like a six month old bear! We hope to be able to raise it.

The night of June 6 should have been spent close to where the Platte forked, somewhere south of present-day North Platte, Nebraska. On the seventh, Father Lempfrit complained about the miserable weather, just like William Porter had on the same day. While being buffeted by another windstorm, Lempfrit described an unexpected visitor in camp:

> 7th June. Today, we came to camp in a place that was entirely devoid of wood, consequently our meal was a wretched affair. The violence of the wind was most disturbing, and it was with great difficulty that we were able to put up our tent. We had to use much stronger pegs, and more of them. About noon we stopped for our customary small meal, and while the caravan was halted we saw a huge herd of buffalo going by. One of them, becoming conscious that one of our cows was in heat, lumbered placidly into the middle of our wagons. Immediately our men surrounded it and the huge animal fell to the ground, pierced by a bullet. As this was a bull the men did not wish to flay it. He had an enormous head and a big beard hanging below his jaws. He had lost almost all of his coat except for the long hair of his hindquarters. This animal somewhat resembles a lion insofar as the shape of its body is concerned.

The wind continued to howl that night, accompanied by a terrible rainstorm:

> We had a terrible storm. The whole evening has been very cold and unfortunately we did not have a stick of wood, not even for roasting a sardine if we had

one! We all had to sleep in our wagons. For our evening meal we had a biscuit,
and nothing but a biscuit!

Wet and miserable, they spent the night of June 7 about six miles southeast of
present Sutherland, Nebraska. Writing under a spell of gloom, the priest complained
about how bitterly cold the next day was, noting that they did not move out of camp
until four in the afternoon on the eighth, perhaps because they needed some extra
rest. As soon as they finally rolled out of camp, they had to stop because one of their
wagon axles broke. They bolted a piece of wood to it and resumed their travels.

The resilience of the adopted buffalo calf seemed to buoy the beleaguered
priest's spirits: "The little buffalo is in excellent shape, and he follows the cow as if
she were his mother." Their camp on the evening of June 8 would have probably been
somewhere south of today's Paxton, Nebraska. June 9 seemed to be a better day:

> This morning we were on our way earlier. I was about two miles ahead of the
> caravan when I came across four wolves, one of whom was white. They did not
> seem to be at all scared, and were eating some roots in a bog. The little buffalo
> is now completely tame and he runs about and plays with O'Neil's children. We
> were able to get a little wood for ourselves today from an island, but we had to
> go across the river for it.

After spending the night of the ninth somewhere south of today's Oglala, the
next day would be an exciting one for the Stone company. The priest described them
crossing the south fork:

> 10th June. We rose quite early as we had to cross over to the other side of the
> River Platte today. At half past ten I arrived at the place where we were to ford
> this famous river that terrifies all the emigrants! I noticed that there was very
> little pasture on the banks, and as I wanted my little pony to have something
> fresh to eat I crossed over to a little grass covered island about thirty metres from
> the bank. There, I started to write up my notes while waiting for the caravan to
> arrive. But to my dismay, my pony abandons me and takes off to rejoin the other
> horses. They had to send me another one to deliver me to from my captivity!
> When everyone had arrived they set about sounding the river bottom so that
> we would be able to avoid the deep places. Unluckily for us the river was greatly
> swollen due to the heavy rains of the day before yesterday, and all the waggon-
> boxes had to be raised up. That having been done, we attempted the crossing,
> using five pairs of oxen for each waggon. I was one of the first to go across. My
> pony did not have to swim, but having reached a spot about four metres away
> from the other bank I noticed he was having a great difficulty extricating himself
> from the quicksands that lie at the bottom of the river. I pulled a little too much
> to the right and there found myself fouled in a sandbank as unstable as feathers.
> Feeling himself being sucked into the sands, my horse made a big effort, sprang

forward, and in so doing covered my back with a fine gravel! Thus I escaped danger. In order to avoid the deep holes we were obliged to cross the river in an oblique direction and as a result, we had to cover a distance of nearly two miles. Each crossing took more than a half an hour. Can you just imagine the racket that ensues from all this: thirty wagons each carrying at least seven to eight people, cows, horses, dogs, all of whom are shouting, barking (etc.). The din almost stuns one. Nevertheless our waggon crossed without any further accidents. I was worrying a great deal about our faulty axel. Our little buffalo was able to swim all the way! At last everyone arrived safe and sound at half past three. We thought we had only six miles to go before reaching our camp site, but to our disappointment we had to travel until 10:30 that evening without finding a single drop of water. We were quite exhausted when we came upon a muddy pond that was almost completely dried up. There were five or six wolves slaking their thirst there. Our dogs chased them off. We then tried to drink this water, but it was so bad that we all agreed to push further on, even if we would have to travel all night. We had covered about two miles when we found a suitable place to camp.

The Stone company was pushing hard, rolling on even after dark, across the dry tableland that separated the North Platte from the South Platte forks. Too exhausted to go any farther, they gave up on reaching Ash Hollow that night. Lempfrit wrote that they found a "suitable place to camp," which might have meant beside a dirty waterhole. The priest had also made a stunning statement in reporting that "thirty wagons" crossed the river. The Stone company had been a party of eleven wagons when it left St. Joseph, and the priest had not mentioned any wagons joining them. On June 10, the day they crossed, the Watt, Walker-Bristow, Purvine, and Smith parties had just departed Scotts Bluff, which was about 130 miles and eight days ahead, and the Chiles company was about twenty-five miles and two days behind them. Edward Smith's list of companies arriving at Fort Laramie notes that the "Hannah company" was the last to arrive before the Stone company, although it arrived a full three days ahead of them. So the identity and source of these additional nineteen wagons that crossed the river as part of the Stone company is an unsolved mystery.

The next morning was Sunday the eleventh:

11th June. As early as four o'clock this morning Mr. Lionnet woke me up with the words "Benedicamus Domino." I responded with "Deo Gratias." We then made our preparations for celebrating the Holy Mass in our tent. Up to now our Protestants have not yet noticed that we have been celebrating the Holy Mass. We left after breakfast and on our way we came across a number of little weasels [prairie dogs]. . . . At 8:45 this morning we go by a former Indian camping ground. It is easy to see where their tents had been pitched. . . . Then we went down a very steep hill and so came into one of the most beautiful little valleys I have ever seen [Ash Hollow]. This, indeed, is the Eden of all Oregon. In the distance, outlined against a verdant green carpet, a field of wild rice comes into view. Its silvery undulating waves had the appearance of a lovely bouquet of flowers adorned with lilies. Both sides of the little valley were flanked by rocks so bizarre that with every forward step new figures could be made out. One of the rocks I saw had the form of a lion recumbent on a pedestal, but nature had deprived him of one paw! Among the shrubs growing in this lovely little valley we noticed a great many red-currant bushes that we call *Gadelles* in Canada. We also found a large number of wild grape vines, a kind of elder tree that has very large berries from which quite good preserves can be made, and a species of hawthorn whose lemon scented fruit grows in clusters. In this lovely valley we saw, for the first time, the red cedar tree. It seemed as if we were entering a sacred grove, so sweet its fragrance. I went and cut a branch of this cedar and then realized that this was the same wood as that used in the manufacture of those pencils that smell so nice. Few people in France know that pencils are made of cedar wood. When the wood is burnt however, its aroma is even more pleasant. There is a great deal of fragrant wood in this country. At noon we left this lovely grove of trees, all my life I shall miss it. At last we arrived at the banks of the river where we were to set up our camp. The men then went out to look for a piece of wood to repair our axle.

Father Lempfrit's description of Ash Hollow reflected his naturally enthusiastic personality. Even in the midst of difficulties, he was ready to marvel at whatever beauty presented itself along the trail. But he was not burdened with struggling oxen, troublesome wagons, or a wife and children. Rather he was often out ahead, enjoying a carefree ride on his little black pony.

It is difficult to know where the Stone company camped on the evening of June 11, but it was likely about ten to twelve miles west of Ash Hollow, south of present-day Oshkosh, Nebraska. The next day, Father Lempfrit wrote:

12th June. We spent the night dreaming of, more exactly, missing the lovely places we had traveled through yesterday. We left after a modest breakfast. We had good water, and plenty of it. This after so many days of deprivation, met all our needs. There was a range of mountains on our left, and we saw some attractive rocks at intervals as we went upstream. It could be said that they had been planted there for the express purpose of providing a foundation for some castle of the Middle Ages. This was very much like the nice country that one finds on the banks of the Moselle between Nancy and Metz. One of the rocks had the form of a great church with its spire, it stood out perfectly against a beautiful horizon. Behind, there was a wood of densely foliaged fir-trees. Then we came into a valley that had a very sandy trail, our animals had great difficulty in making their way out of it. Further on, we discerned a caravan of Indians who had camped in the middle of the prairies.

Edward Smith had reported his encounter with the Sioux on June 5 south of today's Oshkosh. Considering Lempfrit's average rate of travel and his description of the terrain, it appears that his company was about five miles west of present-day Lisco, Nebraska. Since Lempfrit met the Sioux camp there on June 12, the Indian camp must have moved twenty miles farther west during the week after Smith had met them.

Lempfrit was enthralled with the Sioux, and filled his notebook with a lengthy exposition:

The Indians we see are those called the Sioux. . . . [S]oon we saw about a dozen Indians coming towards us with little flags in their hands. Half an hour later we saw their village distinctly. There were about thirty large lodges. Before long we arrived in front of a long line of men, all seated on the ground. There was the Great Chief, decorated with the insignia of his authority, and the head men of the tribe all waiting for us, or waiting for our presents because at the sight of two blankets spread out in front of the Great Chief, two Canadians who were with us told us that every man had to give something. We all gave tobacco, maize flour, and other things like these. I noticed that the Indians really loved maize because when a little of this was set out on the blanket stretched out before the chief's feet, all the women who were standing behind the men demonstrated their satisfaction with prolonged squeals of joy. There were not many Sioux there when we passed by their lodges as they were at war with the Pawnees. This is why so many of them were away from their camp. . . .

After our gifts were presented we continued on our way and set up our camp about a mile beyond their village. Having arrived at our camp site I wanted to get myself a nice buffalo skin that Canadians call a robe. I made use of the time that remained to us before nightfall by doing some trading. I took some trade goods to their village and for a few items of clothing, obtained a really beautiful buffalo robe. As I was going into one of their lodges I noticed a small boy wearing a little cross round his neck which was similar to the one that I have attached to my scapular. I showed this to the head man of the lodge, but at once he noticed my little silver reliquary which he admired very much. Forthwith he asked for it, offering in exchange one, two, even three buffalo robes! I told him that I would not part with it at any price, but he never ceased to pester me for my reliquary without in any way understanding its significance. After this I wandered down the long line of lodges and eventually found myself in front of the Chief's lodge. This was much bigger than the others. Grotesque forms were painted all over it; there were wolves, an enormous turtle, cranes holding snakes in their bills, etc. I confess that the artist had not shown much skill, all the same, it was possible to make out what he had wished to illustrate. . . .

A large number of Indians had followed us to trade in buffalo robes, etc. Often these could be obtained dirt cheap. Could you believe this? For one or two glasses of spirits! . . . They asked everyone for "wiski." On top of this, four Indians were pestering our conductor O'Neil for "wiski."

Like Edward Smith, Lempfrit revealed no fear or apprehension while in the company of the Sioux. Camping that night only a mile from the Indian camp, the Stone company awoke to visitors again the next morning:

13th June. We have been surrounded by Indians since early morning. The small left-overs that we had given them yesterday evening had made our tent popular with them. We again shared our breakfast, after which we left. But this was only to arrive at another Sioux village.

Lempfrit has noted encountering a second Sioux camp, likely the same one that Anderson, Porter, and Smith had reported. At the second camp,

We were told that the Chief we had seen was not the Great Chief, only the second chief! The nearer we drew to the village the more we recognized that what we had been told was indeed the truth. This time is to be the real thing! As we approached the village we saw two flags floating in the breeze. These were the Red Flag and the flag of the United States. On the latter, the eagle of the United States coat of arms could be seen, then, in a scroll, there were two intertwined arms symbolizing the alliance of the Indians with the Whiteman. A deputation from the Supreme Chief had come to meet us. When we arrived before the Great Chief the delegates were lined up in two rows. Then we saw His Highness, adorned with the Insignia of his Supreme Dignity, seated on a mat. He was wearing a French cap and a multicolored shirt fashioned like a short blouse. Hanging around his neck were three large medals, suspended one from the other, and below these was a beautiful crucifix which he told me had been presented to him by Bishop Blanchet the previous year. Pointing up to the sky, he indicated to me that the One fastened to the Cross was the master of Life. I gave him a large medal for himself and for his posterity. He at once hung it around his neck after having kissed it. Once again we had to give our presents, following which the Chief presided over their distribution. Each one had his share. When the ceremony was over the Chief rose to his feet, for he was about to retire to his tent. However, as the entrance was very low he was obliged to treat us to the sight of his posterior—as he was not wearing trousers, only some kind of long hose made from skins. One does not give this a second look!

William Anderson had been very clear that Chief Whirlwind resided in the first camp. Although Lempfrit did not name the chief of each camp, is it possible that Whirlwind was the "Great Chief" referred to in the first camp, while Bad Wound was the "Supreme Chief" that he described in the second? If that is so, then Lempfrit seemed to understand that Bad Wound was now Whirlwind's superior.

Again, an American flag is reported in a Sioux camp. Could this be the same one Thomas Corcoran saw when they sought refuge with the Sioux after being pursued by the Pawnees? And could it be the same one the Sioux brought to the giant Horse Creek Indian Council of 1851?

Before the Stone company left the second camp of Sioux, Mr. O'Neil did some trading of his own. According to Father Lempfrit, "[o]ur conductor [O'Neil] had been stupid enough to trade the little buffalo [calf] for two pairs of buffalo-skin moccasins." This was certain to cause an uproar with O'Neil's little boys: "Everyone was upset about this, especially his little son who was inconsolable." And the calf's adoptive mother wasn't too happy about it either.

> the poor cow, no longer seeing her little bearded foster-child, returned to the Sioux village. The poor beast went six miles—she was brought back, but she never ceased to low the whole day.

With the departure of the Stone company on the morning of June 13, this will be the last that our 1848 diarists will mention the Oglala Sioux. The last wagon train on the Oregon Trail, the Chiles company, will come along a few days later, but oddly enough, Richard May will not mention them at all.

Whirlwind and his people had probably been watching passing emigrants for a few years now, much like watching a circus parade marching through town each spring. Wagon trains had been rumbling through here since 1841, but not in particularly large numbers. Things would change in a dramatic way for the Oglala the following year. Instead of the usual one to three thousand emigrants each year, it would become a swarm of 25,000 gold seekers and emigrants in 1849, and 50,000 in 1850.[48] Not only were the new numbers crushing, but the gold rushers would also manage to infect the Sioux with cholera, smallpox, and measles, causing many deaths. "Many died of cramps" is how the Sioux described the effects of cholera.[49] Despite all this, a precarious peace prevailed between the Sioux and the overland emigrants for the next couple of years. Then, in 1854, the inevitable happened. A few miles east of Fort Laramie, several Sioux warriors discovered and slaughtered a cow that had strayed from a Mormon emigrant. Second Lieutenant John L. Grattan, a young army officer stationed at the fort, had been boasting that he was itching for a chance "to crack it to the Sioux." Now with an excuse, he led twenty-nine of his soldiers into a Sioux camp of almost five thousand, determined to arrest the miscreants. Not surprisingly, the confrontation erupted into a battle that left him, all of his men, and a few Indians dead. The so-called Grattan Massacre was the match thrown into the tinderbox, igniting a fire that would grow each year. The war would not be extinguished until the last of the Sioux were herded off to the Pine Ridge reservation in South Dakota in 1878.[50]

Lempfrit's party left the Sioux camp on June 13 and continued up the trail, but the priest did not report how many miles they traveled that day or where they camped that night. That day, he was enraptured by bizarre geological formations, writing that they passed through

> surroundings [that] could not be more lovely. One would not believe the rock formations to be the work of nature. Everywhere one discerns forts, bastions, redouts, and crenellated towers.

He did not name Courthouse and Jail Rocks, but described them as "an enormous rock, tapered, truncated, and flanked by a tower from which it was separated by only two metres."

Lempfrit's entry for June 14 described traveling during a very windy day. Leaning into the heavy, sand-bearing gusts, their clothing buffeted by Nature's heavy breath, they had to clamp their hats on tight or put them away; otherwise they would never see them again. They pitched their camp that evening near Chimney Rock, which he described as "a sheer cut needle shaped rock several hundred feet high." He had nothing of interest to note on June 15, which is surprising because that afternoon they would have come into view of Scotts Bluff, which Root and McPherson had praised as "romantic." The sixteenth should have sent Lempfrit into poetic ecstasy, as his company would spend the day rolling across the plain toward Scotts Bluff. Upon their arrival at the spring in Robidoux Pass, they undoubtedly refreshed themselves. Yet, the priest wrote nothing about either. Instead, he wrote that "[t]he country is no longer beautiful." Something seems wrong. Ordinarily a profuse writer, an unflagging adventurer, and an unabashed admirer of the land's beauty, the priest's spirit may have finally been dragged down by the endless, arduous days.

In his entry for June 17, Lempfrit recorded that one of their wagons overturned while crossing a gully late that night, then complained that "[t]he aridity of these places does not permit us even a blade of grass. Our cattle are beginning to grow thin." Even though he didn't describe the place where they camped that evening, it likely was at or near Horse Creek.

June 4–17, 1848
Richard May, Chiles company, on the Platte River, just west of Fort Kearny

Lagging behind were the Chiles and Hensley companies, the last parties on the trail this year. They were about eighty miles and five days behind the Stone company. The Chiles company had reached the Platte on June 2, then traveled twelve miles on the third, when they encountered the Colonel L. E. Powell and three companies of his Oregon Battalion. They had just arrrived to begin building Fort Kearny. May did not explain why they stayed in camp on June 4, but it may have been to allow Major Hensley's eighteen wagons and mule train to catch up. One wonders if the delay ignited more grumblings about the dangers of not reaching the Pacific mountains before the deadly snows arrived.

At this point, Richard May took the time to describe Captain Chiles' daily routine for circling his company's wagons:

> [June 4th] when he [Captain Chiles] reaches the intended encampment he turns his horse or mule broadside (as a signal) the gee haw go along as the case may be. The whip is cracked as a token of gladness. We arrived at the place, the foremost wagon drives around the ring and stops so as to be behind the hindmost, each man driving his wagon so as to stretch a chain from one wheel to another, there-by making a good fence by corralling. In the morning the morning guard drives in the cattle, yoke up boys and drive out and take your respective places in the road.

On the fifth, the Chiles company pulled out of camp and rolled another twelve miles up the Platte River Valley. The Chiles party may have passed through here just in time. U.S. Army Captain Van Vliet left the new fort on June 5 with three soldiers. Taking the trail south, they crossed paths with three hundred Cheyenee warriors out searching for Pawnees. The next day, Van Vliet reported overtaking "the whole Pawnee nation—several thousands—migrating south to hunt buffalo."[51] On the evening of June 5, Richard May sat down to write in his journal, beginning with a description of the Platte:

> I rode out to the margin of the river today and had a fine view of it. I would suppose the river to be 1½ miles in width. Its waters are turbid and rolls and boils very much like the Missouri.

The location May described was at or near the "ford" where the Cornwall party crossed from the north side of the Platte to its south side over a month earlier. May then reported that "Major Hensley arrived in our camp this evening, he being one of a mule train that I spoke of some two or three days ago." The Hensley company was not yet joining the Chiles' group, but Hensley may have ridden forward to converse with Chiles.

The Chiles party traveled another twelve miles up the south bank of the Platte on June 6. Earlier that morning, May and a friend stopped to investigate a curious find:

> June 6th, traveled 12 miles. Early this morning one of the company and myself repaired to a newly thrown up mound with a spade dug 3½ feet and found an Indian buried there. He has his implements of war and of taking game in his arms, laying on his right side with his head to the north. This evening 15 or 20 of us repaired to a small mound and dug some 5 feet and found a great many bones and in one of the joints of the spine was a spear which had punctured to the spinal marrow. His head and under jaw was found entire with most of the teeth. In both instances we carefully put the implements in the grave and filled it up.

Chiles' company made sixteen miles on June 7 and twelve miles on the eighth. May described both days as cold and stormy and recorded that there was a "great deal of complaint in camp," although he failed to explain whether the complaints had to do with the weather, the pace, or some other issue. It could have been brought on by little more than boredom. The tedium of traveling day after day through the unchanging scenery of the Platte River bottom could have made people impatient and irritable. But they should not have been complaining; they were traveling the easiest part of their journey.

May mentioned that on June 8,

> Capt. Childs [Chiles] killed a fine buffalo and generously divided [it] among the company. Late this evening the emigrant wagons were just below us on the river. I met in that company David and John Plummons [Plemmons?] who once lived in Cole County, Mo. The only gentleman I have seen since I left Boone County that I was acquainted with, that were traveling to the far west.

It is evident that the Hensley company had finally caught up with Chiles, although they set up camp a short distance downriver.

D. H. Plemmons was one of a few men who signed a petition in St. Louis on May 5, 1848, asking for the issuance of a Masonic charter for California. The charter was granted in St. Louis on May 10.[52] It seems likely that the David Plummons in the Hensley company was the D. H. Plemmons who signed the petition. If so, this suggests that Hensley did not depart Independence until about May 20, since it would take about that long to travel from St. Louis to Independence, whether by steamer or overland by wagon. This would also mean the Hensley had pushed his party four hundred miles in nineteen days, averaging a daunting twenty-one miles per day.

The next day, Hensley's group finally joined them:

> 9th June. We made 20 miles today, and have plenty of buffalo meat in camp having killed four today. We make quite a show after receiving 18 wagons more to our train. The number now is 47 [wagons], near 80 men, quite a formidable force.

Although the combined company had forty-seven wagons, it is still unknown whether Peter Lassen's party of seven wagons from Chariton and Carroll counties started out with Chiles or Hensley.

It has been difficult to estimate where the Chiles party had been camping, as May's estimates of mileage leave something to be desired. But on the tenth, May refers to passing the forks, identifying their company's location:

> 10th June. Made 15 miles today. We have been 7 days on the Nebraska [Platte] and make the crossing tomorrow if nothing prevents. . . . We passed the forks of the river today. We have been in Buffalo Range several days and seen some thousands of them feeding on this entire prairie country. There is scarcely a tree or shrub in sight of encampment. I have just returned from the digging of a well. It affords a sufficiency of water for us all. It is common to dig wells on this river and we never fail to get water. It is always quite good. Several buffalo have been

killed and we have plenty of fresh buffalo which makes a most delicious supper for a wagoner, and a very green one at that. A considerable band of buffalo
crossed our path today, so near as to endanger our teams remaining fast to the
wagons so we loosed them and fired the rifles, without effect.

The forks area still abounded with large buffalo herds migrating between the
river and the prairie above the bluffs. These great herds posed a grave threat to the
wagon trains, and it was virtually impossible to stop them. As much as the buffalo at
the front of the stampede might want to stop, the thousands behind would blindly
keep charging. The emigrants' only hope was to try to steer the leaders of the great
herd around the wagon train.

After traveling eleven miles on June 11, May reported that their train of forty-
seven wagons crossed the South Platte. It appears that the combined Chiles/Hensley
company forded at the "lower crossing," likely the same spot where Wambaugh had
crossed three weeks earlier, perhaps because Chiles had crossed there during his earlier trips in 1841, 1842, 1843, and 1847.

May described the South Fork as "three fourths of a mile wide and from one
to 2 ½ feet deep." It took them "four hours to cross the stream with 47 wagons." He
explained how they had to double up their ox teams on each wagon, "thereby giving
our oxen two trips across this broad flat river." They set up camp that afternoon about
two miles east of present-day Sutherland, Nebraska. The next day, June 12, they continued along the north bank of the South Platte:

> June 12th. Traveled 12 miles. This morning early while all hands were gearing up
> teams a very large buffalo run into camp. Capt. Childs fired on him while running
> and gave him a deadly wound. Men, women and children had to take a look at
> the monster. We geared up and moved one or two miles and a band of buffalo
> broke in upon us from the sand hills and very much alarmed the women. The
> men made a sally and defended with great effect felling one and wounding sev-
> eral deadly. Hooked on our teams, onward and westward we moved. The ground
> over which we passed has the mark of desert although well coated [with] vegeta-
> tion. The sand and pebbles showing very near the surface. I will just remark here
> that in our company there are more general intelligence that I have seen in any
> community I was ever acquainted with. Willows for firewood and buffalo chips.

On the night of the twelfth, they camped near present-day Paxton, Nebraska.
They continued along the north bank of the South Platte on June 13, traveling fifteen
miles that day. But it was a day of great worry. May reported that a member of their
company by the name of Peterson had ridden out of camp the previous day to hunt
buffalo on the plains. He had not returned by the next morning and the camp was
in distress. "Should he not get in," May wrote, "he will be a great loss to the train
and still greater to his wife and children." May felt sick about it, mentioning that Mr.
Peterson had helped him look for his strayed oxen a few weeks earlier and had thereby

"endeared himself to me." That evening they camped near present-day Roscoe, Nebraska, and later that night, the men who had gone in search of Peterson returned with him, safe and sound. He had become disoriented in the vast, featureless prairie and had been unable to get his bearings. It "gave us much jabber," May wrote, "and his family still more."

They continued to roll up the South Fork on June 14, making fifteen miles, and stopped to pitch camp near present-day Brule, Nebraska. This was the location of the "upper crossing" where the Miller, Watt, Walker, Bristow, Purvine, and Stone companies had already forded.

The Chiles-Hensley party laid by on the fifteenth, and May described how they collected firewood during this day of rest:

> 15th June. We laid on the south [north] bank of the south fork of Platte River all day. It is a little amusing to see how the willows are brot to camp for wood. We take a mule or horse which always has a long rope tied to his neck, then cross a slough into an island, cut the willows make them fast to the rope, then make the rope fast to the horn of the saddle, then into the slough, thence to camp. This is the way we make fires to cook and wash. The buffalo grass is [a] blue looking grass and equal to the blue grass of the States. It is very short but very rich in nutriment.... The lads and lassies has a dance on the plains this evening.

The Chiles-Hensley companies left the South Platte on the morning of June 16 and crossed the tablelands between the South and North Plattes. They made it to Ash Hollow by the end of the day, although May hardly gave the place a mention: "16th June. We made 20 miles which places us on the North fork   the bluffs have a wild romantic appearance." He complained that the "grass is poor and just in keeping with the country which we traveled over." Traveling fifteen miles on June 17, mostly "through heavy sand," they departed Ash Hollow and traveled beside the North Platte, camping that evening about six miles west of present Oshkosh, Nebraska.

It was now mid-June. The Wambaugh company was about to cross the North Platte at present-day Casper, Wyoming, while the combined Chiles and Hensley companies were camped west of Ash Hollow. From front to back, the wagon companies were spread along the trail over a distance of roughly three hundred miles.

Table 8: Order of known companies and location as of June 15, 1848

Company (Diarist)	Location
Allsopp	probably had crossed the North Platte River
Greenwood	at North Platte Crossing with Wambaugh
Cornwall	at North Platte Crossing with Wambaugh
Wambaugh (Root)	at North Platte Crossing
Gates	somewhere near North Platte Crossing
Miller (Anderson)	at Deer Creek
12 California wagons	at Deer Creek with Miller
Watt (Belknap)	probably at Horse Shoe Creek
Walker	probably at Horse Shoe Creek
Bristow	probably at Horse Shoe Creek
Purvine (Porter)	at Horse Shoe Creek
Kelly	probably near Horse Shoe Creek
(Edward Smith)	at Fort Laramie
Delaney	at Fort Laramie
Hannah	one day from reaching Fort Laramie
Stone (Lempfrit)	just east of Scotts Bluff
Chiles (May)	at Brule, Nebraska
Hensley	at Brule, Nebraska, with Chiles
Lassen	with Chiles/Hensley

CHAPTER 12

The Sweetness
of the Sweetwater
JUNE 16–30

JUNE 16–27, 1848
Riley Root, Wambaugh company, Mormon Crossing,
North Platte River, Wyoming

The Wambaugh company did not experience any difficulties in crossing to the north side of the North Platte River on June 16. At least Riley Root didn't seem to think so; his short diary entries for June 15 and 16 made the river crossing sound uneventful, almost easy:

> 15th— 5 miles to Platt crossing. At this place the river is about 40 rods wide [660 feet], and has considerable current. The Mormons from Salt Lake had arrivd a few days previous, and prepard a raft for crossing.
> 16th— Crossd the Platt, traveld up the north side of it 2 miles, and encamped.

The Wambaugh party hired the Mormons to ferry their wagons across the Platte, as there was simply no good alternative. Choosing a crossing site for a ferry is usually different from choosing one for fording. With a ferry, one would ordinarily search for a place where the river is narrowest. Narrower means deeper, but with a boat you don't care how deep it is; you just want to get across as quickly as possible.

It would be interesting to know what James Clyman was thinking when his Wambaugh party reached the crossing. He had crossed this dangerous river without the benefit of a ferry; crossing near here a number of times in the 1820s as a trapper, on his way to Oregon in 1844, and again while returning east in 1846.[1] For decades, trappers and traders had crossed it near here as they traveled to and from the Rockies. In the fall and winter, the river was usually low and could be forded in safety. But in the spring and summer months, the runoff from snowmelt, springs, and storms produced a menacing river, causing many men to drown. The trappers often resorted

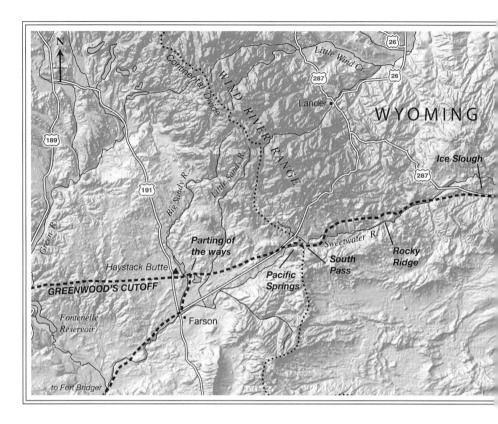

to making "bullboats," flimsy crafts fashioned of buffalo hides stretched over frameworks of bent limbs. When wagons began to appear on the trail, the wagoneers were compelled to construct rafts, but they were unsteady. Strong winds and roiling waters often toppled the top-heavy wagons into the swift, deep-running current. The emigrants' livestock—cattle, horses, and mules—were forced to swim. Most made it, some did not.

When Brigham Young arrived at the North Platte with his company of 150 Mormon pioneers in June 1847, they, like the wagoneers of earlier years, tried different ways of getting their wagons across. Nothing worked well, not even their rafts; they found them too clumsy and unstable. But Young, a nimble-minded visionary, decided there had to be a better way.[2] With organizational aplomb, he decreed that the pioneers would build a large, sturdy ferry, and he sent a detail of carpenters upstream to find a grove of large cottonwoods. Lewis Barney was one of these men and he described the project:

> [At the upper crossing of the Platte River] we had considerable trouble as the river was very high and rapid. Colonel Markham and I made a raft of old dry logs on which we crossed three wagons. There were two or three other rafts

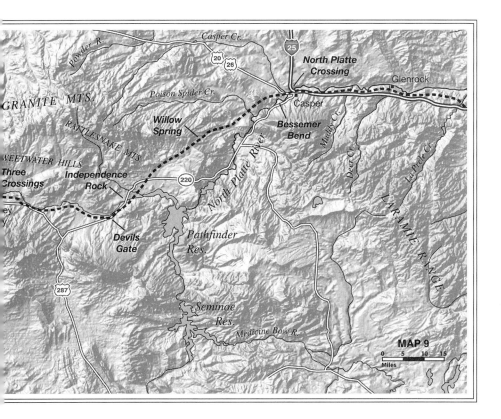

made but the current being too strong the rafts were abandoned. It was decided to make two large canoes and leash them together for a ferry boat. This being decided, myself and several others were sent up the river seven miles, to a grove of large cottonwoods. We selected two large trees, 3 ft through. Of these, we made two large canoes, thirty feet long. We then cut two other trees and hewed them down to two inches thick, and straightened the edges making planks of them 14 inches wide, and 30 ft. long. We then loaded them on our wagons and drove back to camp. We then leashed the two canoes together and fastened the two planks on the canoes lengthwise. Then we launched them in the river and ran a wagon on the planks that were far enough apart to be under the wheels of the wagon. We then ran it across the river which was quickly and easily done. In this way, the wagons were all soon over; the stock we swam across.[3]

Once the Mormon wagons were ferried across, Young ordered nine men to remain behind to assist the main Mormon companies coming along in a few months. In the meantime, however, hundreds of Gentile wagons were now approaching and Young ordered them to ferry the Gentiles across—for a price. By charging $1.50 per wagon, often collected in the form of flour and bacon, the ferry would prove a lucrative source of sustenance for the new settlement they would construct by the Great Salt Lake.[4]

At the end of the emigrant season in 1847, the Mormon ferrymen departed the crossing and continued on to Salt Lake where they spent the fall and winter, but because the ferry operation had been so lucrative, they were ordered to return to the North Platte the following summer. According to Riley Root, the Mormon crew arrived around June 13, just as the first emigrant companies were arriving. Reassembling their ferry and hauling it to the river's edge, the Mormons were ready to do business and the Wambaugh company was among their first customers.

Trail historians differ as to the location of the Mormon ferry in 1847 and 1848.[5] Some trail scholars believed the location of the Mormon ferry was about one-half mile west of where today's Bryan Stock Trail Road crosses the river in Casper (the "lower crossing"). William Clayton, the Mormon pioneer and chronicler of 1847, had devised an odometer for his wagon. A clever device of wooden sprockets and gears, it accurately measured distances, which he included in his 1848 *Latter-Day Saints' Emigrants' Guide*. His mileages from Deer Creek and Muddy Creek to the Mormons' ferry crossing, and from the crossing to locations beyond, such as Mineral Springs, Rock Avenue, and Willow Springs, indicate that Clayton's party was ferried across the Platte near the present-day restored Fort Casper ("upper crossing").[6] Riley Root's estimated mileage (usually pretty accurate) between Deer Creek and the location of the Mormons' "raft" was twenty-five miles. This, and his mileage from the crossing to Willow Springs, is consistent with the ferry operating at the "lower crossing," one-half mile west of the Bryan Stock Trail Road bridge. Hence, for whatever reason, it appears that the Mormons in 1848 had moved their ferry four miles downstream from its 1847 location.

Riley Root's diary makes it sound as if the Wambaugh company crossed the river without delay. He mentioned that the ferry had been in operation for a few days when they arrived. He did not mention any troubles, which, if true, was a testament to how valuable the leadership of experienced men such as Wambaugh, Clyman, Greenwood, and Fallon was to their company.

Leaving their camp on the morning of June 17, Root reported that his company continued along the west side of the river for five miles. To the southwest, on the other side of the river, they could see the Red Buttes, a high-walled escarpment with strata of dazzling vermillion and crimson. The trail then headed away from the river, proceeding southwesterly over a desert highland, a sterile and desolate country with little vegetation. When James Clyman passed through on his way to Oregon in 1844, he described the area as the "most Sterile Barren land imaginable haveing but little vegetation except the wild sage and that not more than Six or eight inches high."[7]

The trail, uneven and crooked, wound past alkali-impregnated springs, creeks, and ponds, and across patches of sodium bicarbonate—baking powder in its native form, which the emigrants called "saleratus." Because it was useful in baking bread, the women sometimes filled containers with it. Where the bicarbonate was dissolved in various ponds and streams, the water didn't taste particularly bad, but it was deadly to livestock. The tainted water would bloat and kill them—they would "burst," as the emigrants put it. As thirsty as their animals were, the men had to keep them away. For a decade, uninformed and careless emigrants had lost a great many animals at these deceptive ponds and streams. Hide-covered ox skeletons lay strewn beside the trail, together with discarded belongings and wagons rendered useless by the death of the oxen that had pulled them.

On June 17, the Wambaugh party rolled across such grimly named streams as Poison Spider Creek and Poison Spring Creek. They trundled by Rock Avenue, a ridge of eerily shaped rocks that some later called the Devil's Backbone.[8] After traveling an exhausting thirty miles, Root reported that they stopped to camp at one of these hellish places: "Encamped 3 miles east of the Willow spring. About 3 miles east of camp is a spring or two, the alkaline properties of which are strong enough in dry seasons to kill cattle, if allowed to drink freely. I was informed that the Mormons the last year lost more than 50 cattle at this place, by drinking the water of these springs."

The forty miles between the North Platte Crossing and the Sweetwater River Valley would be the emigrants' worst stretch of trail so far. Yet, the Wambaugh company must have avoided misfortune, as Root did not record any catastrophes. He certainly didn't report losing any livestock to the water, the mark of a company run by competent leaders. Even Thomas Corcoran, traveling with this company since Fort Laramie, mentioned no difficulties along the trail between Fort Laramie and the Sweetwater.

Root recorded traveling only "7 miles over hilly though smooth road" on June 18. This suggests that they spent some time at midday dawdling at Willow Springs, a free-flowing spring that boasted pure, cold water and good grass, perhaps dozing in the shade under their wagons. The travelers returned to the trail and climbed Prospect Hill, a steep incline just beyond the springs from whose summit they were treated to their first view of the Sweetwater River Valley. Descending, they stopped to camp on the night of the eighteenth by "a small clear spring though somewhat saline," which would be near today's McCleary Reservoir. Now at the edge of the Sweetwater River Valley, Root and his companions had reason to breathe a sigh of relief, assured that they would be traversing a good road for the next one hundred miles, a road that for the most part would be a fairly easy pull, one that would keep them near adequate grass and cold, *sweet* water.

From the North Platte crossing to where the Wambaugh company camped on the evening of the eighteenth, the trail can be followed today by traveling west on Poison Spider Creek Road northwest of Casper, then turning left onto Oregon Trail Road (County Road 319). This dirt road leads across Poison Spider Creek and Poison Spring Creek, past Rock Avenue and Willow Springs, over Prospect Hill, and by McCleary Reservoir. It then joins Highway 220, which leads to Independence Rock a few miles beyond.

Buoyed by prospects of reaching the Sweetwater, with its limpid water and abundant grass, the Wambaugh company should have been in high spirits as they rolled out of camp on the morning of June 19. Advancing across the undulating, sage-covered plain, they crossed the steep-sided Horse Creek, then passed to the west of Steamboat Rock and by a couple of small lakes bordered with crusty deposits of alkali and bicarbonate of soda. Beyond, rising from the valley floor, was Independence Rock. Located just north of the Sweetwater River and between the low mountains on either side of the valley, this large hump of dark granite resembles the back of an enormous whale surfacing from an earthen sea. The first white man to record it was Robert Stuart during his expedition of 1812, but is reputed to have been given its name by a small party of mountain men who camped there on July 4, 1830.[9] In the years that followed, various wagon trains happened to arrive there on July 4, giving them reason to pause for an interlude of merriment. Not only could they celebrate their nation's independence; they could give thanks for surviving that last stretch of dreadful trail, both good reasons to pull out bottles of liquor they had stashed away in their wagons.

Riley Root recorded that on June 19 they had traveled fourteen miles by the time they struck the Sweetwater River. They rolled on another two miles and came to Independence Rock, 1,900 feet long, 700 feet wide, and rising almost 200 feet above the surrounding plain. It was how the rock rose out of the valley floor that made it memorable, a novelty in the midst of the plain, remarkable in its texture and shape, and captivating when one stood beside it. It was something to get excited about after a long monotonous trip across the plains.

Pausing, the travelers parked their wagons in the late afternoon shadow of this intriguing rock formation. One can imagine them approaching it with a sense of awe, anxious to get a close-up view of this rock they had heard so much about. James Clyman had a special fondness for the place, as he and his trapper companions had camped there more than twenty years before. Perhaps he asked the lovely Hannah McCombs to accompany him to a place where he could show her the inscribed names of Thomas Fitzgerald and William Sublette, explaining proudly how these famous mountaineers had been his close friends and companions.[10] Many more names had been added since, some chiseled, some etched, some painted, hundreds upon hundreds of them, mostly by emigrants heading west. Thus Father De Smet had labeled it "The Registry of the Desert."

Not everyone, however, felt the need to carve their name at this place. Rufus Sage, a westbound emigrant in 1842, recorded his thoughts on the matter in his diary: "[H]aving glanced over the strange medley, I became disgusted, and turning away, resolved 'If there remains no other mode of immortalizing myself, I will be content to descend to the grave unhonored and unsung.'"[11]

After the sightseeing, they moved on. They still had a long way to go. Root reported that they left the "Rock" and camped two miles west of it. John McPherson's diary also reports camping two miles beyond Independence Rock, but he went on to

Devil's Gate can be seen as a notch in the ridge beyond. William Henry Jackson (1843–1942), *Independence Rock*. Watercolor painting, 1936. Courtesy of Scotts Bluff National Monument, SCBL-31.

record an incident that Root did not. McPherson and some of the other young men in Wambaugh's company were determined to leave their names on that rock for posterity. McPherson wrote that they stole out of camp later that night:

> About eight o'clock P.M., a few young gentlemen returned to the Rock, for the purpose of inscribing their names. They awaited the appearance of the moon with anxiety. About ten o'clock she was seen ascending gradually from behind the mountain top, casting her silvery beams over the River, and over the massive pile where we sat watching her until in all her splendor, her disk had arrived on the very summit. She there seemed to linger a moment as if to survey the scene she had illumined, and then pursued her night course in the heavens. We returned to Camp about midnight.

Their deed would have been perpetrated in the light of an almost full moon. The moonrise table for this date in 1848 states that a 91 percent illuminated moon would have risen here at 9:56 that night.[12] Perhaps John McPherson's name, or that of other members of the Wambaugh company, can still be found somewhere among the thousands on this great blackboard. Of all the names there, how many others were inscribed under the light of a silvery moon?

The next morning at daybreak, Captain Wambo roused the camp. As they caught up their oxen and hitched them to their wagons, a couple of young men, tired from the night's adventure, may have needed an extra cup of coffee. The oxen, bellies full from a night of grazing beside the river, should have been livelier than usual. The company proceeded up the well-worn trail on the morning of June 20, and after only three miles, came to a towering granite ridge with a narrow fissure known as Devil's Gate. It was only forty feet wide at the bottom and rose perpendicular for three hundred feet on either side, forming a "gate" through which the Sweetwater River rushed. John McPherson described the river rushing over the rocky debris that had tumbled to the bottom of the gap:

> The River, now confined to very narrow limits, summons all its energies to find a proper channel; then dashes with impetuosity, and breaks in foam against the rocks, while the sound reverberating overhead, mingled with the rushing of the wind through the chasm, resembles the roaring of a tempest.[13]

McPherson spotted E. E. Brock clambering high atop one of the cliffs, something one might expect from a thrill-seeking youngster, not from a man who had been selected as one of the company's sergeants:

> [Brock] had ascended from the road to look upon the chasm from above— Admiring the grandeur of the scene he determined to write his name on a prominent place on the vein. With a presence of mind of no ordinary character, he started on his perilous adventure, and would no doubt have accomplished his design, had not the writing material fallen from his hand. . . . His friends below watched his movements with painful anxiety, expecting momentarily to witness his fall. But after an hour's struggle he arrived safely at the bottom, to the gratified astonishment of his companions.[14]

The Brock episode is one of the few incidents that Root described in his book. Mostly consistent with McPherson's version, Root's story concluded with: "[Brock's] comrades stood below looking at him, without daring to speak, with intense anxiety for his safety, till he had accomplished his entire descent."[15] While Brock may have failed in painting his name hundreds of feet above the river (where few would have seen it anyway), he did manage to have his escapade recorded in both Root's and McPherson's chronicles for perpetuity.

To circumvent Devil's Gate, the trail detoured to the left through Rattlesnake Pass, a rocky passage through the ridge. Between 1840 and 1860, over 300,000 people followed the trail through Rattlesnake Pass[16] and beyond, as the road dropped back into the Sweetwater Valley and rejoined the serpentine river as it meandered indecisively across a flat plain. Rarely more than thirty feet wide, it could easily be waded without getting wet above the knees. The trail followed the windings of the river, touching it occasionally, but often drifting a mile or more away when cutting off its wider bends.

William Henry Jackson (1843–1942), *Devil's Gate*. Watercolor painting, 1930. Courtesy of Denver Public Library, Western History Collection, WHJ-10631.

When the road strayed from the river, it rambled over patches of coarse gravel or deep sand, and crossed dry terrain where only sage, greasewood, and occasional clumps of grass would grow. Near the stream, however, there was abundant grass, water, and the occasional clump of willows that were hospitable places for noonings and evening camps, despite the hungry swarms of mosquitoes that attacked the intruders with uncommon eagerness.

Two ranges of hills bordered the five-mile-wide valley, both running parallel to the river. To the north and close to the river were hills of naked granite, separated by coves and tiny indentations. These rock formations, some rounded humps and others huge blocks that came to rest in odd places, were similar in composition and appearance to Independence Rock. The mountains to the south were farther away, but high and covered with timber at the higher elevations.

Today, there is a lookout on Highway 220 overlooking the trail just west of Devil's Gate. It is an imposing, unspoiled scene, with Devil's Gate just to the east, the Sweetwater winding below, and a breathtaking view stretching far to the west. The scene moved J. Quinn Thornton, an 1846 emigrant, to write:

I regard this particular locality as presenting views so exceedingly picturesque, that it felt at once to be more grand, and at the same time, more beautiful, than any other collection of objects within the whole compass of vision.[17]

Root recorded traveling fourteen miles on June 20, twelve of which were west of Devil's Gate. It would appear that they spent the night beside the Sweetwater, just north of Soda Lake. Though difficult to reach today, one can get close to the campsite by taking Turkey Track Road, off Highway 220, and traveling northwest about eight miles. In an 1890 reminiscence, John Trullinger, a twenty-year-old member of the Wambaugh company, related a strange event he claimed had occurred in camp that evening:

[June 20] We were camped on Sweetwater River about twenty miles east [west] of Independence Rock; our corral made, teams out to grass, supper over and all gathered in little groups about the corral talking the things of the day that had just passed. As usual on such occasions upon a beautiful sunset in that lovely country of blue skies in the month of June, everyone was enjoying the beautiful weather and balmy evening. This was the 20th of June, 1848. It was perhaps thirty minutes after sunset when at the horizon in the southwest there began to rise up as it were a gold bronze ball. It looked about the size of a full moon. It very gently arose until it stood at what you would call the eight o'clock mark in the afternoon. There it stood still for a few minutes, then commenced to elongate each way across the horizon until it was in appearance about an inch wide. Then it commenced to crook up, and when it stopped its movement it made the word "mines." . . . It stood there over three hours as plain as any sign over any store in the city of Portland, and as easily read. . . . At that time no one in the plains knew of the discovery of gold in California. There was various comments on this phenomenon for some weeks, but no one could make it out.[18]

According to sunset tables for that location for June 20, 1848, the sun set that evening at 7:57 PM. It could not have been the moon Trullinger saw that night, as it did not rise until 10:34 PM.[19] If this mysterious sight existed in more than Trullinger's imagination, one wonders why the amazing phenomenon did not appear in accounts by Root, Burrows, Corcoran, or Cornwall.

On June 21, Root reported that they "[s]taid at the same place," suggesting perhaps that after weeks of skimpy grass, they had decided to give their livestock an extra day of rest to graze and recruit. Root did not record what was done on this day of rest, but it was common for people to engage in some housekeeping when they lay by. It was a time to unload their wagons, take inventory, and toss aside anything they now deemed unnecessary. After cleaning the wagon box, they would reorganize what they were taking and then reload.

On the morning of June 22, the sound of "Hup, hup, hup" filled the crisp air. The teamsters shouted and cracked their whips as the wagons lurched forward into motion. The Wambaugh company rejoined the trail and continued up the valley, keeping the Sweetwater on their right, not far away. They made twelve miles that day, over what Root described as a "sandy road," and camped on the Sweetwater. During the day, they watched the bald granite hills passing slowly on their right, just to the north of the river. Bulging up from the earth in strange and interesting shapes, some of the formations were given such names as Split Rock and Old Stone Face.

That afternoon, they pitched their camp on the right bank of the Sweetwater, just north of present-day Highway 287/789 and about three miles west of Split Rock. According to Root, it got very cold that night: "Frost and ice." Ordinarily, the night was filled with the sound of tens of thousands of crickets, but as cold nights settled on the high desert, the travelers heard only the eerie howls of nearby wolves.

They traveled through the same kind of scenery during much of the next day. Root wrote: "23d— 14 miles over a sandy road. Grass, no wood. About 3 o'clock, came in full view of the Rocky mountains. Ice formed in our cooking vessels during the night." About eight miles after leaving camp that morning, they reached a point where two paths lay open to the travelers. They could take the right branch, which followed the river through a narrow defile between two rocky hills. Because the wagons had to cross the river three times while traveling through this gap, the branch was called the Three Crossings Route. The southern branch, called the Deep Sand Route, bore to the left, and proceeded over a notch between the two hills, and across a patch of deep, almost dunelike sand. Root's reference to "sandy road" suggests that they took the latter route. Root mentioned that just beyond here they caught their first glimpse of the snow-capped Wind River Mountain Range. Today these routes can be seen by turning north off of Highway 287/789 on to Ore Road (County Road 5) at present-day Jeffrey City and driving about a mile north. Based on Root's estimate of distance, it appears they camped that night about one mile south of Names Cliff and about two miles northwest of Jeffrey City.

June 24 brought more of the same. They made seventeen miles "over an uneven, sandy road," Root explained. Although grass grew beside the river, he wrote that away from it "the country is a barren waste . . . nothing grows but wild sage." During the day, the river drifted north, away from the trail. About five miles out of camp, the trail crossed to the south of present-day Highway 287/789. Soon, it led them through a low, marshy area called Ice Slough. Travel through the Sweetwater Valley had been as good and easy as it could get, but with little variety in the landscape, the emigrants would have been alert to anything different. Ice Slough ought to have provided some interest, for two feet below the surface was permanent ice, kept that way by the insulating effect of the tundra-like turf above it, and over the years, many emigrants stopped to dig up blocks of refreshing ice.

The trail continued south of today's Highway 287/789 until it rejoined the Sweetwater, which is where the Wambaugh party camped on the evening of June

24. This campsite would have been on the river, about a mile and a half southwest of where Highway 135 intersects with Highway 287/789.

Root had little to report on June 25, except that they traveled nine miles along the Sweetwater and at the base of some rocky hills. They camped just below Rocky Ridge, at the mouth of a small, narrow canyon through which the Sweetwater squeezed. This location is difficult to access today, but may be reached by taking a very rough dirt road south off of Highway 287/789 and traveling about ten miles to reach the Rocky Ridge route.

Because the river flowed through the canyon, the company was forced to leave the Sweetwater on the twenty-sixth. According to Root, they dragged their wagons up Rocky Ridge, "over a very hilly road of course, sharp gravel stones." They were forced to proceed at a snail's pace, and Root mentioned encountering large rocks that were a "strain" on the wagons. After their ascent, the land leveled out, and after seventeen miles, they camped near "a fork of the Sweetwater," which would have been Willow Creek. This spot lies about seven miles south of today's Atlantic City, on the Riverview Cutoff Road.

Root did not mention problems with their livestock, but explorers and emigrants had often written about the deplorable conditions through here and how it would cause their horses, mules, or ox to "give out" or "break down." Two years earlier, Edwin Bryant had noted how this stretch of trail had exacted a heavy toll on their oxen. The miles and miles of sharp-edged rocks and coarse sand were all terribly hard on the hooves of their already tenderfooted livestock. Bryant observed a number of ox skeletons strewn beside the road, abandoned because they had become too lame or broken down to continue. The poor oxen became easy prey for the wolves that roamed the area. "Domesticated animals, unprotected," Bryant wrote, "cannot resist the persevering attacks of the wolves, urged on as they are by their appetites."[20]

Something noteworthy occurred on June 26, which Root entirely failed to report. A party of Oregonians mounted on horses and leading a pack of mules was returning to the States, heading east along the trail. Among them was Isaac Pettijohn, whose journal survives. As the Oregon party approached South Pass, Pettijohn began recording encounters with the westbound emigrants. In the following portion of Pettijohn's journal, the names of the companies he likely encountered are indicated in brackets.

> It is 12 oclock [June 23] and we are about to enter the dry stretch [heading east over Greenwood's cutoff] which is 40 miles without grass or water.
>
> Pacific Springs June 24th arrived here this day it being a year and a day from the time I left here. We met one waggon and 5 or 6 men yesterday from the States [Allsopp's scouts] they report a great emigration this season. We expect to meet them tomorrow.
>
> June 25th on the waters of the Sweet water we met to day 43 waggons bound for Oregon and California [Allsopp and first Adams segment].

June 26 met 79 waggons this day [Wambaugh, Greenwood, Cornwall, Gates, Miller].

June 27 met 24 waggons saw some buffalo to day and gave them a chase but caught none . . . [Watt].

June 28 we met 42 waggons this day grass is verry poor on sweet water [Walker-Bristow, Kelly].

June 29 this day we passed the rock independence and left sweet water we met to day 12 wagons [?].

June 30th we are to knight at the crossing of North Platt we have met to day eighty four wagons [Purvine, second Adams segment, Hannah, Delaney].

July the first crossed North Platt to day with thee assistance of the brethren [Mormons] met 11 waggons [Stone].

July the 2nd met 47 waggons to day mostly for California . . . [Chiles, Hensley].

July the 10th this day we met the Brethren [Mormons] or saw them   350 waggons strong.

Pettijohn counted 343 wagons (excluding the Mormons), about twenty fewer than Upper Platte Indian agent Thomas Fitzpatrick had counted when he encountered the westward emigration.[21] Even though the Wambaugh company should have been among the "79 wagons" Pettijohn noted, Root had nothing to say about the encounter.

Root may have been ahead of the other diarists from 1848, but there were other wagon parties ahead of his Wambaugh company. Pettijohn noted that there were forty-four wagons ahead of them. The Allsopp company had arrived at Fort Laramie on May 31, then "rested for a few days" before appointing some "scouts, who were to ride ahead of the party." From Allsopp's statement, it appears that his company departed the fort a few days before the Wambaugh company. The "one waggon and 5 or 6 men" Pettijohn mentioned on June 23 may have been the Allsopp scouts. The "43 waggons bound for Oregon and California," likely included whatever remained of the original twenty-five wagons that had left with the Allsopp party from Independence, but it is impossible to identify with certainty the other twenty or so wagons; however, later journal entries will provide some clues.

The Wambaugh company stirred on the morning of June 27. There was a feeling of excitement in the air. They were drawing near a momentous milestone in their journey—South Pass, the Continental Divide. It seems certain that their leaders had told them this was the day they would cross it. Only four miles out of camp, they encountered the Sweetwater again, a smaller stream now. Upon crossing it, James Clyman rode his horse up a rise just south of the river to a stone marker upon which was inscribed "Jos Barnette— Aug. 26, 1844." No doubt, seeing the marker would have brought back an unpleasant memory.

In 1844, Joseph Barnett traveled with the same Oregon-bound wagon party that Clyman was traveling with. On August 21, 1844, Clyman recorded in his journal that "Mr. Barnette who has been confined 5 or 6 days with a fever has the appearance of being quite dangerous and has been delirious during the whole of the night." Two days later, the company reached this crossing of the Sweetwater. Clyman recorded: "23— Remained in camp to day on the account of Mr. Barnett who we did not expect to live being verry low with a Typhus Fever." The following day, Clyman noted that "poor Mr. Barnett's prospects bad   our circumstances not permitting delay." So Clyman and a few others volunteered to stay and keep the poor man company until he died.

> the camp made early preperations For moveing & all roled out except ourselves who remain to take care of Mr. Barnett, many bid the sick man their last farewell look   a Spade was thrown out & left which looked rather ominous.

Burnett lingered on through the twenty-fifth and the morning of the twenty-sixth: "[A]bout noon, Mr. Barnette commenced with severe Spasms & seemd to be in the gratest agony imaginable . . . & about 10 oclock he departed this life." Clyman and his companions buried him the next morning, made this stone marker, then hastened on to catch up to their wagon party.[22]

Beyond the marker, the Wambaugh company's wagons rolled away from the Sweetwater for the last time, saying goodbye to a benevolent friend that had kept them refreshed and nourished over the last nine days. Traveling nine more miles through sagebrush, the wagons came at last to South Pass. There wasn't much to see. The Wind River Range, its jagged peaks to the north reaching 13,000 feet, had dwindled down to nothing. This passage over the Continental Divide is unusual. Neither a steep mountain summit nor a gap nor a conventional pass, it is a spot that gently ascends and then gently descends. West of the high point was rolling open space with nothing but scrubby sage as far as the eye could see. The notion that rainfall falling west of here would now flow to the Pacific Ocean may have been exciting to some—a symbolic milestone—but some would have only seen great distances ahead. And there was bound to be that cheery soul who had to remind everyone that they were only halfway there and the worst was yet to come.

Five miles past the summit, they came to Pacific Springs, an elongated depression of grass and water. Root had some not particularly inspiring thoughts of his own that day:

> 27th— 18 miles. Traveld 4 miles, and crossd the Sweet Water river. Here we left it, to see it no more. About 9 miles farther, brought us to the South pass or dividing ridge. South of the culminating point, at a little distance, stands a solitary hill, which some call Table rock. On the right, about 12 or 15 miles, are the Wind River peaks, covered in some parts with snow. Traveld 5 miles farther and encamped on Pacific springs, calld so from the fact that their waters run westwardly into the Pacific ocean. Some grass, no wood.

Clyman may have looked at South Pass with a feeling of pride. Perhaps he mentioned that he, along with Jedediah Smith, Thomas Fitzpatrick, Jim Bridger, and seven other men in the Ashley expedition, had crossed here in 1824. He may have understood that they were the first white men to discover this gentle passage to the Far West. Indeed, as he neared South Pass in August 1844, he recorded in his journal that in January 1824, he and his companions "first traversed the now well known South pass."[23] The December 4, 1824, issue of the *Niles Register,* a St. Louis newspaper, announced that "[w]e learn that his [Ashley's] party have discovered a passage by which loaded wagons can at this time reach the navigable waters of the Columbia River." Nevertheless, most historians believe that it was Robert Stuart, traveling east from the Columbia River in 1812, who was the first white man to find this easy way over the Continental Divide.[24] No matter who was first, South Pass was the best way west and, until the transcontinental railroad was completed in 1869, it would remain the primary overland portal for anyone going to the Pacific.

Now on the western side of the Continental Divide, the Wambaugh company settled down for the night of June 27 at Pacific Springs. The livestock were deep in grass, gorging themselves in this spongy, marshlike spot, while families sat beside their campfires, sparks spitting into the night air like excited fireflies. Despite Clyman's reputation as a quiet, humble man, he was proud of his accomplishments and not averse to telling stories about his adventures in this wild country. There had been many places along the trail where he could point to where something interesting had occurred. Anyone listening would have recognized that they were in the presence of someone special and found comfort in his knowledge.

June 16–27, 1848
William Anderson, Miller company, Mormon crossing, North Platte River, Wyoming

On June 16, the Miller company was traveling not far behind Wambaugh. The Miller wagons arrived at the North Platte crossing that afternoon, and William Anderson reported the presence of six Mormon ferrymen:

> June the 16th we traveled 11 miles which brought us to the crossing of the north platte and we camped   here was a grav of a man that was said to have bin drowned in crossing the river   the indians had robed his grave as usual   there was 6 men here with a craft for the purpose of ferrying emigrants across the river.

The Wambaugh company must have just completed their crossing as the Miller company arrived, although Anderson did not mention any company crossing ahead of them. Since it was late in the day and they had about thirty-five wagons to cross, Captain Miller decided to remain on the south side of the river that night. The next morning, June 17, the Miller company crowded their wagons up to the ferry landing, as Anderson described the event:

> June the 17th we were all this day and half the night crossing the river   we swam the cattle and horses and ferried the sheep and wagons for which they charged $1.50 cts per waggon and $1.50 cts a trip for the sheep   we got the wagons and baggage all over by dusk then we had an awful time catching sheep tieing and putting them on the raft (one old sheep the worst one to catch after we tied him to a chunk and left him on the bank while we caught the last one struggled into the river and floated across with the chunk [tied] to him)   from that time until near midnight here the 12 waggons that joined us on the south bank concluded to separate from us on account of the scarcity of grass   we crossed and went a head of them   we stayed all night on the bank of the river after crossing.

Anderson had previously reported that when the twelve California-bound wagons joined them near the South Platte crossing they had become a party of "35 waggons, 275 head of cattle, 300 head of sheep and 35 to 40 horses." The sheep gave them the most trouble because they were unable to swim and had to be caught and tied on the ferryboat. Anderson recounted that the California wagons remained on the near side of the river and did not ferry across until the following morning. Considering the barrenness of the country ahead, it was inadvisable to overtax the limited grass and water at any camping spot.

On June 18, the Miller party traveled fifteen miles, the first five up the river. The trail then left the river and began traversing that barren, desolate stretch that the Wambaugh party had struggled through the day before. After ten miles, Captain Miller stopped to camp at Poison Springs, which Anderson called "mineral springs." Miller's party was not as wise as Wambaugh's; they foolishly allowed their livestock to drink the alkali-tainted water. Anderson groused that "these springs have a kind of alkalie around them which made our cattle sick." But they seemed to know what to do: "[A]s a remedy for this we drenched them with hogs lard and we found it answered a first rate purpose as the cattle got well soon after drenching them."

While the area did not support the large buffalo herds that were found south of the South Platte, there were still some buffalo scattered through here. Anderson reported that their hunters killed a few solitary buffalo bulls loitering near the springs. They caught a buffalo calf as well, but it died. Another bull was spotted approaching the springs and the men organized an ambush. "9 of us hid under a hill a long his path," Anderson wrote, "when within 50 yards we fired of 8 guns   he whirled an ran a piece." Anderson was about to fire when someone in his thoughtless excitement jumped in front of Anderson's rifle:

> I was in the act of pulling [the] trigger   I threw the muzzle up and jumped around him and fired   two got him [the buffalo] by the tail and one by the nose

so with another volley of pistol balls he soon fell to the ground a mass of lifeless flesh for the bear wolves and vultures to feed on.

The next morning, June 19, the Miller wagons continued their crawl through this toxic land, lumbering past Rock Avenue shortly after leaving camp. Eight miles from their morning camp, they crossed Poison Spring Creek. Three miles farther they came to another spring, which he called a "spring and marshy branch." Two miles farther, they arrived at "willow spring," which Anderson acknowledged was a welcome spot with "good watter and wood." He complained, however, that "the grass is not verry good," likely because livestock in the parties ahead had eaten much of what was there. Nevertheless, the company stayed the night at Willow Springs.

Anderson recounted the next day:

[T]he 20th we left these springs [Willow Springs] and ascended a long hill [Prospect Hill]   soon after we started we traveled 13 miles to day and camped on a small swift running stream [Horse Creek] that empties into sweetwater   3 miles from willow springs we came to the soap mines or springs which continued a mile and a half or 2 mile [Alkali Slough]   these mines consists of alkali and salartus watter which has become thick like jelly and has the appearance of soft soap   it is verry poisonous to stock   our road was verry sandy to day we saw hundreds of buffalo to day   we were over taken this evening by a hail storm   it soon abated however until after we camped when it commenced agan and rained verry hard and there was a hard wind   we had to get on the inside of our tents and hold them up   the watter ran under them like a branch and almost floated us and our blankets away.

It must have been a dramatic scene: The women huddled in the wagons, arms wrapped around frightened children, while the hail pummeled the canvas tops and the violent wind threatened to topple the wagons. The oxen would have stood silently with their heads down, with nothing to protect them from the onslaught.

The next day, Anderson reported making it into the Sweetwater River Valley, where they would encounter Independence Rock and Devil's Gate:

June the 21st we traveled 12 miles   4 miles brought us to sweet watter and independence rock   this is a solitary pile of grey granite standing in the open plain   it is about 300 yards long and 120 yards wide and 250 feet high and the south side is sufficiently sloping to be easily ascended   portions of it is covered with inscriptions of travelers names with the dates of ther arrival and departure   some carved some in black paint and some in red   sweet watter a stream heading in the wind river mountains runs along near its south side and empties into north platte 5 miles from this rock   we came to the gap or devels gate where sweet watter breaks through a spur of the mountain which is 2 or 3 hundred feet high   the south side projects over the watter the north side

slopes back a little   this gap is about 5 hundred yards long and 30 or 40 feet
wide   through this the watter rushed like a torrent   this mountain is a naked
rock destitute of vegetation except some small dwarfish cedar and now and then
a wild sage stock shooting up through the crevices of the rock   about 5 hundred yards from this canyon and south of it is another through which the road
pases [Rattlesnake Pass].

From Anderson's mileage, the Miller company stopped to camp on the afternoon of June 21 about three miles beyond Devil's Gate, likely on the banks of the
Sweetwater. With the Wambaugh company staying in camp all day on the twenty-
first, the Miller party was closing in on them, perhaps camping as few as eight miles
behind them that night.

On June 22, the company followed the trail as it passed north of Soda Lake and
stayed close to the Sweetwater. Anderson pointed out that "the road leaves the river
in places for 4 or 5 miles then comes to it again." Traveling over a road that became
"verry sandy," they camped on the Sweetwater about three miles west of Split Rock.
Having made more miles than Wambaugh the last two days, the Miller company's
camp that night was only a mile or two behind Wambaugh, but neither Root nor
Anderson make any mention of another wagon company close by.

While the Wambaugh party had taken the Deep Sand Route, the left branch of
the trail, it is clear that the Miller company chose the right branch, or Three Crossings
route on June 23. This route led them through a meadow, then through a narrow, mile-
long canyon where the Sweetwater weaved back and forth through the tight gap. The
wagoneers were forced to cross it three times before emerging onto an open plain again:

> June the 23rd we travled 15 miles   12 miles brought us to the narrows   here
> the road and sweet watter passess between two mountains which is 25 yards
> wide   the road crosses the creek 3 times . . . in passing through these narrows
> there was one wagon upset with some women and children in it   they all roled
> out into the watter   there was none of them much hurt though they were
> pretty badly scared   it broke the two wagon bows and got some of the things
> wet   was all the injury that it done to the waggon and its load.

They ended the day camping three miles beyond the Three Crossings on the
north side of the river, and about three miles east of Names Cliff. Having taken a
different branch of the trail, the Wambaugh company's camp that night was on the
opposite side of the river, about three miles southwest of the Miller camp.

Remaining on the north side of the river, the Miller company would have passed
Names Cliff the next day:

> June the 24th we traveled 15 miles   at the end of 3 miles we passed through a
> gap in a spur of the mountain that runs out into the plains just as we diverged
> from this gap we came in full view of the snow caped mountains raising there

> while tops almost to the sky as it were   these mountains are caled the wind river mountains or the wind river part of the rocky mountains.
>
> June the 25th we left sweet watter and traveled over a sandy plain a distance of 14 mile without watter when we came to sweet watter agan   we traveled 5 miles up sweet watter and camped making in all 22 miles traveled to day   we saw a dead Indian as we were in or near the crow country   we supposed him to be one of that tribe but what caused his death we did not know.

Names Cliff was on the north side of the gap that Anderson noted, but he did not mention it, probably because it was not so named until the gold rush years, when most of the names were daubed or carved upon it.

Two miles west of the gap, the Sweetwater makes a wide, sweeping bend to the north. To avoid unnecessary miles, the trail did not follow the river, but rather cut off the river's bend by heading almost due west from the gap. After crossing eighteen miles of open plain, including Ice Slough, the trail intersected the river once again.

Anderson indicated that they traveled twelve miles beyond the gap before pitching camp for the night. One would have thought that Miller would have crossed the Sweetwater and followed the trail across the open plain. Twelve miles would have put them slightly past Ice Slough and six miles short of returning to the river. But Anderson made this interesting comment about the following day: "June 25th [the next morning] we left sweet watter agan." This only makes sense if they had followed the Sweetwater on its northward sweep another twelve miles. If they then crossed the river and cut south-westerly across the plain, rejoining the river fourteen miles later, this would have been an unconventional route, one that compelled them to travel twenty-six miles rather than eighteen. It is uncertain whether Captain Miller blazed a different way because of ignorance or because someone had recommended it to him.

Based on Anderson's entry for June 25, the Miller company appears to have camped that evening about three miles east of Rocky Ridge, and about three miles east of where the Wambaugh company was camping that night.

The next day, the twenty-sixth, the Miller company traveled three miles up the Sweetwater. Upon arriving at the canyon through which the Sweetwater flowed, they climbed the trail as it left the river and ascended the dreaded Rocky Ridge:

> June the 26th we traveled 18 miles   after traveling 3 miles the road left the creek and turnd to the right up over a rough hilly and stony country   6 miles further we came to a good spring about 40 yards to the left of the road down a small hollow   camped on a small branch of sweet watter [Rock Creek] and on our left a high clift of perpendicular rocks   it was so cold that we had to draw our overcoats on   to day we met two companys of men from oregon packing to the states on mules and horses one company camped with us at night and had a dance   played the fiddle and sung songs till nearly midnight   some of them

spoke verry highly of oregon and said they were going back agan   others agan
gave it a verry bad name.

Anderson's words fail to convey the difficulty of dragging their wagons up Rocky
Ridge and limping across the plateau that day. The Miller company probably reached
Rock Creek by the evening of the twenty-sixth. With the Wambaugh company camping on Willow Creek that night, Wambaugh would have been about four miles ahead
of Miller.

Of the two parties returning from Oregon that Anderson mentioned, later evidence will suggest that Isaac Pettijohn was traveling with the first group, while the
Miller company camped with the second group on the evening of the twenty-sixth.
Since the Miller company was bound for Oregon, they would have been exceedingly
interested in what the Oregonians had to say about the place. Anderson wrote that
some opinions were positive and others were negative, but he did not record any news
about the Cayuse uprising in Oregon.

The Gates and Miller companies were not far behind Wambaugh. Based on
Root's and Anderson's recorded locations, it appears that the seventy-nine wagons
Pettijohn reported encountering on the twenty-sixth were from the Wambaugh,
Gates, and Miller companies, and perhaps the twelve California-bound wagons. By
this time, a number of wagons would have been abandoned and a few of the slower
and more troubled travelers would have dropped back to join parties behind them.
This could explain why the total number of wagons Pettijohn reported was lower
than the earlier numbers reported in these companies.

The next day, Anderson wrote about their travel beyond Rock Creek: "June
the 27th we traveled 8 miles which brought us to the sweet watter agan   here we
camped   there was a band of traders here from arcansas with cattle and horses to
trade to the emigrants   we found snow here 18 inches deep in places   we killed
3 antelope to day." Their camp on the Sweetwater was near Joseph Barnett's grave
marker. It would be the last the Miller company would see of the Sweetwater.

Mid-June 1848
W. L. Adams, Adams company, just west
of the North Platte Crossing, Wyoming

Another wagon company had recently arrived at the North Platte River crossing, one
for whom we have limited information. W. L. Adams, a member of this party, wrote a
letter on July 8, 1848, from Pacific Springs, 150 miles west of the North Platte crossing. The letter was addressed to his brother in Knox County, Illinois, and it came
to be published in the *Knox Intelligencer*, where the author was identified as W. S.
Adams, but that was a misprint. Adams was the schoolteacher from Knox County
who was part of the fifty-wagon company camping on the Missouri River flats below
Bellevue in early April, where it had been waiting for the spring grass to grow. The

impatient P. B. Cornwall party was unwilling to wait for them and left Bellevue on about April 12. Adams and his company did not leave the Council Bluffs area until two to three weeks later. With no known diarist among them, the first record of their travels comes from the letter Adams penned at Pacific Springs. Because the leader of the company is unknown, we will hereafter call it the Adams company.

> Dear Brother— As I have an opportunity of sending a letter by some traders to Bents Fort Arkansas, from whence I am informed it can be sent to the States, I improved it. I wrote last from the leaving of North Platte, 120 [150] miles back, on the 24th of June. I lost another ox there—supposed to be poisoned by some vegetable. I have two yokes and the cows left. I have hired my books hauled, and [have been] loaned a cow and ox which I work together, and thus make up four yokes, and get along tolerably well. I have lighted some by throwing away one trunk, plates, tumblers, planes &c. We were detained at the ferry on Platte 15 days (which has thrown us much behind) partly by high wind and partly by our cattle running away. They took fright in the night and ran like buffalo, leaving the guard far behind. They continued this for several nights, sometimes running off among the hills for miles and doing themselves much injury. We were compelled to herd them five or six miles from camp in order to get grass.[25]

The earlier letter that Adams sent via Bent's Fort would likely have revealed more about their earlier experiences, but it is sadly missing from the historical record.

One of Adams' more intriguing statements was that his company departed the North Platte River on June 24, having first stalled at the crossing during a wretched ordeal of fifteen days. This suggests that his party first arrived at the North Platte crossing around June 9. Since the various wagon companies were taking between seven and nine days to travel from Fort Laramie to the Platte crossing, Adams' party must have left Fort Laramie around June 1, about a week ahead of Wambaugh's. This means the Adams company had arrived at the fort on or before May 31, making them one of the earlier companies to arrive there.

Riley Root reported his Wambaugh company arriving at the North Platte River crossing on June 15, adding that "[t]he Mormons from Salt Lake had arrivd a few days previous." This indicates that the Adams company arrived at the river crossing almost a week before Wambaugh and a few days before the Mormon ferrymen arrived. A biographical sketch written years later declared that Adams' party had forded all the rivers except the Missouri and the Green.[26] His daughter Inez confirmed it, claiming they had crossed the Platte without the benefit of any Mormon ferry. She also recounted that

> the Platte was so deep and broad it could not be forded so the wagons were caulked water tight and raised and lashed to the standards . . . the men swimming alongside steadying the wagon beds, and reassuring the frightened women and

children, some of whom screamed and covered their faces when the water rose to within a few inches of the edges of their improvised boats.[27]

Adams mentioned how the high winds detained them at the river crossing at first, something that was common at this time of year. Even if it was quiet in the morning, strong winds out of the west usually picked up each afternoon. In fact, it was a wonder that more emigrants didn't lose their hats or develop a permanent lean to their walk while traveling through this wind-plagued country.

With the Adams company stalling at the North Platte crossing because of high winds and cattle running off, and with them fording the river before the Mormon fer-rymen arrived, they must have crossed the North Platte on June 12, give or take a day.

Adams continued to inveigh about how matters worsened after they got across the river:

> The night after we crossed Platte, we guarded them [their cattle] by our wagons intending to start in the morning— some yoked up and chained together. I yoked mine, chained them to wagons and trees, and tied legs together and kept them safe. The cattle frighted in the night and ran terribly. Some came unyoked but still ran. It seems almost impossible for a smart horse to head them. They scatter in all directions. We had almost 400 head, 50 wagons at that time. We followed the trails and found droves of from 10 to 100 head, from 15 to 40 miles from the camp. All this distance they traveled over a desert without grass and water— They were of course much cut down— We rode our horses nearly down in hunt-ing. Our horses were reduced to mere skeletons from want of grass. Some men never found all their cattle. Many people for want of teams are leaving wagons, plows, feather beds, stoves, kettles, harrow teeth, chains, boxes, &c. The road is lined with such articles . . . together with dead cattle. Our cattle have become so weak from the want of grass and hard labor, that 10 hundred [pounds] is a good load for four yoke of cattle on good roads. Emigrants are scattering their [pos-sessions] and such fool appendages to the four winds, sawing off their 12 foot [boxes] to 10 ½, and coupling up shorter. . . . Some are still lucky enough to keep all their cattle and are still hauling their "plunder." One had better a thousand fold start with "NOTHING BUT PROVISIONS AND CLOTHING" than run the risk of wearing out their teams in hauling such stuff as they can do without. . . . During our troubles on Platte, I think it was the darkest time I ever saw. Many stout hearts quailed and faces blanched that seldom turn pale. I trusted alone in Almighty God, and he brought deliverance. . . . We are now traveling in a company of 26 wagons. Large companies cannot be tolerated.
>
>   Adieu, W. S. [L.] Adams

If the Adams company crossed the river on June 12, but did not leave its vicinity until the twenty-fourth, then their tribulations on the west side of the river continued another eleven days after crossing the river. The Wambaugh and Miller companies crossed the river on the sixteenth and seventeenth, respectively, and immediately headed off across the Poison Spider desert, but neither Root nor Anderson mentioned encountering or passing this floundering group.

Adams freely acknowledged that a large company was a mistake. Four hundred head of cattle was far too many hungry mouths to move together through this dry, grassless country. While full bellies usually produced contented, placid cattle, the converse was also true—hungry cattle tended to be agitated and restless, and were much more likely to scatter into the night at the slightest provocation.

Companies that were not competently led usually suffered more that those led by men who knew what they were doing. Some people were simply better at managing or working around livestock than others. There were good and bad ways of guarding them, of tending to their needs for grass and water, of chasing them, of rounding them up, and of calming them down. In contrast to the wretched experience of the Adams company, Riley Root never mentioned difficulties with their livestock in the Wambaugh/Clyman company.

The Adams company had seemed to violate about every precept that an experienced pilot or wagon captain would have laid down: do not travel in too large a party (they had fifty wagons); do not travel with too many livestock (they had four hundred head); and do not overload wagons with nonessentials. Adams chastised their oxen as if they were unruly ingrates. Emigrants tended to mention their oxen only when they are failing or causing trouble, but rarely do we read expressions of appreciation when they are serving as remarkable, four-legged engines of locomotion. As the Adams party continued to chase down its scattered livestock, it was passed by companies such as Watt, Walker-Bristow, and Kelly.

June 16–30, 1848
William Porter, Purvine company, along the North Platte River, north of Horseshoe Creek, Wyoming

William Porter's Purvine company left Fort Laramie on June 13, the same day, according to Edward Smith, as the Watt, Walker/Bristow, and Kelly companies. Together, they would have constituted a considerable procession—about eighty wagons. From here on, Porter's entries in his tiny notebook dried up to the barest essentials, reporting little more than dates, miles traveled, and places camped. On the morning of June 16, his party was about forty miles north of the fort. They traveled sixteen miles that day and camped beside the North Platte, about five miles southeast of present-day Orin, Wyoming, and just east of today's I-25.

On June 17, Porter recorded that they left the river and proceeded up the trail, along the ridge between Indian and Spring Creeks. After eighteen miles, they descended to Big Timber (La Bonte) Creek and camped. They traveled another eighteen miles the next day and camped at Mike's Head (La Prele) Creek. Here, Porter complained of "poor grass" and reported that some of their cattle were poisoned, but he did not say from what. After another eighteen miles on June 19, they made it to Deer Creek. Rolling beside the North Platte on the twentieth, they traveled seventeen miles and stopped to camp eight miles below the Mormon ferry. If Porter's estimate of distance is correct, it would indicate that the Mormon ferry was operating near where the future Fort Casper would be built. Had the Mormons recently moved their ferry four miles upstream to the "upper crossing"?

Porter wrote that his company lay by on June 21 and 22, and remained "8 miles below the ferry waiting for the advance companies to cross the river." His term "advance companies" probably meant the Watt, Walker-Bristow, and Kelly parties. It appears that his Purvine group had to wait their turn. The ferry appeared capable of crossing between thirty and forty wagons in a long day. They needed to get Joe Watt's flock of three hundred sheep across the river as well. With their dense wool, sheep were not good swimmers, not like cattle and horses, so it was advisable to ferry them. Assuming only fifteen sheep could be squeezed on the ferry at a time, it might take twenty trips, the good part of a day, to transport a flock the size of Watt's.

On June 23, Porter wrote that they moved eight more miles toward the ferry. Yet, they still did not cross. Instead, Porter explained that his company "move[d] our cattle to the front of the mountains for grass," presumably waiting for one or more companies to cross ahead of them. With time on his hands, Porter sat down and wrote a lengthy letter to his family on the twenty-fourth:

Crossing of the North Fork of Platte
June 24, 1848
Dear Father, Mother, Brothers and Sisters,
      ... We are all well, and getting on as well as common. Some of our company are a little discouraged on account of fatigues of the journey and the reports in reference to the Indians in Oregon. I have felt a little discouraged sometimes, about the scarcity of the grass, though our cattle look well. As a general thing, there is no difficulty in finding good camping places till you get to Laramie, thence to this place there is but one or two good camps. Grass is not as good this season as it commonly is. . . . This is the fourth day we have been here waiting to cross the Platte. A small company of Mormons from Salt Lake are here with a canoe boat to cross the immigrants. They charge 1.50 per wagon. It will be two days yet till we can cross. . . . There is now a company in our camp from Oregon just arrived. They say grass is very scarce on the route from this on. . . . We have been traveling with Walker and Bristow's Company for some time, but for convenience will separate here till necessity calls us to join again. . . .
      In hopes of seeing you again, I am, William Porter

Again the complaint is made that "grass is not good this season." The emigrants were passing through an ordinarily arid area that seemed to be suffering from a drought that was making matters worse. During the gold rush years, it would be even worse, when infinitely larger numbers of people and livestock would swarm through this desolate landscape.

While waiting their turn to cross the North Platte, things went from bad to worse for Porter's company: "24th, 25th, 26th, 27th. Cattle took a regular stampede every night, losing more or less each time." Hungry and restless, their livestock had become unmanageable. His group was having a terrible time, much like those in the Adams company.

Edward Smith had recorded that the Hannah (Hanna) company left Fort Laramie four days after Purvine, but the Purvine company's troubles gave the Hannah company time to catch up to and cross the river ahead of Purvine, which was trying to collect their scattered livestock. During the next three days, Porter recorded in his notebook:

> 28th. Found cattle enough to move five miles from ferry.
> 29th. Lay by for purpose of hunting cattle.
> 30th. Traveled 28 miles and camped near Willow Springs.

Porter did not specify the day they crossed the river, but since Willow Springs is about twenty-eight miles beyond the river crossing, his entry for the thirtieth suggested that his company left the river that morning. Therefore, it appeared that they crossed on the twenty-ninth, eight days after they first arrived in the vicinity. Porter's mileage of twenty-eight miles to Willow Springs seems to confirm that the ferry was operating at the "upper crossing" when his company used it on the twenty-ninth.

June 18–23, 1848
Edward Smith, at Fort Laramie, Wyoming

Edward Smith and his family crossed the Laramie River on June 11 and set up camp near Fort Platte, just east of Fort Laramie. On June 18, a week later, the Smiths were still there, biding their time. He had already reported the arrival and departure of the Watt, Walker-Bristow, Purvine ("Pike & Scott Co."), Kelly, Delaney, and Hannah companies, but this previously impatient man had not departed with any of them. By June 18, his journal entry was showing an unwillingness to languish at the fort much longer:

> Sun 18— time passes wearily along, and I have concluded to go with the first
> Co that comes today we went down the River about 16 miles to look for a
> Co   found none   Returned about sun set.

The following day, it appeared that Smith's wait might be coming to an end: "Mon 19— about 4 oclock Capt Stone arrived with ten wagons   two Roman Catholic Missionaries came with him." While the Stone party and Father Lempfrit rested at the fort and repaired their wagons on June 20, Smith recorded a few incidents: "tues

20— at day break a wolf came in a few feet of my tent   I fired a pistol at him at about 5 feet and missed him   During the day we killed a Rattlesnake about 5 feet Long." These serpents were why careful emigrants had learned to encircle their beds at night with a coarse horse-hair rope, lest a rattlesnake became their cozy bedfellow.

The next day, Smith reported that the Stone company departed: "wed 21— nothing of importance occurred to day we remained in camp to day   Capt Stones C left at 2 PM." Obviously, Smith did not leave with Stone. Why not? Perhaps because he had heard that another company would be arriving the next day: "June Thur 22— to day Col. Chiles company arrived and encamped about one mile above fort John [Laramie]." Smith had been intending to go to California from the outset, but the companies he watched depart from Fort Laramie had all been Oregon-bound. The Chiles-Hensley party, however, the last wagon train on the trail this year, was going to California. This must have been his reason for waiting. "frid 23" he wrote. "I hauled up my wagon to Mr. Chiles encampment yesterday."

JUNE 18–30, 1848
Father Lempfrit, Stone company, a few miles east of Fort Laramie, Wyoming

Father Lempfrit was last seen when his Stone company was nearing Fort Laramie on June 17. The next day he wrote:

> 18th June. The feast of the Holy Trinity. The captain of the caravan [Stone], hoping to join up with the caravan that was ahead of us, made us leave early in the morning. Thus we were deprived of the joy of celebrating the Holy Mass. We are getting near Fort Laramie.

It is amusing that Captain Stone was still trying to overtake the company ahead, as he had been aspiring, without success, ever since they departed St. Joseph. But the Hannah company arrived on June 16, a full three days ahead of Stone.

Lempfrit had recently sounded downhearted, but he now seemed uplifted by his arrival at Fort Laramie. His diary entry reflects a rejuvenated spirit:

> 19th June. Since early morning I hurried up to get on ahead of the others. I wanted to see Fort Laramie for myself. . . . An hour later Fort Laramie at last came into view. At first sight it looked like a pile of bricks. I was separated from it by the river, however a Spanish house-servant came to meet me and he showed me where I could cross. Then I was at the Fort. Fort Laramie had lost all its splendor! It is nothing but a pile of sun-baked bricks. Not a single room has a roof, all is open to the elements. Our wagons crossed over the river and then we carried on to camp near Fort Jean [Fort John/Fort Laramie] which belongs to the American [Fur] Company. I went and delivered the letters that had been given to me by Mr. Sarpy of St. Louis for the employees at the various forts they have. Mr. Picot[te] and Mr. Bourdeau [Bordeaux] to whom these letters had been addressed

received us most cordially. They invited us to take our meals with them during the two days we have to stay here.

The next day, June 20, Captain Stone oversaw the repair of some of their wagons. Since all of the wagon trains ahead of them had left, they had the fort to themselves (except for Edward Smith, who was still there). While Lempfrit did not exactly gush at the fort's appearance, his journal suggested that he enjoyed the attention of the fort's dignitaries. Francis Parkman reported in 1846 that Pierre Papin was the fort's *bourgeois*, but he was not there. In his absence, the congenial deputy, James Bordeaux, commanded the fort.[28] Consistently acclaimed by other diarists as a friendly and hospitable host, Bordeaux seemed to heap extra attention on Lempfrit. A French Catholic priest rarely passed through here, so it is not surprising that Bordeaux and the other AFC *engagés* of French ancestry treated Lempfrit like a celebrity:

> 20th June. While they were busy making repairs to our waggon we passed two most agreeable days with these gentlemen. This made us forget that our journey had had some unpleasant moments. In a country deficient in everything we were sumptuously treated. We celebrated the Holy Mass in one of the Fort's apartments and these gentlemen attended Mass with great devoutness. We set up our camp below the Fort. However, we had much to suffer from grasshoppers and dust.

Very little occurred on June 21. Lempfrit reported celebrating Mass again. Assured by Bordeaux that Lempfrit's correspondence would be safely conveyed to St. Louis on their next trip east, the priest set about writing several letters to family, friends, and his religious superiors in France.

On the morning of the twenty-second, Lempfrit bid his hosts farewell, and their wagons began rolling away from the fort at 8:30 AM. The priest may have found it difficult to return to the trail. Perhaps sad thoughts engulfed him when he finally lost sight of the fort. It would be the last outpost of civilization he would see for quite some time.

Shortly after leaving the fort, Lempfrit described encountering a poor little lamb. "She belonged to Captain Lhenen who was ahead of us," he wrote. Who was Lhenen? Although Edward Smith had reported the Delaney company arriving at Fort Laramie on the fifteenth, he failed to record when it left. Could it be that the Delaney company was just ahead of Stone? Between Lempfrit trying to spell the name phonetically (which he may have heard as "de Leneh") and/or the translator of the priest's journal perhaps misreading his handwriting, it is easy to see how "Delaney" might have become "Lhenen."

Lempfrit next wrote:

> 22nd June.... Towards midday we were at the foot of a mountain, and there we found a vigorous mineral spring [Warm Springs] that had lukewarm water. The

weather became so cold that we had to put on our overcoats to keep ourselves warm. We are now entering the territory of the Crow Indians. These Indians have the reputation of being dangerous and of being the greatest horse thieves in all the country.

Lempfrit's entries make it appear that his company took the hill route rather than the river route that most of the earlier companies had taken. Captain Stone may have calculated that by taking the lesser-traveled road, they would avoid overcropped grass at their campsites.

During the twenty-third and twenty-fourth the priest reported little, except that along this higher, more mountainous trail, they camped at pleasant spots. "[T]he vegetation is quite marvelous," he reported, remarking that there was plenty of grass, wildflowers, "century-old trees . . . [and] cherries and red currents in abundance." But he also complained of the cold nights: "[W]hen we got up we found two [inches] of ice in our pails that we had filled with water."

On June 25, Lempfrit noted their wagon breaking down and the wind blowing with such ferocity they were unable to put their tent up. For the next five days, the priest's entries seemed subdued and uninspired, as if he had slipped into another dour mood:

> 26th and 27th. Nothing special happened. The men killed a buffalo. We met some people coming from Oregon. During the 28th, 29th, and 30th of June we continued to travel alongside the River Platte. We had very strong winds. We are waiting until tomorrow to cross the River Platte for the second [and last] time.

Lempfrit provided little detail about where they were during these five days. Assuming normal progress, they should have made it to Deer Creek by the afternoon of June 28, and he seems clear that by the thirtieth they had at last arrived at the Mormon ferry on the North Platte River.

June 18–27, 1848
Richard May, Chiles-Hensley company, Chimney Rock, Nebraska

As of June 17, the wagon companies of 1848 were stretched over three hundred miles. The Joseph Chiles party, accompanied by Major Hensley and his train of pack mules and wagons, was lagging far to the rear. Richard May, our sole diarist in the Chiles-Hensley party, had last reported their position on the evening of June 17 as fifteen miles west of Ash Hollow. According to May, they traveled twenty-two miles on the eighteenth, camping within sight of Chimney Rock. May was a poor judge of distance, so it would be useless to speculate where they camped that night. On the eighteenth, May reported that they "passed 2 Indian villages of the Sioux Nation," undoubtedly the camps of Chiefs Whirlwind and Bad Wound, but he failed to mention whether they stopped to bestow gifts, engage in trading, or just passed them by.

It was on June 4 when William Anderson recorded encountering these Sioux camps. Now, two weeks later, the Indian camps had moved about twenty-five miles farther west. On June 19, Richard May reported traveling twenty-four miles, "a hard day's drive," during which time they passed Chimney Rock.

May reported an even longer day of travel on the twentieth, perhaps indicating that their leaders were beginning to worry whether they would reach the Sierras soon enough to beat the deadly winter snows. It was evident that they had picked up their pace:

20th June. Traveled 30 miles, a still harder day's drive. Passed Scott's Bluff. We drove until midnight and in passing over a small branch of Horse Creek broke the reach [tongue] of Capt. Childs' wagon. We came to a dead halt at that late hour without wood . . . . The country through which we passed for the last three days has the most romantic appearance of any my eyes have beheld. The wagoner's language fails to describe the magnificent grandeur of the rocks and hills on the Nebraska [Platte River]. I have taxed my imagination to see if I could add another variety to the different shapes and figures presented to view, in particular on the North fork, but such is the sublime and picturesque scenery that I would as soon undertake to add another tinge to the rainbow.

The actual distance between Ash Hollow and Horse Creek is 110 miles. Yet May reported the distance between these two points as ninety-one miles. He was off by nineteen miles, a significant error of nearly five miles per day.

The Chiles company did not stop to camp until midnight on June 20. Coming on the heels of the two previous long days, it had to have been a killer pace, making it difficult for man and beast to get moving the next morning. Worn out from those exhausting marches, they managed to make only thirteen miles on the twenty-first, although May's attitude seemed positive enough: "The scenery very sublime. The Black Hills was in sight today from a very elevated situation. The grass is not so abundant as wished for."

May reported arriving at Fort Laramie the next day:

22nd June. Traveled 20 miles and passed Fort Laramie. This is built on Laramie Fork of the North fork of the Nebraska [Platte] near 640 miles from Independence, Mo. It has the appearance of neatness above what I had anticipated. There was at this fort near 1000 Indians which annoyed us very much begging and stealing. Several of our surplus ox bows was stolen, hard wood being in demand. They made a demand upon our generosity as did other villages. We gave them a small quantity of tobacco, lead, beans meal, and flour and other things that were useful to them.

Edward Smith, still at the fort on the twenty-third, had also mentioned the Sioux: "The Brulie band of Sioux Indians moved their village to the fort numbering about 150 Lodges." With the exception of Smith and May, no other diarist recorded the presence of Sioux in such numbers at the fort.

According to May, his Chiles company moved their camp to "1½ miles above Fort Laramie" on June 24, perhaps to avoid being pestered so much by the Indians. May visited the fort and described what he saw:

> This fort I visited today [24th] and found it a quadrangular structure and built of dobies, viz, sun dried brick. It covers ½ acre of ground with sentry boxes on the corners and contains within a blacksmith shop and a stable sufficient for 30 horses, also trading rooms one of the proprietors told me that they brought on 25,000 dollars worth of goods annually. I saw no mounted guns. One small piece was say 3 pounds was laying in a portico much neglected. Mr. Burdiew [Bordeaux] is now proprietor of this fort or trading post.

After reporting that John Richard ("Risaw") was carrying on a trading operation at Fort Platte, May went on to confirm that trade at both places "appeared quite brisk... lame cattle were disposed of and all wagons repaired that required it."

Smith mentioned the Chiles company on June 24, noting that they were repairing their wagons. Smith then wrote about an episode with the Sioux:

> Sat 24...to day occurred a singular trait in the Indians character   a young Indian had stolen a horse from one of the Emigrants By the name of Simmons   as soon as his brother found out he was the only Indian missing from the band he went to Simmons and spoke to him as follows My Brother has made me ashamed by stealing your horse but I will not make you ashamed, there is the best horse I have got take that for the one that is stolen, such conduct surely ought not go unrewarded.

Perhaps because Chiles-Hensley was the last company that would pass through the fort this season, Bordeaux threw a party on the evening of the twenty-fourth: "An entertainment was given by Mr. Burdiew this evening," May wrote, "and several young ladies and gentlemen from the train partook of his generosity. Dancing was the entertainment resorted to on this occasion." Smith also noted the party, writing in a tone of disgust: "Last night [the 24th] they had a real fandango at fort John and to their shame be it said some young Laidies Belonging to the Emigrants went to it where some of the Gentlemen got gloriously drunk." Smith was apparently more straitlaced than May.

According to Smith, the Chiles party continued repairing wagons on June 25, while the large band of Brulé Sioux "[l]eft the fort." Smith's entry will be the last reference to the Sioux by our 1848 diarists. In the next three decades, the tribe would face cholera, smallpox, and conflict with both emigrants and the U. S. Army. When Francis Parkman was about to leave Fort Laramie in 1846, following a month of studying the Sioux, he penned a prophetic observation:

With the stream of emigration to Oregon and California, the buffalo will dwindle away, and the large wandering communities who depend on them for support must be broken and scattered. The Indians will soon be abashed by whisky and overawed by military posts; so that within a few years the traveler may pass in tolerable security through their country. [But] its dangers and its charm will have disappeared together.[29]

The Chiles-Hensley party remained at the fort another day, continuing to rest and repair. Like the other parties before them, they probably "lighted" their wagons, discarding the unnecessary. They traded as well, according to Richard May: "25th and 26th June. I visited the fort again and gave 5 lbs. of tobacco for one buffalo robe and 4 lbs. tallow. The tobacco cost me $1 in the States and I sold it for $5."

The Chiles-Hensley company finally pulled away from the fort at nine o'clock on the morning of June 27, and May described their departure:

27th June. This morning we rolled out from Laramie River and took to the black hills and hills they are. We had a very rough road to travel. At noon we came to a large spring [Warm Springs] 12 miles from the fort then traveled 8 miles further and encamped [at Bitter Cottonwood Creek] without grass for our oxen. We was in sight of high hills all day and I several times took it to be a cloud rising, it being in the west and very little to the left of our travel.

Edward Smith and his family had attached themselves to the Chiles-Hensley company and were finally leaving the fort. His entry for June 27 confirmed that they traveled twenty miles that day and camped at sunset on Bitter Cottonwood Creek.

When the Chiles-Hensley company pulled away from the fort on June 27, they not only closed the book on that year's emigrants at the fort, they also closed a colorful, memorable chapter in the lore of the West. This would be the last season when the fort would be under American Fur Company's ownership. Because of congressional legislation in 1846 to establish "military stations on the route to Oregon," the U.S. Army had established Fort Kearny on the Platte in June 1848. In March 1849, the War Department in Washington, DC, issued orders for the establishment of a "second station . . . at or near Fort Laramie." This was followed by a directive to Lt. Daniel Woodbury of the Army Corps of Engineers (the same man who had established Fort Kearny in 1848) that he purchase the buildings of Fort Laramie from the AFC, "provided it can be done at a reasonable price."[30]

In May 1849, Major W. F. Sanderson and Lt. Woodbury led a company of fifty-eight mounted riflemen up the Platte River. On June 16, their long column of canvas-topped army wagons arrived at Fort Laramie. At the time, the fort was no longer overseen by Papin or Bordeaux; Bruce Husband, an AFC lawyer, was in charge then. Woodbury and Husband commenced negotiations and by the next day they had struck a deal, settling on a price of $4,000. It was a sign that the AFC was as anxious to dispose of the falling-down fort as the army was to acquire its location. The army immediately set to work preparing the site as a place to garrison three companies of troops. They commenced building two structures outside the fort's adobe walls: a sutler's store and a barracks ("Old Bedlam"), both of which survive today.[31] The other two army companies arrived a month later.

The new army fort would serve as a welcome way station for massive numbers of gold rushers, Mormons, and other wayfarers in the years to come. In 1850 alone, the army recorded 44,000 persons passing through the fort.[32] But a change in ownership of the fort also presaged a change in the fortunes of the Sioux. Whereas the AFC and the independent traders had a financial interest in keeping the passing white emigrants and the Indians on reasonably good terms, hotheaded army officers fresh out of West Point would come to command the post. Some may have had a different agenda—perhaps to make a name for themselves in order to advance their careers. In 1854, six years hence, the Grattan massacre would occur near here, involving Fort Laramie's Lt. Grattan and his troops.

———————————

As the sun set on June 27, the Wambaugh company was camping at Pacific Springs, three miles west of South Pass. According to the eastbound Oregonian Isaac Pettijohn, the vanguard of the emigration was the "43 waggons bound for Oregon and California" and they were traveling about forty miles ahead of Wambaugh. The back end of the emigration was the Chiles/Hensley party, which had just left Fort Laramie and was camping at Bitter Cottonwood Creek, twenty miles west of the fort. The 1848 wave of the emigration now stretched over 285 miles, and the parties were not even halfway to their destinations. Their livestock were in varying stages of deterioration and their wagons were lighter but were still too heavy. The emigrants must have been dispirited and weary, but they had no choice but to push on. As the old adage goes, "When you are in the middle of the river, you have no choice but to keep swimming."

Table 9: Arrival at Fort Laramie and location of companies on June 27, 1848

Company (Diarist)	Arrived Fort	Left Fort	Location on June 27
Adams	May 30 (est.)	June 1 (est.)	some west of Pacific Springs; some west of North Platte ferry
Allsopp	May 31	June 5 (est.)	west of Pacific Springs
Greenwood	May 9 (est.)	June 7 (est.)	Pacific Springs
Cornwall	May 10 (est.)	June 7	Pacific Springs
Wambaugh (Root)	June 3	June 7	Pacific Springs
Gates	June 4 (est.)	June 8 (est.)	near Pacific Springs
Miller (Anderson)	June 8	June 9	last crossing of Sweetwater
12 California wagons	June 8	June 9	somewhere behind Miller
Watt (Belknap)	June 11	June 13	near Rocky Ridge
Walker	June 12	June 13	west of North Platte crossing
Bristow	June 12	June 13	west of North Platte crossing
Kelly	June 12	June 13	west of North Platte crossing
Hannah	June 15	June 17	west of North Platte crossing
Purvine (Porter)	June 12	June 13	just east of North Platte ferry
Delaney	June 16	June 21 (est.)	somewhere ahead of Stone
Stone (Lempfrit)	June 19	June 22	likely near La Prele Creek
Chiles (May)	June 22	June 27	Bitter Cottonwood Creek
Hensley	June 22	June 27	Bitter Cottonwood Creek
(Smith)	June 11	June 27	with Chiles at Bitter Cottonwood

CHAPTER 13

Les Mauvaises Terres
JUNE 27–JULY 18

JUNE 28–JULY 15, 1848
Riley Root, Wambaugh company, Pacific Springs, Wyoming

As the sun rose on the morning of June 28 and the Wambaugh company began to stir, they could see their cattle grazing across the grassy expanse known as Pacific Springs. There was no risk of the animals wandering off during the night, as there was nothing but dry sagebrush in all directions beyond this patch of green. The springs issued from a slight depression in the terrain, producing an area of abundant grass for almost a mile. Within this hollow, the waters gathered into a narrow brook not more than a few feet wide and meandered in a southwesterly direction. Many emigrants reported experiencing a sensation of rippling, floating, or rolling in this boggy area and there was a danger of oxen getting mired in the muck during the night.

After catching up their oxen, the Wambaugh company left the springs and began a journey across an undulating, treeless desert. As the sun climbed into the sky, its glare caused the far-off landscape to shimmer with heat waves, and created dancing phantom lakes. Now west of South Pass, the travelers entered the domain of the Snake Indians. Edwin Bryant had encountered a hunting party of Snakes just west of Pacific Springs in 1846, and learned how intensely they hated the Sioux. The Snakes called the Sioux "cutthroats," and referred to them in sign language by a slashing motion across the throat.[1]

About nine miles west of Pacific Springs, the Wambaugh company passed just south of Plume Rocks, a small outcropping of red clay with a plume-shaped projection on the top. A mile and a half farther they came to Dry Sandy Creek. Although it was usually dry this time of year, they could have obtained water by digging deep in its sandy bed. But why? The water was so brackish and alkaline it was deadly to stock, and was why knowledgeable guides made sure their livestock drank their fill before leaving Pacific Springs.

They continued traveling through country that grew little besides sage. As the day wore on, the heat from an unremitting sun became their implacable enemy. Nine miles beyond Dry Creek, they came to the twenty-foot-wide Little Sandy Creek. Root called it "a fine stream, of sufficient amount of water to carry 4 run of mill stones. . . . here is no grass, except what borders the stream, a few rods wide on each side of it." He failed to mention the bands of blue lupine and small willows that crowded its steep banks, and the legions of ferocious mosquitoes that eagerly attacked them. After a day of traveling nineteen miles, the company camped here for the night.

Root reported leaving the Little Sandy the next morning:

> 29th— Six miles to Great Sandy [Big Sandy] creek, over a barren clay road. Fine stream. Little grass, no wood except a few willows. . . . This is Greenwood's cut-off, which begins a little east of this river, between the two Sandys. The old road is the one leading to Fort Bridger. It is also the one the Mormons took, when they emigrated to Salt Lake.

Here, between the Little and Big Sandys, the trail forked. The left branch bent slightly to the southwest and led to Fort Bridger, ninety miles away. The right branch, which Root called Greenwood's Cutoff, continued straight, almost due west; it was a shorter, more direct way of getting to the Bear River.

The first emigrant wagon company to open Greenwood's Cutoff was reputed to be the Stephens-Townsend-Murphy company in 1844, piloted by Caleb Greenwood. According to Moses Schallenberger, a member of the Stephens party, the shortcut was not Greenwood's idea, but Isaac Hitchcock's. The sixty-four-year-old Hitchcock had claimed to know a shorter way to the Green River, saying he had been with the Bonneville expedition in 1832, and that they had successfully taken a party of wagons that way.[2] Yet, for some reason, the shortcut was called Greenwood's Cutoff, as Root and most of our 1848 diarists would call it. One of the earliest written references to "Greenwood's Cutoff" appeared in Edwin Bryant's account of his 1846 trip.[3] In later years, people began calling it Sublette's Cutoff even though Sublette had nothing to do with it.

The benefit of taking Greenwood's Cutoff was that it shortened the journey by about fifty miles and three days. The problem was that it forced wagon companies to cross forty-five miles of waterless, grassless desert before they struck the Green River. No doubt Caleb Greenwood would have lobbied for saving fifty miles, dismissing any objectors with a wave of his hand and a rebuke: "Wall, what's a little thirsty spell?"

Root's entry revealed where the trail forked prior to the gold rush: between the Little Sandy and the Big Sandy. Sometime during the gold rush, wagons began heading toward Fort Bridger five miles west of the Dry Sandy and before reaching the Little Sandy. The new split was moved seven miles east of where it forked in 1848. The location of the later "Parting of the Ways" is well established and clearly marked. Even today, the trail ruts are deep and unmistakable.

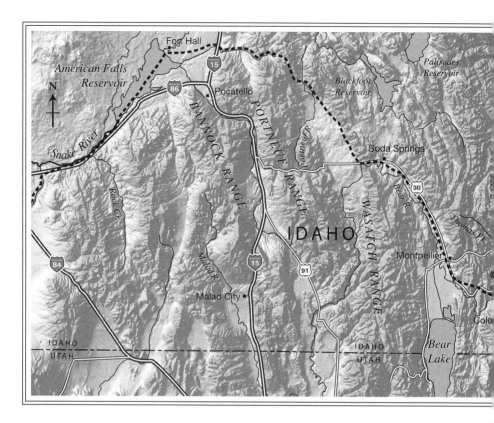

After taking the cutoff, Root wrote that the company stopped at Big Sandy Creek at noon on June 29. Here Root was moved to describe the majestic Wind River Mountains looming to the north, their spectacular snow-capped peaks rising to 13,000 feet. Before setting off across the Little Colorado Desert, the emigrants encouraged their cattle to drink their fill from the Big Sandy and filled every container that would hold water. When the party had rested long enough on June 29, they drew a collective sigh, hitched up their trousers, tugged on their hats, then launched themselves in a defiant march across what French trappers called *les mauvaises terres à travers*—"a bad land to travel across." It would be a foretaste of even worse things to come.

About two miles west of the Big Sandy, the trail passed just north of Haystack Butte, where it can be seen today nine miles north of present-day Farson, and one-half mile east of today's Highway 191. The trail then crossed today's Highway 191 and continued west across the lonely desert.

Root reported that they traveled "[t]he rest of the day and the following night" across a land that was flat, wide, and dusty. During the gold rush years, it was common for large wagon companies to fan out, traveling abreast so they wouldn't have to choke on each other's dust. It is not known whether that is what the Wambaugh company did. Because the road was relatively new, few wagon parties had gone this

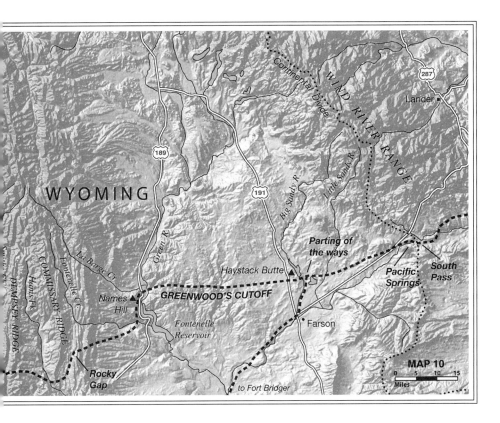

way and the way may not have been well defined. It is remarkable that the party was able to navigate this featureless expanse at night. Even today, it would be virtually impossible to find a single definable trail in the desert west of Highway 191. The land now belongs to the Bureau of Land Management and the poor-quality dirt roads are far from water and help in the event of a breakdown.

Late that night and twenty-six miles after leaving the Big Sandy, the struggling Wambaugh company groped their way through the dark. According to Root, they came to "a deep valley [Buckhorn Canyon] dangerous to go down at night." He seemed critical of his guides, wondering why they couldn't have waited at the Big Sandy until late in the afternoon: "[I]t would be safe to remain at Big Sandy creek till 4 or 4 ½ o'clock in the afternoon in order that daylight may appear before arriving at this valley."

Panting heavily and struggling with the heavy wagons, the oxen pushed on through the dark, moonless night. A moonrise/sunrise table for that date and place reveals that the moon did not rise until 4:51 AM, while the sun rose one minute earlier, at 4:50 AM.[4] With nothing to light the way except faint starlight and perhaps a few lanterns, it would have been like traveling with your eyes shut. Those on horseback and the wagon drivers might have caught themselves nodding off from time to time, but people trudging alongside the wagons had no such luxury. A lucky child might be able to doze in his mother's arms for a while, but for most there was no chance to rest. Crossing rough terrain in the dark would have kept everyone's nerves on edge and watching the horizon for any signs of the coming dawn.

They continued to crawl on until night melted into day. About midday on the thirtieth, after a seemingly endless forty-four-mile *jornada* over what Root described as "a sage plain, destitute of water and grass for our cattle, with four deep and dangerous valleys [the Buckhorn Canyons and their branches]," they came at last to the rim of the bluffs overlooking the Green River Valley.

To get to the river they had to descend a steep drop-off into a gorge, possibly Steed Canyon, locking their back wheels and letting their wagons down by ropes. Root's silence suggests they escaped serious mishaps. In later years, when infinitely larger numbers of wagons descended here, there would be the occasional catastrophe, when a wagon would break free and careen down the slope, smashing into a useless heap of splinters.

Once they reached the bank of the river, the men had to keep their livestock from overdrinking and killing themselves. The company must have suffered no losses, as Root only recorded that "our hearts were gladdened that we were enabld to slake the thirst of our famished cattle." They then faced crossing a swift-running river that was more than a hundred yards wide. The Mormons would send men to ferry emigrants across the Green this year, but Root did not mention any ferrymen present.[5] Although there were several places along the river where wagon parties were known to cross, the most likely place for the Wambaugh company would have been at the foot of Steed Canyon, about two miles north of Names Hill on today's Highway 189.

After crossing the river, Root reported that they "[s]taid at the crossing" the next day, July 1, to rest themselves and their exhausted animals. They likely camped on the extensive meadow stretching along the west bank of the river, just east of Names Hill. Overlooking the river, Names Hill consisted of an overhanging sandstone cliff hundreds of feet long. As early as 1848, there would not have been many names etched upon its face, although there is one old inscription that survives today: "James Bridger—trapper—1844." Since Bridger could not write, either someone inscribed it for him or it is counterfeit.[6]

James Clyman would have recognized familiar terrain when he arrived at the Green River because he had trapped in the area with the Ashley brigade from 1824 through 1827. La Barge Creek flowed into the Green about three miles north of where the Wambaugh company camped on the evenings of June 30 and July 1. While sitting around a campfire at night, Clyman might have told his fellow travelers about when he and three other companions were trapping on the La Barge in 1825. A party of Arapahos stole up on them one night as they slept along the creek and killed their night guard, Joseph La Barge, with a tomahawk chop to the skull. Clyman and the others sprang up and took shelter behind a breastwork of hastily thrown-up stones, where they were well defended. Losing interest, the Indians left and Clyman lived to see another day.[7]

The large grove of tall cottonwoods where the Wambaugh company likely camped can still be seen today just east of Names Hill, on today's Highway 189. As pleasant as the place was, the company needed to get moving again. Refreshed to a small degree, they resumed their journey on the morning of July 2, although Root seemed unsatisfied with the day's progress: "2nd— 9 miles to camp on Salmon Trout branch [Fontenelle Creek], 6 or 8 miles above its union with Green River. We gained but little towards Oregon, to-day, the road being very circuitous and hilly, part of the way."

When they left camp on the second, they first headed south, marching beside the river about four miles. Then they turned west and followed the trail as it climbed out of the river bottom through a ravine and up a ridge called Holden Hill. They traveled along the ridge until they descended into a small valley through which Fontenelle Creek snaked. At the end of the day, one in which they only traveled nine miles, they stayed the night on Fontenelle Creek. It was the right choice because there would be no water beyond the creek for quite some distance.

Root probably did not know it at the time, but in terms of miles, they had just completed the first half of their journey to Oregon. Given what they had endured so far, it is hard to know what Root's state of mind would have been had he known what still lay ahead. Root called Fontenelle Creek "the Salmon Trout," suggesting that Clyman had not informed him that its name should have been Clyman's Fork. Indeed, many branches of the Green River had been named after men in Ashley's brigade in 1825: Ashley's Fork for William Ashley, Smith's Fork for Jedediah Smith, Sublette's Fork for William Sublette, Ham's Fork for Zacharias Ham, La Barge's Fork for Joseph La Barge, and Clyman's Fork for James Clyman.[8]

Clyman was one of the few Ashley men who quit the trapping trade and left the mountains in the fall of 1827. Therefore, he was not there to protect the name of his creek when Lucien Fontenelle, an American Fur Company employee, squatted there in the 1830s. He, or someone, renamed it Fontenelle Creek, the name by which it is known today.

After departing the creek on the morning of July 3, the Wambaugh party ascended a gradually sloping ridge between the dry Willow and Sheep Creeks. They were now gradually ascending a series of treeless, sage-covered hills, ridges, and ravines. For the next few days, they would be traveling across vast stretches of ups and downs. About nine miles after leaving camp, their wagons passed over Slate Creek Ridge, where the hills looked especially bald and desolate. On the other side of the ridge, they probably made it to a small valley in which the upper reaches of Slate Creek ran, but it would have been dry. By then, they had gone sixteen tough, wearing miles. Unable to continue, they stopped to camp. According to Root, there was "[n]o wood, little grass, no water except a small spring."

Climbing a "stony road" on the morning of July 4, they likely picked their way through Rocky Gap, a narrow cleft in the next ridge. The road was rough, hilly, and perfectly bare of grass, the only vegetation being the ubiquitous sage. Then they descended into Pomeroy Basin, crossing Fisher Creek, then went up and over Commissary Ridge at Branley Pass. On the western side, they descended into the Ham's Fork Valley. Root wrote: "4th— 10 miles, over a hilly and stony road, to Ham's fork of Green River. Some grass, no wood but willows. Here were a few Indian lodges of the Snake tribe."

Ham's Fork was a medium-sized stream. It snaked through a pretty little valley, a flat, grass-covered bottom with stunted willows fringing the stream. Rufus Burrows' reminiscence contains a fascinating piece about his Wambaugh party encountering a Snake village, likely the one at Ham's Fork:

> While passing Snake Indian country, we came to a dead Indian warrior laying on his buffalo robe just beside the road. Greenwood, knowing the country well, and being familiar with all the Indian nations, told us he was a warrior of the Snake tribe. His bow, quiver of arrows, war club, tommy-hawk, and scalping knife lay beside him. The train passed on and after a few miles came down in a nice little valley. There beside a nice little stream [Ham's Fork?], we found a big Snake Indian village. These Indians were at peace with the whites. We camped just one-half mile below the village. The Indians were all glad to have the train camp near them as that gave them an opportunity to trade their buffalo robes and moccasins for different articles. Some of the men told the Indians about seeing the dead warrior and they said that they were out on a war raid when they ran on to a large rattlesnake. This Indian, saying he was possessed with the totem or [was a] medicine man and that he could remove the fangs without the snake biting him, picked up the snake and it bit him. The bite soon proved fatal. His faith failing in his Indian belief, his companions would not touch him and left him alone to go to the happy hunting grounds. We passed an Indian grave up in an old cottonwood tree. I presume he was an Indian warrior, as all his possessions were hanging there beside his skeleton. A horse's head, war club, tommy-hawk, bow, quiver and blankets were beside him their belief being that he might need his horse and war outfit on the road to the happy hunting ground.
>
> While camped at the Snake village, Captain Wambo told us we would see some sport. About eighty young Indian warriors were going out to practice on a ridge about three quarters of a mile long near the camp. To this the Indians went, riding their ponies bareback with only a tug in their mouths to guide them. About five would start at a time and at full speed and run their ponies down the ridge, hollowing and yelling and pretending to be escaping from the enemy. But to show how cute they were in warfare, they would split, one half going on one side of the ridge and the other half on the other side, getting out of sight of the first. Then they would go back up the hollow on each side of the ridge and come

in behind the other band, running and yelling, following them up to show how smart they had been. They would keep this up for hours, training their horses and themselves.

This is a valuable narrative, not only because of its colorful description of life with a band of Snakes, but because it confirmed that Caleb Greenwood was traveling with them, presumably since Fort Laramie. It seems odd that neither Root nor Burrows reported the company celebrating the nation's independence on July 4, although it is possible that they did. Most wagon trains found a way to honor it, no matter where on the trail they were.

While at Ham's Fork, Clyman likely kept a vigilant eye on his horses. Indians, likely Snakes, had stolen horses from his trapping party near here in 1824 and it must have made a lasting impression on him. When his wagon party neared Ham's Fork in 1844, he wrote:

> all Subordination and controle haveing been broken up for several days, thinking ourselves out of danger at least out of danger of life But all Savages will Steal & so will the Shoshonees [Snakes] & a party of which are now passing while I am writeing.[9]

The next day, July 5, the Wambaugh wagon train left Ham's Fork and the Snake Indians, ascending steep hills that rose to the west of the valley. Following the trail up a long ridge just north of Quakenasp Canyon, they finally reached the top of the Ham's Fork Plateau, where the trail leveled off for a stretch before plunging down some steep inclines. According to Root, they traveled "14 miles over a very hilly road and part of it very dangerous to pass." Their fourteen miles of travel that day would have been very taxing, but Root's account does not convey the difficulty of traveling this wicked section of trail. Some of our later diarists will do a better job of it.

Root was not clear about where they camped, but based upon his estimate of miles, which is ordinarily quite accurate, there is a good chance that they stopped to camp along Rock Creek where it ran down a long valley between Dempsey Ridge and Rock Creek Ridge. Traveling at almost eight thousand feet elevation, they were experiencing bone-chilling nights. They began to pass north- and east-facing slopes that sheltered groves of quaking aspen. Even today, the area remains quite remote and is difficult to reach. As the crow flies, the campsite for the night of the fifth would have been about six miles east of Highway 30, and about nine miles southeast of modern Cokeville, Wyoming.

The next day, Root wrote:

> 6th— Frost in camp, this morning. To-day, we travld 18 miles and encamped on Bear river, 4 miles west of Smith fork. The hills around us are quite barren. Bear river has a little grass in some places along its bottoms. It is a considerable stream, though not more than three-fourths the water that Green river has at its crossing.

Steep and sudden was the descent off the last hill into the Bear River Valley, and it would have been difficult to keep their eyes on the road; they would have been drawn to the dazzling valley floor below. Grass abounded through much of the three to four-mile-wide river plain. Fields of colorful blue flax abounded and schools of beautiful mountain trout drifted silently in the slow-moving river. After a month of traveling through parched desert, it must have been a grand and refreshing change of scenery. Most of the emigrants were farmers, and some might have felt an urge to unhitch their oxen and stay forever in that enticing place.

In an 1844 entry in his journal, Clyman reminisced about attending the trappers' rendezvous in the Bear River Valley in 1827, noting that the buffalo he had seen then could no longer be found in the valley.[10] Prior to the 1830s, buffalo ranged as far west as here, but white hunters and Indians seeking hides had slaughtered huge numbers. As of 1848, none were to be found west of South Pass.[11]

The trail reached the valley floor about four miles south of modern Cokeville, near Highway 30, and joined the trail coming up from Fort Bridger. Volcanically formed mountains rose up on both sides of the trail and after traveling north for about four miles, the wagon company came to Smith's Fork and crossed it near where it flowed into the Bear River. Believed to be named after Clyman's former trapping leader, Jedediah Smith, the swift-running stream flowed toward the Bear in multiple channels.[12] Lined with aspen, cottonwood, and willow, the fork entered the valley between two mountains, each peaking almost one thousand feet above the valley. The wagon party crossed the stream just east of modern Cokeville and Highway 30.

On July 7, the company marched north eleven miles, staying close to the river. At the end of the day, they crossed a flat meadow and forded Thomas Fork, a deep-channeled stream that entered the Bear River from the northeast. Owing to its steep and muddy banks, the stream's crossing, just east of the modern Highway 30 bridge, was a difficult one. Abundant, lush grass bordered the stream, and they camped there for the night.

The next morning, they traveled thirteen and a half miles, according to Root. From Thomas Fork, they headed northwest, away from the Bear, which had jogged to the southwest for seven miles before heading north again. They followed a shortcut that led them over a series of hills for six miles, somewhat following the route taken by today's Highway 30. At the end of these hills, they had to creep down a very steep slope to return to the Bear. They then turned north and traveled another seven miles, staying near the winding river. Based on Root's estimated distance, they should have stopped to camp near Peg Leg Smith's trading post, although Root mentioned neither him nor his post. This site, where there were four log cabins and some Indian lodges, is estimated to have been about four miles south of today's Montpelier, and between Highway 30 and the river.[13]

Peg Leg had a long and mixed career in the West, beginning as a trapper and mountain man. One emigrant reported meeting Smith at Fort Hall in 1844 and another noted his trading post at the Bear River in 1846.[14] Joe Meek and his east-bound Oregonians were struggling through deep snow when they stumbled into the Bear River Valley in March 1848, just three months before the westbound Wambaugh party reached the area. They encountered Smith's camp beside the almost snow-free Thomas Fork, where he was running cattle. Smith fed them, partied with them, and then got them underway again.[15]

When J. Goldsborough Bruff, a 1849 gold rusher, encountered Peg Leg here in the Bear River Valley, he wrote much of what one needed to know:

> The old mountaineer—"Peg Leg Smith" came into camp: he has a cabin on the bank [of the Bear], some distance below, and trades with cattle, whiskey, &c. His leg was injured and he outed his knife & amputated it himself, and afterward dressed [it], and fortunately recovered. He has fitted a wooden leg—(hence the appellation, by his comrades) and a socket to the stirrup, permits him to ride as smartly as ever.[16]

But Peg Leg had a dark side, too. At one time, he was supposed to have engaged in kidnapping Indian children and selling them as slaves in the Mexico trade. He was reported to have ridden with Bill Williams and a band of Ute Indians, a horse-stealing outfit that savaged California in 1840 by stealing over 3,000 horses from various ranchos between Pueblo de los Angelos and Pueblo de San Luis Obispo. In the spring of 1849, a gold rusher getting ready to depart from Independence, Missouri, claimed to have encountered Smith near a saloon, where Smith had gotten into a drunken brawl and killed two men with his wooden leg and shot a third.[17] Despite his gracious hospitality to former mountain messmate Joe Meek earlier in the year, Smith sounded like someone you shouldn't get riled up. And you might want to keep a close eye on your horse as well.

Root explained that they stayed in camp on July 9 and buried a young man from their company. Root did not report the name of the deceased or what he died from, but it sounds like the company was suffering a small epidemic. Root added that "[t]oday, also, are 14 sick persons in our company." Without a description of the symptoms, it is impossible to say what illness the emigrants were suffering, but one possibility is Rocky Mountain spotted fever, which people were known to have come down with in the area. They may have gotten it from disease-carrying ticks they picked up as their clothing brushed against bushes and tall grasses. The disease can incubate for up to two weeks before showing any symptoms. Another possibility could be food poisoning, common on the trail where, even if the emigrants had known about germs, proper food storage was practically impossible, and a number of emigrants might become sick at the same time.

Trying to make up for lost time, Root wrote that they traveled twenty-five miles on July 10. The traveling was easy, on a nearly level road close to the Bear River. Root praised both the road and the scenery:

10th— 25 miles to camp on Bear river. Passd several fine rills from the mountains, to-day. A very good road down the Bear river bottom. The bottom and mountain lands, to-day, assume a more verdant appearance, though the verdure consists mostly of useless shrubs and weeds, except on the skirts of some of the peaks, where they are clothd with timber sparingly. From this camp, snow is seen on the Bear River mountains.

The company continued rolling through the Bear River Valley on the eleventh. Between today's Montpelier and Soda Springs, the trail pretty much corresponded to the route of today's Highway 30. After traveling eleven miles on July 11, Root wrote that they encamped on the Bear, a mile below Soda Springs:

11th— 10 miles to Soda Springs, and 1 farther to camp, making 11 miles. Have traveld over volcanic rocks to-day, the first I have seen on our route. Near to camp and north of it, near the base of the mountain, the three small craters, apparently, of extinct volcanoes. They may, however, be the craters of some of those silent springs.

There were hundreds of springs in the Soda Springs area, mostly along the north bank of the Bear River. Cones of deposited minerals, ranging in color from white to flesh-colored, and from less than a foot to twenty feet tall, were scattered throughout the area, some oozing water that ran as red as blood. The more memorable curiosities were Soda Springs, Beer Springs, and Steamboat Springs. Soda Springs was located about one and three-quarters miles west of the center of the modern community of that name (and a half mile west of Soda Creek). Its waters were noted for their natural soda taste, while the waters of Beer Springs, a few hundred feet farther west, possessed effervescent gas and a slightly acid, beerlike taste. Another half mile west was Steamboat Springs, not regarded so much for the taste of its water as for the noise it made. It was famous for jetting steaming gas and mineral water out of a three-foot-high rock cone several feet into the air every fifteen seconds, producing a hissing noise that resembled a steamboat boiler releasing steam. Regrettably, these springs have disappeared beneath the waters of Soda Point Reservoir, a man-made lake. A couple of small, rust-colored cones, the only remaining evidence of these fascinating springs, can be found today at the west end of the Soda Springs Country Club golf course.

That night, the travelers pulled close to their campfires and chatted quietly in the cold night air with the sound of Steamboat Springs not far away. At some point apparently, William Fallon approached Thomas Corcoran with a proposal. Thomas explained:

Nothing of note happened until we came to Soda Springs. Fallen [Fallon] and Gunthrie [Guthrie] said they knew a cut-off that would shorten the distance by 200 miles. They knew all the Rocky Mountain country as they had been trading and trapping in this country for the last 25 years. They were going to start next morning as they were tired of stopping and traveling so slow with the oxen drawn wagons. They coaxed me to go with them. The three of us were to start at 6 o'clock the next morning. I bought an Indian pony to carry my clothes and other things. They came after me at the appointed time but I was asleep. Fallen asked Parks to wake me but Parks made some excuse and said that I would not be able to stand the trip. When I awoke, they had already started. I had never slept as long as I did that morning. We heard no more of Fallen or Gunthrie until we got to the Truckee River. There were some Snake Indians who came along with us. As they were out hunting on the river, they came across some wild Indians. They told them that there were two men who came ahead of us and that they had had a fight with the Indians for two days. The Indians had them corralled in a bunch of timber. Somehow, they escaped during the night and were never heard from again. It was supposed that they perished from wounds or starvation.

Corcoran was not the only one to report the Fallon-Guthrie incident. The Cornwall biography described it as well:

This large party [Wambaugh company] moved slowly, and Fallon became restless. With a Scotsman named Guthrie, who had joined them at Fort Hall, he left to proceed more quickly to California. The two were attacked for their supplies by the Hill Indians, and some weeks later, the main party came upon their mutilated bodies by the trail.

Corcoran's lungs should have been improving after almost two months in the dry air, but David Parks felt either that Thomas was not well enough to travel with Fallon or that going off on this venture was too dangerous. No wonder Thomas held Parks in high regard. Not only had the man helped him since they had left Fort Laramie, but he had kept him from joining this fateful party. Ironically, the very disease that threatened Thomas' life may have saved it.

Both Corcoran's and Cornwall's narratives are valuable in that they establish that Fallon, Cornwall, Corcoran, and Parks were traveling together, presumably in the Wambaugh party. And it is another instance in which Corcoran and Cornwall recall the same incident, but with different details. While Corcoran reported Fallon leaving them at Soda Springs, Cornwall suggested that Fallon left the party at or beyond Fort Hall.

Corcoran explained that because Fallon and Guthrie were experienced trappers in the Rockies they knew of a route that would cut off two hundred miles. There was, in fact, a shorter way, but it wasn't nearly two hundred miles. A shortcut for wagons from Soda Springs would become established the following year when J. J. Meyers (in the Chiles party of 1843) and Benoni Hudspeth led a wagon party west from Soda Springs, blazing a new path that bypassed Fort Hall. Known as the Hudspeth Cutoff, it became a popular route among gold rushers, even though it really did not shorten the journey.[18] There were no shortcuts west of Fort Hall that eliminated anywhere near two hundred, one hundred, or even twenty miles. Therefore Corcoran's version about the two men taking a much shorter route makes sense only if they left the trail at Soda Springs. If, as Cornwall asserted, Guthrie did not join the train until Fort Hall, then Corcoran would have been wrong about Fallon and Guthrie leaving the party at the springs. A brief news item appeared in the September 2, 1848, issue of the *Californian*, a San Francisco newspaper:

> Captain O'Fallon, the brave soldier and well known recruiting officer under Col. Fremont during the war in California, left Fort Hall for this territory [a] few days previous to the departure of the party from that place, and from the appearance of the Indians and his non-arrival here, they express the belief that he has been murdered by the Indians on his way hither.

Regrettably, neither Riley Root nor Rufus Burrows mentioned the incident at all, even though both are believed to have been traveling with these men.

Corcoran and Cornwall attribute Fallon's decision to impatience with the slow progress of the wagons, but something more could have played a role in Fallon's decision to leave the train. He was probably a proud man, and with good reason. Historian Bernard DeVoto, in *Across the Wide Missouri*, called Fallon "as fantastic a mountain man as the trade ever produced."[19] But when the Cornwall and Greenwood parties joined Wambaugh at Fort Laramie, Fallon was likely forced to subordinate his role as a guide to either Greenwood or Clyman, which must have wounded his pride. Ever since they left Fort Laramie, he must have felt useless and humiliated; perhaps he had had enough. Traveling through an area where companies joined together for protection against Indians, Fallon and his friend threw prudence to the wind and struck out alone, and they paid the ultimate price. It was an ignominious blow to Fallon's reputation and a sad end to his long career.

Leaving the springs on the morning of July 12, the Wambaugh party marched west along the north bank of the Bear River for three miles until they were opposite Sheep Rock, a high precipice at the northern end of the Bear River Range. The river rounded this cliff, and then made an abrupt turn south as it headed toward the Great Salt Lake. The trail made a right turn at this spot, departed the river valley and proceeded northwesterly just west of high ledges of hardened black lava, then headed across a desolate sagebrush-covered plain west of the Soda Springs Hills and entered the equally desolate Portneuf Valley.

Despite the company resuming travel across a sagebrush desert, the emigrants should have been in high spirits, knowing Fort Hall was not far away. By the end of July 12, the Wambaugh company had made twenty-three miles, and they camped where the trail struck the upper reaches of the Portneuf River, which Root called "very circuitous." They likely camped near the river about one mile west of the present community of Chesterfield, Idaho.

Raising clouds of white dust, the wagon train continued traveling across the Portneuf Valley on the morning of the thirteenth. By midmorning, they were well out of the valley. They followed the trail where it turned into the Portneuf Hills. Wending its way up a ravine, the trail led them over a low place in the hills, then descended toward Ross Fork. Completing twenty-one miles that day, over what Root described as "a mountainous road," they stopped to camp on the Ross Fork, a small creek where Root observed willows but no grass.

With lively anticipation, the people of Wambaugh company rose early on the morning of July 14. Captain Wambaugh probably announced that they would arrive at Fort Hall by day's end. The wagons rocked through a narrow canyon through which Ross Creek snaked. Six miles after leaving their morning camp, they left the hills and emerged onto a long, wide plain. After ten miles of marching across this plain, they inexplicably halted and pitched their camp while still four miles east of the fort. Root did not explain why. The thirty miles of trail between the present-day communities of Chesterfield and Fort Hall passes through the Fort Hall Indian Reservation, and cannot be accessed without permission from the Fort Hall Indian Agency.

The next day, Root wrote in his journal: "15th— 4 miles to Fort Hall, and 2 miles farther to camp, on Portneuf creek." Captain Wambaugh's party of around fifty wagons rolled by the fort on July 15, and camped two miles beyond it on a narrow tongue of land between the Snake and Portneuf Rivers. As usual, Root provided little detail about the fort or what they did there.

Fort Hall had been established along the Snake River in 1834, the same year William Sublette and Robert Campbell built their Fort William stockade along Laramie Fork. Nathaniel J. Wyeth, a young Yankee ice merchant from Cambridge, Massachusetts, had organized a trading expedition to the Far West in 1832. Encouraged by what he found, he returned with a second expedition in 1834. He crossed the Laramie Fork just in time to witness Sublette's and Campbell's fort being constructed. Wyeth must have made mental notes, for when he and his men reached the Snake River, he selected a site on its east bank, and began cutting long cottonwood logs. Like Fort William on the Laramie, they planted the cottonwood logs, palisade-style, two and a half feet in the ground. His compound was eighty-feet square, with twelve-foot-high walls and eight-foot-square bastions at opposite corners.[20]

It was a good place for a trading post, within easy reach of a number of tribes with whom fur trading could be profitably engaged. But it was a risky place to build anything; it was on a floodplain between the mouths of the Bannock and Portneuf Rivers, and sat beside a potentially engulfing, 150-yard-wide river.

Misfortune plagued Wyeth. His venture suffered from desertion, disease, massacres, and stiff competition, and he called it quits and returned to the States in 1836.[21] The following year, he sold his post to his primary competitor, the British-owned Hudson's Bay Company, which commenced a long tenure at the fort.[22] The Hudson's Bay Company renovated the fort, encasing its log walls in adobe bricks.[23] The post not only served the fur trade, but it became an important stopover and trading point on the trail to Oregon.[24] It was overseen during much of its life by the very anti-American Captain Grant. It had a good blacksmith's shop, an abundance of pasturage that supported a large herd of cattle, horses, and mules, and a sizeable herd of milk cows that provided the emigrants with a supply of butter and cheese.[25] Captain Grant had trade goods brought to the fort from Astoria on the Pacific coast, but it was not exactly an emporium. Disgruntled emigrants often condemned it for being ill-provisioned and for charging exorbitant prices.[26]

John Boardman passed through the fort in 1843, sneering that it was "inferior to Fort Laramie." By 1849, a gold rusher thought that its walls were "in a very dilapidated state—and on the N. W. side are shored up with timbers."[27] Another traveler sketched it the same year, and his drawing depicted poles propping up the walls.[28]

Nothing lasts forever, and the Hudson's Bay Company abandoned the fort in 1856. The great flood of 1862—it was bound to happen—came along and swept away what remained. Today, the remote site on the Fort Hall Bottoms is twelve miles west of the community of Fort Hall, marked by a neglected stone monument, largely hidden by chest-high grass. Because the monument is on Fort Hall Indian Reservation land, one must get permission from the Indian Agency in Fort Hall to visit.

June 27–July 15, 1848
William Anderson, Miller company, on Sweetwater,
ten miles east of South Pass, Wyoming

Perhaps not wanting to step on the heels of the Wambaugh and Gates companies just ahead, Captain Miller brought his company to an early halt on the afternoon of June 27, pausing to camp beside the Sweetwater, within sight of Joseph Barnett's grave and about thirteen miles east of Pacific Springs. With no water between these two places, the Gates party must have either spent the night camping with Wambaugh at Pacific Springs, or with Miller here at the Sweetwater, but neither Riley Root nor William Anderson mentioned Gates.

The next day, Anderson reported his company's passage over South Pass and its arrival at Pacific Springs:

> June the 28th we had a heavy frost last night   ice froze ¼ of an inch thick in some buckets that had some watter left in them over night   we bid good bye to sweet watter and traveled 13 miles and pased over the dividing ridge of the rocky mountains into Oregon territory and camped at the pacific springs   here the watter runs the other way or runs into the pacific while the watter east of the ridge runs into the Atlantic ocean.

It should have bolstered their spirits that they had made it to where the creeks and rivers now flowed toward the great Pacific Ocean. Yet, gazing west across that boundless stretch of bleak solitude, and thinking of the great distances and hardships that lay ahead may have been enough to cause some to despair.

The Miller company departed Pacific Springs on June 29 and set out across the great sage desert. After twenty dreary miles traversing a "barren sandy plain," Anderson wrote that they reached Little Sandy Creek where they made camp and stayed the night. The next day, he reported traveling six miles to Big Sandy Creek, where they stopped to spend the night. It was time to let their livestock eat, drink, and rest before embarking across the arduous, forty-five-mile Greenwood's cutoff.

Shortly after noon the next day, the men crawled from beneath the shade of their wagons, yawned, stretched, and yoked up their teams. Anderson climbed into his wagon. When Captain Miller gave the signal, Anderson whistled to his oxen, and they obediently lurched forward. It was a promising start, but they had far to travel across a waterless and grassless distance. Anderson described the trek:

> July 1st . . . [H]aving looked on our map we found we had a long drive without wood watter or grass so we lay by at big sandy till 2 o clock in the evening when we started and traveled all that evening an all night and July the 2nd till 2 oclock PM when we reached green river which we were glad to see it having bin verry warm and dusty   the road was good with the exception of some verry steep hills we started our sheep drivers on ahead this morning with the sheep as they would not travel verry well after night   we overtook them a while before day standing by the side of the road holding their horses and guarding the sheep without anything to eat or drink either for themselves or their animals   we stoped a few minutes and let them get a bight out of the wagons then left them to follow on at day light.

This is the account of a young teamster whose company had spent twenty-four hours creeping across a dry desert, trying to follow an uncertain trail, part of it through a pitch-black night. Despite conditions that would have tried ordinary men's souls, he wrote without a trace of self-pity, in matter-of-fact, understated terms. It was just the way things were. He was, after all, a toughened bullwhacker, and to complain of trivial hardships would have seemed unmanly.

The Miller company rested the afternoon and night of July 2 on the east side of the Green River, then crossed it the following day. "July the 3rd we spent the most of the day in crossing the river and camped on the west side," Anderson wrote, then went on:

> there was a small ferry kept here by the mormons but we found a place where we could ford it by propping the waggon beds up on the bolsters and putting 4 or 8 yoke of oxen to a waggon and hitching a horse before with a man on his back and 2 more riding by the side of the cattle and one in the waggon   in this manner we all got across safe.

Anderson did not explain how they got their sheep across, but revealed that the

Mormon ferrymen were now at the Green River. His Miller company did not use their ferry; perhaps they were trying to save money.

The next day, July 4, the Miller company departed their camp, likely from beneath the grove of cottonwoods just east of Names Hill. They left the river and followed the trail twelve miles up and over Holden Hill to Fontenelle/Clyman Creek. According to Anderson, they pitched their camp there. The Miller group was now two days behind Wambaugh. Like Root, Anderson failed to describe his company celebrating the Fourth of July.

Leaving Fontenelle Creek the next morning, they followed the trail as it slowly ascended the ridge between the dry Willow and Sheep Creeks. Anderson described the way as "verry mountainous," probably referring to the Slate Creek Ridge and Rocky Gap sections. He wrote that they made twenty miles, likely putting them into the Pomeroy Basin by the end of the day. It was cold, he wrote, with snow in sight. "[We] wared our overcoats on buttoned up to the chin." They were at about 7,600 feet, where the air temperature rapidly plummeted when the sun dropped below the mountains. Even though it was summer, at these high altitudes, it could be bitter cold at night. When the camp began to stir the next morning, July 6, the travelers must have been shocked by the icy air when they crawled from beneath their blankets.

According to Anderson, they traveled seven miles that day, over Commissary Ridge and through Branley Pass. Anderson then described them crossing "a small creek caled hams fork of bear [Green] river   here was an Indian village of the snake tribe   they appeared friendly   we stoped and traded with them and pased on." In contrast to Rufus Burrows, Anderson had little to say about the Snakes.

July 7 was probably a hard day, as the Miller company made sixteen miles through mountainous country, crawling up beside Quakenasp Canyon, then leveling out across the Hams Fork Plateau. Crossing Dempsey Ridge and Rock Creek Ridge was next. Anderson commented on passing a "great deal of snow to day." It sounded like they stopped to camp as soon as they reached the Bear River. Anderson wrote,

> here is good grazing   we saw numerous bands of indians but none of them appeared hostile   they seemed to be roving about in search of provisions such as grass hoppers crickets and various other insects.

The Snakes did not have buffalo like the Sioux and had to augment their diet with insects.

The Miller company only traveled eight miles on the eighth, lumbering in close proximity to the river. After crossing Smiths Fork, they camped about five miles north of today's Cokeville. Anderson wrote, "in order to let our cattle refresh themselves a little we camped near an Indian village   there were some whites amongst them with a band of horses and mules for trade."

Anderson described traveling fourteen miles on July 9, crossing Thomas Fork, then climbing over that narrow mountain spur. Shortly after rejoining the river, he recorded that they came to Peg Leg Smith's:

peg leg smith is in command here with a few whites and a band of indians   he
kept a dairy here and as soon as we camped they swarmed around us with butter
and cheese and buck skin pants and mokasens to trade   one of our company
Mr. Miller traded one of his wagons off here for some horses   here is a bottom
of some 4 or 5 miles in width and good grass and some timber.

The Miller company camped at Smith's on the evening of the ninth. Riley Root
had reported that they camped near the same place that same evening. Yet Anderson
did not mention Wambaugh or Gates. Once again, the Miller company had closed in
on the heels of the wagon companies ahead of them, but in this valley of abundant
grass, it would not have been a problem.

While the Wambaugh company traveled twenty-five miles on July 10, Anderson's company traveled only fourteen: "July the 10th we traveled 14 miles down bear
river   we crossed numerous branches to day of clear cold spring watter flowing from
the mountains."

On July 11, the Miller company traveled sixteen miles and caught up to Wambaugh once again. While Root had noted camping that evening one mile beyond
Soda Springs, Anderson wrote that the Miller company camped at Beer Springs:

July the 11th we traveled 16 miles and camped at the beer springs   this watter
sweet and makes a very good drink which tastes some what like soda   one ¼ of a
mile below these springs is the boiling of steamboat spring situated on the bank of
bear river   this water is warm enough for good dish watter and comes up through
a rock and boils up some 2 feet high and runs down into the river   at one side of
this is crevis in the rock where the steem is constantly coming out   the nois of
which resembles that of the scapepipe of a steamboat   here was some indians
and white traders stationed   we had quite a shower of rain to day.

Anderson had mentioned Indians a number of times since they arrived in the Bear
River Valley, while Root had not noted any.

If these companies camped close to one another, as they should have here, one
would expect that a few curious men from one camp would ride over to gossip with
others. But Anderson didn't mention what Root had reported—that the Wambaugh
company was suffering much sickness.

The Miller party left Beer Springs on July 12 and headed northwesterly, following the trail as it quit the Bear River Valley. They traveled fourteen miles that day
according to Anderson, likely stopping to camp when they struck the Portneuf River.

During their travel on the thirteenth, Anderson wrote about encountering some
French traders and Indians heading east. After traveling fifteen miles, the last portion of which was over the Portneuf Hills, they stopped to camp beside a "beautiful
spring" with "a little lake about 10 feet across and 3 feet deep and has several little
speckled trout in it."

On July 14, the Miller company trudged "over sandy ridges almost destitute of vegetation except wild sage," according to Anderson. They descended from the hills and began to move across the wide Snake River plain. Completing a twenty-mile march that day, they, like Wambaugh, stopped short of Fort Hall and camped five miles east of the fort at a place Anderson said had "good grass and water."

Until now, Anderson had made no mention of Fort Hall, as if the prospect of arriving at this oasis of civilization had provoked no feelings of excitement:

> July the 15th we traveled 7 miles   5 miles brought us to fort hall   this fort is situated on the south bank of snake river 150 or 200 yards from the river   we stoped here and had some little repareing done to our wagons and camped 2 miles below the fort on a small tributary of the Portneth [Portneuf] river   here we found 2 other companys waiting for reinforcements having been told at the fort that they must go strong handed through the Cyuse country as they were then at war with the oregon settlers   it was thought to be verry dangerous traveling through their country so there were 3 companys here to gether some for Oregon and some for California   the Californians separated off in one company and the oregon emigrants in 2 companys which made our company number about 50 armed men and 35 waggons.

One might expect that the haggard travelers felt a surge of renewed optimism and resolve when they arrived at Fort Hall, which represented the beginning of the last leg of their journey, but in Root's and Anderson's accounts, we find nothing of the sort. Like Wambaugh, the Miller company moved on to establish their camp beside the Portneuf River about two miles below the fort, joining "2 other companys waiting for reinforcements." One of these would have been Wambaugh's. The other was probably the Gates company, which is believed to have continued traveling just ahead of Miller. These three companies now divided and reassembled into those going to California and those going to Oregon.

June 30–July 4, 1848
Keturah Belknap, Watt Company, beside the Sweetwater, east of South Pass

Keturah Belknap and her family were still traveling with the Watt company on June 30. With Keturah's pregnancy, and with meals and other chores to do at the end of each day, she must have had little time and energy to write in her journal. And when she did, she rarely used dates. This time, however, she gave some meaningful clues as to where they were.

> Here we are; it is almost sundown [June 30th?]. We will have a cold lunch for supper, then shake up the beds and rest after the excitement of the day is over. We will leave the sweet water in the morning and have a long dry drive. We will fill our kegs and everything that will hold water so we will not suffer of thirst. We

stop at noon for an hour's rest. It's very warm; the oxen all have their tongues out panting. George took the wash pan and a bucket of water and let our team wet their tongues and he washed the dust off their noses; some laughed at him but the oxen seemed very grateful. George lays down to catch a little nap; if they start before he wakes the team will start up in their places. Time is up, the word along the line is "Move up." That means 10 miles of dry hot dirt. I have a little water left yet; will have to let the thirsty ox drivers wet their parched lips. It will be hot till the sun goes down, then it will be dusk. That night we got to plenty of water [Pacific Springs?]. I think old Bright's feet hurt; he is standing in the water. We eat a bite and go to bed.

This is a touching vignette about the Belknaps' relationship with their oxen. Not all wagoneers or teamsters treated their teams like this. There were some, however, who, like the Belknaps, held a strong affection for their beasts, knowing how sorely they depended on them. It is interesting how Keturah suggested the oxen were smart enough to start moving on their own initiative when the wagon ahead resumed moving.

If Keturah was referring to her party leaving the Sweetwater for the last time, they would have reached Pacific Springs at the end of the day on July 1. Therefore, her next entry was likely entered the next morning, on July 2, at Pacific Springs: "My little boy is very sick with Mountain Fever and tomorrow we will have to make a long dry drive." One can barely imagine her fear of losing little Jesse. After all, she had already lost three of her children as infants and he was all she had left.

It is certain that the Watt company waited at the Big Sandy River on the following day, July 3, when Keturah wrote: "We will stay here at this nice water and grass till about 4 o'clock. We will cook up a lot of provisions, then will take what is known as 'Greenwoods cutoff' and travel all night. Must fill everything with water."

When four o'clock in the afternoon of the third arrived, the Watt company bravely plunged into the desert. Responding to George Belknap's exhortations, his oxen leaned into their yokes. Traveling that afternoon and all through the night, Keturah described the next morning:

It's morning. [July 4th] I have been awake all night watching the little boy. He seems a little better; has dropped off to sleep. The sun is rising and it shows a lot of the dirtiest humanity ever was seen since the Creation. We just stop for an hour and eat a bite and let the teams breath again. We divide the water with the oxen. George has sat on his seat on the front of the wagon all night and I have held the little boy on my lap on a pillow and tended him as best as I could. I thot in the night we would have to leave him here and I thot if we did I would likely have to stay with him but as the daylight [arrived], we seemed to get fresh courage.

For the rest of the day, the caravan stubbornly pushed on, gradually stringing itself out as those with weaker teams lagged farther and farther behind.

When the Watt company reached the edge of the bluffs overlooking the Green River at the end of their twenty-four-hour ordeal, one can imagine Keturah whispering a grateful prayer. She continued with her narrative:

> We are coming near to the Green River; will have to ferry it with the wagons. The cattle will be unyoked and swim over; some Mormons are here. They have fixed up a ferry and will take us over for a dollar a wagon. It will take all day to get over, it is the 4th of July. While some are getting over, they have got Hawley's wagon over and have got our anvils and are celebrating the Fourth. The Jacksons are doing their best to entertain the crowd; there is three of them. . . . Watts and the sheep pulled out and fell behind. I got the blame for the split. The old Mother Watts said after they got through "Yes, Geo. Belknap's wife [Keturah] is a little woman but she wore the pants on that train." So I came into notoriety. But to return to the trail, they say we are on the last half of the journey now.

The Green River crossing was indeed halfway to Oregon City. The Fourth of July is one of the few dates that Keturah noted during the trip, the day they reached and crossed the Green. It was also the same day William Anderson and his Miller company were leaving it behind, confirming that the Watt company was traveling on the heels of Miller, and why it seemed certain that Isaac Pettijohn was identifying the Watt company when he reported encountering "24 waggons" on June 27. Edward Smith reported that the Watt, Walker-Bristow, Purvine, and Kelly companies all left Fort Laramie on the same day, and likely in that order. Because of Watt's habit of traveling ahead of Walker, etc., it can be assumed that Watt was the first of those companies to cross the Platte. With their wagons and their large flock of sheep, they probably crossed the Platte on June 22 and 23. Thus, the Watt company should have left the North Platte crossing on June 24, and reached Willow Springs that evening. By the twenty-seventh, they should have been traveling past Ice Slough or Rocky Ridge. These facts make it consistent with the speculation that it was the Watt company that Pettijohn recorded passing on the twenty-seventh.

Keturah's comment about the Watt family and their sheep "pulling out and fell behind" is significant. Later evidence will show that, after the Watt family dropped back, George Jackson took over leadership of the group that included the Belknaps and others. Unfortunately, we do not know what precipitated the split, or why Mother Watt felt Keturah was responsible for it.

June 29–July 15, 1848
William Porter, Purvine company, North Platte River crossing, Wyoming

On June 29, William Porter and his Purvine company were finally crossing the North Platte River. They had suffered through a number of discouraging days, some spent waiting their turn to be ferried, and some searching for the cattle that had run off the previous night. In any event, his company had fallen behind. Porter's writings were never lengthy, but once his company crossed the river, his entries became even shorter. He was college-educated and could write well. He may have been tired or despondent, or perhaps it was just that he had brought a very small notebook.

> 30th. Traveled 28 miles and camped near Willow Spring.
>
> July 1st. Samuel Tucker left one wagon, and much valuable property. Traveled fourteen miles and camped within 10 or 12 miles of Independence Rock.
>
> 2nd. Traveled 20 miles, 8 miles past Independence Rock— nooned at said rock.
>
> July 3rd. Traveled 18 miles.
>
> July 4th. Traveled 20 miles. Good grass.
>
> July 5th. Traveled 24 miles.
>
> 6th. Traveled 20 miles.
>
> 7th. Traveled 9 miles and camped at the last camping on sweet water.
>
> 8th. Traveled 12 miles to Pacific Spring. We are now in Oregon.
>
> 9th. Traveled to Little Sandy 20 miles.
>
> 10th. Traveled 6 miles to Big Sandy.
>
> 11th and 12th. Traveled 40 miles [Greenwood's Cutoff] to Green River and crossed.
>
> 13th. Traveled 10 miles to a creek called [Fontenelle] Fork.
>
> 14th. Traveled 10 miles and camped on a spring branch.
>
> 15th. Traveled 20 miles and camped on a creek, Haines' [Hams] Fork.

While Keturah and her Watt company celebrated the Fourth of July on the Green River, Porter and his Purvine company did not reach the Green until the twelfth, putting them eight days behind Watt, even though both parties had left Fort Laramie on the same day.

Porter and his company arrived at Pacific Springs, the same day that W. L. Adams had written his brother a letter from Pacific Springs. Adams' letter explained that when they reached the North Platte River crossing, they had "50 wagons." But at Pacific Springs, he explained that "[w]e are now traveling in a company of 26 wagons. Large companies cannot be tolerated." Adams' statement is ambiguous. He could have meant that he had separated from his fifty-wagon party and had joined Porter's company, increasing the size of the Purvine company to twenty-six wagons. On the other hand, because of Adams' declaration that "large companies cannot be tolerated," it seems more likely that his train of fifty wagons had divided into two segments. The first group may have continued west almost as soon as they crossed the river. The second group, consisting of twenty-six wagons, of which Adams would have been a part, would have remained just west of the river, struggling as Adams had described.

Eastbound Oregonian Isaac Pettijohn recorded encountering forty-four wagons traveling a day or two ahead of Wambaugh. Part of them could have been from the Allsopp party of twenty-five wagons that had left Fort Laramie before Wambaugh.

The Allsopp party probably crossed the North Platte River before Wambaugh did on June 15. The Adams company likely crossed the North Platte on June 12, also ahead of Wambaugh. It is possible that the first segment of the Adams party (about twenty-four wagons) continued west unimpeded shortly after crossing the North Platte on the twelfth. Thus, these westernmost forty-four wagons could have been a combination of these two groups. Besides, there is no evidence of any other wagons traveling ahead of Wambaugh.

June 30–July 18, 1848
Father Lempfrit, Stone company, at North Platte crossing, Wyoming

On June 30, Father Lempfrit and his tiny Stone company were approaching the North Platte crossing. The priest ended the day's entry with "We are waiting until tomorrow to cross over the River Platte for the second time."

"1st July— The River Platte is very deep at this point, and its bed is extremely confined," Lempfrit explained the next day. "This is why it can only be crossed on rafts. We made the crossing without any accidents." His observation confirms that ferry operators look for where the river is narrowest, which is also where it is deepest.

By now, traffic was diminishing for the Mormon ferrymen. July 1 was not a busy day, as Father Lempfrit's party of eleven wagons and Isaac Pettijohn's eastbound party were the only ones to cross, each heading in opposite directions. On that day, Pettijohn recorded passing "11 waggons"—obviously the Stone company.

"After this we had to go through some horrible places before we arrived at our camp site," Lempfrit continued. He did not specify where they camped on the night of July 1, but he was clearly referring to the desert immediately west of the river.

July 2 was spent marching across that bleak domain of poisonous creeks and springs, although Lempfrit did not mention them. He seemed more fascinated instead by the "mountain that had red marble rocks, absolutely fiery red [the Red Buttes]."

Once again, Lempfrit was overtaken with impatience on July 3. As he had often done in the past, he mounted his pony and rode ahead of the slow-creeping train:

> 3rd July— I went ahead so that I could explore the country. About 9 o'clock in the morning the heat became more oppressive than usual, and by noon it was absolutely suffocating. About 3 o'clock the sky grew dark and at that moment I found an abandoned waggon. The storm soon broke, and happy to have this shelter I settled down under the waggon to wait for the storm to finish. At 5:30 our company arrived, and found me quite dry!

The Fourth of July likely meant nothing to the Frenchman, but the day presented some exciting encounters:

> 4th July— Whilst traveling through this country which has no vegetation but absinth [artemisia/sagebrush] we encountered a rattlesnake for the first time.

The sight of this horrible reptile really frightened me. This rattlesnake was nine years old. The age of a rattlesnake can be determined by the number of rings it has on its tail. . . . During the after noon, we killed two more of them, both much bigger than the first one. I began to feel less afraid of this creeping insect, just the thought of which had made me shudder.

At about 5 o'clock that afternoon the captain invited me to accompany him and go with him to look for a good camp site. We came close to the river and it was raining. I had no wish to cross over it to the other side. The captain left me alone under a thicket. I wrapped myself up in a buffalo robe he had left me, also I had his gun which he left with me as he did not wish to take it with him in case it got wet. Just when he had reached the other side of the river I saw a little black heifer coming towards me. At first sight I thought it was one of the animals that belonged to our waggon-train that was coming up to me, but when I saw a large hump on its neck I no longer doubted that this was a young buffalo. I aimed my gun at the animal . . . she was down. I came out of my little thicket and caught sight of the captain who yelled out to me, "Bravo, bravo, Doctor!" (For this is what the people of our caravan called me.) He himself had seen the young buffalo and was hurrying to cross the river so that he could kill it, but I had spared him the trouble. After congratulating me on my good shot he at once took out and cut the animal's throat to let the blood out. The caravan company arrived soon afterwards. I had the buffalo portioned out, reserving a good piece of meat for ourselves. The meat was really delicious and it lasted us for eight days.

"5th July . . . We left about 10 o'clock," Lempfrit recorded the next day, "and on our way, we passed a large rock on which a number of names were engraved. I read those of Fathers De Smet, Point, and Mengarini." The priest had unmistakably identified Independence Rock, but he ignored Devil's Gate, perhaps not finding it worthy of noting. He then reported that two wagons joined them from the company ahead, which could have been the Delaney company.

Regarding the next three days, Lempfrit made only one entry. It contained a number of favorable impressions and clues to their progress through the Sweetwater River Valley:

6th, 7th, and 8th July— We have had very pleasant camp sites these last three days. We had an abundance of wood, water and grass. Fresh pasturage was most welcome. Also, we often had good fortune of having excellent trout to eat, for the river by which we camped was known as the Trout River [Sweetwater]. The trail then took us down a narrow gorge at the bottom of which was a river that we had to cross three times [Three Crossings]. When we emerged from the gorge we saw a range of snow-covered mountains in the distance [Wind River Mountains]. Then we went through a marshy valley [Ice Slough] where we were subjected to the annoyance of thousands of mosquitos. For over an hour I had to urge my pony to the gallop, otherwise he would surely have died for one had to halt for only a couple of minutes for him to be literally covered with those dangerous insects. Eventually we arrived at a very poor camp where there was no wood and no water.

July 9 was Sunday and the two priests planned to say Mass in their tent, but their intentions were thwarted:

9th July— Today, Sunday, we had hoped to celebrate the Holy Mass, but as we had to get up very early to continue on our way we had to renounce this plan. My traveling companion [Father Lionnet] was very displeased and made a wry face. I was accustomed to his sulky behavior.

The Presbyterian minister traveling with them delivered a sermon to the company that evening. Perhaps reacting out of professional jealousy, Lempfrit complained that the preacher "held forth *ex abundantia*." He seemed perversely delighted when he wrote that many in the "congregation" fell asleep during the preacher's marathon oration.

July 10 could have been as sad a day for us readers as for Lempfrit. He had crossed a very small stream and had stopped to write in his notebook. When putting it back in his pocket, it fell out unnoticed. Two miles later, he discovered it missing and desperately retraced his steps. "At last, by a stroke of luck I found my notebook," he wrote. "I came back filled with joy to our people who had been kind enough to wait for me."

The next day, July 11, Lempfrit reported that the Presbyterian preacher came down with a fever so severe that he became delirious. Because of Lempfrit's reputation regarding medical matters, he was summoned to the preacher's side. The sick minister thought a good dose of rhubarb as a purgative would cure him. But the priest disagreed, insisting that he needed a good bleeding instead. "In the end," the priest explained, "he gave in and I bled him. After this he felt better."

Lempfrit noted on July 12 that they "arrived at the height of land [South Pass]. Henceforth, we will find that the rivers have changed course." Upon arriving at camp, presumably Pacific Springs, they discovered that "two waggon-trains had halted the day before. The remains of their fires were still warm." These were likely from the Hannah and Delaney parties. It could not have been from Purvine as they had already made it to the Green River on the twelfth.

According to the priest, they traveled "in easy stages" on July 13 and 14, because a "poor woman is extremely unwell." He did not identify where they camped on those nights, but it was probably on Little Sandy Creek on the thirteenth and Big Sandy on the fourteenth. They stayed at the Big Sandy through the next day until late in the afternoon; then, squinting into the late afternoon sun, they headed off into the desert:

15th July— As we had the longest stage of our journey to make at a single stretch, that is to say forty-five miles without the prospect of finding either water or fodder en route, we remained at the same camping ground until 5:30 in the evening. We readied ourselves for traveling throughout the whole night. When we left at 5:30 we saw the cabins, or rather holes in which some very formidable Indians live. Their only food is the meat of wild sheep and a species of grasshopper called "crickets" here. These Indians hollow out pits in the earth and then cover them with the skins of sheep. After this, we continued on our trail which led through an arid desert. I remained on my pony until about 2 o'clock in the morning, and then, being much afraid of the cold, I asked the lay brother to mount my pony and I went and slept in the waggon. We stopped about 3 o'clock in the morning to make a little something to eat. Our animals did not have even a blade of grass. They looked at us very sadly.

The priest was undoubtedly still exhausted when he wrote these words, which may account for the relative lack of detail, but his observations about the Indian habitations, presumably Snake, are something no other diarist had reported.

On and on the company marched into the next day. Lempfrit wrote:

16th July—We arrived at last at the Green River the same day, 16th July, at 6:30 in the evening. Everyone was exhausted by hunger and thirst. We had traveled forty-five miles in a single day [24 hours].

In spite of their ordeal, he commended the oxen for performing heroically, and noted that the company arrived in surprisingly good shape.

"17th and 18th July— We are not advancing very fast," Lempfrit complained. "We crossed the Green River on quite a good raft," he wrote, suggesting that they used the Mormon ferry to cross the river on the seventeenth. They probably stayed in camp the next day to allow their drained company and exhausted livestock to recuperate.

June 27–July 15, 1848
Edward Smith and Richard May, Chiles-Hensley company, Bitter Cottonwood Creek, Wyoming

The Chiles company, with Major Hensley's pack train and Edward Smith attached, left Fort Laramie on June 27. Our two diarists, Richard May and Edward Smith, were now traveling together and their company stopped that night at Bitter Cottonwood Creek.

The next morning, Smith reported that they left the Bitter Cottonwood at seven AM and traveled fourteen miles, stopping to camp at Horseshoe Creek. Their camp would have been where the creek crosses today's Highway 319, and about two miles south of Glendo, Wyoming. Both men mentioned meeting ten men from Oregon, heading east. May observed that

7 out of the ten disliked the country and was returning home. The other three intended going back and said it was good enough for them. One gave us a bad account of the grass saying it was all dried up this being one of the driest seasons ever known.

On June 29, the Chiles company traveled fourteen miles and camped on the banks of the North Platte, where both men complained of poor grass. Their camp would have been at or near where the companies ahead of them had camped, about three miles southeast of present-day Orin, Wyoming, and east of Highway 319. May noted the current of the Platte as a swift six miles per hour.

The company came to life on July 30 as a new moon, dark and barely visible, floated near the rising sun. According to May, they traveled fifteen miles that day. After leaving the river, they followed the heavily traveled trail as it headed southwest along the ridge dividing Indian and Spring Creeks. They ended the day at La Bonte Creek, the same campsite used by the earlier companies. Both May and Smith reported there was no grass. Since as many as two thousand head of livestock had been in the companies ahead, the grass, scarce in an uncommonly "dry year such as this," had likely been overgrazed. Despite the region's lack of bounty, Richard May saw some value in it:

> In traveling through a country like this, the mind is naturally led to some conclusions as to the worth of it. Having neither timber, water nor soil you would suppose it worthless and so it is individually but it is of great worth to the United States. The furs, the necessaries of life taken in these mountains form a very considerable link in commerce which gives employment to a great number of her enterprising citizens.

North of La Bonte Creek, the company entered the rough but geologically provocative "red earth country." It seems that many diarists, after months of hard travel, had grown tired of making lengthy entries, but Richard May's pen seemed enlivened. Although the region was somewhat desolate, he found a great deal on which to comment:

> 1st July. Traveled 18 miles, the teams under the yoke all the time. Today decidedly the richest scenery surrounded us that we have had the pleasure of seeing on the journey. We traveled through ridges and gorges in the mountains, giving us every veriety of height from the snowy region down to a mole hill. In passing through a gorge we passed a confused pile of rocks 200 feet high appeared to have been thrown up by some powerful convulsion. The rocks laying in every form except a natural one. In view of our road the Buttes showed plainly. The dust is very bad today and is about the color of madder [dark red] now and then some as white as snow. The buttes and hills generally about the color of dark ashes. The rocks are of all colors and of all sizes. What is generally called the Lost

Stone of Missouri is here in abundance. Very little of the flat or round rock to be seen in this region. The wild sage is the only shrub worthy of note. The branches [streams] have some cottonwood and box elder timber, very short and worthless except for firewood. The country appears to have been in a volcanic state at some period or other from the appearance of the rocks and earth. In fact the whole face of it has a volcanic appearance.

Edward Smith used fewer words than May, but he mentioned a few things May did not: "July sat 1st— we started at 8 about noon we met about 20 waggons a going to meet the Mormon Emigrants at fort John   encamped on a creek called Laprel or Box Elder Creek." They camped on La Prele Creek, not Box Elder.

It is odd how this company of twenty Mormon wagons, traveling east from the Great Salt Lake Valley and on their way to meet their westbound Brethren, could have passed all of the westbound companies and not be mentioned by any of our other diarists.

On July 2, Smith wrote that two of their oxen were missing in the morning, and the search caused them to leave camp late and travel only ten miles that day. They pitched camp at what Smith called Fourche Boisee, which was also called Box Elder Creek, where they enjoyed abundant water, grass, and wood. In May's words, they shared their camp that evening with "twenty pack mules and horses returning from Oregon," or in Smith's words, with "20 men from Oregon going to the States." This was Isaac Pettijohn's party, who wrote: "July the 2nd. met 47 wagons to day mostly Californians." Since May and Smith were both heading to California, they would not have been particularly curious about conditions in Oregon, and their entries reflected their indifference. "I had a few minutes conversation with them," May wrote, "but nothing worthy of note."

There were a number of buffalo in the area. May reported that Captain Chiles killed three, while Smith found something more interesting to write about:

the fresh grave of some young person. The wolves had got the corpse as soon as the Emigrants left by the appearance of the bones and hair which lay strewed over the ground the hair was light colored.

William Anderson had passed this place eighteen days earlier and had noted a disturbed grave with light-colored hair strewn about. Was it the same grave? While Smith thought it was "fresh," Anderson did not describe it that way. While Smith thought it was of a "young person," Anderson thought it was of a woman. While Smith thought it had been dug up by wolves, Anderson thought Indians had dug it up to get at the clothing.

Leaving Box Elder Creek on the morning of the third, the company traveled ten miles: four miles to reach the North Platte River, then another six to reach Deer Creek. May wrote that it was a "very pleasant encampment." Smith reported their hunters killing several more buffalo during the day, and mentioned encountering another disturbed grave four miles after leaving Box Elder Creek. Smith described it as being "of a child of 6 years of age." It could have been the same one that Anderson had written about eighteen days earlier, when he encountered a dug-up grave of "a boy probably some 10 or 12 years old" at about the same location.

Taking time at Deer Creek on the evening of July 3 to write in his journal, Richard May described the condition of their livestock and equipment:

> They [the oxen] are all doing tolerable well as yet. Some tenderfootedness manifested on their part and a great deal of solicitude on the part of the owners for their welfare. I have seen wagons mended in every way in the States I thought, but our best mechanics cannot teach a mountaineer a trick in doing up such things. Broke the tongue of a wagon short off and in minutes the wagon is going. So with any other part of it. Fasten tires by driving wedges between it and the rounds. The dexterity with which wagons can be mended would astonish any person not acquainted with the art. Coarse canvass is the best fastening for boxes and should any of your spokes become loose in the hub canvass is the article to fasten them. Draw on your tire and all is right.

Smith described finding another recent grave. After reading the marker, he wrote that "Here on the 24th of June 1848 while Bathing was drowned a young man from Kendal County Illinois Belonging to Capt. Hannahs Co by the name of Hiram Malik aged about 23 years." This is valuable information as it informs us that the Hannah company had reached Deer Creek on June 24, suggesting that Hannah should have reached the North Platte Crossing by the twenty-fifth and likely ferried across the next day or shortly thereafter, depending on what companies were just ahead of them.

The morning of July 4 found the camp stirring beside the fish-filled waters of Deer Creek. They were close to the Mormon ferry and could reach it by day's end, but Captain Chiles deemed it more important to "make meat," as numerous buffalo were in the area. May explained:

> This day we all recollect as the anniversary of our independence and intend enjoying it by taking a buffalo hunt. . . . The hunters have returned and have plenty of buffalo beef, elk and deer, having killed 12 buffalos. Our camp was very well illuminated drying the meat. The manner of drying is very simple. Raise a scaffold about 2 feet high, lay small sticks close together across it, cut the meat in thin slices, then lay it on the sticks, the larger and thinner the pieces the better, build a fire under it so as to dry it in three to four hours. Be careful not to salt it at all. And should you have time and sunshine it will dry in that. It is very good. The Indians live on such meat all summer and in fact all the time it keeps well.

May then mentioned another group of eastbound Oregonians, the third group they had seen in the last few days:

[I] took a stroll up the creek to an encampment of about 20 Oregon gentle-men, rough and rude were their appearance, but their intellectual facultie were good and only parallel with all I have seen from that distant land. A Mr. Umphet returned to camp with me. I found him very social. He was returning to Ohio with the view of going to Oregon next spring.

Both May and Smith reported that they finally departed Deer Creek on July 5. They traveled fifteen miles beside the North Platte, crossing a number of deep chasms and narrow, steep-sided ravines, most of them dry. They stopped to camp six miles below the Mormons' ferry. According to Smith, they were visited that night by "one of the severest hailstorms I have ever seen at this season of the year. The ground was cov-ered one inch thick after the storm was over." May worried that "[t]he captain [Chiles] and two of his men failed to get into camp. There was some uneasiness manifested about them but knowing his familiarity with the mountains I could not be uneasy."

The Chiles-Hensley company was the last one on the trail. It was not even half-way to California and still needed to cross the high Sierras. The people in Chiles' company seemed to derive comfort from their leader's experience and cocky self-assuredness. He had earned their trust and they felt dependent upon him. It was no wonder they were alarmed when he did not show up. Late that night Chiles finally showed up. The next morning, July 6, the company pulled out of camp, even though, according to Smith, "some cattle were gone." After traveling only a few miles, Smith wrote that they stopped to camp for the night "two miles Below the Regular ford."

"Some of our men have gone to the ferry to help out with the boat," May explained. Smith added that "[t]he Mormons Brot their ferry Boat consisting of two dugouts and a few cross Pieces." Interesting. It appears the Mormons were moving their ferry craft two miles downstream. May explained what transpired:

7th July. Late evening the boat arrived near our encampment and all hands were busily employed in making ready to cross the turbid stream, with a strong cur-rent. The captain detailed six hands to dig down the bank on the other side or north bank. . . . This being done our ferry boat began to ply. Our wagons began to land on the opposite bank at the rate of about 4 per hour. All got over except about 3 or 5. The Mormons who are stationed here (4 in number) are quite intelli-gent, and manly. The most of the emigrants in this train paid them in trade. [May mentioned earlier that the Mormons charged $1.50 per wagon] I paid them in coffee at 25 cents per lb. The coffee which paid them cost me 8 cents per pound. Some wagons started for the new encampment. We followed up the river and we had not traveled more than 1 ½ miles before we split into two parties and now it might be said we are in distinct companies. Where I turned in there were nine wagons and the most beautiful encampment I have ever seen. On the north the hills put in very close while on the south the mountain heights are in full view. At the same time the east and west is lined with a very dense growth of young cottonwoods. The little bottom of about 100 acres is covered with a fine sward of grass. Indeed this rural spot has charms that make me forget my weariness. The birds are singing, bells ringing and children playing as if this was a civilized country. So we have pleasures in traveling through this district of America. We have some sick. Mrs. Williams, a lady of fine accomplishments is very sick and in fact dangerously ill. Also Mr. McClelland lies prostrate and some doubt is entertained of his recovery.

Smith's journal reported that on July 7 they crossed "over about 2/3 of the wagons and Quit for the day." They finished ferrying the rest of their wagons "without accident" by ten AM on the morning of the eighth. May praised the Mormons for "being very active and vigilant in their vocation." It is interesting that William Anderson had reported six Mormon ferrymen here when his Miller company arrived on June 16, while May now says there were four. The sick "Mr. McClelland" mentioned by May was probably Mike McClellan, a nephew to mountain man Joseph R. Walker and a brother to Frank McClellan, who was now traveling to California with Wambaugh.

The diarists have been complaining of sickness recently, ailments marked by headaches, aching joints, high fevers, and delirium. There is a good chance it was Rocky Mountain spotted fever or some similar disease, possibly contracted from ticks attaching to peoples' clothes as they strode through the sagebrush and grasses.[29]

After completing the crossing, the company moved up the river a few miles to a spot on the north side of the river at present-day Casper. With the crossing of the Chiles/Hensley party completed, the Mormon crew could take a breather. It would be a few days before the first wagons would arrive from the 1848 wave of the great Mormon emigration.

Smith's journal entry for July 9 began by lamenting that his oxen were gone. The company started late that morning, presumably because they had to track down their strays. According to Smith, they made fourteen miles before stopping to camp at a "spring on Dry Creek [Poison Spider Creek] in sight of the Red Buttes." His description suggests that Chiles led his company toward the river's Bessemer Bend, a more southern route. This was not surprising, as it was a popular route during the earlier years when Chiles traveled through here. Their campsite might have been at Bessemer Bend, just west of today's Highway 220 and west of the river on County Road 308, and at the mouth of Poison Spider Creek.

Even though May was discomforted with his first cold on the trip, he still registered his admiration for the scenery: "tolerable water and grass on a small creek where the hills, mountains and red buttes make a picturesque appearance." He wrote that the cattle drank from the spring waters, but expressed concern "that our cattle would be poisoned."

By the next morning, May was relieved that their cattle were still alive, apparently suffering no ill effects. They made fifteen miles on July 10, the trail winding between low, bleak hills, and barren ridges. They ended the day at Willow Springs, and May praised its water as "good as I have seen on the road." The grass was "good," he added, surprising because of all the livestock that had grazed there during the preceding month. Despite traveling through this desolate country, neither May nor Smith complained much about it, and neither reported the loss of any livestock due to straying or drinking the water.

When Smith arrived at Willow Springs, he reported a fight had erupted:

> this afternoon a most disagreeable fight took place at the Willow Springs Between a man by the name of Carroll Belonging to Capt. Hensleys co of Mules and a man by the name of Hutt from passing jokes they came to blows . . . a few waggons stoping in the Road opposite the Mule Co. it appearing they would rather see a fight then to proceed on their journey.

Smith did not report on the outcome of the fight, but did mention that they passed "the remains of a waggon which had Been left by some Emigrants."

On July 11, the Chiles company departed Willow Springs, their oxen straining mightily up the steep incline of Prospect Hill. Nine miles past the summit, Smith reported that "Mr. McClelland" turned his wagon over in crossing Horse Creek, probably the same McClellan whom May had reported as very sick a few days earlier. Descending into the Sweetwater River Valley, the Chiles company passed Steamboat Rock and the series of small saleratus lakes. After making sixteen miles, Captain Chiles gave his signal and the train of wagons circled at the foot of Independence Rock. Yet neither May nor Smith had much to say about it.

They departed Independence Rock without much fanfare the morning of July 12, the last company to roll past it this year. The rock could now return to its normal state of quietude until the following summer. In the years to come, one could easily climb to the top of the rock and use it as a grandstand seat from which one could see great distances in both directions and watch the huge number of gold rushers moving by.

Major Hensley and his pack train of mules separated from the Chiles company at Independence Rock and hurried ahead to Salt Lake. The eighteen wagons that had been part of Hensley's original party remained with Chiles. Hensley and his pack train would reconnect with the Chiles company later on the California Trail.

The Chiles company next passed Devil's Gate. Smith mentioned the towering cliffs, but only in the context of saying that he had discovered another grave there, that of a young man who had died a year earlier. Smith also reported on abandoned wagons and dead oxen:

> wed 12 . . . [A] little farther [beyond Devil's Gate] we came to where an emigrant family had broke and left there waggon there Being no timber to Repair it where they Buried their Little all in a cache beside the Road and to their shame be it said that some Emigrants Dug it up and took the Property . . . the son of a Baptist Preacher took some of the Property in [the] presence of his Right Reverend

father   a little past them and we came to another waggon which had been
abandoned and Simmeno Lanjanesse a trader from Bridgers fort took it to put in
a part of his load of goods. . . . from the ford of the Platte until here we seen the
carcases of many dead steers.

Smith's account of this section of trail brings to mind W. L. Adams' earlier
description of how their oxen were getting so weak that they had to lighten their loads
in this area:

Many people for want of teams are leaving wagons, plows, feather beds, stores,
kettles, harrow teeth, chains, boxes, &c. The road is lined with such articles . . .
together with dead cattle.

The grim detritus of wagon trains starting to fall apart must have included at
least one piece of handsome but heavy furniture. Imagine the tension when the tough
decision was made to abandon a family heirloom. It calls to mind W. L. Adams' warning to those back home: "One had better a thousand fold start with 'NOTHING BUT
PROVISIONS AND CLOTHING' than run the risk of wearing their teams down in
hauling such stuff as they can do without."

After traveling only ten miles on July 12, the Chiles company stopped early in
the afternoon to camp beside the banks of the Sweetwater, five miles west of Devil's
Gate. Richard May and two companions thought they had time for an excursion to
a high mountain three miles away, possibly Savage Peak to the north. After climbing
two thousand feet in elevation, May described the view as breathtaking. From high
atop the rocky peak, he and his friends could see great distances in all directions.
When they spotted a flock of mountain sheep, they tried killing one, but with no success. The next morning, before breaking camp, May's spirits were still elevated when
he wrote in his journal:

We had a very pleasant encampment, all cheerful and gay. The mountains rising
in majestic grandeur on both sides, the beautiful little Sweet Water, so clear and
limpid in its water and so are the creeks puttin into it, with their gravelly beds
and sandy bottoms.

According to Smith, the company did not leave camp until one thirty in the
afternoon of July 13. In spite of their late start, they still made sixteen miles that day.
They stayed close to the south bank of the Sweetwater and came to rest late that afternoon just west of Split Rock. They would have camped just to the north of modern
Highway 287/789, about ten miles northwest of its junction with Highway 220.

Smith's entry for July 13 makes one wonder if he had a copy of Fremont's *Report
of the Exploring Expedition*, because he recorded his belief that Fremont's group had
camped here on August 9 and 10, 1843, although Fremont's *Report* suggested that
they camped near here on August 3, 1842, and August 6, 1843.[30]

On July 14, the Chiles company traveled fifteen miles, crossing the Sweetwater three times in the Three Crossings canyon. It appears that they camped that afternoon on the west side of the Sweetwater, about one mile west of Names Cliff. Their camp was probably located just north of modern Highway 287/789, thirteen miles east of where Highway 135 today intersects with Highway 287/789. Buffalo were still in the area and May wrote that he went on another hunting excursion. After they finished, he wrote that "[w]e are well supplied with meat," and noted several "dead oxen on the road which had died from other trains." As for the sick emigrants, May reported that they "are mending and will soon be well."

On July 15, the company continued their way across the sage-covered plain, drifting away from the river and passing through the marshy area of Ice Slough, although neither diarist mentioned it. May notes passing "some saleratus lakes," then striking the Sweetwater again and pitching camp after sixteen miles of travel. May complained of a hailstorm that "pelted the poor wagoners, while the aristocracy of the company were secure from the storm. . . . Capt. Childs lost a very valuable steer today." In Smith's words, "J. B. Chiles had to leave his best ox 6 miles from camp. He died of the Bloody [illegible]." This incident serves to remind us that Chiles was taking his four children back to his rancho nestled in the beautiful little Chiles Valley north of Napa. This tall, stern-faced man may have had many responsibilities as captain of this train, but as a thirty-eight-year-old widower with children, wagons, and oxen, he was also dealing with the same family problems and headaches that others in his company faced.

On the evening of July 15, the Wambaugh, Gates, and Miller companies were in the lead, camped two miles below Fort Hall and getting ready to embark on the last leg of their journey. This put them 330 miles ahead of where the Chiles company was encamped on the Sweetwater River, near Rocky Ridge. The next party ahead of Chiles was the Stone company and Father Lempfrit, which was seventy miles west and traveling in the beginning stages of their all-night, all-day journey across Greenwood's cutoff.

In the following table, the number of wagons in each company is based on earlier declarations by diarists, but the numbers had changed as some wagons had pulled ahead, others had dropped back, and some had been abandoned beside the trail. As for the companies for which we have no numbers, they are estimated in light of the total number of wagons observed by Isaac Pettijohn.

Table 10: Location of companies on July 15, 1848

Company	Number of Wagons	Location on July 15
Allsopp	25	probably at Salt Lake City
Adams, first segment	20	probably at Fort Hall
Wambaugh	39	at Fort Hall
Cornwall	4	at Fort Hall
Greenwood	10	at Fort Hall
Gates	10	at Fort Hall
Miller	23	at Fort Hall
12 California wagons	12	perhaps at Fort Hall
Watt	24	perhaps leaving Bear River Valley
Walker/Bristow	24	likely in Bear River Valley
Kelly	23	likely in Bear River Valley
Purvine	24	at Hams Fork
Adams, second segment	26	likely at Hams Fork
Hannah	20 (est.)	probably west of Green River
Delaney	20 (est.)	probably at Green River
Stone	11	crossing Greenwood's cutoff
Hensley (pack train)	0	on way to Salt Lake
Chiles	38	on Sweetwater, near Rocky Ridge
Lassen	9	near Pacific Springs
Total	362*	

*This compares to Pettijohn's count of 342 wagons.

CHAPTER 14

The Great Trail Forked
JULY 16–AUGUST 2

JULY 16, 1848
William Anderson, Miller company, two miles
south of Fort Hall, present-day Idaho

William Anderson was last heard from on July 15 when the Miller company stopped to camp two miles south of Fort Hall "on a small tributary of the Portneth [Portneuf] river." He explained that, in addition to his own company,

> here we found 2 other companys waiting for reinforcements haveing been told at the fort that they must go strong handed through the Cyuse country as they were then at war with the Oregon settlers   it was thought to be verry danger-ous traveling through their country so there were 3 companys here to gether some for Oregon and some for Californa   the Californans separated off in one company and the Oregon emegrants in 2 companys which made our company number about 50 armed men and 35 wagons.

The three companies Anderson was referring to were Wambaugh, Gates, and his own Miller company. With three companies spread across a grassy floodplain on the east side of the Snake River, the area would have been dotted with the dull white can-vas covers of over one hundred wagons, with about four hundred men, women, and children, and probably close to six hundred head of livestock, not counting sheep. Gathered here to reorganize, the assembly would have resembled an immense church camp meeting, except that the people were sunburned, gaunt-faced, and dirty, their wagons were beat up, and their livestock emaciated. Despite their trail-worn appear-ance, however, one might expect to see a trace of jubilation in their faces and swagger in their walk. They had traveled so many miles and endured many hardships. Now they were about to begin the final leg of their long journey.

On June 25, Isaac Pettijohn had reported "43 waggons bound for Oregon and California." Likely from the original Allsopp party and a faster-moving element of the

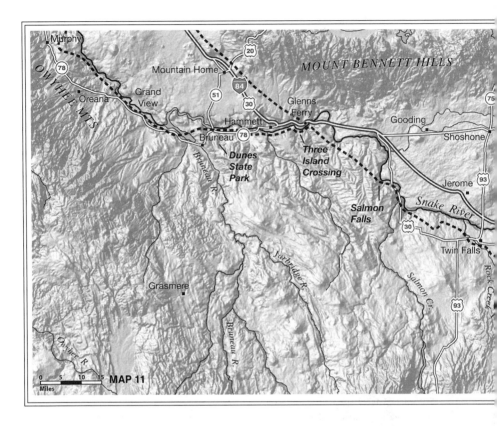

original Adams company, these forty-three wagons had probably remained traveling a day or two ahead of the Wambaugh, Gates, and Miller companies. When these forty-three wagons reached the Parting of the Ways west of Little Sandy Creek, there is no known record of how many (if any) took Greenwood's cutoff, and how many (if any) took the long way through Fort Bridger. As for Allsopp's stag party, he reported that they had headed on to Salt Lake, and no wagons are known to have accompanied them. If these forty-three wagons had taken the longer route via Fort Bridger, they should have arrived at Fort Hall about the same time as the Miller company, but Anderson did not mention any wagon companies there besides Wambaugh, Gates, and Miller. The greater probability was that these forty-three wagons took the shorter Greenwood's cutoff and continued traveling a few days ahead of Wambaugh, Gates, and Miller. Under this scenario, they should have already passed through Fort Hall, and were now on their way to Oregon.

It must also be remembered that Pettijohn had noted that some of these forty-three wagons were "California-bound." Because the original Adams party was considered an Oregon company, any wagons intending to go to California would have

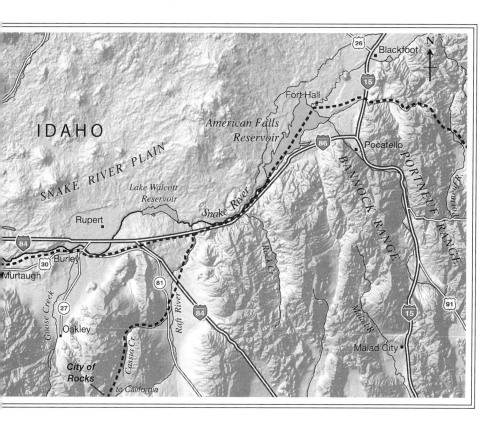

probably come from the Allsopp party. These few California wagons may have paused at Fort Hall to wait for the next California-bound group.

There are two families known to be waiting at Fort Hall when Wambaugh, Gates, and Miller arrived: thirty-six-year-old Hazen Kimball, a disaffected Mormon, with his wife and two young children, and the Pollack family. They had come from Salt Lake in hopes of catching on with a wagon train headed for California. Kimball wrote a letter to a friend in December 1848 from San Francisco.

> I arrived in Salt Lake Valley on the 3d of October 1847, and remained there during the winter. On the 2nd of March [1848], I left in company with one team for Fort Hall—a distance of 200 miles—where a wagon had never been before without a guide without difficulty. On the 15th of July I left Fort Hall with 25 wagons and 34 men, emigrants from the States, for California.[1]

Other evidence suggests that, in addition to Kimball and Pollock, there may have been another fallen-away Mormon by the name of Rogers waiting at Fort Hall.[2]

The Wambaugh company, which probably still included the Cornwall and Greenwood parties, had arrived at Fort Hall as a group of slightly more than fifty wagons. As for the Miller company, Anderson initially reported it as starting out with twenty-three wagons. The twelve California-bound wagons that had joined them along the South Platte had separated from them at the North Platte crossing because of a scarcity of grass. But somewhere in the Sweetwater or Bear River Valleys, where grass was not so scarce, they may have caught up and rejoined the Miller company and hence, may have arrived at Fort Hall with the Miller company and become part of the group assembling for California. It is highly unlikely that they arrived later, because the next groups of wagons to head for California were Peter Lassen's and the Chiles company, who did not leave Fort Hall until about two weeks later; neither group will show the addition of any significant number of wagons.

Table 11: Wagon companies at Fort Hall on July 15, 1848

Company	Number of Wagons
Allsopp	10
Wambaugh	39
Cornwall	4
Greenwood	10
Gates	10
Miller	23
12 California wagons	12
Kimball/Pollock	2
Total	110

William Anderson's entry for the next day:

> July the 16th all things being regulated and organized and as we thought suf-
> ficiently strong to travel through any nation of indians west of the rocky moun-
> tains we roled out on our journey Gates company of 25 waggons before and
> ours next   we traveled 8 miles and camped to let the foremost company get
> ahead a little   we camped on portneth [Portneuf] river just above its junction
> with snake river   here spent the remainder of the day in fishing and gathering
> wild currents.

Anderson's entries for the fifteenth and sixteenth established that the two Oregon-bound companies leaving Fort Hall were Gates, the "foremost company," with twenty-five wagons, and Miller with thirty-five—a total of sixty wagons going on to Oregon.

Riley Root's entry for July 16 mirrored Anderson's. He wrote that they left their camp and traveled south seven miles, stopping to camp near the mouth of the Portneuf River. According to Root, they camped "about 25 rods [400 feet] above its

William Tappan, sketch of Fort Hall, probably 1849. Courtesy of Idaho State Historical Society, 1254-C.

confluence of the Snake River." This placed the Miller company about nine miles below Fort Hall, the same location that Anderson had indicated. Their campsite is presently under the waters of the American Falls Reservoir.

Because the dates and locations of Root's camps from this point coincide with those of William Anderson's, it will be evident that Root had joined the Miller company train. It appears that the large Trullinger family and Peter Cline (from the original Wambaugh company) also joined Miller. In contrast, the Dickens, Patterson, and Houston families, plus John Crooks, Thomas Patton, Dr. D. S. Baker, John Crooks, N. Wilcox, and L. Lanterette (all from the original Wambaugh company) joined the Gates company. The same evidence showed that the Kellogg and Hathaway families, originally members of Cornwall's party, decided to travel with Gates as well.[3]

July 16, 1848
P. B. Cornwall and M. N. Wambaugh, two miles south of Fort Hall, Idaho

P. B. Cornwall's biography corroborated Anderson's report that the emigrants reorganized their companies at Fort Hall. When Cornwall's party, presumably still traveling with Wambaugh, reached the fort, his biography explained that "[t]he original party divided, the Kelloggs going to Oregon, the Cornwalls to California."[4]

Before leaving Missouri, Cornwall had been entrusted with a charter from the Masonic grand lodge of Missouri to establish a new Masonic lodge in Oregon. He had been carrying it west in a "tin cylinder." Both Cornwall and the Kelloggs concurred that it was at Fort Hall that Cornwall handed the charter over to Orrin

Kellogg, asking him to take it on to Oregon. Since Cornwall had started his journey with the intention of going to Oregon, something during the trip had changed his mind, but his reason is not revealed. It will later be seen that the Kelloggs arrived at Milwaukee, Oregon (near Oregon City), on September 8, and they delivered the charter to Oregon City on September 11, thereby establishing Multnomah Lodge, No. 1.[5]

While sixty wagons were going to Oregon, this meant that about forty-five were going to California. Anderson referred to them when he recorded in his journal that the "Californians separated off in one company." We will leave the California wagons for the time being, and follow the progress of the Gates and Miller companies as they leave Fort Hall to commence the final leg of their journey to Oregon.

July 17–31, 1848
Riley Root and William Anderson, Miller company,
Portneuf River, below Fort Hall

On the morning of July 17, the Miller company rolled out of their camp beside the Portneuf River, nine miles south of Fort Hall. The Gates company was some distance ahead. Anderson failed to report whether the California wagons traveled ahead of or behind them. Judging by the short time these companies hung around Fort Hall, it appears everyone was anxious to resume their journey. While their destination might have seemed just beyond the horizon, in reality it was much farther than that. In fact, they were beginning the most difficult leg of the entire trip, and if they were feeling positive, it was probably due to ignorance of what lay ahead.

One mile beyond the Portneuf crossing, the newly constituted Miller train made a difficult crossing of a slough. After another two miles, they experienced another difficult crossing at the one-hundred-yard-wide Bannock Creek with its steep banks, and Anderson noted that "several of the teams [got] stuck at the coming out place." Now traveling with the Miller company, Riley Root wrote that "where the road ascends the first terrace," they left the Snake River bottom. They traveled along the bench for a few miles, then descended and camped along the river. They had completed a day of twelve and a half miles by Root's measurements, and fifteen by Anderson's.

Two miles after leaving camp on the morning of July 18, the Miller wagons lumbered past American Falls. Just above the cascades, the river was about nine hundred feet wide, then narrowed to about two hundred feet where it spilled over a dyke of black volcanic rock, producing a thundering waterfall. Root explained,

> The water of the American falls does not descend perpendicularly but like a cascade. The whole descent from the upper to the lower expanse is from 40 to 50 feet, reckond by perpendicula measurement. . . . The table lands draw to a point

at the falls. Below the falls, the table lands border the river, and being entirely destitute of grass, render encampments difficult.

The eighteenth would be an exhausting day for the oxen as the road was very uneven, with many steep ravines and hills to negotiate. After navigating ten miles across the tablelands mentioned by Root, the trail squeezed between what Root called the "palaisades." He was referring to Massacre Rocks, a black, twisted volcanic mass thrust up from the ground. The rocky formation was not given this name until many years later, when a series of Snake Indian attacks near here on a group of wagon trains in 1862 left a number of emigrants dead. Today, there is a good half-mile-long section of discernable wagon ruts just east of Massacre Rocks, on the south side of Interstate 86.

Six miles beyond the palisades, the Miller company stopped to camp on the eighteenth, on what Root called "Cascade Creek," completing a day of eighteen miles. Anderson called it "beaver dam creek" owing to its many beaver dams. "[T]his is a small stream," Anderson reported, "flowing down a succession of falls which resembles those of a mill dam built of rocks." It is called Fall Creek today and the location of the Miller camp on July 18 was just north of I-86, about two miles east of its exit 21.

The next morning, July 19, the company traveled about two miles along the Snake River. Then the trail ascended, lifting out of the Snake River bottom. Evidence of wagon wheel ruts can again be seen just south of I-86, about one mile west of exit 21. After traveling only eight miles, over a trail that Anderson complained was a "verry dusty road," they came to a three-mile-wide valley through which the Raft River meandered. It was a thirty-foot-wide stream that many called Cassia Creek. They camped on the creek's west side, the trail's next great "parting of the ways." Here, the California road split from the Oregon Trail and headed south, up the west bank of the Raft River. Anderson noted this momentous fork in his journal: "[T]he California trail turns off to the left while the Oregon trail keeps to the right." Anderson and Root again failed to report whether the California wagons were ahead of or behind them. Today, the place where the trail crossed the Raft River can be seen by taking exit 15 off of I-86 and traveling a mile and a half south on Yale Road. From there, look west toward the creek.

The Miller company cattle grazed contentedly through the night on the grass growing beside the riverbank. The next morning, the twentieth, the company caught up their oxen, hitched them to their battered wagons, and began to rolling west out of camp. Some may have tossed a wistful glance at that other trail vanishing in the distance to the south. Even though they had not yet heard about the untold riches that lay in the streams of California, some might have wondered whether they were making the right choice by going to Oregon.

After ascending a sage-covered bluff and leaving the Raft River Valley, the Miller company labored westward across an undulating plain. Their wagons rattled and creaked as they lumbered across a path that Anderson called "verry rough and rocky."

Root also complained about the rock-strewn trail: "20th— 16 miles over a district of basaltic rock, slightly hidden from sight by a thin layer of clay, though in many places they protrude so as to render traveling with wagons irksome."

James Clyman had penned a few uncomplimentary words of his own when he traveled this bleak section of trail in 1844:

> nothing to disturb the monotony of the Eternal Sage plain which is covered with broken cynders much resembling Junks of pot mettal & Now & then a cliff of Black burned rock which looks like Distruction brooding over dispair.[6]

Root and Anderson both reported their company camping on Marsh Creek on the evening of July 20, a place with "plenty of grass." Their campground was located about two and one-half miles south of where I-84 departs and I-86 split, but because the site is presently farmed, there is no visible trace of the campsite.

The company left Marsh Creek on the morning of July 21, taking a route that somewhat followed today's Highway 81. Root reported traveling "11½ miles, over a dry and dusty plain, to camp, to Snake river, about 2 miles above the mouth of Goose creek. Here is a narrow bottom, which furnishes a little coarse grass. No wood. [Snake] River here about ¼ of a mile wide." Their camp beside the Snake River would have been just southeast of present-day Burley, Idaho.

On the morning of July 22, they quit the Snake River, which bent to the north, and toiled over a level plain for the next four miles amidst suffocating clouds of dust before arriving at Goose Creek. Because of upstream dams and irrigation projects, Goose Creek disappeared from here long ago. Anderson reported that "the foremost company [Gates] had camped there [Goose Creek]," probably the previous night. After heading west another eight miles, Miller's party struck the Snake River once again. According to Anderson, they "halted for noon and wattered our cattle   grass was verry scarce."

Resuming their march in the afternoon of the twenty-second, Root complained about the road changing from "good" to "rocky." It was a long day of twenty-one miles that took them over mildly undulating desolation with little to prick the senses other than the strong scent of sage. Anderson wrote that they finally stopped to camp, but it was on a "dry branch there was 1 or 2 small pools of watter but not enough for our stock we had to dig for drinking watter grass was pretty good here." The location of the Miller camp that evening would have been about one-half mile southeast of the present community of Murtaugh, Idaho, and about one mile north of Highway 30. The Snake River was near, but it was inaccessible to the emigrants because it was now running through a deep canyon formed from nearly vertical cliffs of black volcanic rock hundreds of feet deep. At this camp, Root recorded that he had logged a total of 1,200 miles from St. Joseph. Had he known the distance to his destination in Oregon, he would have known that he still had a third of the way to go—probably a very discouraging thought.

For the last few days, the landscape had little to break up its dull uniformity, and the travelers had had nothing interesting to look at save endless stretches of gray-green sagebrush. The country had been as bleak and dreary as any they had traveled through before. Many of the oxen limped badly after days of treading over sharp-edged stones. When the company had met Joe Meek just a hundred miles out of St. Joseph, he had told them of his encounter with a hostile band of Bannocks somewhere in this area and warned them about the Cayuse Indians in Oregon,[7] but he had not told them about this endless passage along the Snake River. One wonders whether the tedium of the endless empty landscape was broken by a sense of relief that at least they saw no Indian war parties. Anderson, however, expressed no sense of apprehension about the Indians. The next day, he wrote:

> July the 23rd we traveled 8 miles and camped on rocky creek [Rock Creek]   here was a pretty good camp   we saw a few indians to day   here a company that was behind came up with us a bout midnight   there were 29 waggons in there company.

The last information from Keturah Belknap was when her company arrived at the Green River one day behind the Miller group. Since she had reported that the Watt family had left their company and dropped back, it appears that this party of twenty-nine wagons was her group, now led by George Jackson.

When the emigrants arrived at Rock Creek, they encountered a narrow stream only twenty feet wide and bordered by willows. With plenty of good water and willows for firewood, Root declared it a "Good camp." Today this site is about five miles south of Highway 30, on Road N 3600 E, then one mile west on Pumpland Road.

Shortly after dawn on July 24, the Miller company left camp and continued northwest along the east side of Rock Creek. For eight miles they did not try crossing it because it meandered through a deep channel between sheer sides of black volcanic rock. They finally came to a place that allowed wagons to creep down a rocky bank to get to the other side. The location of this crossing is southeast of the present town of Twin Falls, Idaho, just southeast of the modern intersection of 3700 North Road and Eastland Drive, but there isn't much to see.

Anderson recorded a lengthy description of the day:

> July the 24th we roled out a head of the 29 waggons [Jackson company?] and traveled 20 miles   8 miles brought us to the crossing of rocky creek in a canyon   here we stopped and wattered our cattle then turned up over the bluff and traveled 12 miles over a dusty sage plain and camped at the dry camp on snake river   the bluffs here exceed 1000 feet in height   we drove our cattle [on] a narrow path and let them go and shift for themselves though the river was near 1 ¼ miles from the camp which was the nearest place they could get watter   here we were badly deceived in the distance to the river as my self and two of our men were verry dry   we concluded we would take some buckets and

go bring some watter so we started about dusk and traveled till about sometime after night when the two that were with me became tired and discouraged
turned back   I traveled on determined to have some watter   at length came
to the river and took a hearty drink and got some in my bucket and made the
best of my way back to the camp where I arrived safe about 10 o'clock at night
with near half a gallon of watter in the bucket which I set in my waggon and lay
down on the sand and slept sound until morning the rest having retired sometime befor I came back from the river   on the opposite side of the river there is
a spring that breaks out some 300 feet from the top of the mountain and runs
almost perpendicular 7 or 8 hundred feet down into the river which we could
see and hear verry distinctly from our camp although it was near 1 ½ miles off.

While Anderson recorded that they camped twelve miles beyond the Rock
Creek crossing, the usually accurate Root wrote that it was only seven miles. In any
event, neither chronicler was happy, Anderson calling the camp "dry" and Root
terming it "miserable." Root's version of driving their cattle to the river for water and
grass was similar:

Our cattle were driven down a narrow and difficult way, much of it very steep,
three-fourths of a mile to the river, where it was bordered in some places by little
patches of grass, often not one rod wide. Our cattle were taken up, next morning, with not a half a supply during the night.

While their mileage estimates are uncertain, it seems most likely that the location of
their awful camp on the night of July 24 was at the head of a deep ravine that ran a
little over a mile to the Snake River. This location is about three miles north of today's
Highway 30, near the intersection of 2000 East Road and 4400 North Road.

"[T]his morning [July 25]," Anderson wrote, "one of our men shot an Indian dog
before we left our camp which was running our sheep." After collecting up their livestock, the Miller company returned to the trail, praying for better conditions ahead.
The trail continued to traverse the sage-covered high bluffs, staying a couple of miles
south of the huge gorge through which the Snake made its determined way. According to Anderson, the emigrants could hear thundering rapids in the distance, perhaps
Kanaka Rapids. Or they could hear the sound of spectacular springs cascading from
the cliffs above the river, places like Crystal Springs, Niagara Springs, and Banbury
Springs. But unless they left the trail and made a side trip, they would not have seen
these scenic treats.

A few miles after leaving camp, they came to a steep, sandy hill. From here they
had a wonderful view of a valley below where Salmon Falls Creek entered the Snake
River. Descending a steep incline, they rolled into the valley and came to "the mouth
of a warm spring branch [Deep Creek]," according to Anderson. "[H]ere we watered
our cattle." After traveling three more miles between the Snake River on the right and
Salmon Falls Creek on the left, Anderson wrote that

we pased by a warm spring on our left   several of our company ran with cups to this spring thinking that after traveling all day through the hot sunshine they would have a good cool drink of watter but they came back verry much disappointed.

Root's entry for the same day focused on something different:

25th— 16 miles. Eleven miles to Warm Spring creek [Deep Creek]. Here is but little grass. About 4 miles farther, to Salmon Fall creek. One mile down the creek, to camp, near its mouth. Here is a very good camp. On the north-east side of the river, along here for several miles, are fine springs issuing from the bluffs [Thousand Springs], some of which would carry the largest flouring mills. They are a curiosity. Supposd to be the waters of the river, spreading out into the country above the American falls, and passing along between the basaltic rock above, and another stratum below, till they arrive at this place, where they are discharged into the river. The evidence that they are the waters of the river appears to be derivd from the fact, that the river between the falls and this place had not more than half the water in it that it has above the falls.

Root made an extraordinarily trenchant observation. Much of the Snake's water did indeed disappear into areas of volcanic rock hundreds of miles upstream, then travel through subterranean channels before bursting from the face of these black cliffs. Gushing out in tremendous volumes, the waters plunged, white and foaming, several hundred feet into the river below. Root usually had little to say, but when it came to geological things, like Thousand Springs, he took the time to write a great deal.

The company camped beside Salmon Falls Creek near its mouth with the Snake on the evening of July 25. The twenty-sixth would be a short day. After fording Salmon Falls Creek, they traveled only five miles, then stopped to make camp beside the Snake at the lower end of Upper Salmon Falls. For almost one hundred miles, the Snake had meandered through deep canyons, making it unapproachable to the wagon trains. Now the emigrants could travel along its banks, even if only for a short distance.

Anderson was enthralled with the scenery at Salmon Falls:

July the 26th we traveled 5 miles which brought us to the salmon falls on snake river   here were several lodges of indians   they were catching fish and drying them in the sun   we bought some of them for which we paid them powder and lead and some old cloths   this is a poor camp   we drove our cattle on to an island in the river [Millet Island?] where they got a little grass soon after leaving camp this morning   we came to the river on the opposite side of which was a lot of springs creeks or rivers [Thousand Springs] the first bursts out from under the ground near the top of the bluff and falls in a sheet 8 feet wide 50 feet

Early photograph of Thousand Springs as it issues from the eastern bank of the Snake River, northwest of Twin Falls, Idaho. Courtesy of Idaho State Historical Society, 69-4.2196.

perpendicular into the river   ¼ of a mile below this is a nother small one   just below this is a nother about 100 yards wide   it also comes out of the bluff and falls in a solid sheet 20 or 25 feet perpendicular into the river   there are some 8 or 10 below this scattered along from 20 to 100 yards apart all on the opposite or north side of the river.

The travelers of 1848 saw very different conditions than we would see today. The Snake River has been dammed at various locations and irrigation water has been pumped from the river and plateaus above, reducing the amount of water in the river and drying up or diminishing many of the springs.

Anderson described their camp as "poor" due to the lack of grass and wood, but it was an ideal place for Indians to spear salmon struggling up the rapids to spawn. When Fremont's expedition camped here in 1843, he had reported seeing Snake Indians spearing salmon here.[8] The Miller company had traded flour, cornmeal, and dried apples to the Sioux for buffalo robes; they now traded powder and lead to these Bannocks or Snakes (he didn't say which) for dried salmon. With their meat stocks largely depleted, the emigrants probably accepted the dried fish with relish. But they had to be careful, as their digestive systems were not accustomed to this protein-rich food.

Root described July 26 in more concise terms:

26th— 6 miles. Five miles to first rapids of Salmon falls, 1 more to camp. But little grass at this place, and that is mostly on a small island or two. Salmon falls is more a cascade than a fall, except in one place, where it falls a few feet perpendicularly. Also calld Fishing falls. The whole cascade is more than a mile in length. To this place the Indians resort to obtain salmon, which at some seasons of the year are tolerably plenty, having come from the ocean up the Columbia river, to the mouth of Snake river, whence they find their way to this place.

The next day the Miller company faced a severe test as the Snake made a dramatic bend to the north and the trail left the river and headed across a cutoff. They first had to draw their wagons up a steep ridge to climb out of the Snake River bottom. Once they reached the bluffs, they rolled onto a dry, undulating high plain, vegetated with the eternal sage. As their wagons lurched across the many ravines, they must have held their breath and prayed that no axles broke and no wagons toppled. Anderson wrote:

July the 27th   this day we traveled 24 miles   soon after starting we ascended a long steep hill on a narrow ridge the river on one side and a deep hollow on the other   here we had a plain view of the falls and river below our road   to day over a hilley sandy sage plain in a bout 11 miles travel we pased a road that turned off to a camp on this river but there was no grass   here were a set of mill irons thrown away   we traveled on about 13 miles and descended a long hill into a dry branch and turned to the wright down the dry branch 1 ¼ miles to the river and camped   grass was verry scarce here   there were lots of old waggons plows and various kinds of implements here that had bin left by the emigrants of the year before.

Root noted the abandoned wagons and other items as well:

27th— 24½ miles to camp, on Snake river. To obtain this camp, we left the road a mile and a half back, and followd a dry branch down to this place. To-day, we traveld over a dry sage plain, though we had a tolerably good road. At this place, and even farther east, are seen the relics of wagons of former emigrants, strewd along the road. Boxes, bands, tires, and all parts of the irons of wagons, left behind.

The Miller company had ended the long, grueling day of July 27 at the Snake River, camping a few miles above Three Island Crossing. The next morning, Root wrote that they traveled two miles downstream to the crossing, which he described as the "old crossing of the Snake river. . . . Encamped 2½ miles farther on, where is little grass. No wood for fuel." Anderson also described their arrival at "the upper crossing" of the Snake River on the morning of the twenty-eighth:

July the 28th we traveled about 5 miles which brought us to the upper crossing of the snake river   just before we came to the crossing we came down a
verry steep mountain   I rugg locked both hind wheels of my waggon but still
the hill was so steep that the waggon cattle slid some 2 or 3 rods without taking a step   we drove down to the river and camped   here is a small bottom
on the river bank and here we over took the foremost company [Gates]   they
had lost one ox since they left fort hall   they were busily engaged here sawing
off there waggon beds   we commenced making our loads lighter as our cattle
were getting very weak   there was several bushels of salt and a stove thrown
away besides a great many other things which we found could be done without
rather than have our teams give out halling them   while we were here the third
company [Jackson] came up   they stated that since they left the salmon falls on
snake river they had lost two oxen and left one waggon one saddle and several
other things   they camped here also making 3 companys here on a small narrow bottom of not verry good grass   here the trail forks one crosses the river
the other keeps down on the left side of the river.

Now that Gates, the "foremost company," had been overtaken, and the "third
company," presumably Jackson's (with Keturah Belknap), had come up from behind,
the river crossing thronged with travelers representing almost ninety wagons and
countless livestock. Like parties in earlier years, they were forced to face reality. The
day before had been a killer. Their oxen may have been remarkable, but there was only
so much they could pull in their weakened state. The men knew they must lighten
their loads again, even to the point of sawing off and shortening their wagon beds.

Anderson had another gruesome detail to report at the river crossing:

here was a grave of a man said to have got drowned, the wolves had scratched
down to his feet but the poles that laid length wayse of him prevented them
from getting him out his feet were naked the flesh partly scratched off.

Anderson's graphic description of the corpse suggests that it was fairly fresh, perhaps
not from an earlier year. Could this be evidence that another company of wagons—
maybe wagons from Allsopp and the faster-moving Adams' segment—had passed
here recently?

As Anderson explained, the trail divided at Three Island Crossing, south of
present-day Glenns Ferry, Idaho. Many wagon companies forded the Snake here and
traveled northwest to Fort Boise, about 115 miles away. The other fork of the trail did
not cross the Snake, but continued to travel along the south bank of the river.

For the wagon trains wanting to take the northerly branch of the trail, Three
Island Crossing was the best place to cross because the river expanded into a wide bay
here, ranging from four hundred to one thousand feet wide, depending on the water
flow. The spot got its name because the trail crossed three islands—actually, grassy
sandbars—situated in the midst of the broad channel. But the crossing could be

dangerous. The current was swift and the water deceptively deep, ranging from four to six feet depending on the river's condition. Drownings were frequent and many wagons were upset or swept away. When Fremont crossed here on October 3, 1843, his howitzer was carried downstream and he nearly lost a number of mules.[9] Indians could also be a danger to the unwary. Three years earlier, two men had crossed the river ahead of their wagon party to hunt, and were later found dead and scalped.[10]

Most companies preferred crossing the Snake and taking the shorter, easier northern route, but if the river's condition was too treacherous or too deep to safely ford, companies were obliged to take the southern route, a less desirable trail that was about ten to fifteen miles longer and traveled through some of the most dreary country imaginable.

Root reported the next day:

[July] 29th— 12 miles, over as rough and stony a road, along the banks of the Snake river, as I ever traveld. One wagon was broken, to-day, and left to be totally destroyd by those that came after us.

His entry revealed that he was traveling along the southern trail, and his camp was just north of modern Highway 78, about fourteen miles west of Glenns Ferry.

Anderson's report for the twenty-ninth reflected the same choice. He described the same difficult trail that Root had complained about:

July the 29th we concluded that we would not cross the river and so the foremost company [Gates] roled out and we followed and traveled 8 miles down on the left bank of the river   our road to day was pretty bad   there several places that there was barely room for our waggons to pass between the river and the bluffs and they were very rocky and sidelong   some waggons came verry near to upsetting and roling some 40 or 50 feet into the river   we pased several small patches of grass to day.

Based on Anderson's mileage, his camp would have been on the south side of the river, about ten miles west of Glenns Ferry.

Neither Root nor Anderson had crossed the Snake, but neither explained their reason for taking the southern route. Perhaps it was high water. Since the Miller company traveled with a band of sheep and there was no ferry to transport them, the decision could have been dictated by their flock.

At this point, the Gates company moved on ahead of the Miller company. Both at Fort Hall and here, the Miller company had closed in on the Gates company, but it seemed rare that a company would let another pass. Did pride play a role in spurring a company to stay ahead? After all, who wanted to feel that they were lesser men than those closing in behind?

Root recorded traveling twelve miles on July 29, while Anderson reported going only eight. These and subsequent journal entries make it evident that Root was now

William Henry Jackson (1843–1942), *Three Island Crossing.* Watercolor painting, 1932–38.
Courtesy of Scotts Bluff National Monument, SCBL-43.
Some wagon companies crossed the Snake River here, while others did not.

traveling with the Gates company, which would remain ahead of Anderson's Miller party. There must have been a reason why Root decided to leave Miller and join Gates at the Three Island Crossing. Was it friction with Captain Miller or a lack of confidence in him? Did he feel the Gates company would get him to Oregon more quickly? Unfortunately, Root continued to report little and explain nothing.

Root recorded traveling eleven miles on July 30, adding, "Grass not very good. About two miles back, grass might be had by driving the cattle on to an island, in the river. Road sandy during forepart of the route, to-day, and during the afterpart, good." The location of their camp would have been about one mile southwest of where Highway 51 today crosses the Snake.

In contrast, the Miller company only traveled seven miles on July30, causing it to lag behind Gates and Root by about eight miles. This was helpful, as neither company would have to compete for grass at the same spot. Anderson explained:

> when we came to where the road left the river and not knowing how far it would
> be before we would come to watter agan we concluded to camp here (here a
> blacksmith who had said all the way he would take his tools through had to give
> it up and buried them with the intention of coming back the next season after
> them)   our road to day was pretty good with the exception of one mile where
> the mountains closed into the river   this was verry rocky and sidelong   the

Modern photograph of Three Island Crossing. Courtesy of Idaho State Historical Society, 69-45.0.

company before us [Gates] broke an axletree and were compeled to leave the waggon.

The Miller camp should have been along the river about one mile north of today's Highway 78, and about seven miles east of where Highway 51 crosses the Snake.

The next day, Root reported that his Gates company reached the Bruneau River:

[July] 31st— 11½ miles. Six and a half miles to Salt Grass creek [Bruneau River], a name given from the abundance of salt grass growing there. A tolerable camp might be had at that place. The creek soon passes among the bluffs, in a northerly direction, and unites with Snake river, about 5 miles below where we campd. Grass is plenty at this place, but it is almost impossible to obtain any thing of which to make fires.

The Miller company continued to travel not far behind, as Anderson explained:

July the 31st we traveled 14 miles   we traveled up a long sand hill and 4 miles from where we left camp we came down into the river bottom agan   here was pretty smart of grass   we traveled a long in this bottom 2 miles and agan left the

river and ascended a long hill   8 miles from this bottom we came to a creek the
name of which none of the company knew nor none of the maps or journals that
we had gave it any name   so I gave it the name of Moss creek [Bruneau River]
there being a great deal of moss in the bottom of it   this was a good camp.

On the thirty-first, both companies struggled through sections of hub-deep sand
and rolled past an area of high sand dunes on their left. They were passing through
what one could describe as a desert within a desert, as one might see in the Sahara.
Today, these dunes are part of Bruneau Dunes State Park.

Root's entry for July 31 specified that his company crossed the Bruneau River
about five miles above its mouth with the Snake, then continued along the Bruneau
and encamped at the Snake. Today, their campsite is covered by the waters of the C.
J. Strike Reservoir. It seems that Anderson's company camped on the Bruneau at a
location also under water today.

July 31, 1848
Keturah Belknap, Jackson company

Keturah Belknap's diary had been quiet. On July 31, she would have been very close
to her due date, and must have been exceedingly uncomfortable, not to mention having her hands full with the hardships and privations of traveling across this rough
wasteland. Because of her silence, we do not know whether the Jackson company
crossed the Snake River at Three Island Crossing or followed the Miller company on
the more difficult southern road. It is also unknown which branch was taken by the
Watt family, traveling somewhere behind, but if the Miller company had not crossed
the river because of its sheep, Joe Watt probably made the same decision.

July 16–31, 1848
William Porter, Purvine company, Bear River Valley, Idaho

William Porter and the Purvine company had been stymied at the North Platte crossing because of their nightly runaways, which put them eight days behind the Watt,
Walker-Bristow, and Kelly companies. On the evening of July 15, they were camped
on Hams Fork. Porter continued his bare-boned entries, beginning with their departure from Hams Fork on July 16:

[July]16th. Traveled 12 miles and came down the big hill [east of Rock Creek].
17th. Traveled 15 miles and camped on Bear River.
18th. Traveled 24 miles and had a runaway scrape [camped near today's Mont-
    pelier].
19th. Traveled 21 miles to Soda Springs.
21st. Traveled 19 miles to running branch [Portneuf River].

22nd. Traveled 10 miles to foot of the mountain and camped on Port Neuf River.

23rd. Traveled 15 miles and camped on a branch of Snake River [Ross Creek].

24th. Traveled 15 miles to Springs on Snake River bottoms.

25th. Traveled 8 miles and camped on Port Neuf, 2 or 3 miles past Fort Hall.

26th. Traveled 16 miles to springs above American Falls.

27th. Traveled 22 miles to Falls Creek or Levy Creek.

28th. Traveled 10 miles to cassia or Cajeux Creek [Raft River].

29th. Traveled 15 miles to big marsh [creek].

30th. Traveled 15 miles to Goose Creek.

31st. Traveled 7 miles to the [Snake] river.

Porter's entry for July 18 reported another runaway, prompting curiosity over what it was about their oxen that caused this recurring problem. It is noteworthy that the Purvine company was averaging significantly more miles than the Wambaugh and Miller companies did along the same section of trail. Perhaps Captain Purvine was feeling pressure to make up some of their lost time.

By July 31, the Purvine company was camping on the Snake River, about one mile north of modern Highway 81 and eight miles west of today's Burley, Idaho. At that point, they were 130 miles and ten days behind Gates, Miller, and Jackson. We have no information about the Watt, Walker/Bristow, Kelly, and Hannah parties, but they should have been rolling along somewhere between Jackson and Purvine.

July 18–August 2, 1848

Father Lempfrit, Stone company, at the Green River, Wyoming

On July 18, the Stone company was resting in camp beneath the cottonwoods on the west side of the Green River, prompting Lempfrit to complain that "[w]e are not advancing fast." It is curious that many of our previous diarists had expressed the same complaint at this location. Since this was the halfway point to Oregon, no one had pointed this out to Lempfrit, otherwise he surely would have noted it.

The Stone company returned to the trail on July 19, the priest reporting that "[w]e went through a nice valley today that was watered by two rivers, full of fish. We caught some salmon-trout." This would have been the two-channeled Fontenelle/Clyman Creek, and it likely explains why Riley Root had called it "Salmon-trout Creek."

The next day, the wagons slowly advanced up the trail. Lempfrit reported that two Indian horsemen appeared. Then more appeared, perhaps a hundred:

[July 20th] . . . We saw we were in the middle of a large nation. I gave several of them tobacco and some biscuits. These Indians were on the war-path, and all were mounted on superb horses. I observed that the women also were going along with their men. One of these poor creatures I saw asked me for some bread for her small child. I asked here where the child was, then she showed it to me, pulling away the little cloth that concealed it. What I saw was a tiny face, absolutely yellow, that one could have taken for a little Egyptian mummy. The child woke up and she at once started to rock the little board to which the child was attached, as if nailed. For the poor little creature could not move an inch. It was imprisoned in a casket shaped like a large boot, the front of which was laced up. The child kept crying all the time, so she took the little box off the saddle-bow and gave it something to drink. But what I saw then was not a breast, but some kind of narrow pendant sheep-skin bag. The poor little thing sucked at it all the same. This unfortunate woman was also carrying all the warlike paraphernalia of her husband, his lance, his quiver, and his shield.

Lempfrit called them Bannocks, but that is not likely, as this was Snake country.

Lempfrit's description of the next day is vague and uninformative. He did not report the distances traveled or the names of places, as was typical of him, but it is probable that his company camped at Hams Fork on the night of the twenty-first. His description of an extremely difficult passage over a steep mountain on July 22 is consistent with the dreadful terrain just west of Hams Fork, especially the descent off Dempsey Ridge into the Rock Creek Valley.

22nd July. We left at 7.30 in the morning. Shortly afterwards we climbed up a hill steeper than any we have met with so far. The trail zigzagged for three-quarters of an hour and then we came to the crest of the mountain. The path was no more than eight feet wide, and on each side were frightful precipices. . . . Towards 1 o'clock we came to a place that Providence had taken pleasure in making beautiful. Oh! What a lovely bed of flowers. Nature was in her finest attire. . . . All too soon we had to leave this earthly Paradise for the steepest trail we have had up till now. For two whole miles, two almost black mountains seemed to want to embrace each other; they left, however, a space wide enough for a waggon to pass between them. It seemed as if we were about to descend into Hell! We had to lock the brakes on all four wheels. The waggons were almost perpendicular. When one was twenty-five feet below, it seemed as if the waggons above would all come hurtling down to crush one. This was not all! Having reached a spot about one hundred metres above the little valley, which, however, was nothing but a pile of broken rocks, the trail was all of a sudden blocked by an enormous boulder, pieces of which had been hacked away so that waggons could get past. . . . [T]he descent was very dangerous. For a waggon had to slide only a couple of inches for it to disappear over the side of the precipice. . . . Two or three fissures in the rock were wide open, ready to swallow you up, and the waggon wheels, whilst going from one edge of the gap to the other, must have smashed to pieces if no precautions had been taken to absorb the shock of the sudden drop. This could be achieved, either by throwing down brushwood under the wheels, or else by unhitching the oxen so that the waggons could be guided over this spot by the men. The captain decided on the latter course of action, and the events that followed demonstrated that he had indeed acted with great prudence.

After having unyoked the oxen the four wheels of the waggons were locked, but much more securely; so that the front wheels could slide, a strong cable was fastened securely to the back of the waggon. Ten men held it fast so that it could move forward only very slowly. Two other ropes were then attached to the right side of the waggon, and six men held it back, and prevented it from sliding too near the edge of the precipice. Two men then held the shaft of the waggon and guided it in its perilous descent. When the first waggon had been safely brought down we all felt like shouting "Hurrah," but then there were so many more to be guided down that our enthusiasm abated. We carried out the same procedure with each waggon and the result was excellent. However, this took a lot of time. It took us nearly three hours to get over this rough spot. . . .

As there was no wood to be found we could not remain here overnight. We therefore had to carry on for a few more miles. It was very late when we reached our camp site. We groped about in the dark, looking for a few sticks of dry wood so that we could heat up a little soup, and then we went to bed.

The following day, while camping beside Rock Creek, Lempfrit described a sad scene:

23rd July Sunday. We celebrated the Holy Mass in our waggon as we have not made use of our tent for some time. During the course of the morning a poor woman I had been treating died. The captain decided that we would stay in this place so that the deceased could be buried. This poor, good woman came from an honorable family and the relatives begged me to come to the funeral, assuring me that this would greatly please them. I told them that I would attend most willingly. My companion [Father Lionnet], with his strange ideas, thought I was doing wrong. Him, they had not asked to come.

Who was this woman the priest seemed to highly regard? He did not identify her, but Edward Smith, traveling in the Chiles company, would pass by her grave marker four days later and would record her name in his journal. Lempfrit reported that they paid their "last respects to this good woman" before leaving camp the next morning. After continuing over a steep ridge on the twenty-fourth, the Stone company descended to the Bear River. "We camped near a most abundant spring where several Canadians came to see us," Lempfrit wrote. "During the night there was a terrible storm."

The next morning, July 25, Lempfrit was summoned to a small settlement of Canadian traders and Indians, probably Snakes, "to baptize two children, a boy and a girl. We were also able to obtain a few items of refreshment we were badly in need of. For in this country, the least little thing is precious."

With the disappearance of the buffalo in recent decades, the Indians of this region, faced with vastly diminished sources of meat, turned to other resources, some of which seemed repugnant to the white man. Lempfrit reported the local Indians preparing a meal of camas root and crickets, which he called grasshoppers:

> These grasshoppers are black and very much bigger than the other kinds, and they measure about a finger's length. . . . This type of grasshopper serves as food for the Indians who heap them up into big holes that they have dug in the ground. After having made the hole really hot they remove all the glowing embers of wood, and then fill it up with grasshoppers, covering the hole with grass to make an oven. Afterwards they pulverize this "roast meat" with stones, making a kind of black flour which they blend with camas, a kind of onion that grows in profusion on ther prairies. The camas is the best vegetable product the Indians eat. It is a kind of onion that tastes like lichen. When the camas is dry one would think that it was real lichen. The Indians dry large quantities of it.

Shortly after leaving camp in the morning of July 26, the priest reported encountering

> several mounted men coming towards us. These were Americans who were on their way to Spanish territory to trade horses. Amongst these gentlemen was a Mr. Smith [Peg Leg] who greeted me in the warmest way even though he was not of the same faith. I can truly say that he is a friend to all the missionaries. He invited me to stop by his establishment and was kind enough to give me a note for his clerks, requesting them to give us some sugar and coffee free of charge, things we had run out of for some time.

On July 27, the company continued through the valley. Lempfrit finally got around to acknowledging the valley's beauty:

> [It is] a splendid little valley. The hills on either side gave us lovely views at each turn, for the hillsides were well wooded and we often saw pretty little mountain streams bursting through the greenery. Soon we came on a spring that was so vigourous that it almost immediately formed a lovely little river flowing to the west. There we found tarragon growing so prolifically that no other plants could be seen. Subsequently we found tarragon in many other places. This plant grows naturally here as does the polypetalous flax also.

Lempfrit complained about the cold night on July 27, noting that ice formed in their water pails. On the twenty-eighth, he recorded that they had reached Soda Springs:

> On top of a small hill, six to eight meters in height, a kind of cone-shaped rather large cap suddenly rises up. . . . The cap is surmounted by a smaller cone that is hollow and from which tepid, sulphureous, vile-smelling soapy water escapes in

large bubbles. . . . I wanted to taste it, but so unpalatable did I find it that I found it impossible to swallow even the smallest drop. Several of our travelling companions were foolish enough to drink it but they paid dearly for this, nearly all of them went down with gastritis. That spring really is a marvel. . . . After exploring the soda spring I wanted to push on ahead. All at once I was hailed by a young American who came to beg me to come and treat a poor sick woman who was critically ill. The man was a member of the caravan that was ahead of us. They had halted four miles further on to wait for me for they knew there was a doctor in our company. On my way there I went through a lovely little forest where all the trees were red cedars.

Apparently Lempfrit's reputation as a healer had spread beyond his own company. Summoned forward, Lempfrit noted passing a grove of cedars, which sounded similar to where the Wambaugh company had camped weeks earlier. Indeed, there is an isolated grove of cedars growing today just south of Highway 30 and about a mile west of the community of Soda Springs. Beyond the grove, Lempfrit encountered another small camp of Indians:

Then I came on six tents which belong to Indians. They were busy smoking the skins of deer and antelope. The sweetness of the perfume of the smoking cedar wood was entrancing. . . . Standing apart from the six tents of the Indians was one more beautiful and spacious than the others. This belonged to a Canadian who, having heard that I was there, came out to ask me if I would bless his union with a young Metis. The girl was barely twelve years old. That evening I went to instruct them and prepare them so that I wuld be able to bless their union the following day.

The term *metis* suggests that the girl was a "half-breed"—half-white, half-Indian. Lempfrit then described arriving at the wagon company ahead:

The poor sick woman I had come to see was so weak that I could hold out little hope that she might recover. For nine days she had been tormented by her illness. In the circumstances I informed her people that there was not much hope for her. The poor lady died. The country around here is extremely beautiful and I passed the time wandering around and exploring it. There are many traces of dried up mineral springs like the one I saw the other day. This proves the existence of subterranean volcanoes. We are staying here for a couple of days and from now on our caravan is combined with the first waggon-train.

At last! Ever since Captain Stone had left St. Joseph, he had sought protection for his tiny company by trying to catch up to the company ahead. Now, after 1,300 miles, he appears to have finally succeeded. Lempfrit mentioned that their combined cavalcade was now "under the command of Captain Lence, a good Irishman" and consisted of thirty-two wagons, suggesting that the company ahead had twenty-one, since Stone had eleven.

They could not have joined William Porter's Purvine party, which was at that time on the Snake River, about 130 miles ahead. And the Walker-Bristow, Kelly, and Hannah companies were still ahead of Purvine. So which companies were left? It was most likely the Delaney company, the one that is believed to have been the last to leave Fort Laramie ahead of Stone. Lempfrit wrote that they were now "under the command of Captain Lence, a good Irishman." This could have been Captain Delaney, also a good Irish name. Upon hearing the name "Delaney," the priest could have thought he heard "D. Lenee," and the translator of Lempfrit's notebook may have misread his handwriting and transcribed it as Lence. In contrast, a Stone company member, James D. Miller, produced a reminiscence in which he recalled that at "Steamboat Springs on Bear River," they encountered "a part of Whitaker's train."[11]

The cattle in the two companies benefited greatly from grazing for two days on the abundant grass in the Bear River Valley; then both companies resumed their travels on July 31 and headed northwest into the Portneuff Valley. "At 1 o'clock in the afternoon," Lempfrit wrote,

> we were traveling through a country that had been devoured by the flames of immense volcanoes that erupted, only God knows, in which epoch. . . . All this country seems to be as old as the world.

That day, they also met the son of Richard Grant, the Hudson's Bay Company's chief trader at Fort Hall. The son had come to escort the priest the remaining twenty-five miles to the fort, as his young wife was a "good Catholic" and was anxious to make her confession. The company camped east of Fort Hall on the evening of August 1, and by nine o'clock on the morning of the second they drew in sight of the fort. "From a distance it looked most attractive," Lempfrit wrote, "but its charm evaporated as we drew close to it."

July 16, 1848
Peter Lassen, Lassen party, Pacific Springs, Wyoming

On July 16, four days after Father Lempfrit and his Stone company had departed Pacific Springs, Peter Lassen and his tiny party stumbled onto this green, grassy flat just west of South Pass. Lassen and his friends from Chariton and Carroll Counties, Missouri, had been traveling with the Chiles-Hensley company. Since Edward Smith had not mentioned any company leaving Fort Laramie during the few days before Chiles left on June 27, it appears that Lassen's group was still traveling with Chiles. On July 2, eastbound Isaac Pettijohn reported passing forty-seven wagons just east of the North Platte Crossing (at today's Casper), a number corresponding to the size of the combined Chiles-Lassen-Hensley party. Perhaps at some point after July 2,

Lassen made his move and boldly detached himself and his followers. On the day Lassen reached Pacific Springs, Chiles' party was two days behind him.

Wanting to inform his "old friends" in Brunswick, Missouri, "of our present situation," Lassen hastily penned a letter that later appeared in the September 9, 1848, issue of the *Brunswicker* newspaper. He handed it over to "four men coming from California and bound for the States." Although these four men may have left California sometime in May, Lassen's letter never mentioned a word about gold, strong evidence that these four men left the territory before learning of the startling discovery.

According to Lassen's letter, his party had

> been very fortunate on our venture journey, met with no accidents, crossed all the rivers in perfect safety, and nooned on the Sweet Water about 4 miles East of this place, crossed the famous South Pass, and camped this afternoon on what is called the Pacific Spring, the first water a traveler meets, after crossing the dividing ridge, and running towards the Pacific. . . . A company of from 15 to 20 wagons are all that are necessary together; they can travel with perfect safety, and have the advantage of finding grass and water plenty, when large companies cannot be accommodated.

This may explain why Lassen decided to detach his small group of followers. "[T]here are but nine wagons in our company," he reported, "we get along easily and feel in perfect safety."

Lassen was keenly aware of the foolhardiness of transporting unnecessaries over the trail. Reminded daily by the articles seen heaved beside the trail, Lassen admonished those back in Missouri to bring nothing

> but what will be absolutely necessary on the road. . . . they will have to throw them out . . . as thousands of others have done. The side of the roads about the mountains are literally covered with such articles.

July 16–31, 1848
Richard May and Edward Smith, Chiles company,
east of Rocky Ridge, Sweetwater River Valley, Wyoming

Continuing to bring up the rear, the Chiles company left camp on the morning of July 16. They were still in the Sweetwater River Valley, about six miles east of Rocky Ridge, and needed to go about thirty-nine miles before reaching South Pass. They were about forty-three miles and two days behind the Lassen party, the nearest train ahead.

When they arose on the morning of the sixteenth, Smith reported that they discovered that "about ½ of the oxen were gone." Oxen were a curious lot. Some were downright devilish, seeming to know that as dawn arrived, it was time to disappear before "catching up time." Others, on the other hand, were a dream to work with, even heading on their own initiative toward the encircled wagons to be yoked. After the company found their troublesome oxen, it proceeded on to Rocky Ridge. Earlier diarists had denounced this section of trail as terribly rough and rocky, but neither Smith nor May seemed to complain much about it. Smith called the road "very hilly," and the buoyant May had mostly good things to say about the day's travel:

> 16th July. Moved forward 16 miles, fine grass and the best of water. . . . The grass is very good except a few places on the north fork of the Platte. We traveled very fast today it being cool and cloudy and some rain fell in the afternoon. . . . Encamped in a beautiful little hollow here. I drank the best water I have ever drank, clear of all mineral influences which is uncommon on the Platte and its tributaries.

Smith reported that their camp on the evening of the sixteenth was "on a branch of the Sweet water," perhaps Strawberry Creek.

On the morning of July 17, Smith wrote that some of their cattle had wandered off again, delaying their start. They nooned on Willow Creek, another branch of the Sweetwater, and after traveling a total of fourteen miles, pitched camp for the last time on the Sweetwater.

May mentioned some disharmony in the ranks. Was it because the company was running so far behind? Not according to him:

> Yesterday [July 16th], there was some discontent in the train in consequence of uproarious gentlemen taking the lead before [their] turn. Today all are in their places and quietude prevails. Orders disobeyed are always attended with bad effects. Encamped on Sweet Water for the last time. The great south pass we shall see tomorrow and I will give you what I can see of it.

The eighteenth would indeed be a landmark day, as May described:

> 18th July. Beautiful morning, clear, calm, and cool. Geared up and made Pacific Spring. In making the travel we passed the South Pass. This is one of the most noted points on the route. This pass divided the water of the Mississippi and those winding their way to the Pacific. For the last three or 4 miles the road leading to this pass does not ascend more than 5 feet to the hundred. On the right as you approach the pass the low hills come within a few hundred yards of the road. The same may be said of the left until you pass the culmination point when they raise quite abruptly and to a considerable height. After passing through we ran down a small hollow some two miles to the Pacific Spring. Wagons making it without locking or any difficulty in holding back. Just suppose thousands of wagons and teams crossing the great ridge dividing the waters of the Atlantic and Pacific without an effort . . . you will come to the conclusion that this pass was washed out by nature's hand for great and noble purposes in days and years yet to roll by.

May's vision was prophetic; thousands of wagons would indeed come rumbling over this pass in the decades to come.

Smith's entry for July 18, however, seems more focused on Pacific Springs, when apparently an oxen got mired in one of its marshy bogs:

> tues 18 this morning we left the Sweetwater and crossed the divide between the atlantic and Paciffic oceans and encamped at the Green Springs [Pacific Springs]   this is a large meadow of many acres covering an immense quagmire   it may well be called the Spring of Springs   Here Charles Young lost an ox.

The company left Pacific Springs on the morning of July 19, and started across the great sage-covered plain to the west. Covering twenty miles, they made it to Little Sandy Creek by the end of the day. May reported: "Those sick a few days ago are well but there still is some sickness in camp though not of a serious character. The nights are cool and the days quite warm."

The next morning, the twentieth, they passed the Parting of the Ways. Since they too were going to take Greenwood's Cutoff, May explained that they continued straight until they came to Big Sandy Creek:

> 20th July. Left camp and drove five miles and encamped on Big Sandy Creek where we shall remain tomorrow, having before us a dry trail of 40 miles which must be made during the evening and morning. We passed the balance of the day in camp. Some are washing, some trading and still a portion hunting. I find men in these mountains that have been here 25 years. A Mr. Kincaid is now in camp trading with our men, he having some 200 head of cattle which we need in some measure. This gentleman removed to these mountains from Boone County, Missouri in the year 1824. He is quite an old man, yet active, although he had been injured in the leg as he is lame. Persons of a weakly constitution should visit these mountains and remain one winter in them and if he has the fire of life in him sufficient to bear a year he will get to be a stout man. If he should not have that fire of life in him, he will fall a victim to his complaint. We see a great many graves on the way, but when we consider the number of sickly habits we should not be surprised. . . . This evening closes the day with all the beauties of a clear and calm evening in the mountains.

The Chiles company spent the rest of the twentieth and much of the next day camped beside the Big Sandy, letting their oxen eat grass, drink, and rest. They would need to be at their best for the dreaded march across the forty-five-mile desert.

When the afternoon of July 21 finally arrived, the wagoneers clucked at their oxen and cracked their whips, and set forth across the dry plain with confidence and determination. Others had made it before them, and they would too. May described the great trek:

[21 July.] This morning quite as calm as the evening preceding. The mountaineers still trading. Capt. Childs informs me he will leave this evening at 4 o'clock and then for a long drive in the night. I will give you the particulars when the drive is over. At 3 o'clock [p.m.] we struck out for Green River. When we had traveled 1 ½ miles from Big Sandy we passed a small butte 45 feet high and having no name. We gave it the name of Smith's Butte [Haystack Butte] in honor of a Mr. Smith who is a fellow wagoner in the train. We drove on until night called a halt and boiled the tea kettle, supped and then drove all night.

[A]t sunrise the 22nd halted for breakfast, after which we moved forward and reached Green River at 3 o'clock [p.m.]. Our cattle very much fatigued and ourselves not very well rested after a sleepless night, having traveled 40 miles in 24 hours. In making down the bluff or mountain I should call it, we found it very steep, in fact we traveled over a very rough road the latter part of the stretch.

One wonders whether "Mr. Smith" was Edward Smith, the other diarist in the company.

The Chiles company had made it across the desert successfully, and like the companies before them, they were exhausted and stayed in camp the next day to recruit. May reported:

23rd July. We lay by today and I have an opportunity of seeing up and down the river and to the buttes on either side which is quite a short view. The buttes on the river are very high and of a graying white sometimes inclined to blue and red. The bottoms are low with lakes and some incrustations of salt. The water in the river good and clear; the current quick at the rate of 6 miles per hour. On some islands in the river there is a beautiful grove of cottonwoods. Timber being very rare in this country, I feel like calling any place beautiful that grows a few trees if they could be indifferent.... We lost two oxen out of the train by death last night. They generally look well. There are some mountaineers here trading with our people, dressed skins, shirts and pantaloons are all the go here. We shall see many traders in this portion of the country. The Snake tribe holds here. I have been two months in the train traveling to the far west and I must say a more heavy business I never performed. Traveling with a family cross this American desert is the very hardest business I have ever followed. I was near forgetting to state that Green River is about 120 yards wide and runs to the left, winding its way to the Gulf of California. The weather had been fine, quite cool at night and warm during the day. It has been smoky for several days preventing a view at a distance.

Smith augmented May's comments by pointing out that where they crossed the river was "a spring of Remarkable cold water within a few yards of warm water."

Somewhat rested, the Chiles company returned to the trail on the morning of July 24. May described the difficult ascent out of the Green River bottom, but he neglected to mention Names Cliff, probably because in 1848 it had virtually no names etched in it:

> 24th July. At 9 o'clock this morning we struck tent and ran down the river about 1 ½ miles and there came to a butte or bluff so very steep as to require two teams to one wagon (this is what we call doubling). We then made it very easy. Then in about two miles further we reached a hollow or deep gorge in the mountain, ran up it some distance and then passed on top of the mountain again and ran back parallel with the road in the hollow, then returning to the right when we made another hollow that led us to the fork of Green River [Fontenelle/Clyman Creek] ran up it so as to make 8 miles and encamped on the best grass I have seen for many days. On this stream we passed a spring, the best or as good as any I ever drank of the water being so cold that it made my teeth ache.

While sitting in camp that evening, May took the time to record his pride at how the wagon journey across the west had transformed him:

> I must here record a fact worthy of note. I weighed 245 lbs when I left the states. I was weighed a few days ago and I only drew 194 lbs so here is a falling off of 49 lbs and more health and strength and action enjoyed than when at the greatest weight. I attribute this falling off to the manner of life rather than anything else. The want of vegetable and proper seasoning contributes very much to reduce me, being of a bilious temperament when fed upon luxuries, has caused a decline of flesh in this abstimous [abstemious] mode of living.

Smith's journal entry for July 24 noted that as they made their way to Fontenelle Creek, they "passed several graves of the emigrants of last year also the Remains of another waggon which had belonged to a man by the name of Rhodes."

How did Smith know the abandoned wagon once belonged to a Rhodes? Was the name inscribed on the wagon somewhere? Did Smith spell the name right? This could be significant because a family named Rhoads passed through here on their way to California in 1846. They had made it across the Sierras just weeks ahead of the ill-fated Donner party. Two Rhoads brothers, John and Daniel, served in one of the relief parties sent to help the stranded party.

May mentioned that his company lingered in camp on the morning of July 25 at Fontenelle Creek, and he used the opportunity to go hunting. When he took up his journal that evening, he returned to his theme of the benefits of life on the trail:

> I took a short hunt this morning. Saw plenty of game, say about 40 antelope, but was unsuccessful in killing any. At a late hour I strode into camp having walked some 7 or 8 miles with my rifle and game taking accoutrements, a journey I could not have performed in 2 days one year ago. This is the effect a mountain life has upon those who are bloated up with disease. I would advise all those who are

slightly troubled with dispepsia [dyspepsia] to take a mountain trip. It is almost sure to cure them.

After departing their Fontenelle Creek camp the next morning, both May and Smith reported that they had gone ten miles when they came to what became known as "Pine Grove campground." Here was a spring that supported a grove of trees and dense undergrowth. It was incongruously green and lush in a land of drab sagebrush. The sun may have still been high, but they pitched camp here nonetheless. The grove wasn't much, but compared to the never-ending expanses of sage, it must have seemed heavenly, a place to wander among the trees, inhaling the fragrant scent of pine and spruce.

Smith described the spot briefly: "tues 25 to day we traveled about 10 miles and encamped at the foot of a mountain at a spruce Pine grove with an undergrowth of quaken aspen   good water   grass scarce." May's description of the grove was more detailed:

> 25th July. We traveled 10 miles today over hill and dale and encamped at or near a spring below which there is quite a grove of fir wood. . . . Inter-mixed with this growth is the small sour cottonwood [Bitter Cottonwoods?] whose leaves are said to be poisonous. It does not grow large at any rate. I have not seen any more than 6 inches in diameter and say 25 feet high. . . . It is quite cool and I look for frost tonight. We are immediately under some tall hills. The wind continued. No frost but there was ice in camp ½ inch thick.

Even though it was summer, with murderously hot days, the emigrants experienced freezing nights at these high elevations, often finding ice in their water buckets in the morning. With such wide swings in temperature and the inflammatory dust, it was a miracle that more people and oxen did not succumb to pneumonia.

The early morning air was crisp when the Chiles company resumed their travels the next morning of the twenty-sixth. Marching into even more mountainous country, they labored eighteen miles and ended the day on Hams Fork. July 26 proved an exceptional day, as Edward Smith reported the appearance of a widely known mountain celebrity:

> wed 26 to day the Road was very hilly, at noon we met Mr. Joseph Walker the celebrated mountaineer well known to the History of the mountain trade He conducted us by a new Route to Hams Fork of Green River to avoid a very bad Mountain.

Richard May reported the same encounter, also recognizing Walker as a noteworthy figure:

> 26th July. Left camp earlier than common and traveled 18 miles. At our noon halt Joseph Walker, the noted mountaineer met us. He is a very fine looking man. The

very picture of health and discourses well on most topics. He continued with the
train through the evening. He conducted us through a pass in these mountains by
which means we avoided a very steep hill both up and down. Mr. Walker appears
to be about 45 years of age and steps with the elasticity of a youth but this much
may be said of any one that has lived in these mountains a few years. To see the
buoyancy of a mountaineer compared to one of Missouri's sons would astonish
the most of men.... We are encamped on a fork of the Green River [Hams Fork].

Walker probably met the company just east of Rocky Gap, a pass through a high,
chalky ridge. Was this gap the new route to which Walker introduced the Chiles
party. Trail historians have cited May's report of Walker appearing here and are
generally of the opinion that Walker took leave of the Chiles company after traveling with them only that day.[12] But they may have been too hasty in concluding that
he disappeared as suddenly as he appeared. When Walker rode up and greeted the
Chiles company, he would have met his nephew, Mike McClellan, who was traveling with Chiles. Joseph Walker was a long-time acquaintance of Chiles. The Walker,
McClellan, and Chiles families were early settlers of Independence, Missouri, and
Chiles had hired Walker in 1843 to help lead him and his wagon party to California.

So why was Walker here on July 26, 1848? Was it an accidental encounter? Not
likely. This place in the mountains near Rocky Gap is remote, and it would have been
a near miraculous stroke of coincidence for Walker to stumble across Chiles that day.
Walker had set out on a trip in September 1847, purportedly heading to California
with his brother, Sam, Sam's son Jeemes, and Joseph's nephew Frank McClellan.[13]
Stopped by deep snows at the Rockies in November, they were forced to spend the
winter not far from here. After Sam died, Jeemes and Frank backtracked to Fort
Laramie in the spring, where they hooked on with the Wambaugh company and
continued their journey on to California. Inexplicably, Joseph had remained in the
mountains and had not been heard from until now.

If Walker wanted to continue on to California, he may have been tracking Chiles
down, for Chiles was leading the last wagon party headed to California this year. If
Walker arrived at the Green River crossing looking for Chiles, he might have learned
that they had already left and were not far up the trail. If he then left the Green River
at dawn on the twenty-sixth, he could have caught these slow-moving wagons by
noon with a little hard riding. Later evidence will indicate that Walker was still with
the Chiles company a month later on the Humboldt River, making it appear that he
remained with the Chiles company for the remainder of the trip to California.

May continued to write with unbridled enthusiasm, even when others may have
been wilting under the rigors of the trip. After remarking about Walker, he then
launched into more praise of mountain life:

There is quite a number of men from the states throughout this mountain wilderness. They tell us there is more real pleasure in one year in the mountains

than a whole lifetime in a dense settled country. There is no political pursuits to tire an weary the limbs and last but not least no law or lawyers to pettifog among them to mar their peace and sow discord among them. Their duties are confined to the horse and gun and when they become tired of one place they remove to another.

Hams Fork was a superb spot for the Chiles company to camp on the evening of the twenty-sixth. With ample water, wood, and grass, the company did not travel on July 27, but remained in camp to give their livestock another opportunity to recruit. In May's eyes, the day was far from dull:

> 27th July. We lay by today [at Hams Fork]. The women are washing and cooking which things are indispensable. The men are trading, the mountain boys having followed us from Green River, buying and selling horses, skins, moccasins, whip thongs, etc. The little girls are merily playing around the camp while the little boys are as much delighted with their fishing and bringing willows to make fire. This morning we had quite a frost though the day is warm for all practicle purposes. The grass is very good. Ham's Fork is about 20 yards wide with plenty of water to run any kind of machinery. The quaking asp shows in all the hills though it is of a dwarfish growth. Our encampment shows quite a stir this evening some five or 8 mountain men here drinking alcohol at $1 a pint and they are very mellow.

Smith composed a much shorter entry for the day: "thur 27 to day we remained in camp   ther was a great many trappers and traders and Indians in camp   Chiles sold much liquor   many got Beastly Drunk." Smith may have been a temperate man, as he had expressed disapproval of a drunken frolic at Fort Laramie, and it seems that he disapproved of Chiles selling liquor here. The mountain traders described by our diarists were neither beggars nor panhandlers, but they did seem to attach themselves to the company like a group of leeches. And why wouldn't they? After all, this was the last company of wagons coming through, and it was their last chance to make some advantageous trades before winter set in.

Refreshed, the Chiles company ascended the ridge west of Hams Fork on the morning of July 28. They topped out on the Hams Fork Plateau, and then came to Dempsey Ridge. They may have approached that ridge with a sense of foreboding, as they knew that a climb up on one side often meant a steep descent on the other. When they teetered at the top of the ridge and eyed the descent, it would have looked distressingly dangerous. Yet, May was not overawed by the difficulty and continued to chirp about this gorgeous high country. He seemed to have a gift for seeing elegance and beauty where others only saw difficulty:

> 28th July. Traveled 11 miles over a very rough road. We climbed a hill some 2000 feet above our encampment and continued on high ground [Hams Fork Plateau]

until noon when we rested our teams a few minutes on the most lovely spot I have seen since I left the States. Flora had covered the mountain tops with her many colored dress and among the variety was seen the blue phlox in full bloom. To the left still higher on the mountain was a beautiful grove of fir encircled with quaking asp. On the right was a grove of asp alone. Near 1 ½ miles from our nooning we passed through a mixed grove of asp and fir and continued upward to the top of the mountain [Dempsey Ridge], then down the mountain and it was certainly a long trip not less than 1 ½ miles and in one place we had to let our wagons down by ropes not depending on the team. We are now encamped in a very romantic spot enclosed by mountains on every side, a small branch leading out [Rock Creek]. The very best of water and tolerable grass. . . . Frost had been seen for four mornings in succession.

Not nearly as positive was Smith, who described the climb over Dempsey Ridge, undoubtedly the same difficult passage Father Lempfrit had so elaborately recounted in his July 22 entry. Smith wrote:

frid 28 to day we traveled about 15 miles we had the worst Hill ascend and descend in all creation   we were compelled after working the Road to let the waggons down with Ropes   we encamped on the head waters of Muddy Creek [Rock Creek]. Between two mountains 1000 feet high here wer two graves of this spring emigration to Oregon one of Eunice Emerick aged 48 the other Mrs. Stone aged 67.

This was where Father Lempfrit had lamented the death and burial of one of his patients: "23rd July . . . During the course of the morning a poor woman I had been treating died." An ever-valuable source of enlightenment, Smith now brings to our attention that, in all probability, the deceased was Mrs. Stone, either the wife or mother of Captain David Stone, Lempfrit's company leader.

A couple of modern markers can be found today that identify some graves along the trail on the Hams Fork Plateau. One mentions that Margaret Campbell was buried there on July 29, 1848. Smith and May reported crossing the plateau on July 28, yet neither mentioned the event. No wagon parties were behind Chiles, although slower moving elements in the Chiles party could have traveled through here on the twenty-ninth. It could have also meant that Margaret was failing and was left behind with a few family members to attend to her until she died.

May and Smith both reported that on July 29 their company crossed the last mountain ridges that stood between them and the Bear River Valley. Upon reaching the Bear, May described it as "a beautiful stream about 80 yards wide, the current not more that 3 miles to the hour." Shortly, they crossed Smiths Fork near where it entered the Bear, then traveled another four miles and stopped to camp at a place of "[g]ood grass and plenty of river water." They had completed an arduous day of twenty miles and had barely begun to set up camp when Peg Leg Smith came riding in. Despite having lost one of his legs, May thought he was "a fine looking Mountaineer." Perhaps arriving from his trading post twenty miles north of here, Peg Leg appeared with "several horses," according to Edward Smith, suggesting that he had come to trade.

The next day, July 30, the company nooned at Thomas Fork, then crossed Thomas Fork and ascended the steep hills that lay in their path. Dropping into a quaint hollow, they stopped to camp beside Sheep Creek, ending a day of thirteen miles. Their campsite would have been in the little valley through which today's Highway 30 passes, and about four miles west of where the highway crosses Thomas Fork.

On the morning of July 31, the company climbed another ridge, one that May described as the "the steepest and longest hill we have met with." Arriving at its summit, one can imagine the emigrants heaving a discouraged sigh when they saw how the trail then dropped away beneath them.

After a short day covering only eight miles, they struck the Bear River once again and camped beside it about two miles south of Peg Leg's trading post. May expressed delight at having "caught a salmon trout today. . . . The health of the camp is now very good. Although all in camp are never well at the same time. We have been very fortunate to lose none by casualty or death." May's comment catches our attention because it suggests that this Margaret Campbell was not a member of the Chiles company. Perhaps the year of death on her modern marker is an error.

Smith's entry for July 31 was negative, complaining that "Millions of Musketoes and green headed horse flies" hounded their camp. That evening a party was held at Peg Leg's, even though May did not mention it. Smith again expressed disapproval of the event, complaining that "the camp had to attend it, to take comfort among their equals, the half breeds, and Drunken Mountaineers."

The month of July came to a drunken end at Peg Leg's. The foremost companies—Gates, Miller, and Jackson—were camped that night three hundred miles, or twenty days of travel, ahead. Was anyone in the Chiles company concerned about their lagging pace? So far, we have seen no evidence of it.

Table 12: Order of companies as of July 31, 1848,
with arrival and departure dates at Fort Hall

Company (Diarist)	Arrived at Fort Hall	Departed Fort Hall
Allsopp	?	?
Adams, first segment	?	?
Wambaugh/Cornwall/ Greenwood (Root)	July 15	July 16
Gates	July 15	July 16
Miller (Anderson)	July 15	July 16
Jackson (Belknap)	July 16 (est.)	July 17 (est.)
Watt	?	?
Walker-Bristow	?	?
Kelly	?	?
Hannah	?	?
Purvine (Porter)	July 25	July 26
Adams, second segment	?	?

The following companies have not yet arrived at Fort Hall:

Delaney

Stone (Lempfrit)

Lassen

Chiles (May and Smith)

Hensley (bypassed Fort Hall; went to Salt Lake City, through Fort Bridger)

CHAPTER 15

Snaking Through
Vulcan's Workshop
AUGUST 1–16

AUGUST 1–16, 1848

Riley Root, Gates company, on the Bruneau River, Oregon Territory

On the morning of August 1, the Gates company left its camp near the mouth of the Bruneau River. With 1,300 miles completed, they still had 500 miles to go over difficult and inhospitable country. As the wagon train advanced, the trail stayed as close to the Snake as it could, and its general direction began to change from westerly to northwesterly. Traveling with the foremost company, Riley Root continued to describe the geology of the land:

> August 1st— 19½ miles, over a very level plain, most of the way, and near to the river, to camp, on Grease Wood [Castle] creek, about a mile above its mouth. No good camp can be had along this day's route, till our present one, which is not very good. Between camp and Snake river, the little stream in which our camp is located passes through two crags of basaltic rock, much crumbled down by time. Rock, east of creek, shows marks of excessive volcanic violence. Volcanic cinders, rocks half melted, chimneys where smoke had issued, and in fact, every mark of Vulcan's blacksmith shop is here displayd.

Castle Creek crosses today's Highway 78 about eleven miles northwest of present Grand View, Idaho. The Gates camp would have been on the creek on August 1, about three miles north of where the highway crosses it.

Root and his Gates company put in a very long, hard day on August 2, traveling twenty-four miles. The trail led through rough, barren country, surrounded by dark buttes and bluffs, tall and sheer. Today's Highway 78 runs an average of four miles west of the trail. During the day, they encountered a hill Root described as "so steep and sandy, that we were obligd to double our teams to surmount it." This

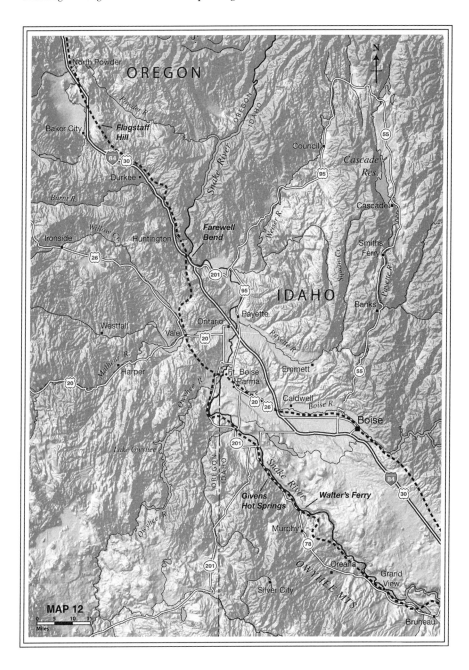

MAP 12

hill was probably located about eight miles southeast of today's Murphy, Idaho. Root described the day's trail as "a very uneven and dusty road," and wrote that they camped "at the mouth of a small dry branch," which he complained afforded "very little grass." Their campsite may have been on Rabbit Creek, east of today's Highway 78, and about four miles southeast of the intersection of Highways 45 and 78.

Because their cattle were famished, Root and his company moved only four miles on August 3. They stopped where the Snake River spread out and drove their cattle onto a small, grass-covered island in the river channel, just south of where the Walters Ferry Bridge is today.

The Gates company traveled nine miles on August 4, most of it continuing beside the Snake. According to Root, they came to a spot during the day where several hot springs (Givens Hot Springs) rose in a flat along the west bank of the Snake. "The water of these Hot springs, at their source, is scalding hot," he recorded. After examining the springs, they continued another mile and a half and camped beside the river east of today's Highway 78.

On August 5, the Gates company made fourteen and a half miles over what Root complained was "a desert plain and dusty road, to camp, on Snake river." For months, the diarists had been complaining of dust, but here the dust was different. The dust here probably consisted mostly of rhyolite tuff, a volcanic ash that had spewed from hundreds of volcanoes over millions of years. Viewed under a microscope, one would see minute particles of jagged-edged rock and glass, not the sort of material anyone would want to inhale. But it filled their mouths, noses, ears, eyes, and lungs. It settled in their hair and beards and covered their faces. It covered their clothes and found a place in every nook and cranny in their wagons. It blanketed their oxen and horses. And they had no idea why it was so irritating, why it reddened their eyes and sent them into fits of coughing. Only those who rode at the front of the column were spared the worst of it, and those bringing up the rear tended to drop back even farther to let the dust clear away. By the end of the trip, many emigrants agreed that the dust, in whatever form, was the worst affliction they had endured on the trail.

Root reported on August 5 that the mountains on either side of the road, principally made of "basaltic rock," began to diminish as they approached "an extensive plain" where the Owyhee and Boisie Rivers converged on the Snake. The fifth was another dispiriting day as the company moved painfully slowly. The wagons were stringing out in little knots along the trail. Unable to keep up, the weaker teams lagged farther to the rear and arrived in camp later in the day. Root expressed concern about their flagging livestock. He ended his August 5 entry with "our cattle are in so starving a condition." His terse statement hardly expresses the seriousness of the situation. Other wagoneers were seeing the same thing: their oxen slowly wasting away, and it alarmed them.

At the beginning of the trip, the oxen had been fat and in good condition. But pulling two-thousand-pound wagons six to eight hours each day, they burned prodigious amounts of energy. Grass is not exactly a high-density source of energy, and the oxen needed to consume large quantities to support the calories they burned. Even with abundant grass, they would not graze all night; they needed to lie down and get off their sore feet. In consequence, they were expending more calories than they were taking in, and drew upon their reserves of fat first. When their fat was gone, their bodies converted protein—muscle—into energy, turning these once-healthy creatures into bone racks with dusty hides stretched over them. They were suffering from *myositis*—where muscles were breaking down completely from malnutrition and exhaustion—and it would be a matter of time before more of them would completely give out. Hitching them to their wagons each morning was becoming more of an uncertain prospect. The emigrants were wondering whether their worn-down creatures would last long enough to take their wagons all the way through.

After pushing nineteen miles on August 6, the Gates company made it to the Owyhee River, then crossed it and set up camp five miles southwest of Fort Boise. But Root grumbled: "Not very good grass at this place." Their camp was on the north bank of the Owyhee, about one mile southwest of where Highway 201 crosses the river. In the meantime, the Miller company had fallen off the pace, setting up camp on the sixth about twenty-four miles behind Gates. Root and his company barely moved on the seventh, moving their camp but a mile and a half farther down the Owyhee River. They were probably looking for new pasturage and trying to give their oxen an easy day.

Root's entry for August 8 explained that Fort Boise was about four miles northeast of their camp,

> located in a pleasant place, on the bank of Snake river, just below the union of the Owyhe and Boyce [Boise River] with the Snake. The river at this place is near to a quarter of a mile wide, and the only means of ferrying it is a canoe brought from the river.

Root did not report whether he ferried the river and visited the mud-walled fort, but his recording that the river was a quarter of a mile wide at the crossing and a canoe was the only ferry across it suggests that he at least visited the crossing. With the Snake so wide here, its current flowed at a sluggish pace, but it was still deep enough to be dangerous. When James Clyman crossed the Snake just northwest of Fort Boise in 1844, he noted that the river's ford was "good & Smoothe but rather deep for wagons." Some of Root's company might have visited the fort, but it is doubtful because taking wagons across and back again would have involved great effort and unnecessary danger.[1]

The Hudson's Bay Company had established Fort Boise as a trading post on the east bank of the Snake River in 1835, near the mouth of the Boise River. Similar in construction to Fort Hall, the original log stockade was later encased in whitewashed adobe bricks.[2] John C. Fremont described the fort when he brought his expedition through here in 1843:

> This [Fort Boise] is a simple dwelling-house on the right bank of Snake River, about a mile below the mouth of *Rivière Boissée* and on our arrival we were

received with an agreeable hospitality by Mr. [Francois] Payette, an officer of the Hudson's Bay Company in charge of the fort, all of whose garrison consisted [of] a Canadian *engagé*. . . . Mr. Payette had made but slight attempts at cultivation, his efforts being limited to raising a few vegetables . . . the post being principally supported by salmon. . . . [O]ur principal inroad was into the dairy, which was abundantly supplied, stock appearing to thrive extremely well; and we had an unusual luxury in a present of fresh butter.[3]

Root and his Gates company did not remain near the fort for long. On August 8 they left their camp on the Owyhee River. Root explained that they traveled sixteen miles that day, first up a dry, treeless hollow, then over "a good road" until they reached the dividing ridge. After that, they slowly descended to the Malheur River. The trail followed the same route followed today by Lytle Boulevard south of Vale, Oregon. The Malheur was a dirty little stream fifty feet wide and about a foot or two deep, running through a mile-wide bottom covered in course grasses and short willows. Root thought it was a good camp, noting "Grass plenty. No firewood but willows."

They left their camp on the Malheur and proceeded northerly along the trail on August 9. After about eight miles, they ascended a plateau, a dividing ridge. For the next fifteen miles, they traveled a good road over a hilly, sage-covered land, traversing harsh and depressingly arid country, then gradually began descending to Birch Creek. After crossing the creek, the party ascended the point of a hill, then descended again to the Snake River. There are many good wagon wheel ruts visible along this section of trail, which can be followed by turning east off of Highway 26 six miles north of Vale and traveling east one mile on Fifth Avenue East, then turning left (north) onto Hill Road. This road follows the trail for the next fifteen miles.

Root wrote an elaborate description of the twenty-five miles over which they traveled on the ninth:

9th— 25 miles to camp, on Birch creek. 13 miles to a sulphur spring, where we noond. This distance is up an arm of the Malheur, though dry at the time. Its course is through a level flat, from one to two miles wide, having high ranges of land on each side. From Sulphur spring, the road ascends rapidly to its highest point, a mile or two farther on, where the country can be viewd for a considerable distance all around. Reflecting upon such a wonderful scenery as is here on every side displayd, the mind can hardly appreciate the amount of dynamics adequate to displace and disrupt the surface of the earth so immensely. It appears like a great harrow, fit only for Hercules to use in leveling off the surface of some planet.

The next day, August 10, Root's company traveled near the Snake River for about three miles, then came to where the trail left it and the Snake continued northerly, winding hundreds of miles between steep, barren mountains as it headed toward its mouth with the Columbia River. Since the trail left the Snake here for the last time, the emigrants called it Farewell Bend. It is about three miles southeast of present-day Huntington, Oregon, and just east of I-84. From Farewell Bend, the Gates company followed the trail northwesterly, along a route corresponding to today's Huntington Highway. Once again, Root described their travels at length, expressing, for the first time, a hint of his emotions:

> 10th— 8 miles to Burnt river (probably from the naked and redden appearance of the mountains through which it passes). Three miles of the morning route brought us once more to Snake river, where we saw it for the last time [Farewell Bend]. Remaining 5 miles over a somewhat hilly road to camp, on Burnt river, but a small stream at this place. On viewing the river and its small flats bordering it, from camp, it appears wholly environd by rugged, jagged mountains, in close contiguity. Oh, when shall I view, once more, a verdant landscape! One thousand miles of naked rocks! Landscape without soil! River bottoms with scarcely enough grass to support emigrant teams.

Leaving camp on the Burnt River about a mile northwest of Huntington, the Gates company continued up the Burnt River Canyon on August 11, fighting for every jarring mile as they tugged their battered wagons over rocks and boulders covering the floor of the narrow canyon.

> 11th— 13 miles to camp on Burnt river. . . . For 5 or 6 miles of our morning route up the river, the road was very rough and stony, and it crosses the creek seven times within that distance. Remainder of the day's travel was more easily performd, though more hilly, yet smooth. . . . Along this stream emigrants have formerly been much intimidated through fear of sudden attacks from Indians. It is very densly shrouded much of the way with balm of Gilead, alder, hawthorn, and various kinds of shrubbery, so that the Indians could secret themselves, till the near approach of an emigrant train, and then with a sudden rush from the thicket, frighten the teams and kill many of the emigrants.

Root revealed that a ripple of fear was beginning to sweep through the company about encountering the murderous savages they had heard so much about.

The Gates company camped on the Burnt River on the evening of August 11, about a mile southeast of the Weatherby Rest Area on I-84. Root wrote very little about the twelfth, only that they made "4 miles over a worse road than yesterday afternoon, and crossd the creek five times." According to Root, August 13 was another daunting day:

> 13th— 16 miles to camp on a tributary of Burnt river. Soon after having started in the morning, we crossed the principal stream of Burnt river, for the last time. A little farther on, we came to a right hand tributary [Sisely Creek] coming from the north, which we followd up about 2 miles, crossing it 8 times. We then left it, winding our way over the mountains westwardly, crossing two or three other

small tributaries, till we arrivd again upon the Burnt river bottoms, not more than 8 miles in a straight line from last night's camp. At this place we nooned, after having passd over a hilly, though smooth road. Here emigrants might tarry for the night. One mile further on we crossd North fork [of Burnt River], and upset one wagon at the crossing. Our course was now nearly west, up a mountain, till we arrivd at a branch of the North fork [Alder Creek]. Passing on a mile or more, we encamped for the night.

Root described how the trail led them out of the Burnt River canyon and up Sisely Creek Canyon. To follow this portion of the trail today, take Sisely Creek Road east of I-84 and continue on it for two miles, then take a left onto Plano Road and follow it until it returns to I-84 at the Burnt River. The trail then follows modern I-84 northwest and past modern Durkee. Root's company camped near the junction of Lawrence and Alder Creeks the evening of the thirteenth, just south of I-84 and about two miles northwest of Durkee.

Leaving camp on the morning of August 14, Root and his party followed the trail as it slowly climbed out of the valley and passed over the hills. Cresting Flagstaff Hill, the emigrants gazed into the beautiful Powder River Valley lying below. After a difficult day of twenty miles, over a "hilly but smooth" road, Root reported following the trail as it rolled down the hill. The valley was green and represented a welcome change. That and the knowledge that they were only three hundred miles from their destination must have had a restorative effect on their minds and bodies.

They stopped in the valley to camp "at Lone Pine stump," where there was "plenty of grass." The "Lone Pine" would have been about one mile east of today's I-84's exit 298. This pine, or what was left of it, had been a well-known landmark to emigrants in earlier years. Standing alone on Baldock Slough, in the midst of this sage-covered valley, it could be seen from far off by approaching wagon trains.[4] Sometime in 1843, however, the beloved landmark was cut down for firewood.[5] Indeed, Clyman had mentioned what was left of it when his party passed through on September 26, 1844: "Nooned at what is called the lone Tree in the middle of a vally & a fine one it had been of the pine Spicies   now cut down & all the branches used for fuel."[6] While Root described it as a "stump" in 1848, a year later even the stump was gone.

By this time, Root had evolved into a more prolific chronicler, and reported their next day's travel in great detail:

15th— 14½ miles to camp, on west branch in west valley of Powder river. Nine miles to Powder river, down by a circuitous route, along the river, 2 miles to first crossing. Thence across the plain to second fork or crossing, 2½ miles. One mile farther to west fork or third crossing. In all, 14½ miles to camp. East valley of Powder river is a spacious plain, very level, and would be as handsome a valley as my foot ever trode upon, were it covered with the rich grasses of the eastern states. At each of the three crossings here mentioned, which unite a short distance below us and form the principal Powder river, is seen in small patches, a luxuriant growth of the well known grass, red top. As we advance, the climate changes. In camp, this morning, was seen ice in our cooking vessels, and by 10 we were uncomfortably warm. On our left, the Powder River mountains, close by which the river finds its way, are clothd with timber, nearly down their declivities to their base. On our right they yet are naked. Indians around us ar burning, as fast as verdure becomes dry enough, which at this time, renders the air so smoky, that we can see but a short distance.

Ramps dug by the emigrants into the banks at the second fork of the Powder River are still visible today. They can be seen a few hundred yards east of where I-84 crosses the North Fork of the River, and just south of the community of North Powder.

The Gates company camped on the "third fork" of the Powder River the evening of the fifteenth, about a mile north of today's town of North Powder. The trail over which they marched on August 15 generally followed the course of I-84.

The next day brought Root's company into country that had a different feel to it—a subtle change in the climate and vegetation. Climbing out of the Powder River Valley, they crossed sage-covered hills until they came to a hill just east of Ladd Canyon. From that vantage point, the emigrants looked into a great round bowl of a valley, almost twenty miles in diameter, full of marshes and golden grass. They called this place the Grand Round, an Americanized version of its French name of *Grande Ronde*. In October 1844, James Clyman described it as occupied by "several hundred" Cayuse Indians and "nearly covered with horses."[7] But in 1848, during the Cayuse War, Root mentioned neither Cayuse nor horses here. They had likely fled to more remote regions to avoid clashing with the Oregon militiamen.

To descend into the valley, Root's party had to creep down an exceedingly long, steep hill, as difficult as any they had faced. They had to break out their ropes, snub them to tree trunks and slowly lower their wagons:

16th— 15 miles to camp, at the head of Grand Round valley [Grande Ronde Valley]. After traveling a short distance, this morning, from the last crossing of Powder river, we ascended a short rise. We then preceeded over a smooth road of moderate descent, till we came to a small branch of Powder river, at the foot of a hill, where several small rivulets are seen to issue from the hills round about [Baylor Springs]. This is about 8 miles from the last crossing. Here is a tolerable encampment. The rest of the way to Grand Round hollow, a distance of 7 miles further, is over a hilly and some part of the way, very stony road. . . . Grand Round vally is extensive. It is surrounded with high hills, covered with bunch grass, except occasional patches of yellow pine. Along our road, this valley is rich, coverd with various kinds of grasses, though entirely dead at this time, no rains having fallen here recently.

Evidence of wagon ruts coming down this hill can be seen today south of the Ladd Canyon Rest Area on I-84. The company camped where the rest area is today at the foot of the hill and along Ladd Creek.

August 1–16, 1848
William Anderson, Miller company, Bruneau River, Idaho

Like the Gates company, the Miller party left the Bruneau River on the morning of August 1. They traveled fifteen miles that day, striking the Snake about six miles after leaving camp, then continued traveling beside it for another nine. "[W]e traveled along on the second bench from the river until night came on," Anderson explained, "then we drove down to the river and camped grass was verry scarce where we first came to the river." Their camp would have been about three miles northwest of today's Grand View and one mile north of Highway 78.

Anderson recorded marching "18 [12] miles" on August 2, noting that "our road to day was a verry dusty sage plain." He explained further that

> 10 miles brought us to a small branch [Castle Creek]   here was a pretty good camp but we passed on 2 miles further to the river where we had a poor camp   we drove the cattle 1 mile down the river to a small patch of grass.

Their camp, surrounded by magnificent rocky buttes, was where the Gates company had camped the day before.

At or near this spot in 1860, a small wagon company with only forty-four men, women, and children would be beset by a band of hostile Snakes. Resisting a two-day siege, twenty-eight of the emigrants died—one of the bloodier Indian attacks on a wagon party along the Snake River.[8] There is a split of opinion, however, over whether this tragic massacre occurred at Castle Creek or at nearby Sinker Creek.[9]

The Miller company left camp beside the Snake on August 3. After seven miles on a rocky, uneven road, they came to a "spring branch [Sinker Creek]," where they stopped. "[W]e drive our stock ¾ of a mile down this branch to the river for grass," Anderson explained. "[I]n going down this branch to the river we pass through a narrow canyon the sides of which were 500 feet high 200 feet perpendicular." Anderson described the surrounding hills, precipitous and barren, as having "a volcanic appearance burnt rock lay scattered around for miles up and down the river and hills in every shape and form." Their campsite was about nine miles southeast of present-day Murphy, Idaho. Access to this site is difficult.

Anderson described August 4 as a long, hard day for his company and their struggling oxen:

> August the 4th we started and traveled 16 miles and came to the river   one mile down the river we camped making 17 miles to day   soon after starting this morning we had a long steep hill to ascend   we put all the cattle to half the

waggons and went up the hill then came back and took the other half of the
waggons up our road   to day was verry dusty and our camp was poor.

Their camp was just south of the intersection of Highways 45 and 78, on the northeast
side of Highway 78. The "steep hill" was just north of Sinker Creek, likely the same one
described by Root on August 2. By pushing hard on the fourth, the Miller company
closed the distance between itself and the Gates company to five miles.

Like the oxen in the Gates company, those in Miller's party were not doing well
either. It was a familiar theme; they were always looking for more browse, so the company traveled only five miles on August 5 and stopped when they "found some grass
by going ¾ of a mile south of the road." They camped just east of today's Highway 78
and about three miles southeast of Givens Hot Springs.

The Miller company traveled ten miles along the Snake River on August 6. There
were "some small patches of grass along the river," Anderson explained. They only
made ten miles, perhaps because they periodically stopped to graze their stock at these
grassy patches. Anderson mentioned passing Givens Hot Springs and described the
water as "warm enough for good dish watter." They again camped on the Snake, this
time one mile east of today's Highway 78 and about three miles southeast of today's
Marsing, Idaho. Because of their slow pace, they fell twenty-four miles behind Gates.

The Miller company lumbered across more arid, flat country on August 7, arriving, after fourteen miles of travel, at "a small branch [Succor Creek] a bout ¼ of a mile
from the river   here was a large bottom of good grass." They stopped and pitched
camp at a spot north of today's Highway 19 and about one mile north of Homedale,
Idaho.

They left their camp beside the Snake on August 8 and traveled about fourteen
miles. They followed the trail as it made a sweep to the west of the river,

passing where the bluff came near the river   we had several deep gulleys to
cross this day   we reached a Creek Caled owihe [Owyhee River]   we crossed
over and camped about 4 miles from fort Boise situated near the mouth of this
creek on snake river.

Their camp was about where the Gates party had camped the night before.

It is remarkable how similarly Root and Anderson estimated their mileage
between the Bruneau and Owyhee Rivers: Root reported traveling 90½ miles, while
Anderson logged 94.

"August the 9th 13 waggons went to the fort to do some trading," Anderson
wrote. "[T]he rest traveled on 15 miles to Malheur Creek and camped   here is a wide
bottom of pretty good grass and several warm springs that break out of the mountain
here." Their camp on the Malheur was just south of Vale, where today Highway 28
intersects with Highway 20.

Anderson reported that those visiting the fort received a bone-chilling warning
of what lay ahead:

> August the 10th we remained in Camp all day [at Malheur River]   in the eavening the waggons we left at the fort came up   they were advised at the fort to beware of the Cyuse Indians whose country they now had to travel through.

This warning had to have been whispered through the camp that night, causing a vague unease. Anderson offered no detail about these warnings, but it is easy to imagine the fort's *engagés* taking a perverse delight in fomenting fear. Anderson did not explain whether the thirteen wagons crossed the Snake to visit the fort, but because of the difficulty and danger of crossing this treacherous river, it seems unlikely that they had done so.

The Miller company left the Malheur River camp on the morning of August 11 and set out on a long day's march. Leaving the trail at today's Highway 26 about three miles north of Vale, they followed the trail as it headed almost due north, across remote uplands. "August the 11th we traveled 24 miles," Anderson explained, "and Camped on a small branch Caled birch creek on the banks of which there were a considerably birch timber this is not a verry good Camp." This camp should have been where the trail crossed Birch Creek, about one mile southwest of where I-84 today crosses the creek. As night fell on the eleventh, the Anderson party was two days behind Gates.

From Birch Creek, the Miller company traveled nine miles on August 12. Anderson reported that they struck the Snake River soon after leaving camp, then traveled beside it to Farewell Bend. From there, they traveled five more miles to camp in a grassy bottom along the Burnt River, just north of present-day Huntington, Oregon.

On August 13, Anderson described a harrowing day traveling up the Burnt River Canyon:

> August the 13th we traveled 11 miles up the river which ran through a canyon nearly all the way   the mountain on each side is from 400 to 800 feet high and verry steep   we Crossed the Creek several times and in some places traveled along it for 80 or 100 yards then out and up over a spur of the mountain which was verry steep and rocky   thus it continued all day making the roughest road we had yet come to   soon after camping this eavening 2 men over took us from a Company behind [Jackson company] stating that the Indians had stole 4 horses from them last night   they followed them some distance up a ravene into the mountains but they being on foot haveing no horses they could not overtake them and so they were obliged to abandon the pursuit.

Although Anderson had just described this narrow, boulder-strewn river canyon as "the roughest road we had yet come to," he reported that conditions became even worse on the fourteenth, forcing them to climb out of the canyon for a distance:

> August the 14th we traveled 10 miles   our road was worse to day than it was yesterday   we kept up burnt river some times in the bed of the river then winding

up along the side of the mountain then down crossing deep and rocky rav-
enes   after 5 miles travel the road turned to the wright up a spring branch in a
narrow bushy Canyon [Sisely Creek Canyon]   while in this Canyon a young man
riding behind the waggons on horseback carrying a loaded gun with the muzzle
foremost when the bush caught the hammer causing it to go off   the ball struck
a front standard of one of the waggons and pased through the iron plate and
standard to the plate on the opposite side and glanced off without doing any
further damage   we traveled 2 miles up this branch then turned to the left and
pased over a bluff one ½ mile to a dry branch then up this ½ mile and turned to
the left over a nother ridge 1 mile to a spring branch down this 1 mile to burnt
river agan   here is a good Camp.

Anderson's entry describes how the company was forced to climb out of the
Burnt River Canyon and make a detour through Sisley Canyon before return to the
river about two miles southeast of Durkee. On the fifteenth, the Miller company
emerged from the inhospitable canyon, and continued to follow a route that corresponds to that of today's I-84, then angled across country east of I-84; today this
section of the trail is not easy to access. Anderson wrote:

August the 15th we traveled a bout 15 miles   the road ran up this branch about
11 miles from where we started this morning crossing one spring branch then
turned up over the bluffs one mile and came to a nother branch up this branch
7 or 8 miles   crossing a small branch that ran into the one we were traveling up
we crossed the main branch twice then turned to the wright up a long hill 2 or
3 miles to a nother small branch   here we camped   our road was pretty good
to day with the exception of some of the branches we had to cross   we had a
pretty smart frost this morning.

About two miles southeast of I-84's exit 317, the trail headed east, away from the
river canyon, and they probably stopped to camp at the end of today's Hixon Road,
which travels east from exit 317.

The Miller company made twenty miles on August 16. Leaving camp, they traveled over hilly country, crossing a multitude of ravines and dry creeks. Finally reaching the "mountain" summit known as Flagstaff Hill, they looked down at the Powder
River Valley. "[W]e camped on a small branch in powder river valley," Anderson
wrote. "[T]his valley is 8 or 10 miles wide the most of it is covered with good grass
after 4 miles in the valley we struck a slue [Baldock Slough] with watter standing
along in muddy pools." According to Anderson, they camped two miles beyond the
slough, likely passing the Lone Pine stump.

It would be interesting to learn how the sheep in the Miller company had been
doing. The last time he mentioned them they were crossing the North Platte River.
But since then, he had been strangely silent about their flock. But no news is good

news; the sheep may not have been good river crossers, but they were probably good travelers and did well on the scant grass.

At this stage in the journey, with about three hundred miles still to go, most of the emigrants' original provisions—flour, beans, rice, corn meal, bacon—had been eaten, but concerns about the condition of their oxen caused some to consider further lightening their loads. If necessary, they could abandon some of their valued wagons and consolidate the contents of two wagons into one. No doubt they were tired, but they had traveled 1,500 miles and the journey had hardened them. As they drew near the end of their journey, their spirits must have been bolstered and their steps more determined.

August 1–16, 1848
William Porter, Purvine company, Dry Creek, near Salmon River

On August 1, the Purvine company had ended the day on Dry Creek, just east of today's Murtaugh, Idaho. They were only one hundred miles behind the front-running Gates company, meaning they had made respectable progress since they had stalled at the North Platte crossing. Porter's journal entries were still short, as he tried to cram his words into his tiny four-by-six-inch notebook:

> August 1st. Traveled 12 miles to dry branch [Dry Creek].
> 2nd. Traveled 12 miles to Rocky Creek [Rock Creek].
> 3rd. Traveled 12 miles to the crossing of Rocky Creek.
> 4th. Traveled 22 miles and camped on Snake River at the mouth of a small branch [Deep Creek].
> 5th. Traveled 6 miles and camped two miles above Salmon Falls Creek.
> 6th. Traveled 5 miles and camped two miles above [below] Salmon [Falls] Creek.
> 7th. Traveled 18 miles and made a dry camp at which two of my oxen gave out and Stephen lost one, to wit, Old Tom.
> 8th. Traveled 12 miles and crossed Snake River.

Porter's entry for August 7 made it clear that they did not make it from the Upper Salmon Falls to Three Island Crossing in one day, but traveled only eighteen miles the first day and spent the night of the seventh in a "dry camp." They then traveled another twelve miles on the eighth before reaching the river at Three Island Crossing. That mean stretch of desert west of Upper Salmon Falls continued to claim victims; Porter lost two oxen and his brother one. Porter failed to say how many oxen he had left.

Porter's company must have found the Snake River fordable at Three Island Crossing on August 8 because he reported crossing it. Porter was the first diarist to cross there and take the northern branch of the trail to Fort Boise. It is regrettable that he recorded no details about the crossing.

As the Purvine company marched on, Porter continued with his concise entries:

9th. Traveled 6 miles up to head of branch [Cold Spring Creek?].

10th. Traveled 8 miles and camped on a small creek [Bennet Creek?].

11th. Traveled 10 miles to a branch from the hot springs and three miles below them.

12th. Traveled 15 miles to rock creek or barrel camp creek.

13th. Traveled 13 miles to a small creek.

14th. Traveled 14 miles to a dry creek and dug some wells for water.

15th. Traveled 15 miles to Boise River.

16th. Traveled 18 miles.

The identities of the creeks Porter noted are uncertain, partly because his estimate of distances was usually inflated. For example, it is 115 miles from Three Island Crossing to Fort Boise by the northern road, but Porter's distances between those two points totaled 132 miles. He did mention a few identifiable landmarks, one being the hot springs that they passed on August 11. To visit these springs today, one must travel seven miles northeast of Mountain Home, Idaho, on Highway 20, then go three miles south on Hot Springs Road. His other known location was where the trail first struck the Boise River, which is three miles southeast of where Highway 21 today crosses the Boise River east of Boise.

August 2–16, 1848
Father Lempfrit, Stone company, Fort Hall, Idaho

Father Lempfrit's Stone company, traveling with what is believed to be the Delaney company, was still the last Oregon-bound wagon train on the trail. When they arrived in view of Fort Hall on the morning of August 2, they were about two hundred miles behind the Gates, Miller, Jackson, and Watt companies, and about one hundred miles behind Purvine. The very last wagon train on the trail, the Chiles company was now traveling through the Bear River Valley, about seventy miles behind Stone/Delaney.

The priest did not describe Fort Hall in particularly flattering terms:

> At 9 o'clock [August 2] I caught sight of Fort Hall. From a distance it looked most attractive, but its charm evaporated as we drew close to it. Fort Hall looks quite impressive when viewed from the other side of the river. As soon as one draws near, however its charm disappears. It is a fort . . . built of sun-baked bricks. They can be overcome, not by cannonballs but by baked apples!

Camping on the Snake River bottom south of the fort on the evening of the second, Lempfrit described the campsite as "most pleasant." He reported local visitors coming to camp early the next morning:

> A large number of Indians known as the Snake Indians came to pay us a visit. They appeared to be well-disposed, friendly, even courteous. They came and

shook hands with everyone. Let anyone tell me that Indians are malicious! Well, not the Snakes. Their open behaviour holds out plenty of promise.

At seven thirty in the morning on August 3, the Stone/Delaney companies bid goodbye to their Snake visitors and departed camp. Ten miles after crossing Bannock Creek, they arrived at American Falls, which Lempfrit concluded were "one of the most beautiful sights in the world. . . . I have seen nothing that comes near to it in all my travels up till now."

Lempfrit's entry for August 4 did not describe the day's travels. Instead, he cited an unspecified source who had told them that the murderous Cayuse Indians "were not very far away from us." Although the Cayuse were dangerous, Lempfrit was told that they had no bone to pick with the French, and he had nothing to fear provided he could explain to them that he was French, not American.

August 5 brought Lempfrit and his caravan to the Raft River:

> 5th August. We did not go far today. We went scarcely twelve miles so that we could set up our camp at the place where the trail divided, with one branch going to California to search for gold. What is absolutely certain is that several people who had been there came back rolling in wealth. Gold can be found everywhere within a sixty mile area; pure gold nuggets, not powdered gold.

Lempfrit's entry is initially stunning. The earlier diarists—Root, Anderson, and Porter—had recently passed through Fort Hall and passed the Raft River. Yet none had reported learning of the discovery of gold in California. May and Smith, traveling with the Chiles company, will not arrive here until August 12, seven days later, and neither of them recorded one syllable about gold. It must be kept in mind that Lempfrit made daily entries in a notebook while on the trail. The following year, drawing from his original notes while on Vancouver Island, he rewrote his journal, the only version that survives. It is almost certain that this entry reflects what he later learned after arriving in Oregon.

For some time, Peter Lassen's small California-bound party had been closing in on the Stone company. Indeed, Lassen was only three days behind Stone when Lassen wrote his letter from Pacific Springs on July 16. When Lassen's fast-moving party turned south at the Raft River toward California, he may have caught up to Stone or been traveling in close proximity. Yet, Lempfrit never mentioned Lassen's group.

The Stone/Delaney company departed the Raft River on the morning of August 6 and headed west across that barren, rocky road. It is likely that the Stone company stayed at Marsh Creek on the evening of the sixth, then traveled along the creek on the seventh. They probably stopped to camp at the end of the day near where the creek emptied into the Snake, north of today's Highway 81, and about six miles east of present Burley, Idaho. Lempfrit described their camp as being on the banks of a little river where there were large numbers of freshwater cray-fish. I went into the river to wash my feet, and two minutes later I noticed more than a score of them hanging to my legs. I harvested over a hundred of them in this manner within a period of half an hour.

After going only a short distance on the morning of August 8, Lempfrit described the company spending the rest of the day in some well-earned recreation:

8th August. Today, we did not travel very far as the Snake River is full of fish, and our Americans had been looking forward to going fishing. We halted after going only seven miles so that every one could fish.

This stop along the Snake could have been either east or west of today's Burley.

On the ninth, Lempfrit described how inaccessible the Snake had become, and he detailed the troubles that this caused them:

9th August. We left quite early in the morning. The further we went the more dif-ficulty we had in finding water. The river here was walled in between two great cliffs over thirty metres in height. The precipices were frightful to look at. All the rocks were black, and it seemed as if it was the River Styx that flowed at the bottom of the gorge. We came near to the edge, and our poor animals, dying of thirst, looked at the foaming water with very sad eyes. We ourselves were suffer-ing from thirst, but no one could bring themselves to attempt going down to the river. It would mean risking one's life. We journeyed on for twelve miles before we found a drop of water. We arrived at our camp site at 7:30 in the evening.

The Stone/Delaney company had pushed on and may have camped on Dry Creek the evening of August 9 near the present-day community of Murtaugh, Idaho. On the tenth, Lempfrit reported that "[n]othing unusual happened today." Even though he gave no clues, there is a good chance his company made it to Rock Creek by the end of the day. Lempfrit made up for his uninformative entry on August 10 by describing in great detail a hellish place he explored on the eleventh:

11th August. Scarcity of water caused several cases of friction. The caravan hardly made any headway. All the same, we departed, but only to come to the most abominable place that exists, I believe, in the whole world. Picture to yourself an immense plateau, baren except for the ever present absinth [sagebrush]. Noth-ing is before ones eyes except for a vast expanse of rock. There are no birds. It seems that if birds would have flown over the precipice they would suffocate in the sulphureous fumes escaping from a dried-up marsh. The way to the marsh is extremely steep and tortuous. We left our wagons on the plateau and then drove our poor animals down, as best we could, so that they could go and drink from this briny water. After we had something to eat I wanted to go down to this horrible place to take a closer look at it. I can assure you, dear readers, that in all my life I have never seen anything that struck such terror in my heart. I imagined I was at the bottom of Hell. A black river flowed at my feet. In several places there were quicksands that seemed ready to threaten the imprudent traveler who would dare to tread upon them. I was frozen with terror, and just as I was about to retreat, an idea came to me. I would push further on. There was a blind alley to my left where it seemed the world would come to an end, for I saw the river being swallowed up under masses of volcanic rock. The valley became narrower all the time, soon there was only space enough for the river. I pressed myself against the calcinated rocks, and as a result of my efforts and the precautions I took I succeeded in getting past the dangerous spots. Beyond, however, new horrors were lying in wait for me. There, four large volcanoes rose up from beneath the rocks. They looked like the openings to four huge furnaces. It appeared that the eruptions here had been extremely violent and that the intense heat had melted both the rocks and the earth. Nearly all the rocks had been reduced to the state of glass like substance, and the earth had been baked like a brick. It seemed that an eruption had probably taken place when everything was white-hot, and that after the lava had ceased to flow, and the craters had cooled off, these four gaping mouths were left to say to posterity, "Just look at what we have done!" This gloomy vally extended a great deal further and I had already gone about two miles in this sinister place. I was heavy of heart, for what numbed me with terror was the deathly silence that reigned everywhere. I did not see even a gnat or a midge, everything was dead in this dark valley.

Where is this place that Lempfrit described? No other diarist had described anything quite like it. No other feature on the established trail quite conforms to his description. Was this elaborate exposition an embellishment of something far less dramatic? As delightful a diarist as Lempfrit was, his failure to report distances and place names makes it difficult to determine where he was. The best guess is that he was describing the plateau northwest of Twin Falls, and his "valley" could have been the Cedar Creek Canyon.

From the sound of it, the Stone company camped beside that horrid place on the night of the eleventh. The next morning they collected up their cattle and moved on:

12th August. I mentioned that we had succeeded, with great difficulty, in getting our animals to go down to the bottom of the Valley Mysterious. On the right side of the valley there was some poor grass and the little water there was not too bad. Out cattle roamed at random, seeking out some tufts of grass with the result that several of them strayed. We had a lot of trouble collecting them up again, consequently it was very late before we were able to get on our way. We, had, however, twenty long miles to go over bad trails, for here, when we emerged from the valley we found only soft ground. The wheels of our waggons sank in up to their axles, also, as from today we lost some of our best oxen.

It is only conjecture, but Lempfrit's entry suggested that after returning to the trail on the twelfth, they descended the very sandy road into the Salmon Falls Creek bottom, with the sandy road becoming too difficult for the weakest of their oxen.

While camping beside Salmon Falls Creek on the evening of the thirteenth, Lempfrit reported:

13th August. Today is Sunday. After celebrating the Holy Mass we had our breakfast and then we left. Our cattle had not had any grass so we had to stop about midday to let them graze. As we arrived in this place we heard the sound of an extraordinary waterfall. Far in the distance I saw a large white streak. We thought that it was snow. I then took a look at this white streak with the aid of my spy-glass. Upon closer examination I saw it was a most beautiful waterfall. It looked as if this was a river or a most powerful spring that gushed from the summit of a rock and then hurled itself down from a height of more than a hundred feet. The column of water split up on some sharp pointed rocks, and then divided up into a thousand very slender sprays. This created a marvelous effect as the water, reflecting the rays of the sun, became a lovely rainbow of a myriad hues. And then I saw a second marvel about one hundred metres further away. This was a round shaped rock leaning back against the mountain. One could have taken it for a tower from the Middle Ages. At its two sides it had two turrets, and then there was a small hill sloping gently downwards. One could see a series of [rock] piles, all pentagonal in shape. These were heaped up one above the other to a height of more than ten metres, twenty metres in certain places. They looked just like a bee's honeycomb. The [rock] piles were all the same size, about two metres in width by a half metre in thickness. I counted eighty-two rows of them which had arranged themselves in the form of a semi-circle in such a way that the river had lapped at their base created a small cove. That same day, in the evening, we came to an even more picturesque sight. This, no longer was a waterfall but a castle, or rather a vast liquid keyboard. Can you believe this! This was a great mass of rocks about two hundred metres wide by twenty metres high [Thousand Springs]. This rock-mass was perforated at its highest point; across the entire stretch of rock clear, limpid water gushed out from the countless openings, forming a small shallow pool which tumbled rhythmically to the river. In my opinion it must have been a river that had carved itself a channel all along the rock since all the other springs that we have seen were of the same height.

Lempfrit must have been describing Banbury Springs and Thousand Springs, and it is evident that the spectacles delighted him. The company probably camped the night of the thirteenth beyond the mouth of Salmon Falls Creek, and a few miles above Upper Salmon Falls on the Snake River. He then described their encounter the next morning with the Indians who had been pulling salmon out of the rapids at Upper Salmon Falls:

14th August. Today several Indians came to visit us, bringing with them an enormous quantity of salmon. I bought one weighing nearly thirty pounds for six fishhooks. We traveled quite near to their cabins. These were made from reeds as are most of the cabins of the Indians who live along the rivers. I went to visit their little village as I wanted to do some trading with them I must admit that these poor Indians are not models of cleanliness—everything one sees in their miserable huts makes the gorge rise. Salmon is their staple food and one sees this spread out to dry in every part of their cabins. The salmon are first of all stretched out so that the eggs can be removed. These are then dried, either in the sun or in the open air. After they have been dried the eggs are interlaced and then packed into bags made from fresh salmon skin where they are stored. Sometimes they are firmed up in the shape of loaves so that they can be eaten during the course of the year. I tasted some of this confection but could not bring myself to swallow even the little that I had in my mouth so revolting was its stench. After the eggs have been removed the salmon is cut up into long slices so that it will dry better. Even the bones that still have some meat on them are preserved. The baskets they use for drawing water are very cleverly woven. They are made from a pliant root and the insides of the baskets are then smeared with salmon fat to make them watertight. The Indians catch their salmon in these parts of the river where the water flows more swiftly. They build a kind of dam over which the salmon must leap in order to make its way up river. The Indians keep watch for them, and at the precise moment that the salmon readies itself to spring forward they spear it with a dart that had been securely fixed to the end of a pole. The point of the dart at its extremity is shaped like an inverted "V," and the moment the point embeds itself in the body of the fish it breaks away from the top of the pole, still however remaining attached by a little line. It looks as if the fish is still free to move at will when it is viewed from a point a few feet lower down the river. This however is not the case. The salmon is assuredly captured, it is just a question of pulling in the line.

Father Lempfrit continued with his lengthy entry for August 14, reporting a short visit to the Indian village beside the rapids. After their visit, his company left the Snake, climbing the steep hill to the west and commencing its toilsome journey across the abominable desert ahead:

[Continuation of August 14] We had halted for about an hour in the small village after which we were again on our way. We had to climb up a very steep hill, and then for more than five minutes the trail led along the brink of a horrible precipice. We had no wood and there was no water. We went nearly thirty miles that day and by 8:30 in the evening I was worn out. At last, at 10 o'clock that evening, we reached our camp site which was situated above a steep gorge, at the bottom of which flowed the river. We remained on top of the hill, and the oxen were led down to the river by a very sandy trail. This took three quarters of an hour. The way down was so steep that the men took the precaution of yoking the animals together. There were ten pairs of oxen and the animals pulled each other up the hill on their way back. We named this camp site "Desolation Camp." We did not have a drop of water and had to send a man down to the river with a small pail to get some. He returned with it half-full as everyone was helping themselves to his water. We could not make a fire to cook our supper—we had just a biscuit to eat and then we went to bed.

Crossing this land of stark desolation, the day's march must have seemed interminable. Even though Lempfrit claimed they made thirty miles that day, it is very likely that they traveled only about twenty miles and camped on a dry plateau overlooking a southward bend of the Snake River. It was likely the same "dry camp" mentioned by William Porter on August 7. As the crow flies, this campsite would have been about four miles due south of today's exit 129 off of I-84, but it was on the south side of the Snake. Today there is no road or bridge across the river to reach it. Instead, one would have to travel about ten miles southeast of I-84's exit 121, over a confusing and obscure series of dirt roads.

The next morning, the impulsive Lempfrit traveled with twelve of the faster wagons, probably from the Delaney company, and left his own Stone company friends and their wagons behind. But his rash impatience led him into an uncomfortable situation:

15th August. This beautiful day of the Assumption had to go by without our being able to celebrate the Holy Mass. As our camping spot was completely destitute of grass and water we had to leave very early in the morning, we got up at 3 o'clock in the morning and were on our way shortly afterwards. We had ten miles to go before finding any pasture for our animals. The most adventurous took the lead. Our waggon was far to the back. I wanted to be in the first group which consisted of twelve waggons. We made a halt at 10 o'clock in the morning. We were all exhausted, and unfortunately there was not a drop of water to be found. We left our waggons behind and pushed on for about six miles before we found the river [Snake]. We had left without breakfast and at noon I was still waiting for our waggon-driver to arrive. Nobody came. I had been hoping that the lay Brother would send me something to eat. By 3 o'clock I was feeling quite weak. I found myself in the middle of strangers all of whom had found me very useful to them at one time or another. They saw me looking quite miserable but nobody fancied that I was, perhaps, lacking some necessity of life. Everyone had eaten both dinner and supper! Then a kind woman noticed me lying down on some dry brushwood and she inquired if anyone had given me anything to eat. She soon learned that I had eaten nothing since the previous evening for not one of them had offered me anything. Everyone had believed that I had been invited to eat with someone else which was why no one had given me a thought. This good woman was most apologetic and before long she brought me an excellent supper that I ate with great appetite. We had to carry on travelling, it already 7:30 in the evening and they were talking of going on another twelve miles. We left. At half past midnight we arrived at our camp site. I was without shelter. There was no waggon, I did not even have a simple blanket. I bided my time until everyone was asleep and then I took two saddles and made myself a kind of coffin with these, using my own horse's saddle as a pillow. I settled down to sleep rigged out in this way and slept perfectly.

Lempfrit did not identify the spot where they stopped late that night of the fifteenth, but it must have been at Three Island Crossing.

The next morning, August 16, Lempfrit suggested that he and his companions remained in camp all day at Three Island Crossing, waiting for the other wagons to catch up:

16th August. It was broad daylight when I awoke— 7 o'clock in the morning. I found myself surrounded by our people who were greatly amused to see me under all this paraphernalia. Five or six Indians were laughing because they saw that everyone else was laughing. This didn't worry me at all, at least I had recovered from my fatigue. This time they did not forget to offer me breakfast! They knew that my wagon had not arrived. I ate with the Captain [Delaney?]. We were in an area where there were large numbers of jackrabbits. The Captain had killed one the previous day and the entrails had been thrown out. Immediately a poor Indian commandeered them and went off to roast them just as they were over a small brazier. Then, as this *fricandeau* was completely covered with ashes he quite simply cleaned them off in the river and then ate it all! Only the gall was discarded. It looked just like a spinach sauce, or, if you prefer, small peas cooked in tripe.

Lempfrit's entry for the sixteenth ended here. But he had not yet reported the arrival of his Stone company or their wagons. Where were they?

August 1–15, 1848

Richard May and Edward Smith, Chiles company, Bear River Valley, Idaho

On August 1, the California-bound Chiles company was still lagging far behind, and was rolling through the Bear River Valley. It was sixty miles behind the Stone/Delaney company. Richard May reported that they left their camp near Peg Leg Smith's trading post on the morning of the first and traveled "over good road, crossing several small streams running into Bear River." After making twenty miles that day, Edward Smith reported that they "encamped late about one mile above Tullicks [Georgetown Creek].... Plenty of wood and water good grass."

They made eighteen miles on August 2, and Smith reported that Captain Chiles "staid Behind to hunt a little." May noted that by the end of the day they had arrived at the renowned Soda Springs area:

[August 2] I have taken some pains to see something of this place. There is a number of springs that are strongly impregnated with the carbon of iron, some as clear and limpid as the purest oil while others are quite the contrary being the color of beer. The waters have a wholesome influence on the system when drank of. These springs are situated on Bear River about 60 miles east of Fort Hall and near 1300 from Independence, Missouri. The Steamboat Spring which is the same class of water is about 300 yards from the present road to the left hand requires a special remark. It issues from a hole in a rock about 6 inches in diameter which rock had been formed by the incrustation of the evaporation of the water in the Bear River and not more that 12 feet distant. It is what might be called a warm spring flowing about 10 gallons per minute. It boils and obulates and even throws 2 ½ and 3 feet high by a current of gas, strongly impregnated as before noted. I laid off my hat and adjusted my clothing so as to bath my face thinking that if it had a wholesome influence on the system when drank it would have a like influence when bathed in. . . . The very ground on which these springs are situated are nicely decorated with the evergreens of the forest. Add to all this the magnificent grandeur of the surrounding mountains covered with pine, cedar, fir and quaking asp. Here everything does allure and must in time attract the capitalist and fashionable as well as the valetudinarians of the land.

On the third, the company stayed in camp all day, allowing their oxen to luxuriate on the grass. It is conspicuous how often Chiles had his company lay by. His earlier trips must have taught him the importance of giving oxen extra time to eat and recruit whenever ample grazing was available. It would pay dividends in the end, even if it resulted in arriving later at the Sierras.

As they relaxed in camp on the third, Smith reported the repairing of "Mr. Beard's waggon in the morning." Both Smith and May used part of the day to explore the area, including a visit to Hooper Spring about a mile and a half north of the trail. Smith wrote that it was "the most highly impregnated of any of the numerous springs   it is about 20 ft in Diameter and 15 feet deep."

On the morning of August 4, people crawled out of their tents and wagons to the sweet smell of sage and cedar filling the chilly morning air. Soon those sweet smells were mingled with the aromas of fires being kindled, coffee boiling, and bacon frying, and the early morning silence was replaced by the sounds of women packing up the family's belongings and men yoking oxen and readying the wagons for another day. The company would be leaving the Bear River Valley today. As some began taking a farewell look at the river valley, they may have wondered if they were making a mistake in leaving this serene, hospitable place. They soon committed themselves to the trail, as May reported:

> 4th August. Geared up and rolled out down Bear River some 6 miles where we left it, turned the spur of a mountain and came to another soda spring, not of equal celebrity of those we had left, but very good. Traveled 18 miles today. Capt. Childs wagon broke down. One of the wheels falling into picas, a printer would say. The tire broke in two places, 4 spokes and two felloes out of the rim. Hallo here come the wagon into camp. The captain has taken a cold meld and the tire and all is made good. The country over which we passed today carries marks of volcanic action. The rocks having the appearance of being burnt and by examination I found them to be very hard and porous. I should not be astonished if in a few years these rocks or similar ones should be used for mill stones instead of sending to France for them. They are hard, sharp and porous, three of the principal qualities of the French stone. . . . Our encampment for the first time is on the waters of Lewis River [Snake River], the principal stream of the Columbia. The little stream close by is called the Portneuff.

Smith's report for August 4 noted that a mile after leaving camp they passed "the grave of Wm Huntly he died on the 29th of July." From Father Lempfrit's journal, we know that the Stone/Delaney companies had camped here on July 29, just six days earlier. The priest had mentioned a sick woman dying here, but had not reported anyone else's death.

Huntly's was not the only grave Smith reported passing on the road that day:

> shortly after our noon halt, we passed the grave of Trimbles Boy   he died   his Drunken father Put the Body under some stones at the head of a spring where it was found a short time after and decently buried by a man named Chapman.

As the company entered the Portneuf Valley on the fourth, Smith described traveling "over a volcanic Region and [it] was very Rough Rocky." Like May, Smith also mentioned Chiles' wagon breaking down: "[I]n the afternoon the wheel of Mr. Chiles waggon Broke about four miles from our evening encampment."

The trail entering the Portneuf Valley pretty much followed today's Oregon Trail Road, and their camp on the evening of August 4 should have been just west of the intersection of 1100 East Road and 2800 North Road.

On August 5, according to May, they

> [t]raveled 18 miles over a good road. It appears to be a basin [Portneuf Valley] in the mountains. The volcanic appearance not so evident today. Encamped at the head of a willow thicket on the small branch [of the Portneuf River]. A very warm and calm evening, but very smoky having the likeness of Indian Summer. It will be cold before morning. Below zero no doubt.

Smith added that they encountered "a few lodges of Whites Indians and half Breeds   in the afternoon continued to travel up the Portneuf and encamped on the stream." They probably camped on the evening of the fifth on the river, about two miles northwest of the north end of Chesterfield Reservoir.

On August 6, May noted that they traveled sixteen miles over a very rough road. They left the Portneuf Valley by ascending a small ravine formed by Jeff Cabin Creek. Smith described the day's travel:

> Sun 6 continued up the stream by a new road   at 12 we crossed the Divide Between Portneuf and Ross creek by one of the most delightful Mountain passes known in any country   noon halt on Ross creek   in the afternoon we traveled late down Ross Creek over very Rough Road and encamped late on Ross Creek   frost.

This entire section of trail is currently on the Indian Reservation.

August 7 was a landmark day, one that members of the company must have been anticipating for some time—they would finally see the much-heralded Fort Hall. Smith explained that they starting early that morning, leaving their camp on Ross Creek and descending toward the Snake River:

> Mon 7 we started early   the Road was very dusty   in about four miles we struck the sandy sage plain and six miles through very bad sand   we came to the Bottoms on which fort Hall stands and found Plenty of good grass and water   encamped about one mile above the fort.

The company remained in camp on the eighth. May described the visit he and his wife made to the fort that day:

> [8 August] Remained in camp all day. I visited the fort. I found Capt. Grant quite communicative. Mrs. Stewart and [Mrs.] May visited in company with me. We had a social conversation with Mrs. Maxwell (whose husband was absent on business to Ft. Vancouver). We found this lady to be intelligent and quite accomplished. . . . Everything appears in order, and carried out according to rule. It is about 80 foot square, the rooms placed inside the outer walls, some of them two stories high. I saw nothing of a warlike character except a rifle or two which are very useful articles in a country like this. Snake River is near 140 yards wide with a smooth gentle current not exceeding 3 miles per hour. The traders follow the train as though their salvation depended on the trade with them. There is at this time not less than a dozen of them around camp and some of them quite rude in their manners. At this fort everything can be had lower than any other point on the road, Horses can be obtained for $25 and good ones at that, but poor horses are much cheaper in California, therefore the emigrants going through should not buy even here.

Oddly, this is the first time May mentioned his wife. As the company remained in camp on the eighth, Smith went on to mention that they did

> some repairing waggons some trading with Indians and Half Breeds Mexicans &c   at the fort found two Mormon families making Butter and Cheese of a good quality   Mr. Grant the gentleman in charge of the fort had a fine stock [of] Cattle Horses &c   here was growing corn Peas and fine Potatoes.

The company departed the fort on August 9, the last party of emigrants to pass the fort until July of the following year, when they would be inundated by a deluge of fevered men heading to the goldfields of California.

According to May, the Chiles company traveled twelve miles on August 9, over a section of trail that had already seen almost three hundred wagons lumber across it during the past month. May wrote:

> 9th August. Traveled 12 miles. . . . crossing several sloughs about 8 miles below the fort, we came to Portneuff again. Here it is quite a river being 800 yards wide, clear and beautiful mountain stream. We are in sight of the Snake River. The plain is several miles wide and fine trees along the banks show the line of the river.

Smith, on the other hand, wrote that on the ninth they traveled "about 15 miles and encamped on the left bank of the Pannuck [Bannock] Creek at the Place where Road leaves the Bottom and Rises to the Plain."

The next day, May reported their company marching along the ravine-crossed highlands beside the Snake:

> 10th August. Traveled 15 miles down Snake or Lewis River. We nooned today one mile above the American Falls. I rode down and took a good look at them. I had been told the fall of water was about 14 feet, but I venture the ascertion, to measure from the bason below to a level of the water above is not less than 24 feet. . . . The river at this place is about 250 yds wide. 90 yds will take in all the fall or nearly so. The water is at a low stage and there is sufficiant to run a quantity of machinery. The misfortune is there is not soil to support a population. No timber near for firewood. The sage brush grows luxuriantly and that tells the story for it only grows in a light sandy, dry soil. The lowlands are generally well set with grass, and the highlands with sage to the exclusion of everything else.

In comparison to May's extended description, Smith only wrote that the falls were "Romantic and Picturesqe   about 35 ft High." After complaining about the grass being "short and scarce," he mentioned a few Indians fishing at the falls.

Smith's account for the eleventh explained how difficult the road had become:

> frid 11 our Road lay along the River up and down the very steepest and Rocky hills ever beheld   dust one foot deep in some places and from 4 to 8 inches in others   we halted at noon on the River one mile below a very Rocky Branch [of]

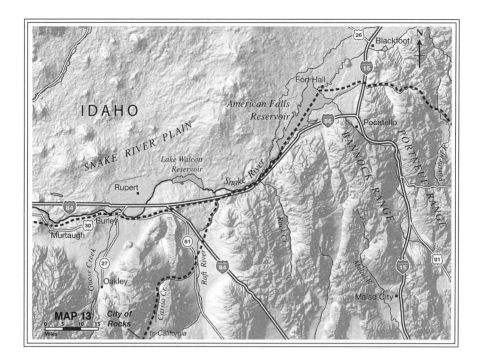

the River for several miles had on its Right Bank high Palisade Rocks Resembling the Right Bank of the Hudson near New York.

May reported traveling thirteen miles on the eleventh, describing the Snake as "600 yards" wide. After complaining about having "a bad road and clouds of dust to contend with," May noted crossing Fall Creek, describing it as "beaver dam after dam and the water pouring over them keeps a continual roaring as though a storm was at hand." They stopped to camp on the west side of the creek, about two miles east of today's exit 21 off of I-86.

Smith and May both complained about the dust. It must have been severe, made worse by the large number of wagons (about thirty-eight) in their company. Despite Chiles' determination to give their oxen extra rest and time to graze, the condition of most of their animals was still precarious. Struggling mile after mile through dense clouds of dust was the last thing these already-weak beasts needed. They might be able to blink enough to keep dust out of their eyes and their noses would have dripped with muddy discharge. Some suffered from what the emigrants called "dust pneumonia," a condition caused by their lungs' literally filling with dirt.

The company traveled only ten miles on August 12, reaching the Raft River. At only thirty feet wide, it was more like a creek than a river. Arriving early in the afternoon, Captain Chiles crossed his company to the creek's west bank, then circled the wagons. The place where the trail crossed the stream, then forked into its Oregon and

California branches, was about one mile west of today's Yale Road and a mile and a half mile south of today's I-86/84's exit 15.

When the wagons came to a stop and the dust finally cleared, the emigrants must have been heartened to know that they had finally left the Oregon Trail and begun the final leg to California. May joyfully recorded:

> 12th August. Traveled 10 miles over a tolerable road for the country. We passed the Oregon road today and encamped on Raft Creek at an early hour. All appears to be cheerful and hiliarity. We are on the way to California for certain.

Although they couldn't see much of the California road from their camp, as it quickly disappeared from view between two low bluffs, the view must have excited an optimism that had been sadly missing lately, and sparked some lively conversation. Captain Chiles might have shared some memories from his trip down that road in late August 1847 as a member of Commodore Robert Stockton's eastbound party. Leaving California in July, his party included Caleb Greenwood and his sons (considered the party's principal guides), M. N. Wambaugh, Major Samuel Hensley, and Peter Lassen. Now, a year later, the Greenwoods, Wambaugh, Lassen, and Chiles were all on this road again, each leading his own party of wagons back to California.

On Sunday morning, August 13, as the eastern sky slowly brightened and the stars blinked out one by one, Captain Chiles rose and roused the camp. He was anxious to get underway. After their usual cup of hot coffee and a few thin slices of broiled bacon, the men went off to catch up, yoke, and hitch the oxen to their wagons. Pulling out of their circle one by one, the wagons began to roll, this time heading south.

After five miles of travel, they came to where today's Yale Road crosses the creek. Here the trail crossed to the creek's east side, then angled up the long, ten-mile-wide Raft River Valley, heading on a southwesterly bearing. The wagons traveled on the east side of the creek for eleven miles across a smooth, grassy plain until the trail led them back to the stream, then crossed to the west side of the creek about one-half mile east of today's I-84 and four miles south of Idahome Lane. The trail continued on a southwesterly bearing for another eight miles before striking Cassia Creek, a branch of the Raft. They stopped to camp for the night on the north bank of the Cassia, just south of today's Highway 77 and four miles west of Highway 81. They had completed an exhausting day of twenty-five miles—perhaps too exhausting, as May suggested:

> Sunday 13th. Traveled 25 miles over quite smooth road on Cajeux [Cassia] or Raft Creek. One ox died and two gave out, but got them in camp. The plain on this creek is large for the size of the stream. In crossing it today the tongue of a wagon was broke entirely out. Then with 3 log chains we made a tongue and [illegible] and done 10 miles. The grass is good with tolerable branch water. I will here remark that branch water in these mountains is as good or better than the water used in Missouri.

After so many days of scarce grass, Smith was pleased that it was plentiful here: "[H]ere was the best grass I have seen since I left the South fork of the Platte," he exulted. "[T]he [road] had the appearance of a heavy shower a day or two before." He also mentioned that they did not arrive at their Cassia Creek campsite until nine in the evening, and reported that the ox that had died earlier in the day belonged to Mr. Moore, while the wagon with the broken tongue belonged to Mr. Beard. It must have been a troublesome wagon, as Smith had noted Beard's wagon needing repairs at Soda Springs on August 3.

The company moved only three miles up Cassia Creek on August 14, probably to where today's Highway 77 comes in from the north. They made it a short day because the previous day had been so arduous and the oxen needed rest. May made a sage comment about the importance of taking care of their oxen:

> Monday 14th. We only moved 3 miles today, almost always after a hard day's drive we lay by in order to rest our cattle. The last 700 miles of the road had been to all appearances much worse on cattle than the forepart of the journey withstanding the teams are better off than when we were at Fort Laramie. There are but few that know the worth of oxen in the states. I am confident if a team of cattle was taken and treated with humanity that they would travel across the continent at the rate of 400 miles a month, but the inhuman treatment of drivers is enough to destroy a number of teams. Men are by ox driving like they are by everything else, some not fit to carry a whip within a mile of a team. Driving is reducing to a system and he that drives to let others know he is driving will soon have no team to drive. The fact is every attention to your cattle is actually necessary to take you through this trip. Oxen are the central object of this route and you belong to them instead of them to you. This evening we made [a] tongue … for the broken wagon [Beard's] in short order and it performs well.

In his entry for August 14, Smith noted that Mr. Stewart's cow had died and that Captain Chiles' "carriage" had broken. Although we knew that Chiles had brought one or more wagons, this is the first reference to his bringing a carriage. Perhaps it was for his youngest children.

According to May, the company continued up Cassia Creek on the fifteenth:

> Tuesday 15th August, 1848, traveled 13 miles, good roads up Cajuix [Cassia] Creek. The scenery bold and rich, peak after peak rising to great height on both sides of our road. The plain on the creek quite narrow but makes a fine mountain pass. Encamped on another branch of the creek [Edwards Creek]. A few of the Digger tribe of Indians in camp selling berries. The mountain black berry is certainly the most delicious of any I ever tasted. They are black when ripe.

Their August 15 camp would have been where Edwards Creek crosses today's Elba-Almo Highway. May's "Digger" Indians were Western Shoshones or Snakes.

Modern photograph of City of Rocks, Idaho, along the California Trail. Courtesy of photographer Jim Olsen, http://utahhikes.net.

About six miles into their travel on the sixteenth, the Chiles company came to an enchanting place, a sanctum sanctorum of uncommon grandeur. The trail entered the northeast corner of a five-mile-long, three-mile-wide oblong basin. The bottom was covered in sagebrush, while the surrounding peaks supported dark-colored pines and cedars, but it was the wondrous rock formations that set the place apart. Made of limestone and granite, these irregularly shaped rocks ranged from 60 to 150 feet in height. The location had been referred to by a number of names: Pyramid Circle and Valley of the Rocks, but because it resembled a gleaming city, it was also called the City of Rocks—the name that finally stuck. May recounted this day in awe-struck prose:

> Wednesday 16th August. Traveled 16 miles and encamped in a basin of the mountains. Here all language I command will not describe the scenery around our encampment. It is rich beyond anything I have ever beheld. Single and isolated rocks standing on the plain from 50 to 200 feet high, encircled by a chain just giving admission to and from our basin. We passed over the roughest piece of road today that had been seen on the journey. Large rocks lying partly under the ground with their edges turned all directions so as to make it very rough. One of the wagons parted [its] coupling pole. If a mountain destroying angel has been dispatched here with power to distroy and scatter the elements of mountains, he could not have done more than he has done here. Rugged peaks, projecting rocks, deep canyons and gorges are all here. I took a mountain stroll

today and saw a few of the curiosities to be found in these stupendous mountains. I am sorry that I have no leisure to take long and frequent tramps in those
places frequented only by the breath of the forest. My mind is ever active, my
eyes always open to those towering heights.

Explaining it in his own simpler way, Smith seemed just as impressed:

wed 16 in the afternoon we traveled about 6 miles   ½ mile the Road was covered with Rocks the Roughest I ever beheld we encamped in a dell surrounded
by Rocks the Roughest and Most Romantic that eyes ever beheld or fancy could
imagine   Broad and lofty domes tall and slender Minerets towering spires &c
which I shall call the City of Rocks.

On the evening of August 15, the Chiles company was camping in the bosom of
the City of Rocks, still five hundred miles from encountering the most formidable
obstacle of the entire journey—the mighty Sierras.

Table 13: Progress of wagon companies as of August 15, 1848

Company (Diarist)	Arrived Fort Hall	Arrived Raft River	Arrived Fort Boise
Oregon-Bound:			
Allsopp/Adams, first segment	before July 14	?	?
Gates (Root)	July 14 (est.)	July 18 (est.)	August 8
Miller (Anderson)	July 15	July 19	August 9
Jackson (Belknap)	July 17 (est.)	July 20 (est.)	August 10 (est.)
Watt	July 17 (est.)	July 20 (est.)	August 10 (est.)
Walker/Bristow	?	?	?
Hannah	?	?	?
Purvine (Porter)	July 25	July 28	August 17
Adams, second segment	July 25 (est.)	July 28 (est.)	August 17 (est.)
Stone/Delaney (Lempfrit)	August 2	August 5	August 28
California-Bound:			
Wambaugh/Cornwall	July 15	July 19 (est.)	—
Lassen	August 2	August 5	—
Chiles (May, Smith)	August 7	August 12	—
Hensley	did not pass through Fort Hall	—	—

CHAPTER 16

Glory, Hallelujah, I Shall Die a Rich Man Yet!
AUGUST 15–SEPTEMBER 8

AUGUST 15, 1848
Thomas Corcoran, Cornwall/Greenwood company,
near Humboldt Sink, Nevada

On the same day that the two Oregon-bound companies, Gates and Miller (representing a total of sixty wagons), left their staging area south of Fort Hall on July 16, about forty-three California-bound wagons left the same area. Riley Root was now traveling with an Oregon company, and John McPherson's journal is lost, so there are no diaries that allow us to monitor the California wagons beyond Fort Hall. In later reminiscences, Cornwall, Corcoran, and Burrows report a few incidences along the California Trail, but they do not give the same day-to-day details that diaries provide.

Either at Fort Hall or sometime thereafter, the forty-three California wagons divided into two parties, each traveling about a day apart. This was a common practice when traveling through arid country because of insufficient grass to satisfy the appetites of large numbers of livestock. James Clyman had acknowledged the problem while traveling east along the Humboldt River in May 1846, and noted in his journal that even a small company needed to divide up.[1]

On August 15, a group of recently discharged members of the Mormon Battalion traveling east from California to rejoin their families met the California-bound wagons at the Humboldt Sink. They encountered the first party, consisting of eighteen wagons, on August 15, and the second, consisting of twenty-five wagons, on the following day. The Mormons did not encounter any other California-bound wagons for another ten days.[2]

The Cornwall biography declared that "Mr. Cornwall had persuaded a number of Oregon immigrants to divert their route to California and the party took the southern route under his leadership." His party, it added, "numbered not less than forty-five men with their families, livestock and some thirty wagons." Thomas Corcoran's biographical sketch, appearing in the 1891 *History of Santa Cruz County*, adds credibility to Cornwall's claim: "The captain of the train was P. B. Cornwall."[3] Corcoran could have meant that Cornwall headed their wagon party between Bellevue and Fort Laramie, but he also could have meant that Cornwall served as captain of this party during the California leg of the journey, just as the Cornwall biography claimed. In spite of fragile health, Corcoran had been allowed by Cornwall to accompany him West, a favor for which Thomas undoubtedly held an abiding sense of indebtedness and loyalty. The Fallon incident at Soda Springs mentioned by both Cornwall and Corcoran is evidence that Corcoran was still traveling with Cornwall at that point, and there is every reason to believe he continued to travel with Cornwall along the California Trail.

If Cornwall was the captain of one of the wagon parties, then who was the captain of the other? In his 1960 biography of James Clyman, Charles L. Camp writes that Wambaugh continued leading his Oregon-bound emigrants on to Oregon,[4] but this is incorrect. Wambaugh owned land in the Santa Clara Valley of California, having purchased it just before returning to Missouri with Commodore Stockton in the spring of 1847. John C. Trullinger, the man who claimed to see the "apparition" in the evening sky west of Devil's Gate, wrote in his 1890 reminiscence that "the company that we traveled with from St. Joseph, on the Missouri River, to Fort Hall was called Wambo's Company." Notice that he said from St. Joseph to Fort Hall, not from St. Joseph to Oregon."[5] But the conclusive evidence was Rufus Burrows' reminiscence, which reported that "Captain Wambo" was their company leader at the time of an accidental shooting along the Humboldt River.

The question of who acted as guides for these two wagon parties must be addressed next. Corcoran's biographical sketch declared that, while his captain was Cornwall, his "pilot was Greenwood, an old Rocky Mountain Guide." As for Wambaugh, it seems certain that his pilot was James Clyman. There is no reason why Clyman would not have continued to travel with Wambaugh and serve as his guide. Stephen Broadhurst drove one of the wagons in Wambaugh's company, and his son, George, explained in a 1953 biography that

> When they were ready to start on [from Fort Hall], thirty wagons were ready to come to California and thirty went on to Oregon. Here it was that Colonel Clyman was chosen to guide the California part of the trail and he brought it through to California.[6]

Now comes the most challenging question of all: Which of the two parties was in the lead when they met the eastbound Mormons at the Humboldt Sink on August 15? Several historians have assumed that the first party was led by Clyman and the second by Cornwall. Camp's 1960 biography of Clyman asserted that the lead company, the one in which Mormon Hazen Kimball was traveling, was led by Clyman,[7] and

Stewart, in his 1962 *The California Trail*, wrote that "This vanguard of migration was probably the company led by Clyman." Stewart continued, "On the next day, August 16, the Mormons continued their march eastward, and on that same day they met twenty-five more wagons, probably Cornwall's company."[8] Both Camp and Stewart fail to cite what led them to believe that Clyman led the first party, while Cornwall led the second. More recent books have continued to make the same assertion, citing only Camp's and Stewart's suppositions as if they were validated facts.[9]

Since the two California parties would travel up the Raft River in order to reach the upper Humboldt—a trail that had become known as the Fort Hall Road, or California Trail—we should consider which guide would most likely have been selected to pilot the first group. Who had the most experience? Indisputably, it would have been Caleb Greenwood and his oldest sons. They had traveled it at least six times (once in '44, twice in '45, twice in '46, and once in '47). Captain Wambaugh, on the other hand, had traveled it once, when he accompanied the Commodore Stockton party east to the States in 1847. Frank McClellan, traveling with Wambaugh in 1848, had been over the trail in 1843 with his uncle, Joseph Walker, when Walker led a party of wagons to California for Joseph Chiles. James Clyman, on the other hand, as experienced and respected a trailsman as he was, had never traveled the Fort Hall Road before. When the parties divided and settled upon who would take the lead, Greenwood might have regarded himself as the appropriate choice. And there is abundant evidence that makes it almost certain that the Cornwall company, led by Caleb Greenwood, was out in front.

The Greenwoods, Cornwalls, Corcoran, and the Mormons (Kimball, Pollack, and Rogers) would have traveled in this lead group of eighteen wagons, although it is difficult to know who else traveled with them. It could have included some wagons from the original Allsopp company—the company of "Oregon and California-bound wagons" that Isaac Pettijohn had reported earlier.

Many who had traveled from St. Joseph under Wambaugh's leadership are known to have gone to California, and it is fair to expect them to continue traveling with him and Clyman. Those with families were E. E. Brock, Lambert McCombs, Levi Hardman, Stephen Broadhurst, Rufus Hitchcock, Street Rice, David Hunsaker, and J. C. Austin. Then there were the single men: Henry Shields, John McPherson, and young Rufus Burrows.[10] There is evidence that the David Parks family continued traveling with Wambaugh/Clyman, and the fact that Thomas Corcoran attached himself to the Cornwall/Greenwood party, suggests that Corcoran had regained his health to the point where he no longer needed the support of the Parks family.

There were others who started with Wambaugh at St. Joseph, such as W. Harper, G. Mullen, H. Sharp, and Levi Lafflair, for whom we have no evidence whether they went to Oregon or California. We can only hope that some diary or journal comes to light in the future that sheds light on the question.

After leaving Fort Hall on July 16, the two California companies would have followed the Oregon Trail beside the Snake River until they came to the Raft River on about July 20. At this point, they veered left and took the trail that led to California. They traveled up the Raft, then up Cassia Creek, then after passing through the picturesque City of Rocks, went over Granite Pass to the Goose River. Then they made their way up the Goose until they entered Thousand Springs Valley and eventually came to the upper Humboldt River in present-day Nevada. The Humboldt would be a longer version of the Sweetwater. It would be their lifeline for the next three hundred miles.

For almost a month, the two companies advanced along the narrow Humboldt that gently wound through parched, sage-vegetated plains and between small, utterly desolate mountain ranges. When James Clyman left California in the spring of 1846, he described this area along the Humboldt as "one of the most Steril Barren countrys I ever traversed."[11]

On August 14, the Cornwall/Greenwood wagons were rumbling in a southwesterly direction and were drawing near the Humboldt Sink. On that day, they met twenty-three eastbound Mormon packers who had left California and were heading toward the Great Salt Lake Valley to join families and friends. Although there were no diarists from either company to record their encounter, according to a source traveling with the Mormon party behind the packers, the packers had informed the westbound company of the recent discovery of gold in California. The stunning news must have set the westbound emigrants' minds spinning with a new reality that must have turned their reasons for going to California upside down. A Mormon reported one old man's reaction:

> One of the [Mormon] men began to explain and, taking his purse from his pocket, poured into his hand perhaps an ounce of gold dust and began stirring it with his finger. One aged man of probably over three score years and ten, who had listened with intense interest, while his expressive eyes fairly glistened, could remain silent no longer; he sprang to his feet, threw his old wool hat upon the ground, and jumped upon it with both feet, then kicked it high in the air, and exclaimed, "Glory, hallelujah, thank God, I shall die a rich man yet!"[12]

It is impossible to know who the old man was, but Caleb Greenwood makes a good candidate. Other than him, there would have been few in the Cornwall party quite as ancient as "over three score years and ten." The packers had other news as well: They had just crossed the Sierras by way of a new and "better" route, a road blazed by a Mormon wagon party just behind them, one that was led by Samuel Thompson.

The following day, August 15, the Cornwall party was approaching the Sink. It was a place where the Humboldt had finally came to die. Because its rate of percolation and evaporation exceeded its inflows, the river had gradually diminished in size and what little water remained was ugly brown and polluted with high concentrations of alkali and salt. The Sink was a lake bed about twelve miles long and four miles wide, but much of it was dry and covered by white, powdery alkali. Portions, however, were bulrush-covered marshes containing foul, brackish water. In short, the Sink was a loathsome place. In earlier times, some explorers had called it Ogden's Lake. When James Clyman passed here in May 1846, he noted that the lake was a "small shallow pond know[n] as Ogdens Lake . . . and has the most thirsty appearance of any place I ever witnessed."[13]

As the Cornwall company traveled along the west side of the Sink near the end of the day, the late afternoon sun beat down upon them and huge, billowing clouds of dust, strongly impregnated with alkali and saleratus, enfolded the strung-out wagon company. Thomas Corcoran's lungs must have vastly improved since he had been traveling through bone-dry air for the last two months, but he probably wasn't taking any chances, and may have been riding at the head of the column to stay ahead of the irritating dust. From this point, Greenwood might have pointed out a faint jagged line about seventy miles distant and barely visible through the blue haze. It was the Sierra Nevadas, a steep, hulking barrier lying across their path. Even from a distance, the barren mountains looked enormous and seemed to stretch on forever. Before they could venture into a rocky pass, they had to cross the "Forty Mile Desert," a waterless, alkali-covered stretch of wasteland every bit as difficult as Greenwood's cutoff in Wyoming. They would be stopping soon to rest their worn-down livestock before beginning the daunting night crawl. No doubt Greenwood knew some of their oxen would not make it across, but to tell the wagoneers might have been needlessly disheartening.

Soon, they would have seen in the distance the camp of the Samuel Thompson company, the one the Mormon packers had told them about. When they rolled into the Thompson camp, they encountered a ragged party of thirty Mormon men, one woman, sixteen wagons, and a large herd of livestock.[14] The story behind these east-bound Mormons is remarkable.

We saw in chapter 10 that in July 1846, Brigham Young had pressured five hundred of his Saints to volunteer for one year of service in the U.S. Army to fight in the war against Mexico. On July 20, 1846, the Mormon Battalion left their camp at Council Bluffs. After being hastily outfitted and trained at Fort Leavenworth, the Battalion marched nine hundred miles along the Santa Fe Trail, suffering fatigue, hunger, thirst, and sickness. When they reached the crossing of the Arkansas River in present-day Colorado, most of the women and about eighty sick were diverted to the little Mexican town of Pueblo to overwinter,[15] and the remaining 420 members of the Battalion continued on. On October 9, the lead companies of the Battalion marched into Santa Fe, but the town had already surrendered without resistance to the recently promoted General Kearney. The rest of the Mormon companies arrived on October 12. General Kearney was gone, having left with a small unit of dragoons to help subdue California. He had left orders for Lt. Colonel Philip St. George Cooke to take command of the Mormon Battalion and lead them on to California.[16] Cooke sent eighty-one of the weakest and sickest back to Pueblo to stay the winter with their fellow church members.[17] Then, on October 19, 1846, Cooke led the remaining 340 men of the Mormon Battalion out of Santa Fe and across the harsh deserts of southern New Mexico, Arizona, and California.[18] It was a miserable march, but they blazed a new, thousand-mile-long wagon road through an unknown wilderness. On January 28, 1847, after a three-month ordeal, the battalion made it to Mission San Luis Rey, an abandoned Spanish mission a few miles from the Pacific Ocean. Once again, the Mormon Battalion did not have go fight, as the Mexican forces had already capitulated and signed a peace treaty. The Mormon Battalion was then split into three parts and assigned to garrison duty at San Diego, San Luis Rey, and Pueblo de los Angelos. By July 1847, the battalion had completed its promised one year of service; its members were gathered together in Los Angeles and on July 16 were mustered out of service.[19]

Not only were these men terribly far from their families, they weren't even sure where their families were. They did know that a group of 230 Mormon colonists led by Sam Brannan had arrived at Yerba Buena (San Francisco) from New York City on the ship *Brooklyn* on July 29, 1846,[20] and had founded a communal farming colony called New Hope Farm in the upper San Joaquin Valley, where they waited for Brigham Young to bring the rest of the Saints to California. Many of the discharged veterans decided to stay in California, anticipating that their families would be arriving soon. Eighty re-enlisted for another six months, and others took jobs at local ranchos in southern California making adobe bricks and digging wells.[21] About 150 battalion veterans had no intention of waiting in California any longer and planned to return east, but not by the trail they had blazed across those horrid southern deserts. In characteristic Mormon fashion, they organized into units of tens and fifties, used their pay to buy horses and cattle from nearby ranchos, and departed the Los Angeles area on July 21. They headed north through Tejon Pass, and entered the southern end of the San Joaquin Valley. They traveled along the valley's east side, hoping to start their journey by going east through Walker's Pass, which some had heard about.[22] Unable to find it, they decided to continue north, and pushed on toward Sutter's Fort. About twenty miles south of the fort, near New Hope Farm, the group learned for the first time that an advance party of Brigham Young's pioneer party had just arrived at the Salt Lake Valley, where he had decided to settle instead of bringing the Saints to California.[23]

Despite the lateness of the year, the battalion veterans were determined to join their loved ones and began departing Sutter's Fort on August 27, 1847. They traveled northeast to Johnson's ranch, then followed the trail over the Truckee Route, as the Donner Pass trail was then called. At Truckee Lake, later called Donner Lake, they encountered the abandoned shanties in which the ill-fated Donner party had spent the previous winter. The Mormon diarists expressed dismay at the sight of human bones scattered on the ground, some broken open so the living could get at

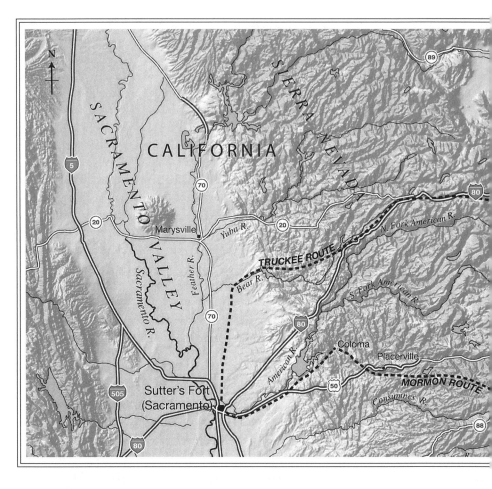

the marrow inside. Sickened, the Mormons reburied the remains and hastened away from this haunting place as quickly as they could.[24]

Continuing down the eastern slope of the mountains, they encountered Sam Brannan, who was returning to California after going east to meet Brigham Young. When Brannan had met Young on the Green River near the mouth of Big Sandy Creek, he had enthusiastically extolled the virtues of California, but his accolades fell on deaf ears. Young had already decided on the Salt Lake region, having decided that Mormons should no longer settle in places that would soon attract scores of Gentiles. Brannan was beside himself. He had planned on enriching himself from the multitudes of Saints he expected would come to California.. The disgruntled Brannan followed Young to the Salt Lake Valley to have a look around, and then left "in a black rage" to return to California.[25] When Brannan encountered the eastbound group of battalion veterans on the Truckee River, he told them he had seen the Salt Lake and denounced the place as an unfortunate mistake: "[I]t froze there every month in the

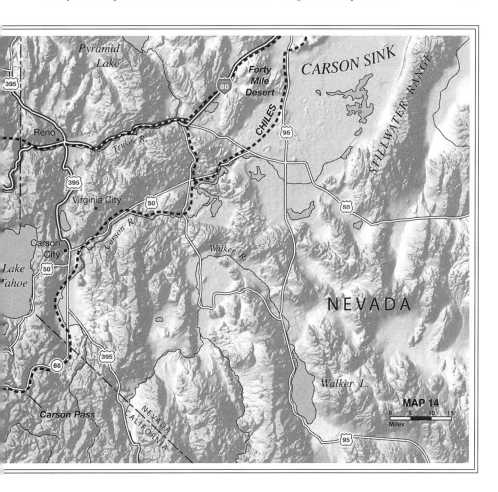

year," and said it was "no place for an agricultural people, and expressed his confidence that the Saints would emigrate to California the next spring."[26]

The Mormon veterans listened to Brannan, but continued traveling east, while a still fuming Brannan continued on to California. The next day, the veterans met Captain James Brown, who had been sent by Brigham Young to warn the discharged men that they were not welcome at the strapped Salt Lake settlement unless they brought enough provisions to last them until the next year's harvest.[27] If they could not they should return to California and get jobs, then return in the spring with provisions purchased from their earnings. About half of the men disregarded the warning and continued on to the Salt Lake anyway. The others, about forty of them, mostly young messmates from the battalion's B and C companies, obediently turned back. They arrived at Sutter's Fort in two groups, one on September 12, and the other on September 14.[28]

For some time, John Sutter had wanted to construct a flouring mill on the south bank of the American River, about six miles upstream from his fort, but he could never find enough workers for the job. Now that a large work force had fallen into his lap, Sutter hired them on the spot and sent them off to begin the project.[29] Two weeks later, on September 28, a man by the name of James Marshall appeared at the grist-mill site and informed the Mormons that he and Captain Sutter had formed a part-nership to build a sawmill thirty-five miles up the south fork of the American River at a place called Coloma.[30] He needed four men. Henry Bigler, Azariah Smith, Israel Evans, and William Johnston, all Mormons, volunteered and followed Marshall to Coloma to join a small number of men already working there.

By late January 1848, the men had completed most of the sawmill's frame at Coloma and had dug much of its mill race. At the end of each workday, they would open the race's headgate to let the water wash away the loosened dirt and gravel dur-ing the night. On the afternoon of January 24, Marshall was out having a look. "This day," Bigler wrote in his pocket diary, "some kind of mettle was found in the tail of the race that looks like goald." It was not until another night's run of water and another close inspection the next morning that Marshall finally came to his employees and declared, "Boys, by God I believe I have found a gold mine!"[31]

Marshall warned the Mormon boys to keep the discovery a secret. Henry Big-ler wrote a letter to three of his former messmates who were working at the flouring mill. In obedience to his employer's warning, Bigler concluded his letter by telling his friends to keep it to themselves.[32] What fun is a secret if you can't tell it? Despite the bar of secrecy, word spread in all directions like a wildfire, it being the nature of men to not keep their mouths shut.

Despite the stunning discovery, Marshall's workers continued their work on completing the sawmill, allowing themselves only Sundays to go off on their own to hunt gold. Once the mill was finished and running, Marshall allowed his employees to dig for gold, provided he got half of all they gathered. The Mormons at the flouring mill were not nearly so loyal and left the mill project to work an unimaginably rich deposit of gold they had found on an upstream sandbar that famously became known as Mormon Island.[33] On April 9, 1848, most of the Mormons gathered to make plans to leave for the Great Salt Lake.[34] Their efforts in the rivers and creeks had been yield-ing abundantly, but even with the strong allure of gold, their love of family was stron-ger. They agreed to continue mining for the next couple of months, as they could use the gold to outfit themselves with wagons, livestock, and provisions, and agreed to meet in the middle of June to begin their trip east.

By the first week of May, hordes of people from throughout California had heard of the gold strike through many sources, including Sam Brannan's newspaper, the *California Star*, and there was a great rush to the goldfields east of Sutter's Fort.[35] Peo-ple left their jobs, trades, and posts, shops were left unmanned, cattle left untended, and crops left in the field. Miners swarmed over the rivers and creeks, and it seemed that they were picking up riches wherever they turned.

In planning their trip east, the Mormon group considered what they had already seen of the Truckee Route. They didn't much care for it, especially the nightmare of its pass or the maddening Truckee River Canyon. Since they were planning to traverse the Sierras two months earlier than westbound emigrants normally did, there would be more unmelted snow to deal with, and their wagons, full to the brim, would be much heavier. They needed to find a shorter, easier way. Someone recalled that John Fremont and Kit Carson, leading an expedition into California in 1844, had crossed the mountains somewhere south of the Truckee Route, so in early May, an impatient group of eight Mormons led by Daniel Browett ventured out on horseback in search of this better way over the mountains. They may have followed a trapper's trail that in turn followed an established Indian trail,[36] but in any event, the scouting party followed the ridge that divided the American River from the Cosumnes River and, it is believed, made it as far as West Pass before being turned back by a heavy snowstorm.[37]

On June 17, Henry Bigler and two friends went to locate a suitable place where their expedition to the Salt Lake could gather.[38] About eight miles southeast of today's Placerville, and not far from the south fork of the American River, Bigler and his companions found a pretty little grass-carpeted basin surrounded by oaks, pines, cedars, and firs, which they called Pleasant Valley. The first Mormon wagons and livestock began arriving at Pleasant Valley on June 21, and on June 25 the impatient Daniel Browett, with Ezra Allen and Henderson Cox, left on another scouting expedition to further explore the best route for their wagons, although some had tried to discourage them from setting out alone. By July 3, seventeen wagons, filled to the brim with tools, seed, and provisions, had assembled in Pleasant Valley, a group consisting of forty men, one woman (wife of one of the members), 250 head of oxen, cattle, and calves, 200 horses and mules, and two small cannons. Virtually everything had been purchased from Captain Sutter with their recently mined gold.[39]

On July 3, the company began leaving Pleasant Valley and climbed a steep ridge to the east. By the fifth, they had arrived at another small valley they called Sly's Park, named after one of their members. Nervous about the failure of the three scouts to return—it had been ten days—they stayed at Sly's Park while ten men went ahead to look for the scouts and explore the country ahead. On July 13, the ten scouts returned to Sly's Park, reporting that they had found a path over the crest of the Sierras and had made it all the way to the Carson Valley in four days. They believed they had found a good route, although it would require a great deal of labor to make it passable for wagons, but they had seen nothing of the three men.[40]

The party, led by Samuel Thompson, began moving out of Sly's Park on July 15, climbing Stonebreaker grade, a ridge dividing the watersheds of the American and the Cosumnes Rivers.[41] The ascent was steep and the trees were so tall and dense they could not see what lay ahead. Work details forged ahead of the wagons to cut trees, move rocks, and slash through thickets of brush, following the top of the ridge as far as it would take them. Their path took them through forests of pine and fir, many two hundred or more feet tall, and trunks eight feet or more in diameter. The ridge was narrow and fell sharply away just a few yards on each side of their line of march, plunging into deep, impassable canyons.

At the end of the day on July 17, the company came to Leek Spring where they encamped. They let the wagons remain in camp on the eighteenth, while a work detail was sent ahead to work on the road. Climbing out of the Leek Spring meadow and crossing a knife-edged ridge, the work crew would have looked to the northeast at a high country of immense scale and vastness. Mostly above the timberline, it was a scene of jagged peaks and naked sheets of boulder-covered granite. They would have to make their way over this.

Near the end of the day on July 18, the work party came to a large spring and discovered a grisly scene. Blood-smeared arrows lay on the ground. Nearby, they found the remains of their missing three-man scout party, their naked, badly mutilated bodies lying in a shallow grave. The wagons were brought forward on the nineteenth, and the company camped at this place they named Tragedy Springs. Fearing attack from the Indians that had killed their friends, they tightly corralled their livestock that night and posted a heavy guard. During the night, their livestock became frightened, as if something were creeping up through the dark. The nervous Captain Thompson ordered one of the cannons unlimbered and loaded. It was fired, and the discharge resounded through the night, echoing from mountain to mountain. Not surprisingly, it did more harm than good. The startled cattle stampeded into the night, and the men spent all of the next day and part of the next searching for them. Except for two mules, they eventually recovered them all.[42]

Today, the Thompson company's route between Pleasant Valley and Tragedy Springs can be followed by picking up Pleasant Valley Road two miles south of Placerville, and following it east into Pleasant Valley. From there, turn left onto Sly Park Road and continue until reaching Johnson Lake at Sly's Park. Just before reaching the lake, turn right onto Mormon Emigrant Road, and follow it to Leek Springs. Shortly thereafter, the road will join Highway 88. From there, travel five miles east on Highway 88 to Tragedy Springs.

On July 21, the Thompson company resumed their travel over high country, with the work crews continuing to clear the route ahead of the wagons. They reached Rock Valley, where Silver Lake sits today, and climbed a seemingly impossible pathway up sheets of slick and boulder-strewn rock. They made it over West Pass at 9,600 feet, then descended into what they called Lake Valley (where Kirkwood is today) and moved across a meadow now covered by Caples Lake.

On July 29, they had worked their way toward the next summit at 8,600 feet (later named Carson Pass), laboring in the thin air up steep slopes and over huge boulders. The company crossed its crest, then began lowering their wagons with ropes down the steepest descent they had yet encountered. "Today the wagons are crossing the back bone [Carson Pass]," Azariah Smith wrote on the twenty-ninth, "and going down the

Mountain on the other side which is very steep, and the men have to hold the wagons to keep them from tiping over."[43] In later years, this dangerous mountainside would often be referred to as the Devil's Staircase.[44] What Smith called the "back bone" was a high mountaintop near the pass. Because of its resemblance to the back of an elephant, it later became known as "the elephant."[45] In later years, it was common for gold rushers to proclaim that they were "going to see the elephant."

The road this party of tough young Mormons pioneered over these two passes took them over majestic but treacherously difficult ridges and across deep snow banks. Even with the road improvements, their wagons were battered unmercifully by the jolting route. Their diaries constantly mentioned broken axles, shattered wagon tongues, tipped wagons, and much time spent in repairing them.[46] At the foot of Carson Pass, they camped beside Red Lake. The next day, they moved their wagons through a beautiful basin they named Hope Valley, stopping to camp at the head of the narrow, steep-sided West Carson Canyon on July 30.[47] For four days, they left their wagons in camp while they sent almost everyone out to work a road through the canyon, perhaps their most difficult obstacle yet. It looked impossible. The tight squeeze at the bottom of the canyon was filled with great rocks that had tumbled down over the ages from the heights above. Sometimes encountering boulders as high as ten feet, they had to build fires on them, using the sudden heat to shatter them into smaller pieces.

While working on the road on August 3, the Thompson company looked up to see a train of thirteen Mormon packers coming up behind. "We were overtaken to day by 13 of our boys with pack animals," Henry Bigler wrote. "They had left the mines 5 days ago." The diaries of Jonathon Holmes and Samuel Rogers, however, said there were fourteen packers.[48] Starting from Pleasant Valley on July 30, the pack train had been able to travel rapidly, largely because of the remarkable road work performed by the Thompson company.

After four grueling days, work on the canyon road was completed. Beginning in the morning of August 4, the pack train, livestock, and all but one of the wagons made it through the five-mile-long canyon and emerged at last onto the broad Carson Valley.[49] Looking at the canyon today, one has to marvel at how these hardy men managed to get their wagons through it at all. At the end of the day, the party was camping along the Carson River about eight miles beyond the mouth of the canyon, having completed one of the most extraordinary achievements of wagon-road pioneering, improvement, and passage ever recorded in western history.

When the Thompson company reached the Carson Valley, they entered a country of yellow-blossomed sage that suffused the air with its overpowering scent. Often passing beneath the shade of tall cottonwoods, they bumped along beside the Carson River. Some of the Mormon diarists called it the Pilot River, while at least one called it the Salmon Trout.[50] For the next seven days, the Thompson company traveled about seventy miles along the river, but their progress was slow, mostly due to the troublesome Paiute Indians, or "Diggers," as the emigrants called them. Bigler mentioned seeing countless fires burning on the mountainsides at night, set by the Indians as signals that there were strangers in the area. Despite the company posting heavy guards around their livestock, the Indians were still able to run off numbers of them almost every night, compelling the men to spend part of the next day searching for them. The Indians would also shoot horses and cattle with poisoned arrows at night. "It seems that it is their calculation," Bigler explained, "that when a horse is shot with a poison arrow, the animal will become so sick that it will be left, and of course will fall into their hands." Nothing seemed safe. Henry Bigler complained on August 11 that one of their small dogs and a calf were running around with arrows sticking in them.[51]

By August 12, the party departed the Carson River and headed north twenty-five miles, across barren hills to reach another cottonwood-lined river, the Truckee.[52] It was here, near present-day Fernley and I-80, that the company encountered the established emigrant trail. On the twelfth, "our packers left us and went ahead," Henry Bigler wrote, although Holmes claimed that the packers left them on the tenth and Rogers wrote that it was the eighth.[53] Ten impatient men from the Thompson company, wanting to travel at a faster pace, joined the pack train and increased its size to twenty-three. This group of packers was the first to encounter the Cornwall/Greenwood company along the Humboldt River on August 14.

The Thompson wagon party remained in camp beside the Truckee River all day on August 13, resting in the shade of the tall cottonwoods and letting their tired animals recruit. On the fourteenth, Henry Bigler reported that they started traveling northeast across the Forty Mile Desert, pausing at Brady Hot Springs about halfway across. One can still see plumes of steam boiling out of these springs about twenty-five miles northeast of Fernley, Nevada, and just south of today's I-80. The men waited at the springs to rest, and did not resume their trip across the desert until eleven o'clock that night. They finally arrived at the Humboldt Sink early the next morning, August 15.

There were five Mormon diarists in the Thompson company who described their encounter with the California-bound companies: Henry Bigler, Samuel Rogers, Ephraim Green, Azariah Smith, and Jonathon Holmes. Henry Bigler described the fifteenth, the day when they met the Cornwall/Greenwood party:

> August 15 . . . At six this morning arrived at the sink of the Humboldt and camped. The water here was not very good. Cattle did not like it. Towards evening, 18 emigrant wagons [Cornwall/Greenwood company] rolled in and camped by us. They had met our packers about forty miles ahead of us and had traveled about one hundred miles without water. These emigrants had come by way of Fort Hall. There was one family in the crowd by the name of Hazen Kimble that had wintered at the Salt Lake and had moved in March to Fort Hall. Kimball said he did not like the Salt Lake country and had left.[54]

Samuel Rogers also recorded that this company had eighteen wagons and he mentioned "Hasel Kimbel," noting that he was "a compleat Apostate or he appears so."[55] Ephraim Green wrote in his notebook that at "thee sink of maris [Mary's] river . . . we met the emagration."[56]Azariah Smith also described the fifteenth:

> The Boys mostly are laying under the wagons in the shade a sleeping, as we did not get to sleep last night. . . . In the afternoon some sixteen wagons came in, on the way to California, from the States, and they got a waybill of us—calculating to take our trail over the mountains.[57]

None of the Mormon diarists identified the pilot, captain, or anyone else in the Cornwall party except for Hazen Kimball. But this is not surprising, as they wouldn't have known any of these men.

When the Cornwall company met the Thompson party on August 15, they had had a day to think about the earth-shaking revelations they had learned from the Mormon packers the day before. They must have peppered the Thompson men with scores of questions. By writing that these wagons were "calculating to take our trail," Azariah Smith suggested that the Cornwall company was showing interest in their new Carson Pass route. The men must have exchanged other news and information, such as warning each other of the troubles each had with the Paiutes along the Humboldt and Carson Rivers.

These two Mormon parties were not the first to carry news of the gold discovery east. Sam Brannan had sent four men east with the news as early as April 1, but they did not arrive at the new Mormon settlement at Salt Lake until July 9. Another group left Sutter's Fort on May 1 and arrived at Salt Lake on July 1.[58] But word of gold did not reach Fort Hall, 150 miles to the north, until after all the emigrant trains had passed through, including the last in line, the Chiles company, which left the fort on August 9.

The Cornwall company could have spent the night of August 15 camping with the Mormons at the Sink, but it is not likely. The two parties had met on the west side of the Humboldt Sink, a place virtually destitute of grass, where the sage was widely spaced and the water was, in the words of Henry Bigler, "not very good." The Mormons alone had about four hundred head of livestock and the Cornwall company had their own animals as well. It was not a spot for any company—let alone two companies with lots of livestock—to linger for long. Before the Cornwall party had met the Mormon packers the day before, they must have been dreading the final barriers to their journey—the throat-parching desert, the menacing Truckee River Canyon, and the dizzying climb over Donner's Pass. But with the stunning news of gold now ringing in their ears, their mood may have utterly changed. For these reasons, it is reasonable to assume that Greenwood had his company resume their travel that evening of the fifteenth after only a few hours of rest. It was the usual practice anyway to strike out across the Forty Mile Desert late in the evening so that much of it could be crossed during the cool of the night.

It would be a long, grim haul. Upon leaving the Sink, the Cornwall party would have ventured across an expanse of fetlock-deep, powdery white alkali, interrupted periodically by stretches of abrasive volcanic gravel. In stark contrast to their moonless trek across Greenwood's cutoff a month and a half earlier, they would have been able to roll all night under the illumination of an almost full moon.[59] Some, spurred on by visions of gold-filled streams and rivers, may have engaged in fevered discourse about goldfields and debated whether to follow the Mormons' waybill over the mountains.

After about eight miles of alkali flats, the company began climbing a section of low, sage-covered hills, reaching the summit about seventeen miles after leaving the Sink, and probably arriving in the early morning at Brady Hot Springs, where they encountered cauldrons of furiously boiling water and columns of white steam spewing into the cool morning air. There was water, but it was deadly hot. If they were willing to be patient, they could bail buckets of scalding water into tubs and let it cool for an hour or so, but it was sulfurous, mean-tasting stuff, and Greenwood had discovered in 1844 that it would make oxen sick.[60] It was also a good idea to keep their thirsty dogs away from the pools, lest they fall in and instantly scald to death as they tried to get a drink. This had happened to one of the Mormon dogs just two days earlier, and James Clyman had lost his beloved spaniel here in the same way when he was returning east from California in 1846.[61]

Leaving the springs, the company descended onto another broad plain that was little more than a sheet of cracked mud and encrusted salt. Even though they would travel the rest of those waterless miles beneath a hot sun, they were encouraged by the sight of a thin dark line of cottonwoods beginning to appear far off in the distance. At last, sometime near the end of August 16, the Cornwall company should have arrived at the Truckee River, near today's Fernley, Nevada, and just north of I-80. It was common for the weakest oxen to perish while crossing this abominable forty-mile desert, compelling the emigrants to abandon some wagons, but we have no diaries or journals describing the Cornwall company's experience crossing this harrowing stretch. The surviving oxen would have been so fatigued that companies probably spent more than a day at the Truckee's edge letting their livestock recruit. It was a true oasis in the wilderness, with abundant grass, a river of cold, clear water, fed by snowmelt from the high Sierras, and plenty of shade beneath the cottonwoods.

From here, Greenwood would have originally planned to lead the company up the established road that he and his sons had traveled many times before: up the Truckee River bottom to the foot of the mountains, and skirting the worst part of the Truckee Canyon before crawling over Donner Pass. But the Mormons' revelation of an allegedly "better" route must have caused considerable consternation, and debate must have continued during their rest at the Truckee. Should they take a known but difficult path or gamble on an unknown but perhaps better trail? The Donner experience could have influenced some, making them reluctant to risk their families on a new, unverified route. Some might have argued that the Donner party had foolishly swallowed the untried promises of a charlatan in following Lansford Hastings' "nigher route." Others might have argued that news of this trail had come from over fifty men whose hale and hearty physical condition was evidence of their success. If there was still doubt, then why not follow the Mormons' fresh wheel and hoof marks to see if they corresponded to their waybill.

In the end, the Cornwall party decided to try the Mormons' new way. We know this partly because of Cornwall's biography:

> Having crossed this [Forty Mile Desert], my father [P. B. Cornwall], fearing the snows in the high mountains in the vicinity of Truckee Pass, decided, without precedent, to take a more southerly route and therefore led the party down to Carson Pass. In the Carson Cañon, progress was very slow, and some days, cutting a way through virgin forests and skirting precipices, not more than half a mile would be covered. The men had often to take the wagons apart and they themselves pack both wagons and supplies up the steep slopes. In this manner they persistently toiled on, climbing ridge after ridge, hoping each would be the last. . . . The descent was easy.[62]

The Cornwall biography's failure to attribute the new way to the Mormons is odd, and its suggestion that it was P. B. who unilaterally decided that the company would travel the new Mormon road does not seem credible. Keeping in mind that the biography was written forty-eight years later by P. B.'s adoring son, it is doubtful that P. B. made the decision by himself. It seems certain that other members of the company were very much involved.

Like Cornwall, Hazen Kimball declared in his December 7, 1848, letter that the company with whom he was traveling came over the new Mormon road.

> We had very good luck— came over the Sierra Nevada by a new route, one the Mormons opened this fall on their way in to the Salt Lake. The road is very good— much better than the old one, it is said by those who have traveled both.[63]

There was a second Mormon wagon company heading east, this one led by Ebenezer Brown. This group of over sixty men, women, and children left Pleasant Valley on August 12, five weeks after the Thompson party. One of its members, John Borrowman, noted in his journal on August 27 that they were making their way through the West Carson Canyon. He described it as

> the worst I ever saw being over larg rocks and down hill so that it wrenched the waggons in a way one would think that something must break yet all passed through without injury . . . we camped tonight by a small river where there is very

little feed for the animals this evening we met a company of emigrants from the states consisting I believe of 19 waggons they told us that we would have 3 miles very bad road and then we would get into the plains and have good roads.[64]

Borrowman's report of passing this party of nineteen wagons in the canyon on August 27 is extremely significant. It was his only report of a California-bound company during this period. He did not report encountering any westbound wagon parties before the twenty-seventh or during the next few weeks. His count of nineteen wagons closely matched the Thompson company's accounts that the first party had eighteen wagons at the Sink on August 15. The Thompson company took eleven days to travel from the mouth of the Carson Canyon to the Humboldt Sink (August 4 to 15). Based on Borrowman's sighting, it also took Cornwall's company eleven days to travel the same distance (August 16 to 27). Moreover, it took Borrowman's Brown company twelve days to make it from the mouth of the canyon to the Sink (August 22 to September 8). All of this evidence leads to the conclusion that it was the Cornwall company that Borrowman met in the Carson Canyon. And with Hazen Kimball being identified as traveling in the front company of eighteen wagons, it is certain that it was Cornwall's party the Thompson company encountered on August 15.

This brings up the next important question: Did Caleb Greenwood remain with the Cornwall company? Caleb and his sons were extraordinarily familiar with the Truckee Route, having traveled it many times, and in the absence of evidence to the contrary, it seems likely that Caleb continued traveling with the Cornwall company. P. B. may have been impetuous and audacious, but it is difficult to imagine him wanting to lead a wagon party over an unfamiliar mountain trail without a guide of Caleb's experience, and other members of Cornwall's party probably felt the same way. Caleb was a professional guide, earning his living by leading people through unfamiliar country. It might not have been difficult to convince Caleb to take the Mormon road. He knew of the difficulty of the Truckee Route as well as anyone, and many of these Mormons had tried the Truckee road the year before and learned how difficult it was. Hazen Kimball had been talking to his Mormon brethren at the Sink on the fifteenth, and was probably referring to them in his December 1848 letter when he wrote: "The road is very good—much better than the old one, it is said by those who have traveled both." Thus, having a basis for comparing, the Mormons' assurances that their new road was better might have been enough to convince Caleb.

Kimball's letter went on to report that "I arrived at the mines on the 3d day of September—on the American fork of the Sacramento."[65] Cornwall's biography recounted where he encountered his first gold miners. "At Mormon Island on the American River . . . the first miners were encountered panning in the stream. My father [P. B.] took one of his tins and did his first mining."[66] As for Caleb, a couple of gold miners wrote in April 1849 that the Greenwood family was living at Sutter's sawmill at Coloma, on the south fork of the American River.[67] Significantly, Coloma was less than ten easy miles from the beginning of the Mormon road, while it was more than forty difficult miles from the Truckee/Donner route.

Having wrung all of the juice out of the available evidence, it seems certain that the Cornwall company, including Kimball, Cornwall, and the Greenwoods, traveled over the new Carson road, and from there hastened to the nearest diggings along the American River. The Cornwall company had completed their odyssey and in doing so, earned the distinction of being the first westbound emigrant company to reach the California goldfields in 1848 and the first to enter via this new road. It is estimated that between 25,000 and 45,000 gold rushers entered California in 1849 by traveling the Carson road, a road that would supplant the Truckee-Donner route, and would remain the principal route into California for years to come. There should be no doubt that the emigrants benefited greatly from the Mormons' pioneering spirit, their valuable route, and their important road improvements.

Not everyone elected to remain with the Cornwall company. There were two—and maybe more—who left the wagon company and chose to take the Truckee-Donner route. Thomas Corcoran was one of them, and he explained the situation in his letter to his sister:

> When we came to the Truckee River, we heard of the discovery of gold in California. I left the wagon train with a man named Greenwood. I gave him one of my horses and he rode the other and we started for the gold diggings. The first night, we stopped in the Sierra Nevada Mountains at Donner Camp. It was here that about half of the emigrants died of starvation during the winter of 1846–47. The next morning, Greenwood showed me six or seven of the skulls lying around. That night, he told me the most horrible story about the starving party. He was sent by Captain Sutter to pilot relief parties to the suffers [sufferers]. He showed me where three of his toes had been frozen off. The first time, they took all of those who were able to travel as well as the young folks and children. They left several of them behind and when they came back again, Mrs. [George] Donner was dead. There was a family with them all that winter who came out on the same ship from Ireland [with the Corcoran family in the 1820s]. . . . I think that they were distant relatives of father's. Their name is Breen. None of that family starved and they came safe to California.

The Greenwood named by Thomas was not Caleb, but rather Britton, Caleb's twenty-year-old son. This is known because Britton had served as the pilot for both the second and fourth Donner relief parties sent by Sutter. As tough as he was, Caleb was too old to endure traveling through the deep snow at the higher elevations, so he and his nine-year-old son, William, had stayed with the horses at a snowline camp. Britton, however, led the other members of the relief parties on snowshoes the rest of the way. During the first of these two trips, Britton suffered severe frostbite, causing him to lose a number of toes, just as Thomas described. In 1888, Britton's daughter recalled her father's exploits, explaining that Britton was asked by Mrs. Graves, one of the women in the Donner party, to accompany her to a place near the stricken camp where she could hide her money. She died soon thereafter, but, according to Britton's daughter, he did not want to be branded a thief, so he never went back to the spot where the money was buried, even though "he could go back to Donner lake rat where he buried that money   its still there."[68]

The original Truckee River route coursed between twenty-five miles of steep, narrow canyons, over and around large boulders, and crossed the stone-filled river as many as twenty-seven times. A few years earlier, the Greenwoods had pioneered a route that circumvented much of this wicked canyon, and Britton undoubtedly took Thomas this easier way.[69] They would have left the Truckee River near present-day Verdi, California, and ascended Dog Creek, then, near the head of Dog Creek Valley, passed over a ridge and descended to the Little Truckee River. Following it for a few miles, they would have then cut over to Prosser Creek (initially named John's Creek, after John Greenwood, its discoverer), and followed the creek to where it flowed into the Truckee River in the Marti Valley. From there it was an easy eight-mile journey across a long meadow to Donner Camp at the foot of Donner Lake. By taking this route, they would have bypassed the worst twenty miles of the Truckee Canyon.

Thomas was still riding his mare, Slipper. The horse he gave Britton might have been his Indian pony, the one he had bought sometime before reaching Soda Springs "to carry my clothes and other things." It is unclear whether Thomas merely loaned the pony or gave it to Britton as compensation for guiding him over the mountains. Thomas also failed to explain whether any other persons accompanied the two of them, or why they chose to take the Donner route rather than remain with the main wagon company. Perhaps they had learned from the Mormons that gold had recently been discovered on the Bear or Yuba Rivers and Britton might have felt that on horseback the Truckee trail would be the quickest way to get there. It is interesting that Thomas claimed a possible relationship to the controversial Breen family. Mr. Breen had earned a place in infamy when he ensured his family's survival by refusing to share provisions with less well-off members of the starving Donner party.

Spurred on by thoughts of riches in the goldfields, and perhaps by the prospect of seeing Ellen Murphy, Thomas eagerly departed the Donner camp with Britton:

> We left Donner Camp next morning about six o'clock and traveled till noon. We were descending a steep hollow with the expectation of finding some water where we could eat lunch. It was all covered with thick timber. When we got into the valley, there were about 500 Indians before us. We unstrapped our rifles and cocked them but as soon as the Indians saw us, they ran away like wild deer excepting some old ones that did not get away until we came right on them. They offered us some roasted grasshoppers and we gave them two biscuits. We rode along leisurely, keeping our eye on them till we got out of sight. Then we galloped as fast as our horses could go. We traveled 'til 11 o'clock that night. We then turned off the

trail so that the Indians could not track us. After we had gone about a quarter of a mile, we came to a halt, took off our saddles and staked our horses out to graze. When we lay down to sleep, we were so tired that we slept until sun-rise. When we looked around, we found that we were on the summit of the Sierra Nevada Mountains. We saw a beautiful little lake called Lake Bigler. We saddled our horses and went back to the trail where we found fresh Indian tracks. We saw no more Indians till we arrived at the gold diggings. Next evening about sunset we came to a camp of white men from California who were going to meet their releatives we had left behind us in the wagon train. It was lucky for us as we only had four biscuits left. When we come to thank them, one of them was Hunsucker [Nicholas Hunsaker] that lived in Nishnabatona [Nishnabatna], Atchison County, Missouri. They were the first to show us gold dust. Next day we arrived at Johnson's Ranch on the Bear River. I bought a hundred weight of flour for $16, some dried beef, a pick, a shovel and a tin pan. We then had to go 16 miles to the Yuba River.

Since it is certain that the Cornwall/Greenwood company was the leading party, and because of the speed with which Thomas and Britton likely traveled on horseback once they left the wagon train, the two young men easily could have been the first men to cross the Sierras into California after the discovery of gold.

The encounter with Nicholas Hunsaker probably explains why Thomas headed to the Yuba goldfields as soon as he got himself outfitted at Johnson's Ranch. Nicholas, a former resident of the community of Nishnabotna, had lived a few miles from Thomas' home at Irish Grove, Missouri, and had traveled to California by wagon train the year before. While living in Benicia, Hunsaker and a few companions heard of gold in the Sierra foothills and traveled to the Yuba River, arriving there on June 6, 1848. They were the first to find gold there, but because they were only making fifty dollars per person per day, they moved on in disgust, thinking that there had to be richer places than this.[70] When Thomas encountered him, Hunsaker was going to meet his parents and brothers, who were traveling as members of the Wambaugh party.[71] One of them had been mentioned by Rufus Burrows back when the Wambaugh train approached the Platte River: "[O]n account of one sick man, Mr. Huntsucker, the train delayed for a while."[72]

August 16–September 8, 1848
Wambaugh/Clyman company, beside the Humboldt River, near its Sink

The Wambaugh/Clyman company had been traveling along the Humboldt River, a day behind the Cornwall/Greenwood party. According to Rufus Burrows' remembrance, a tragic incident took place during that time:

On our way—I think it was the Humboldt River, we had been following and had made our camp—a very sad accident happened. A man by the name of James

[Henry] Shields came to me and wanted to borrow my shotgun, which I told him he might have. He had seen some wild ducks on the river and as we had very little bacon with us, everyone had to get all the wild meat they could, saving the cattle to bring to California.

It was the custom to take the cattle out every evening to graze after we had made camp. This evening while the guards were watching, they saw two Piute Indians crawling through the grass. They surrounded the Indians, rushed in on them and took them captive. The guards kept them until they went to camp, giving them up to Captain Wambo. He said, "we will keep them until morning so they will not go back and inform the rest of the Indians."

In the morning, Shields came to me for the shotgun I had loaned him the evening before. He said, "I do not want any powder, but will take some shot." I gave him some shot and he started to his wagon for his bullet pouch. I went into our tent and was just sitting down to eat breakfast when we heard the report of a gun. We all rushed out of the tent to see Shields lying on his back, blood running from the center of his chin. There was also blood on the back of his head. When he went to his wagon after the bullet pouch and powder, he took hold of his loaded rifle to pull it to one side, and the hammer catching, fired the gun, killing him instantly.

Captain Wambo, knowing it was the custom of all these different tribes of Indians to dig up the graves of all whites that were buried, to get clothing or anything that was found, and having in mind an open grave that we had passed where the bones and hair of a woman, who had been buried the year before and dug up by these savages and left to bleach by the sun and winds, decided to circumvent the Indians in this case and let Shield's body rest in peace.

Captain Wambo took the remains of Shields in the tent, placing it in a box, not letting the two captive Indians know where it was. The body was then put in a wagon and hauled all day. The two Indians were turned loose and allowed to go to their village. When camping time came that evening, the wagons were corralled as usual, going round in a circle, but with this exception, Captain Wambo had carefully picked out a place covered with sod in the center of the circling wagon tracks, here a grave was dug and Shields buried. In the morning, when the train started it was driven several times around in a circle, passing over the grave. This was done to obliterate all signs and to keep the Indians from digging up the remains. Then we started on our way.[73]

Scotsman John McPherson was still traveling with Wambaugh, and he captured the Shields tragedy in a touching poem that was later published in the October 14, 1848, issue of the San Francisco newspaper, the *Californian*:

The following lines were written by Mr. John McPherson, on the death of a Mr. Henry Shields, to whom the writer was sincerely attached. They breathe the spirit of friendship, and he who can read them without a pensive feeling for the unfortunate Shields, cannot appreciate the value of an honorable and dignified intimacy with a man. They are adapted to the plaintive but beautiful air of the "Soldier's Dream." Mr. Shields had shot himself accidentally on Mary's River, and this accident threw a gloom over the company on their journey from the States, which may well be seen in the strain in which the writer indulges in his grief at the loss sustained. —*Ed. Cal*

Oh! sweet was the morning—the sky was serene,
Empurpl'd the mountains, that tower'd far and wide;
The calm river flowed like a youth's happy dream,
Reflecting the scene that we gaz'd on with pride.
We all by the camp-fire were seated, nor dreamed
That danger nor grief could allay our repose,
The jest, and the laugh, told the mirth that then reign'd
In hearts which were bright as the sun when he rose.
Oh! who could then tell of the grief that was nigh,
Those hearts that with pleasure so warmly then thrill'd,
Oh! who could then say, that dear woman's soft eye
So radient with mirth would with tears soon be fill'd.
Alas! ere the sun on his course long had ran
That pleasure and mirth were to sorrow resign'd,
In moments of bliss, oh! how thoughtless is man—
Ne'er dreams he the next may to death be consign'd.
The discharge of a gun now peal'd loud and clear,
Our pulse, as we turn'd whence the sound quick did beat—
Ah! me, 'twas the death knell that rang on the ear,
Of our friend, our companion, who lay at our feet!
Oh! sad was the scene, as we gaz'd on that form
Which a moment before exhulted in health,
Closed now those eyes, late as bright as the morn,
And the voice that we lov'd was for e'er hush'd in death.
With hearts full of sorrow, we made him a grave,
Where the Sun in declining his soft rays shall fling,
Near the bank of the stream, where green willows wave
To the breeze, as it sadly his requiem may sing.
There, gently they laid him in twilight of eve
While pensive we mused, as reclin'd on the sod,
And thought of the friends far away, how they'd grieve
O'er his fate, tho' now happy. His soul is with God![74]

Burrows and McPherson's writings are, in their own way, poignant requiems, but from a trail historian's viewpoint, both are disappointing. They fail to provide much in the way of historical facts other than confirming that they were traveling along the Humboldt with Captain Wambaugh when Henry Shields accidently shot himself.

After Shields' death, the Wambaugh company met the Mormons near the Humboldt Sink, and Burrows' reminiscence recounted the meeting:

> On the desert between the sink of Humboldt and Truckee rivers, we met a company of Mormons returning to Salt Lake. They told us of the discovery of gold by Marshall at Coloma, El Dorado County, on the American River, while building a mill race for Sutter.[75]

Burrows' recollection that they met the Mormons between the Sink and the Truckee was probably a misrecollection caused by the passage of time. According to the Mormon diarists, they met the second company of California emigrants at or north of the Sink. Burrows' suggestion of only meeting one party of Mormons was also probably a misrecollection. Like the Cornwall company, his group should have met the Mormon packers first, followed by meeting the Thompson wagon party the next day.

According to Henry Bigler, his Thompson company had departed their camp at the Humboldt Sink on the morning of August 16, likely after the Cornwall/Greenwood party had already disappeared into the Forty Mile Desert. Bigler reported,

> August 16. Made twenty miles. Road good. At this camp the water is a little better and runs a little. The stock looks bad, not having had much grass since leaving the Truckee. Today we met twenty-five wagons, emigrants for California.[76]

Mormon diarist Samuel Rogers noted the encounter as well, but only counted twenty-four wagons.[77] Azariah Smith wrote, "[16th] [T]oday we met another train of wagons, on the road to California."[78] Ephraim Green reported, "Wednesday, 16 we started this morning and met the rest of the emagration." Jonathon Holmes only noted, "Met another Company of Emigrants going to California."[79] Once again, these Mormon diarists failed to give us the names of any of the Wambaugh company leaders or members.

When the Wambaugh party heard the Mormons' startling revelations, one can only imagine James Clyman's reaction to the news of James Marshall's good fortune. He knew Marshall well, as both had traveled together from Oregon to California in 1845.[80] After taking leave of the Mormon expedition, the Wambaugh company would have made their difficult way across the Forty Mile Desert. Only a day behind Cornwall, they may have met Cornwall and his party recruiting at the Truckee River. If so, the two parties would have surely conferred regarding the startling news they had heard, and would have discussed their plans. Should they take the Truckee Route or the new Mormon road? We know what the Cornwall company decided, and it is similarly clear what the Wambaugh party decided. James Clyman's stance is predictable;

at Fort Laramie he had discouraged James Reed from taking Hasting's "nigher route," and encouraged him to stay on the "regular wagon track" through Fort Hall, even before he learned about what happened to the Donner party after it had gambled on Hastings' ill-advised path.[81] In light of this, Clyman's cautiousness suggests that he would have been against trying the Mormons' new way. Then we have Mormon John Borrowman in the Brown company reporting that they only passed one party, a group of nineteen wagons, along the Carson River. Rufus Burrows' reminiscence is additional evidence that the Wambaugh party took the Donner route:

> On the way we came to Donner Camp at the foot of the summit of the Sierra Nevada mountains. Two cabins had been built late in the fall of 1847 [1846] by this party. We laid over here one day in order to gather up and bury the bones and skeletons of the people that had perished in the winter before. We could see where they had cut off limbs of trees sixty feet high for fuel, this showing that the snow had been sixty feet deep, otherwise these limbs would never have been cut so high. . . . We passed over the mountains and soon arrived at the Sacramento Valley, near Bear Creek, where Wheatland now stands. From here we went to Sutter's Fort, arriving on September 10, 1848.[82]

In mentioning that his Wambaugh company gathered up and buried the bones at Donner Camp, Burrows seems to confirm that Britton Greenwood and Thomas Corcoran were traveling ahead of them. If these two were traveling behind them, it seems unlikely that the bones reburied by the Wambaugh party would have still been found strewn on the ground as Corcoran described them.

The Wambaugh/Clyman party probably followed the route that avoided the worst part of the Truckee Canyon. Both Clyman and Wambaugh were familiar with it. Clyman had traveled east with the Greenwoods in 1846, and had described this route in his journal, and Wambaugh had traveled east with the Greenwoods in the Stockton party in 1847. Confronted with the imposing eastern face of the mountain at the head of Donner Lake, the Wambaugh party had to scale it, wagons and all. This was the famed Truckee or Donner Pass. Prior wagon parties had learned that they had to unload the wagons and carry the cargo up the near-vertical rock face to the summit on packhorses, mules, and people's backs. The livestock, including the oxen, had to be led single-file, switching back and forth, over and around rocks, squeezing through tight fits and along narrow ledges to reach the top of the mountain. Great lengths of logging chains were joined, one end connected to the oxen at the top and the other to an empty wagon at the bottom. The oxen would be goaded into motion, and if all went well, the wagon would be lifted to the top. It was an exhausting and unimaginably dangerous process that had to be tediously repeated for each wagon.

Clyman wrote a letter to his friend, Fred Ross, from Napa Valley in December 1848, in which he wrote that he "arrived *here* on the 5th of September without accident or interruption of any kind worthy of notice." It is uncertain what he meant by "here." Another member of the Clyman party, John McPherson, claimed that he arrived in California on September 5 as well.[83]

Rufus Burrows reported that they arrived at Sutter's Fort on September 10. Perhaps they had paused to spend a few days in the goldfields before continuing on to the fort. Finally, a biographical sketch written about the David Parks family, also traveling with the Wambaugh company, declared that they arrived at the Yuba River goldfields on September 8.[84] From Cornwall, Kimball, Greenwood, Corcoran, Burrows, and Parks, it appears that those who traveled the Mormon/Carson road made their way to the diggings on the American River, while those who traveled the Truckee/Donner route scurried to the nearby goldfields on the Yuba.

When the Cornwall and Wambaugh companies arrived, the gold rush had just begun. Governor Mason had not bothered to make his first trip to see what the fuss in the hills was all about until August 17, 1848, only two weeks before our emigrants arrived. Someone in California wrote a letter from Monterey dated August 29, just days before our wagon companies had arrived, that described the frenzied state: "At present the people are running over the country and picking it [gold] out of the earth here and there, just as a thousand hogs, let loose in a forest, would root up ground nuts."[85]

The Cornwall and Wambaugh companies had safely arrived between September 3 and September 5. Remembering the refrain "Five months to get there," it can happily be reported that their journey took them only four months and a few days. With the exception of Henry Shields, there were no known fatalities in either party, perhaps the reason why James Clyman wrote to his friend in Milwaukee that they had arrived "without accident or interruption of any kind worthy of notice." It is unfortunate that Clyman chose to not keep a journal on this, his last overland trip. John McPherson did, but his journal is lost. Cornwall, Corcoran, and Burrows were able to shed some light on their journey, none of which revealed any serious mishaps besides Shields' death. Traveling overland by wagon train was never easy, but as far as is known, few wagon parties made it to their destination as smoothly, efficiently, and as free of significant hitches as the Wambaugh company had. Wambaugh deserves a share of the credit, but it seems likely that James Clyman was the stalwart guide, the steady hand at the wheel, the calm, unflappable voice, and a well of sage advice. It is clear from Bernard DeVoto's *The Year of Decision: 1846* that his admiration of Clyman was boundless. If there was one man to choose to follow across the West, Clyman would easily be this author's choice.

CHAPTER 17

The Heavenly Scent
of Oregon Pine
AUGUST 17–SEPTEMBER 1

AUGUST 17–31, 1848
Riley Root, Gates company, Grand Round Valley, Oregon

By August 17, the lead companies were deep into Oregon and entering the final stages of their grueling journey. On the morning of the seventeenth, the front-running Gates company left their camp on Ladd Creek, about eight miles southeast of today's La Grande, and made their way through Grand Round Valley, following a route that tracked southwest of present-day I-84. The valley was a beautiful sight, a flat, round basin covered with marshes and waist-high, gold-colored grass. Riley Root described the day's travel:

> 17th— 15 miles to camp, on Grand Round river. Eight miles across the head of the beautiful Grand Round valley, to a small branch, where emigrants might camp for the night, at the foot of the Blue mountains bordering the valley. From thence, we wound our way over the steep and rugged mountains, racking and straining our wagons, the distance of 7 miles farther, to the deep and lonely dell, where the Grand Round river is struggling and forcing its way through its narrow passage, down to the beautiful valley, Grand Round. . . . Where we are encamped, the dell is narrow, and furnishes but little grass. It is remarkable for loudness of sound, when a gun is fired.

Root did not mention it, but about halfway across Grand Round Valley a branch of the trail forked to the right, used by westbound travelers who were either going to or through Whitman's mission. Because of the Whitman murders in November 1847, this trail was effectively abandoned in 1848.[1]

Root explained that after crossing the southwestern part of the valley, they climbed over a section of low hills, then descended into a canyon through which the

351

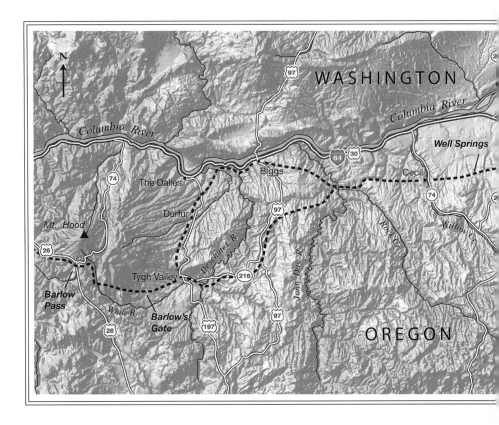

Grande Ronde River emerged from the Blue Mountains. The company stopped to camp on the river, probably at the mouth of Pelican Creek, about a half-mile east of the junction of Highway 244 and I-84.[2] Crossing the fifty-foot-wide river the next morning, the Gates company climbed into the Blue Mountains and followed the trail as it ascended a steep ridge just east of today's I-84. Women and children often collected huckleberries growing here and rewarded the men in the evening with freshly baked pies.[3]

The company found itself creaking through groves of tall pines and firs. After a thousand miles of depressingly endless sage, the sweet scent of evergreens must have been a soothing and welcome change. The usually taciturn Root described the new scenery:

> 18th— 10½ miles, over a very uneven district of volcanic rocks and mountain soils, to camp, on one of the highest peaks of the Blue mountains on our route. Country, to-day, becomes more densely timbered all around and along our road, overshadowing it in many places with yellow pine, fir and spruce hemlock. Have passd several deep cuts, to-day, so steep that teams were necessarily doubld to ascend out of them, and some of them were dangerous and difficult. Our camp

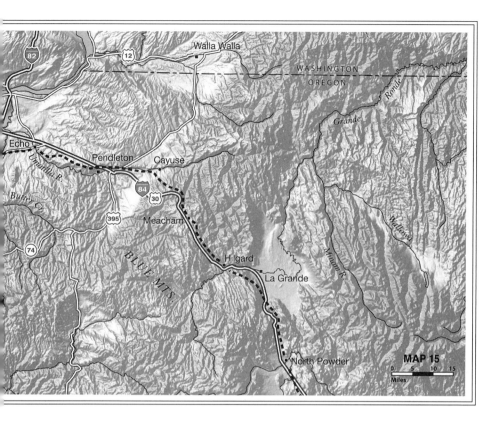

is located on the side of a high ridge, in a small opening, nearly one-fourth of a
mile above its base, where we are obligd to descend, to obtain water for cooking. From this high ridge, it is said, Mt. Hood can be seen, but at this time it is so
smoky, that we can see but a little distance.

They camped at the summit of today's I-84. Had the air been free of smoke, they
should have been able to see Mt. Hood's peak 150 miles away, and had they been told
that their destination was just beyond that distant peak, their mood should have been
elevated by the sight.

Emigrants often wrote about smoke coming from distant fires started by lightning or Indians. Root first mentioned this smoke on August 15, three days earlier,
while they were in the Powder River Valley. When James Clyman traveled through
here in 1844, he had registered the same complaint. For four successive days, he
had bemoaned the dense smoke, reporting that fires had been burning for a month.[4]
Many believed that the air in the west was clear and pristine, but clearly this was not
the case.

In entering the Blue Mountains, the Gates company had entered the southern
fringe of the Cayuse homeland. They were now behind enemy lines. They had been

warned that these murderous savages, undefeated and defiant, could appear at any time in these forested mountains. If Root was afraid, he would not have admitted it, but it seems certain that the travelers would have been in a state of heightened alert.

Root reported that they continued over the Blue Mountains on August 19, descending a "tolerably smooth" road for ten miles. They stopped to camp at "a small opening, a little larger than our carelle [corral, circled wagons], called Lee's encampment." It was located on today's I-84 at Meacham, and named for Jason and Daniel Lee, Baptist missionaries who camped there in 1834.[5] Root reported that his company was visited that evening by two men, likely from the Oregon militia, who assured them that they had nothing to fear from hostile Indians for the rest of their trip. Whether it was believable or not, Root wrote that it "gave great encouragement to the timorous emigrants."

On August 20, Root recorded that his Gates party traveled sixteen and a half miles, the first twelve of which continued through the Blue Mountains, "through a timberd district of pine, hemlock, and fir, loaded, many of them, with pendant moss." They toiled past Emigrants Springs, then through Deadman Pass, both along today's I-84. "On leaving the timber," Root continued, "we ascended a hill, a mile or more, to Mount Prospect [Emigrant Hill]." After pausing to admire the view of the Umatilla Valley below, they switchbacked their way down the treeless, grass-covered slope. At the bottom, they traveled another four and a half miles across dry, yellow grass to the Umatilla River. Today, the trail down Emigrant Hill can be followed on Old Emigrant Road off of I-84.

Descending the bluffs to the river bottom, the Gates company stopped to camp beside the river about two miles west of the present-day community of Cayuse. In those days, westbound travelers wanting to go to the Whitman mission or Fort Walla Walla could leave the main trail here by crossing the Umatilla and traveling north another forty miles.

The Gates company began the next day by traveling along the river bottom. "21st— Down Umatilla river, near to crossing, 10 miles," Root reported. "Country here entirely prairie, and very undulating." James Clyman had reported passing several "Kyuse" farms along the Umatilla in 1844.[6] Four years later, Root made no mention of them, a result of the Cayuse War.

The next day, Root reported that his Gates company crossed the Umatilla:

> 22d— Crossed the river, half a mile below camp, and passed about two miles on the flat. Ascended the bluff, and passd over the prairie about 14 miles, to the river, down the river two miles to camp, making in all 18 ½ miles. Prairie, to-day, uneven, and of poor soil.

They crossed the Umatilla just west of today's Pendleton, about where I-84 crosses the river, then left the river and took a cutoff across dry highlands, descending to the river along today's Reith Road. Traveling two miles down the river, they stopped and camped about five miles southeast of present Echo.

William Henry Jackson (1843–1942), *Blue Mountains*. Watercolor painting, 1930s. Courtesy of Scotts Bluff National Monument, SCBL-44.

According to Root, the company left their camp on August 23 and traveled along the eastern side of the Umatilla for five miles. Then they crossed it for the second time:

> 23rd— 14½ miles to camp, on Alder Creek [Butter Creek]. Five miles to second crossing of Umatilla, 8½ miles to Alder Creek, up the same one mile to camp. Little grass, no wood, but fine willows. In this day's travel, two miles might have been saved, by crossing the river at the camp, but to avoid sandy traveling, emigrants go down the river some farther. This is Whitman's cut-off.

The "second crossing" Root described was about four hundred feet south of today's Echo Bridge. After crossing the river, Root described his company heading west across an arid, treeless upland to a camp on Butter Creek. Today, their campsite can be reached by following the Oregon Trail Highway nine miles west out of Echo. "Whitman's cut-off" refers to the trail taken by those coming from the Willamette Valley and going to the Walla Walla Valley; they would cross the Umatilla River at today's Echo and head northeast.

Leaving camp on Butter Creek on the morning of August 24, Root described how his Gates party continued southwest across dry, rolling country. At noon, after traveling ten miles, they came to a sobering reminder of the Cayuse War—Sand

Hollow. It was here, just six months earlier, that the Oregon regiment of volunteers, over five hundred in number, had engaged a band of Cayuse.[7] Root reported:

> 24th— 18½ miles, over a poor tract of the Columbia River valley, to camp, at the foot of a hill, by a spring, calld Well spring, rising in the center of a large mound of decayd vegetation, and sinking suddenly again, within a few feet of where it issues. Noond, to-day, on the battle-ground of the 24th February, 1848, between Oregon soldiers and the Cayuse Indians. No grass nor water exists along this day's route, where emigrants might refresh themselves and their weary teams. Fire wood is obtained two miles east, in a hollow, where there are a few scattering cedars. The spring at camp should be watchd during the night by a strong guard, to keep thirsty cattle from falling into it, out of which they cannot extricate themselves.

The origin of the Cayuse War went back many years. Dr. Marcus Whitman, a Presbyterian missionary-physician, had been operating his mission among a band of Cayuse along the Walla Walla River since 1835, but tension and mutual distrust between the Americans and the Indians had been brewing for a number of years.[8] The Cayuse had heard rumors that the Americans were planning on eventually killing all of them and taking their lands, while the Americans feared that the allegiant tribes of the region—the Cayuse, Walla Wallas, Nez Percé, Des Chutes, The Dalles, Yakimas, Palouse, etc.—would someday rise up together and mount a full-scale attack on all whites living in Oregon.

As the years progressed, the Cayuse's mood grew darker and more menacing, causing Dr. Whitman to become apprehensive. In fact, he expressed his intention of abandoning his mission, but he waited too long. In November 1847, a measles epidemic, introduced by a passing wagon train, was raging through the Cayuse tribe. Dr. Whitman worked tirelessly to save the sick, but they continued to die and the Indians became convinced that the medicine Whitman was giving to his patients was meant to poison them.[9] Thus, the match was struck that began the war.

On November 29, 1847, Indians attacked the mission and murdered the Whitmans and thirteen other whites. Word of the tragedy reached the residents of the Willamette Valley on December 8, and a regiment of more than five hundred Oregon volunteers was assembled over the next month.[10] Led by Colonel Cornelius Gilliam, the militia left the Willamette Valley and headed east to see what remained of the Whitman mission, intending to confront the out-of-control Cayuse and seize the killers. Joe Meek and his small party was appointed to carry word of the slaughter to Washington, DC.

On February 24th, the militia came across a large band of about five hundred mounted Cayuse warriors at Sand Hollow and a lengthy battle ensued that resulted in five wounded and eight killed among the Cayuse, and five wounded and none killed of the militia. Surprised at the whites' willingness to fight, the Cayuse retreated. The

Oregonians then continued on to Fort Walla Walla, where Col. Gilliam met with some of the Cayuse chiefs and informed them that his regiment had not come to wage war with their nation, but had come to take custody of the murderers and recover all the property, mostly cattle, the Cayuse had stolen from the mission. Despite initial promises of cooperation, the chiefs did not produce the killers. Gilliam's troops searched for the fugitives, but were never able to find or corner them. They remained at large, probably kept hidden by the tribe and out of reach of the overstretched American force. The Cayuse living along the Walla Walla and Umatilla rivers fled, scurrying to hide in the innumerable valleys and canyons of the mountains.[11]

To find the Sand Hollow battleground today, return to Highway 207 from the Butter Creek campground and follow it southwest for about seventeen miles. Turn onto Bombing Range Road and take it north seven miles, then turn east and travel three miles on Lindsay Feedlot Road, which will come to an unmarked place believed to be the site of the battle.

After stopping at the battleground, Riley Root and his Gates company traveled eight miles to Well Springs, where they camped. To visit Well Springs today, return to Bombing Range Road and travel south four and one-half miles. Turn west onto Little Juniper Lane and proceed west five miles, then travel north on Wells Springs Road two and one-half miles, then turn west onto Immigrant Lane. Well Springs is about a half-mile west on, and two hundred feet south of, Immigrant Lane. But be warned— today Well Springs is a disappointment, just a dry depression in the ground.

The next morning, August 25, Root wrote that the Gates company left Well Springs and followed the trail west thirteen miles "over a miserably poor and uneven country" to Willow Creek. Root called it "Quesnell's creek." He then reported traveling "[d]own the creek one mile, in order to obtain water, where camp is located." Immigrant Lane follows the approximate route of the trail, and wagon wheel ruts are occasionally visible today just north of the road for the next thirteen miles. The Gates company's camp on the evening of the twenty-fifth was along the creek at Cecil, on Highway 74. Root reported that they "[s]taid at camp" on August 26 to rest for a day.

August 27 would be a long day. According to Root, they left Willow Creek and headed west over bleak, treeless country:

> 27th— Returnd up the creek to the crossing, though on the west side of the flat. From the east side of the flat, to-day's reckoning commences, and crosses over to Beaver fork [Rock Creek] of John Day's river, a distance of 20½ miles. No camp can be had between the two places, though a small spring [Cedar Springs] exists, two miles east of camp. Most of the way to-day, the road has been good, through a long, level valley.

Much of the first half of the day's travels crossed through country that is presently roadless and therefore inaccessible. The last half of the day's travel, however, can be followed by taking Cedar Springs Road off of Highway 19, then traveling west for about nine miles to Rock Creek, where the Gates company stopped to camp on the evening of August 27. The spring mentioned is on the same road, but is encountered about two miles before reaching Rock Creek. While William Anderson reported that his Miller company managed to overtake the Gates party by the end of the day, and would camp near them on Rock Creek, Root did not record the event.

Root described the next day as one in which they made only seven miles, but they were difficult miles. Root explained: "28th— 7 miles to crossing of John Day's river. Way down Beaver fork [Rock Creek], very rocky, and road crosses it 4 times." Surrounded by bare hills, the trail led down a canyon through which Rock Creek snaked until they came to the John Day River. They stopped at the river to camp for the night. Today, the crossing of the wide but shallow John Day River is remote, accessible by proceeding west on Lower Rock Creek Lane.

Root's entry for the next day contained an unexpected twist:

29th— Down John Day's river, half a mile. Then ascended the bluff, about one mile, up a narrow, winding, rocky ravine, the worst we had ever traveld. On the top of this bluff, the road divides, one leading to the Columbia river. The other, at the left, is the one we took. From the top of this bluff, the road, the remainder of the day, was smooth to camp, at a lone spring among the bluffs. Distance to-day, about fifteen miles. Grass enough for a small band. No wood. About two miles east, up a ravine a short distance to the left, there are two small springs, where a small party might camp for the night. No wood.

Root was describing a fork in the trail that they encountered shortly after climbing a ravine through the bluff on the west side of the river. The right fork had been the usual road taken by emigrants for many years, and that trail headed northwesterly toward the Columbia River. The left fork, however, the one taken by Root's company, is rarely reported by trail historians, and is not found on most maps showing the route of the Oregon Trail, even with its variations. A few sources mention a cutoff, a shorter route to the Barlow Road, but they suggest that this route was not pioneered until 1864.[12] Yet Root is very clear that they took a southern branch and confirms that such a cutoff existed as early as 1848. It may have been pioneered the year before, as it headed toward the Barlow Road, which was opened in 1846. It would be interesting to know who in the Gates party was aware of this branch of the trail.

On the morning of August 30, Root and his Gates company continued along this southern branch. It was a hard, long day of travel:

30th— 25 miles to camp, on the western declivity of the dividing ridge, between John Day's and Deshutes river, at the upper end of a ravine, where was a little grass, but no wood, and no water for cattle. We staid through the night, without supper, and left next morning without breakfast.

The next day, they only had to travel a short distance to reach the Deschutes River:

> 31st— Traveld about 5 miles, to the crossing of Deshutes or Fall river. Here, we breakfasted in a deep chasm, almost as difficult of descent and ascent, as the valley of Sinbad the sailor, with nearly precipitous rocks, from 1000 to 1500 feet high, on every side. Afternoon employd in calking wagonboxes, to ferry our goods across the river.

This southern branch taken by Root's company probably traveled just north of Grass Valley Canyon, then south along a route generally corresponding to today's Highway 97. The route would then have headed westerly at Highway 216, generally following the course of today's highway west until it came to the Deschutes River at today's Sherars Bridge.

Coming to the end of August, Riley Root and his Gates company were in this deep canyon, preparing to ford the treacherous, swift Deschutes River. The good news is that they only had about one hundred miles to go to reach the end of their journey.

August 17–31, 1848

William Anderson, Miller company, Powder River Valley, Oregon

On August 16, William Anderson and his Miller company were encamped at Baldock Slough in the middle of the Powder River Valley. Their camp was about one and one-half miles east of today's exit 298 off I-84. They were about twenty-six miles and two days behind the Gates company.

The next day, Anderson reported that they continued traveling northwest through the valley:

> August the 17th we traveled 14 miles   10 miles further brought us to the crossing of the east fork of powder river   4 miles further took us to the middle fork of powder river   here is a good camp   we camped early on account of a verry sick child in company so the company behind us called Jacksons company passed us shouting and waveing ther hats saying they would go on and lay claims for us by the time we got through   this did not set verry well on the stomachs of some of us especially our captain so we determined to pass them agen.

The Miller company camp ended the day on the middle fork of the Powder River, at the present town of North Powder, where the fork crosses under I-84. The desperately sick child must have cast a dark pall over the camp, yet their pride was offended when the Jackson company passed them, hooting and hollering. It had been assumed that the Jackson company was traveling just behind the Miller party, and this entry confirms it. Keturah Belknap had recorded how the three Jacksons—George and his two brothers—had originally joined the Watt company at St. Joseph, the same time that Keturah and her family had joined. And when the Watt company celebrated the Fourth of July after crossing the Green River, Keturah had reported that "[t]he Jacksons are doing their best to entertain the crowd; there are three of them," adding that "Watts and the sheep pulled out and fell behind," allegedly because of her.

Given their frosty relationship with the Watt family, it seems certain that the Belknaps remained with the Jacksons. When Keturah's party was near Fort Boise on August 10, she had given birth to a son, Lorenzo Walker Belknap, who would have been only seven days old when the Jackson company passed Anderson's group here on the seventeenth.[13]

Anderson went on to describe the next day:

August the 18th Mr. Bullocks child that was sick died last night and was buried and we started an drove the whole train over its grave and traveled 24 miles   1 mile brought us to the west fork of powder river   9 miles further brought us to a spring branch where there was a good camp   here is a range of mountains on the left covered with pine timber a nother with wright destitute of timber and covered with drie bunch grass   from this place we ascended a mountain and traveled 7 miles then down a verry steep sidelong hill [Ladd Canyon Hill] 1 mile to grand round valley   we crossed a small branch and traveled 6 or 7 miles passing Jacksons Company camped at a big spring   we camped at 9 or 10 o clock at night on a small branch at the foot of the blue mountains   here two Indians camped with us   they had a pass or reckemendation from fort wala wala to show that they were friendly Indians.

Perhaps needing an outlet for their grief over the death of the child, the Miller company marched ahead all day, and when the Jackson company stopped to camp for the night in the Grande Ronde Valley, the Miller company pressed on, continuing through the darkness until they passed them.

Based on Anderson's description, his Miller company may have finally stopped late at night on Mill Creek to camp, just west of the present town of La Grande. Having fulfilled their vow to regain their position ahead of the Jackson company, Anderson reported that they returned to their rightful place on the morning of the nineteenth:

August the 19th we ascended a high mountain leaving Jacksons Company behind   we traveled 8 miles over high roling mountains through pine groves and falen timber to grand round river   here the river passes through a deep narrow heavy timbered canyon   here we saw several cyse Indians   they showed no sines of hostility one of our [men] bought a pony of one of them for which he gave a [illegible] but the Indian soon became dissatisfied and wanted to rue   so to keep the peace the man rued back agan and we drove to the top of the mountain and camped   to fire off a gun in this canyon it will roar tremendous along the mountains from one to the other and every time it strikes it seems to make a new report then back to the other and a nother report and so on until it at length dies away in the distance.

By Anderson's account, his Miller company probably crossed the Grande Ronde River and camped in the canyon beyond the present-day settlement of Hilgard. Anderson noticed the same thing Root had—that firing a gun in this canyon would produce a splendid echo.

Anderson identified the Indians encountered as the feared Cayuse, but expressed relief that they did not appear hostile. His comment that one of the emigrants purchased a pony from one of the Cayuse, but had to adjust the bargain "to keep the peace" brings up a significant point. For a number of years, the Indians in the region had been testing the emigrants. The Walla Walla and Cayuse tribes regarded the Americans as "women" because the emigrants tended to react meekly when the Indians confronted them.[14] What they had failed to consider was that the travelers, weary from their trip and burdened with families and livestock, might have been practicing restraint in order to not put their women and children at risk. The Indians' belief that the whites would not fight was one of the reasons why the Cayuse were emboldened to challenge them in 1848. The Indians' portrayal of the emigrants was regrettable; they could not have realized that this insult would serve as a rallying cry in recruiting volunteers to respond to the Whitman massacre. A circular distributed throughout the Willamette Valley in December 1947 read:

> They call us "women," destitute of the hearts and courage of men, and if we allow this wholesale murder to pass by, as former aggressions, who can tell how long either life or property will be secure in any part of the country, or at what moment the Willamette will be the scene of blood and carnage?[15]

On January 29,1848, Governor Abernathy of the Oregon Provisional Government penned a letter to Col. Gilliam, commander of the volunteers, in which he wrote "let them [the Cayuse] know that the Americans are not women." After the militia's first two battles with the Cayuse resulted in routs, Governor Abernathy wrote a congratulatory letter to Gilliam with these words: "The Indians have learned by this time that the Americans are not women."[16]

The Miller company entered the Blue Mountains on August 20, and Anderson described this picturesque portion of the trail:

> August the 20th we traveled 10 miles over the roughest road we have yet traveled   our road was verry mountainous and rocky and verry heavy timbered with pine and fur   the road wound around amongst the standing and falen timber which made it difficult driving   we camped on the side of a mountain and had to carry watter near half a mile from a small branch down of the side of the mountain.

It is obvious that the Miller company camped at the same "high ridge" on the summit on I-84 that Root had described on the eighteenth, two days earlier.

The Miller company continued through the mountains on August 21. Anderson described the day: "August the 21st we traveled 9 miles   our road to day wound its coarse along the side of the mountain which was verry sidelong and rocky occasionly passing through a small plains then through thick groves of pine fur and hemlock." After a total of nine miles, the company came to Lee's Encampment, where the Root party had spent the night on the nineteenth. Anderson reported that

> we camped on a small branch at a place caled lees encampment   to day we
> were met by some of the Oregon soldiers who told us there was not much dan-
> ger of the Indians as they had all the hostile ones run back into the mountains.

The soldiers Anderson mentions might have been the same ones Root had mentioned meeting near here.

Anderson described another long day of travel on the twenty-second, during which they finally emerged from the mountains:

> August the 22nd we travled 20 miles   10 miles brought us to the river umatila
> our road to day was verry good there was one hill that we came down about 4
> miles long [Emigrant Hill]   it was pretty steep in places   we traveled 4 miles
> down this river and camped   here is the ruins of a cyuse villedge   they have
> had a pretty smart farm here once the fences of which wer gone down   there
> was some stalks of wheat a growing about in places   we saw several large
> bands of Indian horses   they were verry wild   her we met a party of Oregon
> soldiers   they were a party from whitmens station a scouting about through
> the country in search of the murderes of whitmen and family.

Anderson's report of the Cayuse village is very different from that of James Clyman, who, when he passed through here in October 1844, reported the Cayuse growing "Potatoes Corn Peas & Squashes," and tending to their "horses of which they have great Quantities."[17] Anderson's accounts of meeting Oregon militiamen were sobering reminders that the Cayuse War was still in progress.

The Miller company traveled twelve miles along the Umatilla River bottom on August 23, on a "verry dusty" trail according to Anderson. Some from the scouting party camped with them that night on the river, where they "had a great dance at night." Anderson went on to mention that "2 or 3 of our company whose teams were verry weak concluded to go to the fort [Walla Walla] with the soldiers and recrute up a little before crossing the cascade mountains." The site of the Miller camp on the evening of August 23 was likely just west of today's Pendleton, near where I-84 crosses the river.

The next morning, Anderson explained that the "verry weak" teams headed north to Walla Walla, while the rest of his company left the river and headed west across a cutoff:

> August the 24th the party that went to the fort struck across the plains north to
> whitmans station and we left the river and traveled 18 miles   10 miles traveled

took us across a plain to the river bottom agan here we pased a spring [Corral Springs] on the wright of the road that is said to be poison watter   we traveled 2 miles further down the river and came to the crossing here   there are two roads one keeps down the river to the wright the other caled whitmens cut off turns to the left and crosses the river   here our company split up on account of the scarcity of grass so 9 waggons camped here at the crossing of the river   the rest of us let our cattle graze awhile and then put in some watter and crossed over and drove 6 miles and camped on the drie perarie without fire or watter with the exception of what little we had in our waggons and a few scattering bunches of dead grass was all that our cattle could get to eat.

The company circled their wagons and made a "dry" camp on the evening of the twenty-fourth at a site about four miles east of today's Highway 207, along Oregon Trail Road, and six miles west of Echo.

The Miller wagons returned to the trail the next morning. Anderson described their long day:

August the 25th we traveled 25 miles   6 miles brought us to alder branch [Butter Creek]   here we stoped and let our cattle graze and got some breakfast and here we divided our company agan making 3 companies out of one   we then traveled 10 miles across a dusty sandy plain to the well spring [Well Springs] which we reached about 10 o clock at night   these springs are verry deep our cattle being verry dry they rushed up to drink and some of them pitched in head foremost and went clear under head and ears and would have drowned if we had not helped them out   this is a poor camp   it was verry dry and dusty around these springs   our cattle rambled off some distance from camp and found some dry bunch grass   at these springs Col. Gilem was shot a few weeks before by the accidental discharge of a gun   he was an officer of the Cyuse war and was on his way to the valley with some of his men after provisions and camped here and was pulling the tent out at the front part of the waggon and it caught on one of the guns and it fired and shot him dead (as some of the soldiers told us).

Anderson did not explain why they divided the rest of the company into three parts. It would have seemed inadvisable in Cayuse country, but perhaps they had taken the militiamen's reassurances to heart. Anderson failed to mention the battleground at Sand Hollow, which they passed that morning, but he knew all about Colonel Gilliam's accident at Well Springs, something Root had failed to note.

Gilliam was a respected leader; he had led a large party of emigrants and eighty-four wagons to Oregon in 1844, and had been selected to lead the Oregon volunteers in the Cayuse War. He and his militia had secured the Walla Walla region in late March 1848, and he and a few men were returning to the Willamette Valley to report when he was killed. The emigrants would not have realized it, but the war east of the Cascade Mountains was part of a calculated strategy. After the Whitman massacre, the settlers of the Willamette Valley realized that their survival hung in the balance. The small number of settlers were widely scattered and understood how easily their Indian enemies could send raiding parties to pick them off at night, one by one.[18]

The Cayuse, Walla Walla, Nez Perce, Spokane, and Snake tribes, all allies, were on the verge of mustering two thousand warriors in 1845 to exact revenge on the whites because an Indian had been murdered.[19] Therefore, when news of the Whitman killings arrived in 1847, the settlers felt vulnerable and decided to send their young men east of the Cascades to keep the Cayuse in turmoil and engaged hundreds of miles away. "We must conquer the enemy in their own country or fight them in our midst," Col. Henry A. G. Lee of the volunteers proclaimed in April 1848. If the other tribes saw evidence of failure or weakness by the settlers, Lee warned, they would join the Cayuse and "we will have ten times their present number to contend with."[20] The Willamette settlers were also poor: their provisional government only had $43.72 in its treasury, and supplies and provisions were hard to come by. As the campaign progressed, the militia used up most of its percussion caps, powder, and lead, and they were desperately looking forward to the arrival of the emigrant wagon trains of 1848, hoping to buy surplus ammunition from the emigrants.[21]

The Miller company left Well Springs on the morning of August 26 and traveled thirteen miles over what Anderson called a "verry dusty" road" to Willow Creek, where they camped just west of today's Highway 74, at a place called Cecil. According to Anderson, they followed the trail west the next morning:

> August the 27th we traveled 21 miles to beaver creek [Rock Creek] and camped   after traveling 10 miles the road went down into a hole and pursued this down to beaver creek [Rock Creek]   here we over took the foremost company [Gates]   our road was verry dusty to day it being 8 inches deep in some places.

This section of the trail headed west from Cecil across remote country, then crossed today's Highway 19 at the Weatherford Monument, just below Shutler. It then continued west, along today's Cedar Springs Road, which leads to where they camped on Rock Creek.

The next day, the Miller company traveled seven miles along the twisty Rock Creek to the John Day River:

> August the 28th we traveled 8 miles   we pursued beaver creek [Rock Creek] down through a verry narrow canyon for 7 miles where it empties into John days river   we crossed this river and traveled one mile down it and camped   here the road turns to the left and goes up a steep hill in a narrow canyon   at the mouth of the canyon we were camped   the other company [Gates company] was camped a little above us on the river.

Anderson's company crossed the John Day River during the afternoon of the twenty-eighth, rattling across the smooth cobblestone-like rocks of its wide bottom before stopping to camp on the river's west side, a mile north of where they crossed at the mouth of Rock Creek. When Anderson explained that the Gates company "camped a little above us," he was indicating that his company had moved past them, probably where Gates was camped at the mouth of Rock Creek. Naturally, Root had ignored mentioning the presence of the Miller company.

Anderson described an incident the next morning that suggests a flaring up of rivalries:

> August the 29th the company above us [Gates] made an attempt to gain this narrow canyon before us so there was a general rush for this narrow canyon   we succeeded in getting our cattle up and yoked by daylight when we saw the other train coming on for the canyon   so we just moved in before them without any breakfast   so we traveled 24 miles and camped on the banks of the great Columbia river.

Although Anderson described a "rush" for the canyon by both companies, Root never so much as hinted at the incident. Despite the many miles they had traveled and the worn-down condition of both men and oxen, it seems as if their competitive juices gave them a resurgence of energy as they neared the end of their journey.

Anderson's entry disclosed that his Miller party did not take the left fork of the trail, as Root and the Gates company had. Rather, they took the right fork, the one that led to the Columbia River. Root did not rejoin his former travel mates in the Miller company when the two companies passed. One wonders whether he had no desire to rejoin them, or whether he was not welcome. Now that the two companies were taking separate roads to the same destination, it will be interesting to see which party made the better choice.

Anderson did not describe the landscape they crossed on August 29, but it was a bleak and gently rolling plateau, unremarkable in all respects. At the end of the day, the trail brought them to a ridge just west of today's Highway 97, a high overlook from which they got their first view of the great and mighty Columbia River. The next day, from their camp beside the river, the Miller company traveled along its south bank:

> August the 30th we traveled 4 miles when we came to the deshutes river at its junction with the columby   here were some Indians with three canoes in which for some old cloths they ferried our loads across and we forded with the teams and empty waggons   the watter was pretty swift and would be in shallow watter and wood pull the waggon out after them in this manner we all got across safe and loaded up and traveled 8 miles up over the bluffs and camped on a small branch [Fifteenmile Creek] some 5 or 6 miles east of the dals [The Dalles] of the Columbia river.

Anderson described the challenging Deschutes River near its mouth with the Columbia. Crossing it was no easy task, for the river was divided into a number of deep, swift channels, where several rapids produced a roaring sound that emigrants often described in their journals. They crossed just south of where I-84 crosses the river today. They likely camped on the evening of the thirtieth on Fifteenmile Creek, the "small Branch" mentioned by Anderson. It would be near where present Petersburg is situated along Fifteenmile Road.

On August 31, Anderson wrote that his company "traveled 10 miles and camped [on] the same branch leaving the dals [The Dalles] of the Columbia on our wright   to day there was one or two left our company for the dals intending to go from there down the Columbia by watter." It appears he meant that the main body of his company left Fifteenmile Creek and proceeded up a smaller branch called Eightmile Creek for ten miles, perhaps camping near where Eightmile Road branches off to the east of Highway 197.

Anderson also explained that the main body of the Miller company had decided to not take the Columbia River route, but rather would head south to take Barlow's Road over the Cascades. Nevertheless, he noted how some in their party would not accompany them over Barlow's Road, but were going to take the Columbia River route. An article appearing in the October 12, 1848, issue of the *Oregon Spectator* reported that eleven wagons had left the main body of the Miller company and gone to The Dalles to travel down the Columbia by raft.

Before the Barlow Road was pioneered in 1845/46, crossing the Cascades with wagons had been unthinkable. Emigrants would arrive at The Dalles, the site of a Hudson's Bay Company trading post and a Methodist mission, and would either pay dearly to hire boatmen to float their wagons down the dangerous Columbia or build their own rafts, which were often not riverworthy. As for their livestock, they drove them overland along a narrow Indian trail that hugged the Columbia's south bank.

AUGUST 17–SEPTEMBER 1, 1848
William Porter, Purvine company, on the Boise River, Idaho

In contrast to the Gates and Miller companies, which did not cross the Snake River at Three Island Crossing, William Porter and his Purvine company must have found the river fordable. He reported them crossing the river there on August 8 and proceeding along the northern branch of the trail. On August 16, they were camped beside the south side of the Boise River, west of today's Boise, about where today's Highway 55 crosses the river. Porter's diary continued to give us very little detail. Although he was a college-educated man who had the ability to write detailed accounts, his diary entries continued to be exceedingly succinct, probably because his tiny notebook provided little room in which to squeeze many words:

> 17th. Traveled 14 miles and crossed Boise River [near where I-84 crosses Boise River].
> 18th. Traveled 17 miles and camped on Boise River [about 1 mile west of Parma,

Idaho].

19th. Traveled 3 miles and crossed the Snake River [just west of Fort Boise].

20th. Traveled 18 miles to the Aux Matthew [Malheur] River [where Highway 26 crosses the river].

21st. Traveled 22 miles to Birch Creek [about 3 miles south of I-84's exit 353].

22nd. Traveled 8 miles to Burnt River [where Burnt River crosses Highway 30, at Huntington, Oregon].

23rd. Traveled 12 miles up Burnt River [along canyon on I-84].

24th. Traveled 13 miles and camped on a small branch near Burnt River [mouth of Sisely Creek on I-84].

25th. Traveled 14 miles [about 3 miles southeast of Durkee, on I-84].

26th. Traveled 22 miles to Powder River valley [likely one mile east of I-84's exit 298].

27th. Traveled 7 miles to first fork of Powder River [about three miles southeast of North Powder, on I-84].

28th. Traveled 14 miles to a small branch and the last branch of Powder River [on Clover Creek, near exit 278 on I-84].

29th. Traveled 14 miles and camped on the west side of Grand Round [likely near Mill Creek, two miles west of exit 265 on I-84].

30th. Traveled 8 miles to Grand Round River [at Hilgard, exit 252 on I-84].

31st. Traveled 14 miles and camped on hill [near exit 243 on I-84].

Sept. 1st, 1848. Traveled 12 miles to Lee's encampment [at Meachum, exit 238 on I-84].

The Purvine company had reached Lee's Encampment in the Blue Mountains on September 1, placing them thirteen days and 160 miles behind the Gates and Miller companies. Father Lempfrit's Stone company was ten days and 115 miles behind Purvine.

AUGUST 17–31, 1848

Father Lempfrit, Three Island Crossing on Snake River, Idaho

On August 16, Father Lempfrit had described himself as uncomfortably languishing on the Snake River at Three Island Crossing. The ever-impatient priest had arrived there by traveling across the waterless, twenty-five-mile cutoff from Upper Salmon Falls with a faster-moving contingent of twelve wagons from what is thought to be the Delaney company. He slept the night of the fifteenth with "strangers," as he termed them, and without his tent or blanket because the Stone company, including the O'Neil wagon in which his belongings were being carried, had been slow in arriving.

The priest's entry for August 17 indicates that the struggling Stone wagons had finally arrived, but he was angry at Mr. O'Neil, whom he had paid fifty dollars in St. Joseph to carry his trunks and other baggage in one of his two wagons:

17th August. Today I ran into trouble with my waggon conductor, O'Neil. This wretched man was absolutely determined to get rid of one of our waggons. He claimed that our agreement referred to only one waggon and that he had every right to dispose of the second waggon that carried some of our belongings as well as his own small chattels. We stacked up all our boxes into a single waggon. The waggon driver threw out all his things and then wanted me to get rid of all our things that were not really needed. Nothing from our big trunks could fit into the waggon that was already fully loaded. I offered up to eight piastres to any of our Americans who would be willing to transport our possessions to Walla Walla, however, I found no one willing to do this. Finally, and after much effort, we managed to find a place for the trunk in the waggon that was already as fully loaded as an egg. The waggon-train company was in dissent. Some wanted to cross the Snake River, the others wanted to push on further ahead. In the end, it was decided that the river, which had three arms [Three Island Crossing], should be crossed. The last arm of the river was widest and the most difficult to negotiate. Our waggon arrived very late. I had supper with the Captain [Captain Stone?].

Frayed nerves and short tempers. The Stone company, which had been struggling to catch up, had finally made it into camp after stumbling across that miserable stretch of desert. We have only Lempfrit's side of the story. Perhaps O'Neil had lost some of his oxen during the crossing or perhaps he had no choice but to jettison one wagon and some cargo because his animals were so weakened that he needed to double them up to pull one wagon. Beset with his own problems, O'Neil may have had enough of this independent priest who was so often not around to lend a helping hand. Now Father Lempfrit was bristling with anger and failing to acknowledge the sacrifices that were needed. His dispute with O'Neil could have been an eruption of a festering conflict, the details of which the priest had not previously shared, or it could have been nothing more than a sudden outburst, as might happen with even the best of men under such stressful circumstances. Notice how when Lempfrit offered to pay others to transport his baggage there were no takers; money loses its value when survival moves to the forefront.

After crossing the Snake on the seventeenth, Lempfrit reported that they camped on the north side of the river the next evening, probably where Three Island Crossing State Park stands today:

18th August. Our waggon-driver was late in arriving, he had to chase after one of his cows. He arrived eventually at 5:30 in the evening. I had a great many sick people to look after and was caring for them from morning to night. A young man had been bitten on the arm by a snake and his whole arm became poisoned. The wound developed gangrene and I was obliged to cut away the infected flesh. The operation was extremely dangerous but was marvelously successful. We were in a very agreeable place and had plenty of pasture and very good water.

His next entry covered the following two days, during which time he continued to care for the sick:

> 19th and 20th August. We were very sorry to have to leave this beautiful camp site. About sixteen miles further on we found a most vigorous mineral spring whose water was so hot that one could not bear one's hands in it for more than two or three seconds. I had no time to analyze it but believe it would prove really healthful for baths. That water must be most beneficial. The air in this place is very pure. I took advantage of these conditions to beg the Captain to allow us to remain here for a short time as my poor patients were sorely in need of rest.

Sixteen miles from their Three Island Crossing camp, the Stone company stopped to camp at these hot springs on the afternoon of the nineteenth. Today the hot springs are on Hot Springs Road, about three and a half miles southeast of Highway 20 (seven miles northeast of Mountain Home, Idaho).

After staying an extra day to tend to the sick, they resumed their travels on August 21. Lempfrit noted:

> There is a sudden change in temperature, consequently we did not stay here any longer. We left. We traveled seventeen miles and on the way came across numberless rocks that were quite grotesque in shape. One of them we saw, pro-truding from the barren earth, had the exact likeness of the bust of a woman wearing a nightcap on her head! I stopped for a few minutes to take a closer look at this oddity.

These "grotesque" rocks were likely somewhere along today's Immigrant Road, west of Highway 20, but it is difficult to be sure where they camped that night. Lempfrit's notion of miles were often inaccurate, and there are a number of small creeks along this stretch where they might have stopped.

Lempfrit's next entry covers both August 22 and 23. He reported "traveling along the banks of the [Boise] river. The escarpment was so precipitous that we could not get down to the river-bed and had to approach it by a long circuitous route in order to get a little water." His entry suggested that they reached the Boise River on the twenty-third, about two miles east of I-84's exit 57, in the general neighborhood of where Highway 21 crosses the river.

The Stone company continued making their way along the south bank of the Boise River on the morning of August 24, and the priest mocked his companions' reaction to warnings of possible Indian attack:

> 24th and 25th August. There was rich pasturage everywhere near the river and this was the cause of many of our cattle straying. It was midday before we could leave. We were visited by several Indians who came to trade some very fine horses with us, taking guns or blankets in exchange. For a very inferior gun one could acquire a very good horse. We obtained a large quantity of salmon for

ourselves. The caravan was on the verge of breaking up today—some wanted to carry on and others wished to remain where we were. A false alarm restored unity and harmony. An Indian warned us that we were running the risk of being attacked by the Indians who just left us and that the moment our company was reduced to only a small number we would be swooped down upon and robbed of everything. No people are more easily alarmed than the Americans. When they run into a dangerous situation they make common cause but as soon as the peril is past they are at one another's throats!

Lemprit had previously explained how his company consisted of thirty-two wagons after his Stone company was joined by what was probably the Delaney party. Because of a disparity in the condition of their oxen, those with the stronger teams may have been frustrated with being held back by those with weaker, slower animals, but it was the fear of Indians that quickly squashed the idea of breaking the train up.

The next day, sickness compelled the company to spend another day in camp:

26th August. We stayed in the same camp. That night I was called out at 2 o'clock in the morning to attend to a poor woman who was dangerously ill. I advised that her condition was such that she must have some rest. The Captain told the company that he was acting on my advice and that we would remain here. During the afternoon the poor woman gave birth to a dead baby. Fear and panic spread among the Americans. Throughout the night the guards were doubled and no one was allowed to light a fire. Apparently we were traveling in the midst of enemies who were coming to devour us like ogres!

Ever since meeting Joe Meek just west of St. Joseph, the members of the Stone company had dreaded the time when they would arrive in Oregon. They understood that they would have to pass through the land of the Cayuse before they reached the Willamette Valley. Although they were still east of the tribe's domain, they may have been informed that the Cayuse had alliances with the Nez Percé and Snakes, and Lempfrit's report of "fear and panic" among his companions likely reflected their uncertainty as to how far east the flames of war had spread. Apparently Lempfrit was unable to empathize with his fellow travelers, but he didn't have the safety of wives and children to consider.

27th August. We have not been able to celebrate the Holy Mass today [Sunday]. My patients are getting better. We left, happy to get away from this place safely as it had been feared that at least half of our caravan company would be massacred! We met two Indians who were bringing us back one of our horses that had strayed. Since it had been rumoured that the Indians had stolen it our people looked rather foolish. See how the poor Indians are maligned? Many Europeans and Americans are not as worthy as the poor Indians of whom they speak so much ill.

The priest seems to have viewed the Indians in a favorable light and free of reproach, an admirable, if not essential, quality for one intending to become an Indian missionary.

On the twenty-eighth, the company finally made it to Fort Boise:

> 28th August. As we were supposed to arrive at Fort Boise today we left really early in the morning in order to reach it. . . . This fort, like all the others, is built with sun-baked bricks. It still belongs to the Hudson's Bay Company. I must not omit to tell you about the generous hospitality that I received at Fort Boise. The Scottish Chief Clerk Mr. Gims Crayer [Jim Craig?] received me with the most dignified kindness and attention. This kind gentleman had only a small supply of sugar and coffee on hand, however he was kind and generous enough to make me a gift most lavish for this country. He sent me a supply of sugar, coffee and tobacco, also an enormous salmon. I met several Canadians and two Creoles in the fort. They informed us that the Indians in whose country we would shortly arrive were called the Cayuse, and that they liked the French very much. They called the French "Tabibo" and I was advised not to forget to tell them I was Tabibo should I be questioned about my nationality. Thereupon I started to sing "Oh, how proud one is to be French when, etc."

The next day, the priest penned a fascinating explication about how the local natives fished the Snake River near the fort:

> 29th August. Several Indians paid us a visit. They brought us a quantity of salmon and other fish. As we were crossing over the river I made a note of the way they caught salmon. . . . They dam the river and set up at intervals a series of stakes or posts in the form of a triangle. A net is fastened to the bottom of this triangular formation of stakes, and then a pole is set firmly in the net. A bunch of straw is tied to the top of the pole. As the water stirs the bottom of the net it agitates the pole and this in turn caused the bunch of straw to wave about, indicating that the net is full of fish. The Indians then go up to it and close the opening to the net. They pull the net out of the water and take out the fish trapped in it. After we had crossed the river we met some Canadian traders who begged us to come and baptize a child. The trail then started to deteriorate badly. We traveled through clouds of dust. Finally, we came to a mountain gorge at the bottom of which flowed the Malheur River. This is where we set up camp.

Lempfrit did not describe their crossing of the Snake River just west of the fort. Ordinarily quite deep and dangerous, the river may have dropped considerably this late in the summer. After crossing, the company left the tall cottonwoods and dense undergrowth along the river, and once again entered sage-covered country. They followed the trail up the gradually ascending Lytle Pass, then descended into the Malheur River Valley, encamping where the town of Vale sits today.

Lempfrit mentioned how bitterly cold it got on the night of August 29. He failed to describe how far they traveled on the thirtieth. On the thirty-first, he only wrote: "Nothing worth recording happened today." By the evening of the thirty-first, Father Lempfrit and his Stone company had probably made it to Birch Creek, not far from Farewell Bend on the Snake River. This put them about one hundred miles behind Porter's Purvine company and only 380 miles from Oregon City.

AUGUST 17–31, 1848
Richard May and Edward Smith, Chiles company, City of Rocks, Idaho

Camping among awe-inspiring geological formations illuminated by the glow of an almost-full moon, the Chiles company spent the evening of August 16 in the City of Rocks. Richard May and Edward Smith both composed glowing tributes to this wondrous place. As the last California-bound train, they were now on the home stretch, but still five hundred miles behind the Cornwall party, which was camping on the Truckee River near today's Fernley, Nevada, and the Wambaugh company, which was nearing the Humboldt Sink. If any company should have been concerned about being trapped in the snows of the high mountains, it was Chiles, but we have no evidence of anyone in his party registering concerns.

Leaving the City of Rocks on the morning of August 17, the Chiles company exited the southern end of the basin by squeezing through a narrow gap called Pinnacle Pass. As the trail departed this amphitheater of stone, it passed the Twin Sisters, two magnificent pillars of granite rising side by side beside the trail. Many emigrants, especially those making their way through here during the gold rush years, paused to engrave their names on some of these rocks, while thousands of wagon wheels wore deep grooves in the rocks over which the trail passed. The most pronounced evidence of such grooves can be seen in Pinnacle Pass.

Both May and Smith reported a long day on the seventeenth, during which they traveled twenty miles. Richard May wrote:

> Thursday, 17th Aug. Started early and traveled 20 miles over a very rough road. Several steep hills to go down. Had to lock 2 wheels 4 times during the day. We encamped on Goose Creek, which makes its way in [to] Lewis [Snake] River. . . . Major Hensley who left us at Independence Rock with the mule train overtook us today. He intended to pass to Fort Bridger and thence south to Salt Lake intending to follow [Hastings'] trail. He passed on without difficulty until he reached the southwestern portion of the Lake and traveled several miles upon an incrustation of salt and unfortunately for the Major and his train (10 in number) there fell a heavy rain which so weakened the encrustation that they were very near perishing in the mire. They were under the necessity of cutting loose the packs to save the animals, in this way they lost their provisions or nearly so with part of their clothing. They were 48 hours without food and water and hard at work

most of the time to save the property. They then retraced their steps to the Mormon City and there replenished their larder. They had been absent from us 36 days.

And Edward Smith wrote:

> Thur 17 we started at 8　our Road ran over hills and through deep valleys as Rough as natures architect could make it　about noon Capt. Hensley of the army with pack mules overtook us　they left us at Rock Independence went to the Salt Lake got lost and nearly starved　we encamped at 6 on goose creek　Distance about 20 miles　good camp　ice in Bucket.

Major Samuel Hensley and his pack train of mules had overtaken the Chiles company somewhere just beyond Pinnacle Pass. Hensley was lucky to be alive after his reckless attempt to cross the salt flats south of the Great Salt Lake. After he and his men struggled back to the new Mormon settlement, they headed west again. This time they pioneered a new route north of the Salt Lake that joined the California Trail just south of Pinnacle Pass. The new route became known as Hensley's Cutoff, and because it bypassed Fort Hall, it became popular during the gold rush years.

The Allsopp company was last mentioned when Isaac Pettijohn reported on forty-three wagons traveling west of South Pass on June 25. It is believed that this was a combination of wagons from Allsopp and from a faster moving coterie from the Adams company, and that most of these wagons remained a few days ahead of Wambaugh and continued on to Oregon. As for Allsopp and his horse-mounted bachelor friends, they traveled south to Fort Bridger and then on to Salt Lake. Allsopp wrote in his memoirs that a number in his stag party, "tired of their celibacy, joined the Brighamite gang, in the hopes of being much married," and added, "I hope they had as many Mormon girls as they could buy calico for. I never saw them again."[22]

Allsopp reported that he and five of his friends finally left the Mormons and continued on their journey west. They "took a SW course through the present State of Nevada, by Humboldt River, passed the Sink, then to Carson [Pass] and soon via Hangtown [Placerville] till we reached the village of Sacramento." He reported that they arrived in San Francisco on December 15, 1848.[23]

Because of the Paiutes, it would have been insane for this small party to travel alone, so they probably joined a larger group. Since Allsopp wrote that they crossed the Sierras by way of the Carson route, it is clear that they had not joined Wambaugh because his company used the Donner road. This leaves Cornwall, Chiles, or Hensley. Since Hensley spent time in Salt Lake, his would have been a possible group for Allsopp to join.

The combined Chiles and Hensley party left Pinnacle Pass behind and descended into a sage-covered basin and crossed Junction Creek, then ascended a ravine, which led them over a rough passage called Granite Pass. On the other side, they had to make a steep and twisting descent to Birch Creek. The descent, described

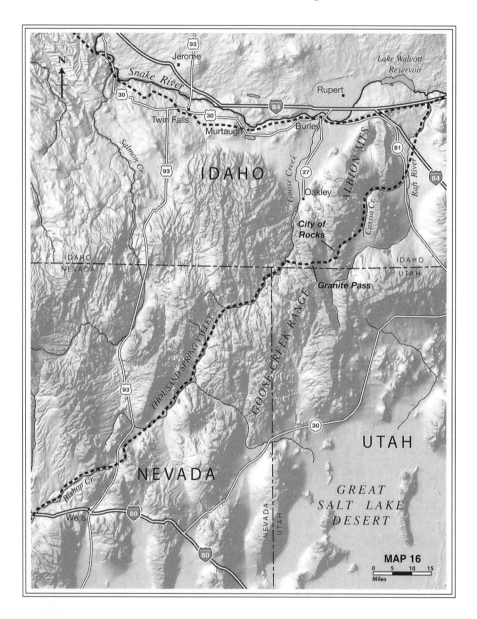

by many emigrants and gold rushers as the worst so far, compelled the men to lock their wheels with chains and use ropes to hold the wagons back as they eased them down a gravelly incline.

Following Birch Creek a few miles, they came to Goose Creek, a fifty-foot-wide, willow-lined stream. After an extremely arduous day, the party encamped on the creek's grassy bottomland, on today's Goose Creek Road, about one mile south of where Birch Creek enters Goose Creek, and about twenty miles south of present-day Oakley, Idaho.

Both May and Smith recorded traveling sixteen miles up the Goose Creek Valley on August 18. It was a pleasant day of travel, during which they rambled along a nearly smooth creek bottom with plenty of good water and grass. The surrounding hills were vegetated with sagebrush and scattered junipers. Near the end of the day, the company came to where Goose Creek snaked through a canyon walled in by sandstone cliffs. During the ensuing gold rush years, scores of men carved their names on some of these rock escarpments, the most prominent of which became known as Record Bluff. The place was not mentioned by our diarists, and it is difficult to reach, accessed only by a private ranch road. Just before stopping to camp at the end of the day, both men described passing a hot springs on the right side of the trail. It got cold that night, and Smith again reported "ice in Bucket."

May reported that they made eighteen miles on August 19, while Smith wrote that they traveled "over a very Rough Road" through Little Goose Creek Canyon. With the canyon walls pressing in, the emigrants were forced to cross the tiny creek several times, bouncing over large boulders in the bottom. During the gold rush years, diarists often noted scores of wagons strewn about, broken and abandoned because of the severe jolting suffered through here.

About five miles beyond the canyon, the company lumbered over a divide that separated the waters flowing to the Snake by way of Goose Creek, from those flowing to the Salt Lake by way of Rock Creek and Thousand Springs Creek. Beyond the divide, the trail meandered across a sage plain, between low, smoothly rounded hills. May observed that the sage "grows in abundance on our line of travel." Smith added that they "encamped for the night in a spring Branch   distance about 18 miles   Poor grass   Hard Frost." Judging by the distances recorded, it seems likely that they camped at Rock Springs, a very remote, bulrush-fringed pool located on Goose Creek Road, and about forty miles east of today's Highway 93 on County Route 765.

August 20 would be another long, punishing day of travel. Smith recorded that they had traveled twenty-two miles. Perhaps Joseph Chiles was finally feeling the need to pick up the pace. The company spent the day rolling through deep dust as they rattled through Thousand Springs Valley, a dreary expanse of stunted sage, bordered by even more barren hills. The trail took them past Emigrant Springs and Chicken Springs—not the best of water. They "traveled until 1/2 Past nine," Smith wrote, "and encamped at good grass and Bad water   the head of the spring is about one mile above called horse spring   hard frost."

Richard May described the twentieth:

Sunday 20th August. Traveled 20 miles, made a late start and encamped at 10 o'clock at night. All the camp were very much displeased at the unusual and unnecessary drive through the night. The dust being so very bad and with the darkness of the night made it dangerous in the extreme to the families who had to go in wagons. The present encampment is without wood and water not abundant. . . . The Digger tribe of Indians are our neighbors for 300 miles and have been for the last 100. They speak the Snake language and are of the same family though distinct in territory. Their territory being in a manner destitute of game they are very poor, almost entirely naked and with all very filthy, living principally upon roots and small insects such as crickets, ants, etc.

May's description of the Digger Indians is interesting and informative, and we will hear a great deal more about them in the weeks to come. The emigrants used the name "Diggers," the short form of the term "Root Diggers," to identify them.[24] This weakest and most destitute branch of the Western Shoshoni had been driven by their Indian neighbors into the least hospitable deserts of the region, and were given this unflattering sobriquet because they principally subsisted on roots, insects, worms, reptiles, and other unappealing food sources dug out of the ground.

The company resumed their travel through the dreary Thousand Springs Valley on the morning of August 21. It had been one tedious day after another, and the jaded emigrants must have wondered when this interminable journey would ever end. Despite the monotonously bleak landscape, the cheerful May continued to express uncommon exuberance with whatever he encountered:

Monday 21st August. Traveled 8 miles and corralled for the day. The road ran along a plain at the upper end of which we found the hot springs, strongly impregnated with sulphur. In looking around the spring I picked out a hole near the large body of water about 2 ounces of sulphur as that purchased at the shops. In taste, smell and by calcimining it proved to be quite pure, but a short distance from the springs runs as pure a little stream of good water as ever I drank of. This is certainly a wonderful country. . . . 5 o'clock, I have just returned from the hot springs and while there I shaved, a great luxury for sure. These springs are spread over an area of an acre. The ground is quite warm. This is another great watering place or is to be in time.

Smith's account of the twenty-first was less positive. He related one incident that May had not—that the Indians had been at work the previous night:

mon 21 we traveled up this valley about nine miles and encamped at the warm springs   good grass all the way from the last camp   here are numerous Sulpher springs nearly boiling hot and cold springs of good water close together   Hard frost   last night the Indians stole a Horse from our Interpreter by the name of Antwine   he started early this morning after it.

The springs both men mention are just above the creek on today's County Route 765, about thirteen miles east of today's Highway 93. As Smith explained, the springs were quite the curiosity: a number of them squeezed into one acre, some hot, some cold.

Leaving the springs in the morning, the company crossed a plain for three miles, then headed up the West Brush Creek ravine. It was another landmark day because this summit divided the Salt Lake and Humboldt River watersheds. Through here they encountered some remarkable sagebrush, some up to six feet tall and with trunks six inches in diameter. On the other side of the divide, the company descended into a basin in which they encountered several artesian springs, or "wells." The springs, likely near where Willow Creek and Bishop Creek merge, were about one-half mile west of today's Highway 93 and thirteen miles northeast of the present town of Wells, Nevada. May composed a detailed account of the day's travel, ending with their arrival at the wells:

> Tuesday 22nd. Traveled 13 miles, good road, water and grass, wood scarce. There is in the vicinity of this camp various pools some of them deep enough to swim in. I saw a yearling pulled out of one and might have drowned if it had remained in the water. This is the first encampment on the waters of Mary River. The springs at this place are worthy of notice. The ground around them is raised from one half to 3 feet and there appears to be a fountain that could supply even a city. You may stand 15 or 20 feet from the center of the low mound (where the water is seen) and by stamping your feet put the water in motion. It appears to be entirely hollow.

Edward Smith's entry for August 22 explained what had happened to Antoine:

> tues 22 this morning Antwine Returned with his horse having rode 24 hours   we started ½ Past 7   traveled 6 miles   halted for noon, and a good spring on the Right side of the Road   good grass   at 4 PM we encamped at the far known springs of marys River in sight of the Canion   good camp   distance about 14 miles   very hard frost.

The fact that they believed that they were now camping on what they called the Mary's River must have been heartening—California could not be far away. As they crowded around their campfires that night, there may have been more merriment on their dirty faces. The water from these springs actually fed into Bishop Creek, which then flowed into the Humboldt. Although the Humboldt was originally named the Mary's or Ogden's, John C. Fremont renamed it in 1845 after the famed European naturalist and explorer, Baron Alexander Von Humboldt.[25] Obviously, not everyone had adopted the new name yet.

Departing the wells the next morning, the company traveled beside the fifteen-foot-wide Bishop Creek on August 23, then entered the throat of a tight, four-mile-long canyon formed by precipitous walls several hundred feet high. Emerging from the canyon, they came to Bishop Flats, where May recorded that they stopped to camp:

> Wednesday 23rd Aug. Traveled 8 miles and passed through a canyon that shall be called the Vale of Horrors. Of all the places that I ever saw a wagon go over, a

part of this canyon is [the] worst, jumping rocks that actually looks unreasonable for a four wheeled carriage to pass, although 32 wagons and 2 carriages passed with entire safety. We are now encamped on a branch of Mary River [Bishop Creek] in a beautiful plain [Bishop Flat] where the grass is abundant. We are taking all possible care of our teams because everything depends on them. Major Hensley left our camp very early this morning with the mule train. It is expected that Mr. H will return to us in the California mountains with supplies, not that we expect to want them but to be sure not to be in danger of suffering. This is a very interesting part of the journey. The many warm springs, the snow capped mountains and the beautiful plains very agreeably decorated with flowers all go to interest the weary wagoner on this tour through the dust that is almost enough to suffocate. A very pleasant evening, quite cool.

Recalling that the Chiles company once boasted forty-seven wagons, it is perplexing that May reported that they only had thirty-four, counting the two carriages.

Smith described August 23:

wed 23 to day we Passed through the canion crossed the stream 11 times and encamped 1 ½ miles below   good camp   one Mile of the Road was as Rough as nature could frame it   hot springs in the Middle of Canion   distance about 6 miles.

The company would have an easy road on August 24, as May described:

Thursday 24th. Traveled down Mary's River 17 miles [Bishop Creek, then Humboldt River]. A rich and beautiful plain the whole distance. The stream is quite small, the water does not cascade. Encampments are to be had at any given point. The grass good but dry for the season. This is our 3rd camp on this stream. We expect to travel slow in order to keep our teams in good order for the mountains. We are getting more watchful knowing this to be the most dangerous river we have passed. To the left is a tall range of mountains [East Humboldt Range] which marks the line of this little river.

To clarify, the company traveled across the plain straddling Bishop Creek for about eight miles, then joined the Humboldt River. The party then continued another ten or so miles down the Humboldt. The river plain was wide, pretty, and had plenty of grass. Lined with willows, the Humboldt averaged about twenty-five feet in width and was two to three feet deep. In mentioning the "dangerous river," May was probably not alluding to the river's width, depth, or current. He was likely referring to Digger Indians ahead.

Smith's entry:

thur 24 started ½ Past 8   traveled down the Level Bottom halted for noon where there was good water and grass   at night we encamped at the junction of the

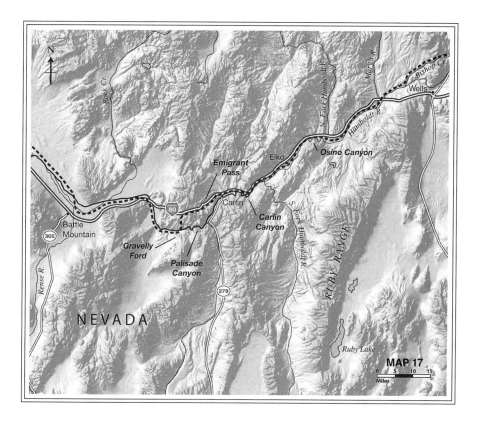

north fork [Mary's River]   to day I lost my young dog Rover   hard frost   distance 20 miles.

The company's camp on the evening of the twenty-fourth was where a small stream called Mary's River joined the Humboldt. The place is near today's Deeth, Nevada, about one mile south of I-80's exit 333. Smith had not mentioned his dog before; it is possible that it fell into the hands of the Indians and became a meal. For quite a few nights, Smith had been mentioning how cold it got: "ice in Bucket," "hard frost," "very hard frost." It seems odd how Smith frequently recorded how cold it got at night, but failed to use even a drop of ink to write how his family was doing.

The next day would be this company's turn to encounter the east-headed Mormon pack train. May wrote of the occasion and of hearing the astonishing news from California:

> Friday 25th Aug. Traveled 15 miles and made our fourth encampment on the Creek of Mary's River [Humboldt]. The best grass that I have seen for many days. The lowland is from 1 to 2 miles wide, which produces a heavy coat of vegetation. We met a train of packs from California, 23 in number. Several of them had specimens of gold lately discovered in that country about 70 miles above Sutters

establishment. They represented the mines as being very rich yielding on an average of two ozs of gold to the days labor and that one man had made 700 dollars in a day. The train giving this information were Mormons bound for the Salt Lake Valley.

Smith's entry for the twenty-fifth also noted the encounter:

frid 25 last night Antwine and Wells lost two horses   at noon we met 20 Mormons with Pack Mules   the[y] left the settlement at Sutters on the 29 of July   about one mile from our camp we Passed the East fork of Mary's River   to night good grass wood & water   distance about 20 miles   Hard frost   good camp.

The meeting with the Mormon packs should have been on the north side of the Humboldt, very near today's exit 328 on I-80, and about halfway between the present communities of Halleck and Deeth, Nevada.

News of the discovery of gold would electrify a nation, so how is it that Smith wrote nothing about it, while May's mention seemed devoid of emotion? It should have made a deep impression. Where is the wonder and astonishment? May had described sagebrush-covered deserts with more exuberance and fanfare.

Disengaging from the Mormon packers, the Chiles company resumed their march westward. At the end of the day, they camped somewhere near today's Elburz Siding, south of exit 321 on I-80. If their dulled minds had been animated with news of gold, you would never know it. May's attention was focused on lurking Indians:

Saturday 26th. Traveled 17 miles, 5th camp on this stream. We cross 3 low hills the river running through as many canyons [Osino Canyon]. In the afternoon we ran down a beautiful plain near eight miles. The mountains [Ruby Mountains] quite bold on the left while they appeared at a distance on the right. The Digger Indians made their appearance but they kept out of camp. A strict guard is around the cattle. A gentleman named Antoine who joined our train on packhorse on Bear River, had three horses stolen from him 2 days ago and he has returned to camp this evening without them. The Digger Indians of all that we have passed through, are the most dangerous. They sulk about the watering places and shoot the stock with their bows and arrows. It was in this nation that Comodore Stockton was wounded last fall while in camp. It would be very pleasant to see timber for I do not know how long it has been since I saw anything that could be called a tree not since we left Lewis River. Fine grass, bad water, willows for firewood.

Like May, Smith was also preoccupied with the Indians:

Sat 26 nothing of note occurred to day   about 10 AM we crossed a saline Branch from the north [North Fork of the Humboldt] and the River entered a canion [Osino Canyon]   here we entered the country of the Real Digger Indians and at night guard for the Cattle was for the first time Mounted   distance about 20 miles   about 6 PM we had a light Shower and disagreeable guarding   good camp.

The North Fork of the Humboldt was a foul stream. Smith called it a "saline Branch"; other emigrants would be less complimentary, one likening its alkali-impregnated water to "pure lye." After crossing the North Fork, the trail moved away from the Humboldt just before it entered Osino Canyon, and crossed some low hills to avoid the canyon's six miles of steep, narrow walls. This stretch of trail corresponds to today's I-80 route between exits 314 and 310.

The company's camp on the evening of August 26 would have been beside the river at the approximate location of today's Elko, Nevada. Diarists, especially those during the gold rush years, frequently complained about the suffocating dust on this section of trail. One had complained that it was so bad that one of his oxen had finally drowned in it and collapsed dead in the road. Marshiness was another problem frequently noted. Many spots beside the Humboldt were so boggy that there was a danger of their livestock sinking up to their bellies when they tried approaching the river to drink.[26]

Judging by May's entry on August 27, the Indians were the travelers' ever-present concern and would remain so for some time:

Sunday 27th August. Traveled 10 miles down Mary's River. We are just at the head of a canyon [Carlin Canyon] through which the river runs. We shall take the hills for our road. The plain continued thus far, also the mountains on the left or southeast of the river. Some of the Digger family are in camp, almost naked. In fact a man grown has to make use of a small piece of skin as a fig leaf or he would be in the state he was born. Our stock guarded day and night and will be until we reach the heights of the California Mountains which are called Sierra Nevada Mountains.

Smith's entry for the twenty-seventh also mentioned the Indians:

Sun 27 in about 3 miles we passed two hot springs in the bed of Mary's River   we traveled about 12 miles and encamped   several digger Indians came into the camp entirely naked except a very small tunic of Rabbit skin   hard frost   good grass.

On the afternoon of the twenty-seventh, they stopped to camp on the river just before it entered Carlin Canyon. The site of their camp was about two miles southwest of today's exit 292 on I-80.

On August 28, the company entered the canyon. During much of the day, the wagons followed the twisting river between towering rock walls that seemed to overhang the travelers' heads in places. Sometimes they were forced to cross the stream. At other times, they had to travel down the streambed itself. Fortunately, the Humboldt was small and ran slow and shallow. Richard May wrote:

Monday 28th. Traveled 16 miles until noon we ran down a canyon crossing the river frequently. . . . This canyon is rather singular in many places. The rocks are perpendicular while in others it slopes back so as to admit a road. . . . The scenery was rich, touching the sublime.

And Edward Smith wrote:

mon 28 to day road ran along the River Bottom through a deep Canion   crossed the River four times   traveled about 15 miles and crossed a fine stream of Mountain water [Maggie Creek] and encamped immediately at the junction near several Indians camps   about one mile below the camp the bed of the River was covered with hot sulpher springs   here one of Christopher Chiles horses was lost   very hard frost   distance about 15 miles   good grass.

Smith makes the first and only mention of Christopher "Kit" Chiles, Joseph Chiles' brother, who had apparently been traveling with the company from the start. The frequency with which May and Smith had been mentioning Diggers reveals the significance of the problem. Since they camped where Maggie Creek joined the Humboldt, and about one mile above the hot springs, their camp was where the community of Carlin is today.

Returning to the trail the morning of August 29, the Chiles company left the river and began an almost steady ten-mile pull up a series of ravines and ridges on their way to Emigrant Pass at the summit. The trail followed the same path as today's I-80. From the heights of the summit, one could see mountains on all sides, barren, sterile, and unfriendly. One reason for taking to the hills was to avoid the fifteen-mile-long Palisade Canyon through which the Humboldt passed; the other was because the hill route was shorter.

Shortly after making it through Emigrant Pass, the company came to Emigrant Springs, where they paused to water their livestock. Beyond the springs the trail took a hard left turn and descended the winding Emigrant Canyon, which took the wagon train back to the river. They crossed the river at Gravelly Ford, a wide, shallow, pebbly spot and came to rest for the night on the river's south side, about four miles southeast of today's Highway 306, and five miles south of I-80's exit 261. Richard May wrote:

Tuesday 29th Aug. Traveled 23 miles through clouds of dust and part of the time rough road. At our encampment we met 17 wagons from California. They had near 100 head of horses and some cattle bound for the Salt Lake being part of Cooks Battalion. They were returning from the services of their country and had with them a small piece of ordinance. I did not inquire but expected it was a trophy they were carrying along won by their arms. The landscape was very beautiful, one mountain upon another in amphitheater style. The valley very level with some sloughs. No wood convenient not even sage brush but willows at a distance and river water. Upon the whole it was a poor camp had not even grass sufficient.

And Edward Smith wrote:

tues 29 this morning we left the River   the road was very hilly crossed a divide about 100 feet high   struck the River again   after dark crossed over and encamped   a co. of Mormon Volunteers were encamped about 2 Miles below on their return from California   very poor grass   distance about 17 Miles   hard frost.

The Chiles group had finally made contact with the Thompson company, the eastbound Mormon wagon party that had met the Cornwall and Wambaugh companies at the Humboldt Sink two weeks earlier. While the Mormons still had their seventeen wagons, May reported a smaller livestock herd. Recalling that the Mormons had started their journey with 250 head of cattle and 200 horses and mules, it shows how badly the clever Indians had decimated their animals during the previous two weeks. The diaries of the Mormons had recorded numerous accounts of Indian depredations.

The Mormon diarists recorded meeting a small westbound train of ten wagons on August 26, the one believed to be led by Peter Lassen. Mormon Samuel Rogers wrote: "Aug 26 we started as usual but had not gone far when we met 10 wagons from the States. They came by way of Salt Lake. A man by the name of Levi E. Riter was with them from Salt Lake. He told us that he was a Bishop of one of the wards."[27] Ephraim Green's journal also mentioned them: "Sat. 26. to day we met another company of emigrants thare was one mormon from salt lake mr riter gives a verry faverable report of the country." In fact, there were three Mormons believed to be traveling with Lassen's company: Levi Riter, John Neff, and John Van Cott. They had left the Salt Lake and had joined Lassen, and were on their way to pick up goods they had shipped to California on the ship *Brooklyn* when they understood that Brigham Young was planning to settle the Saints in California.[28]

By the time the Mormons encountered Lassen's ten wagons on August 26, they were approximately 110 miles west of Chiles. This meant that Lassen had increased his distance ahead of Chiles to seven days. Interestingly, the Chiles party had turned onto the California trail at the Raft River on August 12. Since Father Lempfrit's Stone company passed the Raft River on August 5, seven days earlier, the priest's entry for that day may have vaguely referred to Lassen's group separating from his Stone company at the Raft.

After meeting Lassen on August 27, the Thompson company met Major Hensley and his packers, which had left Chiles' wagons on August 23. Because Hensley had discovered a new route from the new Mormon settlement at Salt Lake to the California Trail just south of the City of Rocks, he encouraged the Mormons to retrace his steps. Mormon diarist Henry Bigler recorded that "he [Hensley] gave us a way bill saying the route was a good one and easy to be found saving at least eight or ten days travel as it was our intention to go by way of fort hall. Mr. Hensley had got defeated in attempting to take Hastings Cutoff and had turned back by so doing discovered this new route and found it to be so much nearer than Hasting's."[29]

The Thompson party then encountered the Chiles wagons on August 29. Mormon diarist Azariah Smith recorded the event in his journal: "Tuesday August the 29th.... this evening another train of wagons came in sight over the hills."[30] Ephraim Green's entry added something very significant: "Weds, the 30th. Last night [29th] there was a company of emgrants came in of thirty six waggons   the captain of the company was mr. waker   we had to in quire about the rout and give directions about ours."[31] Green's reference to "mr. waker" is fascinating, especially since he is referred to as the "captain of the company." The likelihood is very high that "mr. waker" was the celebrated trapper, explorer and guide, Joseph Walker, who joined the Chiles company just west of the Green River in Wyoming. This is significant evidence that Walker, regarded as the man who first pioneered the California Trail in 1833, continued to travel with the Chiles company all the way to California.

Henry Bigler also recorded meeting the Chiles company:

> On the thirtieth [29th] we met Captain Chiles and Company of forty-eight wagons: emigrants. He gave us a way bill purporting to give a still nearer route than that of Hensley. We bought of Captain Chiles's Company some bacon and buffalo meat.[32]

Bigler was wrong on his date and the number of wagons attributed to the Chiles party, but he was correct that Chiles gave them a waybill for a route to the Salt Lake that Chiles claimed was shorter than that of Hensley. Chiles had traveled to California with the Bartleson-Bidwell party in 1841. Searching for a shorter route to the Humboldt River by not traveling as far north as Fort Hall, the Bartleson party tried an uncharted route just north of the Great Salt Lake, but their uncertain wanderings through this waterless, inhospitable country were a near disaster.

Unfortunately, the Thompson company chose to follow Chiles' waybill rather than Hensley's. At least they were cautious about it, sending scouts forward. When they concluded that Chiles' waybill seemed to be sending them into a hellish wasteland, they backtracked and returned to the well-traveled Fort Hall road. They then followed the established trail through Thousand Springs Creek Valley, over to Goose Creek, and then over Granite Pass to the City of Rocks, where they found Hensley's new path forking off to Salt Lake. They followed it and found it to be quite satisfactory.[33]

Chiles knew how miserable the land was that his Bartleson-Bidwell party tried in 1841. He had undoubtedly conversed with Hensley about the new route Hensley had just pioneered and should have understood the superiority of that route. Bigler's entry suggested that Chiles knew that Hensley had already given the Thompson company a waybill. So why did Chiles go ahead and give them different directions over his inferior route and insist that his way was better? It looks like Chiles was up to no good—but why? Was it because Chiles was from Jackson County, Missouri, where the Mormons and Missourians had been at each others' throats for years?

The Chiles company departed the Gravelly Ford area on the morning of August 30, leaving the Mormons to continue their travels east. Chiles and his train traveled beside the crooked, snakelike Humboldt all day. This would be the last year when traveling along the Humboldt plain would seem quiet and peaceful. During the gold rush era, an immense mass of humanity would pour over this dusty trail and diarists would describe dead animals and abandoned wagons littering the trailside. William R. Rothwell colorfully recounted the conditions he passed along the Humboldt in 1850:

> The destruction of property is amazing. There is not a single camping ground from Laramie onward that is not marked by the iron remains of one or more wagons. Thousands of harnesses, chains, saddles, guns, in short everything but provisions, are scattered along the ground.[34]

The travelers even threw away unneeded clothing, giving rise to a standing joke that the trail had become an endless outdoor emporium, where one could pick up a discarded jacket or shirt if it appeared to be better than the one you were already wearing.

In another illustration of how dramatically traffic would increase during the gold rush, Henry C. St. Clair wrote about camping at Gravelly Ford in 1849: "[W]e found about 200 waggons encamped and the grass was all gone. In the morning we found our oxen in a drove of five or six hundred [oxen]. It was some trouble to get them out."[35]

May did not have much to report on August 30, but what he wrote was amusing: "Wednesday 30th. We ran 13 miles. Fine camp. Plenty of dry willows and grass, even water, but the glowing stories of the Mormons of the gold mines nearly ran us all mad." It had been five days since the Mormon packers gave them the news that riches awaited in California and May's silence about the prospect made it seem that he was indifferent . . . until now.

Smith's entry for August 30: "wed 30 we started late traveled about 10 Miles and crossed a sage Point [Shoshone Point] and encamped on the River near a dense thicket of willows there were some diggers in the willows　good grass & water　very hard frost." At the end of the day on the thirtieth, the Chiles company camped on the river in close proximity to Shoshone Point, near exit 254 on I-80.

According to May, the company made fourteen miles on August 31:

> Thursday 31st Aug. Traveled 14 miles . . . grass good, large willows for wood. the mountains are of medium height on both sides of the plain. No timber to be seen nor a shrub of any kind save the willows which line the river in abundance. The mountains appear entirely bare and present a smooth appearance. On this river we anticipated a great deal of sickness. The camp notwithstanding is in better health as at any period since we left the States. Health prevails throughout the camp.

Smith's account for August 31: "thur 31 we traveled down the valley and encamped at 3 oclock   distance about 11 Miles   our teams are failing fearfully fast   very hard frost   James Davidson Burst my shot gun."

In a later entry, Richard May will inform us that James Davidson was Smith's teamster, and that the shotgun exploded while Davidson was on night guard, injuring his face and right hand. The country the team had been traveling had been decent, but Smith noted that their ox teams were failing. They had rambled beside the Raft River, Cassia Creek, Goose Creek, Bishop Creek, and then the Humboldt River, all with reasonably good grass, so one might assume that their oxen would be gaining weight and strength. Not unexpectedly Smith reported the opposite. Hardworking oxen continued to lose weight despite adequate grass at the campsites. After pulling wagons all day, they could not graze all night—they needed time to lie down to rest their feet and fatigued muscles—so they simply could not consume enough energy at night to match what they burned each day. And then there was the poor quality of the Humboldt River water. It was very alkaline, which interfered with the oxen's digestion. Oxen are ruminants and the high pH of the water was injurious to the rumen bacteria they needed to digest the cellulose in the rank grass. So it is understandable why the oxen were continuing to lose weight and grow more fragile.

The Chiles' camp on August 31 would have been on the Humboldt River plain, about seven miles directly east of the present town of Battle Mountain, Nevada. And they were still 350 miles from their final destination.

Table 14: Location of companies as of August 31, 1848

Company (Diarist)	Location
Allsopp	probably arrived in Willamette Valley
Adams, first segment	probably arrived in Willamette Valley
Cornwall	crossing Sierras via Mormon/Carson Pass
Wambaugh	crossing Sierras via Truckee/Donner Pass
Gates (Root)	on Deschutes River, near today's Sharars Bridge, Oregon
Miller (Anderson)	on Eightmile Creek, south of The Dalles, Orgeon
Jackson (Belknap)	likely nearing the Deschutes River
Watt	probably slightly behind Jackson company
Kelly	probably behind Watt company
Walker-Bristow	probably behind Watt company
Hannah	probably behind Watt company
Purvine (Porter)	in the Blue Mountains, Oregon
Adams, second segment	probably traveling with the Purvine company
Stone (Lempfrit)	on Birch Creek, Oregon
Delaney	probably traveling with the Stone company
Lassen	on Humboldt River, probably near today's Winnemucca
Hensley	on Humboldt River, probably near today's Winnemucca
Chiles (May/Smith)	on Humboldt River, near today's Battle Mountain

CHAPTER 18

Time to Pay
the Gatekeeper
SEPTEMBER 1–16

SEPTEMBER 1–12, 1848
William Anderson, Miller company, at Barlow's Gate, Oregon

At the beginning of September 1848, the leading Oregon-bound companies were at the gateway to the Cascade Mountains, their last great obstacle. On the evening of August 31, William Anderson and his Miller company may have been camping on Eightmile Creek, near where today's Eightmile Road branches off of Highway 197, and about ten miles southeast of The Dalles.

The next day, the company traveled south toward Barlow's Road, the route they would take across the mountains. They began the day by traveling up the narrow and difficult Eightmile Creek, ascending a high plateau, and traversing a series of treeless hills and ridges, often in sight of Mount Hood. Late that night, the company groped through the dark, descending a long, steep ridge into a little basin called Tygh Valley. Anderson described it:

> September the 1ste traveled 4 miles up this branch [Eightmile Creek] crossing it several times at the first crossing this morning I had the misfortune to turn my waggon over in the water there was one person in besides myself but neither of us got hurt nor nothing broke we left this branch on our wright and traveled on over a rough and hilly road until after dark when we came to the top of a high mountain where we could see the fires of our camp pickers far below us on Indian creek [Tygh Creek] these fires looked to be visable within half a mile at least but we travled hard until 10 o clock at night before we reached them here were several old wagons left here by emegrants of last year having traveled 18 miles to day and being pretty tired I fried a mess of salmon eat it and lay down.

The trail had led them through where the community of Dufur stands today on Highway 197. They continued southwest, much of the trail following the course of today's J Hix Road until it reached the Tygh Valley. When Anderson mentioned "our camp pickers," he was probably referring to the company's scouts who rode ahead, looking for water and suitable places to spend the night.

As dawn broke on September the 2, the emigrants climbed from under their heavy blankets and buffalo robes and gazed at the Tygh Valley for the first time in the light. As the early morning mists slowly cleared, they could see a tiny valley surrounded by high, bare hills, and the path down the steep hill they had descended in the dark. Beautiful wide-spreading oaks, the first oaks they had seen in a long time, populated the valley bottom. After breakfast and catching up their worn-down oxen, the emigrants were soon climbing "a verry steep mountain near ½ mile high and verry rocky." Other diarists would describe the climb on the south side of the valley as the worst they had yet faced. "[H]ere we had to double team to get up," Anderson wrote, "we were near half the day in getting up this hill." They only went a few miles, but the climb made it an exhausting day. "[W]e camped on a small branch between 2 and 3 miles from this hill," he reported, referring to tiny Threemile Creek. Today, Wamic Road, south of the small community of Tygh Valley, pretty much corresponds to the first two difficult miles traveled by the wagons when they first ascended out of the valley. The trail then drifted southwest another mile to reach the creek where the company camped.

Anderson reported arriving at Barlow's Gate the next day:

September the 3rd we traveled 19 miles [more likely 9] which brought us to what
is caled Barlows gate on a small branch at the entrance of the cascade mountains
we had to drive our cattle 1 mile to the left of the road for grass here Mr. Barlow
was stationed with a few men to take a toll from the emegrants he said to pay
him for working the road through the Cascade mountains for which he charged
5 dollars per waggon which sum some of the emegrants paid and some gave
there notes and others drove right along without doing either.

After 1,800 miles and four months of travel, the Miller company was finally at
Barlow's Gate, the threshold to the Cascades. They spent the night on Gate Creek,
and the next morning would commence a daunting trip over the mountains.

The company found the country around Barlow's Gate arid, but populated with
scattered cedars and pines. Samuel K. Barlow, the father of the road, stood at its
entrance, collecting tolls. It was a bargain by any standard, considering the countless
hours he and his colleagues spent in 1845 and 1846 blazing and improving the route,
clearing it of fallen trees and boulders. Perhaps as many as two hundred wagons would
pass his tollgate this year. Most of the emigrants paid, but some could not. When the
Trullinger family, traveling with the Miller company after Fort Hall, reached Barlow's Gate, they did not have the money and were forced to pay by promise.[1]

The story of Samuel Barlow and his road is a simple one. In the fall of 1845, Barlow
and his small wagon party had arrived at The Dalles where they found a large number of
families waiting for boats to take them down the Columbia. The wait would be long—
only two boats were running the river then—and the trip was expensive, something
not all could afford. Navigating your own raft down the river was dangerous, especially
for those who had never done it before, and Barlow was reluctant to try. Convinced
there had to be a cheaper, safer way to the Willamette Valley, he and his party of seven
wagons headed south looking for a way across the mountains. Joel Palmer, leader of
a company of twenty-three wagons, was traveling just behind Barlow, and decided to
follow them. Together, Barlow and Palmer scouted the mountains, eventually finding
a feasible route just south of Mount Hood. It was too late in the year to improve the
road sufficiently to get their wagons through, so they built a cabin south of Mt. Hood,
later referred to as Palmer's Cabin or Fort Deposit, and left one man to stay the winter
with their wagons. The two parties crossed the mountains on horseback, taking provisions on pack animals. They returned the following summer to complete the road and
recover their wagons. In the falls of 1846 and 1847, a majority of the emigrants would
meet Mr. Barlow, pay him his toll, and use his new road.[2]

On the morning of September 4, Anderson and his Miller company caught up
their dismal-looking oxen and continued on past Barlow's Gate, perhaps recalling
stories of earlier emigrants' troubles during those last hundred miles: food running
out, oxen dying, wagons abandoned, slogging through heavy rains, or getting caught
in deadly snows. Anderson described their first day beyond Barlow's Gate:

September 4th we traveled 16 [13] miles 10 miles traveled brought us to clear cold creek [Cedar Creek] 8 [3] miles further we came to the north fork of the Deshutes river [White River] in going down the hill to the river which was verry steep and rocky my team was so tender hoofed they would not hold back so they ran down like a streak scattering the most of the load out at the fore end of the waggon but did not do much damage . . . when they stoped we loaded up agan and crossed over the river [White River] and camped.

They camped where the road crossed the White River, a brawling mountain torrent, on today's Barlow Road, about fourteen miles south of Highway 35. It appears that Anderson either overestimated the miles as his company proceeded over the twisty, mountainous trail, or the transcriber misread his journal entry.

Anderson described some of their difficulties the next day:

September the 5th we traveled 17 miles our road to day was verry rough and rocky we camped on a small branch [Barlow Creek] that empties into the deshutes [White River] and drove our cattle to the left of the road to grass there were two horses killed to day belonging to one of our company Isaac Winkle his wife and daughter were on them some distance a head of the train when they discovered some watter 30 or 40 yards to the left of the road, so they lighted and hitched there horses it happened there was a large fir tree a fire some 50 yards off which they did not notice and while they were gon it fell and killed both ther horses dead fire gets out in these mountains from the emegrant camps and burns up a great deal of timber I have [seen] acres of green fir timber burnt off smooth.

Weaving between tall, dense firs, the Miller company would have passed Barlow and Palmer's Cabin and crossed the summit of the Cascades at Barlow Pass, although Anderson failed to mention both places. He also failed to mention Summit Meadows shortly beyond the Pass, where they camped on the evening of September 5 and could get their first unobstructed view of Mount Hood only seven miles to the north.

The emigrants were now traveling through an entirely different world: a rain forest, much wetter and lusher than the semiarid forests of the Blue Mountains. Squeezing at times through narrow spaces between trees and boulders, their wagons bumped over stumps, bulging roots, and fallen logs, crashed through impervious thickets of undergrowth, and splashed through muddy holes and marshy bogs. They rolled over feet-thick blankets of rotting fir needles and deadfall, and lumbered beneath thick canopies of immense overhanging firs that kept the ground in perpetual gloom. The penetrating scent of the evergreens should have been invigorating and the sights stunningly beautiful, but how could they enjoy it when they had to focus on their rapidly failing oxen, wondering when the next one would collapse. They had to make it through these mountains as rapidly as possible because it was almost impossible to find any grass for their starving animals in these sun-deprived forests.

The next day, the company temporarily stalled at the infamous Laurel Hill:

Mt. Hood can vaguely be seen in the background. William Henry Jackson (1843–1942), *Barlow Cutoff*. Watercolor painting, 1930. Courtesy of Scotts Bluff National Monument, SCBL-46.

> September the 6th we traveled 16 miles and passed over laurel hill this is a verry long steep mountain to descend some of the emigrants cut trees and chained them to the axletree of their waggons to hold them back we camped on a stream caled sandy in a rocky canyon at the foot of Mount Hood there was not a spear of grass here for our cattle so we chained them up and cut some alder bushes for them to brouse on and then lay down a mongst the rocks and slept sound untill morning.

Laurel Hill was a frightening experience. The emigrants had to descend a dangerously steep incline, as much as a 60 percent slope in places. But it was not just its steepness; the mountainside was covered by a blanket of rocky rubble—tens of thousands of sharp-edged, unstable rocks, many as large as baskets. The only sane method of making it down was to unhitch the oxen and lead them single-file down a narrow, switchback trail. After locking the wheels, the men tied heavy logs to the back of their wagons to serve as drags, then tied ropes to the wagons and snubbed the other ends to trees as they slowly eased them down.

On September 6, Rev. A. M. A. Blanchet, Catholic bishop of Walla Walla, was returning to his St. Peter's mission at The Dalles by way of the Barlow Road, and he reported encountering westbound emigrants, most likely Anderson and his Miller company:

On the 6th [of September] we camp on the Big Prairie [likely Summit Meadows]. To get there one has to cross the Sandy River five times and climb the steepest hill of the entire trail [Laurel Hill]. On that hill we meet the first of the wagons of the emigrants who descend with much difficulty and trouble. We were to meet many others before leaving the mountains and can attest that the crossing of the Cascade mountains is extremely difficult. A great number of animals and wagons must be left behind there because of the scarcity of pasture and the difficulty of the road.[3]

The Miller company was now on the wet, western slope of the mountains. They lumbered through immense groves of fir and thick stands of fern as tall as eight feet. As Anderson pointed out, these mountains grew little grass. Their oxen, who had eaten little in days and were famished, would eat almost anything, so the emigrants fed them alder bushes. But they had to be careful; unsupervised cattle would also eat rhododendrons or hemlock, which grew everywhere and were poisonous to livestock.

Anderson wrote that they camped on the Sandy River on the night of September 6, probably where the trail crossed the river, near today's community of Zigzag on Highway 26.

Over the next four days, Anderson's estimate of miles is difficult to understand and he failed to identify many recognizable features.

September the 7th we traveled 8 miles when we came to some grass on the wright of the road we stopd turned our cattle out and let them grase a while then started on agan and traveled 5 miles further making 13 miles to day.

September the 8th we traveled 14 miles and camped on the side of the mountain and found a spring of watter on the left of the road here one of Isaac Millers best horses gave out and died our road to day was verry mountainous.

September the 9th we traveled 5 miles over some verry steep hills we had a shower of rain this morning which caused the mountains to be verry slippy my waggon slid around at one hill and got before the team and crippled the off lead ox we got them stoped chained the waggon to a tree and took the cattle loose unloaded the waggon and let it down with chains and ropes.

September the 10th we traveled 8 miles which brought us down off the mountains into the Walwametta [Willamette] valley in sight of the habitation of Civilised man having made the trip from St. Josephs on the Missouri river in 4 months and 14 days at Mr. Fosters near whose farm we camped we procured some beef cabbage and potatoes which I thought were the best that I ever ate and here I ate my first raw tomato half green as I pulled it of the vines in Mr. Fosters garden it tasted verry good we were so near starved for vegitables that Cris Millers Wife Mary ann took the colic from eating too much cabage & we thought she would die any way but she got easier awhile after midnight & was able to travel next morning.

In his entries of September 7 through 10, Anderson described following the trail beside the Sandy River along today's Highway 26 until they came to where the present-day community of Alder Creek stands. The trail then led them northwest, away from the river, and traversed a long, high-backed ridge called the Devil's Backbone. Today's Marmot Road pretty much follows the trail over the ridge. Descending from the Backbone, the company returned to the Sandy River, crossing it near the present town of Sandy. They then followed the trail west along the same course as today's Highway 211 to where the town of Eagle Creek now stands, and where Philip Foster's farm and vegetable patch was located. The Miller company had been fortunate avoiding rain and snow as they crossed the mountains; harsh weather was often the last straw for exhausted livestock.

By September 11, the Miller company was traveling through country with plenty of grass and abundant fish:

> On the 11th we started on & crossed the Clackmus [Clackamus] River at a verry shallow Place where the fall Salmon were verry plenty going up stream & we killed all we wanted with sticks & Clubs this stream I afterwards learnt emptied into the Williamett River below oregon City we only traveled a few miles after crossing until we camped & began cooking and eating these fall salmon as they were caled were white meated while the spring salmon were red or pink Collered Meat they were so thick trying to get over this Riffle in the river that they put me in mind of a drove of sheep & I think would weigh from 15 to 20 Pounds.

When the Miller company stopped to camp on the evening of the eleventh, they were but ten miles from Oregon City. The Willamette Valley, the place of their dreams, was all that they had hoped for. It was green and lush with flat areas of black, fertile soil, bordered by tree-covered hills, and water—lots of water. They had completed their epic journey. We may marvel at their accomplishment, but they apparently did not stop to celebrate and they did not roll triumphantly into Oregon City. Instead, they began to split up, each going their separate ways. Anderson's description of September 12 made it sound as if it was a bittersweet time. They were delighted and relieved to have finally reached their destination, but also sad at the splitting up of their company.

> On the 12th we began to separate after a long acquaintance which seemed almost like Parting with Brothers and sisters the Cleaver family and his son in law William Ransom John Ramsay his Mother and two sisters Bullock & his large family started in the direction of Oregon City Isaac Winkle & his large family started for the Yam Hill settlement West of the Willamatt River while the rest of us started up the valley but some would drop Out at most every trail crossing. . . . we all took a rest for a few Days & looked round at the country some looking for land Claims & some looking for game which was quite Plenty Wild Geese sand hill Cranes Ducks Deer Black Bear Grouse quails Rabits squirrels Brants & and lots of other small game & plenty of fish in all the streams. . . . I sught to look out for

The end of the trail. Oregon City, Oregon Territory, as depicted in about 1845. Courtesy of Oregon Historical Society, Portland (OrHi 79 #822).

a job so Isaac Shurt Jacob Sutherland and myself struck out for Oregon city to see if we could strike a job of any kind I left my gun & Cloths with Isaac Miller and Betay his wife that I Drove a Team for from Montgomery County Indiana telling them I wanted to have a house with them in case I should fail to find another.

In a postscript, Anderson added that Isaac Miller and his family ended up settling on the north side of the Santiam River, while Isaac's older brother Christopher [Chris] Miller and his family settled on the south side. Isaac Miller's son-in-law Isaac Wyatt and his brother Thomas located on the south side of the river as well. As for our diarist, William Anderson, the last he wrote about himself was that he was going to look for a job in Oregon City.

Recalling the Miller company's shaky start, it is interesting how the party seemed to get better as they went along. They even passed their rival, the Gates company, near the end. One trail historian who studied hundreds of trail diaries calculated that between 1841 and 1848 it took an average of 169 days to make the trip to Oregon.[4] The Miller company had made it in 134. Their success stands as a testament to the leadership of Captain Miller and to the many good people who traveled with him.

Notwithstanding what Bishop Blanchet suggested, the Miller company was probably not the first wagon party to arrive in the Willamette Valley in 1848. The eastbound Oregonian, Isaac Pettijohn, had reported passing forty-four wagons traveling ahead of Wambaugh, Gates, and Miller. Such a significant number of wagons do not just disappear. This group probably included the twenty-five-wagon Allsopp party that left Independence on April 10, plus some from the Adams company, the Oregon-bound group of fifty wagons that had started from Council Bluffs in mid-April.

A wonderfully valuable article appeared in the September 7 issue of Oregon City's newspaper, the *Oregon Spectator*, reporting that a small party of five packers had arrived at Oregon City. The article did not specify their arrival date, but they probably had arrived just days before September 7:

> **Emigration**. Since our last a small company of Packers, consisting of Messrs. Geo. L. Boone, G. J. Basket, J. A. Ebey, Mo., R. Jay, Iowa, and Wm. Bristoe, Ill., have arrived in this city. We welcome them to Oregon. These gentlemen know of 600 wagons on the way to the Pacific—about 300 of which, they suppose, will go to California. They think that there are only the 600 wagons upon the road, although that it is possible there may be more.
>
> They left St. Joseph, Mo., about the 3rd of May, and met Joseph L. Meek, Esq., bearer of dispatches to Washington, on the 7th of May, between 60 and 70 miles west of St. Joseph. They learned that Mr. Meek arrived at St. Joseph, and took passage for St. Louis on the 10th of May.

Among the names of the five packers, the name of Wm. Bristoe (whose correct spelling was Bristow) appears. He was captain of the small company that left St. Joseph on May 3 and soon merged with Bolivar Walker's party (it was thereafter referred to as the Walker-Bristow company). The Walker-Bristow company began traveling with William Porter's Purvine company along the Platte, then continued traveling with it along the South Platte and North Platte Forks. At the North Platte River crossing, the Purvine party was delayed because of their skittish, unmanageable livestock, and fell behind. Because there no longer was any diarist traveling with Walker-Bristow, we lost track of them, but they probably continued traveling not far behind the Wambaugh, Gates, Miller, and Watt companies.

Since Bolivar Walker led the combined company, William Bristow may have realized his leadership was no longer needed (or wanted), so he and a few friends must have left the company and hastened on to Oregon City on horseback. Traveling at a faster pace than the wagons, they would have eventually passed each company ahead of them, and must have paused long enough to record the identities of the "Heads of Families." The article continued with Bristow and his traveling companions reporting that five wagon companies would soon be arriving in the Willamette Valley:

> They [Bristow, et al] bring the names of the gentlemen composing the 5 forward companies, which will be found below. Probably, the first three companies

are in the Cascade mountains—the fourth and fifth companies are some distance behind. As far as we have been able to learn, the emigration has not been molested by Indians. Some of the teams are getting weak.

FIRST COMPANY [Gates company]—*Heads of Families*—Wm. Brunson, **Thomas Gates**, John Stipp, Riley Root, Ira Patterson, John S. Crooks, Samuel S. Jones, and Dr. D. S. Baker, from Illinois. Reuben Dickens, Reuben Pigg, Wm. M. King, and James Robinson, from Mo. Orrin Kellogg, Daniel Hathaway, Robert Houston and Joseph Kellogg, from Ohio. Elias D. and Nathaniel Wilcox from Iowa. Rineheart and Benjamin Cripe, and Andrew Bowers, from Ind. Lyman Lautarette, from N. Y.; and James Emery, from Vermont.

SECOND COMPANY [Miller company]—J. G. Ramsey, E. Garther, Thos. Burbanks, Leonard Williams, L. Davis, John Davis, Christian Clyne, Illinois. Thos. Wyatt, Peter D. Cline, Isaac Wyatt, Ind. Jacob Miller, John Dennis, John McGee, Daniel Trulinger, Richard Hutchinson, Thos. Adams, Ill. Fendall Sutherlin, John, Nathan and and Gabriel Trulinger, Levi Grant, **Isaac** and Christian **Miller**, Ind. Benj. Cleaver, Isaac Owens, Ill. Horace Rice, David Priestly, Isaac Winkle, Wm. Porter, Mo.

THIRD COMPANY [Jackson company]—Isaac, George [husband of Keturah], C. & H. Belknap, Chapman, David and Jesse Hawley, Abitha, Isaac & Norris Newton, Rev. John Starr, W. Bethers, G. Kittredge, M. Neff, Andrew, Martin and P. Hagey, Anderson De Haven, Adam Cooper, Wm. Armpriest, Iowa. **Geo. W. Jackson** (from Oregon in '47), Benj. B. & Andrew Jackson, John Miller, Henry Moody, Illinois. Burrel Griffin, (and two others whose first names are not given,) John, William and ____ and Edgar Lindsay, Mo. Henry Henninger, Indiana.

FOURTH COMPANY [Kelly company]—Capt. Greenwood, Iowa. Jas. Valentine, Geo. Irvin, Mo. **Clinton Kelley**, Ky. Nathaniel Hamlin, C. Emerick, Mo. Samuel Welch, Illinois. P. Gearhart, John Moore, Iowa. J. A. Cloneinger, J. C. Lane, Mo. P. Hebbert, B. Smith, B. Moore, Illinois.

FIFTH COMPANY [Walker-Bristow/Purvine companies]—William and Stephen Porter, H. N. V. Holmes, Watt Tucker, J. Lewis, ____ Coffey, Mo. **John Pervine** [Purvine], Geo. Graham, ____ Hooker, Ill. **W. B. [Bolivar]** and W. M. **Walker**, Mo. Farley Pierce, Pliny Richison, Simon Markham, Daniel Cushman, Ill. [Isaac] Ball, Mo. A. Prussel, M. Shelley, Iowa. A. B. Holcomb, W. F. [L.] Adams, Illinois.

This article and its list of companies is a delightful treasure trove of information. It identified the names of some of our diarists—Riley Root in the first company, Keturah Belknap's husband, George, in the third company, and William Porter in the fifth company—and our letter writer, W. L. Adams, traveling with the Purvine party. It also included the names of those understood to be the captains of their companies (in bold letters): Thomas Gates in the first company (Gates company), Isaac Miller in the second company (Miller company), George Jackson in the third company (Jackson company), Clinton Kelly in the fourth company (Kelly company), Bolivar Walker in the fifth company (Walker-Bristow companies), and John Purvine in the fifth company (Purvine company). After examining all of our sources, we have some additional information about each company and some of its members.

First Company [Gates]

William Anderson of the Miller company always referred to the party just ahead of them as "the Gates company." The name of Thomas Gates is found here, purportedly the man after whom the company was named. The names of Root, Patterson, Crooks, Baker, Dickens, Houston, Wilcox, and Lanterette were all members of the original Wambaugh company who signed the Mosquito Creek Resolution. While diarist Riley Root joined the Miller company at Fort Hall, he moved ahead and joined the Gates party at Three Island Crossing.

John S. Crooks is listed in the Gates party. John Trullinger, who traveled with the Miller company, claimed in a reminiscence that when the Wambaugh company split up at Fort Hall, "old man Crook" was elected captain of his Oregon-bound party.[5]

The Kellogg family—Orrin (father) and John (son)—also appear in the Gates company. This is the family who joined P. B. Cornwall at Bellevue in early April, and who cooked for Thomas Corcoran and carried his clothing and blankets as far as Fort Laramie. They were the ones whom Cornwall asked to carry Oregon's first Masonic Charter on to Oregon. The Kelloggs arrived at Milwaukie, just west of Oregon City, on September 8, perhaps meaning they passed through Oregon City on or before the seventh, four days ahead of the front-running Miller company. By arriving ahead of Anderson and Root, the Kelloggs demonstrated how companies were fragmenting into smaller segments as they neared the Cascades and as the threat of Indians diminished. People felt free to travel as fast as the condition of their oxen would permit. For many, it became "each man for himself," often resulting in companies arriving in bits and pieces.

Second Company [Miller]

Here are found Thomas Adams, Peter Cline, and the Trullinger family, all members of the original Wambaugh company. The name of our diarist, William Anderson, is not encountered, but the article listed only "Heads of Families," and William Anderson was a bachelor wagon driver.

The Trullingers had been traveling with the Miller company. Yet, in a reminiscence written years later, John Trullinger recalled that his family arrived at Oregon City on September 15.[6] If his date is correct, his family may have fallen off the pace and arrived a couple of days behind the bulk of the Miller party.

Bristow identifying Gates as the "First Company" and Miller as the "Second Company" provides a clue as to where Bristow encountered them. Gates had been ahead of Miller until the two parties reached the John Day River on August 28. At that point, they split and took different forks of the trail. This would indicate that Bristow passed these two parties before August 28, before the parties had reached the John Day River and about 160 miles from Oregon City. If Bristow and his group had left the John Day River on August 28, and averaged twenty miles per day thereafter, he would have arrived at Oregon City on September 5, just two days before the article in the *Spectator* appeared.

Using the assumption that parties on horseback averaged twenty miles per day, while wagon parties averaged thirteen miles per day, Bristow's group should have gained seven miles on the wagons companies for each day after he left his own wagon company. Acknowledging possible errors in these estimates, Bristow and his friends could have left his Walker-Bristow company as early as Fort Hall and as late as Three Island Crossing.

Third Company [Jackson]

The large Belknap family and their friends, Starr, Hawley, Newton, and Beathers, were listed as traveling in the Jackson company. Keturah and her family and friends, together with the three Jacksons, left St. Joseph as members of the Watt company, but separated from the Watt family near the Green River. Oddly, the Watts are not found in any of the companies, making one wonder what became of them and their flock of sheep. People like Chamberlin, Cheadle, Blain, Simonds, Roberts, and Holdridge had all started the journey with Watt, and these names are missing from the Jackson company as well, making it appear that they chose to remain with the Watt family when they broke away.

There is a logical reason why the Watt company was not listed among the companies Bristow passed. Bristow likely crossed the Snake River at Three Island Crossing and took the northern branch of the trail to Fort Boise, but sheep are not good swimmers and Joe Watt's biographical sketch reported that there was a "strong" current when they arrived at Three Island Crossing.[7] Considering the river's great width at this location, Watt probably decided to take the southern route, as the Gates and Miller parties had done, which would explain Bristow's not crossing paths with Watt's party.

Fourth Company [Kelly]

Reverend Clinton Kelly, the leader of this company ever since it left Independence, Missouri, is listed here. Diarist Edward Smith first traveled ahead of him, then with him, then behind him, then ahead of him, then finally behind him. Smith often mentioned the "Kelley co." in his journal, including when it arrived at and left Fort Laramie.

Captain Greenwood of Iowa is found in the Kelly company, but this is not the Caleb Greenwood who went to California. Rather, this Greenwood was mentioned by Richard Cheadle as a member of the original Watt company when they left St. Joseph.

Fifth Company [Walker-Bristow/Purvine]

The names in this group reflect a combination of those from the Walker-Bristow and Purvine companies, including Bolivar Walker, John Purvine, diarist William Porter, and many individuals whom Porter mentioned in his earlier writings. It is interesting that the Purvine company, at one time traveling as much as a week behind Walker-Bristow, had managed to catch up to them again.

There are no wagon companies mentioned after the Fifth Company, but the article conceded "although it is possible there may be more." It is understandable that Bristow would not have known anything about the Hannah, Delaney, and Stone companies, since they had always traveled behind him. The article badly estimates the year's emigration at six hundred wagons, the error stemming from a gross overestimate of three hundred going to California (there were only about ninety).

September 1–13, 1848

Riley Root, Gates company, on Deschutes River, near Shurar, Oregon

Earlier, Riley Root had described how his Gates company chose a southern branch of the trail right after they crossed the John Day River. Three days and forty-five miles later, on August 31, they had arrived at the deep canyon of the Deschutes River. It was near where today's Highway 216 crosses the river. The next day, Root described them crossing this dangerous river:

> Friday, Sept. 1st— All day employd in getting our goods across the river, with the help of several Indians. River at the crossing about seven rods [112 feet] wide, with considerable current.

The next morning, they resumed their trip, traveling over dry country:

> 2d— ... Nine miles from Deshutes, over the rocky bluffs, brought us to another resting-place [Tygh Valley], on an arm of Deshutes [Tygh Creek], flowing from the mountains, in the direction of Mount Hood. Five miles from Deshutes, was a spring, where emigrants sometimes camp, but at this time the Indian ponies had eaten off all the grass. We therefore passd on to our present camp.

By the end of the day, the Gates company had made it to Tygh Valley and camped. They would not have encountered William Anderson's Miller company, which had climbed out of the valley that morning. The next day, Root and his Gates company struggled up the long, steep hill bordering the south side of the valley, and continued until they reached Barlow's Gate:

> 3d— 12½ miles to camp, on a small tributary of Deshutes [Gate Creek], at Barlow's gate— all but the gate, though he was found sitting there at the receipt of custom, allowing each wagon to pass his road through the Cascade mountains,

at the moderately healthy sum of five dollars each, which the government of Oregon has authorized him to receive. But, as miserable a road as it was, thanks be to Mr. Barlow for his energetic movement in opening a way through so rough a district as the Cascade mountains. Several small streams were passd to-day, though no camps could well be made on them for want of grass, except the first, which had very little.

Root suggests that Barlow had no formal gate—only himself collecting tolls. Even though William Anderson had reported arriving at Barlow's Gate on the third, strangely, neither Anderson nor Root mentioned the presence of the other company.

By Anderson's records, the Miller company had taken six days and traveled seventy-six miles between the John Day River and Barlow's Gate. Root recorded that his Gates party had also taken six days, but had traveled sixty-six miles between the same two points. When Root left the Miller company to join Gates at Three Island Crossing, it was probably because he thought Gates was a faster moving party. If so, one wonders if it rankled him that he was behind the Miller company, even if it was by only a few hours.

Root wrote that they "Staid at the same place" on September 4, suggesting that they laid by an extra day at Barlow's Gate. Their oxen could have been on the brink of failure and needed an extra day of rest before they started the difficult Cascade passage, or perhaps it was because a lack of grass made it inadvisable for two large wagon parties to travel the Barlow Road together.

From here on, Root will again revert to his regretfully terse entries, devoid of anything but the bare minimum. Yet, he continued to be better than Anderson in estimating mileage and describing landmarks. Root's company left Barlow's Gate on the morning of September 5, a day after the Miller company:

> 5th— Over the rocky hills, 12 miles to camp, on a muddy arm of Deshutes [White River], flowing from Mount Hood. Ten and a half miles to the arm, 1½ up the same to camp. No grass for our stock.
> 6th— 3 miles up Deshutes valley, to Palmer's cabin. In consequence of having lost some of our cattle in the thick and inpenetrable forest, our day's drive was short.

Root's entries confirmed that Palmer's Cabin [Fort Deposit] was on the White River, just 4 ½ miles beyond where the trail crossed the river. The next day the company passed the summit: "7th— 10 miles, over the dividing ridge [Barlow Pass], to camp, at a small flat prairie [Summit Meadow] on our left, from which Mount Hood is seen a few miles distant, towring high above its neighbor mountains." The Miller company continued a day ahead of Gates, since Miller appeared to have camped at Summit Meadows on the sixth.

Root recorded the next four days:

8th— 10 miles to camp. No grass. Chaind our oxen to trees, and cut a few birch limbs for them. Passd, to-day, what is calld Laurel hill. It is steep and dangerous.

9th— 6 miles, down Muddy fork of Sandy, to camp. Drove our cattle across the stream, and found some grass for them. This has been a rainy day.

10th— 15 miles, most of the way over a good road, especially on the ridge, calld by some, "Devil's Back-Bone."

11th— 8 miles, over a hilly road, down to the first settlement at the west foot of the Cascade mountains. One mile to the last crossing of Sandy Creek, 7 more to camp.

On September 11, Root reported coming to the "first settlement" seven miles beyond the crossing of the Sandy River. This meant they camped that evening at Philip Foster's farm, where the Miller company had camped the night before. Root's entries for the next two days were very short:

12th— 12 miles to camp.

13th— 6 miles to Oregon City. 1846 [miles].

On the twelfth, the Gates company crossed the Clakamas River about two miles beyond Foster's farm, then proceeded another ten miles toward Oregon City. With so few miles to Oregon City, one wonders why they didn't push on into the settlement at the end of the day on September 12. Were their oxen now so weak that they just couldn't make it any farther? The Gates company finally finished their trip on September 13, completing it in 138 days—only four days longer than it took the Miller party.

The city where the emigrants arrived, Oregon City, was first laid out as a town in 1842 by Dr. John McLoughlin, chief factor of the Hudson's Bay Company's Columbia district. It was a dirty little village, seat of the provisional government of Oregon and center of activity for the widely scattered settlers.[8] Its streets alternated between dust and ankle-deep mud, depending on the seasons, but it had far more civilization than the emigrants had seen since they left St. Joseph. Although Root did not describe the town in his last diary entry, he did devote a paragraph to it in the book he later published. Crowded against the Willamette River on the west and the foothills of the Cascades on the east, the roughly five-hundred-person village was described by Root as "containing about 150 buildings, two saw mills, one of which is a double mill, and two grist [flour] mills."[9] The shops and stores offered goods brought in by ships from Boston, one of the reasons the Indians, in addition to other unflattering names, often called the Americans "Bostons."

It was disappointing that Root did not have more to say in his last diary entry of September 13. After journeying 1,846 miles (by his calculations), it would have been nice to know how he felt at finally making it. Or had at least mentioned the names of a few members of his company. Something. Anything.

September 1–15, 1848
William Porter, Purvine company, Blue Mountains, Oregon

On September 1, William Porter's Purvine company was 160 miles behind the Miller and Gates companies, and an unknown number of miles behind the Jackson, Watt, Walker-Bristow, Kelly, and Hannah companies. As William Porter made his way with his company through the forests of the Blue Mountains, he continued with his truncated entries:

> Sept. 1st, 1848. Traveled 12 miles to Lee's encampment [at Meacham, Oregon, on I-84].
>
> 2nd. Traveled 18 miles to Utilla River [on Umatilla River, near Cayuse, Oregon].
>
> 3rd. Traveled 10 miles down Utilla River [at river crossing at Pendleton, Oregon].
>
> 4th. Lay by to recruit cattle.
>
> 5th. Traveled 18 miles and camped on the Utilla [upstream of Echo, Oregon].
>
> 6th. Traveled 12 miles to Springs in Utilla bottom [near Echo, Oregon].
>
> 7th. Traveled 28 miles to Well Springs.
>
> 8th. Traveled 16 miles to Willow Creek [at Cecil, Oregon].
>
> 9th. Lay by to recruit and left another wagon.
>
> 10th. Started at 2 o'clock p.m. and traveled 10 miles and made a dry camp [near Weatherford Monument on Highway 19].
>
> 11th. Traveled 14 miles to John Day River.
>
> 12th. Traveled 12 miles down John Day River.
>
> 13th. Traveled 24 miles to Columbia River.
>
> 14th. Traveled five miles to Deshutes River, crossed it and traveled five miles further to a small creek [Fifteenmile Creek, near Fairbanks, Oregon?].
>
> 15th. Traveled 10 miles to a branch of Deshutes [Eightmile Creek?].

Miller and Gates had each taken a fork of the trail that left the John Day River just west of the river crossing, but when Porter recorded that they traveled "down John Day's River" for twelve miles on September 12, he seemed to be suggesting that his company followed still another variant of the trail.

By September 12, both the Miller and Gates companies had arrived in the Willamette Valley, but William Porter's company was still 140 miles away.

September 1–15, 1848
Father Lempfrit, Stone company, Burnt River Canyon, Oregon

The morning of September 1 found Father Lempfrit and his Stone-Delaney company about 150 miles behind William Porter. Captain Stone was getting his company ready to leave camp, likely on Birch Creek, a couple of miles southwest of Farewell Bend. Since the Stone party was the last Oregon-bound company on the trail, nobody was behind them.

Passing Farewell Bend, the Stone company turned northwest and headed into the challenging Burnt River canyon north of today's Huntington, Oregon, on I-84. Lempfrit complained about the miserable weather on September 1, scribbling the following with numb, freezing fingers: "Throughout the night we had high winds and violent squally weather. It was extremely cold. There was nearly half an inch of ice on our pails. The trail got worse all the time. The mountains here are sheer cut peaks. We camped near the River Brûlée [Burnt River]."

For the next four days, Lempfrit provided few clues about how far they traveled or where they camped. Their travel on the second should have taken them through the Burnt River Canyon. Lempfrit continued to bemoan the cold, noting that they "needed two blankets and a buffalo robe to keep us warm." Near the end of the day, he described coming "to a crater shaped hill. I could not see in which direction the trail was leading us when all of a sudden we made a spiral turn which enabled us to see the long circuitous route we had traveled over the past three miles." His description suggested a winding segment of trail that descended into the Burnt River canyon about one mile northwest of exit 338 on I-84.

After suffering through another bone-chilling night in the Burnt River canyon, Lempfrit described resuming their travels on September 3. Ever since his company had arrived at the Boise River on August 24, he had repeatedly described his fellow travelers as extremely edgy. The company was now approaching the land of the Cayuse, and the priest was again mocking his companions' nervousness, seemingly insensitive to the fear generated by the stories they had heard from Joe Meek and the *engagés* at Fort Boise:

> 3rd September. The night has been very cold. We left at 8 o'clock. About 2 o'clock we witnessed a little comedy! Two of our men who had ridden on ahead of us were waiting for us on top of a small hill. When we saw them one of our Americans said, "Those are Indians, this time it really is the Walla Walla murderers waiting for us. Come on everyone, to arms!" And they at once readied themselves in a defensive position and walked with guns at their sides. A number of our Americans had forgotten the name the Indians call the French and trembling with anxiety they asked me what the name was. I told them they should reply "Tabibo" if questioned. Soon, however, I could laugh at their fear. We recognized our own people. Their gallantry was thus simply denied to them!

At the end of the day on the third, the party may have camped about five miles northwest of Durkee, Oregon. The following day, the Stone company arrived at the top of Flagstaff Hill, where the cold, crisp air afforded them a clear view across the

Powder River Valley. They would soon encounter Indians and what had been simmering anxiety now threatened to boil into full-blown panic.

> 4th September. We had quite a nice camping spot and there was a little spring there that was most refreshing. . . . At 3 o'clock we saw a number of Indians going by at the far end of the patch of prairie. This time it must be the murderers! A brave Canadian who was traveling with us as far as Walla Walla offered to go on ahead and scout out who the Indians might be. His proposal was accepted and he was off like a flash. He was there in ten minutes. We halted so that we could ascertain what the result of his mission would be. If you could only have seen the American ladies! They all believed that they heard the sound of a gunshot! "Look, they are killing the Canadian," and "he will never come back again," said another. "They have massacred him." Fifteen minutes later the Canadian returned in triumph, carrying with him a bow and a handful of arrows. When they saw him these timorous ladies said, "These are the weapons he took from the enemy when he had overcome them." The best part of the story is that the Americans again had to swallow their words. Quite simply, what had happened was that a friend of the Canadian was traveling with some Blackfeet Indians, and the head of this little group had made the Canadian a present of a bow and some arrows! At last we arrived at our camp site at the foot of the Blue Mountains. . . .

There is a good chance they had made it as far as the north end of the Powder River Valley. It would have been north of exit 278 on I-84. The next day:

> 5th September. We left rather late as we did not have far to go— in fact we set up our camp only six miles away. During the evening an Indian came to our camp and spoke with the Canadian who was traveling with us. This Canadian had lived for several years among these Indians and spoke their language fluently. His wife belonged to the Nez Percé Indian nation. The Indian told him that he had been sent by the chiefs of the Nez Percés and Cayuses to find out if there were any Fathers traveling with the caravan. He told them that several days ago they had hidden themselves in the prairie grass in order to watch out for the waggon in which the Fathers were traveling. However, they had not been able to identify it for they thought that the Fathers' waggon must be quite special in appearance. They went back and reported to the Cayuse chief that they hadn't seen any priests and that all the waggons looked exactly alike. The chief then said to another Indian, "you go yourself now, try and speak with the Fathers or anyone else belonging to the caravan company because I am sure that the priests are coming and we wish to see them on their way through this country." I was delighted with the good news this Indian gave to me. He told me that his chief had sent word to the brigands telling them that if any one of them dared to do us any harm or harm any of our company he would have to answer for it to the chief himself. He required that we should all be treated with respect. The Indian

then informed us that our Fathers were no longer at Walla Walla, they were now at Oregon City. Finally, the Great Chief had told him that he had letters from our Fathers to hand over to me. This last piece of news was balm to my soul. I treated the good Indian to my best and gave him some small presents. He hardly waited for my reply and left so abruptly that I must admit that his behaviour caused me some misgivings. The Americans, especially, believed that we were about to fall into a trap. I did the best I could to set their fears to rest but these poor people put the worst possible construction upon this event. . . .

The Stone company was now solidly in Cayuse country, but why would a Cayuse messenger be sent to deliver a message to Father Lempfrit? The answer goes back to the original missionaries. Even though Dr. Whitman had established his mission at Waiilutpu in 1835 among the Walla Walla band of Cayuse, two French Canadian priests, Father F. N. Blanchet and Father Demers, arrived in the region in 1838, intent on converting the local Indians to "the one true faith."[10] Dr. Whitman reacted to the priests as if a pestilence had arrived. Although he was disturbed by priests encroaching upon his territory, it was more than petty jealousy. He perceived that these Indians were subject to heated prejudices, and it was inviting danger to have two competing religions dividing the tribe.[11]

Although Dr. Whitman made his objections known to Catholic missionaries, they were not deterred. They established a mission between Fort Walla Walla and the Whitman mission, which they called St. Rose. Within a few years, about half of the Cayuse converted to Catholicism, finding the elaborate rites and rituals of the Catholic faith irresistible—the Masses, crucifixes, bells, rosary beads, etc.[12] The other half of the tribe remained devoted to Whitman's brand of Christianity. Tauitowe, chief of the Umatilla band of Cayuse, claimed to be a devout Catholic convert, and in 1847 he asked that a Catholic mission be established in his own village on the Umatilla River. Just a few days before the Whitman murders, Oblate Fathers Brouillet and Rousseau arrived at Tauitowe's village and established their mission, calling it St. Anne. After the Whitman killings, the Oregon militia ordered the priests at St. Rose and St. Anne to evacuate and hasten to The Dalles for safety so the priests were not at Oregon City, as Lempfrit had been told.[13]

News that the chiefs wanted to meet the priests seemed to delight Lempfrit, although it must have made his companions uneasy; they regarded these Indians much as one would a strange dog that might bite. The next day, the Stone company advanced into the Blue Mountains and Father Lempfrit filled a number of pages in his notebook describing the day in arresting detail:

6th September. That night we camped on the banks of a little river that was chock-full of salmon and we caught a large number of them. We left at 8 o'clock in the morning and the further we went the more beautiful the country became. The Blue Mountain region is quite delightful. What lovely scenery! How nature smiles here! What lovely groves of trees that nature has kept hidden away until it pleased her to send thither a handful of Europeans to admire some of her most beautiful creations. At 5 o'clock that evening we came to an immense plateau which was about fifteen miles wide by twenty-five miles long [Grande Ronde Valley]. As we were about to make our way down to this plateau we noticed a fine quarry of slate on the slope to the right. The trail that led down to the plateau was very steep with numerous spiral turns [Ladd Canyon Hill]. Those people on foot sometimes took a shortcut, a little path that was extremely steep and therefore very dangerous. I had already reached the prairie that lay at the foot of the plateau when I could not help but admire the courage of an American lady. In order to get down the hill this lady got hold of a plank from an abandoned waggon and after placing her child at one end of it she positioned herself at the other end. Then by making a little movement she set the plank in motion and slid straight down to the foot of the prairie without the slightest mishap. However I shuddered to think of the danger she was courting.

At last we arrived in the middle of this famous plateau called "Le Grand Rond." It is really one of the loveliest places in the whole world. Just imagine an enormous arena measuring about fifteen miles wide by twenty-five miles long, entirely surrounded by the most beautiful wooded mountains and watered by two lovely rivers. The extremely fertile soil supports a luxuriant vegetation and to the south there are some lovely rolling hills that seem to beg to be put under cultivation, being fatigued by producing nothing but trees whose branches fall to the ground from old age.

Two Indian nations have established their lodges at the foot of these lovely hills, the Nez Percés and the Cayuse. Their chiefs are "Le Grand Thuoté [Tauitowe], chief of the Cayuse nation, and "Le grand chef Cinq Corbeaux" [Five Crows] of the Nez Percés. I am going to tell you about these two great chiefs very shortly.

One of the chiefs, Tauitowe (also written as Tawatowe) was phonetically spelled "Thuoté" by Lempfrit. The other was Five Crows, Tauitowe's brother. Both were chiefs of the Umatilla band of Cayuse. Lempfrit was mistaken about Five Crows being a Nez Percé chief.[14]

Lempfrit continued:

We camped on the heights of the Grand Rond by the banks of the smaller of the two rivers that cross this immense prairie from south to north. The time is after dinner, about 4 to 5 in the evening. I go for a walk so that I can explore the country around us. Very soon the Indians come to seek me out to tell me that the two Great Chiefs of this Nation have come with their whole retinue to pay me a visit. "Wait a minute," I said to myself, "this now is the real thing, I am going to find myself in the presence of their Eminences! Well then, let us go and see these Great Chiefs." I set off at a gallop. When I arrived I was told that the chiefs were awaiting me in the tent of the Canadian who would serve as interpreter. Then came the solemn moment! Gathered round a great fire were thirteen Indians. Two of whom were more formally dressed than the others. These Indians were Thuoté [Tauitowe] and Five Crows. Both were dressed in the European fashion. They were wearing caps made from high quality blue cloth. Thuoté sported a green suit, a red waistcoat and pale blue trousers made from a very fine material. Five Crows was also carefully dressed. They took off their caps as they greeted me. I walked around the assembled groups, shaking hands with everyone.

Both Tauitowe and Five Crows had been present at Sand Hollow at the February 24 battle between the Oregon militia and the Cayuse. It had been reported that Five Crows had been shot during the battle, his arm shattered by a militia bullet. It was now six months later, but Lempfrit did not report noticing a problem with Five Crows' arm.[15]

Lempfrit continued:

Then the Great Chief spoke for a short while and the good Canadian immediately repeated in translation the reason for this official visit. "Father we have come especially to see you. We have known for a long time that priests would be coming this way but of you we learned that you are not only a priest, you are a doctor also. Here we are completely forsaken. We have no one who can teach us the beautiful prayer. It is true that we had a Father amongst us but he abandoned us after the revolt [Whitman massacre] of some misguided wretches. You, Father, you must not do the same as the others who have all gone away to the sea [the Willamette Valley]. Stay here with us. We will obey you and we know you will want to instruct our young people and teach them the wonderful things you do beyond the great sea. Look, Father, see those lovely hills. We will cultivate these lands that are so fertile. Tell us where you would like us to establish our village, choose the place for our village yourself. We are hoping that if you remain here with us, the poor misguided people who have rebelled will be sorry for what they have done. We have tried really hard to bring them back but it was useless.

It is important to explain that three months after the November 1847 massacre, representatives of the Oregon government met with the chiefs of the nearby tribes, including Tauitowe and Five Crows, and told them the Americans did not desire war with the Cayuse nation, but were adamant that the tribe must surrender the Whitman murderers and return the stolen property, mostly cattle. Although the chiefs agreed to their demands and continued to profess cooperation, they never produced the killers and seemed to give the militia commanders false information as to their whereabouts.

Because the Catholic priests had moved to The Dalles for their protection, Tauitowe now appeared to miss the attentions of his former priests. Having heard that new priests were coming in this year's emigration, it is evident that he was earnestly courting new ones. Lempfrit continued with his long entry, revealing how he had utterly fallen under the spell of the natives:

> I then took the floor and spoke to them more or less as follows: "Great Chief and all of you who have come to see us. I am very moved to see you hastening here to greet the priests on their way through this country. This eagerness on your part is proof enough that you would be happy to welcome amongst you a priest who could teach you the law of the Great Master of Life. Alas! You have lived your lives up till now in ignorance of this beautiful law. I can assure you that I would be very happy to be able to stay here with you. You are situated in a really enchanting place. I, however, have made myself responsible for really urgent official letters for my superiors and it is absolutely necessary for me to continue my journey to deliver these to them. I promise you, however, that I will do everything in my power to come back here as soon as possible. Indeed, I trust that in about two weeks I will definitely be able to come here and serve you as your priest. It will give me great pleasure to teach your children to know about the Master of Life. They must also learn the skills that are necessary for making life more agreeable and less harsh. Thus, you can rely on me."
>
> When I had finished speaking the Great Chief seemed satisfied. Then he said to the Canadian that he would like to hold a big festival for me on the morrow. It was already very late however. How could he collect all his people together? Immediately he sent off several messengers to the camps that were furthest away. Their orders were to summon everyone to assemble here at 2 o'clock the following day. I stayed with them until 10 o'clock that evening after which I departed. The good Canadian had been ordered not to tell me about the proposed festival but he dropped a hint that enabled me to guess that they wanted to do something special for me.

Lempfrit seemed completely taken by the Cayuse chiefs and their outward demonstrations of affection. Was he sincere when he wrote of his desire to come back as their missionary? Did he not worry that some unintended insult or misunderstanding could provoke them into turning against him? After all, members of this tribe had turned on their previous missionaries and had murdered them. Was Lempfrit being naïve or was he being shrewd by saying that he needed to get himself and his company members safely away from this potentially dangerous band? The answer can be found in his account of the following day, which he recorded at length:

> 7th September. I had a really beautiful night, my imagination lulled to sleep by the loveliness of this picturesque spot. On top of this, the genuine eagerness of these good Indians to have a priest in their midst transported me to the Seventh Heaven. During the morning an ambassador from the Great Chief came to see me. This messenger who knew a little English at once asked me if I was agreeable to receiving a visit from the whole tribe. Having acquiesced, he took me by

the hand and showed me a small hillock on which he asked me to stand without moving away from it. Our Americans had not the least idea what was going to happen. As for myself, I had no fears at all but I must admit that my situation caused me some discomfort. For over an hour I stood there, looking around in all directions but there was nothing to be seen. At last, bathed in a cloud of dust, I perceived a long file of horsemen advancing in orderly fashion. Soon two flags fluttering in the breeze could be seen. Just at this moment however, an Indian of an enemy tribe pointed out to us that we were running the risk of being massacred by this troop of Indians advancing towards us. "Look at these two flags," he said, "the white flag is good but the other one is red, that is the signal for war. They are going to kill you all." Then he went on to demonstrate that they were going to make "poum, poum, poum" on us. This had the effect of making our Americans tremble with apprehension. I tried to reassure them by reminding them that this could not possibly be a war party as an ambassador had been sent to me to announce that a festival was to be held. Then Mr. O'Neil suggested to me that we hoist a flag as a sign of peace and he asked me for a bit of white cloth which he promptly attached to a long stick that Americans use as a horsewhip. The Captain [Stone] who was a pretty poor violin scraper dashed off to his waggon to get his instrument.

We arranged ourselves in a semicircle and then we advanced slowly to meet the procession. Now we are face to face! A dozen Indians mounted on superb horses had small drums that they tapped lightly with little drumsticks. The drums were bound around with horsehair and the sound they produced could either be muffled or very loud according to the wishes of the player. Behind them came the singers beating out the measure by striking the saddles of their horses. We were the first to halt. Then the long line of horses peeled off to the right and to the left and the two flags were brought up and set up beside our own. The white flag had a red cross at its centre and the other flag, the one that had inspired so much fear in the hearts of our Americans, was a red flag emblazoned with the arms of the United States. The Great Chiefs Five Crows and Thuoté came forward while their Indian musicians played a fanfare. They shook hands with us, then several horsemen rode up and circled round our flags and immediately the peace-pipe ceremony got under way. I noticed that in circumstances such as these it is the newcomers who are expected to provide the tobacco. As we were unaware of the etiquette required by this ceremony the Indians let us see the great peace-pipe empty, then a huge amount of tobacco was hastily brought up. Later on the two Great Chiefs requested me to follow them into the Canadian's tent. It was here that they repeated to me in essence what they had said the previous evening but this time I learned that this festival had been prepared especially for me, the objective being to commit me to come and establish my mission amongst their people! Then they brought me a large roll of papers. I thought I would find there the letters they had told me about, but instead, I found fourteen beautifully coloured engravings. These were the fourteen stations of the Road to the Cross. They told me that they had been given them by a Catholic Father. I also found other religious engravings amongst which was a Catholic Ladder. These were the letters they had to deliver to me! I told them to take great care of these things and that we would hang them up in the church I would come and build for them. After this short conversation, I went back to have a look at the festival.

As the Great Chief had earlier announced that trading could take place most of the Indians had gone off to fetch horses and other items of barter. They came back shortly bringing some magnificent horses that we could acquire for very little; for example a very poor gun or a blanket could be exchanged for a horse that in France would cost at least one hundred Louis. I spent a little time walking about among the rows of Indians as I wanted to study the variety of their costumes and more especially the colours of them. I had previously noticed that there were eighty-three horsemen on the right and only about thirty on the left. I was told that the reason why the group on the left was smaller was because many in this group had gone away to their village to fetch horses. Only then did I realize that the group on the right consisted entirely of women while the group on the left were all men.

Shortly afterwards a large number of men and women carrying baskets filled with potatoes and Indian corn arrived. Sometimes there were two riders on the same horse, a man sitting up front and a woman sitting behind on the rump of the animal. This sight called to my mind the observation of an American lady, who came up to me and having separated me from the other people in our party, showed me an Indian woman eating the lice on her man's head! The Indian woman searched for them skillfully and then, with great delicacy, picked them out with her small fingers and nibbled them as we might relish a grain of salt! I have no idea what exquisite taste this good Indian woman could possibly find in this condiment! Perhaps it might have tasted like crab sauce! . . . The festival went on until evening. It was not until about 7 o'clock that the chief's messenger called out to the crowd that the party was over and that everyone should return to their villages. In a few minutes this huge swarm of Indians had vanished.

The next morning, the Stone party was undoubtedly anxious to get underway. Not only did they still have 350 miles to go, but it is possible that the nervous emigrants did not share Lempfrit's exuberance with the Cayuse, and wanted to get through this country quickly. Lempfrit reported their departure:

8th September. As we had to be on our way early that morning I bade farewell to the good Indians after the festival. At first light I was away on my horse so as to be able to explore this attractive country. The further I went the more enchanted I was with what I discovered. Oh! How many castles in Spain did I build while riding past these lovely hills covered with magnificent fir trees. In my imagination I was already established amongst those good Indians as their priest! Soon, however, the trail became very arduous. At about four o'clock there was a very steep hill to go down. I made my way down the hill, leading my horse by the bridle. When I reached the bottom I came on a little American girl who had fallen off her horse. She was lying in a dust-filled, dried-out gully screaming at the top of her voice. I got this poor child out of the hole, luckily she was unhurt, she was just frightened. Then we came to a little valley through which flowed a river abounding in crayfish [the gunshot-echoing Grande Ronde River Canyon]. When our company arrived I showed them a basketful of them. "Well," they said to me, "you go ahead to catch crayfish instead of remaining behind to receive the excellent horse the Great Chief came to give you this morning. Since he did not find you, he went away, taking the horse with him." I confess that I was rather vexed with myself for having departed so precipitately.

Once again, Lempfrit's interest in solitary jaunts had cost him; this time he had missed out on a gift of an "excellent horse." The next morning, the Stone caravan departed their camp, probably near Hilgard, Oregon, and ascended into the Blue Mountains:

9th September. Today we had an excellent camping spot, a very nice situation completely surrounded by tall fir trees. Right beside us flowed a river [Grande Ronde River] abounding in fish and in the shallow parts of the river one could scoop up quantities of crayfish. I went on ahead with the Canadian who was traveling with us. At first we climbed a very steep path, then, having arrived at the summit we saw a group of horsemen riding toward us and shouting at the top of their voices. For a moment I was apprehensive, but was soon reassured when the good Indians came up to us. I much admired their beautiful horses. Soon, however, we had to take leave of them as the provisions they were carrying were putrid! This was indeed a travelling stench as the air was polluted everywhere they had been. We had hoped to find water but we had to go on for twelve more miles before we found any. Our horses were spent, the oxen refused to go any further and the night was about to descend upon us. The Captain wanted us to carry on further. We had three waggons with us, all the rest lagged behind. An unusual stratagem for preventing the Captain from pushing on was conceived by the people in the waggons behind us. All of a sudden one of their guides came galloping up and reported to the Captain that one of their waggons had overturned as it was going down a hill. Two men had been crushed under the weight of the vehicle. Can you imagine more agonizing news! At once I spurred my horse and we all went to the help of these unfortunate men. Soon however we learned that it was only a ruse to make us go back. It was a false alarm!

Despite Captain Stone's determination to push on, the exhausted company had other ideas and they finally stopped to camp in the afternoon at or near the summit of the mountains, but their camp (perhaps a mile or two south of today's exit 238 on I-84) was not adjacent to any stream:

> 10th September. We had a very bad camp site and as a result of this we lost half our animals. Nearly all of them strayed during the night in search of a little water. We had let them graze at random, consequently when morning came we found ourselves without any oxen. We had a great deal of difficulty getting them back. The poor old man who had died the previous evening was buried. Thirteen of our oxen were still missing at 11 o'clock. Finally, we left around noon so that we could make a little headway. On our way out of this area we came on grassy clearings in the forest. The grass was parched and yellowed by the heat of the sun. These patches of prairie looked like fields of fully ripened corn. Then we came upon huge trees which hung long clumps of blackish moss.

On September 11, the Stone company finally left the Blue Mountains by descending Emigrant Hill. They soon reached the Umatilla River:

> 11th September. . . . The trail was extremely rough. We emerged from the lovely fir forests at about 2 o'clock and at last left behind us the long range of mountains. Ahead of us the country was quite flat. Now we had a new horizon. It seemed as though we saw a vast expanse of sea in the distance, for the scorched prairies give the landscape a bluish hue. We camped on the banks of the Umatilla River and there we found the remains of gardens that the poor Indians had cultivated before the Walla Walla revolt. The country is extremely fertile.

Like the diarists preceding him, Lempfrit noticed that the Umatilla river valley was devoid of Cayuse, their villages and gardens unoccupied and unattended. The company camped along the riverbank near the present community of Cayuse.

> 12th September. The Mission established by our Fathers was eighteen miles away, but having learned that they had to abandon this post I decided to leave for Oregon City. Several Americans who wanted to have some fresh meat sent an agent to Fort Walla Walla to buy beef. My patients were all fully convalescent. The pure air they were breathing here contributed greatly to their recovery. We left rather late today. About 2 o'clock in the afternoon there was dissent among our Americans and seven of the waggons of our company left in order to go and join the waggon-train that was one day ahead of us.

What wagon train was he referring to? It could not have been the Purvine company, which was one hundred miles and seven days beyond. It could have been a group of impatient wagons that had left their company and pulled ahead.

The entry of the twelfth confirmed their camp on the evening of the eleventh was near today's town of Cayuse, as this was where westbound travelers crossed the river if they were going to Whitman's mission or the Hudson's Bay Company's Fort Walla Walla. Father Lempfrit had indicated earlier that his original destination was Walla Walla, likely meaning the St. Rose mission near Fort Walla Walla, thirty-five miles northeast of where he was. Therefore, the mission he described as "eighteen miles away" would not have been St. Rose, but was probably the Oblate mission of St. Anne that had recently been established at Tauitowe's village on the Umatilla. The location was on the river a few miles west of today's Pendleton, or about eighteen miles west of the Stone company's camp of the eleventh. Lempfrit understood that he had to go on to Oregon City to find his Oblate Superior. Lempfrit recorded a day of discord on the thirteenth:

> 13th September. I have called this camp the "Make Believe Camp" because although we have changed our camp we traveled only half a mile! Division and dissent reigned in the camp of Israel! Once the danger is over the American cherishes his idea of liberty and submits unwillingly to every kind of constraint. Soon he rejects all obedience to authority. Our company divided up into four groups today and each group elected the captain of his choice.

Was mere dissent turning into something more intense? Lempfrit recorded an interesting transformation in attitudes. The company was in the process of disintegrating, not so much because the emigrants were disputatious, but because they were independent by nature. Having to travel together in one mutually cooperative and dependent unit was in conflict with their natural temperaments and personalities. Their fear of the Cayuse and their perceived need to travel in large parties had probably abated, the terrifying stories and horrific images they had conjured had now largely fled. They had, after all, met this purportedly murderous tribe and found them quite convivial. What was there to fear? Their natural impatience, fermenting for some time, had finally boiled to the surface. The stronger, faster wagons decided that it was time for them to look out for themselves. And the slow-moving plodders who were holding others back should do the same.

In truth, the emigrants were not in much danger. While the tribe had not lost many warriors in battles with the whites, they had suffered significantly in other ways: they had been uprooted from their villages and gardens, and had been forced to keep on the move. They had learned that causing trouble with the whites was an unwise thing.

Father Lempfrit's next entry described the next two days:

> 14th and 15th September. The night has been very cold. Our caravan was now reduced to eleven waggons. At noon we were in sight of the Cascade mountains. They were all snow-covered. The next day [15th] our travel was abominable, deep sand, but sand so unstable that it was only with difficulty that one could

extricate himself. We had taken the wrong road. We should have followed the one on the right. We were thus subjected to awful trails.

Now traveling with eleven wagons, their party had returned to the size it had been when it left St. Joseph. Riley Root had opined earlier that his company should have taken a shortcut by heading directly west from present-day Nolin: "August 23rd two miles might have been savd by crossing the [Umatilla] river at the [Nolin] camp, but to avoid sandy traveling, emigrants go down the river some farther." It sounded like Captain Stone had decided to try the sandy shortcut, another one of his questionable decisions. According to Lempfrit, this route took them through deep sand, something Root said they had purposely avoided.

Father Lempfrit and his dispirited Stone company likely camped on Butter Creek about a mile west of Highway 207, on Oregon Trail Road.

September 1–15, 1848
Richard May and Edward Smith, Chiles company, Battle Mountain, Nevada

The Chiles company continued its monotonous march down the Humboldt River plain. On the evening of August 31, the company had camped, about seven miles east of today's Battle Mountain, Nevada. They were tired and impatient after days of crawling like snails past an endless succession of look-alike, cream-colored mountains and trudging beside this stream that someone had incongruously named a river. While the Cornwall and Wambaugh companies were crossing the high Sierras, the former traveling over the new Mormon/Carson trail and the latter over the older Truckee/Donner road, the Chiles company was still more than three hundred miles from beginning to cross those same mountains.

On September 1, Richard May wrote:

Friday 1st September 1848. Traveled 15 miles and our eleventh camp on Mary's River. The dust had been intolerable bad, rising in clouds from the train as it moved down the plain. A part of the road today was covered with dust so strongly impregnated with saleratus that it caused every living thing to sneeze that inhaled it. If we had been traveling through lime to the same depth it would not have been more disagreeable. The landscape still beautiful, the day very cool with flying clouds and heavy squalls of wind from the northwest.

Edward Smith also complained that "the Road was very dusty," a bit of an understatement considering that the ever-present cloud of dust would have thickly coated everything in a whitish powder and made the emigrants wish they could hold their breath. He reported that they encamped at "3 oclock PM," likely spending the night about two miles southeast of today's exit 222 on I-80. The next day, the company resumed their crawl across the broad river plain just east of Battle Mountain. About ten in the morning, according to Smith, the company crossed to the right (north) bank of the Humboldt and traveled across a flat that, in May's words, was "covered with a saline encrustation." May reported the day as very cold and cloudy. Freezing rain commenced in the afternoon.

Chiles had a delicate balance to maintain: he needed to press forward with all possible haste, as they still had far to go and much to overcome. Speed was important, but too much would be costly. They had to manage their animals wisely. Continuing on until six that evening, they completed eighteen miles, then stopped to camp on a salt-covered plain on the north side of the river, about seven miles northeast of I-80's exit 205.

Snow fell on the mountaintops that night. The next morning, Smith wrote that they looked "as white as silver." It was an alarm: snow had likely fallen in the high Sierras as well, and the company was still weeks away.

They traveled only nine miles on the third. May described the country as a "beautiful plain," and the mountains as "bold and above medium height." They camped at a good spot, which Smith described as "near where some Mountains close in on the River   here the River turns to the Southwest." His entry suggests that their camp was just east of Emigrant Canyon, about five miles northwest of today's I-80, on Highway 789.

Companies that crossed to the other side of the river, like Chiles, avoided Iron Point, a steep, sandy ridge that ran up to the south bank of the river. Some groups chose to stay on the south (and east) side of the Humboldt all the way to the Sink. The Donner party had taken the southern branch of the trail, and the sand hill at Iron Point was where frayed tempers ignited between one of James Reed's teamsters and John Snyder, a driver for another family. Reed intervened; he ended up stabbing and killing Snyder, and was banished from the party.[16]

On September 4, the Chiles company entered Emigrant Canyon, a four-mile-long canyon chiseled along the southern spur of the Osgood Mountains. Once through the canyon, the river turned northwest again, and the trail entered another wide plain. Smith reported,

> Mon 4 our road through a narrow valley   Mr. Peirson found a Paper stating that Capt. S. J. Hensley's co. of Mules Had shot three digger Indians in this canon on the 29th of August   the valley opened to about four miles wide   the Road in this Bottom runs northwest   distance about 10 miles.

It had been five days since May or Smith had mentioned encountering any Indians. From this point on, the company would begin to encounter them again, still calling them Diggers, even through they had passed from the territory of the Shoshoni "Diggers" to that of the Northern Paiute "Diggers." The warning left by the Hensley packers should have encouraged the night guards to renew their vigilance.

May's entry for September 4 described the route as "very good, grass good . . . mountains bold and rugged." He was probably referring to the Sonoma Mountains to the south, rising to over nine thousand feet. After traveling thirteen miles by May's

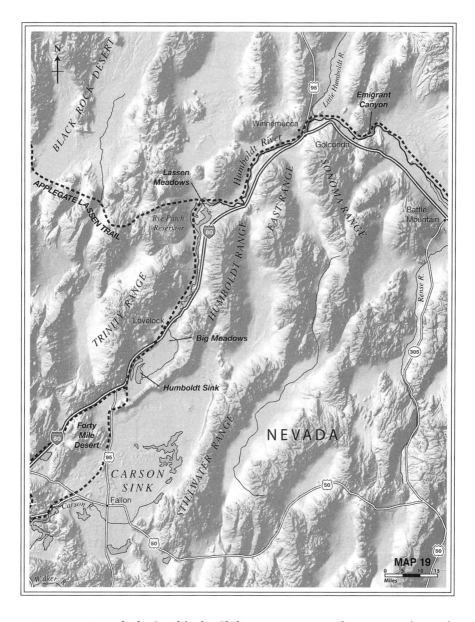

MAP 19

estimates, or ten miles by Smith's, the Chiles company stopped to camp on the north side of the river about three miles due east of today's exit 187 on I-80. Their campsite was a favorite among travelers because the river split into two branches, forming an "island" of thousands of acres, where lush grass grew in abundance, much of it over three feet tall. Especially during the gold rush years, travelers used scythes to harvest tons of grass hay and loaded it in their wagons to feed their stock when they reached the grassless stretches ahead.[17] But there was also the danger of their animals' miring in the swampy bogs that frequented the island.

The company resumed traveling down the river plain the next day, their direction being mostly westerly. Richard May described a disturbing incident that occurred that evening in camp:

> Tuesday 5th Sept. Traveled 15 miles and pitched our 15th camp on this little river. The scenery continues near the same as heretofore. The day very warm, grass good, wood difficult to get at having to cross the river and float it over. At this camp we found a mule belonging to Hensley's Train pierced with arrows so as to prevent it from traveling. It becomes my duty to record an accident which happened this evening while on guard. A pistol in the hands of Mr. Misner unfortunately went off and entered the fleshy part of the arm above midway from the shoulder of Mr. Smith to the elbow. There is some censure attached to the unfortunate Misner but taking all the circumstances together I see no reason for censure whatsoever. The whole camp sympathizes with Mr. Smith and it was certainly a serious affair. His teamster being badly mutilated by the bursting of a shot gun a few days ago leaving him in a rather helpless condition. Mr. Misner who is quite a discreet young man and in bad health is as much cut down from the accident as anyone can be.

Diarist Edward Smith had been shot. While May seems anxious to acquit Misner of blame, in many ways it didn't really matter who was at fault. Any wound, even an apparently minor one, was a frightening thing on the trail. Despite Mrs. Smith's ministrations, infection could set in and an infection could quickly become fatal. No doubt Mrs. Smith kept a watchful eye on her husband over the next days, checking his wound often and trying to hide her worry as she wondered what would become of her and the children if her husband were to die on the trail. Smith, however, seemed to take a stoic approach. He mustered the strength to take up a pen and record his own version of the mishap:

> Tues 5 nothing of note occurred to day   we traveled about 13 miles and encamped   one digger came into camp   good grass   at dark i was wounded in the arm by Isaac Misener   at dusk Isaac Newton Misner shot me through the left arm with a rifle pistol distance about 3 ft   he says it was an accident but I doubt it.

What a strange entry. Even though May reported that Misner was "as much cut down from the accident as anyone can be," Smith conveyed a different impression. Smith chose not to report any more about the incident, and he never explained how he and his family managed. With one of his arms probably useless and his driver Davidson injured, one wonders who caught up his oxen, hitched them to the wagons, and drove.

Not surprisingly, the appearance of Smith's handwriting in his journal changed suddenly on September 5. It became weak and shaky. For the next four days, he only recorded miles traveled. Then for the next nine days, he recorded nothing, as if his wound had worsened to where he could not write at all. On September 15, however, he resumed writing again in a firm, clear hand. His condition had apparently rallied. He then went back in time to write new, more detailed entries for September 7 through 14.

The company's camp on the evening of September 5, where Smith met his accident, was in an area commonly called Upper Meadows, another campsite with abundant grass. The river ran southwesterly here, and their campsite would have been about three miles directly north of today's Winnemucca. According to May, they made twenty miles on the sixth, proceeding south for four miles, then rounding the southern nose of Winnemucca Mountain and continuing southwesterly beside a rush and willow-filled slough that paralleled the river's north bank. These mosquito-infested sloughs, former river channels, were quite common along the Humboldt.

In the afternoon, the company rolled over low bluffs just to the north of the river. The river had washed away at these bluffs and produced steep banks, some as much as one hundred feet deep. This made it difficult for the emigrants to get their livestock to water. The company's campsite on the sixth should have been just beyond the bluffs, on the west side of the river, probably six miles west of today's exit 168 on I-80.

May reported that they continued to follow the river on September 7. They traveled twenty miles, mostly south, then turned due west. "Willows scarce and grass not very plenty," he observed. "The last two days has been quite warm about summers heat. The nights are cool. The mountains rugged and picturesque. An incrustation of saline efflorescence covers the plain almost entirely for the last three days." He was probably referring to the East Range, with peaks that rose in the southeast to over seven thousand feet.

Smith reported that they had traveled eighteen miles on the seventh, in contrast to May's estimate of twenty miles. Smith lamented that his "wound continues to be extremely Painful." At the end of this long day, they camped on the north side of the river, about four miles northwest of today's exit 145 on I-80.

May recorded a short travel day on the eighth:

Friday 8th. Traveled 4 miles and encamped on the river. A general repairing of wagons with the men, the women are washing. All in good humor and high spirits. The grass is good. The mountains bold and rugged. The water bad and we expect it to be no better intil this river leaves us as it will do in a few days more.

The company's campsite on September 8 was likely Lassen Meadows, a narrow river valley with high bluffs on either side. It was also where the Humboldt River made a wide turn to the west, then turned almost due south. The meadow in the river bottom was another excellent spot to camp. It should have been near Pioneer Road (also known as Imlay-Sulphur Road), about eight miles northwest of today's exit 145 on I-80 and probably beneath the waters of Rye Patch Reservoir.

Neither of our diarists commented on the state of their provisions. Large game was scarce in this region, and neither diarist had reported any hunting activity for some time. Aside from what was left of their cured bacon and the occasional frog caught in the river and sloughs, they probably did not have much in the way of meat. They still had flour and beans, but they must have been tired of that bland fare. Bushes grew in the area that yielded a sweet berry that made delicious pies, but the women must have feared wandering far to gather them because of the Indian threat.

Lassen Meadows was another great source of grass that could be cut and loaded into their wagons. Chiles had traveled this trail twice before, in 1841 and 1847, and knew that grassless wastelands lay ahead, yet neither of our diarists report cutting hay. If Chiles had not had his party cut hay here, that would have been an unpardonable failure.

Lassen Meadows was named after Peter Lassen, whose party of ten wagons had encountered the first two companies of eastbound Mormons four days earlier. Although Lassen must have learned from the Mormons about their new Carson road, he had his own agenda and would not be swayed. He left the main trail here and led his small party across what was called the Applegate Trail, named for Jesse Applegate, who, with eleven others, had been sent by the Oregon settlers in 1846 to find a shorter, easier way between Fort Hall and the Willamette Valley. The Applegate party included Black Harris and Colonel Nathaniel Ford, both of whom had also led the party with which James Clyman traveled to Oregon in 1844.[18] Applegate and his companions first traveled south through the Willamette Valley, then wound through the southern Cascades to the Klamath River. Then they headed southeast across the extreme northeast corner of California. After crossing the Black Rock Desert of Nevada, one of the driest, bleakest regions imaginable, they finally struck the Humboldt River at this large meadow. Now in 1848, Lassen led his small band of followers along the Applegate route, entering California just south of Goose Lake, then leaving the Applegate road and heading southwest. They then wandered through uncharted regions of the northern Sierras until they staggered virtually starving into the Sacramento Valley in late October.[19] Suffice it to say, his was not a better route into California and those who followed him came to rue the day they made that decision. In the years following 1848, many a quarrel would erupt at Lassen Meadows, arguing over whether to continue south on the main trail, or head west on the Applegate/Lassen trail.

The Chiles company left camp early on the morning of September 9 and headed south along the main trail on the west side of the Humboldt. With the trail traveling over bluffs high above the deep-cut river, getting to water was difficult. Sometimes they would encounter springs. A gold rusher would later describe a simple criterion used to distinguish good springs from bad: "[I]f it is full of snakes, frogs and other reptiles, it is alright. We drive them out and take a drink ourselves; but if the water looks black and we can't find no water varmint, not even a snake, we let it alone."[20]

At some point while traveling on the ninth, the Chiles party would have seen a plume of dust rising in the distance. It turned out to be a third Mormon party coming from California: "Sat 9 we traveled about 4 miles," Smith wrote, "met some of the Mormons on Pack Horses." May recorded encountering the group:

> Saturday 9th Sept. 1848. Traveled 6 miles and encamped the 19th time. We met another portion of Cooks (it will be remembered they are Mormons) just from California. The glowing gold stories were rehearsed and I have no doubt but what fortunes are realized in a very short time. They were packers.

These packers were members of the Mormon Battalion, commonly called Cooke's Battalion, after its commander, Colonel P. St. George Cooke. The Mormon packers likely recounted the latest news from the goldfields, as well as details of the trail ahead, especially where Digger attacks were to be expected. After they moved on, some members of the Chiles company probably struck up excited conversations about the new stories of gold discoveries. The location of Chiles' camp on the ninth would have been on the west side of the Humboldt, about seven miles northwest of today's exit 138 on I-80.

Many Paiutes lived close to the river, and the company must have sensed it was being watched continuously. According to May, the Diggers were busy the next night:

> Sunday 10th. Traveled 15 miles. At 4 o'clock this morning we were aroused from our slumbers and shortly after daylight it was discovered that some of our cattle were pierced with arrows. The cow beasts and one horse were mortally wounded. We detached six men to watch the animals and the train moved forward and in a few minutes after we started the sound of their rifles was heard. They shot an Indian and suppose they killed him. This is the first time we have been molested by Indians. Nothing but diligence will save our stock in guarding them.

And Smith wrote:

> Sun 10 crossed Mary's River twice and encamped in a nest of diggers in the morning chiles Bull was shot with four arrows 4 cows & steers and one horse was shot antwine [Antoine] shot one digger.

The next day, September 11, the Chiles company encountered Ebenezer Brown's company, the Mormon wagon party that had passed P. B. Cornwall's company when it entered the West Carson Canyon on August 27. This means that Chiles still had two weeks to go before his party would reach the formidable Sierras. Richard May described the day:

> Monday 11th Sept. Traveled 16 miles over what may be termed a salaratus plain and made our 20th camp. We met too, another company bound for Salt Lake.

The glowing stories about the gold mines in Alta California. These wagons, 12 in number, came a new route over the mountains and represent it much better than the old road. Our Indian war yesterday has not proved as yet any disadvantage.

Mormon diarist John Borrowman, still traveling with the Brown company, recorded the Chiles company rolling into their camp that evening. He added details about the Indian incident of the tenth, revealing how the emigrants' frustrations with losing livestock had finally boiled over and provoked them into an act of revenge:

Monday, 11th, we rested in camp   here a company of emegrants came to us and camped with us   they informed us that the Indians had shot several of their cattle at the western crossing of the Marys river and they had also shot one Indian   this they did by 5 men remaining in ambush near their camp after the company had left and when the Indians came into camp as is their custom they shot one.[20]

On the morning of September 12, the two companies parted. According to May, the Mormons recommended their new road, and they no doubt mentioned their encounter with P. B. Cornwall and his company. Borrowman reported buying a gun from someone in the Chiles company, but did not indicate whether Chiles gave his group of Mormons a "waybill" to Salt Lake, as he had with the Thompson company.

The Chiles party crept along under an intense sun and through punishing heat on the twelfth. It remained virtually impossible to reach water as the river meandered through a narrow channel twenty to one hundred feet deep between almost perpendicular banks of clay that turned the water a milky white. May related that they continued on through a moonlit night:

Tuesday 12th. We traveled 35 miles during the day and night and made our 21st camp on this stream. It was 4 o'clock in the morning [of the 13th]. We were forced into this drive for the want of grass. We had a delightful time driving the teams during the night. The moon fulled at an early hour and shone with great clearness, but all at once she appeared to be covered with clouds, it grew quite dark. I looked and behold the shadows of the earth had fallen on her. The eclipse was total and of course lasted for some time. The Indian fires were plainly to be seen on the right and left. It is their custom when strangers get into their neighborhood to do this in order to give warning to their friends of the fact. Our team gave out but rolled in shortly after daylight. We are now encamped near what is termed the sink of Mary's River. . . . This stream takes its rise within the rim of the great Salt Lake bason. . . . the banks are very high in that region, say from 20 to 30 feet, the channel narrow never exceeding forty feet. The plain which is extensive, with some very rich spots, but the greater portion is dry and covered with a mixture of saleratus and other substances which are very offensive to those traveling through this country. . . . [W]ith the exception of a few miles it forms one of the best natural roads that I ever traveled and the only pass known from Fort Hall to upper California. We have dust in quantities on this road which does annoy the members but proves of great utility to the teams saving their feet from being worn down so they could not travel.

Why did Chiles not stop his company that night at "Big Meadows"? It was a grassy oasis where the town of Lovelock, Nevada, presently stands and the Humboldt River meandered through a low area of meadows and tule marshes. It would have been a good spot to rest, cut grass, and let the stock graze. Inexplicably, Chiles kept his weary troop marching on, passing these meadows in the dark and continuing another fifteen miles to the Sink. Was anyone concerned? Chiles didn't seem to be. After all, he had made this trip twice before.

When they reached the Sink in the early morning hours of the thirteenth, after a trek of thirty-five miles, the exhausted, dust-covered company collapsed—but only for eight hours, barely long enough to catch their breath. While much of the Sink was a dry, white alkali flat about twelve miles long and four miles wide, it was also an area of bulrush-filled sloughs, marshes, and shallow ponds filled with a brackish brew of stinking scum, dissolved alkali, sodium bicarbonate (saleratus), and other salts. Grass was almost nonexistent. It was no place to loiter. "Farewell to thee! thou stinking turbid stream," a disgruntled traveler wrote when he bid goodbye to the Humboldt and its Sink in 1852.[22]

At noon, Chiles ordered his company to move out again. He had decided on taking the Mormons' new Carson road over the Sierras, but instead of following the Mormons' route by first crossing the Forty Mile Desert to the Truckee River, then heading south twenty-five miles to the Carson River, he decided to head directly south from the Sink. He had traveled that way in 1841 as part of the Bartleson-Bidwell party, and knew they could reach the Carson River in thirty-five miles.[23] All he had to do was locate the old wagon tracks. By skipping the Forty Mile Desert and heading directly to the Carson River, he must have reasoned that he would replace a forty-five-mile leg and a twenty-five-mile leg (a total of seventy) with just one leg of thirty-five miles, a savings of thirty-five miles over waterless desert.

After barely eight hours of rest, the company began crossing this cheerless stretch of abject desolation, a place that an 1850 gold rusher warned: "Expect to find the worst desert you ever saw, and then find it worse than you expected."[24] May described the harrowing trek:

Wednesday 13th and night following, at noon today we left the sink of Mary's River where we had poor grass and the worst water we have met with on the road it being very salty and scowering our cattle and several fasted in consequence of that disease. We moved on until 10 o'clock [P. M. on the 13th]. Stopped without water until 2 o'clock in the morning then run on until the sun had risen

we called a halt. You must recollect from the sink we took a new route aiming to
strike Salmon Trout River [Carson River].

After leaving the Sink at noon, the company continued a long march of ten hours
across a plain of deep sand and powdery alkali, with no trees, little grass, and few
sage. The only water would have been the occasional toxic pool. They finally had to
stop for a breather at ten o'clock that night, but they could not pause long, as the cattle
desperately needed to reach good water. After resting only four hours, the company
resumed their march at two o'clock in the morning. With teamsters cracking their
whips to keep the dull-eyed oxen moving, they marched for three more hours. When
the sun rose, they were forced to stop again as they came to a section of deep sand
dunes where one ox after another collapsed in the deep sand and wagons quickly
became bogged down. They were still eleven miles from the river, but could not go
another step. Hadn't Chiles foreseen that this would be too much to expect of them?

The livestock were in serious trouble. May mentioned how the cattle had been
scouring ("scowering"), meaning that they were suffering from diarrhea induced by
the brackish water they drank at the Sink. Ingesting a salty solution produces a laxa-
tive effect in cattle, which these already dehydrated creatures could ill afford. Further-
more, May described their animals as "fasting," meaning they had lost their appetites,
or "gone off their feed." Cattle are ruminants and depend on millions of rumen bacteria to digest otherwise indigestible plant fiber. Too much salt-infused water dras-
tically changes the pH in their rumens from acidic to alkaline, kills most of their
fiber-digesting bacteria, and causes their digestive systems to effectively shut down.

Edward Smith stressed their hardships in his entry on that dismal day:

> Wed 13 about 4 o clock this morning we arrived at the Sink having traveled about
> 40 miles without stopping to graze   the cattle look very bad   here is no grass
> and the water fetid   started about 3 PM   in 4 miles we turned to the south and
> south east in about 6 more miles   we found water and grass but it was so salty
> the cattle would not eat it   the Road is strewn with given out Cattle, halted
> about 2 hours   traveled through the sand and sage   about one 8th of the
> cattle have given out and the same amount of wagons have been left   I went
> about 3 miles on a hill [probably the Upsal Hogsback] to take a look at the Coun-
> try   I saw timber in the South about 10 miles distant   some waggons went on
> while 15 waggons corralled and sent the cattle under guard to the timber which
> appeared to be cottonwood a sure indication of water   chiles has not returned
> at night   a little water arrived in camp.

Smith must have climbed the Upsal Hogsback, a solitary hill about twenty-four miles
south of the Sink and eleven miles north of the Carson River. From these heights,
he could see a narrow ribbon of dark green—cottonwoods lining the Carson River.

Smith's entry was generally consistent with May's, except that he reported
leaving the Sink at three o'clock in the afternoon on September 13, while May had

As tough as oxen were, even they had their limits. Charles Nahl (1818–78), *Crossing the Plains*. Oil on canvas, 1856. Courtesy of the Iris & B. Gerald Cantor Center for Visual Arts of Stanford University; Stanford Family Collections.

reported leaving at noon. It may suggest that their wagon train was strung out, with not everyone traveling together as one unit.

Their cattle were rapidly giving out. It was insane to think that these broken-down creatures, after weeks of little to eat, bad water, and insufficient rest, suffering from dehydration and massive digestive collapses, could pull wagons seventy miles in the space of forty-eight hours. Most teams were being unhitched from their wagons so they could be led to the river to drink. Smith reported that oxen were dropping all along this horrid expanse, but it was a wonder that any survived. Only a few ox teams were strong enough to pull their wagons all the way. Most teams were being unhitched from their wagons so they could be led to the river to drink. The teamsters whose wagons did reach the river filled kegs with desperately needed water and returned to the miserable remains of their company still stranded in the desert, which included Smith and May.

And where was Captain Chiles? May noted that he was "ahead of us explored the road." Smith complained that "chiles has not returned at night [the 13th]." Admittedly, there was value in scouting ahead, but as captain of this company, perhaps he should have been among his stricken people, looking after their needs.

On September 14, Smith recorded that some of their party returned from the river with water, but it was not nearly enough:

Thur 14 about one oclock a m [on the 14th] Mr. Moore came in with two small kegs of water and about 10 [AM?] Mr. Hallenbecks boy arrived with two more kegs of water   about 3 p m [on the 14th] Jerome came in with 2 more and at sun set the cattle came   at 9 p m [on the 14th] we started once more on our wearisome journey which I shall call the forlorn hope   our cattle travel very well through the sand in many places one foot deep all the way [to] 6 inches   I arrived in camp [on the Carson River] in daylight [on the 15th] two waggons were left in camp   2 more along the Road   the cattle comes in slowly   we are still hunt-ing for our cattle   those oxen have been shot at this camp by Indians   I have lost from Mary [Humboldt] Sink 3 cows strayed off and one ox given out   sent back to near the Sink to hunt the cows this morning   Mr. Slater and St. Francisco Returned without finding anything of the cows   we are now encamped on the Salmon Trout [Carson] River Running East and west which we intend to follow to the mountains   last night the Indians Killed 7 Head of cattle   the camp Looks bad and gloomy   I still remember the darkest hour is just before daylight to night another of my oxen was killed.

What a gloomy picture Smith had painted, like something out of Dante's Eighth Circle of Hell. When Smith finally made it to the river, four wagons still remained in the desert, perhaps from the lack of oxen to pull them. Most of the animals that had been turned loose earlier—usually the "given out" ones—had wandered off in search of water. Some made it to the river, but being unguarded, many fell prey to the lurking Paiutes. As for Smith's own animals, four cows had wandered off or been abandoned in the desert since they left the Sink. He sent someone back to look for them, but they returned empty-handed.

Richard May also described their camp on the Carson River. It was probably near where Ragtown was later established west of today's Fallon, Nevada:

Friday 15th Sept. This day was spent in getting up our fatigued cattle. The most of the teams reached camp on the Salmon Trout River some 10 miles west of a lake of the same name and formed by the river, thus you see this water runs east and is within the great Salt Lake bason. . . .

Sat. 16th. Lay in camp waiting for the wagons and cattle to come in. There are a few trees on the Salmon Trout. Generally cottonwood, some of them 9 feet in circumference. This is the first timber seen since we left Lewis River. The weather is very warm. We have (that is the train) some 25 or 30 head of work cattle. Since we left the sink of Mary's River, the salaratus scowering them and the drive being rather long in such a contingency.

Are we to understand that this company only had twenty-five to thirty oxen left? At one yoke per wagon, that would barely be enough to pull twelve wagons. It was an unqualified mess. We must wonder whether the last two days could have been handled better. Was it an avoidable calamity that could have been mitigated by smarter decisions, better management, and more inspired leadership? Why did Chiles not have his company halt at Big Meadows to recruit their teams on its lush grass and decent water before moving on to the Sink, fifteen miles away? For some reason Chiles instead forced his company to endure two back-to-back thirty-five-mile marches, separated only by an eight-hour rest at a place of the worst possible water. Although there is not a single word of criticism from May or Smith, Chiles' decisions appear to be incompetent.

The legendary Joseph Walker was probably traveling with the Chiles company. Believed to have been the first white man to pioneer this route between the Sink and the Carson River when he led an exploration party for Captain Bonneville into California in 1833, he would have been familiar with it. He crossed it again when returning from California in 1834; then in 1843, while working for Chiles, he led a party of mule-drawn wagons across it again.[24] Did Walker protest this madness? Perhaps, but even if he did, is it possible Chiles rebuffed him, believing his own experience made him at least Walker's equal? One has to wonder if the snowfall on September 2 had unsettled Chiles more than we realize, prompting him to push forward despite the dangers.

This route was destined to become an integral part of the Carson Road, the main thoroughfare to the California diggings in the years to come. Consider the losses suffered by the Chiles company; then multiply it by a factor of two hundred to four hundred to get an idea of what occurred during a typical gold rush year, when this trail would be strewn with the remains of fallen beasts, abandoned wagons, and discarded goods.

Table 15: Status of companies as of September 16, 1848

Company (Diarist)	Location
Allsopp	journey completed (Oregon)
Adams, first segment	journey completed (Oregon)
Cornwall	journey completed (California)
Wambaugh	journey completed (California)
Miller (Anderson)	journey completed (Oregon)
Gates (Root)	journey completed (Oregon)
Jackson (Belknap)	journey probably completed (Oregon)
Watt	journey probably completed (Oregon)
Walker-Bristow	probably at the eastern foot of the Cascades
Kelly	just left The Dalles
Purvine (Porter)	just crossed the Deschutes River, Oregon
Adams, second segment	with the Purvine company
Hannah	probably nearing the Cascades
Delaney	probably near Well Springs, Oregon
Stone (Lempfrit)	on Butter Creek, Oregon
Hensley	at the foot of the Sierras
Lassen	in the Black Rock Desert, Nevada
Chiles (May, Smith)	on the Carson River, Nevada

CHAPTER 19

The End of the Journey
SEPTEMBER 16–OCTOBER 15

SEPTEMBER 16–OCTOBER 1, 1848
William Porter, Purvine company, on Eightmile Creek, Oregon.

William Anderson and his Miller company had arrived in the Willamette Valley on September 11, while Riley Root and his Gates company had arrived in Oregon City on September 13. Because Keturah Belknap had ceased making journal entries and there were no known diarists in the next few companies, there is no date for the arrival of the Jackson company. It is known, however, that the Belknaps took the Columbia River route instead of Barlow's Road, sending their women and children down the river in canoes piloted by Indians and floating their wagons down on rafts, while the livestock were driven by the men along the trail beside the river's south bank.[1]

The Watt family and their flock of sheep should have been not far behind, even though the *Spectator* article omitted any mention of them. Members of the Kelly, Walker-Bristow, and Purvine companies would have arrived over the next few weeks. William Porter recorded that his Purvine company crossed the Deschutes River on the Columbia on September 16 and headed south, on their way to Barlow's Gate. Porter continued to cram bare-boned entries into his diminutive notebook, his mileage estimates usually inflated:

> [Sept.] 16th. Traveled 10 miles up said branch [Eightmile Creek].
>
> 17th. Lay by to rest oxen.
>
> 18th. Traveled 16 miles to Village Creek [Tygh Creek in Tygh Valley].
>
> 19th. Traveled 3 miles going up the worst hill on the road.
>
> 20th. Traveled 12 miles to Barlow's Gate.
>
> 21st. Lay by to recruit cattle.
>
> 22nd. Traveled 16 miles to 4th crossing of Deshutes [White River].
>
> 23rd. Traveled 12 miles to foot of Summit Hill.
>
> 24th. Traveled 10 miles to prairie [Summit Meadows] near foot of Mount Hood.

25th. Traveled 19 miles to 3rd crossing of Zigzag.

26th. Traveled 12 miles to first crossing of Sandy [River].

27th. Traveled 15 miles to 2nd crossing of Sandy [River].

28th. Traveled 15 miles to 3rd house in the settlements.

29th. Lay by to recruit our cattle.

Oct. 1st. Traveled 10 miles passing through the City of Oregon and camped on a small creek near Mr. Armpriest.

The September 7 *Oregon Spectator* article confirmed that when Bristow and his friends left their wagon company, the Purvine company was traveling with Walker-Bristow. Porter never mentioned this, nor did he indicate whether this large combined group separated at any point thereafter. Porter's entries show that they rested their cattle three times during the final two weeks, a sign that their animals were desperately in need of it. It seemed to pay off, as they made good mileage during those final days of travel through the Cascades.

W. L. Adams, Adams company, traveling the Barlow Road

W. L. Adams, the schoolteacher from Galesburg, Illinois, had left Council Bluffs in late April with his wife, Olivia, their two baby daughters, a wagon, four oxen, and a milk cow ("Old Rose"). In July, he had written a downhearted letter to his brother from Pacific Springs, describing the terrible times they endured at the North Platte River crossing. In late September, Adams had finally reached the Cascades, and he reported his experience in crossing them in great detail in an 1889 biographical sketch:

Des Chutes was the most dangerous stream they [Adams] forded on the route. It was forded a few hundred yards above its junction with the Columbia. The bottom was full of huge boulders. The water was deep enough to swim the small cattle and the team. The Indians rode in and showed the immigrants how deep it was. The company was afraid to venture. Adams hired the Indians to pilot them over, giving them a shirt for each team in the company. The wagon beds were propped up nearly to the tops of the standards. Adams volunteered to take the lead. The waters roared over the rocks so as to drown an ordinary voice. In crossing, the water ran near to the tops of the wagon-beds; and the frightened women covered their heads with bed-clothing and screamed. . . .

Before reaching Barlow's gate—a toll gate at the entrance of the road cut over the Cascade Mountains by S. K. Barlow—the company had split up into many squads. Their teams were weak and jaded, and reduced almost to skeletons. The faces of the immigrants were peeled and scaled by the alkali of the sage plains. Here lay before them the hardest part of the trip. The rain had rendered the road almost impassable. The whole route was lined with dead horses and cattle lost by immigrants who had gone before. Adams concluded to make the trip across the mountains by himself. He was ten days in making it to [Philip] Foster's—the first house he had seen in six months. The mud up many mountains was knee deep; and the cattle were barely able to get on with the empty wagon. He and his wife carried the babes and the entire load up several mountains, wading through mud nearly knee deep, and then went back and drove up the team. On reaching Foster's they camped to rest. Foster, on learning that he had no money, generously gave him a peck of potatoes, and offered him every accommodation for the winter if he would stop there and teach school. Adams did not like the country and pushed farther on. In Oregon City he was met by friends, who invited his family to dinner.[2]

Inez Eugenia Adams was one of the Adams' two daughters. She was two and a half years of age at the time of the trip, too young to remember much, but she later wrote a reminiscence in which she related some of the stories told by her parents:

Arrived at last at the Cascade Mountains, weary and worn; we found the road almost impassable from mud caused by the recent heavy warm rains incident to the Pacific coast climate. Here Brindle, our third ox, mired and died, leaving us but one ox, "Old Bright," and our cow [fourteen-year-old Old Rose].

The scene is clear before me now of poor old Brindle lying beside the mud hole from which he had been extracted, his big dark eyes rolled back, and his chest painfully heaving with his last feeble breaths. . . . Now it would seem as though my parents would despair of ever reaching their destination; but not so. My father hitched up our cow [Old Rose] with the remaining ox [Old Bright] and she gallantly bore the yoke, and helped us into the land of mighty forest trees, pure and abundant water, green grass and genial climate.

At its gateway, at the foot of the last mountain lived Philip Foster, a pioneer rancher, who generously shared his abundant crops, raised for a small price if able to pay—free if any were left as was my father, with but ten cents to his name. . . . We reached this seeming paradise on the 1st day of October, 1848.[3]

Because Adams and Porter were at Pacific Springs on the same day in July, because "W. F. Adams" appeared in the "Fifth Company" (Walker-Bristow/Purvine company) of the September 7 *Spectator* article, and because Adams and Porter both arrived at Oregon City on October 1, it seems undeniable that Adams had traveled from Pacific Springs to Oregon with the Purvine company.

The Adams biography claimed that the group had separated into small "squads" when they approached the Cascades. This phenomenon of wagon parties breaking apart at the end of the trail will continue to be seen. Slower groups lagged farther behind and parties began to separate on the basis of friendships or speed as self-interest seemed to replace principles of mutual support and group loyalty.

Reverend Clinton Kelly, Kelly company, traveling the Barlow Road

The *Spectator* article designated the Kelly company as the "Fourth Company" and showed it as being ahead of the Walker-Bristow and Purvine companies. By the time these companies arrived at the Cascades, however, it appears that the Kelly party had fallen behind Walker-Bristow/Purvine. A biographical sketch written about Reverend Kelly explained why:

> He [Kelly] arrived at The Dalles late in September, having suffered the loss of some stock, some of the heavier goods and one wagon, abandoned on Snake River, but without loss of life. From The Dalles a portion of the household goods and farming implements, about two thousand five hundred pounds, were transported by water to Oregon City, under the supervision of Dr. Saffaran. After remaining a few days, to permit the cattle to recuperate somewhat, the remainder, with the family, crossed the Cascade mountains, the most trying part of the journey, by the Barlow pass, which was little more than an elk trail over apparently the most precipitous ground. The entire first day of October, just five months from Indian Creek was spent in descending what was called the "backbone" [Devil's Backbone], a hill on the opposite side of Sandy from Revenue. Rain had fallen the night previous and the mountain road was so slippery and precipitous that for the cattle to keep their feet was simply impossible. Many devices were resorted to to overcome the difficulty—hitching cattle behind the wagons, dragging logs behind, letting the wagons down by ropes, etc. . . . After a halt of a few days at [Philip] Foster's, the journey was resumed to Oregon City.[4]

Based on the above, the Kelly family seems to have arrived at Oregon City a couple of days after Porter and Adams.

After the Walker-Bristow, Purvine, and Kelly parties had all arrived, the "Hannah company" should have arrived next. The name "S. Hanna" appeared on a list of 1848 Oregon emigrants appearing in H. H. Bancroft's 1886 *History of Oregon*.[5] Since there was no other Hanna or Hannah listed among 1848 Oregon emigrants, it is probable that he was the captain of the company.

Most emigrants, when they entered the Willamette Valley, had fewer animals than they had started with and those that remained were in miserable condition. In desperate attempts to lighten their loads, emigrants had often thrown out seed and tools of agriculture along the trail. In many cases, the emigrants arrived in late fall with little or no food and money, and just as the cold, wet season was setting in. They might secure a claim of land, but how would they survive until they had cleared, plowed, planted, and harrowed their land, built a cabin, and harvested their first crop? And how could they clear, plow, plant, and harrow with no tools or seed? And how could they purchase them if they had no money? The emigrants' difficulties were far from over when they arrived.

September 16–October 12, 1848

Father Lempfrit, Stone company, at Butter Creek, Oregon

The last Oregon-bound party, the Stone company, was camping at Butter Creek on the afternoon of September 15. Because they had taken a difficult, sandy shortcut, their camp on Butter Creek was probably at the end of today's Eagle Ranch Road, a mile west of Highway 207 and about two miles south of where the Gates company had camped on August 24.

On the morning of September 16, the company headed west across dry, rolling country. It would be a long day during which they made twenty miles and passed the Sand Hollow battleground. Father Lempfrit's long entry detailed a day of hardships and privations:

> 16th September. We had a very good night [on Butter Creek]. The Captain [Stone] announced that as we had a long distance to travel before finding any water we must make an early start. We were still traveling in deep sand and the trail became worse all the time. . . . We were in a most distressing situation and we all suffered terribly from thirst. Between noon and 2 in the afternoon the heat was absolutely unbearable. . . . At noon, a waggon belonging to a German family from Pennsylvania was forced to remain behind. These poor people had lost almost all of their oxen and their food was spent. We had to share our food with them to prevent them from starving to death. We halted at noon to eat a little something after which we were on our way. We traveled until 5 o'clock in the evening and were quite exhausted when we saw in the distance something that looked like a little river [perhaps Sand Hollow]. The Captain went on ahead with two men. At 6:30 that evening we came to a small gorge where there were numerous sweetly smelling trees. I cut one or two branches of these and delighted in their fragrance. [Root had earlier described a "hollow" just two miles east of Well Springs in which cedars grew.] There was no water, at 7 o'clock in the evening we were all dying of thirst and my heart was breaking as I heard the poor children crying out for water.
>
> As the Captain had not yet returned we decided to wait for him where we were. This is why we decided to camp without unhitching our oxen. I lay down, covered with my buffalo robe and stretched myself out in the sand. . . . At 11 o'clock that evening we set out to continue our nocturnal journey. . . . At last we arrived at a wide stretch of land in the middle of which was a little hill enclosed by a kind of wall. We took a look at it, here there was water and very good water [Well Springs]. We gulped it down thirstily and in the meantime the rest of the company arrived. Everyone drank their fill. A little calf, however, thought he would end his life there. He tumbled into the water and it was only with the greatest of difficulty that we succeeded in getting him out of the water hole. The time was about 2 o'clock in the morning. The Captain had still not appeared. Then we

had the idea of firing a few shots into the air. The Captain, who had taken shelter a short distance away heard the shots and immediately acknowledged our signal by firing a shot from his own gun. . . . [I]n less than half an hour we found the Captain camped near two springs bubbling over with clean water. . . . The day we named "The Day of Disaster."

The waterhole where they camped must have been Well Springs. Traveling for fourteen hours and covering twenty miles, they were clearly moving at a slow pace—about a mile and a half per hour. Their oxen must have been so weakened and the sandy trail so difficult that this was the best they could manage. Lempfrit did not explain how Captain Stone managed to lose contact with his party and got lost in the dark, but it is hard to envision how he could have wandered away from a heavily traveled, clearly marked trail.

The Stone company had to make fifteen miles the next day to reach Willow Creek, their next source of water. Yet, for some reason it seemed to take them forever. Eventually, the ever-impatient Lempfrit would again leave the company to range ahead:

17th September. . . . We left early in the morning. Unfortunately we were soon without water. We felt so sorry for our poor animals. The heat was absolutely suffocating. We found very little grass and on top of this what there was all dried out and growing in little tufts. Our animals nevertheless devoured it, poor as it was. At noon I drank a few drops of the polluted water we had brought with us, for in spite of the little calf's having fallen into the pool, everyone had provided themselves with a little of this water, revolting as it looked. At 5 o'clock in the evening . . . I set out to look for the river. At 6 o'clock that evening, as I was descending a ravine, my pony saw a green spot in the distance. After a few minutes I was in the meadow [at Willow Creek] in spite of the tortuous and difficult path that led down to it. Once arrived in the meadow I saw some horsemen in the distance. I thought they were Indians but little by little, as I got nearer I saw that there were also waggons. When finally I came up to them I found out that these wagons belonged to the caravan that was ahead of us [Delaney company?]. They were making preparations for travel throughout the night. Further on I met some characters who looked like brigands. They told me they were soldiers! Well, they certainly looked the part! They were a troop of volunteer militiamen that the government had stationed in the nearby fort [probably Fort Waters, east of Fort Walla Walla] to disperse large gatherings of hostile Indians.

On September 18, the Stone company remained in camp to rest and recruit in the meadow beside Willow Creek. "I used the time to explore the country around us," the priest reported. Father Lionnet, the companion priest with whom Lempfrit had never gotten along, left with the militiamen. "As Mr. Lionnet wanted to go on ahead,"

Lempfrit explained, "he decided to take advantage of the company of the soldiers and he left me at 11 o'clock that evening to go to The Dalles."

While remaining in camp on the nineteenth, Lempfrit reported that "I was able to help a poor woman who thought she was going to die. I delivered her baby." Since they had to go seventeen miles to reach Cedar Springs, their next source of water, and because it promised to be another miserably hot day, Lempfrit reported that the company did not leave their Willow Creek camp until two in the afternoon. Then:

> [we] traveled all night without the slightest mishap. About midnight we went through a little valley where the cold was intense. At 5 o'clock in the morning we reached a creek [Rock Creek]. We took advantage of this by getting our horses to drink a little water but as there was no fodder we carried on for another seven miles and encamped on the John Day River.

After completing an exhausting day of twenty-six miles on September 19, the Stone company camped on the east side of the John Day River, just below the mouth of Rock Creek and close to where the Miller and Gates companies had camped three weeks earlier. They stayed in camp the next day. "We were exhausted by fatigue and lack of sleep," Lempfrit noted. "Luckily we were in a good camping spot and our animals had plenty of grass. The Indians came to bring us some delicious salmon."

The next day they would try to reach the Columbia River, another major milestone in their long journey: "21st September. We had a good restful night in spite of the very high wind. At 8 o'clock the Captain gave the departure signal. We forded the [John Day] river and carried on travelling for a long time."

Lempfrit then described meeting an eastbound priest on the trail. It was Father Accolti, the superior for all the Jesuit missionaries in the Pacific Northwest. He was a good friend of Father Pascal Ricard, the superior in charge of all oblate missions in the region and the one to whom Lempfrit would report.[6] Accolti likely informed Lempfrit that Ricard was at Fort Vancouver, while Blanchet, bishop of Walla Walla, was at The Dalles. The two priests parted and Accolti continued on, probably returning to one of the Jesuit missions in northern Idaho. Lempfrit continued his description of the day's travel:

> We had thought that we would soon be arriving at the Columbia River bank but we were mistaken. We had to carry on traveling until 11 o'clock that night. Our poor animals were exhausted by fatigue and were at the point of collapse from inanition. They had not a single blade of grass to eat all day. About midnight we reached the longed for Columbia River, but alas! what a disappointment. We had thought that we would find the Promised Land, we had set our hopes on a new Eden! Not so! We found a dry and arid land where there was not a piece of wood, not even a stick, and where a violent wind carried clouds of dust with it. . . . We had to take shelter behind our waggons to avoid being buried in the sand that

the wind hurled at us with unbelievable violence. We ate a few biscuits and slept as best we could.

After an exhausting day of twenty-six miles on September 21, Lempfrit described the company arriving at the lip of a high bluff overlooking the Columbia River in the middle of the night (just west of today's Biggs, Oregon). Instead of describing one of the spectacular vistas along the trail, the priest could only report darkness and misery:

> . . . a very bad night. We had to use dried horse dung for fuel. We baked a few slices of salmon but immediately they became blackened with dust. However, what will one not eat when one is famished?

The next morning, they completed their breakfast at ten, then returned to the trail beside the river. After what Lempfrit thought was eight miles, they came to "a branch of the Columbia to cross." The Deschutes River was swift-running and regarded by most emigrants as extremely difficult and dangerous, but Lempfrit did not describe it that way:

> [September 22nd] . . . This [the Deschutes] was not very deep. An Indian pointed out to us a place where the river was fordable. After we got across the river we stopped for a few moments to debate whether we should push on further ahead. We were faced with a very steep hill to climb. The Captain [Stone] decided that he wanted to carry on and our conductor [O'Neil] who was very friendly with him wanted to go with him. Thus we were reduced to two waggons, the four others remained behind. The Captain was the first to get up the hill and so he had to use our four pairs of oxen as well as his own. Thus he had eight pairs and despite this long string of oxen he had the utmost difficulty in reaching the top of the hill. After this he came down for us and we managed to get up the hill quite well. When we arrived at the summit we found a nice little spot to set up our camp. A little spring furnished us with very good water and this was most welcome. We had some salmon which I prepared and cooked myself for supper.

Lempfrit had been reporting evidence of rebellion within the Stone/Delaney party ever since Three Island Crossing on the Snake on August 17. From that point on, groups of wagons had been splintering off. The last time we heard of the company losing wagons was on September 15 when they were left with eleven. Now they were down to six wagons and the tiny group was breaking up again. Stone had been pushing hard over the last three weeks; perhaps his pace no longer suited the four wagons remaining behind. Or maybe they no longer respected his leadership because of questionable decisions, such as taking the exceedingly sandy cutoff or getting lost while trying to find Well Springs. Father Lempfrit had no choice but to travel with Stone and O'Neil because his baggage was being carried in O'Neil's wagon.

On the morning of September 23, Stone, O'Neil, their two wagons, and the priest left their camp at six-thirty, traveling six miles to "a little river," probably Fifteenmile Creek near present-day Fairbanks, Oregon. Lempfrit wrote:

> Towards evening, I saw two horsemen riding towards us at a fast trot. These gentlemen were Mr. Lionett [Lempfrit's former companion] and Mr. Roussean [one of Chief Tauitowe's former missionaries], a young priest who was in the personal service of the Bishop of Walla Walla. They were coming to take delivery of the letters that we had brought for the two Bishops and also to let us know that we had taken the wrong trail. These gentlemen stayed with us and did not leave us until the next morning.

The "two Bishops" would have been Rev. F. N. Blanchet, archbishop of Oregon (based at the St. Paul's mission south of Oregon City), and his brother, Rev. A. M. A. Blanchet, bishop of Walla Walla (based at St. Peter's mission at The Dalles).

The next morning, September 24, Lempfrit handed Lionnet and Rousseau "the letters addressed to the Bishops as well as the letters for other people in the Willamette," and the two priests departed to return to The Dalles while Lempfrit remained behind with the slow-moving wagons. Lempfrit explained that "I did not want to leave our wagon driver [O'Neil] in case there was an accident." This incident was confirmed in Bishop A. M. A. Blanchet's diary entry of September 24th: "Rev. Rousseau went ahead of the wagons, brought letters to me."[7]

The party left their camp, but the unsteady priest did not remain with the wagons for long. Despite his penchant for getting lost, he wrote that "I went on ahead on my pony thinking we would arrive at The Dalles in a few hours," and he headed off on another one of his solitary junkets, another one he would regret.

> [September 24] . . . I first came to a little valley where I stopped for a short time. I noticed that there were several trails that crossed each other. Undecided as to which trail to take, I asked some Indians where the Bishop's house [was]. . . . They pointed out a hill on my left but as this was so far away I thought they were mistaken, so I carried on along the trail I was following thinking that our waggons were coming on along behind me. I rode for six more hours without seeing the slightest sign of a dwelling. I had eaten practically nothing that morning. I had not brought any food with me and night was falling. "Where am I," I said to myself. "Alone with my pony." I don't know what had become of the caravan— come now, I will have to make up my mind to spend the night under a tree!

Would this priest ever learn? One can hardly feel sorry for him. From his vague descriptions, it is impossible to ascertain where he was, but as he neared The Dalles, he reported encountering many trails leading hither and yon. Instead of following the Indian's instructions on how to get to The Dalles, he likely took what appeared to be the heavily traveled trail, the one toward Barlow's Gate.

[24th, cont.] I looked around then for a fairly comfortable place where I could find shelter. I found a tree which had large roots that created a little niche and I filled this up with dry leaves. I decided to wait there for the caravan. I tethered my horse to a kind of shrubby tree that was near my little nest and as I did not have a gun of any kind to defend myself in case of need, I armed myself with my horsewhip and set this down beside me. Then I took my horse's saddle to serve me as a pillow and the horse blanket to cover me.

After midnight I was awakened by the howls of a huge wolf that was attacking my poor little horse. Luckily I had not tied him up very firmly so he was able to get away. I heard him bolting at the gallop and scrambling back up the hill. Imagine, dear readers. Just think of my predicament! The horse had escaped from the wolf but the wolf smelt other prey! Alas, he would come after me! I was now on the alert and armed with the whip I waited for daybreak.

It was a miracle he survived again. He went on to relate the events of the following morning:

25th September. About 4 o'clock in the morning the first glimmerings of dawn were appearing. I went to examine the spot where my pony had been tethered and when I noticed a few drops of blood there I came to the conclusion that my poor horse had been injured. So I climbed to the top of the hill to see if I could see where he had gone but there was no trace of him no matter in what direction I looked. I crossed over to the opposite side of the river and then, when I reached the top of the river bank, I saw my pony ambling peacefully along the path I had followed yesterday.

Lempfrit had to pursue his little horse for six miles before it would finally let him grab its halter. The rest of his day went somewhat better, and we see, at last, some acknowledgment of his flaw!

[September 25th cont.] It would be better I thought to go and find the caravan for I had no idea which way it would have gone. Once again I found myself in the little valley that I had been through the previous day. . . . I said to myself, "I am a donkey, this is what I am always doing, I go on ahead and then I get lost." I had to find consolation. . . . I tied my horse up at the edge of the river and set out to look for the wheel-tracks of our waggons. About a hundred paces away I discovered fresh tracks. I saw that they had crossed over the river, and a short distance away I came on two fires that were still smoking a little. This was a message from Heaven as I was now sure that the caravan had halted there. I then returned to where I had left my horse on the other side of the river and led him along the path to my right which, if I had heeded what the Indians I met yesterday had told me, would have taken me straight to The Dalles. I lit my pipe. This was another piece of good fortune for me because it was more than a day since I had been able to smoke. . . .

We climbed a long hill and went at least six miles without seeing anything. But my mind was at ease as we were following the tracks of our waggons. At last, about 2 o'clock in the afternoon I reached the crest of a hill and then I saw our waggons halted in a little valley. Our people soon saw me and came up to me asking questions. "Oh, please give me something to eat," I said, "I am absolutely famished." Afterwards, I told them all about my unfortunate adventure.

Nearing the end of his long journey, Lempfrit was determined to find the bishop, so the next day he again rode ahead of the company. He never learned, did he?

26th September . . . I was most anxious to get to the Bishop's Palace as soon as possible so, in spite of my unfortunate adventures I decided that I would once more take the risk of going on alone. . . . There were several hills to climb and descend however before I could get to this place. As I was going up the last hill I saw in the distance the enchanting banks of the Columbia River whose waters pour into the ocean so many miles ahead. In this pretty little valley I came on a forest of magnificent oak-trees luxuriant with acorns more beautiful than any I have seen. . . . I decided not to push further ahead. Yesterday's adventure had made me prudent! I waited patiently for our waggons to arrive. At last, just as I was writing these few lines, I heard the sound of our waggons coming down the hill. It was 5 o'clock in the evening. I was happy. "At least I will have supper this evening and need not fear being devoured by wolves," I said to myself. Towards evening we saw a fairly high building surrounded by a strong palisade. We were told that this was a fort the Americans had built to protect themselves from the incursions of the Indians. We made our way toward the fort. Night had fallen by the time we arrived there. We went all round this wooden fortress but found it completely shut up.

The fort was Fort Lee, originally a Methodist mission built among the Deschutes Indians in 1838. Consisting of two dwellings, a schoolhouse, and a barn, it also served as a resting place for emigrants as they got ready to transport their wagons down the Columbia on rafts. Within weeks of the Whitman massacre, the first company of Oregon Volunteers arrived to fortify the mission by encircling its buildings with hastily thrown-up log palisades, quickly transforming it into a makeshift military garrison.[8] By the time Lempfrit's party showed up at the fort, the heat of the Cayuse War had largely dissipated and the Oregon militia was mostly disbanded. Some volunteers had been discharged so they could return to the Willamette Valley to harvest their crops; others simply abandoned their posts. Writing from his mission at The Dalles, Bishop Blanchet explained on September 8: "I learn that all Volunteers are coming down [the river]; that they are abandoning all the interior forts because they have nothing to wear and little to eat."[9] When word of gold in California arrived, many of the few remaining volunteers left for the diggings, explaining why the Stone party found Fort Lee deserted.[10]

From local Indians, Lempfrit learned that the bishop's residence was on the other side of Mill Creek, about a mile and a half west of the fort. Since night had fallen and the creek's current was swift and dangerous, they camped on the fort side of the creek and waited until daylight to cross.

> 27th September. We arrived early in the morning at the residence of the Bishop of Walla Walla. He was saying mass at the time of our arrival. He welcomed us with kindness and invited us to stay with him until we were able to arrange for a barge to transport us to Fort Vancouver. The Bishop's residence is not grand, far from it. It is a little wooden cabin about twelve feet by fifteen. Such is his little manor house! On one side of it another house is being built for him but as there are no workmen it remains uninhabitable.

A month later, Bishop Blanchet's new house would be done, a grand thirty-by-twenty-four-foot structure that would serve as both church and residence.[11] When Lempfrit visited Bishop Blanchet, he was informed that he would have to go on to Fort Vancouver to meet with his superior, Father Ricard. With the unsettled Indian situation, he was also probably advised that it was unlikely he would be assigned to a mission among the Cayuse or any other tribe in the immediate area, so his dream of returning to the beautiful Grande Ronde Valley to establish a mission among Chief Tauitowe's Cayuse would not come true.

The next morning, Lempfrit found "our Americans were camping" along the banks of the Columbia. He probably meant that Captain David Stone, David O'Neil and his two children, and perhaps others were arranging for rafts to float their wagons down the river. Lempfrit and his fellow priest Father Lionnet "found a young American" who would transport them and their baggage to Vancouver by canoe:

> At 5:30 this same evening [on September 28] we entrusted our fate to a small canoe that was to transport us to Fort Vancouver. I feared greatly for my baggage that had already got wet before this. Our canoe was heavily loaded, we had four Indians to row us and a fifth man, the young American, who was our skipper. We wanted to go about a dozen miles before nightfall but as we descended the Columbia a strong wind got up so we landed on the right bank of the river to camp there overnight.

Since the earlier wagon companies had used the Barlow Road to reach the Willamette Valley, why did the Stone party choose the river route? Lempfrit and Lionnet came to The Dalles to see the bishop, but we can only speculate why Stone and his party came here. Perhaps they had learned that recent rains in the Cascades had rendered the Barlow Road virtually impassable, as described by W. L. Adams and Rev. Kelly.

Lempfrit did not specify who else traveled in the canoe besides the two priests, the young American, and the four Indian rowers, but because he described the canoe as "small" and "heavily loaded," it did not sound as if there would have been room for anyone else. And oddly, Lempfrit never again mentioned his black pony, failing to pen a single word about the stalwart little steed that had carried him almost two thousand miles, and making one wonder what had become of it.

The priests began their ninety-mile descent of the Columbia to reach Fort Vancouver. The river had been used for transportation for many years, but the trip was neither easy nor smooth; rather it was another harrowing experience. "There were violent gusty winds throughout the night [of September 28]," Lempfrit complained, adding that he was forced to spend the night tightly wrapped in his buffalo robe. The next morning,

> nearly all our baggage was swamped, and my medicine chest particularly had suffered a great deal. This caused me great concern for how could one procure medicaments in this wild country? Nearly all my other things had been soaked.

They returned to the river, then stopped about midmorning for breakfast, making soup from the eggs taken from a large salmon caught by one of the Indian oarsmen. They also "roasted the rest of it on a skewer." Resuming their trip down the river, the priest's mood improved and he praised the slowly passing scenery:

> What a lovely country! A new panorama comes into view at every turn. The lovely mountains are clothed in majestic fir-trees and spruce-trees. . . . As the river-bed is extremely constricted between rocks here one can discern the different high-water marks where the river has risen in time of spate. Some of the marks I saw were six, eight, ten, even up to eighteen feet above the river.

At noon, they passed an island (perhaps Walls Island, north of today's exit 62 on I-84), on which a large Indian village was situated, and Lempfrit noted a number of Indian dugout canoes plying the river. The wind again rose to dangerous levels, and they returned to the riverbank that afternoon to spend the night.

After "feasting" on salmon that night and the next morning, they set off again on the morning of September 30. They barely managed to get through a dangerous section of rapids churned up by rocks just beneath the surface and camped that night along the riverbank. Lempfrit noted that their "provisions were completely exhausted by now. All we had left were a few pounds of biscuit all crumbled up and just about two pounds of smoked bacon fat."

Resuming their journey on October 1, Lempfrit wrote that his hunger made him exceedingly "anxious to reach our destination." At nine o'clock that evening they reached "La Chute," also called the Cascade, or Great Falls of the Columbia. These powerful rapids were too dangerous to navigate, so river traffic was forced to portage about five miles past this impossible stretch of river. Lempfrit wrote that since "[o]ur skipper was not able to take us any further," they would have "to stay here for a few days until a canoe of some kind could be found to transport us." He and his fellow travelers spent the night camping somewhere along the portage, at a place where he complained about hordes of insufferable fleas.

Still waiting at the portage on October 2, the priest again complained that "our provisions were completely exhausted." Unable to abide his hunger and idleness, he went hunting and explored the surroundings, and while ambling through a "lovely little meadow entirely surrounded by the forest," he purred that it gave him a "great deal of pleasure." He then reported something very confounding: "Here we remained until it pleased Divine Providence to send us a canoe that will transport us down the river for our skipper and Master O'Neil could not agree on the price for our voyage." Where did O'Neil come from? Lempfrit had not suggested that O'Neil and his children were also passengers in his canoe. Perhaps they had recently arrived at the portage on a raft with their wagon. Lempfrit wrote as if O'Neil was currently part of Lempfrit's party, but where was O'Neil's wagon if he was trying to make arrangements to travel on a small canoe? And what had become of Captain Stone and his wagon?

Still stranded at the portage on October 3, Lempfrit was beginning to sound desperate: "We were without flour and we did not have a morsel of meat. What would become of us? We had no idea how long we would remain in this place." The next day, Lempfrit reported happily that "[t]oday [October 4th] two rafts carrying our Americans arrived. A kind American lady gave me a whole loaf of bread." Then he reported that a canoe landed that carried provisions for the Americans. They all ate well that night, but Lempfrit continued to grumble about the pesky fleas.

Lempfrit had nothing to report on October 5 and 6, except that they were still stuck at the portage, and that "each day a canoe or a barge full of our Americans arrived. It was high time that we were on our way." Although Lempfrit did not elaborate, it is possible that the "Americans" he mentioned were some of those who had once traveled in the Stone/Delaney company.

After being marooned for six days on this flea-ridden strip of riverbank, the two priests were finally able to resume their journey on October 7:

> At last we found an American who would take us to Fort Vancouver. We arranged for places in a strongly built boat but it was inadequate for all our baggage so a second canoe was then obtained, loaded up, and left. During the evening we set out to meet the boat five miles lower down the river.... We then descended the Columbia, most of the time going with the river's current. We traveled throughout the night.

The river route had the advantage of avoiding steep slopes and muddy roads across the Cascades, and, under good circumstances, it could be quick, but it could be problematic as well—with high winds, treacherous rapids, and the possibility of getting stranded at the portage for extended periods.

After traveling through the night, Lempfrit and Lionnet finally arrived at Fort Vancouver at nine o'clock on the morning of October 8. Lempfrit described the place as "a magnificent establishment . . . most charming," and explained that the place consisted of "a Governor's house, the assistant officer's house, the Presbytery, the Post Office, and numerous shops." It was a large fort—six hundred feet long and three hundred feet wide—surrounded by "a strong palisade of wooden timbers ten and more inches thick and over thirty feet in height." First established in 1824 by John McLoughlin of the Hudson's Bay Company, Fort Vancouver was built as the company's western headquarters and main trading post in the Pacific Northwest.[12] It was situated on a grassy prairie above the northern bank of the Columbia, about six miles above the mouth of the Willamette River. Under the able management of Dr. McLoughlin and his successor, James Douglas, the fort had supplied the Oregon emigrants with provisions during the 1840s, including giving aid to the desperate and destitute. It was not the shabby-looking establishments that Fort Laramie, Fort Hall, and Fort Boise were. Thanks to its able superintendents, the fort was universally praised for being in a high state of order and repair.[13]

A few buildings stood outside the fort walls, including a small Catholic church. Upon their arrival, Lempfrit and Lionnet were taken to the church to meet Father Délivaut, a young French priest who attended to the fort's Catholic employees and nearby Indians. Délivaut introduced them to the fort's chief factor, James Douglas, who had replaced Dr. McLoughlin in 1846.

Lempfrit learned that his oblate superior, Father Ricard, had recently left for a oblate mission called St. Joseph's, near where the city of Olympia, Washington, would later be established. On October 10, Father Lionnet left for his assignment at the oblate mission of St. Paul's south of Oregon City, and on the twelfth, Lempfrit left with James Douglas and his entourage to travel one hundred miles north to meet Father Ricard at St. Joseph's.

Father Lempfrit traveled for five difficult months with Captain Stone, Mr. O'Neil, and the rest of the Stone company, many of whom had at one time or another helped him when he got into one of his many scrapes. But just as he did not mention his pony upon their separation, he also failed to record a single word about his former companions when they parted ways. On this note of unfathomable silence, Father Lempfrit left the trail and entered into his career as an Indian missionary.

The arrival of the Stone company brought an end to the Oregon emigration of 1848. In its issue of October 12, 1848, the *Oregon Spectator* made only a brief comment: "All the immigrants who took the northern route [to Oregon], including some waggons in Captain Miller's company, who took water at The Dalles, have arrived in this valley in safety, numbering 177 wagons." Based on what was reported and estimated, about 370 wagons departed Missouri and Council Bluffs. About ninety intended to go to California, with the remainder heading to Oregon. This suggests that of the 280 wagons originally headed for Oregon, close to 100 apparently did not make it to the end.

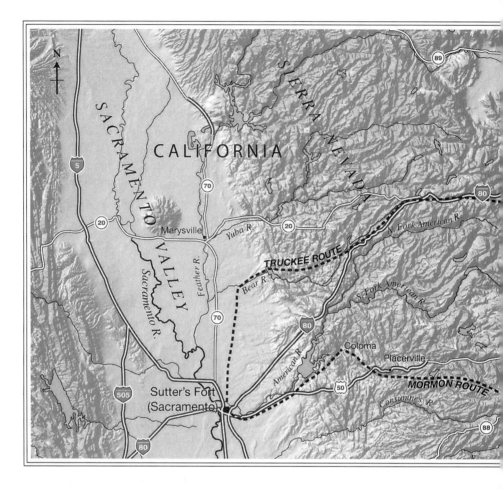

September 17–October 15, 1848

Richard May and Edward Smith, Chiles company,
on the Carson River, Nevada

On September 17, the Chiles company remained in camp along the hundred-foot-wide Carson River and licked its wounds. Some of the men returned to the desert to bring in stranded wagons and whatever surviving livestock could still be found, and some had been assigned to protect the animals from the Paiutes hiding in the dense willow thickets along the river. They did not always succeed, as Richard May complained: "[d]uring our stay at the first camp, the Indians made beef of several of our work cattle."

Although the Mormons had recently brought news of the discovery of gold in California, there was little evidence of gold fever in the company. They had lost a sizeable number of oxen and their surviving animals were a mess, and the emigrants were

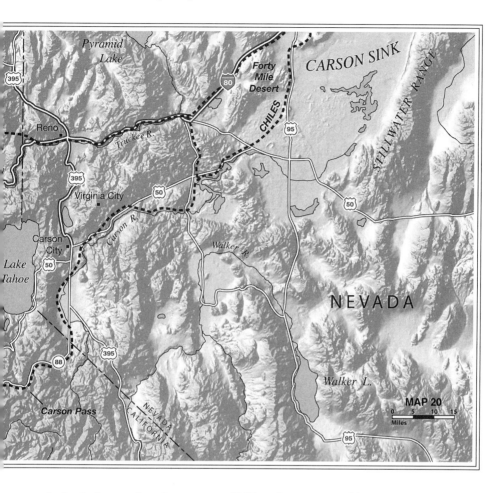

drained of strength and energy as well. "It is almost impossible to get some men up to their duty," May wrote on September 17.

Smith reported on September 17 that they "sent back Pack animals after Mr. Beard's things. Mr. Bennett gave him his wagons." Afterwards, they managed to move their camp only two miles up the river. The Paiutes continued to shadow and plunder. The night of September 17, according to Smith, was another bad one: "Mr. Beards waggon had been Robbed by the Indians last night," he wrote the next day. "Mr. McClellens [Mike McClellan] horse was shot in the neck." This is the second time the diarists mentioned Mike McClellan, Joseph R. Walker's nephew and brother to Frank McClellan. Brother Frank had already arrived in California with the Wambaugh company.

Smith also recorded that on the morning of the eighteenth the pack animals sent to get Mr. Beard's things had returned. May's entry for the eighteenth contained the observation that "[o]ur cattle are in bad condition and require more nursing." Yet, the company moved up the Carson River eight miles and May wrote that they camped "in a grove of large cottonwoods," near the east end of today's Lahontan Reservoir.

According to Smith, the company made ten miles on September 19, passing through a canyon of the Carson River, where Smith spotted "two Indian fish dams." Continuing to call the Carson the "Salmon Trout River," May observed: "the weather very warm, good grass." That night, their camp was likely beneath the waters of today's Lahontan Reservoir, perhaps two miles east of present-day Silver Springs, Nevada.

On the morning of September 20, the company left a bend in the river. Four miles after leaving camp, Smith wrote that they "Struck the Mormon trail or new road to California." It was here, near today's Silver Springs, where the eastbound Mormons had left the Carson and traveled twenty-five miles north to the Truckee River. "[I]n the afternoon," Smith continued, "we traveled about ten miles over a Sandy plain and encamped again on the River   Capt. Chiles filly got in the river and the Indians drove Francisco and Dick from her   to night Mr. Williams ox was shot while watering."

The company followed the Mormons' trail on the afternoon of September 20, its course corresponding to the route of today's Highway 95, between Highway 50 and Fort Churchill Road. About ten miles southwest of Silver Springs, the company again struck the Carson and camped that evening near where the army would establish Fort Churchill in 1860.[14] Smith noted how difficult it was to protect their livestock from the Paiutes. While the country on both sides of the river was barren and sterile, the river bottom grew tall sagebrush and dense willows, making it virtually impossible to detect hiding Indians, especially at night. May and Smith both described another maddening experience with the Indians the next day.

> [Richard May]: Thursday 21st. Traveled 11 miles and encamped on S. T. [Salmon Trout] River. The mountains are bold and rather low to be called mountains. We have intercepted the Mormon's road. We are on our way up the great Sierra Nevada range of mountains. Just after sun down an ox was shot within a few rods of camp.

> [Edward Smith]: thur 21 this morning Mr. Staten Coryell Nelson and francisco went back to get the [Chiles] filly   the Indians had killed her and carried her nearly all away   they followed the trail overtook and killed one Indian   Brot the Bow and arrows in camp   we traveled about two miles and encamped for the day.

After traveling eleven miles on the twenty-first, May's group camped between the river and today's Fort Churchill Road, about three miles east of Highway 50. Smith, on the other hand, reported that they traveled only two miles that day, likely because he and his group waited for those sent back to recover Chiles' filly. May's entry for September 22 described the filly incident of the previous day:

Friday 22nd Sept. . . . I neglected to mention that on yesterday two of our men returned a few miles for a mare mired. While on the tour they fell in with a party of Diggers and killed 2 of them and came into camp unhurt. A party was detailed to bring in the mare this morning. They fell also in with Diggers and killed one so there has been two Indian battles in as many days. Three killed on one side and on the other not a hair molested. Traveled 14 miles this morning. We paid our first and last debt of gratitude to a little infant of Mr. Bernett's which was born and lived only a few minutes. It is supposed to be a premature birth. What consolation it should give the parents to be taken by the [*illegible*] who gave it to enjoy blissful eternity. Their loss is surely its gain.

May reported that his group moved only two miles up the river on September 23, while Smith's group, lagging behind, traveled fourteen. In doing so, they likely caught up to May and the main body. If so, the combined company would have camped near the river, about two miles southwest of where today's Fort Churchill Road heads east from Highway 50. Smith pointed out that, because of the abundant cottonwoods, the Mormons had named the area Cottonwood Valley. Leaving a river bottom choked with tall sage and dense willows, and entering an area with less undergrowth, the company guards would enjoy improved visibility and could more effectively protect their livestock. From here on, the company would no longer be pestered by Indian depredations.

The early morning quiet of September 23 was disturbed by men catching up their rail-thin oxen. After the animals were yoked and hitched to the battered wagons, the discordant sounds of creaking, clanking wagons, and the teamsters' "hup, hup, hup," soon filled the air. Smith reported that the company continued through Cottonwood Valley, passing where Dayton, Nevada, is today. In the afternoon, they "crossed a stony point," completing a day of eight miles and entering what the Mormons called Shoshonee Valley, where they camped among the cottonwoods near the river a couple of miles east of present-day Carson City.

The company's westward march along the Carson was drawing them ever closer to the eastern front of the Sierras. From a distance, the Sierras were impressive, but as the emigrants drew closer, the scale and steepness of these massive escarpments would become frighteningly apparent. They seemed utterly impenetrable. As far as the emigrants could see, there appeared to be no gap, no pass, that would take them through the mountains. Some might have begun to wonder whether those Mormons had pulled a trick on them.

Traveling another eight miles on September 24, the company camped on the west side of the Carson River a few miles south of today's Carson City. Richard May had little to add, other than "Good road though dull and uninteresting." He did not appear overly alarmed by the mountains, and after almost two months of barren, treeless landscapes, his delight at the dramatic change in scenery is not surprising:

"We came into view of the timbered mountains. I must say it gave me pleasure to see timber at a distance."

The next day the company turned south, continuing south through the wide, flat Carson Valley, which Smith described as "a beautiful valley with Broad and fertile Bottoms." Here, the river spread across the valley in a number of divided channels, creating a broad expanse of lush meadows and soggy marshlands, so the pioneering Mormon party had blazed their trail along the base of the mountains and over the sage-covered higher ground west of the valley floor.

During the morning of September 25, while bumping through the sagebrush, Smith recorded that they "met a co of Mormons," although no information has been found about this party. Even though Smith did not mention it, they would have passed Walley's Hot Springs during their day's march, just south of today's Genoa, Nevada. They "traveled late" that day, covering about twenty-two miles and crossing several small, snowmelt-fed streams issuing from the mountains on their right. Smith complained that "several of our oxen gave out." Smith also reported that "Hollenback Preston and Winters went on." Like so many of the other companies nearing their final destination, the company's stronger teams were moving at a faster pace and were beginning to pull away from the main body. Smith said that they ended their day "in a fine Bottom area a spring Branch and very large Pine trees on the fork." This spring branch could have been Luther Creek, on today's Highway 88, about six miles south of Minden, Nevada.

Smith's entry for September 26 reported that they continued to follow the trail south, paralleling the Carson River, until they finally encountered a gap in the mountains through which the river rushed. Here they entered and the scenery turned startlingly different. Passing beneath stately pines that rose over two hundred feet into the air, the familiar smell of sage gave way to the perfumed scent of cedar and pine. After making seven miles that day, they came to the narrow West Carson Canyon. Sheer rock walls rose high above them and on the ground, they beheld huge granite boulders that had over the ages dislodged from above choked the canyon floor. In years to come, many gold rushers would regard this as the worst section of trail between the Missouri River and Sutter's Fort. The trail seemed impassable and some may have wondered whether the Mormons had directed them onto a road to nowhere. Some in the party were undaunted, however, and Smith reported that "15 wagons went on." The men who went first must have been reassured by the sight of wagon wheel scrapes and marks across the rocks ahead. If others could make it, so could they.

While the rest made their way into the canyon, Smith, May, and a few others decided to camp for the night at the canyon's mouth, settling in a cool grotto covered with pine needles and bracken fern. The site of their camp today is near Woodford on Highway 88.

Their entry into the Sierras could not have come at a worse time for the usually optimistic May. He was weakened from a recent illness and felt inadequate to face this undertaking. His wife was ill, too, but he did not explain the nature of either of their ailments:

> 26th Sept. We cut out this morning and ran up to the mouth of a canyon and half the train is now in it. But if it was pleasure to see timber at a distance it must give joy to be in timber, large pine timber. The mountains are very tall and rugged, covered to the summit with a bold little mountain stream running by, the whistling of winds in the trees all conspire to make one cheerful, but under the circumstances I cannot feel so. We have an awful road before us. Mrs. May is quite sick and unable to do camp duty. Myself just setting up from disease and feel that the hardships before me are more than I should undergo.

It is not known how many wagons the company had abandoned in the desert and along the Carson because of the loss of many oxen; thus, we do not know how many wagons they had left. If Smith was correct that "15 wagons went on" at the canyon and May was correct that "half the train is now in it," then their company now consisted of approximately thirty wagons. This is compared to "32 wagons and 2 carriages" that May reported on August 23, and "36 wagons" that Mormon Ephraim Green had noted when his Thompson company encountered the Chiles company on August 30.

May combined two days in his next journal entry:

> 27th and 28th Sept. Traveled 5 miles all the way in a canyon and truly it may be called a canyon. The timbered mountains are what I expected in the mountains throughout. The different kinds of pine and cedar and some quaking asp are the only kind of timber found here.

Their wagons could not simply be rolled through the canyon; they had to be heaved, lifted, pried, and pushed over a jumble of jagged boulders, and that required strong men. They had to cross the icy, waist-deep river a number of times. And all the time, the sheer cliffs overhead threatened to rain rocks down upon them. With May and his wife sick, and Smith and his driver healing from gunshot wounds, they would have needed help from their fellow travelers, but with so many wagons gone ahead, one wonders if lack of help is why May and Smith were among those falling behind. Had the company lost their spirit of cooperation and assistance? There is no evidence that Chiles tried to force the company to stay together. Would the companies have begun to fall apart if there had been no news of gold? Judging by what happened to the Oregon-bound companies when they arrived at the Cascades, it is likely the same thing happened with the Chiles company.

Smith reported making two miles through the dreaded canyon on September 27, writing that "I upset my waggon" and noting that "Chiles went on." Making it through the final two miles of canyon the next day, they finally emerged at the foot of Hope Valley, a handsome alpine basin, and Smith plaintively added that "all of the waggons have left except 8."

On September 29, these eight wagons advanced through the serene meadows of Hope Valley, a beautiful area seven thousand feet above sea level and cradled between soaring granite peaks on all sides. The May family trundled through the eight-mile-long valley that day, alternatively crossing slabs of exposed granite, expanses of sage and grass, and groves of pine and cedar. Even though May was still weak from his illness, he recorded delight in the suddenly changed scenery:

> 29th. Ran 8 miles above the canyon to what is called Hope or Lake Valley and immediately at the foot of the mountain which will take us one day to make the top. I succeeded in getting one of my wagons on the mountain. I suppose we have not raised less than 3000 feet today. We are now in the snowy region. The mountains there towering above us and snow in every direction in the deep ravines. This is truly a beautiful mountain and different kinds of pine and cedar are the only timber. The rocks are quite picturesque, but the most lovely sight is the beautiful little lakes of fresh water surrounded by meadows that afford grass in abundance for our many stock.

May's family had made it to Red Lake at the head of Hope Valley by the end of the day. The tiny lake, then only about a half-mile long and a quarter-mile wide, has been dammed and is larger today. At the west end of the lake rose an intimidating mountain, which they would have to scale to reach Carson Pass at its summit. Later called the "Devil's Staircase," the mountain ascended over a thousand feet. Because it was impossible to go straight up, the route switched back and forth. The usual practice was to unload a wagon and haul it upward in short segments, pushing the empty wagon from behind and pulling from the front by long ropes or chains connected to double and triple teams of oxen or to blocks-and-tackles tied to trees. Ropes were often wrapped around sturdy trunks to snug the wagon in place as oxen and ropes were repositioned for another pull. In places, the wagon was dragged almost straight up, and in other places it was rolled laterally across the face of the mountain, often along narrow rock ledges. There were some places where, if a wagon slipped from a ledge, it could fall a hundred feet without touching anything. Once a wagon made it to the summit, its contents had to be hauled up on the backs of men and animals. Over the years, diarists universally swore that this mountain was by far the most difficult obstacle on the entire trail.

Our diarists had no way of knowing this, but upon making it over this 8,600-foot-high pass, they had crossed another geological divide, one that separated the waters of the Great Basin from those of the Pacific. Today a breathtaking view of the route up this mountain can be seen from Highway 88 at both its top and bottom.

This party of eight wagons separated on August 29, as Smith and his family did not keep up with May and his two wagons. Instead, Smith traveled only four miles up Hope Valley:

frid 29 this morning we succeeded getting the last wagons out of the canion, and traveled about 4 miles   encamped at Mormons carrel   all the co. have left except 5 waggons this morning   Rc'd a message from Capt Chiles that for our money he would help us out of the Canion and a good pile at that or we might stay   this of course was indignantly refused.

The Smith party was being left behind. Chiles' attempted extortion was a despicable breach of the noble duty that a wagon train captain owes to each member of his company. But for some time, Smith's entries had suggested there was something about Chiles that was less than honorable.

The next day, May reported dragging his second and last wagon up the mountain:

30th Sept. (That day I am 46 years old and on the highest mountain in North America) [not true]. This day we succeeded in getting all the wagons but 6 on the mountain and ran 3 miles and encamped on one of those beautiful little lakes.

After getting both of his wagons up the mountain, May reported traveling three miles beyond the windswept Carson Pass and into Lake Valley, another beautiful basin with a small lake in its bottom (where Kirkwood and Caples Lake are today).

Left to fend for themselves, Smith's small group had to push on alone: "Sat 30 to day 6 Miles Brot us to the foot of the Mountain." Perhaps he meant that they made it the rest of the way through Hope Valley and stopped at the foot of the mountain at Red Lake. He added, "the Company had not all got up and we succeeded in getting two waggons." Smith seems less clear than usual; perhaps his mind was dulled by fatigue, by confusion brought on by the thin air in the mountains, or by a combination of both.

The next day, October 1, Smith reported that they "got the other three waggons up and Brot 4 in Red Lake Valley." This could mean that he and others returned to Hope Valley to haul their last three wagons up to Red Lake, or that they dragged the three wagons up the mountain. Or was he saying that of their five wagons, they were forced to leave one behind? In any case, they made little progress in those two days.

In the meantime, May and his family remained in their Lake Valley camp on October 1: "We lay in camp all day recruiting our teams. We are in what is called Lake Valley. This is quite a pleasant place good water, grass and plenty of wood that makes a blazing fire." Because Caples Lake has been dammed, it is considerably larger now than it was in 1848, and the site of their camp is likely underwater today. Note that May and Smith use the names given by the Thompson company, evidence that the Mormons had given Chiles a map or "waybill" on which they had written these names.

The next day, May and most of the company resumed their travel, beginning another steep climb. They were aiming for a low spot in a ridge that was southwest of and about a thousand feet above their Lake Valley camp. Today called West Pass, it is over nine thousand feet high. As they approached the pass, massive snow-clad crags stared down at them. May wrote:

> "Oct. 2nd. Traveled 4 miles and made the mountain height. We are now near 13,000 feet above the level of the Gulf of Mexico [he was in error]. We also have to run down that height in about 50 miles. Let me tell you I have seen the elephant in the way of mountains. We passed the snow in the mountains and eat of it and it may have fallen there many years ago. The top of the mountain is entirely bare of vegetation. Below the snow the pine grows luxuriantly."

Perhaps May was too tired to describe his trip over West Pass with his usual superlatives, but from the top of this great range of mountains, above the timberline, they would have had spectacular views of unconquered granite peaks as far as the eye could see. The scenery was grand, but the company could not dawdle here gawking; they had to get off this mountain as soon as possible. The oxen must have been gasping in the thin air as they strained at the wagons, slipping and staggering across uneven, glacier-sculpted rock and treacherous sheets of ice and snow. After crossing the pass just south of Thimble Peak, the trail descended westerly into what the Mormons named Rock Valley (where man-made Silver Lake is today). In later years, the trail beyond West Pass would change, and would head south and creep along a series of knife-edged ridges that bounded Rock Valley to the south and southeast.

While May and others were crossing over West Pass, Smith and his small group remained behind in Lake Valley:

> mon 2   this morning the co. left us again   we sent 2 men to bring in the other waggons   they Returned at sunset with the waggons   Dr. Fredrick had not unyoked his oxen and in consequence two yoke were lost   I urged the necessity of Making a Cache of all his load except Beding and clothing   this he and his wife refused.

Smith was still not being clear; the thin air may have been muddling his mind. Had they left some of their wagons at Carson Pass, then spent the night with the main body of the company at the Lake Valley camp? If so, the two men were probably sent to bring these wagons forward. Dr. Fredrick and his wagon may have been left behind in Hope Valley or at Red Lake because some of his oxen had died due to his foolish mistake. It also sounded like Smith and his small group spent a second night at the Lake Valley camp.

The next morning, Smith and his party, down to four wagons, began their ascent of West Pass:

> tues [October] 3   to day, we had another mountain to rise of about 4000 ft.   succeeded in getting our 4 waggons on the summit at dark   descended about one mile and encamped with Mr. Hallenbeck   we were obliged to leave

> Dr. Fredrick and wife to their fate in the valley called by the Mormons Red
> Lake   night very cold.

In leaving behind Dr. and Mrs. Frederick, was Smith beginning to behave like the others? In fairness, Smith was responsible for the safety of his wife and children, and some blame should be assigned to Dr. Fredrick for refusing to lighten his wagon or leave it behind.

Smith's entry for October 3 suggests they stopped to camp just a mile beyond the summit of West Pass. Perched at an altitude of over nine thousand feet on a treeless, windswept mountain, they had picked a dangerous place to spend the night. His entry for the third was, for the first time, written in pencil. Had he run out of ink, or had it frozen during that "very cold" night? Smith and his small party made it off the western face of West Pass on the fourth and descended six miles into Rock Valley, which he incorrectly called "Lake Valley":

> Wed 4   this morning the Road was very Hilly and Rough, and about one mile
> we met Slater Patton & Stuart Young party after Dr. Fredricks waggon   after a
> distance of about 6 miles we encamped in Lake Valley.

Was this rescue party a sign that someone was finally concerned about those struggling behind?

The Smith group had successfully made it over the highest pass on the trail, but still had fifty miles of hard mountain travel to go. He reported traveling five miles on the fifth as they continued making their way down from West Pass:

> Thurs [October] 5 to day we traveled about 5 miles and encamped at Rock Lake
> James Killed a Duck for Dinner Provisions is extremely Scarce I borrowed 14 lbs of
> flour which must last until AM all returned to day Hillenbeck killed a deer James
> came in at night he killed a deer and hung it in a tree about 3 miles from camp
> the people look Better.

They likely camped at Rock Creek that evening, somewhere beneath the waters of today's man-made Silver Lake. When Smith wrote "all returned to day," he was probably referring to Slater, Patton, Stuart, and Young returning with Dr. Fredrick and his wife and their wagon and team.

In the meantime, Richard May dashed off a journal entry covering three days:

> 3rd, 4th and 5th Oct. Traveled 30 miles over hill and dale in the Sierra Nevada
> Mountains and on a new route just opened by the Latter Day Saints. We have
> experienced a great deal of hardships in getting this far though. The timber of
> this region is pine and cedar, the undergrowth laurel, ivy and I saw today some
> oak bushes. It is quite cool, the weather clear. There is a great deal of game in
> these tallest of mountains.

After crossing West Pass on the second, May must have been getting tired of writing as he failed to give much detail about the land features he passed on these three days. From here on, the trail for the most part would travel along narrow ridges that would eventually lead them to the diggings. They would have also passed Tragedy Springs, and perhaps camped there, but May's silence about the location may indicate that he did not know about the place or what had happened there. They probably camped the next night at Leeks Springs, on today's Mormon Emigrant Trail Road, about two miles west of Highway 88. Then they likely camped at Camp Valley on the evening of the fifth, another eight miles west and near the Mormon Emigrant Trail Road. By October 5, May was still traveling along the ridge, fifteen miles east of Sly's Park. On the sixth, he reported descending into Sly's Park. The nearest gold diggings were not far away.

The trail had been easy the last few days. The worst was behind them, and May sounded like he was in good spirits. His entry for the sixth reflected a return to his usual bubbling, exuberant voice:

> October 6th. Traveled 15 miles and camped on Sly's Park and it should be called anything but a park, having no resemblance to any such thing. The timber in this portion of the mountains is delightful. The tall red woods and pine and hemlock with some oak give the country more beauty than where nothing but bare, arid mountains make their appearance. The birds whistle and sing in every glen and hollow while the evergreen both great and small have an air of cheerfulness that can be found only in a timbered country.

On October 6, Edward Smith was on the trail at some unspecified location a few miles west of Rock Valley, perhaps was even resting at Tragedy Springs. He reported on the men who had gone to rescue Dr. Franklin's wagon:

> Mr. Slater Mr. Patten Mr. Stuart when they went after Dr. Fredrick had nothing to eat with them and eat up all the Provisions Dr. Fredrick had he [Fredrick] had killed 2 young fawns and [they] now Refuse to Repay.

Should we credit Chiles with a redemptive act of mercy by sending these three men? Hardly.

> Sat Oct 7   this morning we Descended Rapidly full 3000 ft and after a distance of 16 miles we encamped without grass at camp valley   in the evening all the co. came in   Capt. Chiles exacted from Dr. Fredrick His waggon & team to haul about 600 lbs to the settlements   these were the only conditions or he might Perish in the mountains   he having only the 8 lbs of flour I obtained from Mr. Hollenbeck was obliged to accept of these Hard Conditions or Starve in the mountains   the waggon and team was worth at least $250 in Missouri.

Smith's explanation of the situation continues to show the color of Chiles' character. He had simply taken Dr. Fredrick's wagon and team from him by forcing him to either accept these stiff terms or be left in the mountains. Smith thought that the wagon and ox team was worth $250, which he considered a hefty sum, but he would later find out that in this gold-rich country a wagon and team would bring over $1,000. Chiles' behavior seems beneath contempt, a tawdry act of larceny that should forever stain his place in history.

On October 8, Smith reported a long day of travel that ended with their arrival at Sly's Park: "Sun 8   we started at 8 traveled until dark   encamped at Slys Park   no water within ½ mile and 3 miles to grass   very poor."

Traveling was now easier as they descended from the mighty Sierras, and it couldn't have come at a better time for their played-out oxen. A descending road and thoughts of gold must have quickened their pace over the gently rounded foothills covered with dry grass that was as golden in color as the precious metal being found in nearby streams and rivers.

Richard May and his family had left Sly's Park the day before, on October 7, and were traveling along the ridge that separated the American and Cosumnes Rivers. They were on their way to Pleasant Valley, where the pioneer Mormons had started three months earlier:

> 7th October. Traveled 8 miles and encamped on a high ridge in the mountains it being the divide between the [Cosumnes] and American Rivers. We are several thousand feet lower than when on the back bone of this range of mountains, in fact the climate tells me that we are in the neighborhood of being through this highest of mountains in North America. The weather has been very cool for several days in consequence of our great height.

> Sunday the 8rd Oct. Traveled 10 miles through the hills and [emerged] on the plain bordering on the Sacramento River. The timber is very indifferent, the pine and cedar giving way to oak principally.

By the end of the eighth, May was in Pleasant Valley, although he did not call it that, effectively coming to the end of the trail. When they left Independence on May 12, they believed they had five months to get to California. Well, they did it in five months—150 days to be exact. They had cleared the high mountains before a major storm could trap them. Now fifty miles from Sutter's Fort and only spitting distance from the diggings, there should have been evidence of mounting excitement. Yet, there is not:

> 9th October. Traveled 4 miles and encamped on a small branch of Weaver's [Webber] Creek which is noted for its richness of gold mines though not richer than any other little creek in this whole region of country.

May was probably referring to Ringold Creek, just north of today's County Road E-16 and about three miles east of today's Diamond Springs. Just a few miles further was Webber Creek, named after Charles Weber, a German emigrant who had come to California with the Bartleson-Bidwell wagon party in 1841, and had gone to work for Captain Sutter before he obtained his own Mexican land grant. Shortly after learning of the discovery of gold at Coloma, Weber began exploring this creek and found gold in abundance. But May would not dig gold for long, blaming it on his poor health. He sold his wagon and teams, discovering that they were worth a great deal:

> Here Weaver [Webber] Creek near the diggings, I unloaded my wagon on the 10th of October and proceeded on to Fort Sutter without delay intending to bring back supplies for the winter, being gone two weeks and finding provisions very high I determined to sell my wagon and teams and done so. They brought me 1,100 dollars and in the meantime my health so much endangered that I did not think it advisable to remain in the gold mines. As soon therefore as I could make it convenient I rolled out for the Sacramento River. I remained in the mining district two weeks after my return from the Fort digging a little gold but very feeble indeed, being reduced down to 160 pounds or something lower, having lost 86 lbs. of flesh on the travel.

Mike McClellan, who had traveled with the Chiles party, sent a letter home to a friend, explaining that "[w]e arrived at the gold mines on Weaver's [Webber's] Creek, a branch of the American fork of the Sacramento, where my family is at this time, after a toilsome, tedious and perilous journey of five months and five days."[15]

In the meantime, Edward Smith was still at Sly's Park on October 9, because "one yoke of My oxen was gone." The next day, he left Sly's Park with only one of his wagons and traveled to "a Spring in Pleasant Valley without grass in the afternoon we traveled about 2 miles encamped at a small spring near the Road." This was probably today's Diamond Springs, on County Road E-16. With little fanfare, the Smiths had also finally reached the end of their journey.

On October 11, Smith and his small party traveled a few more miles. "Arrived at the gold mines," he wrote, "which in Productiveness far exceeds Aladdins fancy Dream." Despite being in this wonderfully rich country, Smith did not seem interested in staying there. He and his family traveled on to Sutter's Fort, and arrived there on October 15.

It is regrettable that Smith recorded practically nothing about his impressions of California, his reasons for eschewing gold mining, or his thoughts of what he intended to do next. It would have been interesting to read how May and Smith felt about completing their journey and their impressions of this new land. But their last entries—short, shallow, and unrevealing—are disappointing. They were probably tired of writing, or just plain tired. Their minds had already moved on to an entirely new set of concerns. Like the other recent arrivals in Oregon and California, May and

Smith had to focus on the challenges of where they should go and what they should do in order to ensure their families' survival in the coming months.

For many emigrants, it would be years before they would sit down to reflect upon their trip and recall their memories. They would remember it with pride, but it was unlikely that any would wish to repeat it. Their epic journey demonstrated that human endeavor is rarely executed perfectly. Mistake, misfortune, and misadventure are part of human experience, some caused by recklessness, foolishness, stupidity, or bad judgment, and some are just bad luck. In the end, the 1848 experience demonstrated that, with steadfast determination, all could be overcome.

The overland emigration of 1848 had come to a close. In the history of the Oregon-California Trail, 1848 was the end of an era. The next year would be the beginning of another era as a tidal wave of gold-seekers would swamp the trail for years to come.

Epilogue

Many of the emigrants whose travels we have been following settled into their new homes and were not heard from again, but others left behind records of their trail westward and their new life on the western frontier. Some were already well known before 1848 and some became prominent citizens or at least left some record of their lives. After following the adventures of some of the emigrants who traveled in 1848, it is natural that we are curious about what became of some of those who played prominent roles in our story.

OREGON EMIGRANTS

Riley Root

When the Gates company arrived at Oregon City on September 12, 1848, Riley Root remained there through the fall and winter. In the spring of 1849, he boarded a ship and arrived in San Francisco on May 7. He was astonished by the large number of ships anchored in the Bay, remarking that most of their crews had charged off to the diggings.[1]

He spent the next five months in various gold camps, then returned to San Francisco and boarded a sailing ship that left for Panama on October 21, 1849. Eventually, he passed through New Orleans, taking a steamer up the Mississippi River and returning to his hometown of Galesburg, Illinois, on January 8, 1850. Later that year, he published a small book containing his journal entries and an account of his travels through Oregon and California. Root was a multitalented man; he invented and obtained patents on a number of devices, including a rotary snowplow to clear train tracks. He died in Galesburg in 1870 at seventy-five years of age.[2] His original journal resides in the Coe Collection at the Yale University Library.

William Wright Anderson

Very little is known about the fate of William Wright Anderson, the bachelor who drove a wagon for Isaac Miller. Shortly after Anderson and his Miller company arrived in the Willamette Valley, he went looking for a job in Oregon City. "[T]imes were verry Dul in Oregon," he complained. "not much going on   a great many had gone to the Gold mines." He failed to explain whether he, like many others, went to California, but it is known that sometime later he returned to Indiana. During the remaining years of his life, he probably often recounted his 1848 journey to Oregon to family and friends. His original journal has disappeared, but not before it was transcribed in typewritten form. This transcription resides in the Lilly Library at Indiana University–Bloomington, in Bloomington, Indiana.

Keturah Belknap

On arriving in the Willamette Valley, George and Keturah Belknap took up a donation claim for 640 acres. They and their extended family settled just south of Monroe, Oregon, in today's Benton County. Their first imperative was to build a log house for shelter before winter set in. A year later, George and some of his friends traveled to the goldfields of California and did well. They returned shortly with enough gold dust to purchase livestock and farm equipment.

Keturah's three-year-old son, Jesse, recovered from the illness Keturah described when they crossed Greenwood's cutoff in Wyoming. Jesse grew up, married, and had a child, but he and his wife both died in 1871, when he was only twenty-six. They were survived by their two-year-old daughter.

Keturah was pregnant during the journey, and her son Lorenzo was born on the trail near Fort Boise on August 10, 1848. The infant survived and lived a long life. Lorenzo died in 1926 at seventy-eight years of age.

Keturah lived until 1913, and died at the age of ninety-three.[3]

William Porter

William Porter neglected to report that his wife was seriously ill with "mountain fever" when they arrived in the Willamette Valley. She died within a few weeks later. William acquired a donation claim located two and a half miles south of what became the community of Aumsville, Oregon. With four small children, he needed to find them a new mother. He married his deceased wife's sister, Martha, in 1849, and she bore him three more children.

In addition to farming, the well-educated Porter served as county assessor and commissioner, and was elected to the first territorial legislature. During the Civil War, he spent three years in the U.S. Army, and served in eastern Oregon, Washington, and Idaho. Porter continued to live on his farm until he died in 1899 at eighty-six years of age.[4] His original journal is in the possession of William's great-grandson Kenneth Porter.

W. L. Adams

After reaching Oregon City on October 1, the same day William Porter arrived, Adams and his family crossed the Willamette River and headed thirty-five miles west to Yamhill. He arrived in Yamhill with but ten cents in his pocket, but soon lost it through a hole in his pocket. He sold his wagon and used the money to buy ten cows. He stayed with friends over the winter, and sustained his family by setting up a school and teaching the settlers' children. In the spring, he traveled to California's gold mines, while his wife took over his teaching duties. He returned in the fall with enough gold dust to clear his debts and buy an existing farm with a log house.

He was elected county probate judge in 1850 and state senator in 1856. He bought the *Oregon Spectator* newspaper in 1855, and penned rousing editorials, especially those that condemned slavery. With all that, he remained a farmer until 1873, when, with a restless mind and boundless talent, he traveled east to Pennsylvania at fifty-two years of age to attend medical school and then law school. After graduation, he returned to Oregon and established a medical practice in Portland. During his spare moments he wrote and published a book on the history of medicine.

His daughter Inez, only two when they made the trip in 1848, wrote a wonderful reminiscence in 1925 about her childhood in Oregon. She recounted many details, but one thing that stood out was her observation that "the poorest people of today would consider our pioneer life one of unbearable hardship, yet no people were ever happier or healthier than we were." She reserved a few kind words for Rose, their old milk cow, who lived another ten years on their farm, and died at the age of twenty-four years, an uncommon age for any cow.

Adams' daughter Helen, only an infant during the 1848 journey, grew up and married John Johnson, the first president of the University of Oregon.[5]

Father Honoré-Timothée Lempfrit, O.M.I.

Father Lempfrit's uncanny gift for getting himself into distressing predicaments seemed to stay with him even after he arrived in the Northwest. Seven months after arriving at St. Joseph's Mission, he was sent by his oblate superior, Father Ricard, to Vancouver Island to serve the Catholics and Indians at the Hudson's Bay Company's newly established Fort Victoria.[6] An Anglican minister did not welcome the French priest's intrusion and made matters difficult. Anxious to escape the tension, Lempfrit accepted the offer of a Scottish gentleman who was establishing a new settlement nearby, and moved there to serve the settlers and Indians of the area. He seemed to be getting along well at first, but the constant wet and cold and the harsh, primitive accommodations caused his health to deteriorate.

Like Dr. Whitman, Father Lempfrit seemed incapable of appreciating the unsteady temperament of the Indians—how their superstitions and distrust could unexpectedly rise up and transform fervent acolytes into dangerous threats. When the Hudson's Bay Company's James Douglas began receiving reports in 1852 that Lempfrit's safety was threatened by the local tribe, he did not hesitate to send men to take Lempfrit away from there.[7]

Back at St. Joseph's Mission, Father Ricard received a request from the bishop of Monterey, California, complaining of the difficulty of keeping his priests from running off to the gold mines. The bishop asked for an oblate priest and Ricard sent Lempfrit in June 1852.[8] Lempfrit was assigned to the old Spanish mission at Santa Ynez, but he would serve there only a year. Disheartened and still unwell, he returned to France. He sent Father Ricard a bitter letter from San Francisco dated September 23, 1853. It was evident that he had had enough of the West, including his once beloved Indians. "Thank God I am finally out of this dreadful place," he wrote of the Mission. "I really believe, my dear Father, that it will not be long before you will all follow me [back to France] for, if you call Oregon a sad country, what would you say about California where they know no other God but gold?"[9]

Upon arriving in France, Lempfrit was appointed parish priest for the village of Vého, then for the nearby village of Morville-les-Vic. He died in 1866 at only sixty-three years of age. One wonders if the hardships he had suffered in the West from 1848 to 1853 had permanently ruined his health.[10]

CALIFORNIA EMIGRANTS
Captain M. N. Wambaugh

There is every reason to believe that the members of Captain Wambaugh's company held their wagon master in high regard, but they probably had not heard about an incident that occurred in 1847, while Wambaugh was still in California. Intending to join Commodore Robert Stockton's party as it prepared to head east in the spring of 1847, Wambaugh was asked to deliver a shipment of government silver to the commodore's camp at Johnson's Ranch on the Bear River. Wambo showed up empty-handed, claiming he had been robbed by bandits, and he displayed a bullet hole in his hat to prove it, but there were skeptics. "[H]ad not Providence caused the missile to curve over the top of his head," one of the skeptics scoffed, "it must necessarily have passed through the center of the brain." A few years later, evidence emerged that Wambaugh had stopped at William Gordon's rancho on Cache Creek while on his way to the Bear River, and it was later learned that shortly thereafter Gordon exchanged a large quantity of silver for gold.[11]

Even though Wambaugh had purchased land in the Santa Clara Valley in 1847, he did not return there straightaway after he and his company arrived in California in September 1848. Rather, he became part of the gold-searching jamboree. In 1849, he discovered a rich deposit on the north side of the Yuba River, at the mouth of Dead-wood Creek, about forty-three miles east of Marysville. The place became known as "Wamba's Bar." He took up residence the following year at Fremont, a small settlement in Yolo County on the west side of the Sacramento River, and was elected to represent Yolo and Colusa counties in the State Senate in 1853.[12]

James Clyman

Although James Clyman may have paused momentarily to try his hand at gold panning, he did not remain in the gold country for long. It was the Napa Valley that had drawn him back to California. Even though Pulitzer Prize-winning historian Bernard DeVoto extolled Clyman as one of his heroes, Clyman had managed to remain quietly obscure during this 1848 trip, although his steady hand and unobtrusive experience surely played a prominent role.

Clyman's 1846 letter praising the Napa Valley had inspired Lambert McComb, the family patriarch, to take his family there and the McCombses followed Clyman to Napa and settled on land where the city of Napa stands today. Fifty-seven-year-old Clyman continued to court Lambert's twenty-seven-year-old daughter, Hannah, and the couple was married on August 22, 1849.

Clyman purchased land a few miles south of the McCombses' and established a ranch with a fruit orchard and small herd of dairy cows. He and Hannah had five children, although four of them died as youngsters in 1866 of scarlet fever. Only a daughter, Lydia, survived.

Even as Clyman grew older and feebler, he managed to occasionally make it into the nearby hills to hunt deer and grizzly bear, but old age waits for no man. Eyesight failed, quickness departed, strength fled; the old mountain man died on his ranch in 1881 at eighty-nine-years of age.[13]

David Parks

The Parks family had been kind enough to take Thomas Corcoran under their wing at Fort Laramie. They had fed him and carried his blankets in their wagon. Most significantly, Parks saved Thomas' life by keeping him from accompanying William Fallon when he left Soda Springs and headed off on his fatal encounter with the Paiutes.

The Parks family was large, with seven sons. When they came to the end of the Truckee/Donner Trail, they headed for the gold-rich Yuba River. According to the family's biographical sketch, they arrived at the Yuba on September 8. Thomas Corcoran's letter explained how he was panning gold on the Yuba for three weeks when he came across "my old friend, Park.... He had just got to the mines."

The Parks family settled along the north bank of the Yuba River, about fifteen miles upriver from what would later become the town of Marysville. Being one of the first to work this exceptionally rich area, the Parks family was soon feverishly pulling large quantities of gold out of the sand and gravel. The place became known as Parks' Bar and scores of miners were drawn to the spot. A town sprung up, with stores, hotels, and saloons. Although the Parkses had been doing well at mining, they also opened a store and sold supplies to miners and Indians alike. It was difficult to not make lots of money, especially when they discovered that the Indians, unaware of the relative value of things, would happily trade a tin cup of gold dust for a tin cup of glass beads. After four prosperous years, David Parks gathered up his family and returned to Indiana with over $85,000 in gold. His three oldest sons remained in California for another two years to further enrich themselves.

Although David Parks had been very kind to Corcoran, he was a classic example of the restless, never-satisfied type. He had moved three times between getting married in 1827 and leaving for California in 1848. A few years after returning to Indiana in 1852, he left his wife of thirty-five years for a younger woman. He moved to Wisconsin, then to Minnesota, then finally settled in Oregon. He died in Oregon in 1875 at seventy years of age.[14]

John McPherson

This immensely talented Scotsman, another Wambaugh party member, did not tarry in the gold country for long. By October 14, the first of his journal excerpts appeared in the San Francisco *Californian*. People recognized his considerable ability as a writer, and he became a journalist and freelance writer, producing poetry and stories about early California pioneers for newspapers, usually writing under the pen name of Juanita. While traveling in the Wambaugh party he became friends with Jeemes Walker and his cousin Frank McClellan. In later years, he interviewed Joseph Walker at length and produced a series of articles about the legendary mountain man that appeared in the *Oakland Transcript* in 1873. But McPherson was bedeviled by a drinking problem, and his career ended when he fell through the trestlework of a railroad bridge over the Tuolomne River in 1880 while intoxicated and was killed.[15] The fate of his sorely missed journal is unknown.

Richard M. May

Richard May was trying to recover from his illness when his Chiles company arrived at the goldfields. He had explained how, despite his weakened condition, he tried his luck, but his formerly robust weight of 246 pounds had dwindled to 160. After a short period of prospecting in the chilled waters of creeks and streams, he concluded that his frail body was not up to it. He and his family left the gold country and headed for Sutter's Fort. After leaving the fort on November 8, they boarded a small vessel on the banks of the Sacramento River and arrived in San Francisco three days later.

May appears to have been another one of those restless spirits. He and his family lived in San Francisco for only three months. He moved his family to San Jose, but that did not last long. In October 1850, they moved to Oak Grove, a community not far away. In August 1852, he moved again, taking his family to Salem, Oregon. He acquired a land claim and moved his family onto a farm. But it did not suit him, and he moved his family back into Salem. At this point, we lost track of him.[16]

Edward Smith

When Smith and his family finally made it down from the mountains, he reported that gold was being found in abundance wherever one turned, but he did not seem to be entranced by the life of a gold miner. Just as we had observed his disapproving attitude toward liquor, he may have viewed the lust for gold as another vice to be avoided. Smith hustled his family through the gold country and hastened on to Sutter's Fort. On October 15, he put his family on a boat at the Sacramento River bank. While his family made their way down the Sacramento River, Smith ferried his wagon and team across and drove them overland to Benicia, where he rejoined his family. They sailed across the bay and moved into a house in San Francisco.

Probably referring to his earlier gunshot wound, Smith noted in his journal on October 30 that "my Hand continues very Painful." On November 3, he again complained, "The pain in my hand increases." His daily journal entries then ceased, but Smith survived. His journal contained notations that he was appointed postmaster of San Juan Bautista, Monterey County, in 1850, and that he was a surveyor for Monterey County in 1851 and 1852. The 1850 census showed Edward at age forty-three living in San Juan Bautista with his wife, Jane, and four children ranging in age from fifteen to four.[17] The last entry in his journal was starkly piercing: "1853 Estate of E. Smith, Deceased." He had died. His wife Jane had become a widow much too soon after all, maybe because of the lingering effects of Smith's old gunshot wound.

Smith's wonderfully illuminating journal is owned by the Fresno City and County Historical Society, to which I am indebted for their willingness to let me examine it at length. I will always fondly recall turning the journal's brittle pages, and often encountering particles of grit and fragments of sagebrush pressed between the pages—tiny artifacts from the trail. It was as if the past had traveled through time and reappeared in the present.

Caleb and Britton Greenwood

In April 1849, two separate gold miners mentioned in their diaries that the Greenwood clan was living in a log cabin at Coloma, next door to gold-discoverer James Marshall. One of these men related the story about making the mistake of calling Caleb a liar. To keep the old man from shooting him, he had to bow, scrape, eat crow, and give Caleb a small keg of whiskey.[18]

While the Greenwoods lived at Coloma in 1849, Angelina, one of Caleb's little daughters, died. Later that year, the Greenwood family moved fifteen miles northeast to a small valley that was later named Greenwood Valley.[19] During the cold, wet winter of 1849/50, Caleb's toughness failed him and he died somewhere in the open between the Bear and Yuba Rivers, at the age of about eighty-seven. One gold miner wrote in March 1850 that "[t]his unfortunate wretch was recently found under a tree; liquor was his executioner."[20] That might be true and then again it might not. After all, at eighty-seven, he may have just died of old age. A gentler version of the story was written years later that "[t]his old man died . . . somewhere near Oroville. I heard a report that he insisted on lying out of doors, with his rifle at his side, and would not allow even a tent over him to obscure the sky—threatening to shoot the man who should attempt to put a shelter over him. And thus he died out of doors."[21]

As for Caleb's son, Britton, he spent most of his remaining years raising sheep in Mendocino and Humboldt Counties. He died a very poor man in Humboldt County in 1888, at sixty years of age.[22]

Pierre Barlow (P. B.) Cornwall

P. B. Cornwall was an uncommonly gifted and driven young man whose later life could fill a book. In fact, it did: the biography written by his son in 1906. During P. B.'s journey west, it was evident that he was possessed of an impatient, cocksure personality; hence, his future in California would not come as anything startling. Despite the rigors of the journey, he appeared to have arrived in California with undiminished energy and ambition. Although he tried his hand at gold panning at Mormon's Bar, he did not remain there long. Having once operated a store in Ohio, he foresaw that much greater profits could be had by supplying the miners.

He used his gold pannings to purchase supplies, then transported them to the goldfields. He purchased some small vessels and used them to ship supplies from San Francisco to the riverbank near Sutter's Fort. By December 1848, a mere four months after his arrival in California, he had earned the means to purchase a one-third interest in the mercantile firm of Priest, Lee & Co. At first operating a store within the walls of Sutter's Fort, it quickly expanded into banking and real estate as soon as the future town of Sacramento City was surveyed and divided into lots.

In the late summer and early fall of 1849, thousands upon thousands of forty-niners spilled over the Sierras. In December 1849, Cornwall married an attractive young woman whose family had just arrived with one of the 1849 wagon companies. By April 1850, a mere year and a half after he had arrived, P. B. sold his interest in the Priest, Lee firm for $650,000. He reinvested much of the cash in Sacramento lots and took the rest as a promissory note from his former partner. He had become an enormously wealthy young man almost overnight.

While P. B. and his bride traveled to the East Coast by ship to enjoy their new wealth, an epidemic of cholera spread through Sacramento and the mining camps. The Sacramento real estate bubble burst, and P. B. and his bride hurried back to salvage what they could. Sacramento was then ravaged by a series of fires and floods, further reducing the value of his lots. His wealth had vanished. He took his family to San Francisco in 1858, where he became a notary public to support his family over the next few years.

He was eventually hired to manage the San Francisco office of the Bellingham Bay Co., a coal mining and shipping firm from Bellingham, Washington. Their operations included shipping thousands of tons of coal to San Francisco. In recognition of Cornwall's drive and talents, he was eventually promoted to president of the company. He foresaw other opportunities and established new companies for Bellingham. Under his management, the company prospered and he was able to purchase sizeable amounts of company shares.

Once again financially substantial, Cornwall set up a real estate development company in San Francisco. He also founded the California Electric Light Co. in 1879, which established San Francisco's first electric light system.

In 1904, at eighty-three years of age, Cornwall contracted pneumonia and died. As an interesting sidenote, P. B.'s son, Bruce Cornwall (author of P. B.'s biography), became a lawyer and started a law firm in San Jose by the name of Cornwall, Coldwell, and Banker. Years later, after Cornwall retired, the firm specialized in real estate sales and expanded into a national company that is today called Coldwell, Banker.

Thomas Corcoran

Thomas Corcoran is the person I began this book with and the one I will end it with. He was my great-great-great-uncle and the reason I wrote this book. I thank Thomas for providing the inspiration that launched me on this thoroughly rewarding project.

After Thomas descended from Donner Pass with Britton Greenwood and arrived at Johnson's Ranch on the Bear River in late August 1848, they had already heard that gold had been discovered on the Yuba River. Thomas bought some dried beef and flour, and a pick, shovel, and tin pan for washing gold, then headed for the Yuba, only sixteen miles north. He turned his mare, Slipper, and his packhorse loose to graze, and commenced washing sand and gravel from beside the riverbank. Three weeks later, he came down with a fever and decided that it was time to suspend gold panning and travel south to find his former neighbors, the Murphys. "I was so taken up with the gold that I never thought of Slipper," he explained. "When I went to look for her and the packhorse, they had strayed away. I never saw either of them again."

While looking for his horses along the Yuba, he wrote that he came across "[m]y old friend, Park," the family he had traveled with since Fort Laramie. Being the generous man that he was, Parks loaned Thomas a mare, telling him that if he ever lost her, he was "to pay him $200 whenever I should see him. I never saw him afterwards," Thomas explained, "but I saw his wife and son in Sacramento two years later and I paid her the $200."

Thomas sold his rifle for $100 and his overcoat for six ounces of gold. With that and three weeks of gold washings, he had "got together about $1000 in gold dust." He departed the Yuba River and headed for Sutter's Fort. There, he met Edmond Bray, a former neighbor from Irish Grove who had traveled to California with the Murphys in 1844 and who had been a Sutter employee ever since. "He was very glad to see me," Thomas wrote. "He had the keys to the fort." Thomas spent the night at the fort. In the morning, he discovered that someone had stolen his $1,000 in gold dust from his bundle of belongings while he slept. Undaunted, "I started for Martin Murphy's ranch on the Cosumnes River."

When Thomas arrived at the Cosumnes, about eighteen miles south of Sutter's Fort, he came to Martin Murphy Jr.'s adobe house. After arriving in California in 1844, the Murphy family had settled in the Santa Clara Valley.[23] Martin Jr., however, acquired Rancho de Ernesto, a large Mexican rancho, along the Cosumnes and began raising wheat and cattle. Thomas discovered that the brothers, John and Daniel Murphy, were up in the hills getting rich. Right after news of gold leaked out in March 1848, the Murphy brothers began exploring the streams and rivers south of Coloma. When they came to a small tributary of the Calaveras River, they found gold in large quantities. Sources differ, but it was estimated that the Murphys removed between $1.5 and $2 million worth of gold from Murphy's Flat by the winter of 1848. There are reports that in December 1849, John Murphy left Murphy's Flat with six mules loaded to the gills with all the gold that they could carry. With their wealth, the Murphy brothers bought large tracts of land, also in the Santa Clara Valley. In an odd twist, John married Virginia Reed, daughter of James Reed, of the Donner party.

The Murphys were now considered the richest family in California. As for the sister, Ellen Murphy, she was reported as "so attractive that early travelers wrote about meeting her." Another wrote, "because of her beauty and Irish gift for words, [Ellen] stood out as one of the most eligible women in California." In 1850, she married Charles Weber, a good friend of the Murphys and the founder of the town of Stockton. He had also become very wealthy through his early gold ventures. Was Thomas devastated with Ellen's engagement and marriage to Weber? He never said.

Thomas explained that during his 1848 journey he had "coughed up blood until I got to the Rocky Mountains. Then I got better, but I never got over the effects of that sickness that I had in Missouri." Perhaps because of his infirmity, he did not resume his gold digging career and went into the supply business instead. A "friend" (perhaps one of the Murphys) loaned him money to purchase two packhorses and a load of blankets and shoes. With his profits, he traded his packhorses for a freight wagon and team and hauled supplies, mostly flour, to the mines.

In 1853, Thomas' brother and sister-in-law, Owen and Catherine Corcoran (my great-great grandparents) left their farm in Wisconsin and brought Catherine's younger sister, Bridget, to California by sailing ship. Thomas married Bridget, while Owen and Catherine returned to Wisconsin. In 1854, Thomas and Bridget built a general mercantile store in the small gold town of San Andreas, then sold the store in 1858 and bought a six-hundred-acre wheat ranch six miles east of Stockton. Here they farmed and raised their family. They had seven children, four of them dying young. Bridget died in 1886.

Since Thomas was illiterate and never learned to read or write, he always had someone else transcribe his dictated letters. He mentioned that Ellen Murphy transcribed one of his letters in 1849, and she may have transcribed others. As he grew older, he let his son run the ranch. When only sixty-seven, he may have suffered a stroke, as he complained of numbness on one side and having to use crutches.

Thomas was a good Irish Catholic. In 1904, he wrote a letter to his sister in which he related an incident in 1879 when he had traveled east by train to pay a visit to his old home in Irish Grove, Missouri. Visiting his father's grave, he recounted that, "I knelt down and said my prayers. I had a cold and cough when I knelt down and after saying my prayers, I was well." He brought that last letter to an end by writing, "I send my love to you and hope we will meet in heaven." He died eight months later at seventy-nine years of age, coincidentally the same year in which his former travel mate, P. B. Cornwall, died.

Thomas had made the right choice in coming to California. Although he had not prospered like the Murphys, Charles Weber, or P. B. Cornwall, he had licked his lung fever, had avoided being scalped, and in the end had done all right for himself.

Notes

Introduction (pp. xiii–xx)

1. DeVoto, *Across the Wide Missouri*, 9.
2. Unruh, *Plains Across*, 119–20.

Chapter 1, Just Five Months to Get There (pp. 1–13)

1. U.S. Department of Health and Human Services, Center for Disease Control and Prevention, "Histoplasmosis, General Information." (http://www.cdc.gov/nczved/divisions/dfbmd/diseases/histoplasmosis/).
2. Thomas Corcoran to Elizabeth Lonergan, August 23, 1877. A rough draft of the letter is in Thomas' old copybook, now in the possession of one of Thomas' great-grandchildren.
3. Ibid.
4. Edward Corcoran, Corcoran family genealogy (1974), 4.
5. The word "malaria" springs from the Latin *mala aria*, meaning "bad air." During the nineteenth century, it was commonly believed that malaria was caused by deadly vapors from swamps and wetlands.
6. *History of Holt and Atchison Counties, Missouri*, 643.
7. Barry, *Beginning of the West*, 435; Schmidt, *Who Were the Murphys*, 5, 7; Stewart, *California Trail*, 56.
8. Thomas Corcoran to Elizabeth Lonergan, August 23, 1877; Edward Corcoran, Corcoran family geneaology, 4.
9. Thomas Corcoran to Elizabeth Lonergan, August 23, 1877.
10. Cornwall, *Life Sketch of P. B. Cornwall*, 1, 13.
11. DeVoto, *Year of Decision*, 52.
12. Cornwall, *Life Sketch of P. B. Cornwall*, 14–27.
13. Barry, *Beginning of the West*, 345, 428.
14. *St. Joseph Gazette*, June 25, 1847.
15. Root, *Journal of Travels from St. Josephs to Oregon*, 3.
16. Barry, *Beginning of the West*, 509; Camp, *James Clyman, Frontiersman*, 59, 62–64.
17. Cornwall, *Life Sketch of P. B. Cornwall*, 15. A Tom Fallon lived in San Jose, California, between 1850 and 1885, and was mayor of the town at one time. Cornwall lived near there and may have misrecollected William's name as Tom.
18. Bancroft, *History of California*, 3:734; Kelly and Morgan, *Old Greenwood*, 81.
19. DeVoto, *Across the Wide Missouri*, 239.
20. Bancroft, *History of California*, 3:734; Camp, *James Clyman, Frontiersman*, 320n108; Kelly and Morgan, *Old Greenwood*, 80; Nidever, *Life and Adventures of George Nidever*, 24.
21. Barry, *Beginning of the West*, 287, 448; Camp, *James Clyman, Frontiersman*, 67, 312n41.
22. Bancroft, *History of California*, 3:734; DeVoto, *Year of Decision*, 443; Thornton, *Oregon and California in 1848*, 2:232–39; Barry, *Beginning of the West*, 711.
23. Cornwall, *Life Sketch of P. B. Cornwall*, 16, 23.
24. Ibid., 15.

25. Bancroft, *History of California*, 5:452–53; Tyler, *Mormon Battalion in the Mexican War*, 301–2.

26. *History of Holt and Atchison Counties, Missouri*, 725. The original settlement of Irish Grove was a quarter of a mile from a later community called Milton. The Corcoran farm, as described in a U.S. land grant issued to Thomas Corcoran on January 1, 1849, was probably one mile west of Irish Grove.

27. Barry, *Beginning of the West*, 511; *History of Holt and Atchison Counties*, 613; Stewart, *California Trail*, 56.

28. Ellen Murphy's early photos depict a young woman of uncommon attractiveness.

29. Simmons, *La Belle Vue*, 1.

30. Cornwall, *Life Sketch of P. B. Cornwall*, 15.

31. Parker, "Early Recollections of Oregon Pioneer Life," 17.

32. Evans, *History of the Pacific Northwest: Oregon and Washington*, 2:186.

33. Cornwall, *Life Sketch of P. B. Cornwall*, 16.

34. Bennett, *Mormons at the Missouri*, 254n13; Gale, *Peter A. Sarpy and Early Bellevue*, 10.

35. Kelly and Morgan, *Old Greenwood*, 95; Stewart, *California Trail*, 57.

36. Gale, *Peter A. Sarpy and Early Bellevue*, 13; Shallcross, *Romance of a Village*, 37.

37. Bennett, *Mormons at the Missouri*, 47–48, 253n9; Ramsey and Shrier, *Silent Hills Speak*, 15.

38. Ramsey and Shrier, *Silent Hills Speak*, 5, 32.

39. Simmons, *La Belle Vue*, 31; Barry, *Beginning of the West*, 373.

40. Barry, *Beginning of the West*, 239, 249, 426.

41. Simmons, *La Belle Vue*, 150.

42. Cornwall, *Life Sketch of P. B. Cornwall*, 15, 16.

43. Hines, *Illustrated History of the State of Oregon*, 1037.

44. *History of the Pacific Northwest*, 399; "Biographical—Capt. Orrin Kellogg," 111; *Portrait and Biographical Record of Portland and Vicinity, Oregon*, 102.

45. Cornwall, *Life Sketch of P. B. Cornwall*, 16; Thomas Corcoran to Elizabeth Lonergan, August 23, 1877.

Chapter 2, St. Joseph, a Rising Star (pp. 14–21)

1. Camp, *James Clyman, Frontiersman*, 46.

2. Barry, *Beginning of the West*, 139; Camp, *James Clyman, Frontiersman*, 39, 67.

3. Camp, *James Clyman, Frontiersman*, 229.

4. Ibid., 235.

5. Barry, *Beginning of the West*, 743.

6. Kurz, *Journal*, 27.

7. Camp, *James Clyman, Frontiersman*, 316.

8. Kurz, *Journal*, 29.

9. Ibid., 30.

10. Logan, *Old St. Jo*, 19, 24; Willoughby, *Robidoux's Town*, 20.

11. Barry, *Beginning of the West*, 133, 271; Logan, *Old St. Jo*, 13–16; Willoughby, *Robidoux's Town*, 15.

12. Barry, *Beginning of the West*, 271; Logan, *Old St. Jo*, 13–16; Willoughby, *Robidoux's Town*, 15.

13. Logan, *Old St. Jo*, 24.

14. Ibid., 24, 31.

15. Lewin and Taylor, *St. Joe Road*, 5.

16. Logan, *Old St. Jo*, 49.

17. Shallcross, *Romance of a Village*, 62.

18. Camp, *James Clyman, Frontiersman*, 26–28, 35.

Chapter 3, Load the Wagons (pp. 22–30)

1. Keturah Belknap. A typewritten transcription of "Kitturah Penton Belknap's Journal," copied from the original, is in Washington State University Libraries, Pullman, WA, Cage 1680, #132. See also Holmes, *Covered Wagon Women*, 1:189–229. Many of her entries are undated and judging by events and locations, some of the entries in the transcription appear to be out of chronological order. Her name is variously spelled Kitturah, Ketturah, and Keturah; the last spelling will be used in this book.

2. Camp, *James Clyman, Frontiersman*, 119, 328n149, 334–35n200.

3. Belknap diary, 9.

4. Robertson, "Pioneer Captain of Industry in Oregon," 150–67.

5. Richard Cheadle letter to unidentified party, 1896. A typewritten transcription is available at http://www.oregonpioneers.com/Cheadle_Letter.htm.

6. Root, *Journal of Travels*, 1, 2; "Root Invented Model Rotary Snow Plow," 18; *Daily Register Mail* (Galesburgh, IL), May 16, 1950.

7. Lewin and Taylor, *St. Joe Road*, 5.

8. Ibid., 6, 10.

9. Willoughby, *Robidoux's Town*, 27.

10. Cheadle letter.

11. William Wright Anderson, typewritten transcription of original diary entitled "Diary of William Wright Anderson from St. Joseph, Missouri to Oregon City in the Year 1848," Manuscripts Department, The Lilly Library, Indiana University–Bloomington; *Portrait and Biographical Record of the Willamette Valley, Oregon*, 986.

12. Walker, Purvine letters. May be accessed at http://www.oregonpioneers.com/PurvineWalkerpapers.

13. *Oregon Spectator*, September 7, 1848; William Porter, letter to family, June 24, 1848. Original in possession of Kenneth Porter, great-grandson of William Porter. May be accessed at http://www.oregonpioneers.com/porter.htm.

14. William Porter, letter to family, June 24, 1848. Original in possession of Kenneth Porter, great-grandson of William Porter. May be accessed at http://www.oregonpioneers.com/porter.htm.

15. William Porter, diary; Steeves, *Book of Remembrance of Marion County, Oregon, Pioneers, 1840–1860*, 170, 175–76, 178.

16. Willoughby, *Robidoux's Town*, 38.

17. Lewin and Taylor, *St. Joe Road*, 6.

Chapter 4, The Talk Before the Walk (pp. 31–39)

1. Lewin and Taylor, *St. Joe Road*, 24.

2. Wambaugh's name appeared in the May 12, 1848, *St. Joseph Gazette* three times, once as M. N. Wombaugh and twice as M. N. Wambaugh. It appeared as M. Warnbaugh in James Clyman's 1844 journal (Camp, *James Clyman, Frontiersman*, 79), as M. M. Warnsbough in Bancroft's *History of California*, 4:361, and as Wornbaugh in the April 30, 1846, *Oregon Spectator*.

3. Hansen, *Wagon Train Governments*, 11; Pritchard, *Overland Diary of James A. Pritchard*, 63.

4. *St. Joseph Gazette*, May 12, 1848.

5. Steeves, *Book of Remembrance of Marion County, Oregon, Pioneers*, 170, 172.

6. McCormick, *Our Proud Past*, 1:66.

7. Burrows, *Long Road to Stoney Creek*, 23.

8. Hines, *Illustrated History of the State of Oregon*, 621.

9. Bancroft, *History of California*, 4:726; Gilbert, *Westering Man*, 325.

10. Camp, *James Clyman, Frontiersman*, 338n209.

11. Ibid., 239, 338n209.

12. Ibid., 316n82.

13. Bancroft, *History of California*, 5:526n2, 766; Burrows, *Long Road to Stony Creek*, 64.

14. Camp, *James Clyman, Frontiersman*, 224.

15. Ibid., 283; and Burrows, *Long Road to Stony Creek*, 22.

16. Steeves, *Book of Remembrance of Marion County, Oregon, Pioneers*, 174.

17. *Portrait and Biographical Record of the Willamette Valley*, 986.

18. William G. Porter family tree.

19. Steeves, *Book of Remembrance of Marion County, Oregon, Pioneers*, 174; *Spectator*, September 7, 1848; William Wright Anderson diary, September 12, 1848.

20. *Spectator*, September 7, 1848.

21. Lewin and Taylor, *St. Joe Road*, 24.

CHAPTER 5, A VAST GREEN SEA (PP. 40–57)

1. Lewin and Taylor, *St. Joe Road*, 27–28.

2. Root, *Journal of Travels from St. Josephs to Oregon*, 6–7.

3. The best resources for ascertaining the locations and routes of the trails are Lewin and Taylor, *St. Joe Road*; Franzwa, *Maps of the Oregon Trail*, 3rd ed.; Franzwa, *Maps of the California Trail*; and Brock, *Emigrant Trails West*, 4th ed.

4. Lewin and Taylor, *St. Joe Road*, 22.

5. *Prairie: A Natural History*, by Candace Savage, is a wonderful book about the flora and fauna of the western prairie.

6. Pritchard, *Overland Diary*, 59.

7. Bryant, *What I Saw in California*, 41.

8. Lewin and Taylor, *St. Joe Road*, 25.

9. Brandon, *The Men and the Mountain*, 54–91.

10. Barry, *Beginning of the West*, 861; Camp, *James Clyman, Frontiersman*, 64, 320n106.

11. Lewin and Taylor, *St. Joe Road*, 33.

12. Ebbert, "Joe Meek Trip to Washington, 1847–48," 266.

13. Victor, *River of the West*, 2:85, 139, 151.

14. Tobie, "Joseph L. Meek: A Conspicuous Personality," 260–62.

15. Ebbert, "Joe Meek Trip to Washington, 1847–48," 267; Tobie, "Joe Meek: A Conspicuous Personality," 263.

16. *Gazette*, May 12, 1848; Lempfrit, *Oregon Trail Journal and Letters*, 56.

17. McCormick, *Our Proud Past*, 65.

18. Ebbert, "Joe Meek Trip to Washington," 266; Victor, *River of the West*, 2:196, 200.

19. Lempfrit, *Oregon Trail Journal and Letters*, 56; *Spectator*, September 7, 1848.

20. Robertson, "Pioneer Captain of Industry in Oregon," 160.

21. Lemprit, *Oregon Trail Journal and Letters*, 15.

22. Victor, *River of the West*, 2:202–31.

23. Miller, "Early Oregon Scenes," 57.

24. Ibid., 57.

25. Steeves, *Book of Remembrance of Marion County, Oregon, Pioneers*, 170.

26. Miller, "Early Oregon Scenes," 58.

27. *Gazette*, June 25, 1847.

Chapter 6, Indian Troubles (pp. 58–72)

1. Stegner, *Gathering of Zion*, 84.

2. Clayton, *Latter-Day Saints' Emigrants' Guide*, 41.

3. Stegner, *Gathering of Zion*, 174.

4. Clayton, *Latter-Day Saints' Emigrants' Guide*, 44–45.

5. Haines, *Historic Sites Along the Oregon Trail*, 65.

6. Cornwall, *Life Sketch of Pierre Barlow Cornwall*, 17.

7. Thomas Corcoran, letter.

8. Cornwall, *Life Sketch of Pierre Barlow Cornwall*, 17.

9. "Biographical—Capt. Orrin Kellogg"; Evans, *History of the Pacific Northwest*, 399; *Portrait and Biographical Record of the Willamette Valley*, 102.

10. Cornwall, *Life Sketch of Pierre Barlow Cornwall*, 17–19.

11. Ibid., 21–23.

12. Barry, *Beginning of the West*, 848; Mattes, *Great Platte River Road*, 492.

13. Cornwall, *Life Sketch of Pierre Barlow Cornwall*, 23.

14. Barry, *Beginning of the West*, 644–45, 757; *Gazette*, June 9, 1848.

15. Burrows, *Long Road to Stony Creek*, 23–24.

16. Bryant, *What I Saw in California*, 247.

17. Kelly and Morgan, *Old Greenwood*, 169.

18. Ibid., 22, 84, 88.

19. Barry, *Beginning of the West*, 511; Kelly and Morgan, *Old Greenwood*, 91, 102.

20. Bryant, *What I Saw in California*, 247; Kelly and Morgan, *Old Greenwood*, 84–85, 101, 132, 134, 141, 151, 227.

21. Camp, *James Clyman, Frontiersman*, 228; and Kelly and Morgan, *Old Greenwood*, 184, 189, 200, 211–14, 232, 245–55.

22. Barry, *Beginning of the West*, 722; Kelly and Morgan, *Old Greenwood*, 258.

23. Kelly and Morgan, *Old Greenwood*, 97; Stegner, *Gathering of Zion*, 127.

24. Barry, *Beginning of the West*, 511; Kelly and Morgan, *Old Greenwood*, 102.

25. Hyde, *Pawnee Indians*, 364.

26. Olson and Naugle, *History of Nebraska*, 25; Hyde, *Red Cloud's Folk*, 4–6.

27. Ambrose, *Undaunted Courage*, 154; Hyde, *Red Cloud's Folk*, 29,

28. Hafen, *Broken Hand*, 139–40; Hyde, *Red Cloud's Folk*, 44–46.

29. Hyde, *Red Cloud's Folk*, 46.

30. Hyde, *Pawnee Indians*, 137–39.

31. Ibid., 181, 197–201; Hyde, *Red Cloud's Folk*, 47–50.

32. Barry, *Beginning of the West*, 391; Hyde, *Pawnee Indians*, 202, 364.

33. Barry, *Beginning of the West*, 489, 597, 707; Hyde, *Pawnee Indians,* 208–10, 227; Hyde, *Red Cloud's Folk*, 60–61.

34. Barry, *Beginning of the West*, 759.

35. Camp, *James Clyman, Frontiersman*, 225, 273, 275, 338n208.

36. Hyde, *Pawnee Indians*, 229.

CHAPTER 7, INDEPENDENCE, A STAR IN DECLINE (PP. 73–85)

1. Edward Smith, "A Journal of Scenes and Incidences on a Journey from Missouri to California in 1848." Mss. 18, Fresno Historical Society Archives.

2. Haines, *Historic Sites Along the Oregon Trail*, 33.

3. Gilbert, *Westering Man*, 72, 75.

4. Barry, *Beginning of the West*, 144, 325; Gilbert, *Westering Man*, 88; Hafen, *Broken Man*, 70–71.

5. Barry, *Beginning of the West*, 136–37; Camp, *James Clyman, Frontiersman*, 39.

6. Barry, *Beginning of the West*, 139–40.

7. Ibid., 428–29; Giffen, *Trail-Blazing Pioneer*, 7, 9; Hafen, *Broken Hand*, 174; Stewart, *California Trail*, 6–18.

8. Barry, *Beginning of the West*, 447–48, 476; and Mattes, *Great Platte River Road*, 484.

9. Barry, *Beginning of the West*, 509–10; Camp, *James Clyman, Frontiersman*, 79.

10. J. P. C. Allsopp, reminiscence, Bancroft Library, University of California, Berkeley, microfilm BANC MSS C-D 25.

11. Franzwa, *Oregon Trail Revisited*, 3rd ed., 134; Haines, *Historic Sites Along the Oregon Trail*, 34.

12. Kelly, "Rev. Clinton Kelly," 57–58.

13. Barry, *Beginning of the West*, 726; Schmidt, *Who Were the Murphys*, 5; Thomas Corcoran, letter.

14. Haines, *Historic Sites Along the Oregon Trail*, 35.

15. Barry, *Beginning of the West*, 544.

16. Haines, *Historic Sites Along the Oregon Trail*, 39.

17. Fremont, *Report of the Exploring Expedition to the Rocky Mountains*, 6.

18. Bryant, *What I Saw in California*, 22–23; Haines, *Historic Sites Along the Oregon Trail*, 39–40.

19. Fremont, *Report of the Exploring Expedition to the Rocky Mountains*, 7.

20. Camp, *James Clyman, Frontiersman*, 74–75.

21. Barry, *Beginning of the West*, 732.

22. Haines, *Historic Sites Along the Oregon Trail*, 44.

23. Bryant, *What I Saw in California*, 26, 28, 31.

24. Giffen, *Trail-Blazing Pioneer*, 3.

25. Barry, *Beginning of the West*, 428; Bidwell, *Journey to California, 1841*, 9; Giffen, *Trail-Blazing Pioneer*, 7.

26. Camp, *James Clyman, Frontiersman*, 294–96; Gilbert, *Westering Man*, 88, 229, 235. McClellan's name appears several times in Richard May's diary.

27. Personal communication with Larry Schmidt, a descendant of John Preston, July 10, 2010.

28. Giffen, *Trail-Blazing Pioneer*, 69; Stewart, *California Trail*, 207.

29. May, *Sketch of a Migrating Family to California in 1848*. Original diary is in Bancroft Library.

30. Bancroft, *History of California*, 5:360; Barry, *Beginning of the West*, 722; Chambers and Wells, *History of Butte County*, 2:76.

31. Bancroft, *History of California*, 4:708; *Brunswick* [Mo.] *Brunswicker*, November 4, 1847, and May 4, 1848.

CHAPTER 8, THROUGH THE TALLGRASS PRAIRIE (PP. 86–109)

1. Camp, *James Clyman, Frontiersman*, 79.
2. Ibid., 83.
3. Ibid., 83; Hyde, *Pawnee*, 110, 139.
4. Camp, *James Clyman, Frontiersman*, 28, 226.
5. Barry, *Beginning of the West*, 755–56.
6. Root, *Journal of Travels from St. Josephs to Oregon*, 7.
7. Burrows, *Long Road to Stony Creek*, 24–25.
8. Ibid., 25.
9. Bryant, *What I Saw in California*, 49.
10. Bidwell, *Journey to California*, 13.
11. Bryant, *What I Saw in California*, 47.
12. Ambrose, *Undaunted Courage*, 153.
13. *Californian*, October 21, 1848.
14. Haines, *Historic Sites Along the Oregon Trail*, 77; Kelly and Morgan, *Old Greenwood*, 31; Mattes, *Great Platte River Road*, 264.
15. Bryant, *What I Saw in California*, 36.
16. Miller, "Early Oregon Scenes," 57–58. It is likely that Miller misnamed the Nemaha as the "Little Blue River."
17. Ibid., 58.

CHAPTER 9, BLACK BEASTS, BLACK FACES (PP. 110–135)

1. Root, *Journal of Travels from St. Josephs to Oregon*, 8–9.
2. Victor, *River of the West*, 2:199–200.
3. Bennett, *Mormons at the Missouri*, 96; Hyde, *Pawnee*, 209–27; Hyde, *Red Cloud's Folk*, 48.
4. Fremont, *Report of the Exploring Expedition to the Rocky Mountains*, 51; Hafen, *Broken Hand*, 181–83.
5. Barry, *Beginning of the West*, 545–46; Hyde, *Red Cloud's Folk*, 58; Parkman, *Oregon Trail*, 151. See also Parkman, *Oregon Trail*, 71.
6. Hyde, *Pawnee*, 217.
7. Camp, *James Clyman, Frontiersman*, 46.
8. Root, *Journal of Travels from St. Josephs to Oregon*, 8; Parkman, *Oregon Trail*, 71.
9. Camp, *James Clyman, Frontiersman*, 233–34.
10. Root, *Journal of Travels from St. Josephs to Oregon*, 8.
11. Parkman, *Oregon Trail*, 122.
12. Hyde, *Red Cloud's Folk*, 30, 85, 106, 119.
13. Parkman, *Oregon Trail*, 83.
14. Mattes, *Great Platte River Road*, 305.
15. DeVoto, *Year of Decision*, 115.
16. Parkman, *Oregon Trail*, 59.
17. Ibid., 58–59, 72, 100.
18. Ibid., 59.
19. Hyde, *Red Cloud's Folk*, 29, 307.
20. Ibid., 53, 58; Parkman, *Oregon Trail*, 95–96.
21. Hyde, *Red Cloud's Folk*, 52.
22. Ibid., 53–55, 57, 313; Parkman, *Oregon Trail*, 95–96; Parkman, *Journals*, 2:446.

23. Hyde, *Red Cloud's Folk*, 59; Parkman, *Journals*, 2:445, 2:630n135; Parkman, *Oregon Trail*, 74.

24. Parkman, *Oregon Trail*, 74, 93.

25. Camp, *James Clyman, Frontiersman*, 233.

26. Bryant, *What I Saw in California*, 67.

27. Parkman, *Oregon Trail*, 86–150, quote at 127–28.

28. Bryant, *What I Saw in California*, 68.

29. Hyde, *Red Cloud's Folk*, 59; Parkman, *Oregon Trail*, 83–84.

30. Parkman, *Oregon Trail*, 84.

31. Parkman, *Journals*, 2:458.

32. Parkman, *Oregon Trail*, 122.

33. Hyde, *Red Cloud's Folk*, 59; Parkman, *Journals*, 2:448.

34. Root, *Journal of Travels from St. Josephs to Oregon*, 14.

35. Bryant, *What I Saw in California*, 48.

36. *Californian*, October 28, 1848.

37. Ibid.

38. Camp, *James Clyman, Frontiersman*, 89.

39. Steeves, *Book of Remembrance of Marion County, Oregon, Pioneers*, 172.

40. Haines, *Historic Sites Along the Oregon Trail*, 105; Mattes, *Great Platte River Road*, 451.

41. Parkman, *Oregon Trail*, 84.

42. Hafen, *Broken Hand*, 284–301; Hyde, *Red Cloud's Folk*, 65; Mattes, *Great Platte River Road*, 517.

43. Hafen, *Broken Hand*, 290.

44. Haines, *Historic Sites Along the Oregon Trail*, 133; Mattes, *Great Platte River Road*, 482.

45. Bidwell, *Journey to California*, 14.

46. Fremont, *Report of the Exploring Expedition to the Rocky Mountains*, 17.

47. Camp, *James Clyman, Frontiersman*, 85.

48. Parkman, *Oregon Trail*, 54; Parkman, *Journal*, 2:434.

49. Bryant, *What I Saw in California*, 52–53.

50. Haines, *Historic Sites Along the Oregon Trail*, 80.

51. Mattes, *Great Platte River Road*, 308.

52. Steeves, *Book of Remembrance of Marion County, Oregon, Pioneers*, 174.

53. Parkman, *Oregon Trail*, 59, 92.

54. Hyde, *Red Cloud's Folk*, 67.

55. Bryant, *What I Saw in California*, 66; Parkman, *Oregon Trail*, 60–61.

56. Haines, *Historic Sites Along the Oregon Trail*, 124.

57. Parkman, *Oregon Trail*, 61.

58. Haines, *Historic Sites Along the Oregon Trail*, 97–98.

59. Parkman, *Oregon Trail*, 73, 125.

60. Mattes, *Great Platte River Road*, 404; Hill, *California Trail*, 113.

61. Cheadle letter.

62. Steeves, *Book of Remembrance of Marion County, Oregon, Pioneers*, 177.

63. Bryant, *What I Saw in California*, 59; Russell, *Journal of a Trapper*, 139.

64. Steeves, *Book of Remembrance of Marion County, Oregon, Pioneers*, 177.

65. Fremont, *Report of the Exploring Expedition to the Rocky Mountains*, 176.

66. Ibid., 177.

67. Bidwell, *Journey to California*, 14.

68. Bryant, *What I Saw in California*, 49.

69. Ibid., 49; Hyde, *Red Cloud's Folk*, 62.

70. Hyde, *Red Cloud's Folk*, 62; Root, *Journal of Travels from St. Josephs to Oregon*, 9–10.

71. Hyde, *Red Cloud's Folk*, 61.

72. Haines, *Historic Sites Along the Oregon Trail*, 63–64; Mattes, *Great Platte River Road*, 167.

CHAPTER 10, COME, COME YE SAINTS (PP. 136–150)

1. Stegner, *Gathering of Zion*, 19.

2. Ibid., 23.

3. DeVoto, *Year of Decision*, 82–85.

4. Ibid., 80.

5. Bennett, *Mormons at the Missouri*, 16; Stegner, *Gathering of Zion*, 31–32.

6. Bennett, *Mormons at the Missouri*, 18; DeVoto, *Year of Decision*, 79.

7. Bennett, *Mormons at the Missouri*, 18, 20.

8. Ibid., 14–15.

9. Stegner, *Gathering of Zion*, 38–40.

10. Bennett, *Mormons at the Missouri*, 22–25; Stegner, *Gathering of Zion*, 40–42.

11. Bennett, *Mormons at the Missouri*, 25; Stegner, *Gathering of Zion*, 43.

12. Stegner, *Gathering of Zion*, 51; Bennett, *Mormons at the Missouri*, 27.

13. Bennett, *Mormons at the Missouri*, 31, 224n28.

14. Ibid., 37; Devoto, *Year of Decision*, 93; Stegner, *Gathering of Zion*, 51.

15. Bennett, *Mormons at the Missouri*, 37; Stegner, *Gathering of Zion*, 60–62, 66.

16. Bennett, *Mormons at the Missouri*, 45–46.

17. Ibid., 46.

18. Ibid., 46, 252n2; Stegner, *Gathering of Zion*, 84; Tyler, *Concise History of the Mormon Battalion*, 88.

19. Barry, *Beginning of the West*, 271; Bennett, *Mormons at the Missouri*, 101.

20. Bennett, *Mormons at the Missouri*, 47, 49.

21. Ibid., 47.

22. Ibid., 21–22, 53–54; Stegner, *Gathering of Zion*, 74.

23. Bennett, *Mormons at the Missouri*, 54.

24. Ibid., 54.

25. Ibid., 56.

26. Ibid., 56; Stegner, *Gathering of Zion*, 83–84.

27. Bennett, *Mormons at the Missouri*, 58, 60; Stegner, *Gathering of Zion*, 77.

28. Bennett, *Mormons at the Missouri*, 58–59; Stegner, *Gathering of Zion*, 78.

29. Stegner, *Gathering of Zion*, 78–79.

30. Bennett, *Mormons at the Missouri*, 61; Stegner, *Gathering of Zion*, 82–83.

31. Bennett, *Mormons at the Missouri*, 65–66.

32. Aitchison, "Mormon Settlements in the Missouri Valley," 9; Bennett, *Mormons at the Missouri*, 70–72, 93, 95–96.

33. Bennett, *Mormons at the Missouri*, 73, 75–76, 79.

34. Ibid., 81, 83–84.

35. Ibid., 89–90.

36. Ibid., 94.

37. Ibid., 96.

38. Ibid., 96.

39. Ibid., 99–100.

40. Ibid., 102.

41. Ibid., 101, 104–5.

42. Ibid., 106.

43. Ibid., 107–8.

44. Ibid., 116.

45. Ibid., 116, 127–28.

46. Ibid., 112–13, 125; Tyler, *Concise History of the Mormon Battalion*, 174.

47. Bennett, *Mormons at the Missouri*, 114, 121.

48. Ibid., 134–35.

49. Ibid., 137, 149–41, 145.

50. Ibid., 143–44.

51. Ibid., 147.

52. Ibid., 123.

53. Ibid., 150.

54. Ibid., 148.

55. Ibid., 148.

56. Ibid., 149, 157, 160–61.

57. Ibid., 161.

58. Ibid., 149, 161; Stegner, *Gathering of Zion*, 117, 119.

59. Stegner, *Gathering of Zion*, 153.

60. Ibid., 156.

61. Ibid., 157–58.

62. Aitchison, "Mormon Settlements in the Missouri Valley," 20.

63. Ibid., 21.

Chapter 11, The Babylon of the West (pp. 151–192)

1. Bryant, *What I Saw in California*, 247.

2. *Californian*, 28 October 1848.

3. Mattes, *Great Platte River Road*, 480.

4. Ibid., 481.

5. Bryant, *What I Saw in California*, 68; Fremont, *Report of the Exploring Expedition to the Rocky Mountains*, 48; Mattes, *Great Platte River Road*, 482.

6. Haines, *Historic Sites along the Oregon Trail*, 143; Mattes, *Great Platte River Road*, 482–83.

7. Fremont, *Report of the Exploring Expedition to the Rocky Mountains*, 47–48.

8. Haines, *Historic Sites along the Oregon Trail*, 142; Mattes, *Great Platte River Road*, 484.

9. Camp, *James Clyman, Frontiersman*, 90.

10. Fremont, *Report of the Exploring Expedition to the Rocky Mountains*, 48; Mattes, *Great Platte River Road*, 483.

11. Bryant, *What I Saw in California*, 68; Parkman, *Oregon Trail*, 65.

12. Haines, *Historic Sites along the Oregon Trail*, 144.

13. Mattes, *Great Platte River Road*, 487.

14. Parkman, *Oregon Trail*, 69–70.

15. *Californian*, 28 October 1848.

16. Camp, *James Clyman, Frontiersman*, 103, 323n132; Sullivan, *Martin Murphy Jr.*, 34nn15–16.

17. Camp, *James Clyman, Frontiersman*, 228; DeVoto, *Year of Decision*, 503; Kelly and Morgan, *Old Greenwood*, 200.

18. Camp, *James Clyman, Frontiersman*, 213–16.

19. Ibid., 41, 335–36n202.

20. Barry, *Beginning of the West*, 722.

21. Cornwall, *Life Sketch of Pierre Barlow Cornwall*, 23.

22. Barry, *Beginning of the West*, 715; Gilbert, *Westering Man*, 228.

23. Barry, *Beginning of the West*, 714; Cornwall, *Life Sketch of Pierre Barlow Cornwall*, 23; Gilbert, *Westering Man*, 228–29.

24. Kelly and Morgan, *Old Greenwood*, 84–88.

25. Isaac Pettijohn diary, microfilm 106:14, Bancroft Library, UC Berkeley.

26. Meldahl, *Hard Road West*, 77.

27. Ibid., 77.

28. Haines, *Historic Sites along the Oregon Trail*, 156.

29. Bryant, *What I Saw in California*, 73.

30. Camp, *James Clyman, Frontiersman*, 90; *Plant Guide*, USDA National Plant Data Center.

31. Camp, *James Clyman, Frontiersman*, 284.

32. Stegner, *Gathering of Zion*, 146.

33. Ibid., 145.

34. Haines, *Historic Sites along the Oregon Trail*, 170; Hill, *California Trail*, 123.

35. Fremont, *Report of the Exploring Expedition to the Rocky Mountains*, 62.

36. Camp, *James Clyman, Frontiersman*, 92.

37. Stegner, *Gathering of Zion*, 146.

38. Mattes, *Great Platte River Road*, 426–27.

39. Haines, *Historic Sites along the Oregon Trail*, 135.

40. Mattes, *Great Platte River Road*, 489.

41. Parkman, *Journals*, 2:448.

42. Camp, *James Clyman, Frontiersman*, 284.

43. Unruh, *Plains Across*, 516n75; Haines, *Historic Sites along the Oregon Trail*, 376; Mattes, *Great Platte River Road*, 82; Webb, *Great Plains*, 149.

44. Steeves, *Book of Remembrance of Marion County, Oregon, Pioneers*, 176.

45. Parkman, *Oregon Trail*, 70.

46. Bancroft, *History of Oregon*, 1:751.

47. Parkman, *Oregon Trail*, 64; Parkman, *Journal*, 2:440, 2:443.

48. Unruh, *Plains Across*, 120.

49. Hyde, *Red Cloud's Folk*, 63.

50. Ibid., 303.

51. Barry, *Beginning of the West*, 759.

52. Ibid., 743; Camp, *James Clyman, Frontiersman*, 238, 339n214.

CHAPTER 12, THE SWEETNESS OF THE SWEETWATER (PP. 193–225)

1. Camp, *James Clyman, Frontiersman*, 27, 39, 93, 224.

2. Haines, *Historic Sites Along the Oregon Trail*, 189; Stegner, *Gathering of Zion*, 148.

3. Haines, *Historic Sites Along the Oregon Trail*, 191–92.

4. Stegner, *Gathering of Zion*, 148–49.

5. Franzwa, *Maps of the Oregon Trail*, 125; Haines, *Historic Sites Along the Oregon Trail*, 191.

6. Clayton, *Latter Day Saints' Emigrants' Guide*, 67.

7. Camp, *James Clyman, Frontiersman*, 95.

8. Clayton, *Latter Day Saints' Emigrants' Guide*, 66–67.

9. Wyoming Recreation Commission, *Wyoming: A Guide to Historic Sites*, 169.

10. Camp, *James Clyman, Frontiersman*, 95.

11. Haines, *Historic Sites Along the Oregon Trail*, 206.

12. U.S. Naval Observatory, Moon and Sun Tables.

13. *Californian*, 28 October 1848.

14. Ibid.

15. Root, *Journal of Travels from St. Josephs to Oregon*, 11.

16. Unruh, *Plains Across*, 119–20.

17. Thornton, *Oregon and California in 1848*, 1:131.

18. McCormick, *Our Proud Past*, 65–66.

19. U.S. Naval Observatory, Moon and Sun Tables.

20. Bryant, *What I Saw in California*, 84.

21. Hafen, *Broken Hand*, 261.

22. Camp, *James Clyman, Frontiersman*, 97–98, 324n135.

23. Ibid., 96.

24. Barry, *Beginning of the West*, 70, 115.

25. *Burlington* [Iowa] *Hawk-eye*, 22 March 1849, reprint of article appearing in *Knox* (Illinois) *Intelligencer*.

26. Evans, *History of the Pacific Northwest*, 186.

27. Parker, "Early Recollections of Oregon Pioneer Life," 17.

28. Parkman, *Oregon Trail*, 65.

29. Ibid., 121.

30. Mattes, *Great Platte River Road*, 486–87.

31. Franzwa, *Oregon Trail Revisited*, 235–37; Mattes, *Great Platte River Road*, 491, 497–98.

32. Mattes, *Great Platte River Road*, 502–3.

Chapter 13, *Les Mauvaises Terres* (pp. 226–260)

1. Bryant, *What I Saw in California*, 88.

2. Kelly and Morgan, *Old Greenwood*, 105–6; Stewart, *California Trail*, 60.

3. Bryant, *What I Saw in California*, 87.

4. U.S. Naval Observatory, Moon and Sun Tables.

5. Haines, *Historic Sites Along the Oregon Trail*, 266–67, 271.

6. Ibid., 270.

7. Camp, *James Clyman, Frontiersman*, 38, 222, 265.

8. Ibid., 37.

9. Ibid., 26, 100.

10. Ibid., 101.

11. Fremont, *Report of the Exploring Expedition to the Rocky Mountains*, 174–75.

12. Haines, *Historic Sites Along the Oregon Trail*, 287.

13. Franzwa, *Oregon Trail Revisited*, 292.

14. Haines, *Historic Sites Along the Oregon Trail*, 289.

15. Victor, *River of the West*, 2:198–99; Ebbert, "Joe Meek Trip to Washington, 1847–48," 265.

16. Haines, *Historic Sites Along the Oregon Trail*, 290.

17. Franzwa, *Oregon Trail Revisited*, 293; Gilbert, *Westering Man*, 180.

18. Stewart, *California Trail*, 250–53.

19. DeVoto, *Across the Wide Missouri*, 239; Thornton, *Oregon and California in 1848*, 2:232–39.

20. Barry, *Beginning of the West*, 265–66; Haines, *Historic Sites Along the Oregon Trail*, 305, 307.

21. DeVoto, *Across the Wide Missouri*, 241.

22. Ibid., 241; Galbraith, *Hudson's Bay Company*, 107.

23. Haines, *Historic Sites Along the Oregon Trail*, 307–9.

24. Barry, *Beginning of the West*, 307.

25. Haines, *Historic Sites Along the Oregon Trail*, 310.

26. Ibid., 309.

27. Ibid., 313.

28. Hill, *California Trail*, 178.

29. Stegner, *Gathering of Zion*, 157.

30. Fremont, *Report of the Exploring Expedition to the Rocky Mountains*, 76, 150–51.

CHAPTER 14, THE GREAT TRAIL FORKED (PP. 261–295)

1. Camp, *James Clyman, Frontiersman*, 287.

2. Korns, "Salt Lake Cutoff," 260–61n24; Bigler, *Gold Discovery Journal of Azariah Smith*, 137n40, 139n44.

3. Hines, *Illustrated History of the State of Oregon*, 1037; *Spectator*, September 7, 1848.

4. Cornwall, *Life Sketch of Pierre Barlow Cornwall*, 25.

5. Ibid., 25; Evans, *History of the Pacific Northwest*, 399.

6. Camp, *James Clyman, Frontiersman*, 103.

7. Victo, *River of the West*, 2:196.

8. Fremont, *Report of the Exploring Expedition to the Rocky Mountains*, 212–14.

9. Ibid., 214.

10. Haines, *Historic Sites Along the Oregon Trail*, 341.

11. Miller, "Early Oregon Scenes," 60.

12. Gilbert, *Westering Man*, 230.

13. Ibid., 228.

CHAPTER 15, SNAKING THROUGH VULCAN'S WORKSHOP (PP. 296–325)

1. Camp, *James Clyman, Frontiersman*, 106.

2. Galbraith, *Hudson's Bay Company*, 106; Haines, *Historic Sites Along the Oregon Trail*, 351.

3. Fremont, *Report of the Exploring Expedition to the Rocky Mountains*, 219–20.

4. Haines, *Historic Sites Along the Oregon Trail*, 365.

5. Franzwa, *Oregon Trail Revisited*, 346.

6. Camp, *James Clyman, Frontiersman*, 107.

7. Ibid., 108, 110.

8. Franzwa, *Maps of the Oregon Trail*, 226.

9. Haines, *Historic Sites Along the Oregon Trail*, 344.

CHAPTER 16, GLORY, HALLELUJAH, I SHALL DIE A RICH MAN YET! (PP. 326–350)

1. Camp, *James Clyman, Frontiersman*, 211.

2. Bagley, *Road From El Dorado*, 28; Gudde, *Bigler's Chronicle of the West*, 121–22; Bigler, *Gold Discovery Journal of Azariah Smith*, 137–38.

3. Cornwall, *Life Sketch of P. B. Cornwall*, 25; Harrison, *History of Santa Cruz County*.

4. Camp, *James Clyman, Frontiersman*, 283.

5. McCormick, *Our Proud Past*, 65.

6. Camp, *James Clyman, Frontiersman*, 284.

7. Ibid., 287.

8. Stewart, *California Trail*, 201.

9. Bagley, *Road From El Dorado*, 28; Bigler, *Gold Discovery Journal of Azariah Smith*, 137n40.

10. Camp, *James Clyman, Frontiersman*, 283.

11. Ibid., 210.

12. Tyler, *Mormon Battalion in the Mexican War*, 340.

13. Camp, *James Clyman, Frontiersman*, 210.

14. Pratt, *Journal of Addison Pratt*, 342.

15. Ibid., 21–28; Tyler, *Mormon Battalion in the Mexican War*, 138–48, 157.

16. Bigler, *Gold Discovery Journal of Azariah Smith*, 42–43; Tyler, *Mormon Battalion in the Mexican War*, 164, 173.

17. Tyler, *Mormon Battalion in the Mexican War*, 167, 169.

18. Bigler, *Gold Discovery Journal of Azariah Smith*, 43–68; Tyler, *Mormon Battalion in the Mexican War*, 174–75.

19. Gudde, *Bigler's Chronicle of the West*, 48; Bigler, *Gold Discovery Journal of Azariah Smith*, 72; Tyler, *Mormon Battalion in the Mexican War*, 263, 267, 273, 298.

20. Stegner, *Gathering of Zion*, 158.

21. Gudde, *Bigler's Chronicle of the West*, 60–61; Tyler, *Mormon Battalion in the Mexican War*, 298, 328, 330.

22. Brown, *Giant of the Lord*, 102–3, Gudde, *Bigler's Chronicle of the West*, 62, 67; Tyler, *Mormon Battalion in the Mexican War*, 306, 309.

23. Bigler, *Gold Discovery Journal of Azariah Smith*, 98–100; Gudde, *Bigler's Chronicle of the West*, 68–70; Stegner, *Gathering of Zion*, 168; Tyler, *Mormon Battalion in the Mexican War*, 310.

24. Bigler, *Gold Discovery Journal of Azariah Smith*, 101; Gudde, *Bigler's Chronicle of the West*, 71–73; Tyler, *Mormon Battalion in the Mexican War*, 311–315.

25. Gudde, *Bigler's Chronicle of the West*, 77.

26. Tyler, *Mormon Battalion in the Mexican War*, 315.

27. Ibid., 315.

28. Gudde, *Bigler's Chronicle of the West*, 80; Sutter, *New Helvitia Diary*, 77–78; Tyler, *Mormon Battalion in the Mexican War*, 316.

29. Gudde, *Bigler's Chronicle of the West*, 81.

30. Ibid., 82; Sutter, *New Helvitia Diary*, 81.

31. Gudde, *Bigler's Chronicle of the West*, 88n2, 89.

32. Ibid., 101.

33. Ibid., 107; Owens, *Gold Rush Saints*, 125, 141n12.

34. Gudde, *Bigler's Chronicle of the West*, 106; Owens, *Gold Rush Saints*, 157.

35. Bigler, *Gold Discovery Journal of Azariah Smith*, 115; Gudde, *Bigler's Chronicle of the West*, 109–10.

36. An 1845 map drawn by an engineer of Fremont's showed a trappers' trail heading east, just south of the South Fork of the American River.

37. Owens, *Gold Rush Saints*, 162; Sutter, *New Helvitia Diary*, 134.

38. Gudde, *Bigler's Chronicle of the West*, 112.

39. Ibid., 112–13; Owens, *Gold Rush Saints*, 166; Ellsworth, *Journals of Addison Pratt*, 342.

40. Bigler, *Gold Discovery Journal of Azariah Smith*, 126; Gudde, *Bigler's Chronicle of the West*, 113.

41. Bagley, *Road From El Dorado*, 19; Gudde, *Bigler's Chronicle of the West*, 113.

42. Ellsworth, *Journals of Addison Pratt*, 345; Gudde, *Bigler's Chronicle of the West*, 114–16; Bagley, *Road From El Dorado*, 21.

43. Bigler, *Gold Discovery Journal of Azariah Smith*, 132–33.

44. Bagley, *Road From El Dorado*, 23.

45. Owens, *Gold Rush Saints*, 181n39.

46. Bigler, *Gold Discovery Journal of Azariah Smith*, 132; Bagley, *Road From El Dorado*, 23; Gudde, *Bigler's Chronicle of the West*, 116–17.

47. Bagley, *Road From El Dorado*, 23–24; Bigler, *Gold Discovery Journal of Azariah Smith*, 133; Gudde, *Bigler's Chronicle of the West*, 118.

48. Gudde, *Bigler's Chronicle of the West*, 118; Jonathon Harriman Holmes, diary, LDS Church Archives, MS 1673, 22; Samuel Hollister Rogers, diary, reminiscences, LDS Church Archives, MS 883, 127.

49. Bagley, *Road From El Dorado*, 25; Gudde, *Bigler's Chronicle of the West*, 118.

50. Bigler, *Gold Discovery Journal of Azariah Smith*, 134; Ellsworth, *Journals of Addison Pratt*, 347; Gudde, *Bigler's Chronicle of the West*, 118.

51. Gudde, *Bigler's Chronicle of the West*, 120, 122.

52. Bagley, *Road From El Dorado*, 27; Bigler, *Gold Discovery Journal of Azariah Smith*, 136; Gudde, *Bigler's Chronicle of the West*, 120.

53. Gudde, *Bigler's Chronicle of the West*, 120; Holmes, "Diary. Transcription of original Diary, MS 1673," 22; Samuel Hollister Rogers, diary, reminiscences, LDS Church Archives, MS 883, 128.

54. Gudde, *Bigler's Chronicle of the West*, 120–21.

55. Samuel Hollister Rogers, diary, reminiscences, LDS Church Archives, MS 883, 129.

56. Bagley, *Road From El Dorado*, 28.

57. Bigler, *Gold Discovery Journal of Azariah Smith*, 137.

58. Bagley, *Road From El Dorado*, 52n26.

59. U. S. Naval Observatory, Moon and Sun Tables.

60. Kelly and Morgan, *Old Greenwood*, 120.

61. Bagley, *Road From El Dorado*, 28; Camp, *James Clyman, Frontiersman*, 208; Ellsworth, 349; Gudde, *Bigler's Chronicle of the West*, 120.

62. Cornwall, *Life Sketch of Pierre Barlow Cornwall*, 26–27.

63. Camp, *James Clyman, Frontiersman*, 287.

64. John Borrowman, transcription of original journal in LDS Church Historian's Office, Vol. 3, Joel E. Ricks Collection of Transcriptions, Utah State Agricultural College Library, 55.

65. Camp, *James Clyman, Frontiersman*, 287.

66. Cornwall, *Life Sketch of Pierre Barlow Cornwall*, 27.

67. Kelly and Morgan, *Old Greenwood*, 279–81, 283–84, 298.

68. Ibid., 251, 254–55; Thornton, *Oregon and California in 1848*, 2:215.

69. Camp, *James Clyman, Frontiersman*, 209; Kelly and Morgan, *Old Greenwood*, 137–38.

70. Chamberlin, *History of Yuba County, California*, 88.

71. Hines, *Illustrated History of the State of Oregon*, 621.

72. Burrows, *Long Road to Stony Creek*, 23.

73. Ibid., 27–28.

74. *Californian*, 14 October 1848.

75. Burrows, *Long Road to Stony Creek*, 30.

76. Gudde, *Bigler's Chronicle of the West*, 121.

77. Samuel Hollister Rogers, diary, reminiscences, LDS Church Archives, MS 883, 129.

78. Bigler, *Gold Discovery Journal of Azariah Smith*, 137–38.

79. Bagley, *Road From El Dorado*, 28; Holmes, Holmes, "Diary. Transcription of original Diary, MS 1673," 22.

80. Camp, *James Clyman, Frontiersman*, 170.

81. Ibid., 266, 335n202.

82. Burrows, *Long Road to Stony Creek*, 29–30.

83. According to the records of the San Francisco Chapter of the Society of California Pioneers, McPherson joined their society in 1864, at which time he claimed that he had arrived in California on September 5, 1848.

84. Chamberlin, *History of Yuba County, California*, 88.

85. Thornton, *Oregon and California in 1848*, 2:302.

CHAPTER 17, THE HEAVENLY SCENT OF OREGON PINE (PP. 351–387)

1. Franzwa, *Oregon Trail Revisited*, 349.

2. Haines, *Historic Sites along the Oregon Trail*, 374.

3. Franzwa, *Oregon Trail Revisited*, 351.

4. Camp, *James Clyman, Frontiersman*, 107–8.

5. Haines, *Historic Sites along the Oregon Trail*, 375–76.

6. Camp, *James Clyman, Frontiersman*, 110–11.

7. Haines, *Historic Sites along the Oregon Trail*, 388; Victor, *Cayuse War*, 128–29.

8. Barry, *Beginning of the West*, 286; DeVoto, *Across the Wide Missouri*, 265; Victor, *Cayuse War*, 27.

9. Victor, *Cayuse War*, 72–76.

10. Ibid., 78, 94–95.

11. Ibid., 123, 125–26, 128–32, 136–56.

12. Haines, *Historic Sites along the Oregon Trail*, 392.

13. Holmes, *Covered Wagon Women*, 193, 229.

14. Victor, *Cayuse War*, 66, 129.

15. Ibid., 103.

16. Ibid., 121, 142.

17. Camp, *James Clyman, Frontiersman*, 110.

18. Victor, *Cayuse War*, 71, 172–73.

19. Ibid., 65.

20. Ibid., 145.

21. Ibid., 98, 146.

22. Allsopp, *Reminiscence*.

23. Ibid.

24. Brock, *Emigrant Trails West*, 111.

25. Ibid., 76.

26. Ibid., 86.

27. Rogers, *Diary* [transcript], 130.

28. Bagley, *Road from El Dorado*, 31, 55n74.

29. Gudde, *Bigler's Chronicle of the West*, 123.

30. Bigler, *Gold Discovery Journal of Azariah Smith*, 140.

31. Bagley, *Road from El Dorado*, 32.

32. Gudde, *Bigler's Chronicle of the West*, 123–24.

33. Ibid., 125–27.

34. Brock, *Emigrant Trails West*, 150.

35. Ibid., 103.

Chapter 18, Time to Pay the Gatekeeper (pp. 388–428)

1. McCormick, *Our Proud Past*, 67.

2. Bailey, "Barlow Road," 289–92; Barlow, "History of the Barlow Road," 73–79; Barlow, "Reminiscences of Seventy Years," 260–68.

3. Kowrach, *Journal of a Catholic Bishop on the Oregon Trail*, 102.

4. Unruh, *Plains Across*, 403.

5. "John Corse Trullinger," 285.

6. Ibid., 285.

7. Robertson, "Pioneer Captain of Industry in Oregon," 161–62.

8. Haines, *Historic Sites Along the Oregon Trail*, 423.

9. Root, *Journal of Travels from St. Josephs to Oregon*, 47.

10. Kowrach, *Journal of a Catholic Bishop on the Oregon Trail*, 125n67.

11. Victor, *Cayuse War*, 34.

12. Ibid., 33–34; Lempfrit, *Oregon Trail Journal and Letters*, 189n4.

13. Victor, *Cayuse War*, 74–75; Lempfrit, *Oregon Trail Journal and Letters*, 190n9.

14. Victor, *Cayuse War*, 47.

15. Ibid., 129.

16. Brock, *Emigrant Trails West*, 134.

17. Ibid., 139, 143.

18. Victor, *Cayuse War*, 69; Stewart, *California Trail*, 144.

19. Burnett, *Old California Pioneer*, 157–61.

20. Brock, *Emigrant Trails West*, 170.

21. Borrowman, *Journal* [transcript], 59.

22. Brock, *Emigrant Trails West*, 198.

23. Bidwell, *Journey to California*, 32; Stewart, *California Trail*, 205.

24. Brock, *Emigrant Trails West*, 197.

25. Gilbert, *Westering Man*, 124, 133, 196; Stewart, *California Trail*, 49.

Chapter 19, The End of the Journey (pp. 429–457)

1. Holmes, *Covered Wagon Women*, 193.

2. Evans, *History of the Pacific Northwest*, 2:186–87.

3. Parker, "Early Recollections of Oregon Pioneer Life," 18–19.

4. Kelly, "Rev. Clinton Kelly," 58.

5. Bancroft, *History of Oregon*, 1:751.

6. Kowrach, *Journal of a Catholic Bishop on the Oregon Trail*, 136n93; Lempfrit, *Oregon Trail Journal and Letters*, 190n11.

7. Kowrach, *Journal of a Catholic Bishop on the Oregon Trail*, 103.

8. Haines, *Historic Sites Along the Oregon Trail*, 396–97.

9. Kowrach, *Journal of a Catholic Bishop on the Oregon Trail*, 102.

10. Victor, *Cayuse War*, 175–76.

11. Kowrach, *Journal of a Catholic Bishop on the Oregon Trail*, 103.

12. Galbraith, *Hudson's Bay Company*, 182.

13. Haines, *Historic Sites Along the Oregon Trail*, 422.

14. Hill, *California Trail*, 202.

15. Camp, *James Clyman, Frontiersman*, 294.

EPILOGUE (PP. 458–468)

1. Root, *Journal of Travels from St. Josephs to Oregon*, 92–95.

2. *Pioneer Journal* (Galesburgh, IL), Summer 1984, 18–19; Root, *Journal of Travels from St. Josephs to Oregon*, 97–130; May 16, 1950 *Daily Register Mail* (Galesburgh, IL).

3. Holmes, *Covered Wagon Women*, 191–93.

4. Steeves, *Book of Remembrance of Marion County, Oregon, Pioneers, 1840–1860*, 177.

5. Lockley, *History of the Columbia River Valley*, 835–37; Evans, *History of the Pacific Northwest: Oregon and Washington*, 2:187–90.

6. Lempfrit, *Oregon Trail Journal and Letters*, 31.

7. Ibid., 35–36.

8. Ibid., 36–37.

9. Ibid., 232.

10. Ibid., 38.

11. Burrows, *Long Road to Stony Creek*, 64.

12. Ibid., 63–66; Bancroft, *History of California*, 4:21, 766.

13. Camp, *James Clyman, Frontiersman*, 239–43.

14. Chamberlain, *History of Yuba County, California*, 88; Chambers and Wells, *History of Butte County, California*, 122; Goebel, "David Parks," in *Yuba County Biographies*.

15. Gilbert, *Westering Man*, 325; Bancroft, *History of California*, 4:726.

16. May, *Sketch of a Migrating Family to California*, 54–64.

17. Research done by Ruth Lang, Fresno City and County Historical Society.

18. Kelly and Morgan, *Old Greenwood*, 301–2.

19. Ibid., 301, 308.

20. Ibid., 309.

21. Ibid., 310.

22. Ibid., 319.

23. Sullivan, *Martin Murphy, Jr., 1844–1884*, 11; Schmidt, *We Were the Murphys*, 27–32.

Works Cited

PRIMARY SOURCES

Allsopp, J. P. C. "Reminiscence." Microfilm, BANC MSS C-D 25, Bancroft Library, University of California, Berkeley.

Anderson, William Wright. "Diary of William Wright Anderson From St. Joseph, Missouri, to Oregon City in the Year 1848." Typewritten transcript. Manuscripts Department, Lilly Library, Indiana University–Bloomington.

Belknap, Keturah. "History of the Life of My Grandmother, Kitturah Penton Belknap; as copied from the original. Typewritten transcription of her journal." Cage 1680, no.132, Washington State University Libraries, Pullman.

Blanchet, Augustine Magloire Alexander. *Journal of a Catholic Bishop on the Oregon Trail: The Overland Crossing of the Rt. Rev. A. M. A. Blanchet, Bishop of Walla Walla, from Montreal to Oregon Territory, March 1847 to January 23, 1851.* Translated by Edward J. Kowrach. Fairfield, WA: Ye Galleon Press, 1978.

Borrowman, John. "John Borrowman Journal, typescript, 1846 Dec. 23–1870 Mar." Original in Mormon Church Historian's Office, Salt Lake City. Also in Vol. 3 of *Joel E. Ricks collection of transcriptions [from diaries and journals of pioneers who settled in Cache Valley].* Logan: Library of the Utah State Agricultural College, 1955.

Bryant, Edwin. *What I Saw In California: Being the Journal of a Tour, By the Emigrant Route and South Pass of the Rocky Mountains, Across the Continent of North America, The Great Desert Basin, and Through California, in the Years 1846, 1847.* New York: D. Appleton, 1848. Reprint, Crabtree, OR: The Narrative Press, 2001.

Cheadle, Richmond. Letter to unidentified party, 1896. Typewritten transcription available at http://oregonpioneers.com/Cheadle_Letter.htm.

Clayton, William. *The Latter-Day Saints' Emigrants' Guide: Being a Table of Distances from Council Bluffs to the Valley of the Great Salt Lake.* Edited by Stanley B. Kimball. St. Louis, MO: Republican-Steam Power Press, 1848. Reprint, Tucson: Patrice Press, 1983.

Corcoran, Edward. "Corcoran Family Geneaology, 1974." Unpublished.

Corcoran, Thomas. Letter to Elizabeth Lonergan, August 23, 1877. A pencil rough draft is in Corcoran's copybook, presently in possession of one of Corcoran's great-granddaughters.

Fremont, John C. *Report of The Exploring Expedition to the Rocky Mountains In The Year 1842, and To Oregon and North California in The Years 1843–44.* 1845. Reprint, Santa Barbara: Narrative Press, 2002.

Green, Ephraim. *A Road From El Dorado: The 1848 Trail Journal of Ephraim Green.* Edited by Will Bagley. Salt Lake City: Prairie Dog Press, 1991.

Hastings, Lansford W. *The Emigrants' Guide to Oregon and California.* Cincinnati: G. Conclin, 1845. Reprint, Bedford, MA: Applewood Books, 1996.

Holmes, Jonathon Harriman. "Diary." Transcription of original diary. MS 1673, 19–25. Mormon Church Archives, Salt Lake City, Utah.

Kurz, Rudolph Friederich. *Journal of Rudolph Friederich Kurz: An Account of His Experiences Among Fur Traders and American Indians on the Mississippi and the Upper Missouri Rivers*

During the Years 1846 to 1852. Translated by Myrtis Jarrell. Edited by J. N. B. Hewitt. Smithsonian Institution, Bureau of American Ethnology, Bulletin 115. Washington, DC: US Government Printing Office, 1937.

Lempfrit, Honoré-Timothée. *His Oregon Trail Journal and Letters From the Pacific Northwest, 1845–1853.* Translated by Patricia Meyer and Catou Lévesque. Edited by Patricia Meyer. Fairfield, WA: Ye Galleon Press, 1983.

Nidever, George. *The Life and Adventures of George Nidever, 1802–1883.* Edited by William Henry Ellison. Berkeley: University of California Press, 1937. Reprint, Tucson, AZ: Southwest Parks and Monument Association, 1984.

Parker, Inez Eugenia Adams. "Early Recollections of Oregon Pioneer Life." *Fifty-Sixth Annual Reunion: Oregon Pioneer Association* (1928): 16–35.

Parkman, Francis. *The Journals of Francis Parkman,* Vol. 2. Edited by Mason Wade. New York: Harper & Brothers, 1947.

——. *The Oregon Trail: Adventures on the Prairie in the 1840s.* N.d. Reprint, Santa Barbara: Narrative Press, 2001.

Pettijohn, Isaac. "Diary." Microfilm, BANC MSS P-A 336 A, Bancroft Library, University of California–Berkeley.

Porter, William. Letter from North Platte Crossing, June 24 1848. Transcript is available at http://oregonpioneers.com/porter2.htm.

——. "William Porter's 1848 Trail Diary." Original in possession of Kenneth Porter, great-grandson of William Porter. Transcript available at http://oregonpioneers.com/porter.htm.

Pratt, Addison. *The Journals of Addison Pratt: Being a Narrative of Yankee Whaling in the Eighteen Twenties, A Mormon Mission to the Society Islands, and of Early California and Utah in the Eighteen Forties and Fifties.* Edited by S. George Ellsworth. Publications in Mormon Studies 6. Salt Lake City: University of Utah Press, 1990.

Preuss, Charles. *Exploring with Fremont: The Private Diaries of Charles Preuss, Cartographer for John C. Fremont on His First, Second and Fourth Expeditions to the Far West.* Translated and edited by Erwin G. Gudde and Elisabeth K. Gudde. Norman: University of Oklahoma Press, 1958.

Pritchard, James A. *The Overland Diary of James A. Pritchard from Kentucky to California in 1849.* Edited by Dale L. Morgan. Denver: Old West Publishing, 1959.

Rogers, Samuel Hollister. "Diary." Transcript of original diary. MS 883, frames 169–77. LDS Church Archives, Salt Lake City, UT.

Root, Riley. *Journal of Travels from St. Josephs to Oregon with Observations of that Country: Together with a Description of California, its Agricultural Interests, and a Full Description of its Gold Mines.* Galesburg, IL: Gazetteer and Intelligencer Press, 1850. Reprint, Oakland, CA: Biobooks, 1955.

Smith, Azariah. *The Gold Discovery Journal of Azariah Smith.* Edited by David L. Bigler. Publications in Mormon Studies 7. Salt Lake City: University of Utah Press, 1990.

Smith, Edward. "A Journal of Scenes and Incidences on a Journey from Missouri to California in 1848." Original journal in Fresno City and County Historical Society, Fresno, California.

Stockton, Robert F. *A Sketch of the Life of Com. Robert F. Stockton.* New York: Derby and Jackson, 1856. Reprint, Ann Arbor: Making of America Project, University of Michigan, n. d.

Newspapers

Brunswick (MO) *Brunswicker*
Burlington (IA) *Hawkeye*

(Galesburgh, IL) *Daily Register Mail*
Oregon Spectator
San Francisco *Californian*
St. Joseph (MO) *Gazette*

Secondary Sources

Aitchison, Clyde B. "The Mormon Settlements in the Missouri Valley." Paper presented before the Annual Meeting of the Nebraska Historical Society, January 11, 1899. Nebraska State Historical Society Library.

Ambrose, Stephen E. *Undaunted Courage: Meriwether Lewis, Thomas Jefferson, and the Opening of the American West.* New York: Simon & Schuster, 1996.

Bailey, Walter. "The Barlow Road." *Oregon Historical Quarterly* 13 (September 1912): 287–96.

Bancroft, Hubert Howe. *History of California.* 7 vols. San Francisco: History Company, 1886.

———. *History of Oregon.* 2 vols. San Francisco: History Company, 1886.

Bagley, Will, ed. *A Road From El Dorado: The 1848 Trail Journal of Ephraim Green.* Salt Lake City: Prairie Dog Press, 1991.

Barlow, Mary S. "History of Barlow Road." *Oregon Historical Quarterly* 3 (March 1902): 71–81.

Barlow, William. "Reminiscences of Seventy Years." *Oregon Historical Quarterly* 13 (September 1912): 240–86.

Barry, Louise. *The Beginning of the West: Annals of the Kansas Gateway to the American West, 1540–1854.* Topeka: Kansas State Historical Society, 1972.

Bennett, Richard E. *Mormons at the Missouri: Winter Quarters, 1846–1852.* Norman: University of Oklahoma Press, 1987, 2004.

Bidwell, John. *Echoes of the Past.* New York: Citadel Press, 1962. Originally published as *Echoes of the Past: An Account of the First Emigrant Train to California, Fremont in the Conquest of California, the Discovery of Gold and Early Reminiscences.* Chico, CA: Chico Advertiser, 1850.

———. *A Journey to California, 1841: The First Emigrant Party to California by Wagon Train.* 1843. Reprint, Berkeley: Friends of the Bancroft Library, 1964.

"Biographical–Capt. Orrin Kellogg." *Oregon Native Sons* (May 1899): 111.

Brandon, William. *The Men and the Mountain: Fremont's Fourth Expedition.* New York: William Morrow Company, 1955.

Brock, Richard K. ed. *Emigrant Trails West: A Guide to the California Trail: From the Raft River to the Humboldt Sink.* 4th ed. Reno, NV: Trails West, 2000.

Brown, James S. *Giant of the Lord: Life of a Pioneer.* 1904. Reprint, Salt Lake City: Bookcraft, Inc., 1960.

Burlington (Iowa) *Hawkeye* 22 (March 1849). Republished article from Knox (IL) *Intelligencer* of unknown date.

Burnett, Peter H. *An Old California Pioneer.* 1880. Reprint. Oakland, CA: Biobooks, 1946.

Burrows, Rufus. *A Long Road to Stony Creek.* London: Yendall & Company/Ashland, OR: Lewis Osborne, 1971.

Camp, Charles L., ed. *James Clyman: Frontiersman: The Adventures of a Trapper and Covered Wagon Emigrant As Told in His Own Reminiscences and Diaries.* Portland: Champoeg Press, 1960.

Chamberlain, William Henry. *History of Yuba County, California: With Illustrations Descriptive of its Scenery, Residences, Public Buildings, Fine Blocks and Manufactories from Original Sketches by Artists of the Highest Ability.* 1879. Reprint, Volcano, CA: California Traveler, 1970.

Chambers, W. L., and Harry L. Wells. *History of Butte County, California.* 1882. Reprint, Berkeley, CA: Howell–North Books, 1973.

Cornwall, Bruce. *Life Sketch of Pierre Barlow Cornwall.* San Francisco: A. M. Robertson, 1906.

Dary, David. *The Oregon Trail: An American Saga.* New York: Alfred A. Knopf, 2004.

DeVoto, Bernard. *Across the Wide Missouri.* 1947. Reprint, Boston: Houghton Mifflin Company, 1998.

———. *The Year of Decision: 1846.* 1942. Reprint, New York: St. Martin's Press, 2000.

Dawson, Joseph C. III. *Doniphan's Epic March: The 1st Missouri Volunteers in the Mexican War.* Lawrence : University Press of Kansas, 1999.

Down, Robert Horace. *A History of Silverton* [Oregon] *Country.* Portland: Berncliff Press, 1926.

Ebbert, George Wood. "Joe Meek Trip to Washington, 1847–48." *Quarterly of the Oregon Historical Society* 19 (1918): 263–267.

Evans, Elwood. *History of the Pacific Northwest: Oregon and Washington.* 2 vols. Portland: North Pacific History Company, 1889.

Flora, Stephenie. *The Oregon Territory and its Pioneers.* http://www.oregonpioneers.com

Franzwa, Gregory M. *Maps of the California Trail.* Tucson: Patrice Press, 1999.

———. *Maps of the Oregon Trail.* 3rd ed. St. Louis: Patrice Press, 1990.

———. *The Oregon Trail Revisited.* 3rd ed. Gerald, MO: Patrice Press, 1983.

Galbraith, John S. *The Hudson's Bay Company as an Imperial Factor, 1821–1869.* Berkeley: University of California Press, 1957.

Gale, Kira. *Peter A. Sarpy & Early Bellevue.* Omaha, NE: River Junction Press, 1999.

Giffen, Helen S. *Trail-Blazing Pioneer: Colonel Joseph Ballinger Chiles.* San Francisco: John Howell-Books, 1969.

Gilbert, Bil. *Westering Man: The Life of Joseph Walker.* New York: Atheneum, 1983. Reprint, Norman: University of Oklahoma Press, 1985.

Goebel, T. "David Parks." In *Yuba County Biographies and Family Ties, Yuba Roots: Genealogy and History.* http://www.yubaroots.com/bios/parks.htm

Gudde, Erwin G. *Bigler's Chronicle of the West: The Conquest of California, Discovery of Gold, and Mormon Settlement as Reflected in Henry William Bigler's Diaries.* Berkeley: University of California Press, 1962.

Hafen, LeRoy R. *Broken Hand: The Life of Thomas Fitzpatrick; Mountain Man, Guide and Indian Agent.* Denver: Old West Publications, 1931. Reprint, Lincoln: University of Nebraska Press, 1981.

Haines, Aubrey L. *Historic Sites Along the Oregon Trail.* Tucson, AZ: Patrice Press, 1981.

Hansen, Barbara Julia. "Wagon Train Governments." MA thesis, University of Colorado, 1962.

Harrison E. S. *History of Santa Cruz County.* San Francisco: Pacific Press Publication Company, 1891.

Hill, William E. *The California Trail: Yesterday and Today: A Pictorial Journey Along the California Trail.* 2nd ed. Boise, ID: Tamarack Books, 1993.

Hines, H. K. *An Illustrated History of the State of Oregon.* Chicago: Lewis Publishing Company, 1893.

History of Holt and Atchison Counties, Missouri. St. Joseph, MO: National Historical Company, 1882.

Holmes, Kenneth L., ed. *Covered Wagon Women: Diaries & Letters from the Western Trails: 1840–1849.* Vol 1. Glendale, CA: A. H. Clark, 1983. Reprint, Lincoln: University of Nebraska Press, 1995.

Horn, Hosea B. *Horn's Overland Guide From the U. S. Indian Sub-Agency, Council Bluffs, on the Missouri River to the City of Sacramento, in California.* 1852. Reprint, Ann Arbor, MI: Books on Demand, 2008.

Hyde, George E. *The Pawnee Indians*. Denver: University of Denver Press, 1951. Reprint, Norman: University of Oklahoma Press, 1974.

———. *Red Cloud's Folk: A History of the Oglala Sioux Indians*. Norman: University of Oklahoma Press, 1937, 1975.

"John Corse Trullinger." *Oregon Native Son and Historical Magazine* 1, no. 5 (Sept. 1899).

Kelly, Charles, and Dale Morgan. *Old Greenwood: The Story of Caleb Greenwood, Trapper, Pathfinder and Early Pioneer*. Georgetown, CA: The Talisman Press, 1965.

Kelly, Dr. Richmond. "Rev. Clinton Kelly." *Fifteenth Annual Reunion: Oregon Pioneer Association* (1887): 52–63.

Korns, J. Roderic. "The Salt Lake Cutoff." *Utah Historical Quarterly* 19 (1951): 248–68.

Lewin, Jacqueline A., and Marilyn S. Taylor. *The St. Joe Road: Emigration Mid–1800s: A Travelers' Guide from the Missouri River to the Junction of the St. Joe and Independence Roads*. St. Joseph, MO: St. Joseph Museum, 1992.

Lockley, Fred. *History of the Columbia River Valley: From The Dalles to the Sea*. 3 vols. Chicago: S. J. Clarke Publishing, 1928.

Logan, Sheridan A. *Old St. Jo: Gateway to the West, 1799–1932*. 2nd ed. Edited by Alberto C. Meloni. St. Joseph, MO: St. Joseph Museum, Inc., 2002.

Mattes, Merrill J. *The Great Platte River Road: The Covered Wagon Mainline Via Fort Kearney To Fort Laramie*. Lincoln: Nebraska State Historical Society, 1969.

May, Richard Martin. *A Sketch of A Migrating Family To California in 1848*. Fairfield, WA: Ye Galleon Press, 1991.

McCormick, Gail J. *Our Proud Past: A Complied History of the Families That Settled at the End of the Oregon Trail*. Vol. 1. Mulino, OR: Gail J. McCormick Publishing, 1993.

McLynn, Frank. *Wagons West: The Epic Story of America's Overland Trails*. New York: Grove Press, 2002.

Meldahl, Keith Heyer. *Hard Road West: History and Geology Along the Gold Rush Trail*. Chicago: University of Chicago Press, 2007.

Miller, James D. "Early Oregon Scenes: A Pioneer Narrative. Part 1. Overland Trail, 1848." *Oregon Historical Quarterly* 31 (1930): 55–68.

Morgan, Dale. *Overland in 1846: Diaries and Letters of the California-Oregon Trail*. Vol. 1. Georgetown, CA: Talisman Press, 1963. Reprint, Lincoln: University of Nebraska Press, 1993.

Olson, James C. and Ronald C. Naugle. *History of Nebraska*. 3rd ed. Lincoln: University of Nebraska Press, 1997.

Owens, Kenneth N. *Gold Rush Saints: California Mormons and the Great Rush for Riches*. Norman: University of Oklahoma Press, 2005.

Portrait and Biographical Record of Portland and Vicinity, Oregon: Containing Original Sketches of Many Well Known Citizens of the Past and Present. Chicago: Chapman Publishing, 1903.

Portrait and Biographical Record of the Willamette Valley, Oregon: Containing Original Sketches of many Well Known Citizens of the Past and Present. Chicago: Chapman Publishing, 1903.

Ramsey, William E. and Betty Dineen Shrier. *Silent Hills Speak: A History of Council Bluffs, Iowa*. Omaha, NE: Barnhart Press, 2002.

Robertson, James R. "A Pioneer Captain of Industry in Oregon." *Quarterly of the Oregon Historical Society* 4 (1903): 150–167.

"Root Invented Model Rotary Snow Plow." *Prairie Journal* (Summer 1984): 18–19.

Rohrbough, Malcolm J. *Days of Gold: The California Gold Rush and the American Nation*. Berkeley: University of California Press, 1997.

Russell, Osborne. *Journal of a Trapper, 1834–1843*. Edited by Aubrey L. Haines. Lincoln: University of Nebraska Press, 1965.

Savage, Candace. *Prairie, A Natural History.* Vancouver, Canada: Greystone Books, 2004.

Schmidt, Earl F. *Who Were the Murphys: California's Irish First Family.* Murphys, CA: Mooney Flat Ventures, 1992.

Shallcross, William J. *Romance of a Village: Story of Bellevue the First Permanent Continuous Settlement in Nebraska.* Omaha, NE: Roncha Bros. Printers, 1954.

Shebel, James. *Weber! The American Adventure of Captain Charles M. Weber.* Lodi, CA: San Joaquin Historical Society, 1993.

Simmons, Jerold L., ed. *La Belle Vue: Studies in the History of Bellevue, Nebraska.* Bellevue, NE: Jerold L. Simmons, 1976.

Smith, Clarence and Wallace Elliott. *Illustrations of Napa County, California: With Historical Sketch.* 1878. Reprint, Fresno, CA: Valley Publishers, 1974.

Stegner, Wallace. *The Gathering of Zion: The Story of the Mormon Trail.* New York: McGraw-Hill, 1964, 1971.

Steeves, Sarah Hunt. *Book of Remembrance of Marion County, Oregon, Pioneers, 1840–1860.* Portland: Berncliff Press, 1927.

Stewart, George R. *The California Trail: An Epic With Many Heroes.* New York: McGraw-Hill, 1962.

Sullivan, Sister Gabrielle. *Martin Murphy, Jr.: California Pioneer, 1844–1884.* Stockton, CA: University of the Pacific, 1974.

Sutter, John A. *New Helvitia Diary.* San Francisco: Society of California Pioneers, 1939.

Sutter, John A., Jr. *The Sutter Family and the Origins of Gold-Rush Sacramento.* Edited by Allen R. Ottley. 1943. Reprint, Norman: University of Oklahoma Press, 2002.

Thornton, J. Quinn. *Oregon and California in 1848.* Vol. 1 and 2. 1849. Reprint, New York: Arno Press, 1973.

Tobie, H. E. "Joseph L. Meek: A Conspicuous Personality." *Oregon Historical Quarterly* 40 (1939): 243–64.

Tortorich, Frank, Jr. *Gold Rush Trail: A Guide to the Carson River Route of the Emigrant Trail.* Pine Grove, CA: Wagon Wheel Tours, 2006.

Tyler, Daniel. *A Concise History of the Mormon Battalion In the Mexican War: 1846–1847.* 1881. Reprint, Chicago: Rio Grande Press, 1964.

Unruh, John D., Jr. *The Plains Across: The Overland Emigrants and the Trans-Mississippi West, 1840–1860.* Urbana: University of Illinois Press, 1993.

Vestal, Stanley. *Joe Meek: The Merry Mountain Man.* Caldwell, ID: Caxton, 1952. Reprint, Lincoln: University of Nebraska Press, 1963.

Victor, Frances Fuller. *The Early Indian Wars of Oregon Complied from the Oregon Archives and Other Original Sources: with Muster Rolls.* Vol. 1, *The Cayuse War.* 1894. Reprint, Corvallis, OR: Taxus Baccata Books, 2006.

———. *The River of the West: The Adventures of Joe Meek.* 2 vols. 1870. Reprint, Missoula, MN: Mountain Press Publishing Company, 1983 (vol. 1) and 1985 (vol. 2).

Webb, W. P. *The Great Plains.* Boston, n. p., 1931

Willoughby, Robert J. *Robidoux's Town: A Nineteenth-Century History of St. Joseph, Missouri.* St. Joseph, MO: St. Joseph Museum, Inc., 2006.

Wyoming Recreational Commission. *Wyoming: A Guide to Historic Sites.* Casper, WY: House of Printing, 1976.

Index

bold indicates map or image

A

abandoned possessions, 169–70, 214, 258, 273, 274, 285, 432
Abernathy, George, 361
Accolti, Father (priest), 435
Across the Wide Missouri (DeVoto), 238
Adams, Helen, 460
Adams, Inez Eugenia, 10, 213–14, 431, 460
Adams, Thomas, 33
Adams, W. L., 10, 212–15, 258, 430–31, 440, 460
Adams company, 205, 212–15, 261–62, 373, 431
A Guide to the California Trail to the Humboldt River (Trails West), xv
Alcove Springs, KS, 100, 107
Alder Creek, OR, 302, 355, 394
Alexandria, NE, 51
Alkali Lake, NE, 98
Alkali Slough, WY, 209
Allen, James, 142, 145
Allen County, Ohio, 22
Allsopp, J. P. C., 8, 121, 159
Allsopp company
    Adams company and, 261–62, 373
    formation of, 8
    at Fort Laramie, 62, 157
    member departures of, 373
    progress of, 43, 62, 72, 77, 100, 121, 169, 204–5
American Falls, ID, 265, 266–67, 271, 310, 320
American Fur Company
    buffalo robe shipments of, 130–31
    Fort Laramie purchase of, 154, 223–24
    and Joseph Robidoux, 17
    and Lucien Fontenelle, 231
    Rocky Mountain Fur Company purchase, 50
    Sioux Indians trade of, 71
    and William O. Fallon, 7
    and William Sublette, 76
American Indian Mission Association (Baptist), 72, 79, 354
American Indians. *See* Plains Indians
Anderson, William Wright (Miller company)
    on bad weather, 48–49, 209

on Barlow's Gate, 389–90, 391
on the Blue Mountains, 361–62
buffalo hunting, 121–23, 171, 208–9
on the Burnt River Canyon, 306–7
on Cayuse territory travel, 261
on Chimney Rock, 128
on disturbed graves, 253–54, 274
epilogue, 458–59
experience of, 168–69
on the Indian Chief of Mosquito Creek, 37
on Indians in Bear River Valley, 242–43
on Laurel Hill, 392
on livestock confinement, 46
on load lightening, 169–70, 276–77
on Miller company progress, 36–37, 45, 47, 51, 97, 168, 170–72, 209–10, 211–12, 240, 266, 358, 359, 360–66, 392–95
on Miller company split, 394–95
on Miller company wagon numbers, 264
at the Mormon crossing, 207–8, 241–42
on Pawnee encounter, 94–95
on river crossings, 123–24
at Rock Creek, 269–70
at Scott's Bluff, 167
on sheep, 241
on Sioux Indian encounters, 125–27, 185, 221
on the Snake River area, 273–74, 275, 304–5
on tainted water, 209
on Tygh Valley, 388–89
animals, domestic
    behavior of, 203, 204, 245, 286
    care of, 104, 156–57, 168, 173, 215, 219, 245, 308, 323
    collapse of, 386, 425–26
    confining and corralling, 45–47, 49, 214
    death of, 45, 49, 194, 213, 214, 259, 287, 308, 340, 390–91, 393, 421–22, 430
    difficult river crossings of, 208, 216
    dogs, 32, 126, 173, 182, 340, 379
    food scarcity for, 217, 252, 298–99, 393
    illnesses of, 323, 386, 424–26
    Indian kills of, 421–22, 426